A SOCIOLOGICAL READER ON COMPLEX ORGANIZATIONS

A SOCIOLOGICAL READER ON COMPLEX ORGANIZATIONS

SECOND EDITION

AMITAI ETZIONI
COLUMBIA UNIVERSITY

HOLT, RINEHART AND WINSTON, INC.
New York   Chicago   San Francisco   Atlanta
Dallas   Montreal   Toronto   London   Sydney

First published in 1961 under the title *Complex Organizations:*
A Sociological Reader

Copyright © 1961, 1969 by Holt, Rinehart and Winston, Inc.
All rights reserved
Library of Congress Catalog Card Number: 69–12451
03–072335–3
Printed in the United States of America
1 2 3 4 5 6 7 8 9

PREFACE
TO THE
SECOND EDITION

Since the publication of the first edition of this volume under the title *Complex Organizations: A Sociological Reader,* my conviction that organizational analysis is of central interest to students of our society has been further strengthened. In addition to exploring the important role that organizations themselves play, organizational analysis seems to provide a key to the understanding of modern society and its transformation.* In line with this view, we have extended in this volume the space devoted to the societal aspects of organizations.

The volume includes two new sections—on cross-cultural research of organizations and on the organization of knowledge—reflecting two fields of study that gained in attention over the last years. In other sections new articles have been introduced to replace or add to those included in the earlier edition. Altogether, twenty-two articles are new. Again, we included here several articles not published before as well as some especially revised for this edition.

More space than in the earlier edition is devoted to "hard" data; hence the considerable increase in the number of tables, charts, and formulas. This hopefully reflects a growing "hardness" of the field. We have nevertheless retained a high proportion of theoretical and methodological selections, on the assumption that they provide analytic tools by which the vast material that we could not include may be explored. As the field

---

* While many selections included in this volume provide elements of such a perspective, see especially those included in the section Organizations and Society and the selection from Wolin's important book. Our own view is elaborated in *The Active Society: A Theory of Societal and Political Processes* (New York: The Free Press, 1968), especially pp. 104ff.

v

grows, the frustration of selecting some material to the exclusion of other arises; the articles presented here are at best a fair sample of the torrent of work recently published. We hope that these pages will open the doors to organizational study; they cannot replace it.

I am grateful to comments of W. Richard Scott and to the research assistance of Frederick L. DuBow and Linda Thalberg in preparing this edition.

A. E.

January 1969
New York, N.Y.

PREFACE
TO THE
FIRST EDITION

Complex organizations constitute one of the most important elements which make up the social web of modern societies. Most citizens of modern societies are born in a hospital, educated in a school, work in one organization or another; and to the degree that they participate in religious and political activities, these too, frequently, take place in complex organizations. In short, members of modern societies obtain a large part of their material, social, and cultural satisfactions from large-scale organizations. The way to the understanding of modern man and the society in which he lives leads, therefore, to the study of complex organizations. This volume is devoted to a review of some of the ideas, theories, and research findings concerning organizations, and concludes with a brief examination of some of the methods used in studying these social units.

By "organizations" we mean, following Parsons, social units which are predominantly oriented to the attainment of specific goals. The major types of organizations to be discussed are those which have bureaucratic characteristics, as specified by Weber. Thus, although our journey will lead us to the study of both formal and informal aspects of organizations, we shall not embark on the much longer voyage of presenting studies of "social organizations" in which all forms of patterned, regulated, or "organized" social behavior are explored.*

Some of our contributors, especially Howard S. Becker and Erving Goffman, refer to "institutions" when discussing the same category of social units designated here as organizations. Morris Janowitz sees the

---

* For a recent discussion of this concept, see Scott A. Greer, *Social Organization* (New York: Doubleday, 1955), especially pp. 5–10.

military as an "establishment." Whatever the term, the denotation seems to be similar. All the contributors discuss organizations—factories, prisons, offices, hospitals, churches, schools, military organizations, newspapers, voluntary associations, ships, trade-unions, governmental agencies, and universities—each of which is examined in detail by at least one contributor.

These readings were taken, as is customary, from a considerably large body of literature. One obvious criterion of selection was that of finding writings of high quality which were brief enough to be included or could be excerpted without becoming incomprehensible or distorting the author's thesis.* More specifically, an attempt was made to select material which could serve as a substitute for, or supplement to, a textbook for courses in organizational analysis. At the same time, efforts were made to refrain as much as possible from reprinting once more articles or parts of books which could be found on nearly everyone's desk. It is for this reason that some of the "classics" were not included. Omitting some of the standard selections left more room for newer contributions. Of thirty-nine selections collected here, seven have not been published before or have been revised for this volume. Many of the other excerpts are not easily available. A number of works have been reprinted from journals and publications which have only a limited circulation or do not regularly come to the attention of students of organizations.

These readings draw considerably on recent material because in the last decade organizational analysis has rapidly developed and expanded. For the same reason, young and somewhat less well-known authors are highly represented.

This collection, like others before it, does not lay claim to completeness. Quite a few aspects of organizational study are not represented, and many approaches could not be illuminated. An effort has been made to bring into the limelight new tendencies and recent developments. Considerable space has been devoted to the study or organizational *goals* and to the application of *research techniques* to organization research. Care has been taken to call attention to three dimensions or organizational analysis which still seem to be relatively neglected. These are the study of interaction between *organization and society*; intracultural *comparative* study of organizations; and analysis of *organizational change*.

The editor benefited from extensive comments offered by his colleagues at Columbia University and at the University of California at Berkeley. Their knowledge, generous advice, and encouragement—which are herewith gratefully acknowledged—made these readings possible. I

---

* The more important omissions are marked in the text by ellipsis dots (. . .).

am especially indebted to Robert K. Merton, Philip Selznick, and Erving Goffman for their valuable comments on earlier outlines of this volume. The advice of John W. Riley, Jr., was most helpful, as well as the suggestions made by Renate Mayntz. Eva Etzioni served concomitantly as consultant, assistant, and companion.

A. E.

New York, N.Y.
December 1960

CONTENTS

A SOCIOLOGICAL READER ON COMPLEX ORGANIZATIONS

I

Modern Theories of Organization

Finding a balance between the rational and non-rational elements of human behavior is a cardinal issue of modern life and thought. It is also the central problem of organizational theory. All the scholars presented in this section make it their starting point or touch upon it in one way or another. The basic question is how best to coordinate human activities in order to make a highly rational unit, and at the same time to maintain social integration, the normative commitments of participants, and their motivation to participate.

Weber sees three modes that authority, and in this sense, organizational structure, may take: traditional and charismatic authority, which represents the nonrational elements, and the legal-rational or bureaucratic type of authority which of course represents the rational element. Each one of these modes of authority "is connected with a fundamentally different sociological structure of executive staff and means of administration."

Whereas Weber emphasizes the rational aspects of legal-rational or bureaucratic organizations, Barnard, examining a similar set of complex organizations, places greater emphasis on the psychological and social aspects. He sees organizations, first of all, as *cooperative* systems. Barnard's interest in conscious coordination of activities parallels Weber's interest in the systematic division of tasks and authority and in the rational control of performance. At the same time, however, Barnard focuses on the motivational and nonrational aspects of behavior.

1

How can actors be motivated to participate, to comply, and to perform?

Where Weber focuses on the sources and forms of rational structures and Barnard is more concerned with their nonrational aspects, Selznick's theory rests on both foundations. Selznick studies organizations not only as economies and adaptive structures but also as cooperative systems. This compound approach leads Selznick to examine the formal roles of participants as well as their personalities as a whole. It enables him to cast new light on phenomena such as leadership, informal relations, and the dynamics of interchange between personality and organization. The second part of Selznick's contribution is devoted to an examination of the structural-functional approach and its application to organizational analysis.

Parsons presents a general but elaborated model for the structural-functional analysis of organizations. He points out that organizations differ from other social units by being predominantly oriented to the attainment of specific goals. Two main reference points are adopted as central to the examination of these units: first, the cultural and institutional patterns and, second, various role clusters which make up the organizational structure. The key processes of organizations are defined as recruitment, allocation, and the coordination of activities. The selection included here (which constitutes the first part of Parsons' article on organizations) ends with a discussion of the ways in which the integration of the organization is established and maintained. A comparison of this article with Parsons' other work shows that the basic question illuminated is the special form or structure which organizations employ in "solving" the generic functional problems of social units. The question of balance recurs: the instrumental processes of adaptation to the environment and of goal implementation have to be balanced by the expressive processes of social and normative integration.

All the selections presented up to this point are concerned primarily with organization as such and deal with individuals from the viewpoint of their effect on the organization. Merton focuses on the articulation between the personality as a system and the organization as a social unit. An examination of the *bureaucrat* leads Merton to modify the rationalistic model of bureaucracies by pointing out their inherent dysfunctions. The specialized knowledge of the bureaucrat spells "trained incapacity" when the situation changes; discipline leads to devotion to means rather than devotion to ends; impersonal treatment of clients and cases is carried out by interacting persons who develop primary relations. These relations in turn may have dysfunctional effects. The study of organizations, it follows, is incomplete without a study of the participants as persons rather than as simply incumbents of organizational roles.

Etzioni sees the central variable for characterizing difference among organizations as the relationship between those in control and those under control. The means of control and the reactions to them seem so essential that organizations that differ on these two dimensions differ on most others.

March and Simon assert that "the Barnard-Simon theory of organization equilibrium is essentially a theory of motivation." As such it deals with the conditions under which participation is assured, including willingness to be recruited and trained, willingness to perform adequately in terms of quality and quantity, and willingness to obey. The organization is seen as an exchange system in which *inducements* are handed out in exchange for *contributions* supplied. The present selection examines mainly the participation criterion of employees. The extension of this analysis to other groups of participants is suggested by the authors. These groups include buyers, suppliers, agents, and investors.

Hirschman and Lindblom, bringing economic theory to bear on the subject, view organizations as pluralities of actors which relate to each other much more loosely and "individualistically" than is often assumed by other theoreticians. In particular they are concerned with the question of how a multitude of actors is capable of acting in some coordinated fashion when engaged in decision-making. Drawing on data from three quite different fields, Hirschman and Lindblom find that the actors behave in line with the pluralistic ("disjoint incrementalism") theory developed in their previous works and cited in the present selection.

At the root of economic theories is a utilitarian-rationalistic exchange model. Levine and White apply a sophisticated version of it to organizational analysis. A similar line of analysis is being developed by Homans and Blau.[1] From this perspective

---

[1] George C. Homans, *Social Behavior* (New York: Harcourt, 1961); Peter M. Blau, *Exchange and Power in Social Life* (New York: Wiley, 1964).

organizations are studied not only internally, but also in relation to one another. Levine and White focus their analysis on the relations between community health and welfare organizations where the "goods" exchanged are clients, services, and other resources. Their theory also highlights how the flow of these goods between the organizations and their environments affects the capacity of organizations to attain their respective goals. (See also the article by Litwak and Hylton.)

Taken together, these two articles raise a quite different view of organizations than the prevailing "downward" centralized one. Organizations are not treated as islands or isolated tribes but as related members of larger systems, and these systems are viewed as significantly affected by their members rather than by supra-units and their attributes. Dechert, discussing the subject from the standpoint of cybernetics, takes the opposite track. Cybernetics developed as the technology of communication advanced and man sought to control machines of his own making. The application of cybernetics to social systems, especially to organizations, is useful but incomplete. The application is useful because it provides a model for the conceptualization of communication and control links from directing centers to acting units, using concepts such as "feedback," communications, revisions of instructions, "noise" on the line, and so forth. But, in our opinion, the application is incomplete because cybernetic studies do not adequately take into account the fact that the human actors subject to control in social systems have capacities similar in principle to those of actors in control. They too have goals, emit communications, and exercise power. Hence, for both moral and practical reasons the consensus of the subjects must be won—or the goals the organization can hope to realize will be limited in scope and achieved only at a high human (and often economic) cost.

Wolin, a political scientist, raises radical questions about organizational analysis. Theories have ideological consequences; they affect the view actors have of themselves, their relations with others, and their capacity to transform others. Wolin holds that some of the prevailing organizational theories have a conservative effect, or are destructive to any kind of self-consciousness and political action. The questions raised by Wolin are subject to wide controversy,[2] but whatever position one

[2] On his side, see Alvin Gouldner, "Metaphysical Pathos and the Theory of Bureaucracy," *American Political Science Review*, **49** (1955), 496–

takes, they cannot be avoided: What effects do various organizational theories have on those who draw on them for their
perspective?

---

507. Reinhard Bendix and Lloyd H. Fisher, "The Perspectives of Elton
Mazo," *Review of Economics and Statistics,* **31** (1949), 312–319. For
the counter position see George C. Homans, "Some Corrections to the
Perspectives of Elton Mayo," 319–321; William F. Whyte, "Human Relations—a Progress Report," *Harvard Business Review,* **34** (1956), 125–
132, and Edgar H. Schein, *Organizational Psychology* (Englewood Cliffs,
N.J.: Prentice-Hall, 1965).

THE THREE TYPES
OF LEGITIMATE RULE

Translated by Hans Gerth

Max Weber

Authority means the probability that a specific command will be obeyed. Such obedience may feed on diverse motives. It may be determined by sheer interest situation, hence by the compliant actor's calculation of expediency; by mere custom, that is, the actor's inarticulate habituation to routine behavior; or by mere affect, that is, purely personal devotion of the governed. A structure of power, however, if it were to rest on such foundations alone, would be relatively unstable. As a rule both rulers and rules uphold the internalized power structure as "legitimate" by right, and usually the shattering of this belief in legitimacy has far-reaching ramifications.

There are but three clear-cut grounds on which to base the belief in legitimate authority. Given pure types each is connected with a fundamentally different sociological structure of executive staff and means of administration.

I

Legal authority rests on enactment; its pure type is best represented by bureaucracy. The basic idea is that laws can be enacted and changed at pleasure by formally correct procedure. The governing body is either elected or appointed and constitutes as a whole and in all its sections rational organizations. A heteronomous and heterocephalous sub-unit we shall call "public authorities" (Behörde). The administrative staff consists of officials appointed by the ruler; the law-abiding people are members of the body politic ("fellow citizens").

Obedience is not owed to anybody personally but to enacted rules and regulations which specify to whom and to what rule people owe obedience. The person in authority, too, obeys a rule when giving an order, namely, "the law," or "rules and regulations" which represent abstract norms. The person in command typically is the "superior" within a functionally defined "competency" or "jurisdiction," and his right to govern is legitimized by enactment. Specialization sets limits with regard to functional purpose and required skill of the office incumbent.

The typical official is a trained specialist whose terms of employment are contractual and provide a fixed salary scaled by rank of office, not by amount of work, and the right to a pension according to fixed rules of advancement. His administration represents vocational work by virtue of impersonal duties of office; ideally the administrator proceeds *sine ira et studio,* not allowing personal motive or temper to influence conduct, free of arbitrariness and unpredictability; especially he proceeds "without regard to person," following rational rules with strict formality. And where rules fail he adheres to "functional" considerations of expediency. Dutiful obedience is channeled through a hierarchy of offices which subordinates lower to higher offices and provides a regular procedure for lodging complaints. Technically, operation rests on organizational discipline.

1. Naturally this type of "legal" rule comprises not only the modern structure of state and city government but likewise the power relations in private capitalist enterprise, in public corporations and voluntary associations of all sorts, provided that an extensive and hierarchically organized staff of functionaries exists. Modern political bodies merely represent the type pre-eminently. Authority of private capitalist organization is partially heteronomous, its order is partly prescribed by the state, and it is completely heterocephalous as regards the machinery of coercion. Normally the courts and police take care of these functions. Private enterprise, however, is autonomous in its increasingly bureaucratic organization of management. The fact that, formally speaking, people enter into the power

relationship (*Herrschaftsverband*) voluntarily and are likewise "free" to give notice does not affect the nature of private enterprise as a power structure since conditions of the labor market normally subject the employees to the code of the organization. Its sociological affinity to modern state authority will be clarified further in the discussion of the economic bases of power and authority. The "contract" as constitutive for the relations of authority in capitalist enterprise makes this a pre-eminent type of "legal authority."

2. Technically, bureaucracy represents the purest type of legal authority. No structure of authority, however, is exclusively bureaucratic, to wit, is managed by contractually hired and appointed officials alone. That is quite impossible. The top positions of the body politic may be held by "monarchs" (hereditary charismatic rulers), or by popularly elected "presidents" (hence plebiscitarian charismatic rulers), or by parliamentary elected presidents. In the latter case the actual rulers are members of parliament or rather the leaders of the prevailing parliamentary parties. These leaders in turn may stand close to the type of charismatic leadership or to that of notabilities. More of this below.

Likewise the administrative staff is almost never exclusively bureaucratic but usually notables and agents of interest groups participate in administration in manifold ways. This holds most of all for the so-called self-government. It is decisive that regular administrative work is predominantly and increasingly performed by bureaucratic forces. The historical development of the modern state is identical indeed with that of modern officialdom and bureaucratic organization (cf. below), just as the development of modern capitalism is identical with the increasing bureaucratization of economic enterprise. The part played by bureaucracy becomes bigger in all structures of power.

3. Bureaucracy does not represent the only type of legal authority. Other types comprise rotating office holders or office holders chosen by lot or popularly elected officers. Parliamentary and committee administration and all sorts of collegiate and administrative bodies are included under the type if and when their competency rests on enacted rules and if the use they make of their prerogative follows the type of legal administration. During the rise of the modern state collegiate bodies have made essential contributions to the development of legal authority, especially the concept of "public authorities" (Behörde) originated with them. On the other hand, elected officialdom has played an important role in the prehistory of the modern civil service and still does so today in the democracies.

II

Traditional authority rests on the belief in the sacredness of the social order and its prerogatives as existing of yore. Patriarchal authority represents its pure type. The body politic is based on communal relationships, the man in command is the "lord" ruling over obedient "subjects." People obey the lord personally since his dignity is hallowed by tradition; obedience rests on piety. Commands are substantively bound by tradition, and the lord's inconsiderate violation of tradition would endanger the legitimacy of his personal rule, which rests merely upon the sacredness of tradition. The creation of new law opposite traditional norms is deemed impossible in principle. Actually this is done by way of "recognizing" a sentence as "valid of yore" (the *Weistum* of ancient Germanic law). Outside the norms of tradition, however, the lord's sway in a given case is restricted only by sentiments of equity, hence by quite elastic bonds. Consequently the rule of the lord divides into a strictly tradition-bound sphere and one of free favor and arbitrariness where he rules at pleasure as sympathy or antipathy move him, following purely personal considerations subject especially to the influence of "good turns."

So far as principles are followed in administration and settlement of disputes, they rest on substantive considerations of ethical equity, justice, or utilitarian expediency, not on formal considerations characteristic of the rule of law. The lord's administrative staff proceeds in the same way. It consists of personally dependent men (members of the household or domestic officials), of relatives, of personal friends (favorites), or associates bound by personal allegiance (vassals, tributary princes). The bureaucratic concept of "competency" as a functionally delimited jurisdictional sphere is absent. The scope of the "legitimate" prerogatives of the individual servant is defined from case to case at the pleasure of the lord on whom the individual servant is completely dependent as regards his employment in more important or high ranking roles. Actually this depends largely on what the servant may dare do opposite the more or less docile subjects. Personal loyalty of the faithful servant, not functional duty of office and office discipline, control the interrelationship of the administrative staff.

One may, however, observe two characteristically different forms of positional relationships, the patriarchal structure and that of estates.

1. In the purely patriarchal structure of administration the servants are completely and personally dependent on the lord; they are either purely patrimonially recruited as slaves, bondsmen-serfs, eunuchs, or extra patrimonially as favorites and plebeians from among strata lacking all rights.

Their administration is entirely heteronomous and heterocephalous, the administrators have no personal right to their office, there is neither merit selection nor status honor; the material means of administration are managed under, and on account of, the lord. Given the complete dependency of the administrative staff on the lord, there is no guarantee against the lord's arbitrariness, which in this set-up can therefore have its greatest possible sway. Sultanistic rule represents the pure type. All genuine "despotism" was of this nature. Prerogatives are considered . . . ordinary property rights of the lord.

2. In the estate system the servants are not personal servants of the lord but independent men whose social position makes them presumably socially prominent. The lord, actually or according to the legitimacy fiction, bestows office on them by privilege or concession; or they have contractually, by purchase, tenancy or lease, acquired a title to their office which cannot be arbitrarily taken away from them; hence within limits, their administration is autocephalous and autonomous. Not the lord but they dispose over the material means of administration. This represents estate rule.

The competition of the officeholders for larger bailiwicks (and income) then determines the mutual delimitation of their actual bailiwicks and takes the place of "competency." Privilege often breaks through the hierarchic structure (*de non evocando, non apellando*). The category of "discipline" is absent. Tradition, privilege, feudal or patrimonial bonds of allegiance, status honor and "good will" regulate the web of inter-relations. The power prerogatives of the lord hence are divided between the lord and the privileged administrative staff, and this division of powers among the estates brings about a high degree of stereotypy in the nature of administration.

Patriarchal rule (of the family father, sib chief, father of his people [*Landesvater*]) represents but the purest type of traditionalist rule. Any "authorities" who claim legitimacy successfully by virtue of mere habituation represent the most typical contrast, on the one hand, to the position of a contractually employed worker in business enterprise; on the other, to the way a faithful member of a religious community emotionally relates to a prophet. Actually the domestic group [*Hausverband*] is the nucleus of traditionalist power structures. The typical "officials" of the patrimonial and feudal state are domestic officers with originally purely domestic tasks (dapifer, chamberlain, marshal, cupbearer, seneschal, major domo).

The co-existence of the strictly tradition-bound and the free sphere of conduct is a common feature of all traditionalistic forms of authority. Within the free sphere, action of the lord or of his administrative staff must be bought or earned by personal relations. (This is one of the origins of the institution of fees.) It is decisive that formal law is absent and that substantive principles of administration and arbitration take its place. This likewise is a common feature of all traditionalist power structures and has far-reaching ramifications, especially for economic life.

The patriarch, like the patrimonial ruler, governs and decides according to the principles of "cadi justice": on the one hand, decisions are strictly bound by tradition; however, where these fetters give leeway, decisions follow juristically informal and irrational considerations of equity and justice from case to case, also taking individual differences into account. All codifications and laws of patrimonial rulers embody the spirit of the so-called "welfare state." A combination of social ethical with social utilitarian principles prevails, breaking through all rigor of formal law.

The sociological distinction between the patriarchal power structure and that of the estates in traditionalist rule is fundamental for all states of the pre-bureaucratic epoch. (The contrast will become fully clear only in connection with its economic aspect, that is, with the separation of the administrative staff from the material means of administration or with their appropriation by the staff.) This has been historically decisive for the question whether and what status groups existed as champions of ideas and culture values.

Patrimonial dependents (slaves, bondsmen) as administrators are to be found throughout the Mideastern orient and in Egypt down to the time of the Mamelukes; they represent the most extreme and what would seem to be the most consistent type of the purely patriarchal rule devoid of estates. Plebeian freemen as administrators stand relatively close to rational officialdom. The administration by literati can vary greatly in accordance with their nature: typical is the contrast between Brahmins and Mandarins, and both in turn stand opposite Buddhist and Christian clerics—yet their administration always approximates the estate type of power structure.

The rule of estates is most clearly represented by aristocracy, in purest form by feudalism, which puts in the place of the functional and rational duty of office the personal allegiance and the appeal to status honor of the enfeoffed.

In comparison to patriarchalism, all estate rule, based upon more or less stable appropriation of administrative power, stands closer to legal authority as the guarantees surrounding the prerogatives of the privileged assume the form of special "rights" (a result of the "division of power" among the estates). This rationale is absent in patriarchal structures, with their administration completely dependent on the lord's arbitrary sway. On the other hand, the strict discipline and the lack of rights of the administrative staff within patriarchalism is more closely related to the discipline of legal authority than is the administration of estates, which is fragmented and stereotyped through the appropriation of the means of administration by the staff. Plebeians (used as jurists) in Europe's princely service have been pacemarkers of the modern state.

III

Charismatic authority rests on the affectual and personal devotion of the follower to the lord and his gifts of grace (charisma). They comprise especially magical abilities, revelations of heroism, power of the mind and of speech. The eternally new, the non-routine, the unheard of and the emotional rapture from it are sources of personal devotion. The purest types are the rule of the prophet, the warrior hero, the great demagogue. The body politic consists in the communal relationship of a religious group or following. The person in command is typically the "leader"; he is obeyed by the "disciple." Obedience is given exclusively to the leader as a person, for the sake of his non-routine qualities, not because of enacted position or traditional dignity. Therefore obedience is forthcoming only so long as people ascribe these qualities to him, that is, so long as his charisma is proven by evidence. His rule falls if he is "forsaken" by his god[1] or deprived of his heroic strength, or if the masses lose faith in his leadership capacity. The administrative staff is selected according to charisma and personal devotion, hence selection does not consider special qualification (as in the case of the civil servant) nor rank and station (as in the case of administration by estates) nor domestic or other forms of personal dependency (as, in contrast to the above, holds for the patriarchal administrative staff). The rational concept of "competency" is lacking as is the status idea of "privilege." Decisive for the legitimation of the commissioned follower or disciple is alone the mission of the lord and his followers' personal charismatic qualification. The administration—so far as this word is adequate—lacks all orientation to rules and regulations whether enacted or traditional. Spontaneous revelation or creation, deed and example, decision from case to case, that is—at least measured against enacted orders—irrational decisions are characteristic of charismatic authority. It is not bound to tradition: "It is written but I say unto

---

[1] Translator's note: This allusion to Jesus' death and its interpretation as a downfall of his charismatic authority comes out more strongly in Weber's "Sociology of Charismatic Authority" ("Charismatismus," *Wirtschaft und Gesellschaft*, in *From Max Weber: Essays in Sociology*, H. H. Gerth and C. Wright Mills, trans. (New York: Oxford, 1946), p. 248. In his later work, *Ancient Judaism*, Hans H. Gerth and Don Martindale, trans. (New York: Free Press, 1952), p. 376, Weber reversed his position.

you" holds for the prophet. For the warrior hero the legitimate orders vanish opposite new creations by power of the sword, for the demagogue by virtue of his annunciation or suggestion of revolutionary "natural law." In the genuine form of charismatic justice and arbitration the lord or "sage" speaks the law and the (military or religious) following gives it recognition, which is obligatory, unless somebody raises a counter claim to charismatic validity. This case presents a struggle of leaders which in the last analysis can solely be decided by the confidence of the community; only one side can be right; the other side must be wrong and be obliged to make amends.

A. The type of charismatic authority has first been developed brilliantly by R. Sohm in his *Kirchenrecht* for the early Christian community without his recognizing that it represents a type of authority. The term has since been used repeatedly without recognition of its bearing.

Early history shows alongside a few beginnings of "enacted" authority, which are by no means entirely absent, the division of all power relationships under tradition and charisma. Besides the "economic chief" (sachem) of the Indiaɴs, an essentially traditional figure, stands the charismatic warrior prince (corresponding to the Germanic "duke") with his following. Hunting and war campaigns, both demanding a leader of extraordinary personal endowments, are the secular; magic is the "sacred" place of charismatic leadership. Throughout the ages charismatic authority exercised by prophets and warrior princes has held sway over men. The charismatic politician—the "demagogue"—is the product of the occidental city state. In the city state of Jerusalem he emerged only in religious costume as a prophet. The constitution of Athens, however, was completely cut out for his existence after the innovations of Pericles and Ephialtes, since without the demagogue the state machine would not function at all.

B. Charismatic authority rests on the "faith" in the prophet, on the "recognition" which the charismatic warrior hero, the hero of the street or the demagogue, finds personally, and this authority falls with him. Yet, charismatic authority does not derive from this recognition by the subjects. Rather the reverse obtains: the charismatically legitimized leader considers faith in the acknowledgement of his charisma obligatory and punishes their violation. Charismatic authority is even one of the great revolutionary forces in history, but in pure form it is thoroughly authoritarian and lordly in nature.

C. It should be understood that the term "charisma" is used here in a completely value-neutral sense. For the sociologist the manic seizure and rage of the Nordic berserk, the miracles and revelations of any pettifogging prophecy, the demagogic talents of Cleon are just as much "charisma" as the qualities of a Napoleon, Jesus, Pericles. Decisive for us is only whether they were considered charismatics and whether they were effective, that is, gained recognition. Here, "proof" is the basic prerequisite. The charismatic lord has to prove his being sent "by the grace of god" by performing miracles and being successful in securing the good life for his following or subjects. Only as long as he can do so will he be recognized. If success fails him, his authority falters. Wherever this charismatic concept of rule by the grace of god has existed, it has had decisive ramifications. The Chinese monarch's position was threatened as soon as drought, floods, military failure or other misfortune made it appear questionable whether he stood in the grace of Heaven. Public self-impeachment and penance, in cases of stubborn misfortune, removal and possible sacrifice threatened him. Certification by miracles was demanded of every prophet (the Zwickau people demanded it still from Luther).

So far as the belief in legitimacy matters for the stability of basically legal structures of authority, this stability rests mostly on mixed foundations. Traditional habituation of "prestige" (charisma) fuse with the belief in formal legality which in the last analysis is also a matter of habit. The belief in the legitimacy of authority is shattered alike through extraordinary misfortunes whether this exacts unusual demands from the subjects in the light of tradition, or destroys the prestige or violates the usual formal legal correctness. But with all structures of authority the obedience of the governed as a stable condition depends above all on the availability of an administrative staff and especially its continuous operation to maintain order and (directly or indirectly) enforce submission to the rule. The term "organization" means to guarantee the pattern of conduct which realizes the structure of authority. The solidarity of its (ideal and material) interests with those of the lord is decisive for all important loyalty of the staff to the lord. For the relation of the lord to the executive staff it generally holds that the lord is the stronger opposite the resisting individual because of the isolation of the individual staff members and his solidarity with the lord. The lord is weak opposite the staff member as a whole when they band themselves together, as has happened occasionally in the past and present. Deliberate agreement of the staff is requisite in order to frustrate the lord's action and rule through obstruction or deliberate counter action. Likewise the opposition requires an administrative staff of its own.

D. Charismatic rule represents a specifically extraordinary and purely personal relationship. In the case of continued existence, however, at least when the personal representative of charisma is eliminated, the authority structure has the tendency to routinize. This is the case when the charisma is not extinguished at once but continues to exist in some form and the authority of the lord, hence, is transferred to successors. This routinization of charisma proceeds through

1. Traditionalization of the orders. The authority of precedents takes the place of the charismatic leader's or his staff's charismatic creativity in law and administration. These precedents either protect the successors or are attributed to them.
2. The charismatic staff of disciples or followers changes into a legal or estate-like staff by taking over internal prerogatives or those appropriated by privilege (fiefs, prebends).
3. The meaning of charisma itself many undergo a change. Decisive in this is the way in which the problem of successorship is solved, which is a burning question for ideological and indeed often material reasons. This question can be solved in various ways: the merely passive tarrying for a new charismatically certified or qualified master usually gives way to an active search for a successor, especially if none readily appears and if any strong interests are vested in the continuity of the authority structure.

ORGANIZATIONS AS SYSTEMS OF COOPERATION

Chester I. Barnard

A cooperative system is a complex of physical, biological, personal, and social components which are in a specific systematic relationship by reason of the cooperation of two or more persons for at least one definite end. Such a system is evidently a subordinate unit of larger systems from one point of view; and itself embraces subsidiary systems—physical, biological,

Reprinted in part from Chester I. Barnard, *The Functions of the Executive* (Cambridge, Mass.: Harvard University Press, 1938), pp. 65–74, by permission of the author and publisher. Copyright 1938 by the President and Fellows of Harvard College.

etc.—from another point of view. One of the systems comprised within a cooperative system, the one which is implicit in the phrase "cooperation of two or more persons," is called an "organization."

The number of cooperative systems having more or less definite purposes, and of sufficient duration to enlist attention and description or identification, is very large. They may be broadly classified by character of purpose or objective into a few groups which are widely different, such as churches, political parties, fraternal associations, governments, armies, industrial enterprises, schools, families. Between organizations classified in any one of these groups there are also wide differences.

The variations in concrete cooperative situations may be assigned to four preliminary classes: (a) those that relate to aspects of the physical environment; (b) those that relate to aspects of the social environment; (c) those that relate to individuals; (d) other variables.

a. An inspection of the concrete operations of any cooperative system shows at once that the physical environment is an inseparable part of it. To the extent that there are variations in the physical aspects of cooperative systems an adjustment or adaptation of other aspects of cooperation is required. Whether such variations are significant for the general study of cooperation, or whether for most purposes the physical environment may be treated as a constant, is the first question at issue. By physical environment so far as we mean geographical aspects—that is, mere location, topography, climate, etc.—it will readily be accepted that it may well be excluded from consideration for nearly all general purposes.[1] That part of the environment, however, which is regarded as the property of an organization is of different status; and that part which consists of structures, improvements, tools, machines, etc., pertains still more specifically to the organization which owns or works with them. All aspects of the physical environment are then regarded or most conveniently treated as the elements of other, physical and technical, systems between which and organizations the significant relationships may be investigated as may be required for the purpose in hand.

b. It is in most cases evident that the social elements are an important aspect likewise of a concrete cooperative situation. The social factors may be regarded as entering into the situation by several routes: (1) through being components of the individual whose activities are included in the system; (2) through their effect upon individuals, whose activities are not included, but who are hostile to the system of cooperation or whose activities potentially are factors in any way; (3) through

---

[1] In special cases, however, this is not true; for example, where two manufacturing operations otherwise alike are conducted in two different climates. Climate may then be the most significant variable.

contact of the system (either cooperative or otherwise) with other collateral cooperative systems and especially with (4) superior systems; and (5) as inherent in cooperation itself. Indirectly, social factors, of course, are also involved in the changes of the physical environment, particularly as effected by prior or other existing cooperative systems. . . .

We shall exclude all of the social environment as such from the definition of organization.

c. The exclusion of the physical and social environments from the definition of organization for general purposes will on the whole conform to ordinary usage and common sense, and will be accepted without great difficulty as a method of approach to a scientifically useful concept of organization. The question of persons, however, offers greater difficulty and doubt. Though with much vagueness and many exceptions, some of which have been already indicated, the most usual conception of an organization is that of a *group* of persons, some or all of whose activities are coordinated. The concept of the group as the dominant characteristic of cooperative systems is certainly also frequent in the literature of sociology, anthropology, and social psychology, although, as shown by Parsons,[2] systems in which at least the emphasis is upon *action* have been fundamental in the conceptual schemes of Durkheim, Pareto, and Weber.

As a working concept it may be made clear that "group" contains so many variables as to restrict the number and the firmness of any generalizations. It is unmanageable without the use of some more restricted concept. Hence, to the present writer, discussions of group cooperation often give the impression of vagueness, confusion, and implicit contradiction. The reason for this is apparent from the fact that both group and person require explicit definition. A group is evidently a number of persons plus some interrelationships or interactions to be determined. When the nature of these interrelations or interactions is described or defined, it at once appears that "person" is a highly variable thing, not merely in the sense that persons differ in many respects, but more especially because the extent and character of their participation in groups also widely varies. . . .

Now if, with reference to a particular system of cooperative action to which a person contributes, one examines all the acts of any person for even one day it will be at once evident in nearly all cases that many of these acts are outside *any* system of cooperation; and that many of the remainder are distributable among at least several such cooperative systems. The connection of any "member" with an organization is necessarily intermittent, and there is frequent substitution of persons. Again it is

[2] Talcott Parsons, *The Structure of Social Action* (New York: McGraw-Hill, 1937).

almost impossible to discover a person who does not "belong"—taking into account the intermittent character of his participation—at the same time to many organizations. . . .

It is evident from the foregoing that if persons are to be included within the concept "organization," its general significance will be quite limited. The bases or terms' upon which persons are included will be highly variable—so much so that even within very restricted fields, such as a particular industry, "organizations" will mean a wide variety of entities. Hence, here again as when we included a part of the physical environment within the definition, the inclusion of persons may be most useful in particular instances, but of limited value for general purposes.

It nevertheless remains to consider whether it would actually be useful to adopt a definition from which persons as well as physical and social environments are excluded as components. If this is done, an organization is defined as *a system of consciously coordinated personal activities or forces*. It is apparent that all the variations found in concrete cooperative systems that are due to physical and social environments, and those that are due to persons or to the bases upon which persons contribute to such systems, are by this definition relegated to the position of external facts and factors,[3] and that the organization as then isolated is an aspect of cooperative systems which is common to all of them.

Organization will then mean a similar thing, whether applied to a military, a religious, an academic, a manufacturing, or a fraternal cooperation, though the physical environment, the social environment, the number and kinds of persons, and the bases of their relation to the organization will be widely different. These aspects of cooperation then become external to organization as defined, though components of the cooperative system as a whole. Moreover, the definition is similarly applicable to settings radically different from those now obtaining, for example, to cooperation under feudal conditions. Such a definition will be of restricted usefulness with reference to any particular cooperative situation, being only one element of such a situation, except as by its adoption we are enabled to arrive at general principles which may be usefully applied in the understanding of specific situations.

It is the central hypothesis of this book that the most useful concept for the analysis of experience of cooperative systems is embodied in the definition of a formal organization as a *system of consciously coordinated*

---

[3] That is, external to the organization but not external to the related cooperative system. It is to be borne in mind that we are dealing with *two* systems: (1) an inclusive cooperative system, the components of which are persons, physical systems, social systems, and organizations; and (2) organizations, which are parts of cooperative systems and consist entirely of coordinated human activities.

activities or forces of two or more persons. In any concrete situation in which there is cooperation, several different systems will be components. Some of these will be physical, some biological, some psychological, etc., but the element common to all which binds all these other systems into the total concrete cooperative situation is that of organization as defined. If this hypothesis proves satisfactory it will be because (1) an organization, as defined, is a concept valid through a wide range of concrete situations with relatively few variables, which can be effectively investigated; and (2) the relations between this conceptual scheme and other systems can be effectively and usefully formulated. The final test of this conceptual scheme is whether its use will make possible a more effective conscious promotion and manipulation of cooperation among men; that is, whether in practice it can increase the predictive capacity of competent men in this field. It is the assumption upon which this essay is developed that such a concept is implicit in the behavior of leaders and administrators, explaining uniformities observed in their conduct in widely different cooperative enterprises, and that its explicit formulation and development will permit a useful translation of experience in different fields into common terms.

FOUNDATIONS OF THE THEORY OF ORGANIZATION

Philip Selznick

Trades unions, governments, business corporations, political parties, and the like are formal structures in the sense that they represent rationally ordered instruments for the achievement of stated goals. "Organization," we are told, "is the arrangement of personnel for facilitating the accomplishment of some agreed purpose through the allocation of functions and

Reprinted in part from *American Sociological Review,* **13** (1948), 25–35, by permission of the author and the publisher, The American Sociological Association.

responsibilities."[1] Or, defined more generally, formal organization is "a system of consciously coordinated activities or forces of two or more persons."[2] Viewed in this light, formal organization is the structural expression of rational action. The mobilization of technical and managerial skills requires a pattern of coordination, a systematic ordering of positions and duties which defines a chain of command and makes possible the administrative integration of specialized functions. In this context *delegation* is the primordial organizational act, a precarious venture which requires the continuous elaboration of formal mechanisms of coordination and control. The security of all participants, and of the system as a whole, generates a persistent pressure for the institutionalization of relationships, which are thus removed from the uncertainties of individual fealty or sentiment. Moreover, it is necessary for the relations within the structure to be determined in such a way that individuals will be interchangeable and the organization will thus be free of dependence upon personal qualities.[3] In this way, the formal structure becomes subject to calculable manipulation, an instrument of rational action.

But as we inspect these formal structures we begin to see that they never succeed in conquering the non-rational dimensions of organizational behavior. The latter remain at once indispensable to the continued existence of the system of coordination and at the same time the source of friction, dilemma, doubt, and ruin. This fundamental paradox arises from the fact that rational action systems are inescapably imbedded in an institutional matrix, in two significant senses: (1) the action system—or the formal structure of delegation and control which is its organizational expression—is itself only an aspect of a concrete social structure made up of individuals who may interact as *wholes,* not simply in terms of their formal roles within the system; (2) the formal system, and the social structure within which it finds concrete existence, are alike subject to the pressure of an institutional environment to which some over-all adjustment must be made. The formal administrative design can never adequately or fully reflect the concrete organization to which it refers, for the obvious reason that no abstract plan or pattern can—or may, if it is to be useful—exhaustively describe an empirical totality. At the same time, that which is not included in the abstract design (as reflected, for ex-

---

[1] John M. Gaus, "A Theory of Organization in Public Administration," in *The Frontiers of Public Administration* (Chicago: University of Chicago Press, 1936), p. 66.
[2] Chester I. Barnard, *The Functions of the Executive* (Cambridge, Mass.: Harvard University Press, 1938), p. 73.
[3] Cf. Talcott Parsons' generalization (after Max Weber) of the "law of the increasing rationality of action systems," in *The Structure of Social Action* (New York: McGraw-Hill, 1937), p. 752.

ample, in a staff-and-line organization chart) is vitally relevant to the maintenance and development of the formal system itself.

Organization may be viewed from two standpoints which are analytically distinct but which are empirically united in a context of reciprocal consequences. On the one hand, any concrete organizational system is an *economy;* at the same time, it is an *adaptive social structure.* Considered as an economy, organization is a system of relationships which define the availability of scarce resources and which may be manipulated in terms of efficiency and effectiveness. It is the economic aspect of organization which commands the attention of management technicians and, for the most part, students of public as well as private administration.[4] Such problems as the span of executive control, the role of staff or auxiliary agencies, the relation of headquarters to field offices, and the relative merits of single or multiple executive boards are typical concerns of the science of administration. The coordinative scalar, and functional principles, as elements of the theory of organization, are products of the attempt to explicate the most general features of organization as a "technical problem" or, in our terms, as an economy.

Organization as an economy is, however, necessarily conditioned by the organic states of the concrete structure, outside of the systematics of delegation and control. This becomes especially evident as the attention of leadership is directed toward such problems as the legitimacy of authority and the dynamics of persuasion. It is recognized implicitly in action and explicitly in the work of a number of students that the possibility of manipulating the system of coordination depends on the extent to which that system is operating within an environment of effective inducement to individual participants and of conditions in which the stability of authority is assured. This is in a sense the fundamental thesis of Barnard's remarkable study, *The Functions of the Executive.* It is also the underlying hypothesis which makes it possible for Urwick to suggest that "proper" or formal channels in fact function to "confirm and record" decisions arrived at by more personal means.[5] We meet it again in the concept of administration as a process of education, in which the winning of consent and support is conceived to be a basic function of leadership.[6] In short,

[4] See Luther Gulick and Lydall Urwick (editors), *Papers on the Science of Administration* (New York: Institute of Public Administration, Columbia University, 1937); Lydall Urwick, *The Elements of Administration* (New York: Harper & Row, 1943); James D. Mooney and Alan C. Reiley, *The Principles of Organization* (New York: Harper & Row, 1939); H. S. Dennison, *Organization Engineering* (New York: McGraw-Hill, 1931).

[5] Urwick, *The Elements of Administration, op. cit.*, p. 47.

[6] See Gaus, *op. cit.* Studies of the problem of morale are instances of the same orientation, having received considerable impetus in recent years from the work of the Harvard Business School group.

it is recognized that control and consent cannot be divorced even within formally authoritarian structures.

The indivisibility of control and consent makes it necessary to view formal organizations as *cooperative* systems, widening the frame of reference of those concerned with the manipulation of organizational resources. At the point of action, of executive decision, the economic aspect of organization provides inadequate tools for control over the concrete structure. This idea may be readily grasped if attention is directed to the role of the individual within the organizational economy. From the standpoint of organization as a formal system, persons are viewed functionally, in respect to their *roles,* as participants in assigned segments of the cooperative system. But in fact individuals have a propensity to resist depersonalization, to spill over the boundaries of their segmentary roles, to participate as *wholes.* The formal systems (at an extreme, the disposition of "rifles" at a military perimeter) cannot take account of the deviations thus introduced, and consequently break down as instruments of control when relied upon alone. The whole individual raises new problems for the organization, partly because of the needs of his own personality, partly because he brings with him a set of established habits as well, perhaps, as commitments to special groups outside of the organization.

Unfortunately for the adequacy of formal systems of coordination, the needs of individuals do not permit a single-minded attention to the stated goals of the system within which they have been assigned. The hazard inherent in the act of delegation derives essentially from this fact. Delegation is an organizational act, having to do with formal assignments of functions and powers. Theoretically, these assignments are made to roles or official positions, not to individuals as such. In fact, however, delegation necessarily involves concrete individuals who have interests and goals which do not always coincide with the goals of the formal system. As a consequence, individual personalities may offer resistance to the demands made upon them by the official conditions of delegation. These resistances are not accounted for within the categories of coordination and delegation, so that when they occur they must be considered as unpredictable and accidental. Observations of this type of situation within formal structures are sufficiently commonplace. A familiar example is that of delegation to a subordinate who is also required to train his own replacement. The subordinate may resist this demand in order to maintain unique access to the "mysteries" of the job, and thus insure his indispensability to the organization.

In large organizations, deviations from the formal system tend to become institutionalized, so that "unwritten laws" and informal associations are established. Institutionalization removes such deviations from the realm of personality differences, transforming them into a persistent structural aspect of formal organizations.[7] These institutionalized rules and modes of informal cooperation are normally attempts by participants in the formal organization to control the group relations which form the environment of organizational decisions. The informal patterns (such as cliques) arise spontaneously, are based on personal relationships, and are usually directed to the control of some specific situation. They may be generated anywhere within a hierarchy, often with deleterious consequences for the formal goals of the organization, but they may also function to widen the available resources of executive control and thus contribute to rather than hinder the achievement of the stated objectives of the organization. The deviations tend to force a shift away from the purely formal system as the effective determinant of behavior to (1) a condition in which informal patterns buttress the formal, as through the manipulation of sentiment within the organization in favor of established authority; or (2) a condition wherein the informal controls effect a consistent modification of formal goals, as in the case of some bureaucratic patterns.[8] This trend will eventually result in the formalization of erstwhile informal activities, with the cycle of deviation and transformation beginning again on a new level.

The relevance of informal structures to organizational analysis underlines the significance of conceiving of formal organizations as cooperative systems. When the totality of interacting groups and individuals becomes the object of inquiry, the latter is not restricted by formal, legal, or procedural dimensions. The *state of the system* emerges as a significant point of analysis, as when an internal situation charged with conflict qualifies and informs actions ostensibly determined by formal relations and objectives. A proper understanding of the organizational process must make it possible to interpret changes in the formal system—new appointments or rules or reorganizations—in their relation to the informal and unavowed ties of friendship, class loyalty, power cliques, or external commitment. This is what it means "to know the score."

The fact that the involvement of individuals as whole personalities tends to limit the adequacy of formal systems of coordination does not mean that organizational characteristics are those of individuals. The

---

[7] The creation of informal structures within various types of organizations has received explicit recognition in recent years. See F. J. Roethlisberger and W. J. Dickson, *Management and the Worker* (Cambridge, Mass.: Harvard University Press, 1941), p. 524; also Barnard, *op. cit.,* c. ix; and Wilbert E. Moore, *Industrial Relations and the Social Order* (New York: Macmillan, 1946), chap. xv.

[8] For an analysis of the latter in these terms, see Philip Selznick, "An Approach to a Theory of Bureaucracy," *American Sociological Review,* Vol. VIII, No. 1 (February, 1943).

organic, emergent character of the formal organization considered as a cooperative system must be recognized. This means that the *organization* reaches decisions, takes action, and makes adjustments. Such a view raises the question of the relation between organizations and persons. The significance of theoretical emphasis upon the cooperative *system* as such is derived from the insight that certain actions and consequences are enjoined independently of the personality of the individuals involved. Thus, if reference is made to the "organization-paradox"—the tension created by the inhibitory consequences of certain types of informal structures within organizations—this does not mean that individuals themselves are in quandaries. It is the nature of the interacting consequences of divergent interests within the organization which creates the condition, a result which may obtain independently of the consciousness or the qualities of the individual participants. Similarly, it seems useful to insist that there are qualities and needs of leader*ship,* having to do with position and role, which are persistent despite variations in the character or personality of individual leaders themselves.

Rational action systems are characteristic of both individuals and organizations. The conscious attempt to mobilize available internal resources (e.g., self-discipline) for the achievement of a stated goal—referred to here as an economy or a formal system—is one aspect of individual psychology. But the personality considered as a dynamic system of interacting wishes, compulsions, and restraints defines a system which is at once essential and yet potentially deleterious to what may be thought of as the "economy of learning" or to individual rational action. At the same time, the individual personality is an adaptive structure, and this, too, requires a broader frame of reference for analysis than the categories of rationality. On a different level, although analogously, we have pointed to the need to consider organizations as cooperative systems and adaptive structures in order to explain the context of and deviations from the formal systems of delegation and coordination.

To recognize the sociological relevance of formal structures is not, however, to have constructed a theory of organization. It is important to set the framework of analysis, and much is accomplished along this line when, for example, the nature of authority in formal organizations is reinterpreted to emphasize the factors of cohesion and persuasion as against legal or coercive sources.[9] This redefinition is logically the same as that which introduced the conception of the self as social. The latter helps make possible, but does not of itself fulfill, the requirements for a dynamic theory of personality. In the same way, the definition of authority as

[9] Robert Michels, "Authority," *Encyclopedia of the Social Sciences* (New York: Macmillan, 1931), pp. 319 ff.; also Barnard, *op. cit.,* c. xii.

conditioned by sociological factors of sentiment and cohesion—or more generally the definition of formal organizations as cooperative systems— only sets the stage, as an initial requirement, for the formulation of a theory of organization.

STRUCTURAL-FUNCTIONAL ANALYSIS

Cooperative systems are constituted of individuals interacting as wholes in relation to a formal system of coordination. The concrete structure is therefore a resultant of the reciprocal influences of the formal and informal aspects of organization. Furthermore, this structure is itself a totality, an adaptive "organism" reacting to influences upon it from an external environment. These considerations help to define the objects of inquiry; but to progress to a system of predicates *about* these objects it is necessary to set forth an analytical method which seems to be fruitful and significant. The method must have a relevance to empirical materials, which is to say, it must be more specific in its reference than discussions of the logic or methodology of social science.

The organon which may be suggested as peculiarly helpful in the analysis of adaptive structures has been referred to as "structural-functional analysis."[10] This method may be characterized in a sentence: *Structural-functional analysis relates contemporary and variable behavior to a presumptively stable system of needs and mechanisms.* This means that a given empirical system is deemed to have basic needs, essentially related to self-maintenance; the system develops repetitive means of self-defense; and day-to-day activity is interpreted in terms of the function served by that activity for the maintenance and defense of the system. Put thus generally, the approach is applicable on any level in which the determinate "states" of empirically isolable systems undergo self-impelled and repetitive transformations when impinged upon by external conditions. This self-impulsion suggests the relevance of the term "dynamic," which is often used in referring to physiological, psychological, or social systems to which this type of analysis has been applied.[11]

---

[10] For a presentation of this approach having a more general reference than the study of formal organizations, see Talcott Parsons, "The Present Position and Prospects of Systematic Theory in Sociology," in Georges Gurvitch and Wilbert E. Moore (eds.), *Twentieth Century Sociology* (New York: Philosophical Library, 1945).

[11] "Structure" refers to both the relationships within the system (formal plus informal patterns in organization) and the set of needs and modes of satisfaction which characterize the given type of empirical system. As the utilization of this type of analysis proceeds, the concept of "need" will require further clarification. In particular, the imputation of a "stable set of needs" to organizational systems must not function as a new instinct theory. At the same time, we cannot avoid using these inductions as to

It is a postulate of the structural-functional approach that the basic need of all empirical systems is the maintenance of the integrity and continuity of the system itself. Of course, such a postulate is primarily useful in directing attention to a set of "derived imperatives" or needs which are sufficiently concrete to characterize the system at hand.[12] It is perhaps rash to attempt a catalogue of these imperatives for formal organizations, but some suggestive formulation is needed in the interests of setting forth the type of analysis under discussion. In formal organizations, the "maintenance of the system" as a generic need may be specified in terms of the following imperatives:

1. The Security of the Organization as a Whole in Relation to Social Forces in Its Environment

This imperative requires continuous attention to the possibilities of encroachment and to the forestalling of threatened aggressions or deleterious (though perhaps unintended) consequences from the actions of others.

2. The Stability of the Lines of Authority and Communication

One of the persistent reference-points of administrative decision is the weighing of consequences for the continued capacity of leadership to control and to have access to the personnel or ranks.

3. The Stability of Informal Relations within the Organization

Ties of sentiment and self-interest are evolved as unacknowledged but effective mechanisms of adjustment of individuals and sub-groups to the conditions of life within the organization. These ties represent a cementing of relationships which sustains the formal authority in day-to-day operations and widens opportunities for effective communication.[13] Conse-

---

generic needs, for they help us to stake out our area of inquiry. The author is indebted to Robert K. Merton who has, in correspondence, raised some important objections to the use of the term "need" in this context.

[12] For "derived imperative" see Bronislaw Malinowski, *The Dynamics of Culture Change* (New Haven, Conn.: Yale University Press, 1945), pp. 44 ff. For the use of "need" in place of "motive" see the same author's *A Scientific Theory of Culture* (Chapel Hill, N.C.: University of North Carolina Press, 1944), pp. 89–90.

[13] They may also *destroy* those relationships, as noted above, the need remains, generating one of the persistent dilemmas of leadership.

quently, attempts to "upset" the informal structure, either frontally or as an indirect consequence of formal reorganization, will normally be met with considerable resistance.

4. The Continuity of Policy and of the Sources of Its Determination

For each level within the organization, and for the organization as a whole, it is necessary that there be a sense that action taken in the light of a given policy will not be placed in continuous jeopardy. Arbitrary or unpredictable changes in policy undermine the significance of (and therefore the attention to) day-to-day action by injecting a note of capriciousness. At the same time, the organization will seek stable roots (or firm statutory authority or popular mandate) so that a sense of the permanency and legitimacy of its acts will be achieved.

5. A Homogeneity of Outlook with Respect to the Meaning and Role of the Organization

The minimization of disaffection requires a unity derived from a common understanding of what the character of the organization is meant to be. When this homogeneity breaks down, as in situations of internal conflict over basic issues, the continued existence of the organization is endangered. On the other hand, one of the signs of "healthy" organization is the ability to effectively orient new members and readily slough off those who cannot be adapted to the established outlook.

This catalogue of needs cannot be thought of as final, but it approximates the stable system generally characteristic of formal organizations. These imperatives are derived, in the sense that they represent the conditions for survival or self-maintenance of cooperative systems of organized action. An inspection of these needs suggests that organizational survival is intimately connected with the struggle for relative prestige, both for the organization and for elements and individuals within it. It may therefore be useful to refer to a *prestige-survival* motif in organizational behavior as a short-hand way of relating behavior to needs, especially when the exact nature of the needs remains in doubt. However, it must be emphasized that prestige-survival in organizations does not derive simply from like motives in individuals. Loyalty and self-sacrifice may be individual expressions of organizational or group egotism and self-consciousness.

The concept of organizational need directs analysis to the *internal relevance* of organizational behavior. This is especially pertinent with respect to discretionary action undertaken by agents manifestly in pursuit of formal goals. The question then becomes one of relating the specific act of discretion to some presumptively stable organizational need. In other words, it is not simply action plainly oriented internally (such as in-service training) but also action presumably oriented externally which must be inspected for its relevance to internal conditions. This is of prime importance for the understanding of bureaucratic behavior, for it is of the essence of the latter that action formally undertaken for substantive goals be weighed and transformed in terms of its consequences for the position of the officialdom.

Formal organizations as cooperative systems on the one hand, and individual personalities on the other, involve structural-functional homologies, a point which may help to clarify the nature of this type of analysis. If we say that the individual has a stable set of needs, most generally the need for maintaining and defending the integrity of his personality or ego; that here are recognizable certain repetitive mechanisms which are utilized by the ego in its defense (rationalization, projection, regression, etc.); and that overt and variable behavior may be interpreted in terms of its relation to these needs and mechanisms—on the basis of this logic we may discern the typical pattern of structural-functional analysis as set forth above. In this sense, it is possible to speak of a "Freudian model" for organizational analysis. This does not mean that the substantive insights of individual psychology may be applied to organizations, as in vulgar extrapolations from the individual ego to whole nations or (by a no less vulgar inversion) from strikes to frustrated workers. It is the *logic,* the *type* of analysis which is pertinent.

This homology is also instructive in relation to the applicability of generalizations to concrete cases. The dynamic theory of personality states a set of possible predicates about the ego and its mechanisms of defense, which inform us concerning the propensities of individual personalities under certain general circumstances. But these predicates provide only tools for the analysis of particular individuals, and each concrete case must be examined to tell which operate and in what degree. They are not primarily organs of prediction. In the same way, the predicates within the theory of organization will provide tools for the analysis of particular cases. Each organization, like each personality, represents a resultant of complex forces, an empirical entity which no single relation or no simple formula can explain. The problem of analysis becomes that of selecting among the possible predicates set forth in the theory of organization those which illuminate our understanding of the materials at hand.

The setting of structural-functional analysis as applied to organizations requires some qualification, however. Let us entertain the suggestion that the interesting problem in social science is not so much why men act the way they do as why men in certain circumstances *must* act the way they do. This emphasis upon constraint, if accepted, releases us from an ubiquitous attention to behavior in general, and especially from any undue fixation upon statistics. On the other hand, it has what would seem to be the salutary consequence of focusing inquiry upon certain necessary relationships of the type "if . . . then," for example: If the cultural level of the rank and file members of a formally democratic organization is below that necessary for participation in the formulation of policy, then there will be pressure upon the leaders to use the tools of demagogy.

Is such a statement universal in its applicability? Surely not in the sense that one can predict without remainder the nature of all or even most political groups in a democracy. Concrete behavior is a resultant, a complex vector, shaped by the operation of a number of such general constraints. But there is a test of general applicability: it is that of noting whether the relation made explicit must be *taken into account* in action. This criterion represents an empirical test of the significance of social science generalizations. If a theory is significant it will state a relation which will either (1) be taken into account as an element of achieving control; or (2) be ignored only at the risk of losing control and will evidence itself in a ramification of objective or unintended consequences.[14] It is a corollary of this principle of significance that investigation must search out the underlying factors in organizational action, which requires a kind of intensive analysis of the same order as psychoanalytic probing.

A frame of reference which invites attention to the constraints upon behavior will tend to highlight tensions and dilemmas, the characteristic paradoxes generated in the course of action. The dilemma may be said to be the handmaiden of structural-functional analysis, for it introduces the concept of *commitment* or *involvement* as fundamental to organizational analysis. A dilemma in human behavior is represented by an inescapable commitment which cannot be reconciled with the needs of the organism or the social system. There are many spurious dilemmas which have to do with verbal contradictions, but inherent dilemmas to which we refer are of a more profound sort, for they reflect the basic nature of the

---

[14] See R. M. MacIver's discussion of the "dynamic assessment" which "brings the external world selectively into the subjective realm, conferring on it subjective significance for the ends of action." *Social Causation* (Boston: Ginn, 1942), chaps. 11, 12. The analysis of this assessment within the context of organized action yields the implicit knowledge which guides the choice among alternatives. See also Robert K. Merton, "The Unanticipated Consequences of Purposive Social Action," *American Sociological Review*, I, 6 (December, 1936).

empirical system in question. An economic order committed to profit as its sustaining incentive may, in Marxist terms, sow the seed of its own destruction. Again, the anguish of man, torn between finitude and pride, is not a matter of arbitrary and replaceable assumptions but is a reflection of the psychological needs of the human organism, and is concretized in his commitment to the institutions which command his life; he is in the world and of it, inescapably involved in its goals and demands; at the same time, the needs of the spirit are compelling, proposing modes of salvation which have continuously disquieting consequences for worldly involvements. In still another context, the need of the human organism for affection and response necessitates a commitment to elements of the culture which can provide them; but the rule of the super-ego is uncertain since it cannot be completely reconciled with the need for libidinal satisfactions.

Applying this principle to organizations, we may note that there is a general source of tension observable in the split between "the motion and the act." Plans and programs reflect the freedom of technical or ideal choice, but organized action cannot escape involvement, a commitment to personnel or institutions or procedures which effectively qualifies the initial plan. *Der Mensch denkt, Gott lenkt.* In organized action, this ultimate wisdom finds a temporal meaning in the recalcitrance of the tools of action. We are inescapably committed to the mediation of human structures which are at once indispensable to our goals and at the same time stand between them and ourselves. The selection of agents generates immediately a bifurcation of interest, expressed in new centers of need and power, placing effective constraints upon the arena of action, and resulting in tensions which are never completely resolved. This is part of what it means to say that there is a "logic" of action which impels us forward from one undesired position to another. Commitment to dynamic, self-activating tools is of the nature of organized action; at the same time, the need for continuity of authority, policy, and character is pressing, and requires an unceasing effort to master the instruments generated in the course of action. This generic tension is specified within the terms of each cooperative system. But for all we find a persistent relationship between *need* and *commitment* in which the latter not only qualifies the former but unites with it to produce a continuous state of tension. In this way, the notion of constraint (as reflected in tension or paradox) at once widens and more closely specifies the frame of reference for organizational analysis.

For Malinowski, the core of functionalism was contained in the view that a cultural fact must be analyzed in its setting. Moreover, he apparently conceived of his method as pertinent to the analysis of all aspects of cultural systems. But there is a more specific problem, one involving a principle of selection which serves to guide inquiry along significant lines. Freud conceived of the human organism as an adaptive structure, but he was not concerned with all human needs, nor with all phases of adaptation. For his system, he selected those needs whose expression is blocked in some way, so that such terms as repression, inhibition, and frustration became crucial. All conduct may be thought of as derived from need, and all adjustment represents the reduction of need. But not all needs are relevant to the systematics of dynamic psychology; and it is not adjustment as such but reaction to frustration which generates the characteristic modes of defensive behavior.

Organizational analysis, too, must find its selective principle; otherwise the indiscriminate attempts to relate activity functionally to needs will produce little in the way of significant theory. Such a principle might read as follows: *Our frame of reference is to select out those needs which cannot be fulfilled within approved avenues of expression and thus must have recourse to such adaptive mechanisms as ideology and to the manipulation of formal processes and structures in terms of informal goals.* This formulation has many difficulties, and is not presented as conclusive, but it suggests the kind of principle which is likely to separate the quick and the dead, the meaningful and the trite, in the study of cooperative systems in organized action.[15]

The frame of reference outlined here for the theory of organization may now be identified as involving the following major ideas: (1) the concept of organizations as cooperative systems, adaptive social structures, made up of interacting individuals, sub-groups, and informal plus formal relationships; (2) structural-functional analysis, which relates variable aspects of organization (such as goals) to stable needs and self-defensive mechanisms; (3) the concept of recalcitrance as a quality of the tools of social action, involving a break in the continuum of adjustment and defining an environment of constraint, commitment, and tension. This frame of reference is suggested as providing a specifiable *area of relations* within which predicates in the theory of organization will be sought, and at the same time setting forth principles of selection and relevance in our approach to the data of organization.

It will be noted that we have set forth this frame of reference within the over-all context of social action. The significance of events may be defined by their place and operational role in a means-end scheme. If functional analysis searches out the elements important for the maintenance

[15] This is not meant to deprecate the study of organizations as *economies* or formal systems. The latter represent an independent level, abstracted from organizational structures as cooperative or adaptive systems ("organisms").

of a given structure, and that structure is one of the materials to be manipulated in action, then that which is functional in respect to the structure is also functional in respect to the action system. This provides a ground for the significance of functionally derived theories. At the same time, relevance to control in action is the empirical test of their applicability or truth.

SUGGESTIONS FOR A SOCIOLOGICAL APPROACH TO THEORY OF ORGANIZATIONS

Talcott Parsons

For the purposes of this article the term "organization" will be used to refer to a broad type of collectivity which has assumed a particularly important place in modern industrial societies—the type to which the term "bureaucracy" is most often applied. Familiar examples are the governmental bureau or department, the business firm (especially above a certain size), the university, and the hospital. It is by now almost a commonplace that there are features common to all these types of organization which cut across the ordinary distinctions between the social science disciplines. Something is lost if study of the firm is left only to economists, of governmental organizations to political scientists, and of schools and universities to "educationists."[1]

This is the first article of a two-part series, reprinted in part from *Administrative Science Quarterly*, 1 (1956), 63–85, by permission of the author and the publisher, Cornell University.

[1] There is already a considerable literature on organization which cuts across disciplinary lines. It is not the intention of this paper to attempt to review it. Three writers have been particularly important in stimulating the author's thinking in the field: Max Weber, Chester I. Barnard, and Herbert Simon. See particularly, Weber, *Theory of Social and Economic Organization* (New York, 1947), ch. iii; Barnard,

The study of organization in the present sense is thus only part of the study of social structure as that term is generally used by sociologists (or of "social organization" as ordinarily used by social anthropologists). A family is only partly an organization; most other kinship groups are even less so. The same is certainly true of local communities, regional subsocieties, and of a society as a whole conceived, for example, as a nation. On other levels, informal work groups, cliques of friends, and so on, are not in this technical sense organizations.

THE CONCEPT OF ORGANIZATION

As a formal analytical point of reference, *primacy of orientation to the attainment of a specific goal* is used as the defining characteristic of an organization which distinguishes it from other types of social systems. This criterion has implications for both the external relations and the internal structure of the system referred to here as an organization.

The attainment of a goal is defined as a *relation* between a system (in this case a social system) and the relevant parts of the external situation in which it acts or operates. This relation can be conceived as the maximization, relative to the relevant conditions such as costs and obstacles, of some category of *output* of the system to objects or systems in the external situation. These considerations yield a further important criterion of an organization. An organization is a system which, as the attainment of its goal, "produces" an identifiable something which can be utilized in some way by another system; that is, the output of the organization is, for some other system, an input. In the case of an organization with economic primacy, this output may be a class of goods or services which are either consumable or serve as instruments for a further phase of the production process by other organizations. In the case of a government agency the output may be a class of regulatory decisions; in that of an educational organization it may be a certain type of "trained capacity" on the part of the students who have been subjected to its influence. In any of these cases there must be a set of consequences of the processes which go on within the organization, which make a difference to the functioning of some other subsystem of the society; that is, without the production of certain goods the consuming unit must behave differently, i.e., suffer a "deprivation."

The availability, to the unit succeeding the organization in the series, of the organization's output must be subject to some sort of terms, the

---

The Functions of the Executive (Cambridge, Mass., 1938); Simon, *Administrative Behavior: A Study of Decision Making Processes in Administrative Organization* (New York, 1951).

settlement of which is analyzable in the general framework of the ideas of contract or exchange. Thus in the familiar case the economic producer "sells" his product for a money price which in turn serves as a medium for procuring the factors of production, most directly labor services, necessary for further stages of the productive process. It is thus assumed that in the case of all organizations there is something analogous to a "market" for the output which constitutes the attainment of its goal (what Chester I. Barnard calls "organization purpose"); and that directly, and perhaps also indirectly, there is some kind of exchange of this for entities which (as inputs into it) are important means for the organization to carry out its function in the larger system. The exchange of output for input at the boundary defined by the attainment of the goal of an organization need not be the only important boundary-exchange of the organization as a system. It is, however, the one most directly involved in defining the primary characteristics of the organization. Others will be discussed later.

The existence of organizations as the concept is here set forth is a consequence of the division of labor in society. Where both the "production" of specialized outputs and their consumption or ultimate utilization occur within the same structural unit, there is no need for the differentiation of specialized organizations. Primitive societies in so far as their units are "self-sufficient" in both economic and other senses generally do not have clear-cut differentiated organizations in the present sense.

In its internal reference, the primacy of goal-attainment among the functions of a social system gives priority to those processes most directly involved with the success or failure of goal-oriented endeavors. This means essentially the decision-making process, which controls the utilization of the resources of the system as a whole in the interest of the goal, and the processes by which those responsible for such decisions can count on the mobilization of these resources in the interest of a goal. These mechanisms of mobilization constitute what we ordinarily think of as the development of power in a political sense.

What from the point of view of the organization in question is its specified goal is, from the point of view of the larger system of which it is a differentiated part or subsystem, a specialized or differentiated function. This relationship is the primary link between an organization and the larger system of which it is a part, and provides a basis for the classification of types of organization. However, it cannot be the only important link.

This article will attempt to analyze both this link and the other principal ones, using as a point of departure the treatment of the organization as a social system. First, it will be treated as a system which is characterized by all the properties which are essential to any social system. Secondly, it will be treated as a functionally differentiated sub-system of a larger social system. Hence it will be the other subsystems of the larger one which constitute the situation or environment in which the organization operates. An organization, then, will have to be analyzed as the special type of social system organized about the primacy of interest in the attainment of a particular type of system goal. Certain of its special features will derive from goal-primacy in general and others from the primacy of the particular type of goal. Finally, the characteristics of the organization will be defined by the kind of situation in which it has to operate, which will consist of the relations obtaining between it and the other specialized subsystems of the larger system of which it is a part. The latter can for most purposes be assumed to be a society.

THE STRUCTURE OF ORGANIZATIONS

Like any social system, an organization is conceived as having a describable structure. This can be described and analyzed from two points of view, both of which are essential to completeness. The first is the "cultural-institutional" point of view which uses the values of the system and their institutionalization in different functional contexts as its point of departure; the second is the "group" or "role" point of view which takes suborganizations and the roles of individuals participating in the functioning of the organization as its point of departure. Both of these will be discussed, as will their broad relations to each other, but primary attention will be given to the former.

On what has just been called the cultural-institutional level, a minimal description of an organization will have to include an outline of the system of values which defines its functions and of the main institutional patterns which spell out these values in the more concrete functional contexts of goal-attainment itself, adaptation to the situation, and integration of the system. There are other aspects, such as technical lore, ideology, and ritual symbolization, which cannot, for reasons of space, be taken up here.

The main point of reference for analyzing the structure of any social system is its value pattern. This defines the basic orientation of the system (in the present case, the organization) to the situation in which it operates; hence it guides the activities of participant individuals.

In the case of an organization as defined above, this value system must by definition be a subvalue system of a higher-order one, since the organization is always defined as a subsystem of a more comprehensive social system. Two conclusions follow: First, the value system of the organization must imply basic acceptance of the more generalized values of the superordinate system—unless it is a deviant organization not integrated into the superordinate system. Secondly, on the requisite level of generality, the most essential feature of the value system of an organization is the evaluative *legitimation* of its place or "role" in the superordinate system.

Since it has been assumed that an organization is defined by the primacy of a type of goal, the focus of its value system must be the legitimation of this goal in terms of the functional significance of its attainment for the superordinate system, and secondly the legitimation of the primacy of this goal over other possible interests and values of the organization and its members. Thus the value system of a business firm in our society is a version of "economic rationality" which legitimizes the goal of economic production (specified to the requisite level of concreteness in terms of particular goods and services). Devotion of the organization (and hence the resources it controls) to production is legitimized as is the maintenance of the primacy of this goal over other functional interests which may arise within the organization. This is Barnard's "organization purpose."[2] For the business firm, money return is a primary measure and symbol of success and is thus *part* of the goal-structure of the organization. But it cannot be the primary organization goal because profit-making is not by itself a function on behalf of the society as a system.

In the most general sense the values of the organization legitimize its existence as a system. But more specifically they legitimize the main functional patterns of operation which are necessary to implement the values, in this case the system goal, under typical conditions of the concrete situation. Hence, besides legitimation of the goal-type and its primacy over other interests, there will be legitimation of various categories of relatively specific subgoals and the operative procedures necessary for their attainment. There will further be normative rules governing the adaptive processes of the organization, the general principles on which facilities can be procured and handled, and there will be rules or principles governing the integration of the organization, particularly in defining the obligations of loyalty of participants to the organization as compared with the loyalties they bear in other roles.

A more familiar approach to the structure of an organization is through its constituent personnel and the roles they play in its functioning. Thus we ordinarily think of an organization as having some kind of "management" or "administration"—a group of people carrying some kind of special responsibility for the organization's affairs, usually formulated as

[2] Barnard, *op. cit.*, pt. II, ch. vii.

"policy formation" or "decision-making." Then under the control of this top group we would conceive of various operative groups arranged in "line" formation down to the lowest in the line of authority. In a somewhat different relation we would also think of various groups performing "staff" functions, usually some kinds of experts who stand in an advisory capacity to the decision-makers at the various levels, but who do not themselves exercise "line" authority.

It seems advantageous for present purposes to carry through mainly with the analysis of the institutional structure of the organization. Using the value system as the main point of reference, the discussion of this structure can be divided into three main headings. The primary adaptive exigencies of an organization concern the procurement of the resources necessary for it to attain its goal or carry out its function; hence one major field of institutionalization concerns the modes of procurement of these resources. Secondly, the organization will itself have to have institutionalized procedures by which these resources are brought to bear in the concrete processes of goal-attainment; and, finally, there will have to be institutional patterns defining and regulating the limits of commitments to this organization as compared with others in which the same persons and other resource-controllers are involved, patterns which can be generalized on a basis tolerable to the society as a whole.

THE MOBILIZATION OF FLUID RESOURCES

The resources which an organization must utilize are, given the social structure of the situation in which it functions, the factors of production as these concepts are used in economic theory. They are land, labor, capital, and "organization" in a somewhat different sense from that used mainly in this paper.[3]

The factor of land stands on a somewhat different level from the other three. If we treat an organization, for purposes of analysis, as an already established and going concern, then, like any other social system, we can think of it as being in control of certain facilities for access to which it is not dependent on the maintenance of short-run economic sanctions. It has full ownership of certain physical facilities such as physical land and relatively nondepreciating or nonobsolescing buildings. It may have certain traditions, particularly involving technical know-how factors which are not directly involved in the market nexus. The more fully the market nexus is developed, however, the less can it be said that an organization has very important assets which are withdrawn from the

[3] This possibly confusing terminological duplication is retained here because organization as a factor is commonly referred to in economic theory.

market. Even sites of long operation can be sold and new locations found and even the most deeply committed personnel may resign to take other positions or retire, and in either case have to be replaced through the labor market. The core of this aspect of the "land" complex is thus a set of commitments of resources on value grounds.

The two most fluid factors, however, are labor and capital in the economic sense. The overwhelming bulk of personal service takes place in occupational roles. This means that it is *contracted for* on some sector of the labor market. It is not based on ascription of status, through kinship or otherwise, but depends on the specific terms settled between the management of the organization and the incumbent. There are, of course, many types of contract of employment. Some variations concern the agents involved in the settlement of terms; for example, collective bargaining is very different from individual bargaining. Others concern the duration of commitments, varying all the way from a casual relation terminable at will, to a tenure appointment.

But most important, only in a limiting case are the specific *ad hoc* terms—balancing specifically defined services against specific monetary remuneration—anything like exhaustive of the empirically important factors involved in the contract of employment. The labor market cannot, in the economic sense, closely approach being a "perfect market." It has different degrees and types of imperfection according to whether the employer is one or another type of organization and according to what type of human service is involved. A few of these differences will be noted in later illustrations. Here the essential point is that, with the differentiation of functionally specified organizations from the matrix of diffuse social groupings, such organizations become increasingly dependent on explicit contracts of employment for their human services.

Attention may be called to one particularly important differentiation among types of relation existing between the performer of services and the recipients of the ultimate "product." In the typical case of manufacturing industry the typical worker works within the organization. The end result is a physical commodity which is then sold to consumers. The worker has no personal contact with the customer of the firm; indeed, no representative of the firm need have such contact except to arrange the settlement of the terms of sale. Where, however, the "product" is a personal service, the situation is quite different; the worker must have personal contact with the consumer during the actual performance of the service.

One way in which service can be organized is the case where neither performer nor "customer" belongs to an organization. Private professional practice is a type case, and doctor and patient, for example, come to constitute a small-scale solidary collectivity of their own. This is the main basis of the sliding scale as a pattern of remuneration. A second mode of organization is the one which assimilates the provision of service to the normal pattern involved in the production of physical commodities; the recipient is a "customer" who pays on a value-of-service basis, with prices determined by commercial competition. This pattern is approached in the case of such services as barbering.

But particularly in the case of professional services there is another very important pattern, where the recipient of the service becomes an operative member of the service-providing organization. The school, university, and hospital are type cases illustrating this pattern. The phrase "member of the university" definitely includes students. The faculty are in a sense dually employed, on the one hand by their students, on the other by the university administration. The transition is particularly clear in the case of the hospital. In private practice the patient is unequivocally the "employer." But in hospital practice the hospital organization employs a professional staff on behalf of the patients, as it were. This taking of the customer *into* the organization has important implications for the nature of the organization.

In a society like ours the requirements of an organization for fluid resources are in one sense and on one level overwhelmingly met through financing, i.e., through the provision of money funds at the disposal of the organization.[4] This applies both to physical facilities, equipment, materials, buildings, and to the employment of human services—indeed, also to cultural resources in that the rights to use patented processes may be bought. Hence the availability of adequate financing is always a vital problem for every organization operating in a monetary economy no matter what its goal-type may be; it is as vital for churches, symphony orchestras, and universities as it is for business firms.

The mechanisms through which financial resources are made available differ enormously, however, with different types of organization. All except the "purest" charitable organizations depend to some extent on the returns they receive for purveying some kind of a product, be it a commodity, or a service like education or music. But even within this range there is an enormous variation in the adequacy of this return for fully meeting financial needs. The business firm is at one pole in this respect. Its normal expectation is that in the long run it will be able to finance itself adequately from the proceeds of sales. But even here this is true

---

[4] Weber, *op. cit.*, ch. iii.

only in the long run; investment of capital in anticipation of future proceeds is of course one of the most important mechanisms in our society.

Two other important mechanisms are taxation and voluntary contributions. In a "free enterprise" economy the general principle governing financing by taxation is that organizations will be supported out of taxation (1) if the goal is regarded as important enough but organizations devoted to it cannot be made to "pay" as private enterprises by providing the service on a commercial basis, e.g., the care of large numbers of persons from the lower income groups who (by current standards) need to be hospitalized for mental illnesses, or (2) if the *ways* in which the services would be provided by private enterprise might jeopardize the public interest, e.g., the provision of military force for the national defense might conceivably be contracted out, but placing control of force to this degree in private hands would constitute too serious a threat to the political stability of the society. Others in these categories are left to the "voluntary" principle, if they are publicly sanctioned, generally in the form of "nonprofit" organizations.

It is important to note that financing of organizations is in general "affected with a public interest" and is in some degree to be regarded as an exercise of political power. This consideration derives from the character of an organization as a goal-directed social system. Every subgoal within the society must to some degree be integrated with the goalstructure of the society as a whole, and it is with this societal goal-structure that political institutions are above all concerned.[5]

The last of the four factors of production is what certain economists, notably Alfred Marshall, have called "organization" in the technical sense referred to above. This refers to the function of *combining* the factors of production in such ways as to facilitate the effective attainment of the organization's goal (in our general sense, in its "economic" or factorconsuming aspects). Its input into the organization stands on a level different from that of labor services and financing, since it does not concern the direct facilities for carrying out defined functions in a relatively routine manner, but instead concerns readjustment in the patterns of organization itself. It is, therefore, primarily significant in the longer-run perspective, and it is involved in processes of structural change in the organization. In its business reference it is what J. A. Schumpeter referred to as "entrepreneurship."[6] Organization in this economic sense is, however, an

---

[5] This general thesis of the relation between financing and political power and the public interest has been developed by Parsons and Smelser, *Economy and Society* (London, 1956), especially in chapters ii and iii.
[6] J. A. Schumpeter, *The Theory of Economic Development* (Cambridge, Mass., 1934).

essential factor in *all* organizational functioning. It necessarily plays a central part in the "founding" stages of any organization. From time to time it is important in later stages, since the kinds of adjustments to changing situations which are possible through the routine mechanisms of recruitment of labor services, and through the various devices for securing adequate financial resources, prove to be inadequate; hence a more fundamental structural change in the organization becomes necessary or desirable. This change would, in the present frame of reference, require a special input of the factor of organization in this technical sense.

The more generalized equivalent of the land factor is treated, except for the longest-run and most profound social changes, as the most constant reference point of all; its essential reference base is the stability of the value system in terms of which the goal of the organization is defined and the commitments involved in it are legitimized. It is from this reference base that the norms defining the broadly expected types of mechanism in the other respects will be derived, particularly those most actively involved in short-run operations, namely, the recruitment of human services through the labor market and the financing of the organization.

THE MECHANISMS OF IMPLEMENTATION

The problem of mobilizing fluid resources concerns one major aspect of the external relations of the organization to the situation in which it operates. Once possessing control of the necessary resources, then, it must have a set of mechanisms by which these resources can be brought to bear on the actual process of goal-implementation in a changing situation. From one point of view, there are two aspects of this process. First is the set of relations to the external situation centering around the problem of "disposal" of the "product" of the organization's activities. This involves the basis on which the scale of operations is estimated and on which the settlement of terms with the recipients of this product is arrived at. In the economic context it is the problem of "marketing," but for present purposes it is necessary to generalize this concept to include all products of organization functioning whether they are "sold" or not; for example, the products of a military organization may be said to be disposed of immediately to the executive and legislative branches of the government and through them to the public, but of course in no direct sense are they sold. The second aspect of the process is concerned with the internal mechanisms of the mobilization of resources for the implementation of the goal. For purposes of the present analysis, however, it will not be necessary to treat these internal and external references separately. Both, as distinguished from the mobilization of resources, can be treated together as governed by the "operative code" of the organization.

This code will have to have an essential basis in the value system which governs the organization. In the case of mobilization of resources, this basis concerns the problem of the "claims" of the organization to the resources it needs and hence the settlement of the terms on which they would be available to it. In the operative case it concerns the manner of their utilization within the organization and the relation to its beneficiaries. We may speak of the relevant value-implementation as centering about the question of "authorization" of the measures involved in carrying through the processes of utilization of resources.

There is an important sense in which the focus of all these functions is the process ordinarily called "decision-making." We have assumed that goal-attainment has clear primacy in the functioning of the organization. The paramount set of decisions then will be, within the framework of legitimation previously referred to, the set of decisions as to how, on the more generalized level, to take steps to attain the goal. This is what is generally thought of as the area of *policy* decisions. A second set of decisions concerns implementation in the sense of decisions about the utilization of resources available to the organization. These are the *allocative* decisions and concern two main subject matters: the allocation of responsibilities among personnel, i.e., suborganizations and individuals, and the allocation of fluid resources, i.e., manpower and monetary and physical facilities in accord with these responsibilities. Finally, a third set of decisions concerns maintaining the *integration* of the organization, through facilitating cooperation and dealing with the motivational problems which arise within the organization in relation to the maintenance of cooperation. The first two sets of decisions fall within the area which Barnard calls the problem of "effectiveness"; the third is the locus of the problem of "efficiency" in his sense.[7] Let us consider each of these decision areas in more detail.

Policy Decisions

By policy decisions are meant decisions which relatively directly commit the organization as a whole and which stand in relatively direct connection to its primary functions. They are decisions touching such matters as determination of the nature and quality standards of "product," changes

---

[7] Barnard, *op. cit.*, pt. I, ch. v.

in the scale of operations, problems of the approach to the recipients of the product or service, and organization-wide problems of modes of internal operation.

Policy decisions as thus conceived may be taken at different levels of generality with respect to the functions of the organization. The very highest level concerns decisions to set up a given organization or, conversely, to liquidate it. Near that level is a decision to merge with one or more other organizations. Then the scale descends through such levels as major changes in type of product or in scale of operations, to the day-to-day decisions about current operation. Broadly, this level of generality scale coincides with a scale of time-span of the relevance of decisions; the ones touching the longer-run problems of the organization tend to be the ones on a higher level of generality, involving a wider range of considerations and leading to more serious commitments. An important task for the theory of organization is a systematic classification of these levels of generality of decisions.

As has been noted, the critical feature of policy decisions is the fact that they commit the organization as a whole to carrying out their implications. This area of decisions is the focus of the problem of responsibility. One but only one major aspect of responsibility in turn lies in the fact that all operations of organization to some extent involve risks, and the decision-maker on the one hand is to some extent given "credit" for success, and on the other hand is legitimately held responsible for unfavorable consequences. One of the major features of roles of responsibility is the handling of these consequences; this becomes particularly complicated psychologically because it is often impossible to assess accurately the extent to which success or failure in fact stem from particular decisions or result from factors outside the control or predictive powers of the decision-maker. On high levels of responsibility conflicts of moral value may also operate.[8]

Because of the commitment of the organization as a whole, and through this of the interests of everyone participating in the organization to a greater or lesser degree, authorization becomes particularly important at the policy-decision level. This clearly connects with the value system and hence with the problem of legitimacy. It concerns not simply the content of particular decisions, but the right to make them.

Different organizations, according to scale and qualitative type, of course, have different concrete ways of organizing the policy-making process. Often the highest level of policy is placed mainly in the hands

[8] *Ibid.*, ch. xvii.

of some kind of a board; whereas "management" has responsibility for the next highest levels, with the still lower levels delegated to operative echelons.

Allocative Decisions

Higher policy decisions will concern the general type and quantity of resources brought into the organization and the more general policies toward personnel recruitment and financing. But the operative utilization of these facilities cannot be completely controlled from the center. There must be some allocative organization by which resources are distributed within the organization, and responsibility for their utilization in the various necessary operative tasks is assigned. This means that specialization in the functions of administration or management precludes the incumbents of these functions from also carrying out the main technical procedures involved in the organization-goal, and hence making the main operating decisions at the "work" level. Thus, a commanding general cannot actually man a particular aircraft or command a particular battery of artillery; a university president cannot actively teach all the subjects of instruction for which the university is responsible.

From one point of view, these mechanisms of internal allocation may be treated as "delegations of authority," though this formula will have to be qualified in connection with various cross-cutting considerations of types of competence and so forth. Thus a general, who by training and experience has been an artilleryman, when he is in command does not simply "delegate" authority to the air element under his command; he must in some way recognize the special technical competence of the air people in a field where he cannot have such competence. Similarly a university president who by academic training has been a professor of English does not merely delegate authority to the physicists on his faculty. Both must recognize an independent technical basis for "lower" echelons performing their functions in the ways in which their own technical judgment makes advisable. The technical man can reasonably be held responsible for the *results* of his operations; he cannot, however, be "dictated to" with respect to the technical procedures by which he achieves these results.

Seen in this light, there are two main aspects of the allocative decision process. One concerns mainly personnel (organized in suborganizations, for example, "departments"), the other financial and, at the requisite level, physical facilities. In the case of personnel the fundamental consideration is the allocation of responsibility. Using decisions as the reference point, the primary focus of the responsibility problem is allocation of the responsibility to decide, i.e., the "decision who should decide," as Barnard puts it. Technical operations as such may then be treated as controlled by the allocation of responsibility for decisions.

The second main aspect of the allocation process is the budget. Though generally formalized only in rather large and highly differentiated organizations, analytically the budget is a central conception. It means the allocation of fluid financial resources which in turn can be committed to particular "uses," namely, acquisition of physical facilities and employment of personnel. Allocation of responsibility is definition of the *functions* of humanly organized subsystems of personnel. Budget allocation is giving these suborganizations access to the necessary means of carrying out their assignment. There is a certain important crisscrossing to the two lines in that at the higher level the decision tends to be one of budget, leaving the employment of the relevant personnel to the subsystem to which funds are allocated. The people responsible at the level in question in turn divide the resource stream, devoting part of it to personnel the employment of whom is, subject to general policies, under their control, another part to subbudget allocation of funds to the uses of personnel they employ. This step-down series continues until the personnel in question are given only various types and levels of control or use of physical facilities, and not control of funds.

Coordination Decisions

Two types of operative decisions have so far been discussed, namely, policy decisions and allocative decisions. There is a third category which may be called "decisions of coordination," involving what Barnard has called the problems of "efficiency." These decisions are the operative decisions concerned with the integration of the organization as a system. Our two types of fundamental resources have a sharply asymmetrical relation to these decisions as they do to the allocative decisions. Funds (considered apart from their lenders or other suppliers) and physical resources do not have to be motivated to cooperate in organizational tasks, but human agents do. Decisions of policy and decisions of the allocation of responsibility still leave open the question of motivation to adequate performance.

This becomes an integrative problem because the special types of performance required to achieve the many complex contributions to an organization goal cannot be presumed to be motivated by the mere "nature" of the participants independently of the sanctions operating in the organizational situation. What is coordination from the point of view of the operation of the organization is "cooperation" from the point of view of the personnel. The limiting case of noncooperation is declining to continue employment in the organization, a case of by no means negligible importance where a free labor market exists. But short of this, relative to the goals of the organization, it is reasonable to postulate an inherent centrifugal tendency of subunits of the organization, a tendency reflecting pulls deriving from the personalities of the participants, from the special adaptive exigencies of their particular job situations, and possibly from other sources.

In this situation the management of the organization must, to some degree, take or be ready to take measures to counteract the centrifugal pull, to keep employment turnover at least down to tolerable levels, and internally to bring the performances of subunits and individuals more closely into line with the requirements of the organization than would otherwise be the case. These measures can take any one or a combination of three fundamental forms: (1) coercion—in that penalties for noncooperation are set, (2) inducement—in that rewards for valued performance are instituted, and (3) "therapy"—in that by a complex and judicious combination of measures the motivational obstacles to satisfactory cooperation are dealt with on a level which "goes behind" the overt ostensible reasons given for the difficulty by the persons involved.[9]

[9] The famous phenomenon of restriction of production in the informal group as reported by F. J. Roethlisberger and W. J. Dickson (*Management and the Worker* [Cambridge, Mass., 1939], pt. IV) is a case of relative failure of integration and hence, from one point of view, of failure of management in the function of coordination. It could be handled, from the present point of view, neither by policy decisions (e.g., not to hire "uncooperative workers") nor by allocative decisions (e.g., to hold the shop boss strictly responsible for meeting high production quotas), but only by decisions of coordination, presumably including "therapeutic" measures.

BUREAUCRATIC STRUCTURE AND PERSONALITY

Robert K. Merton

A formal, rationally organized social structure involves clearly defined patterns of activity in which, ideally, every series of actions is functionally related to the purposes of the organization.[1] In such an organization there is integrated a series of offices, of hierarchized statuses, in which inhere a number of obligations and privileges closely defined by limited and specific rules. Each of these offices contains an area of imputed competence and responsibility. Authority, the power of control which derives from an acknowledged status, inheres in the office and not in the particular person who performs the official role. Official action ordinarily occurs within the framework of pre-existing rules of the organization. The system of prescribed relations between the various offices involves a considerable degree of formality and clearly defined social distance between the occupants of these positions. Formality is manifested by means of a more or less complicated social ritual which symbolizes and supports the pecking order of the various offices. Such formality, which is integrated with the distribution of authority within the system, serves to minimize friction by largely restricting (official) contact to modes which are previously defined by the rules of the organization. Ready calculability of others' behavior and a stable set of mutual expectations is thus built up. Moreover, formality facilitates the interaction of the occupants of offices despite their (possibly hostile) private attitudes toward one another. In this way, the subordinate is protected from the arbitrary action of his superior, since

[1] For a development of the concept of "rational organization," see Karl Mannheim, *Mensch und Gesellschaft im Zeitalter des Umbaus* (Leiden: A. W. Sijthoff, 1935), esp. 28 ff.

the actions of both are constrained by a mutually recognized set of rules. Specific procedural devices foster objectivity and restrain the "quick passage of impulse into action."[2]

THE STRUCTURE OF BUREAUCRACY

The ideal type of such formal organization is bureaucracy and, in many respects, the classical analysis of bureaucracy is that by Max Weber.[3] As Weber indicates, bureaucracy involves a clear-cut division of integrated activities which are regarded as duties inherent in the office. A system of differentiated controls and sanctions is stated in the regulations. The assignment of roles occurs on the basis of technical qualifications which are ascertained through formalized, impersonal procedures (e.g., examinations). Within the structure of hierarchically arranged authority, the activities of "trained and salaried experts" are governed by general, abstract, and clearly defined rules which preclude the necessity for the issuance of specific instructions for each specific case. The generality of the rules requires the constant use of categorization, whereby individual problems and cases are classified on the basis of designated criteria and are treated accordingly. The pure type of bureaucratic official is appointed, either by a superior or through the exercise of impersonal competition; he is not elected. A measure of flexibility in the bureaucracy is attained by electing higher functionaries who presumably express the will of the electorate (e.g., a body of citizens or a board of directors). The election of higher officials is designed to affect the purposes of the organization, but the technical procedures for attaining these ends are carried out by continuing bureaucratic personnel.[4]

Most bureaucratic offices involve the expectation of life-long tenure, in the absence of disturbing factors which may decrease the size of the organization. Bureaucracy maximizes vocational security.[5] The function of security of tenure, pensions, incremental salaries and regularized procedures for promotion is to ensure the devoted performance of official

[2] H. D. Lasswell, Politics (New York: McGraw-Hill, 1936), 120–121.
[3] Max Weber, Wirtschaft und Gesellschaft (Tübingen: J. C. B. Mohr, 1922), Pt. III, chap. 6; 650–678. For a brief summary of Weber's discussion, see Talcott Parsons, The Structure of Social Action, esp. 506 ff. For a description, which is not a caricature, of the bureaucrat as a personality type, see C. Rabany, "Les types sociaux: le fonctionnaire," Revue générale d'administration, 1907, 88, 5–28.
[4] Karl Mannheim, Ideology and Utopia (New York: Harcourt, 1936), 18n., 105 ff. See also Ramsay Muir, Peers and Bureaucrats (London: Constable, 1910), 12–13.
[5] E. G. Cahen-Salvador suggests that the personnel of bureaucracies is largely constituted by those who value security above all else. See his "La situation matérielle et morale des fonctionnaires," Revue politique et parlementaire (1926), 319.

duties, without regard for extraneous pressures.[6] The chief merit of bureaucracy is its technical efficiency, with a premium placed on precision, speed, expert control, continuity, discretion, and optimal returns on input. The structure is one which approaches the complete elimination of personalized relationships and nonrational considerations (hostility, anxiety, affectual involvements, etc.)

With increasing bureaucratization, it becomes plain to all who would see that man is to a very important degree controlled by his social relations to the instruments of production. This can no longer seem only a tenet of Marxism, but a stubborn fact to be acknowledged by all, quite apart from their ideological persuasion. Bureaucratization makes readily visible what was previously dim and obscure. More and more people discover that to work, they must be employed. For to work, one must have tools and equipment. And the tools and equipment are increasingly available only in bureaucracies, private or public. Consequently, one must be employed by the bureaucracies in order to have access to tools in order to work in order to live. It is in this sense that bureaucratization entails separation of individuals from the instruments of production, as in modern capitalistic enterprise or in state communistic enterprise (of the midcentury variety), just as in the post-feudal army, bureaucratization entailed complete separation from the instruments of destruction. Typically, the worker no longer owns his tools nor the soldier, his weapons. And in this special sense, more and more people become workers, either blue collar or white collar or stiff shirt. So develops, for example, the new type of scientific worker, as the scientist is "separated" from his technical equipment—after all, the physicist does not ordinarily own his cyclotron. To work at his research, he must be employed by a bureaucracy with laboratory resources.

Bureaucracy is administration which almost completely avoids public discussion of its techniques, although there may occur public discussion of its policies.[7] This secrecy is confined neither to public nor to private bureaucracies. It is held to be necessary to keep valuable information from private economic competitors or from foreign and potentially hostile political groups. And though it is not often so called, espionage among competitors is perhaps as common, if not as intricately organized, in systems of private economic enterprise as in systems of national states. Cost figures, lists of clients, new technical processes, plans for production

---

[6] H. J. Laski, "Bureaucracy," *Encyclopedia of the Social Sciences.* This article is written primarily from the standpoint of the political scientist rather than that of the sociologist.

[7] Weber, *op. cit.*, 671.

—all these are typically regarded as essential secrets of private economic bureaucracies which might be revealed if the bases of all decisions and policies had to be publicly defended.

THE DYSFUNCTIONS OF BUREAUCRACY

In these bold outlines, the positive attainments and functions of bureaucratic organization are emphasized and the internal stresses and strains of such structures are almost wholly neglected. The community at large, however, evidently emphasizes the imperfections of bureaucracy, as is suggested by the fact that the "horrid hybrid," bureaucrat, has become an epithet, a *Schimpfwort*.

The transition to a study of the negative aspects of bureaucracy is afforded by the application of Veblen's concept of "trained incapacity," Dewey's notion of "occupational psychosis" or Warnotte's view of "professional deformation." Trained incapacity refers to that state of affairs in which one's abilities function as inadequacies or blind spots. Actions based upon training and skills which have been successfully applied in the past may result in inappropriate responses *under changed conditions*. An inadequate flexibility in the application of skills, will, in a changing milieu, result in more or less serious maladjustments.[8] Thus, to adopt a barnyard illustration used in this connection by Burke, chickens may be readily conditioned to interpret the sound of a bell as a signal for food. The same bell may now be used to summon the trained chickens to their doom as they are assembled to suffer decapitation. In general, one adopts measures in keeping with one's past training and, under new conditions which are not recognized as *significantly* different, the very soundness of this training may lead to the adoption of the wrong procedures. Again, in Burke's almost echolalic phrase, "people may be unfitted by being fit in an unfit fitness"; their training may become an incapacity.

Dewey's concept of occupational psychosis rests upon much the same observations. As a result of their day to day routines, people develop special preferences, antipathies, discriminations and emphases.[9] (The term psychosis is used by Dewey to denote a "pronounced character of the mind.") These psychoses develop through demands put upon the individual by the particular organization of his occupational role.

The concepts of both Veblen and Dewey refer to a fundamental

---

[8] For a stimulating discussion and application of these concepts, see Kenneth Burke, *Permanence and Change* (New York: New Republic, 1935), pp. 50 ff.; Daniel Warnotte, "Bureaucratie et Fonctionnarisme," *Revue de l'Institut de Sociologie*, 1937, 17, 245.
[9] *Ibid.*, 58–59.

ambivalence. Any action can be considered in terms of what it attains or what it fails to attain. "A way of seeing is also a way of not seeing—a focus upon object A involves a neglect of object B."[10] In his discussion, Weber is almost exclusively concerned with what the bureaucratic structure attains: precision, reliability, efficiency. This same structure may be examined from another perspective provided by the ambivalence. What are the limitations of the organizations designed to attain these goals?

For reasons which we have already noted, the bureaucratic structure exerts a constant pressure upon the official to be "methodical, prudent, disciplined." If the bureaucracy is to operate successfully, it must attain a high degree of reliability of behavior, an unusual degree of conformity with prescribed patterns of action. Hence, the fundamental importance of discipline which may be as highly developed in a religious or economic bureaucracy as in the army. Discipline can be effective only if the ideal patterns are buttressed by strong sentiments which entail devotion to one's duties, a keen sense of the limitation of one's authority and competence, and methodical performance of routine activities. The efficacy of social structure depends ultimately upon infusing group participants with appropriate attitudes and sentiments. As we shall see, there are definite arrangements in the bureaucracy for inculcating and reinforcing these sentiments.

At the moment, it suffices to observe that in order to ensure discipline (the necessary reliability of response), these sentiments are often more intense than is technically necessary. There is a margin of safety, so to speak, in the pressure exerted by these sentiments upon the bureaucrat to conform to his patterned obligations, in much the same sense that added allowances (precautionary overestimations) are made by the engineer in designing the supports for a bridge. But this very emphasis leads to a transference of the sentiments from the *aims* of the organization onto the particular details of behavior required by the rules. Adherence to the rules, originally conceived as a means, becomes transformed into an end-in-itself; there occurs the familiar process of *displacement of goals* whereby "an instrumental value becomes a terminal value."[11] Discipline,

[10] *Ibid.*, 70.
[11] This process has often been observed in various connections. Wundt's *heterogony of ends* is a case in point; Max Weber's *Paradoxie der Folgen* is another. See also MacIver's observations on the transformation of civilization into culture and Lasswell's remark that "the human animal distinguishes himself by his infinite capacity for making ends of his means." See Merton, "The unanticipated consequences of purposive social action," *American Sociological Review*, 1936, 1, 894–904. In terms of the psychological mechanisms involved, this process has been analyzed most fully by Gordon W. Allport, in his discussion of what he calls "the functional autonomy of motives." Allport emends the earlier formulations of Woodworth, Tolman, and William Stern, and arrives at a statement of the process from the standpoint of

readily interpreted as conformance with regulations, whatever the situation, is seen not as a measure designed for specific purposes but becomes an immediate value in the life-organization of the bureaucrat. This emphasis, resulting from the displacement of the original goals, develops into rigidities and an inability to adjust readily. Formalism, even ritualism, ensues with an unchallenged insistence upon punctilious adherence to formalized procedures.[12] This may be exaggerated to the point where primary concern with conformity to the rules interferes with the achievement of the purposes of the organization, in which case we have the familiar phenomenon of the technicism or red tape of the official. An extreme product of this process of displacement of goals is the bureaucratic virtuoso, who never forgets a single rule binding his action and hence is unable to assist many of his clients.[13] A case in point, where strict recognition of the limits of authority and literal adherence to rules produced this result, is the pathetic plight of Bernt Balchen, Admiral Byrd's pilot in the flight over the South Pole.

> According to a ruling of the department of labor Bernt Balchen . . . cannot receive his citizenship papers. Balchen, a native of Norway, declared his intention in 1927. It is held that he has failed to meet the condition of five years' continuous residence in the United States. The Byrd antarctic voyage took him out of the country, although he was on a ship carrying the American flag, was an invaluable member of the American expedition, and in a region to which there is an American claim because of the exploration and occupation of it by Americans, this region being Little America.
>
> The bureau of naturalization explains that it cannot proceed on the assumption that Little America is American soil. That would be *trespass on international questions* where it has no sanction. So far as the bureau is concerned, Balchen was out of the country and *technically* has not complied with the law of naturalization.[14]

---

individual motivation. He does not consider those phases of the social structure which conduce toward the "transformation of motives." The formulation adopted in this paper is thus complementary to Allport's analysis; the one stressing the psychological mechanisms involved, the other considering the constraints of the social structure. The convergence of psychology and sociology toward this central concept suggests that it may well constitute one of the conceptual bridges between the two disciplines. See Gordon W. Allport, *Personality* (New York: Holt, Rinehart and Winston, Inc., 1937), chap. 7.

[12] See E. C. Hughes, "Institutional office and the person," *American Journal of Sociology*, 1937, 43, 404–413; E. T. Hiller, "Social structure in relation to the person," *Social Forces*, 1937, 16, 34–43.

[13] Mannheim, *Ideology and Utopia*, 106.

[14] Quoted from the *Chicago Tribune* (June 24, 1931, p. 10) by Thurman Arnold, *The Symbols of Government* (New Haven, Conn.: Yale University Press, 1935), 201–202. (My italics.)

STRUCTURAL SOURCES OF OVERCONFORMITY

Such inadequacies in orientation which involve trained incapacity clearly derive from structural sources. The process may be briefly recapitulated. (1) An effective bureaucracy demands reliability of response and strict devotion to regulations. (2) Such devotion to the rules leads to their transformation into absolutes; they are no longer conceived as relative to a set of purposes. (3) This interferes with ready adaptation under special conditions not clearly envisaged by those who drew up the general rules. (4) Thus, the very elements which conduce toward efficiency in general produce inefficiency in specific instances. Full realization of the inadequacy is seldom attained by members of the group who have not divorced themselves from the meanings which the rules have for them. These rules in time become symbolic in cast, rather than strictly utilitarian.

Thus far, we have treated the ingrained sentiments making for rigorous discipline simply as data, as given. However, definite features of the bureaucratic structure may be seen to conduce to these sentiments. The bureaucrat's official life is planned for him in terms of a graded career, through the organizational devices of promotion by seniority, pensions, incremental salaries, *etc.*, all of which are designed to provide incentives for disciplined action and conformity to the official regulations.[15] The official is tacitly expected to and largely does adapt his thoughts, feelings and actions to the prospect of this career. But *these very devices* which increase the probability of conformance also lead to an over-concern with strict adherence to regulations which induces timidity, conservatism, and technicism. Displacement of sentiments from goals onto means is fostered by the tremendous symbolic significance of the means (rules).

Another feature of the bureaucratic structure tends to produce much the same result. Functionaries have the sense of a common destiny for all those who work together. They share the same interests, especially since there is relatively little competition in so far as promotion is in terms of seniority. In-group aggression is thus minimized and this arrangement is therefore conceived to be positively functional for the bureaucracy. However, the *esprit de corps* and informal social organization which typically develops in such situations often leads the personnel to defend their entrenched interests rather than to assist their clientele and elected higher officials. As President Lowell reports, if the bureaucrats believe that their status is not adequately recognized by an incoming elected

---

[15] Mannheim, *Mensch und Gesellschaft*, 32–33. Mannheim stresses the importance of the "Lebensplan" and the "Amtskarriere." See the comments by Hughes, *op. cit.*, 413.

official, detailed information will be withheld from him, leading him to errors for which he is held responsible. Or, if he seeks to dominate fully, and thus violates the sentiment of self-integrity of the bureaucrats, he may have documents brought to him in such numbers that he cannot manage to sign them all, let alone read them.[16] This illustrates the defensive informal organization which tends to arise whenever there is an apparent threat to the integrity of the group.[17]

It would be much too facile and partly erroneous to attribute such resistance by bureaucrats simply to vested interests. Vested interests oppose any new order which either eliminates or at least makes uncertain their differential advantage deriving from the current arrangements. This is undoubtedly involved in part in bureaucratic resistance to change, but another process is perhaps more significant. As we have seen, bureaucratic officials affectively identify themselves with their way of life. They have a pride of craft which leads them to resist change in established routines; at least, those changes which are felt to be imposed by others. This non-logical pride of craft is a familiar pattern found even, to judge from Sutherland's *Professional Thief*, among pickpockets who, despite the risk, delight in mastering the prestige-bearing feat of "beating a left breech" (picking the left front trousers pocket).

In a stimulating paper, Hughes has applied the concepts of "secular" and "sacred" to various types of division of labor; "the sacredness" of caste and *Stände* prerogatives contrasts sharply with the increasing secularism of occupational differentiation in our society.[18] However, as our discussion suggests, there may ensue, in particular vocations and in particular types of organization, the *process of sanctification* (viewed as the counterpart of the process of secularization). This is to say that through sentiment-formation, emotional dependence upon bureaucratic symbols and status, and affective involvement in spheres of competence and authority, there develop prerogatives involving attitudes of moral legitimacy which are established as values in their own right, and are no longer viewed as merely technical means for expediting administration. One may note a tendency for certain bureaucratic norms, originally introduced for technical reasons, to become rigidified and sacred, although, as Durkheim would say,

---

[16] A. L. Lowell, *The Government of England* (New York, 1908), I, 189 ff.
[17] For an instructive description of the development of such a defensive organization in a group of workers, see F. J. Roethlisberger and W. J. Dickson, *Management and the Worker* (Boston: Harvard School of Business Administration, 1934).
[18] E. C. Hughes, "Personality types and the division of labor," *American Journal of Sociology*, 1928, 33, 754–768. Much the same distinction is drawn by Leopold von Wiese and Howard Becker, *Systematic Sociology* (New York: Wiley, 1932), 222–225 *et passim*.

they are *laïque en apparence*.[19] Durkheim has touched on this general process in his description of the attitudes and values which persist in the organic solidarity of a highly differentiated society.

PRIMARY VERSUS SECONDARY RELATIONS

Another feature of the bureaucratic structure, the stress on depersonalization of relationships, also plays its part in the bureaucrat's trained incapacity. The personality pattern of the bureaucrat is nucleated about this norm of impersonality. Both this and the categorizing tendency, which develops from the dominant role of general, abstract rules, tend to produce conflict in the bureaucrat's contacts with the public or clientele. Since functionaries minimize personal relations and resort to categorization, the peculiarities of individual cases are often ignored. But the client who, quite understandably, is convinced of the special features of *his* own problem often objects to such categorical treatment. Stereotyped behavior is not adapted to the exigencies of individual problems. The impersonal treatment of affairs which are at times of great personal significance to the client gives rise to the charge of "arrogance" and "haughtiness" of the bureaucrat. Thus, at the Greenwich Employment Exchange, the unemployed worker who is securing his insurance payment resents what he deems to be "the impersonality and, at times, the apparent abruptness and even harshness of his treatment by the clerks. . . . Some men complain of the superior attitude which the clerks have."[20]

Still another source of conflict with the public derives from the

---

[19] Hughes recognizes one phase of this process of sanctification when he writes that professional training "carries with it as a by-product assimilation of the candidate to a set of professional attitudes and controls, *a professional conscience and solidarity. The profession claims and aims to become a moral unit.*" Hughes, *op. cit.*, 762 (italics inserted). In this same connection, Sumner's concept of *pathos*, as the halo of sentiment which protects a social value from criticism, is particularly relevant, inasmuch as it affords a clue to the mechanism involved in the process of sanctification. See his *Folkways*, 180–181.

[20] " 'They treat you like a lump of dirt they do. I see a navvy reach across the counter and shake one of them by the collar the other day. The rest of us felt like cheering. Of course he lost his benefit over it. . . . But the clerk deserved it for his sassy way.' " (E. W. Bakke, *The Unemployed Man*, 79–80). Note that the domineering attitude was *imputed* by the unemployed client who is in a state of tension due to his loss of status and self-esteem in a society where the ideology is still current that an "able man" can always find a job. That the imputation of arrogance stems largely from the client's state of mind is seen from Bakke's own observation that "the clerks were rushed, and had no time for pleasantries, but there was little sign of harshness or a superiority feeling in their treatment of the men." In so far as there is an objective basis for the imputation of arrogant behavior to bureaucrats, it may possibly be explained by the following juxtaposed statements. "Auch der moderne, sei es öffentliche, sei es private, Beamte erstrebt immer und geniesst meist den Beherrschten gegenüber eine spezifisch gehobene, 'ständische' soziale Schätzung." (Weber, *op. cit.*, 652.) "In

bureaucratic structure. The bureaucrat, in part irrespective of his position within the hierarchy, acts as a representative of the power and prestige of the entire structure. In his official role he is vested with definite authority. This often leads to an actually or apparently domineering attitude, which may only be exaggerated by a discrepancy between his position within the hierarchy and his position with reference to the public.[21] Protest and recourse to other officials on the part of the client are often ineffective or largely precluded by the previously mentioned *esprit de corps* which joins the officials into a more or less solidary in-group. This source of conflict *may* be minimized in private enterprise since the client can register an effective protest by transferring his trade to another organization within the competitive system. But with the monopolistic nature of the public organization, no such alternative is possible. Moreover, in this case, tension is increased because of a discrepancy between ideology and fact: the governmental personnel are held to be "servants of the people," but in fact they are often superordinate, and release of tension can seldom be afforded by turning to other agencies for the necessary service.[22] This tension is in part attributable to the confusion of the status of bureaucrat and client; the client may consider himself socially superior to the official who is at the moment dominant.[23]

Thus, with respect to the relations between officials and clientele, one structural source of conflict is the pressure for formal and impersonal treatment when individual, personalized consideration is desired by the

---

persons in whom the craving for prestige is uppermost, hostility usually takes the form of a desire to humiliate others." K. Horney, *The Neurotic Personality of Our Time*, 178–179.

[21] In this connection, note the relevance of Koffka's comments on certain features of the pecking-order of birds. "If one compares the behavior of the bird at the top of the pecking list, the despot, with that of one very far down, the second or third from the last, then one finds the latter much more cruel to the few others over whom he lords it than the former in his treatment of all members. As soon as one removes from the group all members above the penultimate, his behavior becomes milder and may even become very friendly. . . . It is not difficult to find analogies to this in human societies, and therefore one side of such behavior must be primarily the effects of the social groupings, and not of individual characteristics." K. Koffka, *Principles of Gestalt Psychology* (New York: Harcourt, 1935), 668–669.

[22] At this point the political machine often becomes functionally significant. As Steffens and others have shown, highly personalized relations and the abrogation of formal rules (red tape) by the machine often satisfy the needs of individual "clients" more fully than the formalized mechanism of governmental bureaucracy.

[23] As one of the unemployed men remarked about the clerks at the Greenwich Employment Exchange: " 'And the bloody blokes wouldn't have their jobs if it wasn't for us men out of a job either. That's what gets me about their holding their noses up.' " Bakke, *op. cit.*, 80. See also H. D. Lasswell and G. Almond, "Aggressive behavior by clients towards public relief administrators," *American Political Science Review*, 1934, 28, 643–655.

client. The conflict may be viewed, then, as deriving from the introduction of inappropriate attitudes and relationships. Conflict with*in* the bureaucratic structure arises from the converse situation, namely, when personalized relationships are substituted for the structurally required impersonal relationships. This type of conflict may be characterized as follows.

The bureaucracy, as we have seen, is organized as a secondary, formal group. The normal responses involved in this organized network of social expectations are supported by affective attitudes of members of the group. Since the group is oriented toward secondary norms of impersonality, any failure to conform to these norms will arouse antagonism from those who have identified themselves with the legitimacy of these rules. Hence, the substitution of personal for impersonal treatment within the structure is met with widespread disapproval and is characterized by such epithets as graft, favoritism, nepotism, apple-polishing, etc. These epithets are clearly manifestations of injured sentiments.[24] The function of such virtually automatic resentment can be clearly seen in terms of the requirements of bureaucratic structure.

Bureaucracy is a secondary group structure designed to carry on certain activities which cannot be satisfactorily performed on the basis of primary group criteria.[25] Hence behavior which runs counter to these formalized norms becomes the object of emotionalized disapproval. This constitutes a functionally significant defence set up against tendencies which jeopardize the performance of socially necessary activities. To be sure, these reactions are not rationally determined practices explicitly designed for the fulfillment of this function. Rather, viewed in terms of the individual's interpretation of the situation, such resentment is simply an immediate response opposing the "dishonesty" of those who violate the rules of the game. However, this subjective frame of reference notwithstanding, these reactions serve the latent function of maintaining the essential structural elements of bureaucracy by reaffirming the necessity for formalized, secondary relations and by helping to prevent the disintegration of the bureaucratic structure which would occur should these be

---

[24] The diagnostic significance of such linguistic indices as epithets has scarcely been explored by the sociologist. Sumner properly observes that epithets produce "summary criticisms" and definitions of social situations. Dollard also notes that "epithets frequently define the central issues in a society," and Sapir has rightly emphasized the importance of context of situations in appraising the significance of epithets. Of equal relevance is Linton's observation that "in case histories the way in which the community felt about a particular episode is, if anything, more important to our study than the actual behavior. . . ." A sociological study of "vocabularies of encomium and opprobrium" should lead to valuable findings.

[25] *Cf.* Ellsworth Faris, *The Nature of Human Nature* (New York: McGraw-Hill, 1937), 41 ff.

supplanted by personalized relations. This type of conflict may be generically described as the intrusion of primary group attitudes when secondary group attitudes are institutionally demanded, just as the bureaucrat-client conflict often derives from interaction on impersonal terms when personal treatment is individually demanded.[26]

PROBLEMS FOR RESEARCH

The trend towards increasing bureaucratization in Western Society, which Weber had long since foreseen, is not the sole reason for sociologists to turn their attention to this field. Empirical studies of the interaction of bureaucracy and personality should especially increase our understanding of social structure. A large number of specific questions invite our attention. To what extent are particular personality types selected and modified by the various bureaucracies (private enterprise, public service, the quasi-legal political machine, religious orders)? Inasmuch as ascendancy and submission are held to be traits of personality, despite their variability in different stimulus-situations, do bureaucracies select personalities of particularly submissive or ascendant tendencies? And since various studies have shown that these traits can be modified, does participation in bureaucratic office tend to increase ascendant tendencies? Do various systems of recruitment (e.g., patronage, open competition involving specialized knowledge or general mental capacity, practical experience) select different personality types?[27] Does promotion through seniority lessen competitive anxieties and enhance administrative efficiency? A detailed examination of mechanisms for imbuing the bureaucratic codes with affect would be instructive both sociologically and psychologically. Does the general anonymity of civil service decisions tend to restrict the area of prestige-symbols to a narrowly defined inner circle? Is there a tendency for differential association to be especially marked among bureaucrats?

[26] Community disapproval of many forms of behavior may be analyzed in terms of one or the other of these patterns of substitution of culturally inappropriate types of relationship. Thus, prostitution constitutes a type-case where coitus, a form of intimacy which is institutionally defined as symbolic of the most "sacred" primary group relationship, is placed within a contractual context, symbolized by the exchange of that most impersonal of all symbols, money. See Kingsley Davis, "The sociology of prostitution," *American Sociological Review*, 1937, 2, 744–755.
[27] Among recent studies of recruitment to bureaucracy are: Reinhard Bendix, *Higher Civil Servants in American Society* (Boulder, Colo.: University of Colorado Press, 1949); Dwaine Marvick, *Career Perspectives in a Bureaucratic Setting* (Ann Arbor, Mich.: University of Michigan Press, 1954); R. K. Kelsall, *Higher Civil Servants in Britain* (London: Routledge, 1955); W. L. Warner and J. C. Abegglen, *Occupational Mobility in American Business and Industry* (Minneapolis, Minn.: University of Minnesota Press, 1955).

The range of theoretically significant and practically important questions would seem to be limited only by the accessibility of the concrete data. Studies of religious, educational, military, economic, and political bureaucracies dealing with the interdependence of social organization and personality formation should constitute an avenue for fruitful research. On that avenue, the functional analysis of concrete structures may yet build a Solomon's House for sociologists.

A BASIS FOR COMPARATIVE ANALYSIS OF COMPLEX ORGANIZATIONS

Amitai Etzioni

A DEFINITION OF COMPLIANCE

Compliance is universal, existing in all social units. It is a major element of the relationship between those who have power and those over whom they exercise it.[1] Despite its universality, it has been chosen as a base for this comparative study because it is a central element of organizational structure. The emphasis on compliance within the organization differentiates the latter from other types of social units. Characteristics of organizations such as their specificity, size, complexity and effectiveness each enhances the need for compliance. And in turn, compliance is systematically related to many central organizational variables.

Compliance refers both to a relation in which an actor behaves in accordance with a directive supported by another actor's power, and to the orientation of the subordinated actor to the power applied.[2]

Reprinted with permission of The Macmillan Company from *A Comparative Analysis of Complex Organizations,* by Amitai Etzioni. Copyright © The Free Press of Glencoe, Inc., 1961, pp. 3–21.

[1] G. Simmel, "Superiority and subordination as subject matter of sociology," *Amer. J. Sociol.,* 1896, **2,** 167–189, 392–415.
[2] For other usages of the term see R. Bendix, "Bureaucracy: The problem and its setting," *Amer. sociol. Rev.,* 1947, **12,** 502–507, and H. L. Zetterberg, "Compliant actions," *Acta Sociologica,* 1957, **2,** 179–201.

By *supported* we mean that those who have power manipulate means which they command in such a manner that certain other actors find following the directive rewarding, while not following it incurs deprivations. In this sense, compliance relations are asymmetric (or "vertical"). But it is not assumed that the subordinates have no power, only that they have less.[3]

The power-*means*, manipulated to support the directives, include physical, material, and symbolic rewards and deprivations. Organizations tend to allocate these means systematically and strive to ensure that they will be used in conformity with the organizational norms.

The *orientation of the subordinated actor* can be characterized as positive (commitment) or negative (alienation). It is determined in part by the degree to which the power applied is considered legitimate by the subordinated actor, and in part by its congruence with the line of action he would desire. We refer to this orientation, whether positive or negative, as *involvement* in the organization. In sum, there are two parties to a compliance relationship: an actor who exercises power, and an actor, subject to this power, who responds to this subjection with either more or less alienation or more or less commitment.

The next task is to use compliance as here defined to develop an analytical base for the classification of organizations. This is done in three steps. First, three kinds of *power* are differentiated; then, three kinds of *involvement* are specified; and finally, the associations of kinds of power with kinds of involvement are indicated. These associations— which constitute *compliance relationships*—then serve as the basis of our classification of organizations.

THREE KINDS OF POWER:
A COMPARATIVE DIMENSION

A Classification of Power

Power is an actor's ability to induce or influence another actor to carry out his directives or any other norms he supports.[4] Goldhamer and Shils state that "a person may be said to have power to the extent that he influences the behavior of others in accordance with his own intensions."[5]

---

[3] T. Parsons, "The distribution of power in American society," *World Politics*, 1957, **10**, 139; cf. R. Dahrendorf, *Class and class conflict in industrial society* (Stanford, Calif.: Stanford University Press, 1959), p. 169.
[4] See T. Parsons, *The social system* (New York: Free Press, 1951), p. 121.
[5] H. Goldhamer and E. A. Shils, "Types of power and status," *Amer. J. Sociol.*, 1939, **45**, 171.

Of course, "his own intentions" might be to influence a person to follow others' "intentions" or those of a collectivity. In organizations, enforcing the collectivity norms is likely to be a condition determining the power-holder's access to the means of power.

Power positions are positions whose incumbents regularly have access to means of power. Statements about power positions imply a particular group (or groups) who are subject to this power. For instance, to state that prison guards have a power position implies the subordination of inmates. In the following analysis we focus on power relations in organizations between those higher and those lower in rank. We refer to those in power positions, who are higher in rank, as *elites* or as organizational *representatives*. We refer to those in subject positions, who are lower in rank, as *lower participants*.

Power differs according to the *means* employd to make the subjects comply. These means may be physical, material, or symbolic.[6]

Coercive power rests on the application, or the threat of application, of physical sanctions such as infliction of pain, deformity, or death; generation of frustration through restriction of movement; or controlling through force the satisfaction of needs such as those for food, sex, comfort, and the like.

Remunerative power is based on control over material resources and rewards through allocation of salaries and wages, commissions and contributions, "fringe benefits," services and commodities.

Normative power rests on the allocation and manipulation of symbolic rewards and deprivations through employment of leaders, manipulation of mass media, allocation of esteem and prestige symbols, administration of ritual, and influence over the distribution of "acceptance" and "positive response." (A more eloquent name for this power would be persuasive, or manipulative, or suggestive power. But all these terms have negative value connotations which we wish to avoid.)

There are two kinds of normative power. One is based on the manipulation of esteem, prestige, and ritualistic symbols (such as a

---

[6] We suggest that this typology is exhaustive, although the only way we can demonstrate this is by pointing out that every type of power we have encountered so far can be classified as belonging to one of the categories or to a combination of them.

Boulding, Neuman, and Commons have suggested similar typologies. Boulding has developed a typology of "willingness" of persons to serve organizational ends which includes identification, economic means, and coercion. He suggests, however, that identification should be seen as an "economic" way of inducing willingness, a position which we believe is unacceptable to most sociologists. See K. E. Boulding, *The organizational revolution*, New York: Harper & Row, 1953, p. xxxi; and R. Niebuhr, "Coercion, self-interest, and love," *ibid.*, pp. 228–244.

flag or a benediction); the other, on allocation and manipulation of acceptance and positive response.[7] Although both powers are found both in vertical and in horizontal relationships, the first is more frequent in vertical relations, between actors who have different ranks, while the second is more common in horizontal relations, among actors equal in rank—in particular, in the power of an "informal" or primary group over its members. Lacking better terms, we refer to the first kind as *pure normative power,* and to the second as *social power.* Social power could be treated as a distinct kind of power. But since powers are here classed according to the means of control employed, and since both social and pure normative power rest on the same set of means—manipulation of symbolic rewards—we treat these two powers as belonging to the same category.

From the viewpoint of the organization, pure normative power is more useful, since it can be exercised directly down the hierarchy. Social power becomes organizational power only when the organization can influence the group's powers, as when a teacher uses the class climate to control a deviant child, or a union steward agitates the members to use their informal power to bring a deviant into line.

Organizations can be ordered according to their power structure, taking into account which power is predominant, how strongly it is stressed compared with other organizations in which the same power is predominant, and which power constitutes the secondary source of control.[8]

Neutralization of Power

Most organizations employ all three kinds of power, but the degree to which they rely on each differs from organization to organization. Most organizations tend to emphasize only one means of power, relying less on the other two. Evidence to this effect is presented below in the analysis of the compliance structures of various organizations. The major reason for power specialization seems to be that when two kinds of power are emphasized at the same time, over the same subject group, they tend to neutralize each other.

Applying force, for instance, usually creates such a high degree of alienation that it becomes impossible to apply normative power successfully. This is one of the reasons why rehabilitation is rarely achieved in

---

[7] T. Parsons, *The social system, op. cit.,* p. 108.
[8] Two methodological problems raised by such an ordering are discussed in Chapter XII of Amitai Etzioni, *A comparative analysis of complex organizations* (New York: Free Press, 1961), pp. 297–298.

traditional prisons, why custodial measures are considered as blocking therapy in mental hospitals, and why teachers in progressive schools tend to oppose corporal punishment.

Similarly, the application of renumerative powers makes appeal to "idealistic" (pure normative) motives less fruitful. In a study of the motives which lead to purchase of war bonds, Merton pointed out that in one particularly effective drive (the campaign of Kate Smith), all "secular" topics were omitted and the appeal was centered on patriotic, "sacred" themes. Merton asked a sample of 978 people: "Do you think that it is a good idea to give things to people who buy bonds?"

> Fifty per cent were definitely opposed in principle to premiums, bonuses and other such inducements, and many of the remainder thought it a good idea only for "other people" who might not buy otherwise.[9]

> By omitting this [secular] argument, the authors of her scripts were able to avoid the strain and incompatibility between the two main lines of motivation: unselfish, sacrificing love of country and economic motives of sound investment.[10]

It is possible to make an argument for the opposite position. It might be claimed that the larger the number of personal needs whose satisfaction the organization controls, the more power it has over the participants. For example, labor unions that cater to and have control over the social as well as the economic needs of their members have more power over those members than do unions that focus only on economic needs. There may be some tension between the two modes of control, some ambivalence and uneasy feeling among members about the combination, but undoubtedly the total control is larger. Similarly, it is obvious that the church has more power over the priest than over the average parishioner. The parishioner is exposed to normative power, whereas the priest is controlled by both normative and remunerative powers.

The issue is complicated by the fact that the *amount* of each kind of power applied must be taken into account. If a labor union with social powers has economic power which is much greater than that of another union, this fact may explain why the first union has greater power in sum, despite some "waste" due to neutralization. A further complication follows from the fact that neutralization may also occur through application of the "wrong" power in terms of the cultural definition of what is appropriate

---

[9] R. K. Merton, *Mass persuasion: The social psychology of a war bond drive* (New York: Harper & Row, 1946), p. 47.
[10] *Ibid.*, p. 45.

to the particular organization and activity. For example, application of economic power in religious organizations may be less effective than in industries, not because two kinds of power are mixed, but because it is considered illegitimate to use economic pressures to attain religious goals. Finally, some organizations manage to apply two kinds of power abundantly and without much waste through neutralization, because they segregate the application of one power from that of the other. The examination below of combat armies and labor unions supplies an illustration of this point.

We have discussed some of the factors related to the tendency of organizations to specialize their power application. In conclusion, it seems that although there can be little doubt that such a tendency exists, its scope and a satisfactory explanation for it have yet to be established.

THREE KINDS OF INVOLVEMENT: A COMPARATIVE DIMENSION

Involvement, Commitment, and Alienation

Organizations must continually recruit means if they are to realize their goals. One of the most important of these means is the positive orientation of the participants to the organizational power. *Involvement*[11] refers to the cathectic-evaluative orientation of an actor to an object, characterized in terms of intensity and direction.

The intensity of involvement ranges from high to low. The direction is either positive or negative. We refer to positive involvement as *commitment*[12] and to negative involvement as *alienation*.[13] (The advantage

---

[11] *Involvement* has been used in a similar manner by Nancy C. Morse, *Satisfactions in the white-collar job* (Ann Arbor, Mich.: Survey Research Center, University of Michigan, 1953), pp. 76–96. The term is used in a somewhat different way by students of voting, who refer by it to the psychological investment in the outcome of an election rather than in the party, which would be parallel to Morse's usage and ours. See, for example, A. Campbell, G. Gurin, and W. E. Miller, *The voter decides* (Evanston, Ill.: Row, Peterson & Company, 1954), pp. 33–40.

[12] Mishler defined *commitment* in a similar though more psychological way: "An individual is committed to an organization to the extent that central tensions are integrated through organizationally relevant instrumental acts." Cited by C. Argyris, *Personality and organization* (New York: Harper & Row, 1957), p. 202.

[13] We draw deliberately on the associations this term has acquired from its usage by Marx and others. For a good analysis of the idea of alienation in Marxism and of its more recent development, see D. Bell, "The 'rediscovery' of alienation," *J. Phil.*, 1959, **56**, 933–952, and his *The end of ideology* (New York: Free Press, 1960), pp. 335–368.

of having a third term, *involvement*, is that it enables us to refer to the continuum in a neutral way.) Actors can accordingly be placed on an involvement continuum which ranges from a highly intense negative zone through mild negative and mild positive zones to a highly positive zone.[14]

Three Kinds of Involvement

We have found it helpful to name three zones of the involvement continuum, as follows: *alienative*, for the high alienation zone; *moral*, for the high commitment zone; and *calculative*, for the two mild zones. This classification of involvement can be applied to the orientations of actors in all social units and to all kinds of objects. Hence the definitions and illustrations presented below are not limited to organizations, but are applicable to orientations in general.

ALIENATIVE INVOLVEMENT. Alienative involvement designates an intense negative orientation; it is predominant in relations among hostile foreigners. Similar orientations exist among merchants in "adventure" capitalism, where trade is built on isolated acts of exchange, each side trying to maximize immediate profit.[15] Such an orientation seems to dominate the approach of prostitutes to transient clients.[16] Some slaves seem to have held similar attitudes to their masters and to their work. Inmates in prisons, prisoners of war, people in concentration camps, enlisted men in basic training, all tend to be alienated from their respective organizations.[17]

---

[14] Several sociologists have pointed out that the relationship between intensity and direction of involvement is a curvilinear one: the more positive or negative the orientation, the more intensely it is held. L. Guttman, "The Cornell technique for scale and intensity analysis," *Educ. & psychol. Measurement*, 1947, **7**, 247–279. By the same author see "The principal components of scale analysis" in S. A. Stouffer *et al.*, *Measurement and prediction* (Princeton, N.J.: Princeton University Press, 1950), pp. 312–371, and "The principal components of scalable attitudes." In P. F. Lazarsfeld (ed.), *Mathematical thinking in the social sciences* (New York: Free Press, 1954), pp. 229–230. See also E. A. Suchman, "The intensity component in attitude and opinion research," in S. A. Stouffer *et al.*, *Measurement and prediction, op. cit.*, pp. 213–276; and E. L. A. McDill, "A comparison of three measures of attitude intensity," *Social Forces*, 1959, **38**, 95–99.
[15] H. H. Gerth and C. W. Mills, *From Max Weber: Essays in sociology* (New York: Oxford, 1946), p. 67.
[16] K. Davis, "The sociology of prostitution," *Amer. sociol. Rev.*, 1937, **2**, 748–749.
[17] For a description of this orientation see D. Clemmer, *The prison community* (New York: Holt, Rinehart, and Winston, 1958), pp. 152 ff. Attitudes toward the police, particularly on the part of members of the lower classes, are often strictly alienative. See, for example, E. Banfield, *The moral basis of a backward society* (New York: Free Press, 1958).

CALCULATIVE INVOLVEMENT. Calculative involvement designates either a negative or a positive orientation of low intensity. Calculative orientations are predominant in relationships of merchants who have continuous business contacts. Attitudes of (and toward) permanent customers are often predominantly calculative, as are relationships among entrepreneurs in modern (rational) capitalism. Inmates in prisons who have established contact with prison authorities, such as "rats" and "peddlers," often have predominantly calculative attitudes toward those in power.[18]

MORAL[19] INVOLVEMENT. Moral involvement designates a positive orientation of high intensity. The involvement of the parishioner in his church, the devoted member in his party, and the loyal follower in his leader are all "moral."

There are two kinds of moral involvement, pure and social. They differ in the same way pure normative power differs from social power. Both are intensive modes of commitment, but they differ in their foci of orientation and in the structural conditions under which they develop. Pure moral commitments are based on internalization of norms and identification with authority (like Riesman's inner-directed "mode of conformity"); social commitment rests on sensitivity to pressures of primary groups and their members (Riesman's "other-directed"). Pure moral involvement tends to develop in vertical relationships, such as those between teachers and students, priests and parishioners, leaders and followers. Social involvement tends to develop in horizontal relationships like those in various types of primary groups. Both pure moral and social orientations might be found in the same relationships, but, as a rule, one orientation predominates.

Actors are means to each other in alienative and in calculative relations; but they are ends to each other in "social" relationships. In pure moral relationships the means-orientation tends to predominate. Hence, for example, the willingness of devoted members of totalitarian parties or religious orders to use each other. But unlike the means-orientation of calculative relationships, the means-orientation here is expected to be geared to needs of the collectivity in serving its goals, and not to those of an individual.

As has been stated, the preceding classification of involvement can

---

[18] G. M. Sykes, *The society of captives* (Princeton, N.J.: Princeton University Press, 1958), pp. 87–95.
[19] The term "moral" is used here and in the rest of the article to refer to an orientation of the actor; it does not involve a value position of the observer. (See T. Parsons, E. A. Shils *et al.*, *Toward a general theory of action* (Cambridge, Mass.: Harvard University Press, 1952), pp. 170 ff.

be applied to the orientations of actors in all social units and to all kinds of objects. The analysis in this book applies the scheme to orientations of lower participants in organizations to various organizational objects, in particular to the organizational power system. The latter includes (1) the directives the organization issues, (2) the sanctions by which it supports its directives, and (3) the persons who are in power positions. The choice of organizational power as the prime object of involvement to be examined here follows from a widely held conception of organization as an administrative system or control structure. To save breath, the orientation of lower participants to the organization as a power (or control) system is referred to subsequently as *involvement in the organization.* When other involvements are discussed, the object of orientation—for example, organizational goals—is specified.

Organizations are placed on the involvement continuum according to the modal involvement pattern of their lower participants. The placing of organizations in which the participants exhibit more than one mode of involvement is discussed in a later chapter.

COMPLIANCE AS A COMPARATIVE BASE

A Typology of Compliance

Taken together, the two elements—that is, the power applied by the organization *to* lower participants, and the involvement in the organization developed *by* lower participants—constitute the compliance relationship. Combining three kinds of power with three kinds of involvement produces nine types of compliance, as shown in the accompanying table.[20]

A Typology of Compliance Relations

Kinds of Power	Kinds of Involvement		
	ALIENATIVE	CALCULATIVE	MORAL
Coercive	1	2	3
Remunerative	4	5	6
Normative	7	8	9

[20] A formalization of the relationship between rewards allocation (which comes close to the concept of power as used here) and participation (which, as defined, is similar to the concept of involvement) has been suggested by R. Breton, "Reward structures and participation in an organization." Paper presented to the Eastern Sociological Society, April 1960.

The nine types are not equally likely to occur empirically. *Three—* the diagonal cases, 1, 5, and 9—*are found more frequently than the other six types.* This seems to be true because these three types constitute *congruent* relationships, whereas the other six do not.

THE CONGRUENT TYPES. The involvement of lower participants is determined by many factors, such as their personality structure, secondary socialization, memberships in other collectivities, and so on. At the same time, organizational powers differ in the kind of involvement they tend to generate. When the kind of involvement that lower participants have because of other factors[21] and the kind of involvement that tends to be generated by the predominant form of organizational power are the same, we refer to the relationship as *congruent.* For instance, inmates are highly alienated from prisons; coercive power tends to alienate; hence this is a case of a congruent compliance relationship.

Congruent cases are more frequent than noncongruent ones primarily because congruence is more effective, and organizations are social units under external and internal pressure to be effective. The effective application of normative powers, for example, requires that lower participants be highly committed. If lower participants are only mildly committed to the organization, and particularly if they are alienated from it, the application of normative power is likely to be ineffective. Hence the association of normative power with moral commitment.

Remuneration is at least partially wasted when actors are highly alienated, and therefore inclined to disobey despite material sanctions; it is also wasted when actors are highly committed, so that they would maintain an effective level of performance for symbolic, normative rewards only. Hence the association of remuneration with calculative involvement.

Coercive power is probably the only effective power when the organization is confronted with highly alienated lower participants. If, on the other hand, it is applied to committed or only mildly alienated lower participants, it is likely to affect adversely such matters as morale, recruitment, socialization, and communication, and thus to reduce effectiveness. (It is likely, though, to create high alienation, and in this way to create a congruent state.)

THE INCONGRUENT TYPES. Since organizations are under pressure to be effective, the suggestion that the six less effective incongruent types are not just theoretical possibilities but are found empirically calls for an explana-

[21] "Other factors" might include previous applications of the power.

tion. The major reason for this occurrence is that organizations have only limited control over the powers they apply and the involvement of lower participants. The exercise of power depends on the resources the organization can recruit and the license it is allowed in utilizing them. Involvement depends in part on external factors, such as membership of the participants in other collectivities (e.g., membership in labor unions[22]); basic value commitments (e.g., Catholic versus Protestant religious commitments[23]); and the personality structure of the participants (e.g., authoritarian[24]). All these factors may reduce the expected congruence of power and involvement.

A DYNAMIC HYPOTHESIS. Congruent types are more effective than incongruent types. Organizations are under pressure to be effective. Hence, to the degree that the environment of the organization allows, *organizations tend to shift their compliance structure from incongruent to congruent types* and *organizations which have congruent compliance structures tend to resist factors pushing them toward incongruent compliance structures.*

Congruence is attained by a change in either the power applied by the organization or the involvement of lower participants. Change of power takes place when, for instance, a school shifts from the use of corporal punishment to stress on the "leadership" of the teachers. The involvement of lower participants may be changed through socialization, changes in recruitment criteria, and the like.

Because the large majority of cases falls into the three categories representing congruent compliance, these three types form the basis for subsequent analysis. We refer to the coercive-alienative type as *coercive compliance;* to the remunerative-calculative type as *utilitarian compliance;* and to the normative-moral type as *normative compliance.* Students of organizational change, conflict, strain, and similar topics may find the six incongruent types more relevant to their work.

---

[22] On the effect of membership in labor unions on involvement in the corporation, see B. Willerman, "Overlapping group identification in an industrial setting." Paper presented to the American Psychological Association. Denver, September 1949, p. 4.
[23] See W. F. Whyte et al., *Money and motivation* (New York: Harper & Row, 1955), pp. 45–46. Protestants are reported to be more committed to the values of saving and productivity, whereas Catholics are more concerned with their social standing in the work group. This makes for differences in compliance: Protestants are reported to be more committed to the corporation's norms than Catholics.
[24] For instance, authoritarian personality structure is associated with a "custodial" orientation to mental patients. See Doris C. Gilbert, and D. J. Levinson, " 'Custodialism' and 'humanism' in staff ideology." In M. Greenblatt, D. J. Levinson, and R. H. Williams (eds.), *The patient and the mental hospital* (New York: Free Press, 1957), pp. 26–27.

Compliance and Authority

The typology of compliance relationships presented above highlights some differences between the present approach to the study of organizational control and that of studies conducted in the tradition of Weber. These studies tend to focus on authority, or legitimate power, as this concept is defined.[25] The significance of authority has been emphasized in modern sociology in the past, in order to overcome earlier biases that overemphasized force and economic power as the sources of social order. This emphasis, in turn, has led to an overemphasis on legitimate power. True, some authority can be found in the control structure of lower participants in most organizations. True, authority plays a role in maintaining the long-run operations of the organization. But so does nonlegitimated power. Since the significance of legitimate power has been fully recognized, it is time to lay the ghost of Marx and the old controversy, and to give full status to both legitimate and nonlegitimate sources of control.

Moreover, the concept of authority does not take into account differences among powers other than their legitimacy, in particular the nature of the sanctions (physical, material, or symbolic) on which power is based. All three types of power may be regarded as legitimate by lower participants: thus there is normative,[26] remunerative, and coercive authority (differentiated by the kind of power employed, for instance, by a

[25] For various definitions and usages of the concept, see C. J. Friedrich (ed.), *Authority* (Cambridge, Mass.: Harvard University Press, 1958). For a formalization of the concept in relation to power and leadership, see A. H. Barton, "Legitimacy, power, and compromise within formal authority structures—a formal model" (Bureau of Applied Social Research, Columbia University, 1958). Mimeographed.

[26] The concept of "normative authority" raises the question of the difference between this kind of authority and normative power. There is clearly a high *tendency* for normative power to be considered legitimate and thus to form an authority relationship. The reason for this tendency is that the motivational significance of rewards and deprivations depends not only on the objective nature of the power applied, but also on the meaning attached to it by the subject. Coercive and remunerative means of control are considerably less dependent on such interpretations than normative ones. Most actors in most situations will see a fine as a deprivation and confinement as a punishment. On the other hand, if the subject does not accept as legitimate the power of a teacher, a priest, or a party official, he is not likely to feel their condemnation or censure as depriving. Since normative power depends on manipulation of symbols, it is much more dependent on "meanings," and, in this sense, on the subordinate, than other powers. But it is by no means necessary that the application of normative power always be regarded as legitimate.

A person may, for example, be aware that another person has influenced his behavior by manipulation of symbolic rewards, but feel that he had no right to do so, that he ought not to have such power, or that a social structure in which normative powers are concentrated (e.g., partisan control over mass media; extensive advertising) is unjustified. A Catholic worker who feels that his priest has no right to condemn him because of his vote for the "wrong" candidate may still fear the priest's condemnation and be affected by it.

leader, a contractor, and a policeman.) But these powers differ in the likelihood that they will be considered legitimate by those subjected to them. Normative power is most likely to be considered legitimate; coercive, least likely; and remunerative is intermediate.

Finally, it is important to emphasize that involvement in the organization is affected both by the legitimacy of a directive and by the degree to which it frustrates the subordinate's need-dispositions. Alienation is produced not only by illegitimate exercise of power, but also by power which frustrates needs, wishes, desires. Commitment is generated not merely by directives which are considered legitimate but also by those which are in line with internalized needs of the subordinate. Involvement is positive if the line of action directed is conceived by the subordinate as both legitimate and gratifying. It is negative when the power is not granted legitimacy and when it frustrates the subordinate. Involvement is intermediate when either legitimation or gratification is lacking. Thus the study of involvement, and hence that of compliance, differs from the study of authority by taking into account the effects of the cathectic as well as the evaluative impact of directives on the orientation of lower participants.

LOWER PARTICIPANTS
AND ORGANIZATIONAL BOUNDARIES

Before we can begin our comparisons, the following questions still remain to be answered. Why do we make compliance of lower participants the focus of the comparison? Who exactly are "lower participants"? What are the lower boundaries of an organization? In answering these questions, we employ part of the analytical scheme suggested above, and thus supply the first test of its fruitfulness.

Why Lower Participants?

Compliance of lower participants is made the focus of this analysis for several reasons. First, the control of lower participants is more problematic than that of higher participants because, as a rule, the lower an actor is in the organizational hierarchy, the fewer rewards he obtains. His position is more deprived; organizational activities are less meaningful to him because he is less "in the know," and because often, from his position, only segments of the organization and its activities are visible.[27] Second,

---

[27] The term "visible" is used here and throughout this article as defined by Merton: "the extent to which the norms and the role performances within a group are readily open to observation by others." *Social theory and social structure*, rev. ed. (New York: Free Press, 1957), pp. 319 ff.

since we are concerned with systematic differences among organizations (the similarities having been more often explored), we focus on the ranks in which the largest differences in compliance can be found. An inter-organizational comparison of middle and higher ranks would show that their compliance structures differ much less than those of the lower ranks.

Who Are Lower Participants?

Organizational studies have used a large number of concrete terms to refer to lower participants: employees, rank-and-file, members, clients, customers, inmates.[28] These terms are rarely defined. They are customarily used to designate lower participants in more than one organization, but none can be used for all.

Actually, these terms can be seen as reflecting different positions on at least three analytical dimensions.[29] One is the *nature* (direction and intensity) of the actors' *involvement* in the organization. Unless some qualifying adjectives such as "cooperative" or "good" are introduced, *inmates* implies alienative involvement. *Clients* designates people with alienative or calculative involvement. *Customers* refers to people who have a relatively more alienative orientation than clients; one speaks of the clients of professionals but not ordinarily of their customers. *Member* is reserved for those who have at least some, usually quite strong, moral commitment to their organization. *Employee* is used for people with various degrees of calculative involvement.

A second dimension underlying these concrete terms is the degree to which lower participants are *subordinated* to organizational powers. Inmates, it seems, are more subordinated than employees, employees more than members, and members more than clients. A study in which subordination is a central variable would take into account that it includes at least two subvariables: the extent of control in each area (e.g., "tight" versus remote control); and the scope of control, measured by the number of areas in which the subject is subordinated. Such refinement is not required for our limited use of this dimension.

A third dimension is the amount of *performance* required from the

---

[28] For one of the best discussions of the concept of participation, its definition and dimensions, see J. H. Fichter, *Social relations in the urban parish* (Chicago: University of Chicago Press, 1954), Part I, *passim*.

[29] The difference between concrete and analytic membership in corporations has been pointed out by A. S. Feldman, "The interpenetration of firm and society." Paper presented at the International Social Science Council Round Table on Social Implications of Technical Change. Paris, 1959.

participants by the organization: it is high for employees, low for inmates, and lowest for clients and customers.[30]

Using concrete terms to designate groups of participants without specifying the underlying dimensions creates several difficulties. First of all, the terms cannot be systematically applied. Although "members" are in general positively involved, sometimes the term is used to designate lower participants with an alienative orientation. Archibald, for instance, uses this term to refer to members of labor unions who are members only *pro forma* and who see in the union simply another environmental constraint, to which they adjust by paying dues.

> Most workers entered the yards not merely ignorant of unions, but distrustful of them. . . . They nonetheless joined the unions, as they were compelled to do, with little protest. They paid the initiation fees, averaging not more than twenty dollars, much as they would have bought a ticket to the county fair: it cost money, but maybe the show would be worth the outlay. As for dues, they paid them with resignation to the principle that all joys of life are balanced by a measure of pain.[31]

The term *customers* suggests that the actors have no moral commitments to their sources of products and services. But sometimes it is used to refer to people who buy from cooperatives, frequent only unionized barbers, and remain loyal to one newspaper—that is, to people who are willing to suffer some economic loss because they see in these sources of service something which is "good in itself"—people who, in short, have some moral commitments.

Any moral commitment on the part of mental patients, designated as *inmates,* is viewed either with surprise or as a special achievement of the particular mental hospital; on the other hand, members of labor unions are "expected" to show moral commitment and are labeled "apathetic" if they do not. The fact that some mental patients view their hospital as their home, and thus are positively involved, whereas labor union members may see their organization as a secondary group only, is hidden by the terminology employed. The same point could be made for differences in performance and in subordination.

[30] Participants of a social unit might also be defined as all those who share an institutionalized set of role-expectations. We shall not employ this criterion since it blurs a major distinction, that between the organization as such and its social environment. Members of most groups share such role-expectations with outsiders.

A criterion of participation which is significant for other purposes than ours is whether lower participants have formal or actual powers, such as those reflected in the right to vote, submit grievances, or strike.

[31] Katherine Archibald, *Wartime shipyards* (Berkeley and Los Angeles: University of California Press, 1947), pp. 131–132.

Although the use of such concrete terms leads to overgeneralization, by implying that all lower participants of an organization have the characteristics usually associated with the label, they can also impede generalization. An illustration is supplied by studies of parishioners. Many of these studies focus on problems of participation, such as "apathy," high turnover, and declining commitment. But rarely are comparisons drawn, or insights transferred, from the study of members of voluntary associations and political organizations. Actually, all these organizations are concerned with the moral commitment of lower participants who have few performance obligations and little subordination to the organization.

Another advantage of specifying the analytical dimensions underlying these concepts is that the number of dimensions is limited, whereas the number of concrete terms grows continuously with the number of organizations studied. Thus the study of hospitals introduces patients; the analysis of churches brings up parishioners; and the examination of armies adds soldiers. Following the present procedure, we can proceed to characterize the lower participants of additional organizations by the use of the same three dimensions.

Specifying the underlying dimensions enables us not only to formulate analytical profiles of a large variety of lower participants, but also to compare them systematically with each other on these three dimensions. For instance, "soldiers" (in combat) are high on all three dimensions, whereas inmates are high on subordination and alienation but low on performance; employees are medium in involvement and subordination, but high on performance obligations. The import of such comparisons will become evident later.

Finally, whereas concrete terms tend to limit analysis to participants at particular levels, analytical terms such as alienative, calculative, and moral can be applied equally well to participants at all levels of the organizational hierarchy.

Ideally, in a book such as this, we should refer to lower participants in analytical terms, those of various degrees of involvement, subordination, and performance obligations. Since this would make the discussion awkward, the concrete terms are used, but only to refer to *typical* analytical constellations. *Inmates* are lower participants with high alienation, low performance obligations, and high subordination. The term will not be used to refer to other combinations which are sometimes found among lower participants in prisons. *Members* is used to refer only to lower participants who are highly committed, medium on subordination, and low on performance obligations; it is not used to refer to alienated lower participants in voluntary associations. Similarly, other terms are used as specified below.

Analytical Specifications of Some Concepts
Referring to Lower Participants*

Lower Participants	Nature of Involvement (Intensity and Direction)	Subordination	Performance Obligations
Inmates	High, negative	High	Low
Employees	Low, negative or positive	Medium	High
Customers	Low, negative or positive	None	Low
Parishioners	High, positive	Low	Low
Members	High, positive	Medium to Low	Low
Devoted Adherents	High, positive	High	High

* This table contains a set of definitions to be used. It is not exhaustive, either in concepts referring to lower participants or in possible combinations of "scores" on the various dimensions.

Lower versus Higher Participants

Higher participants have a "permanent" power advantage over lower participants because of their organizational position. Thus, by definition, higher participants as a group are less *subordinated* than lower participants. Often, though not in all organizational types, they are also more *committed,* and have more *performance obligations* (if we see decision making and other mental activities as performances). Thus the three dimensions which serve to distinguish among various types of lower participants also mark the dividing line between lower and higher participants. These very dimensions also enable us to suggest a way to delineate the organizational boundaries—that is, to distinguish between participants and nonparticipants.

Organizational Boundaries

Students of organizations must often make decisions about the boundaries of the unit they are studying: who is a participant, who an outsider. March and Simon, for example, take a broad view of organizational boundaries: "When we describe the chief participants of most business organizations, we generally limit our attention to the following five major classes: employees, investors, suppliers, distributers, and consumers."[32]

[32] J. G. March and H. Simon, *Organizations* (New York: Wiley, 1958), p. 89.

We follow a narrower definition and see as participants all actors who are high on at least one of the three dimensions of participation: involvement, subordination, and performance. Thus, students, inmates, soldiers, workers, and many others are included. Customers and clients, on the other hand, who score low on all three criteria, are considered "outsiders."

We should like to underscore the importance of this way of delineating the organizational boundaries. It draws the line much "lower" than most studies of bureaucracies, which tend to include only persons who are part of a formal hierarchy: priests, but not parishioners; stewards, but not union members; guards, but not inmates; nurses, but not patients. We treat organizations as collectivities of which the lower participants are an important segment. To exclude them from the analysis would be like studying colonial structures without the natives, stratification without the lower classes, or a political regime without the citizens or voters.

It seems to us especially misleading to include the lower participants in organizational charts when they have a formal role, as privates in armies or workers in factories, and to exclude them when they have no such status, as is true for parishioners or members. This practice leads to such misleading comparisons as seeing the priests as the privates of the church and teachers as the lowest-ranking participants of schools, in both cases ignoring the psychological import of having "subordinates." One should not let legal or administrative characteristics stand in the way of a sociological analysis. However, the main test of the decision to delineate the organization as we have chosen follows: it lies in the scope, interest, and validity of the propositions this approach yields. . . .[33]

[33] A preliminary review of research conducted since the first publication of these lines by a number of scholars. See Amitai Etzioni, "Organizational Dimensions and Their Interrelations: a Theory of Compliance," in Bernard Indik and S. Kenneth Berien, eds., *People, Groups and Organizations* (New York: Teachers College Press, 1968; Columbia University Press, 1968), pp. 94–109.

THE THEORY OF ORGANIZATIONAL EQUILIBRIUM

James G. March and Herbert A. Simon

The Barnard-Simon theory of organizational equilibrium is essentially a theory of motivation—a statement of the conditions under which an organization can induce its members to continue their participation, and hence assure organizational survival. The central postulates of the theory are stated by Simon, Smithburg, and Thompson as follows:

1. An organization is a system of interrelated social behaviors of a number of persons whom we shall call the *participants* in the organization.
2. Each participant and each group of participants receives *from* the organization *inducements* in return for which he makes *to* the organization *contributions*.
3. Each participant will continue his participation in an organization only so long as the inducements offered him are as great or greater (measured in terms of *his* values and in terms of the alternatives open to him) than the contributions he is asked to make.
4. The contributions provided by the various groups of participants are the source from which the organization manufactures the inducements offered to participants.
5. Hence, an organization is "solvent"—and will continue in existence —only so long as the contributions are sufficient to provide inducements in large enough measure to draw forth these contributions.[1]

Reprinted in part from James G. March and Herbert A. Simon, *Organizations* (New York: Wiley, 1958), pp. 84–93, 106, 107–108, by permission of the authors and the publisher. Copyright 1958 by John Wiley & Sons.

[1] H. A. Simon, D. W. Smithburg, and V. A. Thompson, *Public Administration* (New York: Knopf, 1950), pp. 381–382.

The theory, like many theoretical generalizations, verges on the tautological. Specifically, to test the theory, and especially the crucial postulate 3, we need independent empirical estimates of (a) the behavior of participants in joining, remaining in, or withdrawing from organizations; and (b) the balance of inducements and contributions for each participant, measured in terms of his "utilities."

The observation of participants joining and leaving organizations is comparatively easy. It is more difficult to find evidence of the value of variable (b) that does not depend on the observation of (a). Before we can deal with the observational problem, however, we must say a bit more about the concepts of inducements and contributions.

INDUCEMENTS

Inducements are "payments" made by (or through) the organization to its participants (e.g., wages to a worker, service to a client, income to an investor). These payments can be measured in units that are independent of their utility to the participants (e.g., wages and income can be measured in terms of dollars, service to clients in terms of hours devoted to him). Consequently, for an individual participant we can specify a set of inducements, each component of the set representing a different dimension of the inducements offered by the organization. Thus, each component of the inducement can be measured uniquely and independently of the utilities assigned to it by the participants.

INDUCEMENT UTILITIES

For each component in the set of inducements there is a corresponding utility value. For the moment we will not be concerned with the shape of the utility function; but we do not exclude from consideration a step function. The utility function for a given individual reduces the several components of the inducements to a common dimension.

CONTRIBUTIONS

We assume that a participant in an organization makes certain "payments" to the organization (e.g., work from the worker, fee from the client, capital from the investor). These payments, which we shall call contributions, can be measured in units that are independent of their utility to the participants. Consequently, for any individual participant we can specify a set of contributions.

CONTRIBUTION UTILITIES

A utility function transforming contributions into utilities of the individual contributor can be defined in more than one way. A reasonable definition of the utility of a contribution is the value of the alternatives that an individual foregoes in order to make the contribution. As we shall see below, this definition of contribution utilities allows us to introduce into the analysis the range of behavior alternatives open to the participant.

These definitions of inducements and contributions permit two general approaches to the observational problem. On the one hand, we can try to estimate the utility balance directly by observing the behavior (including responses to pertinent questions) of participants. On the other hand, if we are prepared to make some simple empirical assumptions about utility functions, we can make predictions from changes in the amounts of inducements and contributions, without reference to their utilities.

To estimate the inducement-contribution utility balance directly, the most logical type of measure is some variant of individual satisfaction (with the job, the service, the investment, etc.). It appears reasonable to assume that the greater the difference between inducements and contributions, the greater the individual satisfaction. However, the critical "zero points" of the satisfaction scale and the inducement-contribution utility balance are not necessarily identical. The zero point for the satisfaction scale is the point at which one begins to speak of degrees of "dissatisfaction" rather than degrees of "satisfaction." It is, therefore, closely related to the level of aspiration and is the point at which we would predict a substantial increase in search behavior on the part of the organism.

The zero point on the inducement-contribution utility scale, on the other hand, is the point at which the individual is indifferent to leaving an organization. We have ample evidence that these two zero points are not identical, but, in particular, that very few of the "satisfied" participants leave an organization, whereas some, but typically not all, of the "unsatisfied" participants leave.[2]

How do we explain these differences? The explanation lies primarily in the ways in which alternatives to current activity enter into the scheme (and this is one of the reasons for defining contribution utilities in terms of opportunities foregone). Dissatisfaction is a cue for search behavior. Being dissatisfied, the organism expands its program for exploring alternatives. If over the long run this search fails, the aspiration level is gradually

[2] L. G. Reynolds, *The Structure of Labor Markets* (New York: Harper & Row, 1951).

revised downward. We assume, however, that the change in aspiration level occurs slowly, so that dissatisfaction in the short run is quite possible. On the other hand, the inducement-contribution utility balance adjusts quickly to changes in the perception of alternatives. When fewer and poorer alternatives are perceived to be available, the utility of activities foregone decreases; and this adjustment occurs rapidly.

Consequently, we can use satisfaction expressed by the individual as a measure of the inducement-contribution utility balance only if it is used in conjunction with an estimate of perceived alternatives available. Speaking roughly, only the desire to move enters into judgments of satisfaction; desire to move *plus* the perceived ease of movement enters into the inducement-contribution utility measure. Many students of mobility (particularly those concerned with the mobility of workers) have tended to ignore one or the other of these two facets of the decision to participate.[3]

Direct observation of the inducement-contribution utilities, however, is not the only possible way to estimate them. Provided we make certain assumptions about the utility functions, we can infer the utility balance directly from observations of changes in the inducements or contributions measured in nonutility terms. Three major assumptions are useful and perhaps warranted. First, we assume that the utility functions change only slowly. Second, we assume that each utility function is monotonic with respect to its corresponding inducement or contribution. Although we may not know what the utility of an increase in wages will be, we are prepared to assume it will be positive. Third, we assume that the utility functions of fairly broad classes of people are very nearly the same; within a given subculture we do not expect radical differences in values. Also, we can expect that if an increase in a given inducement produces an increase in utility for one individual, it will produce an increase for other individuals.

There are other reasonable assumptions about individual utility functions; some will be indicated below when we relate individual participation to other factors. These three assumptions, however, in themselves lead to a variety of estimation procedures. Under the first assumption the short-run effect of a change in inducements or contributions will be uncontaminated by feedback effects. By the second assumption (particularly in conjunction with the third) a host of ordinal predictions can be made on the basis of knowledge of changes in the inducements and contributions. The third assumption permits us to estimate some of the cardinal prop-

[3] J. M. Rice, M. Hill, and E. L. Trist, "The Representation of Labour Turnover as a Social Process," *Human Relations*, 3 (1950), 349–372; J. Behrend, "Absence and Labour Turnover in a Changing Economic Climate," *Occupational Psychology*, 27 (1953), 69–79.

erties of the inducements-contributions balance, avoiding the problem of interpersonal comparison of utilities.

Assumptions such as those listed have some a priori validity, but it is more important that much of the evidence currently available on the behavior of participants is consistent with them. Thus, predictions are frequently and often successfully made by businessmen as to the feasibility of proposed organizational plans.

Consider the analysis of a businessman exploring the feasibility of a business venture. His first step is to construct an operating plan showing what activities and facilities are required to carry on the proposed business, including estimates of the quantities of "inputs" and "outputs" of all categories. In the language of economics, he estimates the "production function." In the language of organization theory, the production function states the rates of possible conversion of contributions into inducements.[4]

His second step is to estimate the monetary inducements that will be needed to obtain the inputs in the amounts required, and the monetary contributions that can be exacted for the outputs—i.e., the prices of factors of production and of product. In estimating these monetary inducements, predictions are being made as to the inducements-contributions balances of various classes of participants. Let us give some hypothetical examples:

SALARIES AND WAGES. Information is obtained on "going rates of wages" for similar classes of work in other companies in the same area. An implicit *ceteris paribus* assumption is made with respect to other inducements, or (if the work, say, is particularly unpleasant, if proposed working conditions are particularly good or bad, etc.) the monetary inducement is adjusted upward or downward to compensate for the other factors. If the problem is to attract workers from other organizations, it is assumed that a wage differential or other inducement will be required to persuade them to change.

CAPITAL. Information is obtained on "the money market"—i.e., the kinds of alternative investment opportunities that are available, the weight attached to various elements of risk, and the levels of interest rates. It is then assumed that to induce investment, the terms (interest rates, security, etc.) must be at least equal to the inducements available in alternative investments.

The same procedure is followed for the inducements to other participants. In each case, information is required as to the alternative inducements offered by other organizations, and these establish the "zero level"

---

[4] H. A. Simon, "A Comparison of Organizational Theories," *The Review of Economic Studies*, 20 (1952–1953), 40–48.

of the net inducement-contribution balance. If nonmonetary factors are not comparable among alternatives, an estimated adjustment is made of the monetary inducements by way of compensation. Of course, the adjustment may just as well be made in the nonmonetary factors (e.g., in product quality).

If the planned inducements, including the monetary inducements, give a positive balance for all groups of participants, the plan is feasible. If the plan is subsequently carried out, a comparison of the actual operations with the estimates provides an empirical test of the assumptions and the estimates. If the outcomes fail to confirm the assumptions, the businessman may still choose which of the two sets of assumptions he will alter. He may interpret the result as evidence that the basic inducements-contributions hypothesis is incorrect, or he may conclude that he has estimated incorrectly the zero points of one or more of the inducements-contributions balances. The fact is, however, that such predictions are frequently made with substantial success.

The testing of the theory is not confined to predicting the survival of new enterprises. At any time in the life of an organization when a change is made—that (a) explicitly alters the inducements offered to any group of participants; (b) explicitly alters the contributions demanded from them; or (c) alters the organizational activity in any way that will affect inducements or contributions—on any of these occasions, a prediction can be made as to the effect of the change on participation. The effects may be measurable in terms of turnover rates of employees, sales, etc., as appropriate.

THE PARTICIPANTS

The theory of organizational equilibrium, as we have formulated it here, implies a structure—an organization—underlying the equilibrium. Specifically, there must exist a social system involving the participants that exhibits both a high degree of interrelationship and substantial differentiation from other systems within the total social milieu.

Up to this point, we have not tried to be precise in defining participation. In fact, we must necessarily be somewhat arbitrary in identifying some particular individuals as participants in a given organization. A number of individuals other than those we will identify as principal participants in a business organization receive inducements from the organization and provide contributions to its existence, and under special circumstances such "participants" may assume a dominant role in determining the equilibrium of the organization. But when we describe the chief participants of most business organizations, we generally limit our attention to the following five major classes: employees, investors, suppliers, distributors, and consumers.

Most obvious in any catalogue of organizational participants are the employees, including the management. Ordinarily, when we talk of organizational participants what we mean are workers, and membership in a business organization is ordinarily treated as equivalent to employment. Employees receive wages and other gratuities and donate work (production) and other contributions to the organization. As will become obvious below, employment is the area of participation in organizations in which the most extensive research has been executed.

The role of investors as participants in the organization is explicit in the economic theory of the firm but has rarely been included in other analyses of organizational behavior. A close analogue is found in some treatises on public administration where external power groups are dealt with specifically.[5] Although the participation of investors in the activities of business firms is frequently less active than that of political power groups in the management of governmental units, the behavior of investing participants is not so insignificant in the general American business scene as to warrant excluding them from consideration.

The distinction between units in a production-distribution process that are "in" the organization and those that are "out" of the organization typically follows the legal definition of the boundaries of a particular firm. We find it fruitful to use a more functional criterion that includes both the suppliers and the distributors of the manufacturing core of the organization (or its analogue where the core of the organization is not manufacturing). Thus, in the automobile industry it is useful to consider the automobile dealers as component parts of an automobile manufacturing organization.

Finally, the role of consumers in an organization has, like the role of investors, been generally ignored except by economic theorists. Since consumers are clearly part of the equilibrating system, organization theory must include in its framework the major components of a theory of consumption.

Taken too literally, this concept of organizations incorporates almost any knowledge about human behavior as a part of organization theory. However, we will limit our primary attention here to the participation of employees. Labor mobility has been studied at some length by both economists and social psychologists. Consequently, we will be able to find at least some evidence for the propositions cited. In general, the areas of

[5] Simon, Smithburg, and Thompson, op. cit.; D. B. Truman, The Government Process (New York: Knopf, 1951); J. L. Freeman, The Political Process, Executive Bureau–Legislative Committee Relations (New York: Random House, Inc., 1955).

investment behavior, supplier behavior, and middleman behavior are less well developed; and their propositions less well documented. Consumer behavior presents a somewhat different case, being the subject of considerable research.[6] Nevertheless, we will limit ourselves in this area to the general observations made below.[7]

EMPLOYEE PARTICIPATION:
THE PARTICIPATION CRITERION

In one respect an employee's relation to the organization is quite different from that of other participants. In joining the organization he accepts an authority relation; i.e., he agrees that within some limits (defined both explicitly and implicitly by the terms of the employment contract) he will accept as the premises of his behavior orders and instructions supplied to him by the organization. Associated with this acceptance are commonly understood procedures for "legitimating" communications and clothing them with authority for employees. Acceptance of authority by the employee gives the organization a powerful means for influencing him—more powerful than persuasion, and comparable to the evoking processes that call forth a whole program of behavior in response to a stimulus.

On the assumption that employees act in a subjectively rational manner, we can make some predictions about the scope of the authority relation from our knowledge of the inducements and contributions of the employees and other organization members.[8] An employee will be willing to enter into an employment contract only if it does not matter to him "very much" what activities (within the area of acceptance agreed on in the contract) the organization will instruct him to perform, or if he is compensated in some way for the possibility that the organization will impose unpleasant activities on him. It will be advantageous for the organization to establish an authority relation when the employee activities that are optimal for the organization (i.e., maximize the inducement utility to other participants of the employee's activity) cannot be predicted accurately in advance.

These propositions can be restated in a form that permits them to be tested by looking at terms of the employment contract. A particular aspect of an employee's behavior can be (a) specified in the employment contract (e.g., as the wage rate usually is), (b) left to the employee's discretion (e.g., sometimes, but not always, whether he smokes on the

[6] L. H. Clark (ed.), *Consumer Behavior* (New York: New York University, 1958).
[7] See "Extension to Other Participants."
[8] Simon, *loc. cit.*

job), or (c) brought within the authority of the employer (e.g., the specific tasks he performs within the range fixed by the job specification). The conditions that make it advantageous to stipulate an aspect of behavior in the contract are sharp conflict of interest (e.g., as to wage level) and some uncertainty as to what that interest is. It is advantageous to leave to the employee's discretion those aspects that are of little interest to the employer but great interest to the employee; and to subject the employee to the organization's authority in those aspects that are of relatively great interest to the employer, comparatively unimportant to the employee, and about which the employer cannot make accurate predictions much in advance of performance. . . .

To construct a series of hypotheses relating employee participation to external variables, we must first establish a criterion for "participation." Three methods of measuring participation yield substantially different results. First, we can measure the quantity of production by the individual worker. Second, we can use an absence criterion. Permanent physical absence associated with leaving the company payroll represents the extreme value on the low side. Differences in on-the-job productivity are not captured by the absence criterion, but employees are distinguished by their absence rates as well as their turnover rates. Third, we can use a turnover criterion: we can identify participation with the all-or-none phenomena of being on or off the organization payroll.

Although it may appear at first blush that these measures simply reflect different degrees of disassociation from the organization and, therefore, are simply different points on a common continuum, the available empirical evidence indicates no consistent relation among measures of production, absences, and voluntary turnover.[9] The correlations are sometimes high, sometimes low; and the antecedent conditions for each result are difficult to specify. Some reasons for these findings are suggested by the available research, although substantiation is difficult.

First, under what conditions should we expect to find low absence (and/or productivity) associated with high voluntary turnover? We might expect that if extreme penalties are imposed for absence (relative to those generally expected in the group employed), absence rates will tend to be low among those who choose to stay on the job. But we should also expect to find a high rate of exit from the job. Similarly, where the

[9] The Action Society Trust, *Size and Morale* (London: The Trust, 1953); N. C. Morse, *Satisfactions in the White-Collar Job* (Ann Arbor, Mich.: Survey Research Center, University of Michigan, 1953); A. H. Brayfield and W. H. Crockett, "Employee Attitudes and Employee Performance," *Psychological Bulletin*, 52 (1955), 396–424.

ability to leave the organization is restrained (e.g., by governmental fiat), we should expect to find low voluntary turnover rates but (particularly if labor is scarce) relatively high absence rates.[10]

Second, under what conditions should we expect to find a positive relation between absence and turnover? Assume (1) that motivation to avoid the demands (i.e., contributions) of the job situation stems primarily from dissatisfaction with the inducements-contributions balance, (2) that for most people motivation to seek relief through temporary absence occurs at a point related consistently to the point at which motivation to quit occurs, and (3) that the factors contributing to individual dissatisfaction are general to the population of workers rather than specific to individual workers. Under these assumptions absence and voluntary turnover will be positively related when the penalties associated with absence and withdrawal are "normal."

Although we have scarcely touched the complexity of the relation among absenteeism, sickness, and turnover, we can see that the choice of a criterion of participation will significantly affect the propositions about participation. We propose here to use a turnover criterion, both because there is some intuitive sense in which such a criterion is most meaningful and because we have already dealt with the production criterion (which is closely related, at least conceptually, to the absence criterion) in the previous chapter. At the same time, however, we will attempt to point out how an absence criterion would support similar or different propositions.

[10] E. Mayo and G. F. Lombard, *Teamwork and Labor Turnover in the Aircraft Industry of Southern California* (Cambridge, Mass.: Division of Research, Harvard University, 1944).

ECONOMIC DEVELOPMENT, RESEARCH AND DEVELOPMENT, POLICY MAKING: SOME CONVERGING VIEWS

Albert O. Hirschman and Charles E. Lindblom

When, in their pursuit of quite different subject matters, a group of social scientists independently of each other appear to converge in a somewhat unorthodox view of certain social phenomena, investigation is in order. The convergence to be examined in this paper is that of the views of Hirschman on economic development, Burton Klein and William Meckling on technological research and development, and Lindblom on policy-making in general. These three independent lines of work appear to challenge in remarkably similar ways some widely accepted generalizations about what is variously described in the literature as the process of problem solving and decision making. Before discussing the interrelations of these views, we will give a brief description of each.[1]

HIRSCHMAN ON ECONOMIC DEVELOPMENT

A major argument of Hirschman's *Strategy of Economic Development* is his attack on "balanced growth" as either a *sine qua non* of development or as a meaningful proximate objective of development policy. His basic

Reprinted from *Behavioral Science*, 7 (1962), 211–222, with omissions.

[1] Another line of related work is represented in Andrew Gunder Frank's "conflicting standards" organization theory. It is sufficiently different to fall outside the scope of the present article but sufficiently similar to be of interest to anyone who wishes to explore further the areas of unorthodoxy described here. A. G. Frank, Goal ambi-

defense of *unbalanced growth* is that, at any one point of time, an economy's resources are not to be considered as rigidly fixed in amount, and that more resources or factors of production will actually come into play if development is marked by sectoral imbalances that galvanize private entrepreneurs or public authorities into action. Even if we know exactly what the economy of a country would look like at a higher plateau, he argues, we can reach this plateau more expeditiously through the path of unbalanced growth because of the additional thrusts received by the economy as it gets into positions of imbalance.

Take an economy with two sectors that are interdependent in the sense that each sector provides some inputs to the other and that the income receivers of each sector consume part of the other sector's final output. With *given* rates of capital formation and increase in the labor supply, it is possible to specify at any one time a certain pair of growth rates for both sectors that is optimally efficient from the points of view of resource utilization and consumer satisfaction. This is balanced growth in its widest sense. Unbalanced growth will manifest its comparative initial inefficiency through a variety of symptoms: losses here, excess profits there, and concomitant relative price movements; or, in the absence of the latter, through shortages, bottlenecks, spoilage, and waste. In an open economy, a possible direct repercussion is a balance-of-payment deficit. In other words, sectoral imbalances will induce a variety of sensations—presence of pain or expectation of pleasure—in the economic operators and policy makers, whose reactions should all converge toward increasing output in the lagging sector.

To the extent that the imbalance is thus self-correcting through a variety of market and nonmarket mechanisms, the economy may be propelled forward jerkily, but also more quickly than under conditions of balanced expansion. Admittedly, the process is likely to be more costly in terms of resource utilization, but the imbalances at the same time *call forth* more resources and investment than would otherwise become available. The crucial, but plausible, assumption here is that there is some "slack" in the economy; and that additional investment, hours of work, productivity, and decision making can be squeezed out of it by the pressure mechanisms set up by imbalances. On the assumption of a given volume of resources and investment, it may be highly irrational not to attempt to come as close as possible to balanced growth; but without these assump-

---

guity and conflicting standards: an approach to the study of organization. *Human Organization*, 1959, 17, 8–13; see also A. G. Frank and R. Cohen, Conflicting standards and selective enforcement in social organization and social change: a cross cultural test. Paper read at the American Anthropological Association meeting in Mexico City, December, 1959.

tions there is likely to exist such a thing as an "optimal degree of imbalance." In other words, within a certain range, the increased economy in the use of given resources that might come with balanced growth is more than offset by *increased resource mobilization* afforded by unbalanced growth. . . .

KLEIN AND MECKLING ON
RESEARCH AND DEVELOPMENT

Another apparently converging line is represented in the work of Klein and Meckling, who have for several years been studying military experience with alternative research and development policies for weapons systems.[2] They allege that development is both less costly and more speedy when marked by duplication, "confusion," and lack of communication among people working along parallel lines. Perhaps more fundamentally, they argue against too strenuous attempts at integrating various subsystems into a well-articulated, harmonious, general system; they rather advocate the full exploitation of fruitful ideas regardless of their "fit" to some preconceived pattern of specifications.

Suppose a new airplane engine is to be developed and we know that it ought to have certain minimal performance characteristics with respect to, say, range and speed. A curve such as SS in Figure 1 may represent this requirement. Is anything to be said here in favor of approaching the goal through an unbalanced path, rather than through shooting straight at the target?

The first and perhaps most important point made here by Klein and Meckling is that there is no single point to shoot at, but a great number of acceptable combinations of the two performance characteristics (shown in Figure 1 by the set of all points lying to the northeast of the curve SS). It is perfectly arbitrary for anyone to pick out a point such as S' as *the* target to shoot at even though this point may be in some sense the expected value of the desired technological advances. The argument then proceeds to show that because of this wide range of acceptable outcomes, and because of the uncertainty as to what is achievable, *any* advance in the northeasterly direction (such as PP') should be pushed and capitalized on, rather than bent at great effort in the direction of any arbitrarily predetermined target.

[2] B. Klein, A radical proposal for R and D. *Fortune*, May 1958, 112; The decision-making problem in development. Paper No. P-1916, The RAND Corporation, Santa Monica, California, February 19, 1960. See also B. Klein and W. Meckling, Application of operations research to development decisions. *Operations Res.*, 1958, 6, 352–363.

The assumption here is that inventions and technical progress follow a "path of their own" to which we should defer: in other words, instead of getting upset at an early stage of development with the "lack of balance" between the two performance specifications (the engine that is being developed is all speed and very little range), we should go on developing it as best we can without reference to point S'. The simplest reason for this is that we may land anyway with a combination of the two characteristics that is acceptable for the purpose at hand: at P'' we have much more speed than we originally bargained for and enough range.

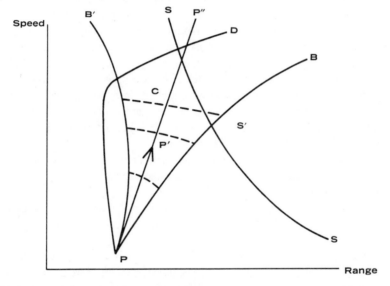

FIGURE 1.   *Alternative paths of development of two performance characteristics.*

But then there may be other, more interesting reasons why "a wise and salutary neglect" of the balance between the two performance requirements may be desirable in the earlier stages of research and development. A second possibility is that, as an invention or technological advance matures and is fully articulated, possibilities of adjustment may appear that are not present earlier. In Figure 1 we represent this phenomenon by two boundaries PB and PB' that limit the range within which trade-offs between the two characteristics (along the dotted curves) are possible. If these boundaries diverge as shown in our figure, then we should postpone our attempt at trade-offs until we reach the range of greater flexibility (point C).

Third, sometimes the new product that is being developed and which at one stage seemed to be so top-heavy with one of our two requirements will veer around along the path *PD* and, in the course of its "natural" development, will acquire the required amount of the second characteristic. To be sure, to assume that this will inevitably happen would require that one places his faith in some basic harmonies, similar to the Greek belief that the truly beautiful will possess moral excellence as well.[3]

Most of what has been said for products with several characteristics applies also to systems with several complementary components. But some of the problems in which we are interested come into sharper focus when we deal with systems where individual components can be independently worked at and perfected. Here also Klein and Meckling advocate full articulation of the components, even though this may mean uneven advances in their development and disregard for their over-all integration into the system at an early stage.

Once again, a principal reason is uncertainty. The final configuration of the system is unknown, and knowledge increases as some of the subsystems become articulated. In the first place, knowledge about the nature of one subsystem increases the number of clues about the desirable features of another, just as it is easier to fit in a piece of a jigsaw puzzle when some of the surrounding pieces are already in place. Second, if two pieces (subsystems) have been worked at independently, it is usually possible to join them together by small adjustments: what is important is to develop the pieces, even though they may not be perfectly adjusted to each other to start with.

Obviously if the subsystems are being perfected fairly independently from one another it is likely that one of them will be fully developed ahead of the others, a situation quite similar to that where one sector of the economy races ahead of another. Also it is likely that even if they reach the point of serviceability together, some of them will be "out of phase" with the others, as in the case of a hi-fi system with an amplifier that is far too good for the loudspeaker.[4]

---

[3] To assume the existence of such basic harmonies may be foolish, but it certainly helps us in making crucial decisions such as choosing a wife or a profession.

[4] Klein (1960, *op. cit.*) gives a straightforward exposition of the logical and empirical differences between development decisions and decisions to maximize the use of existing resources. He again advocates looseness in goal-setting and gradual, oblique, or multiple approaches to the goal. In doing so, Klein now emphasizes the contrast between the decision maker in established production processes who accepts the relatively small uncertainties he faces as a datum, and the development decision maker whose chief purpose is to reduce the huge variance of the initial estimates so that successive investment and production decisions can be made with increasing degrees of confidence. In addition, he argues that it is of rather secondary interest to the developer to achieve an efficient combination of inputs. His main interest is achieving a breakthrough to a new product or to radically improved performance characteristics.

LINDBLOM ON POLICY MAKING

A third converging line is represented in Lindblom's papers on policy-making processes.[5] These papers aspire to fairly large-scale generalizations or to what, in some usages, would be called theory construction; while the points of departure of Hirschman and Klein and Meckling are two widely different, but still fairly specific, problem-solving contexts. The differences among the studies in this respect make the convergences all the more noteworthy.

Lindblom's point of departure is a denial of the general validity of two assumptions implicit in most of the literature on policy making. The first is that public policy problems can best be solved by attempting to understand them; the second is that there exists sufficient agreement to provide adequate criteria for choosing among possible alternative policies. Although the first is widely accepted—in many circles almost treated as a self-evident truth—it is often false. The second is more often questioned in contemporary social science; yet many of the most common prescriptions for rational problem solving follow only if it is true.

Conventional descriptions of rational decision making identify the following aspects: (1) clarification of objectives or values, (2) survey of alternative means of reaching objectives, (3) identification of consequences, including side effects or by-products, of each alternative means, and (4) evaluation of each set of consequences in light of the objectives. However, Lindblom notes, for a number of reasons such a *synoptic* or comprehensive attempt at problem solving is not possible to the degree that clarification of objectives founders on social conflict, that required information is either not available or available only at prohibitive cost, or that the problem is simply too complex for man's finite intellectual capacities. Its complexity may stem from an impossibly large number of alternative policies and their possible repercussions from imponderables in the delineation of objectives even in the absence of social disagreement on them, from a supply of information too large to process in the mind, or from still other causes.

It does not logically follow, Lindblom argues, that when synoptic decision making is extremely difficult it should nevertheless be pursued as far as possible. And he consequently suggests that in many circumstances

---

[5] C. E. Lindblom: Policy analysis. *Amer. econ. Rev.*, 1958, 48, 298–312; Tinbergen on policy making. *J. polit. Econ.*, 1958, 66, 531–538; The handling of norms in policy analysis. In M. Abramovitz (ed.), *Allocation of economic resources.* Stanford, Calif.: Stanford University Press, 1958, 160–179; The science of "muddling through." *Pub. Admin. Rev.*, 1959, 19, 79–88; Decision making in taxation and expenditure. In Universities-National Bureau of Economic Research, *Public finances; needs, sources, and utilization.* Princeton, N.J.: Princeton University Press, 1961.

substantial departures from comprehensive understanding are both inevitable and on specific grounds desirable. For the most part, these departures are familiar; and his exposition of them serves therefore to formalize our perceptions of certain useful problem-solving strategies often mistakenly dismissed as aberrations in rational problem solving.

These strategies, which we shall call "disjointed incrementalism," are the following:

A. Attempt at understanding is limited to policies that differ only incrementally from existing policy.

B. Instead of simply adjusting means to ends, ends are chosen that are appropriate to available or nearly available means.

C. A relatively small number of means (alternative possible policies) is considered, as follows from A.

D. Instead of comparing alternative means or policies in the light of postulated ends or objectives, alternative ends or objectives are also compared in the light of postulated means or policies and their consequences.

E. Ends and means are chosen simultaneously; the choice of means does not follow the choice of ends.

F. Ends are indefinitely explored, reconsidered, discovered, rather than relatively fixed.

G. At any given analytical point ("point" refers to any one individual, group, agency, or institution), analysis and policy making are serial or successive; that is, problems are not "solved" but are repeatedly attacked.

H. Analysis and policy making are remedial; they move *away* from ills rather than *toward* known objectives.

I. At any one analytical point, the analysis of consequences is quite incomplete.

J. Analysis and policy making are socially fragmented; they go on at a very large number of separate points simultaneously.

The most striking characteristic of disjointed incrementalism is (as indicated in I) that no attempt at comprehensiveness is made; on the contrary, unquestionably important consequences of alternative policies are simply ignored at any given analytical or policy-making point. But Lindblom goes on to argue that through various specific types of partisan mutual adjustment among the large number of individuals and groups among which analysis and policy making is fragmented (see J), what is ignored at one point in policy making becomes central at another point. Hence, it will often be possible to find a tolerable level of rationality in decision making when the process is viewed as a whole in its social or political context, even if at each individual policy-making point or center analysis remains incomplete. Similarly, errors that would attend overly ambitious attempts at comprehensive understanding are often avoided by the remedial and incremental character of problem solving. And those not avoided can be mopped up or attended to as they appear, because analysis and policy making are serial or successive (as in G).

While we cannot here review the entire argument, Lindblom tries to show how the specific characteristics of disjointed incrementalism, taken in conjunction with mechanisms for partisan mutual adjustment, meet each of the characteristic difficulties that beset synoptic policy making: value conflicts, information inadequacies, and general complexity beyond man's intellectual capacities. His line of argument shows the influence of pluralist thinkers on political theory, but he departs from their interest in the control of power and rather focuses on the level of rationality required or appropriate for decision making.

POINTS OF CONVERGENCE

If they are not already obvious, specific parallels in the works reviewed are easy to illustrate. Compare, for example, an economy that is in a state of imbalance as the result of a sharp but isolated advance of one sector and a weapons system that is out of balance because a subsystem is "too good" in relation to the capacity of another system. Just as for a sector of the economy, it is possible that a completed subsystem is "too advanced" only in comparison with some preconceived notion, and that actually its unexpectedly high performance level is quite welcome, either because it improves upon over-all system performance or because it happily compensates for the lag of some other component behind the norms originally set. On the other hand, a component can be "too advanced" in a real sense; as in a hi-fi set, where the performance of a component depends not only on its capacity but also on inputs from other components. This situation corresponds exactly to that of an economy in structural imbalance. The laggard components turn into bottlenecks for the full utilization of the *avant-garde* component's capacity. Yet even though such a system or economy represents in itself an inefficient utilization of inputs, it may nevertheless be a highly useful configuration if it is conceived as a stage in the development process. For it may be expected that attempts will be made to improve the weaker subsystems or sectors so that the capability of the stronger ones may be fully utilized. In the process, the weaker systems or sectors may be so improved that they become the stronger ones, and the stage thus set for a series of seesaw advances which may carry the over-all "goodness" of our system or economy beyond what might have been achieved by maintaining balance.

For both economy and weapons system we are talking in terms of probabilities. There can be no certainty that with one *avant-garde* sub-system readied the others will dutifully be put in place or improved. The existence of the Maginot line along the French-German border failed to call forth a corresponding effort along the Belgian frontier to guard against the possibility of a German strategy aimed at circumventing the Line.

This example illustrates an important point: a "system" or economy is never quite finished. Today's system or economy-inbalance is likely to turn into tomorrow's subsystem or economy-out-of-balance, because of unforeseeable repercussions, newly emerging difficulties, unanticipated counterstrategies, changing tastes or techniques, or whatever other forces with which the system or economy has to deal.[6] But these repercussions, difficulties, and counterstrategies could not possibly be fully visualized in advance. The transportation system consisting of highways, gasoline and repair stations, and automotive vehicles is found incomplete; first because of inadequate accident prevention, and later also because of smog. The new system of defense against infections through antibiotics is suddenly "out of balance" because of the development of new varieties of drug-resistant micro-organisms. In these cases, it would have been impossible to foresee the imbalance and incompleteness that emerged clearly only after the new system had been in operation for some time.

Once it is understood that a system is never complete or will never stay complete, the case against spending considerable effort on early integration and simultaneous development of subsystems is further strengthened. For if we do achieve early integration and simultaneity, we are much more likely to succumb to the illusion that our system is actually complete in itself and needs no further complements and watchfulness than if we had built it up as a result of seesaw advances and adjustments which do not provide for a natural resting place.[7]

As another specific illustration of convergence, consider the sequence

[6] It is hardly necessary to mention the similarity, in this respect, between the Maginot line and some of our present defense systems such as the DEW Line.
[7] The examples of the Maginot line, of automobile traffic, and of antibiotics bring up an additional problem. In the latter two cases, the incompleteness of the system is forcefully brought to our attention through accidents and eye irritation, and through new types of infection. The trouble with some other systems that turn into subsystems is that the mutation may not be so easily detected, or that it may be detected only when it is too late, as was precisely the case wih the Maginot line.
There is real difficulty about the meaning of "too late." The imperfections of automobile traffic and antibiotics were discovered too late for the victims of accidents and new-type infections, but not too late, we hope, for the rest of us. The defects of the Maginot line were discovered too late to save France in 1940, although not too late to win the war against Hitler. This suggests that there may be cases where we cannot afford to do our learning about the imperfections and imbalances of a system through the failures, irritations, and discomforts that are the natural concomitants

of moves in problem solving as described, on the one hand, in developmental terms by Hirschman, Klein and Meckling and, on the other hand, in political terms by Lindblom. Recall the picture of desired progress where we wished to move from one fixed point (the present) to another fixed point in a 2-dimensional diagram. From existing levels of output in industry and agriculture (or range and speed in aircraft) we wished to move to higher levels for both. Imagine a situation in which two parties with different preferences want to go off in two different directions. Lindblom argues that in this situation the best way to make progress is through "mutual adjustment," i.e., by a series of moves and countermoves in the course of which a higher plateau can be reached even without prior agreement about the eventual goal. "Individuals often agree on policies when they cannot agree on ends. Moreover, attempts to agree on ends or values often get in the way of agreements on specific policies."[8] Furthermore, it is possible, and even likely, that the value systems of the two parties will move more closely together once an advance that is tolerable to both has been achieved. "The decision-maker expects to learn about his values from his experiences and he is inclined to think that in the long run policy choices have as great an influence on objectives as objectives have on policy choices."[9]

Lindblom's reasoning reinforces the others. It parallels Klein and Meckling's emphasis on the inevitability of moving forward through move and countermove, in what appears an arbitrary, somewhat aimless fashion, rather than Hirschman's stress on the efficiency of such a sequence in squeezing out additional resources. Nevertheless, the idea that unbalanced or seesaw advances of this kind are efficient in some sense is also present. Instead of focusing on the limited supply of decision makers and on the desirability of placing some extra pressures behind investment decisions, Lindblom emphasizes the limited supply of knowledge and the limited area of agreement that exists among the various powerholders, and visualizes a series of sequential adjustments as a way to maximize positive

---

and signals of the imbalance. Such situations present us with a well-nigh insoluble task, similar to the one which would face a child who had to learn to walk without being permitted to fall. Here the temptation is particularly strong to prepare in advance a perfect theoretical solution. Yet we know from all that has been said that reliance on such a solution would be most likely to bring about the failure one is seeking to avoid. One way of dealing with situations in which we feel we cannot afford to learn the "hard way" is to develop institutions whose special mission it is to be alert to and to detect existing and developing system imbalances: in a democracy, some institutions of this kind are a free press and an opposition party. For national defense a certain amount of interservice rivalry may serve the same purpose, as each service has a vested interest in pointing out the "holes" in the other services' systems.

[8] Lindblom, 1958, *op. cit.*, p. 534.
[9] Lindblom, 1961, *op. cit.*, p. 309.

action in a society where ignorance, uncertainty, and conflict preclude not only the identification, but even the existence, of any "best" move.

But we can do better than illustrate parallels. We can explicitly identify the principal points of convergence.

1. The most obvious similarity is that all insist on the rationality and usefulness of certain processes and modes of behavior which are ordinarily considered to be irrational, wasteful, and generally abominable.

2. The three approaches thus have in common an attack on such well-established values as orderliness,[10] balance, and detailed programming; they all agree with Burke that some matters ought to be left to a "wise and salutary neglect."[11]

3. They agree that one step ought often to be left to lead to another, and that it is unwise to specify objectives in much detail when the means of attaining them are virtually unknown.

4. All agree further that in rational problem solving, goals will change not only in detail but in a more fundamental sense through experience with a succession of means-ends and ends-means adjustments.

5. All agree that in an important sense a rational problem solver wants what he can get and does not try to get what he wants except after identifying what he wants by examining what he can get.

6. There is also agreement that the exploration of alternative uses of resources can be overdone, and that attempts at introducing explicitly certain maximizing techniques (trade-offs among inputs or among outputs, cost-benefit calculations) and co-ordinating techniques will be ineffective and quite possibly harmful in some situations. In a sense more fundamental than is implied by theories stressing the cost of information, the pursuit of certain activities that are usually held to be the very essence of "economizing" can at times be decidedly uneconomical.

7. One reason for this is the following: for successful problem solving, all agree it is most important that arrangements exist through which decision makers are sensitized and react promptly to newly emerging problems, imbalances, and difficulties; this essential ability to react and to improvise readily and imaginatively can be stultified by an undue preoccupation with, and consequent pretense at, advance elimination of these problems and difficulties through "integrated planning."

8. Similarly, attempts at foresight can be misplaced; they will often result in complicating the problem through mistaken diagnoses and

---

[10] Hirschman's "model of optimum disorderliness." A. O. Hirschman, *The strategy of economic development* (New Haven, Conn.: Yale University Press, 1958, p. 80.
[11] An even higher authority might be invoked, namely the Sermon on the Mount: "Take therefore no thought for the morrow, for the morrow will take care of the things of itself."

ideologies. Since man has quite limited capacities to solve problems and particularly to foresee the shape of future problems, the much maligned "hard way" of learning by experiencing the problems at close range may often be the most expeditious and least expensive way to a solution.

9. Thus we have here theories of successive decision making; denying the possibility of determining the sequence *ex ante,* relying on the clues that appear in the course of the sequence, and concentrating on identification of these clues.

10. All count on the usefulness for problem solving of subtle social processes not necessarily consciously directed at an identified social problem. Processes of mutual adjustment of participants are capable of achieving a kind of co-ordination not necessarily centrally envisaged prior to its achievement, or centrally managed.

11. At least Hirschman and Lindblom see in political adjustment and strife analogues to self-interested yet socially useful adjustment in the market.

12. All question such values as "foresight," "central direction," "integrated overview," but not in order to advocate *laissez faire* or to inveigh against expanded activities of the state in economic or other fields. They are in fact typically concerned with decision-making and problem-solving activities carried on by the state. In their positive aspects they describe how these activities are "really" taking place as compared to commonly held images; and insofar as they are normative they advocate a modification of these images, in the belief that a clearer appreciation and perception of institutions and attitudes helpful to problem-solving activities will result.

Although many of these propositions are familiar, they are often denied in explicit accounts of rational decision making; and at least some of them challenge familiar contrary beliefs. Either the convergences are an unfortunate accident, or decision-making theory has underplayed the degree to which "common sense" rational problem-solving procedures have to be modified or abandoned. Account must be taken of man's inertia, limited capacities, costs of decision making, and other obstacles to problem solving, including uncertainty, which is the only one of the complicating elements that has been given sustained attention. And most investigations of uncertainty have been within the narrow competence of statistical theory.

POINTS OF DIFFERENCE

These similarities in approach, with their widely different origins, structures, and fields of application, are even better understood if their remaining points of difference are identified.

The basic justification for rejecting traditional precepts of rationality, planning, and balance is somewhat different for the three approaches here examined. For Lindblom it is *complexity,* i.e., man's inability to *comprehend* the present interrelatedness and future repercussions of certain social processes and decisions, as well as imperfect knowledge and *value conflicts.* For Klein and Meckling it is almost entirely *future uncertainty,* i.e., man's inability to *foresee* the shape of technological breakthroughs, or the desirability of letting oneself be guided by these breakthroughs if and when they occur, instead of following a predetermined sequence. For Hirschman it is the difficulty of mobilizing potentially available resources and decision-making activity itself; the *inadequacy of incentives* to problem solving, or conversely, the need for *inducements* to decision making.

Although Klein's and Meckling's concern with future uncertainty could formally be viewed as a special case of Lindblom's problem of inadequate information, their treatment of the research and development problem is different enough from Lindblom's treatment of information inadequacies to argue against its being so viewed. Hirschman's concern with inducements to problem-solving activity is quite different from either Lindblom's or Klein's and Meckling's concern with limits on cognitive faculties. He argues not that men lack knowledge and capacity to solve problems in an absolute sense, but that there is always some unutilized problem-solving capacity that can be called forth through a variety of inducement mechanisms and pacing devices. These different reasons for supporting the same conclusions make the conclusions more rather than less persuasive, for the reasons supplement rather than invalidate each other.

That they are complementary reasons is, of course, indicated by the overlap of the Lindblom and the Klein-Meckling approaches on the problem of imperfect information, and by some Hirschmanlike concern for research and development *incentives* in the Klein-Meckling study. It is also true that Hirschman develops as a secondary theme the difficulties of ignorance and uncertainty in economic development. For instance, his partiality toward "development via social overhead capital shortage" is based in part on the position that shortages and bottlenecks remove uncertainty about the direction of needed overhead investments. Similarly, he emphasizes the importance of unforeseen or loose complementarity repercussions, such as "entrained wants" that arise in the course of development, and asserts that imports are helpful in inducing domestic production because they remove previous doubts about the existence of a market.

From the differences in the main thrust of the respective arguments, certain other major differences emerge, differences which do not deny the convergences, but which, on the other hand, ought not to be submerged by them. For example, Hirschman's argument that a very heavy reliance on central planning will often be inappropriate for underdeveloped countries looks superficially parallel to Lindblom's argument that *partisan* mutual adjustment can sometimes achieve efficiencies that could not be achieved through over-ambitious attempts at central omniscience and control. Yet on closer scrutiny, Hirschman's cautions about centralism only secondarily refer to the *general* difficulties of managing complex affairs that strain man's incentives and intellectual capacities. Instead he argues that a conventional, centrally planned attempt to define and achieve a balance among many varied lines of development will be less helpful than a similarly central attempt to estimate and manage the critical linkages through which economic growth is forced or induced.[12]

Hirschman's explicitly declared view of decision making for economic development is almost entirely one of central planning, or at least problem solving by persons—such as planning board managers or officials of international agencies—who assume some general responsibility toward the economy as a whole, and whose point of view is therefore that of a central planner. Hirschman's policy maker or operator is, with only a few exceptions, such a person or official; and Hirschman's prescriptions are always addressed to such a person. By contrast, Lindblom's policy maker is typically a partisan, often acknowledging no responsibility to his society as a whole, frankly pursuing his own segmental interests; and this is a kind of policy maker for whom Hirschman, despite his between-the-lines endorsement of him, makes no explicit place in his formulation of the development process.

A further important point of difference between Hirschman and Lindblom appears to lie in Hirschman's emphasis on discovering and utilizing the side-effects and repercussions of development decisions, as compared to Lindblom's readiness to recommend at any given "point" neglect of such repercussions. It is indeed a major thesis of Hirschman that analysis of a prospective investment project should above all try to evaluate its effect on further development decisions instead of conventionally concentrating on its own prospective output and productivity. Specifically, every decision should be analyzed to discover its possible "linkages" with other decisions that might follow it. For example, a prospective decision to encourage the importation of some consumer goods, such as radios, should consider not simply the economy's need for these goods but the probability that their importation will in time lead to a decision by domestic investors to assemble them locally, as well as

---

[12] This argument against the attempt at balanced growth is quite different from Hirschman's other argument that balance in growth is not desirable even if achieved.

the "linkage effects" of such assembly operations on further domestic production decisions.

Hirschman's book is both an attempt to uncover such linkages and a prescription that developers seek to uncover them in every possible case. Lindblom suggests that this kind of by-product, the indirect consequences of a decision that flow from the decision's effect on still other decision makers will often escape the analyst in any case; hence he should not try to always anticipate and understand it, but instead should deal with it through subsequent steps in policy making, if and when it emerges as a problem. Since, as Lindblom sees it, policy making is not only *remedial* and *serial* but also *fragmented,* both intentionally and accidentally neglected consequences of chosen policies will often be attended to either as a remedial next step of the original policy makers or by some other policy-making group whose interests are affected. Hence policy as a complex social or political process rises to a higher level of comprehensiveness and rationality than is achieved by any one policy maker at any one move in the process.

The contrast between Hirschman and Lindblom on this point can be overdrawn, however. For one thing, Hirschman feels that calculations which purport to give greater rationality to investment planning may often interfere with development, because they typically do not and cannot take the "linkages" into account; whereas more rough-and-ready methods may be at least based on hunches about such linkages. Second, Hirschman's practical advice to policy makers is similar to Lindblom's when he tells them to go ahead with unintegrated and unbalanced projects on the ground that, in an interdependent economy, progress in some sectors will serve to unmask the others as laggards and will thereby bring new pressures toward improvement. In his general prescription, more implicit than explicit, that development planners try to move the economy wherever it can be moved, that is, seize on readiness to act wherever it can be found, Hirschman is endorsing Lindblom's suggestion that many consequences can best be dealt with only as they actually show themselves.

As a further point of difference, it is implicit in what has been said in the preceding paragraphs that Hirschman's thinking about secondary effects is preoccupied with possible bonuses to be exploited, Lindblom's with possible losses to be minimized. Again, the difference is easy to overstate: Hirschman too is at times concerned with possible losses, even if Lindblom has not explored at all the possibility of bonuses. Hirschman, however, relies on correct diagnosis of linkages for protection from damaging side effects; and his position is therefore parallel to his position on exploiting bonus effects. Only secondarily does he count on Lindblom's remedial, serial, and fragmented kind of process for minimizing losses.

CONCLUDING REMARKS

As Hirschman would now give uncertainty, complexity, and value conflict a more central place in justifying his conclusions on economic development policy, so also Lindblom's and Klein's and Meckling's analyses could be strengthened by taking into account the fact that the policies they defend could also be justified because they permit mobilization of resources and energies that could not be activated otherwise. Perhaps these latter analyses could go beyond the statement that the processes of research and development and of policy making are of necessity piecemeal, successive, fragmented, and disjointed; they could try to define typical sequences and their characteristics, similar to Hirschman's "permissive" and "compulsive" sequences. Once the intellectual taboo and wholesale condemnation are lifted from some of the policies Klein, Meckling, and Lindblom defend, it becomes desirable to have a closer look at the heretofore incriminated processes and to rank them from various points of view. It is useful to ask questions such as the following: as long as we know that a system is going to be out of balance anyway when the subsystems develop, what type of imbalance is most likely to be self-correcting? An answer to this question could affect the desirable distribution and emphasis of the research and development effort. Detailed descriptions of types of incremental meandering would also be interesting; perhaps this would more clearly differentiate between a sequence that leads to reform and another that leads to revolution.

One problem deserves to be mentioned again. The processes of economic development, research and development, and policy making must all rely on successive decision making because they all break new, uncertain ground. Therefore these processes must let themselves be guided by the clues that appear en route. Snags, difficulties, and tensions cannot be avoided, but must on the contrary be utilized to propel the process further. The trouble is that the difficulties are not only "little helpers," but may also start processes of disintegration and demoralization. An intersectoral imbalance sets up a race between the catching-up, forward movement of the lagging sector and the retrogression of the advanced one. The greater the pressure toward remedial positive action, the greater is the risk if this action does not take place. There is a corresponding situation in systems development. The more a system is out of balance, the greater will presumably be the pressure to do something about it, but also the more useless is the system should no action be forthcoming.

All three approaches therefore have one further characteristic in common: they can be overdone. There are limits to "imbalance" in economic development, to "lack of integration" in research and development, to "fragmentation" in policy making which would be dangerous to pass. And it is clearly impossible to specify in advance the optimal doses of these various policies under different circumstances. The art of promoting economic development, research and development, and constructive policy making in general consists, then, in acquiring a feeling for these doses.

This art, it is submitted by the theories here reviewed, will be mastered far better once the false ideals of "balance," "co-ordination," and "comprehensive overview" have lost our total and unquestioning intellectual allegiance.

THE DEVELOPMENT OF CYBERNETICS

Charles R. Dechert

The term "cybernetics" derives from the Greek word *kybernetes* which means steersman. Plato uses it to describe the prudential aspect of the art of government.[1] Ampere in his *Essay on the Philosophy of Science* used the term *cybernétique* for the science of civil government.[2] The Latin term *gubernator* is derived from the Greek, and hence also our word governor. In English we use the term governor in at least two ways: first in the traditional sense of a public steersman or political decision-maker; second to refer to the self-adjusting valve mechanism on a steam engine which keeps the engine at a constant speed under varying conditions of load. In the steam engine governor, a valve linked to the engine's output shaft increases steam flow into the engine as the output

The original version of this paper was presented at a symposium on the Social Implications of Cybernetics held at Georgetown University, Washington, D.C., November, 1964. Reprinted from *The American Behavioral Scientist*, June 1965, vol. 8, no. 10, pp. 15–20. By permission of the author and *The American Behavioral Scientist* division of Sage Publications, Inc.

[1] Plato, *Republic*, I, 346 B.C.
[2] A. M. Ampere, *Essay on the Philosophy of Science* (1838).

speed decreases, raising the speed to the level desired, or reduces steam flow if the speed exceeds the pre-established level. Maxwell analyzed this control phenomenon mathematically in his paper on governors published in 1868.[3] What is essentially involved in steering behavior or control behavior of the type illustrated by the steam engine governor is a feedback loop through which the output of the system is linked to its input in such a way that variations in output from some pre-established or "programmed" norm results in compensatory behavior that tends to restore the system output to that norm.

An analogous process occurs in organisms subjected to internal or external changes that might disrupt metabolism. By the turn of this century physiologists such as Claude Bernard were fully aware of this process of "homeostasis" whereby an organism acts so as to restore its internal equilibrium. Cannon's *Wisdom of the Body* is a classical exposition of these phenomena in the autonomic processes of men. The self-regulatory aspect of neurophysiological phenomena was treated by such men as Sherrington in his work on reflexes, McCulloch in his analysis of neural networks, and Rosenblueth in his studies of psychomotor disorders. By the early 1940's physicists, electrical engineers, and mathematicians were at work on servo-mechanisms, self-regulating systems that could be used for such military purposes as gun laying. A broad range of disciplines had been at work on analogous problems of self-regulation. Institutionally, the interdisciplinary study of self-regulation in the animal and the machine began at a meeting held in New York in 1942, sponsored by the Josiah Macy Foundation.

BEHAVIOR AND PURPOSE

One result was a paper on "Behavior, Purpose and Teleology" which serves as a watershed in which the breadth of the analogy was realized.[4] In 1943 *Philosophy of Science* published this article by Norbert Wiener, Arturo Rosenblueth and Julian Bigelow. The authors distinguish between the "functional analysis" of an entity and a "behavioristic approach." In the former ". . . the main goal is the intrinsic organization of the entity studied, its structure and its properties . . ." ". . . The behavioristic approach consists in the examination of the output of the object and of the relations of this output to the input." Wiener in his subsequent works largely restricted himself to ". . . the behavioristic method of study

---

[3] J. C. Maxwell, *Proceedings of the Royal Society* (London), 1868, XVI, 270–283.
[4] Josiah Macy Foundation Conference on Cerebral Inhibition, May, 1942. A. Rosenblueth, N. Wiener, and J. Bigelow, "Behavior, Purpose and Teleology," *Philos. Sci.*, 1943, X, 18–24.

[which] omits the specific structure and intrinsic organization of the object." The authors assign the term "servomechanism" to designate machines with "intrinsic purposeful behavior." Purposeful behavior is directed at ". . . a final condition in which the behaving object reaches a definite correlation in time or space with respect to another object or event." All purposeful behavior may be considered to require negative feedback," that is ". . . the behavior of an object is controlled by the margin of error at which the object stands at a given time with reference to a relatively specific goal." The authors conclude on the note that "purposefulness [is] a concept necessary for the understanding of certain modes of behavior . . . ," and define teleology as "purpose controlled by feedback." The authors reject the concept of teleology as implying a "cause subsequent in time to a given effect."

In this model the key elements of self-regulation were reduced to a form amenable to mathematical analysis, and the knotty problem of consciousness so relevant to human behavior was bypassed. The novelty of this mode of conceptualizing purposive behavior lies in its implicit distinction between energy and information. " 'Control' is a special kind of relation between two machines or parts of machines, such that one part regulates the operation of the other. . . . The essential point is that the source of energy is dissociated from the source of instructions."[5] The transformation of relatively high energic inputs into goal-oriented outputs is subject to relatively low energies characterized by a formal content whose programmed interaction with these high energies produces the purposive transformation.

The principal characteristic of a self-regulating system is the presence of a control loop whereby system comportment may be modified on the basis of information inputs regarding performance and the comparison of performance with a criterion value. The control loop may be a "closed loop" existing within the boundaries of the system, or it may be an "open loop." In open loop feedback, part of the control information flow takes place outside the system boundary. The interaction of a self-regulating system with its external environment characteristically involves an open loop. Effector elements on the system boundary manipulate the environment to achieve certain objectives. Sensor elements (receptors) perceive environmental changes which are transmitted to a decision making element that compares this percept with the objective and transmits new orders to the effector elements in terms of the difference between objective and achievement.

Basically, self-regulation requires a functional distinction between

5 G. T. Guilbaud, *What is Cybernetics*. New York: Grove Press, 1960, p. 11.

perception, decision-making, and action. This is normally achieved by a structural distinction between perceptor elements, control elements and effecter elements in the system. Behaviorally, system may be defined as a "black box" characterized by a given set or range of inputs and outputs. Adequate knowledge of any system requires both structural-functional analysis and behavioral analysis. Where very large numbers of inputs and/or outputs are involved or where the system is composed of a large number of components, statistical techniques are required and behaviors are analyzed probabilistically. It is entirely possible, of course, that structurally diverse systems may effect identical transformations, and that structurally identical systems of a sufficient degree of complexity may produce very different outputs on the basis of identical inputs. The "sensitivity" of a system refers to the degree of departure of the output from a programmed norm that invokes an adjustive response. "Rapidity of response" refers to the speed with which a given system will correct behavior that does not correspond to the norm. "Stability" refers to the ability of a system to maintain a given behavioral posture over time. Normally there is a rather close formal relation between these aspects of systems behavior. The more sensitive a system, the less likely it is to be stable over a broad range of inputs and outputs. The more rapid the response of the system to an error signal, the more likely it is to overshoot the norm—to overadjust, and so invoke a counter-adjustment, to overadjust, and so forth. This behavior may lead to oscillation destructive of the entire system.

INFORMATION AND MESSAGES

It is clear at this point of our discussion that control involves the communication of information. In an operational sense, information is that which can or does influence the comportment of another. Information is conveyed as a message, that is, as a configuration of signal elements borne by a medium having actual or potential meaning for the recipient (destination). By the late 1920's communications engineers, concerned with the problems of interference (noise) and channel capacity, had begun to develop measures of information.[6] This work culminated in 1948 in a paper of Shannon entitled, "The Mathematical Theory of Communication."[7] Shannon's study does not concern itself with meaning,

[6] H. Nyquist, "Certain Factors Affecting Telegraph Speed," *Bell System Technical J.*, April, 1924, 324; "Certain Topics in Telegram Transmission Theory," *A.I.E.E. Transactions*, 47, April, 1928, 617; R. V. L. Hartley, "Transmission of Information," *Bell System Technical J.*, July, 1928, 535.
[7] C. E. Shannon and W. Weaver, *The Mathematical Theory of Communication*. Urbana: University of Illinois Press, 1949.

that is, with the semantic aspects of communication but with the technical problems of the accuracy of transmission of various types of signals. Clearly, the purely technical problems of coding, transmitting, and decoding signal sequences are of critical importance in designing and understanding self-regulating systems. The actual comportment of such systems, however, is a function of the semantic content of these signal sequences. The "quantity of information" as a measure of the improbability of a signal sequence has no *necessary* relation to the amount of semantic information conveyed by a statement.[8]

In 1948 Wiener published *Cybernetics or Control and Communication in the Animal and the Machine* which formalized much of the thinking up to that time and suggested potentially fruitful areas for further inquiry. With the quantification of signal transmission and the formalization of control system theory a new and broadly applicable science of communications and control had become a reality. In its strict applications, communications and control theory has become a major factor in contemporary technology and lies at the base of the "second industrial revolution." In the "first industrial revolution" prime movers largely replaced human energy while men performed a control function. Under automation, process and production *control* is relegated to servomechanisms while the human operator programs, monitors, and maintains the automated system.

SCOPE OF CYBERNETICS

In the United States, scientists and engineers working in the theory and applications of self-regulation tend to avoid the term cybernetics which deals to a considerable degree with isomorphisms among various types of self-regulating systems. Since only a very limited range of systems and communications processes are presently amenable to mathematical formalization and manipulation, there has been a tendency to institutionalize fairly narrow disciplines concerned with limited formal or material applications of these concepts, such as computer engineering, bionics, and control systems engineering. In the Soviet Union, on the other hand, the term "cybernetics" is used quite broadly, ". . . not as the doctrine of Wiener, Shannon, Ashby, *et al.,* but as the general science of the control over complex systems, information, and communications. . . ."[9] Elsewhere in the Soviet literature we find cybernetics defined as ". . . the new science of purposeful and optimal control over complicated processes and

---

[8] Y. Bar-Hillel, "An Examination of Information Theory," *Philos. Sci.,* 22, 1955.
[9] N. A. Bershteyn, "New Lines of Development in Physiology and Their Relation to Cybernetics" in *Problems of Philosophy,* 1962, 8, 78–87 (JPRS; 17,117).

operations which take place in living nature, in human society, and in industry."[10]

Cybernetics extends the circle of processes which can be controlled—this is its special property and merit. It can help control life activity in living nature, purposeful work of organized groups of people, and the influence of man on machines and mechanisms.

We shall divide cybernetics into three large subdivisions: theoretical cybernetics which includes mathematical and philosophical problems; the cybernetics of control systems and means which includes the problems of collecting, processing, and output of information, and also the means for electronic automation; finally, the field of the practical application of the methods and means of cybernetics in all fields of human activity.[11]

Many of the basic concepts of this science are relevant to an understanding of social groups. Norbert Wiener realized their applicability and suggested many insightful applications, but was concerned about potential abuses owing to the complexity of social processes and the limited applicability of existing methods of mathematical analysis. On the other hand, he also pointed out that the application of cybernetic concepts to society does not require that social relations be mathematicizable in esse, but only in posse—that is, the conceptual clarification of the formal aspects of social relations can make a positive contribution to the science of society.[12]

More recent definitions of cybernetics almost invariably include social organizations as one of the categories of system to which this science is relevant.[13] Indeed, Bigelow has generalized to the extent of calling cybernetics the effort to understand the behavior of complex systems.[14] He pointed out that cybernetics is essentially interdisciplinary and that a focus at the systems level, dependent upon mixed teams of professionals in a variety of sciences, brings one rapidly to the frontiers of knowledge in several areas. This is certainly true of the social sciences. The term "cybernetics" is used here in the more extended sense discussed above. It is entirely appropriate that this should be done, not only because of the traditional political and social connotation of the term governance, but because of the role played by the social and behavioral sciences in the explication and development of models of social control and decision

---

[10] "Biological Aspects of Cybernetics," Moscow, 1962 (JPRS; 19,637, p. 17).
[11] Ibid., p. 19.
[12] N. Wiener, God and Golem, Inc. Cambridge, Mass.: M.I.T. Press, 1964, p. 88.
[13] Encyclopedia of Science and Technology. New York: McGraw-Hill, 1960. "Cybernetics: The Science of control and communication in all of its various manifestations in machines, animals, and organizations."—"an interdisciplinary science."
[14] J. Bigelow, Address at Founders' Dinner, American Society for Cybernetics, October 16, 1964, Washington, D.C.

making. The first modern calculating machine was made by Charles Babbage, whose classic study (*On the Economy of Machinery and Manufactures*) was published in 1832 and anticipated by fifty years or more the beginnings of scientific management.[15] Organizational theory, political science, cultural anthropology and social psychology have for many years analyzed social groups as complex communications nets characterized by a multiplicity of feedback loops. Organizational decision-making was given a quantitative base, again at the time of World War II, by the development of the techniques of operations research. Von Neumann and Morgenstern succeeded in analyzing strategic optima in certain types of decision processes. In 1936 Leontief produced the first input-output matrix. Von Bertalanffy has pointed out analogies (isomorphisms) characterizing all systems, including social systems.[16]

ROLE OF COMPUTERS

Let us now examine certain aspects of the popular view of cybernetics. In one view, cybernetics is identified with the development and use of large digital computers. Computers are, of course, of fundamental importance to cybernetics, first because they embody so much communications and control technology, and second because they oblige us to sort out vague ideas and feelings from clearly formulated univocal ideas and relations if we wish to manipulate them by machine, and finally because once ideas are clarified the machine permits the rapid execution of long and detailed logical operations otherwise beyond human capability. In many cases these logical operations performed by machine permit a rationality in decision-making or precision of control hitherto unattainable. Until a few years ago it was impossible to compare very large numbers of decisional alternatives to find an optimum. Decision techniques and aids such as linear and dynamic programming, critical path analysis, large scale input-output matrices, network analysis, factor analysis, simulation, and so forth are largely dependent upon computers.

Computer technology, of course, lies at the base of the automatic factory, of sophisticated inventory control systems, and of the increasing

[15] C. Babbage, *On the Economy of Machinery and Manufactures*. London: 1832. For a very recent application of advanced analytic techniques to management see: S. Beer, *Cybernetics and Management*. New York: Wiley, 1959; "Toward the Cybernetic Factory" in Von Foerster and Zopf (eds.), *Principles of Self-Organization*. New York: Pergamon, 1962, p. 25.
[16] L. Von Bertalanffy, "General Systems Theory," *General Systems*, vol. I (1956); "General Systems Theory: A Critical Review," *General Systems*, vol. VII (1962); J. G. Miller, "Toward a General Theory for the Behavioral Sciences," *Amer. Psychol.*, X, 1955.

automation of routine paper work. Fundamentally, any information handling operation that can be reduced to rule and rote is amenable to computer performance. Considered abstractly, this means that virtually every human job activity that does not require intellectual or artistic creativity or some human emotivity in its performance is potentially susceptible of automation. Under our existing institutional "rules of the game" the only limiting factor will be the cost of the machine as opposed to the cost of people.

It now seems increasingly likely that computer networks will be formed, first on a local, then a regional, and finally a national scale which will make unused computer capacity available, perhaps on a rental basis—and which as a unit will be capable of data processing tasks of hitherto inconceivable magnitude. Eventually each citizen may have access to computers and a vast complex of data storage centers on a rental-use basis. Computers might be used to handle such routine chores as tallying adding machine tapes, making out Christmas mailing lists and preparing income tax returns. At a more sophisticated level perhaps our citizen may use his machine to analyze interpersonal relations in his office sociometrically in order to optimize strategies for personal effectiveness. He may have access to a wide range of factual or bibliographic information; he may, perhaps, run machine searches of newspaper files or gather genealogical data. From a purely practical economic viewpoint there would be obvious benefits to American business to be gained from centralized insurance files, credit reports, accident reports, academic and job records, public opinion surveys, market surveys, and so forth. All of these would enhance predictability, and so also increase businesses' capacity for rational decision-making. The principal question that will arise in this process of increasing centralized information storage concerns the values in terms of which the information will be utilized in making decisions. Profit maximization? a politically imposed values-mix? or might new institutional forms permit more decentralized decision on the basis of widely varying criteria? In the not very distant future some hard public decisions must be made regarding who shall have access to what information and for what purposes, and perhaps as to what types of information may legitimately be collected and employed.

APPLICATIONS TO SOCIAL SYSTEMS

Let us return to our basic model of a self-regulating system, examine some of its fundamental operations a little more closely, and try to see wherein it is applicable to the study of social relations.

A system is an organized collection of interrelated elements characterized by a boundary and functional unity. The concept of system emphasizes the reality of complex relational networks and permits the analysis of mutual causal processes involving large numbers of interacting entities. Although systems of ideas and systems of symbols play a critical role in human society, we shall here treat of social systems as real composite entities in continuing self-regulated interaction with their environment(s). Social systems comprise every level of complexity from the family or primary work group through large scale formal organizations to the nation-state or even the whole human race conceived of as an interacting human community. Primary groups and ultimately all groups are composed of self-regulating persons as their components. Large social systems normally consist of functional groups as their component subsystems. The integrated activity of large social groupings is the product of effective internal communication and a willingness on the part of decision-makers in their component social subsystems and ultimately of their component persons to respond in a predictable and programmed manner to a defined range of perceptual inputs.

Fundamentally, a model of self-regulation requires a functional distinction between perception, decision-making, and action. This is normally achieved by a structural distinction between receptor elements, decision-making elements, and effector elements in the system. As social systems increase in size and complexity, these functions and the related communications functions tend to become concentrated in component social subsystems.[17]

If we apply these basic concepts in a very much simplified way to the political sphere they may help to systematize certain basic relations that are the traditional matter of political science, such as the constitution and the separation of powers.[18] Basically, a constitution is a program defining the nature (activities) and inter-relations of the formal loci of political power. The outputs of the political system are enforceable laws defining the inter-relations of persons and groups within the society. Demands on the political system are communicated by petition, by representatives of organized groups, by publicists, and other means including elections. Legislative decisions are made in the form of laws and resolutions. The executive puts the laws into effect and the judiciary serves a control function by comparing specific individual actions with the law that programs such action. Even judicial review in the United States is

[17] See K. Deutsch, *The Nerves of Government,* p. 258; C. Dechert, "A Pluralistic World Order," *Proceedings* of the American Catholic Philosophical Association, 1963, pp. 167–186.
[18] See D. Easton, "An Approach to the Analysis of Political Systems," *World Politics,* (IX) 1957, pp. 383–400; R. Dahl, *Modern Political Analysis.* Englewood Cliffs: Prentice-Hall, 1963.

fundamentally a comparison of legislative action (output) with a constitutional norm.

Similarly in the conduct of foreign affairs, information on the international environment in the form of foreign intelligence is communicated to the foreign policy decision-makers—ultimately, in the United States, the President. The challenges of the environment are met by policy decisions allocating resources of the state to effector elements of the executive branch for the achievement of national objectives by various techniques: diplomacy, foreign assistance, propaganda, military action, and so forth.

If we apply the concepts of sensitivity and stability to political systems we see distinct analogies even at an elementary level. The founding fathers of the United States wanted the legislature (decision-maker) sensitive to public opinion, so they introduced a House of Representatives elected biennially on the basis of population. But they did not want the decision process too sensitive to public opinion, so they introduced a Senate elected on a different basis for a different term of office whose concurrence is necessary to legislation. In order to introduce further stability into the system they decoupled the legislative (decision-maker) from the executive (effector) branch and introduced an independent control element in the form of a Supreme Court. The inherent stability of the system has been proved over the past 175 years. It is interesting to note that most of the proposals for "reform" recommended by political scientists are directed at increasing the sensitivity of the system to public opinion.

Each entity in our experience, whether physical object or person or social group, exists in time and interrelates with others in time. In the temporal order what will occur cannot provide a real input into antecedent action—but as a foreseen possibility it may provide an imputed information input. If we conceive of the current state of a system as determined by its antecedent states, the future states of that system are a set of probabilities dependent on the possible future states of its environments, and for self-regulating systems upon their actions in the "now." Insofar as the self-regulating system can know not only its actual state and the state of its environment in the "now," but can project and "know" alternative trajectories that are possible as realizable in the future, to this extent the future can be an input into decisional processes. While recognizing and attempting to predict the future states of key variables over which there is no effective control, individual and social planning consists essentially in: a) projecting alternative trajectories as functions of direct action by the system and of the indirect effects of action by the system on its environment; and in b) choosing the set of actions which, on the basis of past experience or subjectively assigned probabilities, seems most likely to bring about a future state conceived of as desirable. It is perfectly clear that the actions undertaken to achieve a future state of the system may *determine* to a considerable degree that future state. Hence it follows that in the reality of human affairs means and ends can never be separated.

Social systems not only respond to an existing environmental challenge, but they may foresee such challenges and plan to forestall them or cope with them in the future. In brief men and societies are provident—they respond not only to perceptions of reality but to the extrapolation of reality into possible future states. Much social choice depends upon the image of the future deemed desirable by a society and it is for this reason that the abstract ideology or the utopia expressed in concrete terms plays a critical role in defining social purpose and hence in conditioning social decisions. The range of possible response to an existing challenge is normally quite limited, while the range of autonomous action becomes increasingly broad as increasingly long future time-spans are anticipated. As given future goals become increasingly clear, that is concretely defined, social behavior may increasingly resemble that of a servomechanism in which guidance is reduced to control ". . . by the margin of error at which the object stands at a given time with reference to a relatively specific goal." Action may then become a routine problem of technical administration.

Action upon the environment is regulated by a continuing process of perception in which the perceived external reality is compared with an end state to be achieved. Now in this process it is clear that we are dealing with focused perceptions—that is a set of sensory inputs to which attention adverts selected from the innumerable alternative sets to which the person or group might advert. In an evolutionary sense only reasonably adequate criteria of perceptual relevance permit survival of a given biological species. For men whose criteria of perceptual relevance are largely cultural, only cultures having reasonably adequate criteria of relevance can survive. Similarly the norms of behavior of the person, the criterion values on the basis of which action is undertaken, are crucially important to behavior and to survival. These too are largely a matter of culture. In the history of mankind certain patterns of value have proved to possess a higher survival value than others. Within the range of viable systems of value and perceptual relevance (ideologies) there have been diverse degrees of success as measured by the extent of their diffusion and survival. In man we are dealing with a broad range of potential criteria of action and the possibility of self-conscious choice among sets of alternative criteria. Hence in dealing with social systems in which men form the ultimate self-regulating components, we must deal with the problem of the adequacy of perception and of value to effective action within a natural and human environment. The analysis of men and societies as self-regulating systems brings us back to the perennial philosophic problems of the Good and the True.

MAN-MACHINE SYSTEMS

Let us now conceive of the individual's environmental system in terms of a man-machine relationship. The machine is essentially a projection of the personality, normally subject to direct or indirect human control, capable of converting a given input or set of inputs into an output or set of outputs having greater imputed utility.

In its simplest form this is the man-tool relation in which the person serves as both a source of energy and of control. In more sophisticated man-machine systems prime movers may provide energy and man the control. At a more advanced stage the machine is in whole or part self-regulating and human control is exercised only in the programming phase. As we move to "learning machines" the human control interface may be reduced to the direct or indirect construction of the machine (indirect construction might involve programming a machine to produce a machine) and the direct or indirect programming of the criterion values on the basis of which decisions affecting output will be made. There is also a man-machine interface at the output since, presumably, the machine serves some human value. The most sophisticated man-machine systems today are basically extenders of human perceptive, data processing, and motor capabilities.

In some sense complex organizations, especially economic organizations, are man-machine systems in which the components are both men and artifacts in programmed interaction to convert input values into output values having a higher (ascribed) value. Within such an organization both persons and things are subject to decisions and the output values may or may not directly serve the human component of the system itself.

As we move from the realm of machines controlling machines, to men controlling machines, and to men controlling men in society we subtly shift the meaning of the term "control." In machine controls the message either actuates some multiplying device such as a relay or by combining with energic inputs modifies their characteristics. In human control of a machine, the person observes directly, or indirectly through an instrument display, the comportment of the machine in its environment and manipulates control devices. Here our man-machine "interface" basically consists of displays and controls. Social control is the capacity (often based on control of material or financial resources) to manipulate the internal and/or external environments of other persons or groups so as to achieve a preconceived end. This normally involves selected changes in their information inputs designed to change in some way their perceptions or values so that they respond in the desired manner. It is largely concerned with "evoking" an "autonomous" response. Even the social effectiveness of negative sanctions in controlling behavior is contingent upon their being perceived and then evaluated more negatively than noncompliance. Basically, when dealing with objects as complex and autonomous as persons, control is reduced to presenting a challenge so structured that it evokes the desired response. Since social action normally involves a feedback loop, the socially controlled in some sense also control the controller; indeed this is the major characteristic of political decision-making in a democracy. Greniewsky points out: ". . . all control is communication. But on the other hand all communication is control. . . ."[19]

SYSTEM INTERFACES

A system interacts with its environment at the system boundary. Inputs move into the system across this boundary. Outputs move across this boundary into the system's environment. The area of contact between one system and another is termed an "interface." Operationally systems, and subsystems within systems, may be identified by the transactional processes that occur across their boundaries. For social groupings these transactional processes may involve the transfer of energy, material objects, men, money, and information.

The outputs of one social system are normally inputs for one or more other systems. These inter-relations are amenable to analysis for economic sectors (and even for firms) by the use of input-output matrices. Quesnay in his *Tableau Economique* saw the national economy as an integrated system of monetary exchanges and exchanges of goods and services. The political system may be analyzed in terms of input demands and supports and an output of authoritative decisions that program the inter-relations of persons and organized groups within the state. By extending our analysis to comprehend the five categories of exchange noted above, we are in a position to view the entire world as a (relatively) closed system of inter-related social components linked together by these transactional processes.

Communications and control technologies are already being extensively applied for purposes of social organization within the more advanced countries. The Soviet economy is now being organized on the basis of very extensive input-output matrices and computer programs designed to optimize resource utilization. These techniques may also help resolve

[19] H. Greniewsky, *Cybernetics without Mathematics.* New York: Pergamon, 1960, p. 52.

the problem inherent in the limited use of market mechanisms to determine prices. By ascribing more or less arbitrary value to primary resource inputs (including the categories of human labor) all other prices in the economy can be made consistent. In the French indicative plan, a political decision, based on a consensus among all interested groups as to a future national mix of economic values, is reduced to an investment program that generates a high level of business confidence. The result has been an increasing tendency to reduce government to administration in terms of the technical achievement of concrete objectives. In the United States, the Social Security system has provided a means for national population control and is at the base of the new Internal Revenue Service computer system in which wage-earners and salaried persons are posted on a bi-weekly or monthly basis. Given the increasing use of Electronic Data Processing in our banks, plus the sophistication and widespread use of credit facilities, it is quite conceivable that all monetary transactions over say twenty dollars could be posted in a national accounting system (at least aggregate) through the use of cascaded computers. This would, of course, largely do away with the possibility of robbery—but above all would provide a rapid running account of inter-regional and intersectoral exchanges that would permit the use of indirect controls at strategic points to effect very rapid adjustments of the economy in terms of programmed goals such as full employment and planned rates of economic growth. Such a system would also permit more equitable taxation by doing away with unrecorded transfers.

I would suggest that cybernetics today possesses great relevance for the social scientist. First it has begun to provide conceptual tools of the greatest importance for the analysis of complex systems and their interrelations. It establishes a focus on the critical importance of control and communications relations, of individual and institutional modes of perception and values. Certainly this view of men and societies as complex self-regulating systems, interacting among themselves within complex environments should prove conducive to a more holistic approach to the social and behavioral sciences in all their multivariate complexity, and provides us with a more solid foundation for systematic scientific formalization than existed in a past in which "science" *par excellence* comprised the simplified model of a clockwork universe governed by the laws of classical mechanics. Second, the social scientist must examine closely the actual and potential relations of cybernetic modes of thought and technologies to social institutions. Cybernetics has profound implications both as an ideology and as regards ideology. This is already abundantly clear in the works of both the Russians and the Anglo-Americans. Cybernetic technologies lie at the root of the quantum shift in economic relations called automation and cybernation. Computer based "optimum" decisions based on cost-effectiveness analysis have begun to replace the interplay of interest in some key areas of political decision—specifically in U.S. military spending. These techniques are potentially applicable to the whole budget process.

Certainly the political sphere will be a major forum for the resolution of the problems of value and social philosophy that can no longer be ignored. Even in the absence of sophisticated competitive economic and social systems and competitive concepts of a good life, such as those of Russia and France, these decisions could not long be postponed. What must now be demonstrated is the capacity of a democratic society to understand, confront, and resolve very complex problems of social organization in such a way as to retain traditional freedoms and consultative political institutions while moving into new patterns of economic and social relations in which we realize that our relation to the machine has become quasi-symbiotic.

EXCHANGE AS A CONCEPTUAL FRAMEWORK FOR THE STUDY OF INTERORGANIZATIONAL RELATIONSHIPS

Sol Levine
and Paul E. White

Sociologists have devoted considerable attention to the study of formal organizations, particularly in industry, government, and the trade union field. Their chief focus, however, has been on patterns within rather than between organizations. Studies of interrelationships have largely been confined to units within the same organizational structure or between a pair of complementary organizations such as management and labor.

Reprinted from *Administrative Science Quarterly*, 5 (1960), 583–601.

Dimock's study of jurisdictional conflict between two federal agencies is a notable exception.[1] Another is a study of a community reaction to disaster by Form and Nosow in which the authors produce revealing data on the interaction pattern of local health organizations. The authors observe that "organizational cooperation was facilitated among organizations with similar internal structures."[2] March and Simon suggest that interorganizational conflict is very similar to intergroup conflict within organizations but present no supporting data.[3] Blau has commented on the general problems involved in studying multiple organizations.[4] In pointing up the need to study the organization in relation to its environment, Etzioni specifies the area of interorganizational relationships as one of the three meriting further intensive empirical study.[5]

Health and social welfare agencies within a given community offer an excellent opportunity for exploring patterns of relationship among organizations. There are an appreciable number of such organizations in any fairly large urban American community. Most of them are small so that relatively few individuals have to be interviewed to obtain information on their interaction. Within any community setting, varying kinds of relations exist between official and voluntary organizations concerned with health and welfare. Thus welfare agencies may use public health nursing services, or information on the status of families may be shared by such voluntary organizations as the Red Cross and the Tuberculosis and Health Association.

Facilitating communication between local organizations has been a major objective of public health administrators and community organizers. Their writings contain many assertions about the desirability of improving relationships in order to reduce gaps and overlaps of medical services to the citizens, but as yet little effort has been made to appraise objectively the interrelationships that actually exist within the community.

In the following pages we should like to present our theoretical interpretation of interorganizational relationships together with a discussion of our research approach and a few preliminary findings, pointing up some of the substantive areas in organizational sociology for which our

[1] Marshall E. Dimock, "Expanding Jurisdictions: A Case Study in Bureaucratic Conflict," in Robert K. Merton, Ailsa P. Gray, Barbara Hockey, Hanan C. Selvin, eds. *Reader in Bureaucracy* (New York, 1952).
[2] William H. Form and Sigmund Nosow, *Community in Disaster* (New York, 1958), p. 236.
[3] James G. March and H. A. Simon, *Organizations* (New York, 1958).
[4] Peter M. Blau, Formal Organization: Dimensions of Analysis, *American Journal of Sociology*, 63 (1957), 58.
[5] Amitai Etzioni, New Directions in the Study of Organizations and Society, *Social Research*, 27 (1960), 223–228.

study has relevance. Our present thinking is largely based on the results of an exploratory study of twenty-two health organizations in a New England community with a population of 200,000 and initial impressions of data on a more intensive study, as yet unanalyzed, of some fifty-five health organizations in another New England community of comparable size.

The site of our initial investigation was selected because we found it fairly accessible for study and relatively independent of a large metropolis; moreover, it contained a range of organizations which were of interest—a full-time health department, a welfare department, autonomous local agencies, local chapters or affiliates of major voluntary health and social welfare organizations, and major community hospitals. Of the twenty-two health organizations or agencies studied, fourteen were voluntary agencies, five were hospitals (three with out-patient clinics and two without) and three others were official agencies—health, welfare, and school. Intensive semistructured interviews were conducted with executive directors and supervisory personnel of each organization, and information was obtained from members of the boards through brief semistructured questionnaires. In addition, we used an adaptation of an instrument developed by Irwin T. Sanders to locate the most influential leaders in the community for the purpose of determining their distribution on agency boards.[6] The prestige ratings that the influential leaders assigned to the organizations constituted one of the independent variables of our study.

EXCHANGE AS A CONCEPTUAL FRAMEWORK

The complex of community health organizations may be seen as a system with individual organizations or system parts varying in the kinds and frequency of their relationships with one another. This system is enmeshed in ever larger systems—the community, the state, and so on.

Prevention and cure of disease constitute the ideal orientation of the health agency system, and individual agencies derive their respective goals or objectives from this larger orientation. In order to achieve its specific objectives, however, an agency must possess or control certain elements. It must have clients to serve; it must have resources in the form of equipment, specialized knowledge, or the funds with which to procure them; and it must have the services of people who can direct these resources to the clients. Few, if any, organizations have enough access to all

[6] Irwin T. Sanders, The Community Social Profile, *American Sociological Review*, 25 (1960), 75–77.

these elements to enable them to attain their objectives fully. Under realistic conditions of element scarcity, organizations must select, on the basis of expediency or efficiency, particular functions that permit them to achieve their ends as fully as possible. By function is meant a set of interrelated services or activities that are instrumental, or believed to be instrumental, for the realization of an organization's objectives.

Although, because of scarcity, an organization limits itself to particular functions, it can seldom carry them out without establishing relationships with other organizations of the health system. The reason for this are clear. To fulfill its functions without relating to other parts of the health system, an organization must be able to procure the necessary elements—cases, labor services, and other resources—directly from the community or outside it. Certain classes of hospitals treating a specific disease and serving an area larger than the local community probably most nearly approximate this condition. But even in this case other organizations within the system usually control some elements that are necessary or, at least, helpful to the carrying out of its functions. These may be money, equipment, or special personnel, which are conditionally lent or given. Usually agencies are unable to obtain all the elements they need from the community or through their individual efforts and, accordingly, have to turn to other agencies to obtain additional elements. The need for a sufficient number of clients, for example, is often more efficiently met through exchanges with other organizations than through independent case-finding procedures.

Theoretically, then, were all the essential elements in infinite supply there would be little need for organizational interaction and for subscription to co-operation as an ideal. Under actual conditions of scarcity, however, interorganizational exchanges are essential to goal attainment. In sum, organizational goals or objectives are derived from general health values. These goals or objectives may be viewed as defining the organization's ideal need for elements—consumers, labor services, and other resources. The scarcity of elements, however, impels the organization to restrict its activity to limited specific functions. The fulfillment of these limited functions, in turn, requires access to certain kinds of elements, which an organization seeks to obtain by entering into exchanges with other organizations.

Interaction among organizations can be viewed within the framework of an exchange model like that suggested by Homans.[7] However, the few available definitions of exchange are somewhat limited for our purposes because they tend to be bound by economics and because their referents

[7] George C. Homans, Social Behavior as Exchange, *American Journal of Sociology*, 63 (1958), 597–606.

are mainly individual or psychological phenomena and are not intended to encompass interaction between organizational entities or larger systems.[8] We suggest the following definition of organizational exchange: *Organizational exchange is any voluntary activity between two organizations which has consequences, actual or anticipated, for the realization of their respective goals or objectives.* This definition has several advantages. First, it refers to activity in general and not exclusively to reciprocal activity. The action may be unidirectional and yet involve exchange. If an organization refers a patient to another organization which then treats him, an exchange has taken place if the respective objectives of the two organizations are furthered by the action. Pivoting the definition on goals or objectives provides for an obvious but crucial component of what constitutes an organization. The co-ordination of activities of a number of individuals toward some objective or goal has been designated as a distinguishing feature of organizations by students in the field.[9] Parsons, for example, has defined an organization as a "special type of social system organized about the primacy of interest in the attainment of a particular type of system goal."[10] That its goals or objectives may be transformed by a variety of factors and that, under some circumstances, mere survival may become primary does not deny that goals or objectives are universal characteristics of organizations.

Second, the definition widens the concept of exchange beyond the transfer of material goods and beyond gratifications in the immediate present. This broad definition of exchange permits us to consider a number of dimensions of organizational interaction that would otherwise be overlooked.

Finally, while the organizations may not be bargaining or interacting on equal terms and may even employ sanctions or pressures (by granting

---

[8] Weber states that "by 'exchange' in the broadest sense will be meant every case of a formally voluntary agreement involving the offer of any sort of present, continuing, or future utility in exchange for utilities of any sort offered in return." Weber employs the term "utility" in the economic sense. It is the "utility" of the "object of exchange" to the parties concerned that produces exchange. See Max Weber, *The Theory of Social and Economic Organization* (New York, 1947) p. 170. Homans, on the other hand, in characterizing interaction between persons as an exchange of goods, material and nonmaterial, sees the impulse to "exchange" in the psychological make-up of the parties to the exchange. He states, "the paradigm of elementary social behavior, and the problem of the elementary sociologist is to state propositions relating the variations in the values and costs of each man to his frequency distribution of behavior among alternatives, where the values (in the mathematical sense) taken by these variables for one man determine in part their values for the other." See Homans, *op. cit.*, p. 598.
[9] Talcott Parsons, Suggestions for a Sociological Approach to the Theory of Organizations—I, *Administrative Science Quarterly*, 1 (1956), 63–85.
[10] *Ibid.*, p. 64.

or withholding these elements), it is important to exclude from our definition, relationships involving physical coercion or domination; hence emphasis is on the word "voluntary" in our definition.

The elements that are exchanged by health organizations fall into three main categories: (1) referrals of cases, clients, or patients; (2) the giving or receiving of labor services, including the services of volunteer, clerical, and professional personnel, and (3) the sending or receiving of resources other than labor services, including funds, equipment, and information on cases and technical matters. Organizations have varying needs of these elements depending on their particular functions. Referrals, for example, may be seen as the delivery of the consumers of services to organizations, labor services as the human means by which the resources of the organization are made available to the consumers, and resources other than labor services as the necessary capital goods.

THE DETERMINANTS OF EXCHANGE

The interdependence of the parts of the exchange system is contingent upon three related factors: (1) the accessibility of each organization to necessary elements from sources outside the health system, (2) the objectives of the organization and particular functions to which it allocates the elements it controls, and (3) the degree to which domain consensus exists among the various organizations. An ideal theory of organizational exchange would describe the interrelationship and relative contribution of each of these factors. For the present, however, we will draw on some of our preliminary findings to suggest possible relationships among these factors and to indicate that each plays a part in affecting the exchange of elements among organizations.

Gouldner has emphasized the need to differentiate the various parts of a system in terms of their relative dependence upon other parts of the system.[11] In our terms, certain system parts are relatively dependent, not having access to elements outside the system, whereas others, which have access to such elements, possess a high degree of independence or functional autonomy. The voluntary organizations of our study (excluding hospitals) can be classified into what Sills calls either corporate or federated organizations.[12] Corporate organizations are those which delegate authority downward from the national or state level to the local level.

[11] Alvin W. Gouldner, Reciprocity and Autonomy in Functional Theory, in Llewellyn Gross, ed., *Symposium on Sociological Theory,* (Evanston, Ill., 1959); also The Norm of Reciprocity: A Preliminary Statement, *American Sociological Review,* 25 (1960), 161–178.
[12] David L. Sills, *The Volunteers: Means and Ends in a National Organization,* (New York, 1957).

They contrast with organizations of the federated type which delegate authority upward—from the local to the state or national level.

It appears that local member units of corporate organizations, because they are less dependent on the local health system and can obtain the necessary elements from the community or their parent organizations, interact less with other local agencies than federated organizations. This is supported by preliminary data presented in Table 1. It is also suggested that by carrying out their activities without entering actively into exchange relationships with other organizations, corporate organizations apparently are able to maintain their essential structure and avoid consequences resulting in the displacement of state or national goals. It may be that corporate organizations deliberately choose functions that require minimal involvement with other organizations. An examination of the four corporate organizations in our preliminary study reveals that three of them give resources to other agencies to carry out their activities, and the fourth conducts broad educational programs. Such functions are less likely to involve relationships with other organizations than the more direct service organizations, those that render services to individual recipients.

An organization's relative independence from the rest of the local health agency system and greater dependence upon a system outside the community may, at times, produce specific types of disagreements with the other agencies within the local system. This is dramatically demonstrated in the criticisms expressed toward a local community branch of an official state rehabilitation organization. The state organization, to justify its existence, has to present a successful experience to the legislators— that a minimum number of persons have been successfully rehabilitated. This means that by virtue of the services the organization has offered, a certain percentage of its debilitated clients are again returned to self-supporting roles. The rehabilitative goal of the organization cannot be fulfilled unless it is selective in the persons it accepts as clients. Other community agencies dealing with seriously debilitated clients are unable to get the state to accept their clients for rehabilitation. In the eyes of these frustrated agencies the state organization is remiss in fulfilling its public goal. The state agency, on the other hand, cannot commit its limited personnel and resources to the time-consuming task of trying to rehabilitate what seem to be very poor risks. The state agency wants to be accepted and approved by the local community and its health agencies, but the state legislature and the governor, being the primary source of the agency's resources, constitute its significant reference group. Hence, given the existing definition of organizational goals and the state agency's relative independence of the local health system, its interaction with other community agencies is relatively low.

TABLE 1. *Weighted rankings* of organizations classified by organizational form on four interaction indices*

Interaction index	Sent by	N	Sent to					Total interaction sent
			Voluntary		Hospitals			
			Corporate	Federated	Without clinics	With clinics	Official	
Referrals	Vol. corporate	4	4.5	5	3.7	4.5	5	5
	Vol. federated	10	3	4	3.7	3	4	3
	Hosps. w/o clinics	2	4.5	3	3.7	4.5	3	4
	Hosps. w. clinics	3	1	1	1.5	2	1	1
	Official	3	2	2	1.5	1	2	2
Resources	Vol. corporate	4	5	2	1	4	5	3.5
	Vol. federated	10	4	3	3	4	4	3.5
	Hosps. w/o clinics	2	2	4.5	4.5	5	3	5
	Hosps. w. clinics	3	1	1	2	1	2	1
	Official	3	3	4.5	4.5	2	1	2
Written and verbal communication	Vol. corporate	4	5	3	2	4	5	4
	Vol. federated	10	3	1	3	3	3	2.5
	Hosps. w/o clinics	2	2	5	4.5	5	4	5
	Hosps. w. clinics	3	4	4	4.5	1	1.5	2.5
	Official	3	1	2	1	2	1.5	1
Joint activities	Vol. corporate	4	4.5	4	3	5	3.5	5
	Vol. federated	10	3	3	5	3	1	3
	Hosps. w/o clinics	2	2	5	1	2	3.5	4
	Hosps. w. clinics	3	4.5	2	2	1	5	1.5
	Official	3	1	1	4	4	2	1.5

* Note: 1 indicates highest interaction; 5 indicates lowest interaction.

The marked difference in the interaction rank position of hospitals with out-patient clinics and those without suggests other differences between the two classes of hospitals. It may be that the two types of hospitals have different goals and that hospitals with clinics have a greater "community" orientation and are more committed to the concept of "comprehensive" care than are hospitals without clinics. However, whether or not the goals of the two types of hospitals do indeed differ, those with out-patient departments deal with population groups similar to those serviced by other agencies of the health system, that is, patients who are largely ambulatory and indigent; thus they serve patients whom other organizations may also be seeking to serve. Moreover, hospitals with out-patient clinics have greater control over their clinic patients than over those in-patients who are the charges of private physicians, and are thereby freer to refer patients to other agencies.

The functions of an organization not only represent the means by which it allocates its elements but, in accordance with our exchange formulation, also determine the degree of dependence on other organizations for specific kinds of elements, as well as its capacity to make certain kinds of elements available to other organizations. The exchange model leads us to explain the flow of elements between organizations largely in terms of the respective functions performed by the participating agencies. Indeed, it is doubtful whether any analysis of exchange of elements among organizations which ignores differences in organizational needs would have much theoretical or practical value.

In analyzing the data from our pilot community we classified agencies on the basis of their primary health functions: resource, education, prevention, treatment, or rehabilitation. Resource organizations attempt to achieve their objectives by providing other agencies with the means to carry out their functions. The four other agency types may be conceived as representing respective steps in the control of disease. We have suggested that the primary function determines an organization's need for exchange elements. Our preliminary data reveal, as expected, that treatment organizations rate highest on number of referrals and amount of resources received and that educational organizations, whose efforts are directed toward the general public, rate low on the number of referrals (see Table 2). This finding holds even when the larger organizations—official agencies and hospitals—are excluded and the analysis is based on the remaining voluntary agencies of our sample. As a case in point, let us consider a health organization whose function is to educate the public about a specific disease but which renders no direct service to individual clients. If it carries on an active educational program, it is possible that some people may come to it directly to obtain information and, mistakenly, in the hope of

TABLE 2. Weighted rankings* of organizations, classified by function on four interaction indices

Interaction index	Received by	N	Received from					Total interaction received
			Education	Resource	Prevention	Treatment	Rehabilitation	
Referrals	Education	3	4.5	5	5	5	5	5
	Resource	5	3	4	2	4	1	3
	Prevention	5	2	1	3	2	2.5	2
	Treatment	7	1	2	1	1	2.5	1
	Rehabilitation	2	4.5	3	4	3	4	4
Resources	Education	3	4.5	5	4	5	4.5	5
	Resource	5	1.5	3	3	4	3	3.5
	Prevention	5	1.5	4	2	3	4.5	3.5
	Treatment	7	3	2	1	2	2	1
	Rehabilitation	2	4.5	1	5	1	1	2
Written and verbal communication	Education	3	4	5	4.5	5	5	5
	Resource	5	3	2	2	3	2	2.5
	Prevention	5	2	4	3	4	4	3
	Treatment	7	1	1	1	2	3	1
	Rehabilitation	2	5	3	4.5	1	1	2.5
Joint activities	Education	3	4	4	1	3	4.5	4
	Resource	5	2	1	3	4	1	3
	Prevention	5	1	2	2	2	3	1
	Treatment	7	3	3	4	1	2	2
	Rehabilitation	2	5	5	5	5	4.5	5

* Note: 1 indicates highest interaction; 5 indicates lowest interaction.

receiving treatment. If this occurs, the organization will temporarily be in possession of potential clients whom it may route or refer to other more appropriate agencies. That such referrals will be frequent is unlikely however. It is even less likely that the organization will receive many referrals from other organizations. If an organization renders a direct service to a client, however, such as giving X-ray examinations, or polio immunizations, there is greater likelihood that it will send or receive referrals.

An organization is less limited in its function in such interagency activities as discussing general community health problems, attending agency council meetings or co-operating on some aspect of fund raising. Also, with sufficient initiative even a small educational agency can maintain communication with a large treatment organization (for example, a general hospital) through exchanges of periodic reports and telephone calls to obtain various types of information. But precisely because it is an educational agency offering services to the general public and not to individuals, it will be limited in its capacity to maintain other kinds of interaction with the treatment organization. It probably will not be able to lend or give space or equipment, and it is even doubtful that it can offer the kind of instruction that the treatment organization would seek for its staff. That the organization's function establishes the range of possibilities for exchange and that other variables exert influence within the framework established by function is suggested by some other early findings presented in Table 3. Organizations were classified as direct or indirect on the basis of whether or not they provided a direct service to the public. They were also classified according to their relative prestige as rated by influential leaders in the community. Organizations high in prestige lead in the number of joint activities, and prestige seems to exert some influence on the amount of verbal and written communication. Yet it is agencies offering direct services—regardless of prestige—which lead in the number of referrals and resources received. In other words, prestige, leadership, and other organizational variables seem to affect interaction patterns within limits established by the function variable.

An obvious question is whether organizations with shared or common boards interact more with one another than do agencies with separate boards. Our preliminary data show that the interaction rate is not affected by shared board membership. We have not been able to ascertain if there is any variation in organizational interaction when the shared board positions are occupied by persons with high status or influence. In our pilot community, there was only one instance in which two organizations had the same top community leaders as board members. If boards play an active role in the activities of health organizations, they serve more to link the organization to the community and the elements it

TABLE 3. *Weighted rankings* of organizations classified by prestige of organization and by general type of service offered on four interaction indices*

Interaction index	Received by	N	Received from				Total interaction received
			High Prestige		Low Prestige		
			Direct service	Indirect service	Direct service	Indirect service	
Referrals	High direct	9	1	1	1	1	1
	High indirect	3	3	3.5	3	3.5	3
	Low direct	6	2	2	2	2	2
	Low indirect	4	4	3.5	4	3.5	4
Resources	High direct	9	2	2	2	2	2
	High indirect	3	3	3	3	3.5	3
	Low direct	6	1	1	1	1	1
	Low indirect	4	4	4	4	3.5	4
Written and verbal communication	High direct	9	2	2	3	1	2
	High indirect	3	3	3	1	3	3
	Low direct	6	1	1	2	2	1
	Low indirect	4	4	4	4	4	4
Joint activities	High direct	9	1	1.5	2	2	2
	High indirect	3	2	1.5	1	1	1
	Low direct	6	4	3	3	4	3
	Low indirect	4	3	4	4	3	4

* Note: 1 indicates highest interaction; 5 indicates lowest interaction.

possesses than to link the organization to other health and welfare agencies. The board probably also exerts influence on internal organizational operations and on establishing or approving the primary objective of the organization. Once the objective and the implementing functions are established, these functions tend to exert their influence autonomously on organizational interaction.

ORGANIZATIONAL DOMAIN

As we have seen, the elements exchanged are cases, labor services, and other resources. All organizational relationships directly or indirectly involve the flow and control of these elements. Within the local health agency system, the flow of elements is not centrally co-ordinated, but rests upon voluntary agreements or understanding. Obviously, there will be no exchange of elements between two organizations that do not know of each other's existence or that are completely unaware of each other's functions. Even more, there can be no exchange of elements without some agreement or understanding, however implicit. These exchange agreements are contingent upon the organization's domain. The domain of an organization consists of the specific goals it wishes to pursue and the functions it undertakes in order to implement its goals. In operational terms, organizational domain in the health field refers to the claims that an organization stakes out for itself in terms of (1) disease covered, (2) population served, and (3) services rendered. The goals of the organization constitute in effect the organization's claim to future functions and to the elements requisite to these functions, whereas the present or actual functions carried out by the organization constitute *de facto* claims to these elements. Exchange agreements rest upon prior consensus regarding domain. Within the health agency system, consensus regarding an organization's domain must exist to the extent that parts of the system will provide each agency with the elements necessary to attain its ends.

Once an organization's goals are accepted, domain consensus continues as long as the organization fulfills the functions adjudged appropriate to its goals and adheres to certain standards of quality. Our data show that organizations find it more difficult to legitimate themselves before other organizations in the health system than before such outside systems as the community or state. An organization can sometimes obtain sufficient elements from outside the local health system, usually in the form of funds, to continue in operation long after other organizations within the system have challenged its domain. Conversely, if the goals of a specific organization are accepted within the local agency system, other organizations of the system may encourage it to expand its functions and to realize its goals more fully by offering it elements to implement them. Should an organization not respond to this encouragement, it may be forced to forfeit its claim to the unrealized aspect of its domain.

Within the system, delineation of organizational domains is highly desired.[13] For example, intense competition may occur occasionally between two agencies offering the same services, especially when other agencies have no specific criteria for referring patients to one rather than the other. If both services are operating near capacity, competition between the two tends to be less keen, the choice being governed by the availability of service. If the services are being operated at less than capacity, competition and conflict often occur. Personnel of referring agencies in this case frequently deplore the "duplication of services" in the community. In most cases the conflict situation is eventually resolved by agreement on the part of the competing agencies to specify the criteria for referring patients to them. The agreement may take the form of consecutive handling of the same patients. For example, age may be employed as a criterion. In one case three agencies were involved in giving rehabilitation services: one took preschool children, another school children, and the third adults. In another case, where preventive services were offered, one agency took preschool children and the other took children of school age. The relative accessibility of the agencies to the respective age groups was a partial basis for these divisions. Another criterion—disease stage—also permits consecutive treatment of patients. One agency provided physical therapy to bedridden patients; another handled them when they became ambulatory.

Several other considerations, such as priorities in allocation of elements, may impel an organization to delimit its functions even when no duplication of services exists. The phenomenon of delimiting one's role and consequently of restricting one's domain is well known. It can be seen, for instance, in the resistance of certain universities of high prestige to offer "practical" or vocational courses, or courses to meet the needs of any but high-status professionals, even to the extent of foregoing readily accessible federal grants. It is evidenced in the insistence of certain psychiatric clinics on handling only cases suitable for psychoanalytic treatment, of certain business organizations on selling only to wholesalers, of some retail stores on handling only expensive merchandise.

The flow of elements in the health system is contingent upon solving the problem of "who gets what for what purpose." The clarification of organizational domains and the development of greater domain consensus contributes to the solution of this problem. In short, domain consensus is a prerequisite to exchange. Achieving domain consensus may involve

[13] In our research a large percentage of our respondents spontaneously referred to the undesirability of overlapping or duplicated services.

negotiation, orientation, or legitimation. When the functions of the interacting organizations are diffuse, achieving domain consensus becomes a matter of constant readjustment and compromise, a process which may be called negotiation or bargaining. The more specific the functions, however, the more domain consensus is attained merely by orientation (for example, an agency may call an X-ray unit to inquire about the specific procedures for implementing services). A third, less frequent but more formalized, means of attaining domain consensus is the empowering, licensing or "legitimating" of an organization to operate within the community by some other organization. Negotiation, as a means of attaining domain consensus seems to be related to diffuseness of function, whereas orientation, at the opposite extreme, relates to specificity of function.

These processes of achieving domain consensus constitute much of the interaction between organizations. While they may not involve the immediate flow of elements, they are often necessary preconditions for the exchange of elements, because without at least minimal domain consensus there can be no exchange among organizations. Moreover, to the extent that these processes involve proffering information about the availability of elements as well as about rights and obligations regarding the elements, they constitute a form of interorganizational exchange.

DIMENSIONS OF EXCHANGE

We have stated that all relationships among local health agencies may be conceptualized as involving exchange. There are four main dimensions to the actual exchange situation. They are:

1. *The parties to the exchange.* The characteristics we have thus far employed in classifying organizations or the parties to the exchange are: organizational form or affiliation, function, prestige, size, personnel characteristics, and numbers and types of clients served.

2. *The kinds and quantities exchanged.* These involve two main classes: the actual elements exchanged (consumers, labor services, and resources other than labor services), and information on the availability of these organizational elements and on rights and obligations regarding them.

3. *The agreement underlying the exchange.* Every exchange is contingent upon a prior agreement, which may be implicit and informal or fairly explicit and highly formalized. For example, a person may be informally routed or referred to another agency with the implicit awareness or expectation that the other organization will handle the case. On the other hand, the two agencies may enter into arrangements that stipulate the exact conditions and procedures by which patients are referred from one

to another. Furthermore, both parties may be actively involved in arriving at the terms of the agreement, or these terms may be explicitly defined by one for all who may wish to conform to them. An example of the latter case is the decision of a single organization to establish a policy of a standard fee for service.

4. *The direction of the exchange.* This refers to the direction of the flow of organizational elements. We have differentiated three types:

a. Unilateral: where elements flow from one organization to another and no elements are given in return.

b. Reciprocal: where elements flow from one organization to another in return for other elements.

c. Joint: where elements flow from two organizations acting in unison toward a third party. This type, although representing a high order of agreement and co-ordination of policy among agencies, does not involve the actual transfer of elements.

As we proceed with our study of relationships among health agencies, we will undoubtedly modify and expand our theoretical model. For example, we will attempt to describe how the larger systems are intertwined with the health agency system. Also, we will give more attention to the effect of interagency competition and conflict regarding the flow of elements among organizations. In this respect we will analyze differences among organizations with respect not only to domain but to fundamental goals as well. As part of this analysis we will examine the orientations of different categories of professionals (for example, nurses and social workers) as well as groups with varying experiences and training within categories of professionals (as nurses with or without graduate education). . . .

A CRITIQUE OF ORGANIZATIONAL THEORIES

Sheldon S. Wolin

ORGANIZATIONAL THEORY:
RATIONALISM VERSUS ORGANICISM

Today there are two distinct schools of thought concerning the nature of organizational life. There are those who picture an organization as a social organism which has evolved over time. An organization, whether it is a business corporation or a governmental bureaucracy, represents a complex response to a particular historical environment, an institution which constantly adjusts to the needs, sentiments, and emotions of its members, and the members to it. The primary function of these organizations is not to produce profits in the most rational manner possible, nor to delight the production engineer by virtue of its efficiency. Instead, it is to promote the values of social stability, cohesion, and integration. We shall call this group the "organicists."

The second group, in contrast, views organizations as rationally arranged structures designed for specific purposes, such as making goods or "making" decisions. For this group of writers, efficiency is primary. They will have none of the Burkean bias against rational, self-conscious planning. We shall call them the "rationalists."

The representatives of rationalism, including writers like Herbert Simon and Chester Barnard, speak a matter-of-fact language; Simon, in particular, has a fondness for the spare metaphors of mechanics. Thus an organization is "a system in equilibrium, which receives contributions in the form of money or effort, and offers inducements in return for these contributions."[1] In the thinking of this group there is no trace of romanticism, no fondness for modes of natural growth, only a world of hard

[1] Simon, *Administrative Behavior*, p. 122.

rationalism: "Organizations are the least 'natural,' most rationally contrived units of human association."[2] "Formal organization is that kind of cooperation that is conscious, deliberate, purposeful."[3] The rationalists are most impressed by the capabilities of an organization for focusing human energy and pooling human talents; they see its primary values in efficiency of operation and the ability to survive rather than in communal solidarity. For Simon, the "principle that is implied in all rational behavior" is "the criterion of efficiency." Efficiency, however, carries broader implications than the coordination of different operations for a prescribed end. Its aim is to create a special environment which will induce the individual to make the best decision—and "best," in this context, means a decision most helpful to the needs and ends of the organization.[4] It involves setting limits to individual actions and attitudes, exposing behavior to a "well-conceived plan" initiated by a "controlling group."

Highly revealing of the rationalists' outlook is the way they have handled the problem of authority. Their theory can rightly be called Hobbesian. In Simon's writings, for example, the discussion of authority centers on the ability to command subordinates; no concessions are made to eliciting consensus or agreement among the members. There is a no-nonsense quality about authority: its presence is felt whenever a subordinate accepts the decision of a superior and "holds in abeyance his own critical faculties." The superior does not try to convince his underling but only "obtain his acquiescence." Authority, in brief, is "the power to make the decisions which will guide the actions of another."[5] There is no sentimentalizing over the need to create a sense of participation or belonging. To be sure, loyalties are desirable, but mainly in the form of "organizational loyalties," which smooth the way for the decision of authority. The ideal member is one who has been conditioned to permit "the communicated decision of another to guide his own choices . . . without deliberation on his part on the expediency of those premises"—which is to define "choice" in a curious way, as action without deliberation.[6] The organization emerges as a triumph of collective rationality which extends rationality to each member insofar as he responds to its stimuli:

> Since these institutions largely determine the mental sets of the participants, they set the conditions for the exercise of docility, and hence of rationality in human society.[7]

2 Simon, *Models of Man*, p. 199.
3 Barnard, *Functions of the Executive*, p. 4.
4 Simon, *Administrative Behavior*, pp. 14, 38–39, 109, 118–119.
5 Simon, *Administrative Behavior*, pp. 11, 125, 126.
6 *Ibid.*, p. 125.
7 *Ibid.*, p. 101. See pp. 102–103 for the various ways an organization instills loyalties and creates identifications.

The theory of the rationality of organizational behavior presented by this school has some further resemblances to Hobbes. The "final test" of any organization, Barnard declares, is "survival."[8] But more important, the organization is regarded as a contrived world, one as "artificial" as the Hobbesian universe, resting on nothing more than man's affirmation that it shall exist. It is also rational and can be understood rationally because men have made it. Like Leviathan, it is the response to chaos. These points are illustrated in Simon's remarkable contrast between "economic man" and "administrative man":

> Economic man deals with the "real world" in all its complexity. Administrative man recognizes that the world he perceives is a drastically simplified model of the buzzing, blooming confusion that constitutes the real world. He is content with the gross simplification because he believes that the real world is mostly empty—that most of the facts of the real world have no great relevance to any particular situation he is facing, and that most significant chains of causes and consequences are short and simple.[9]

In reaction to the rationalist position there has emerged in recent years a protest against the austerely efficient approach to organization. One example of this is the pioneering writings of Elton Mayo. The bulk of his work centered on the relationship between productivity and worker morale, and he concluded that morale was largely a function of the health of the small social group organized around specific jobs. In one sense Mayo's ideas fall in the tradition of small community theorizing, and they recall at many points the concerns of Fourier and Owen.

More significant, however, is the recent attempt to discover communal values in the large corporation and administrative organization. The ideas of Burke and the philosophy of organicism are pressed into service to explain the world of giant bureaucracies. The major theorist of this development is Philip Selznick. The starting point is one which denies that "formal" organization theory can ever fully capture the subtleties and rich social life of a living structure. Just as Burke had ridiculed the notion that a rationalistic and abstract theory of a political constitution could ever provide a faithful abridgement of the life of a nation, Selznick takes issue with the contemporary heirs of Sieyès and Paine: formal organizations "never succeed in conquering the non-rational dimensions of organizational behavior . . . No abstract plan or pattern can—or may, if it is to be useful—exhaustively describe an empirical reality." The members

---

[8] Chester I. Barnard, *Dilemmas of Leadership in the Democratic Process* (Princeton: Princeton University Press, 1939) p. 7.
[9] Simon, *Administrative Behavior*, pp. xxv–xxvi.

of an organization "have a propensity to resist de-personalization, to spill over the boundaries of their segmentary roles, to participate as *wholes*."[10] Admittedly an organization can be viewed as a rational, formal structure, an "economy" governed by the criteria of "efficiency and effectiveness," but from another perspective it appears as an "adaptive social structure" with certain "needs" radically different from the narrow ones of an "economy." These "needs" are ones which Burke would have applauded, for they are couched in the delicate language of organic growth: like any organism, an organization requires "security" in its environment, "stability" in its lines of authority, subtle patterns of informal relationships, modes of communication, "continuity" in its policies, and "homogeneity" in its outlook.[11]

In Selznick's later writings, the organic aspects of an organization are separated even more sharply from the strictly rational ones. The word "organization" is reserved for what is a "technical instrument" useful in directing human energies towards a fixed goal; it is a tool, rationally designed for specific technical ends, and, like any tool, expendable. The social aspects of the organization are then sorted out and designated an "institution": an institution "is more nearly a natural product of social needs and pressures, a responsive adaptive organism." Its adaptations are identical with Burke's evolutionary view of society; they are "natural and largely unplanned." "As an organization acquires a self, a distinctive identity, it becomes an institution."[12] To understand an "institution" requires a mode of cognition different from the logic of the engineer. "We must draw upon what we know about natural communities," for we are dealing with precious, living aggregates. To the degree that organizations evolve into "natural communities" they become valued for their own

---

[10] Philip Selznick, "Foundations of the Theory of Organization," *American Sociological Review*, Vol. XII, pp. 23–35 (1948), pp. 25–26 (Copyright (1948) by the University of Chicago); *Leadership in Administration*, pp. 8–9. The writings of E. W. Bakke are in the same tradition as Selznick. The members of an organization, he writes, "create a social system and a society which has a reality greater than the sum of its parts at any particular time." *Bonds of Organization*, pp. 200–201, 203. See also his notion of the "organizational charter," *ibid.*, pp. 152 ff. For the same point of view but in terms of small groups, see Kurt Lewin, *Field Theory in Social Science*, ed. D. Cartwright (New York: Harper & Row, 1951) p. 146. The juxtaposition of empirical reality versus preconceived pattern appears also in Jacob Talmon's critique of democratic radicalism, *The Rise of Totalitarian Democracy* (Boston: Beacon, 1952); and see Talmon's explicitly Burkean theory of politics at pp. 1–6, 253–255. For a subtler presentation of this same general position, but without the admiration for bureaucracy, see the two essays by Michael Oakeshott, "Political Education," in *Philosophy, Politics and Society*, ed. Peter Laslett (Oxford: Blackwell, 1956) pp. 1–21; "Rationalism in Politics," *Cambridge Journal*, Vol. I (1947) pp. 81–108, 145–157.

[11] Selznick, "Foundations of the Theory of Organization," *loc. cit.*, p. 29.

[12] Selznick, *Leadership in Administration*, pp. 5, 21.

sakes, for "to institutionalize" is "to *infuse with value* beyond the technical requirements of the task at hand."[13]

Thus far the pure language of Burke: spontaneity, natural processes, adaptative organisms, and non-rational behavior. But, it must be remembered that Selznick is describing not a rural and pre-industrial society, a world of squires, manor houses, and faithful retainers, but the world of General Motors, the Pentagon, and the large public university. To liken a corporation to a natural community evokes the question: what does it mean to be a member of such a community? where is the natural aristocracy of Burke and where is the natural relationship, evolving slowly and unconsciously over time, between the members and the governing elite? The answers that Selznick gives are cast, not in the language of Burke, but in that of Saint-Simon. Words like "spontaneous" are used to describe the relationship between member and the controlling group, but they have been divested of all unpremeditation and serve only as the shell to manipulation.

"Maintenance of social values," Selznick writes, "depends on the autonomy of elites," and hence participation is "prescribed" for the members "only when there is a problem of cohesion." Despite Selznick's avowal that one of the felt needs of the members was not to feel "manipulated," and that the loyalties of the members were vital ingredients infusing the bare structure of an organization with a human warmth, he discovers that these "commitments" and "identifications" cause difficulties; they limit "the freedom of the leadership to deploy its resources."[14] The tension is neatly resolved by arranging for a conjunction between the aims and requirements of leadership and the sentiments of those led. By some alchemy, "spontaneity" and "manipulation" are rendered compatible:

> When we say that policy is built into the social structure of an organization, we mean that official aims and methods are *spontaneously protected* or *advanced*. The aspirations of individuals are so stimulated and controlled, and so ordered in their mutual relations, as to produce the desired balance of forces.[15]

Now Selznick's conclusion is in no significant sense different from that reached by the "rationalist" Simon. "Human behavior . . . gets its higher goals and integrations from the institutional setting in which it operates and by which it is molded." Once the proper "attachment or loyalty to the organization" has been bred in the member, it is "auto-

---

[13] *Ibid.*, pp. 12–13, 16–17. (Italics in the original.)
[14] *Ibid.*, pp. 8, 18.
[15] *Ibid.*, p. 100. (Italics in the original.)

matically" guaranteed that "his decisions will be consistent with the organization objectives"; that is, he will have an "organization personality."[16]
The convergence of the two theories at the point of manipulation faithfully mirrors one of the fundamental points of agreement between nearly
all writers of recent times: the belief that the world created by organizational bureaucracies is and should be run by elites. And at this point the
challenge to the political becomes explicit, and now we turn to how it
has been posed. . . .

Elite and mass: action in the age of organization. Selznick's argument, which is a highly sophisticated and literal example of what can be
found among many writers, is not concerned solely to establish the political
character of business organizations. Rather the more general aim is to
demonstrate that the politicalness of a corporation does not come from
the fact that the corporation is a business enterprise, but from the fact
that it is a large and powerful organization. In other words, the organization is the dominant and ubiquitous phenomenon of society, and whether
it carries the adjective "business," "government," "military," or "educational" is largely irrelevant. All organizations are inevitably "political" in
character, or, conversely, what is most politically significant in the modern
world is contained in organizational life.

This being the case, the question naturally arises, how do these
theorists view politics? A partial answer is that they perceive political
problems from an elitist position. In Selznick's words, elites are "objectively necessary" for the maintenance and development of social institutions and culture.[17] The form of elitism expressed in this literature has
certain superficial affinities with, say, Platonism: it believes that those
few who have the qualifications for exercising the highest social functions
should be in the positions of highest authority. Fundamentally, however,
contemporary elitism is indebted to a far different and more recent conception; namely, that an elite is a group whose superiority rests on its
excellence in manipulation. The *locus classicus* of this formulation was in

---

[16] Simon, *Administrative Behavior*, pp. 101, 109; Barnard, *Functions of the Executive*,
pp. 187–188. Compare also the following from a writer who belongs to the organicist
group: "A society is free so far as the behavior it makes appropriate and natural
for its citizens—the behavior they feel is good—is also the behavior its controls
demand of them." Homans, *The Human Group*, p. 333.

[17] V. Pareto, *The Mind and Society*, trans. A. Bongiorno and A. Livingstone, 4 vols.
(New York: Harcourt, 1935) Vol. I, par. 246; III, pars. 2025–2057; IV, pars. 2183–
2184, 2244–2267; R. Michels, *Political Parties*, trans. Eden and Cedar Paul (New
York: Free Press, 1958) pp. 49–59, 80–90; G. Mosca, *The Ruling Class*, ed. A. Livingstone (New York: McGraw-Hill, 1938) pp. 65–69, 168, 171–173, 394–395, 415–427;
and see the recent study by J. H. Meisel, *The Myth of the Ruling Class* (Ann Arbor:
University of Michigan Press, 1958).

the writings of Pareto, but it has become commonplace in a wide variety of twentieth-century theorists: in Lenin's theory of the party elites; in Nazi and Fascist ideologies; in the various theorists of managerialism; and in Mannheim's conception of the role of social scientists in the planned society.[18] Now the crucial theme in all of these writings, and the one which supplies the dialectical counterpoint to the elitist strain, is the emergence of the "masses." The concept of the masses haunts modern political and social theory: to disenchanted liberals like Ortega y Gasset, it represented the dreaded enemy of culture; to others, like Lenin and, more particularly, Fascist and Nazi writers, the masses represented the pliable stuff of revolutionary opportunity. Although there are a wide variety of definitions of the "masses," Selznick has given one which describes fairly well what most writers have in mind: "When the normal inhibitions enforced by tradition and social structure are loosened . . . the undifferentiated mass emerges."[19] This kind of definition sets the stage for the dramatic confrontation between the "elite" and the "mass": the elite is a sharply defined group, possessing clear qualifications and performing a vitally useful role in the social system. The concept of the elite fits naturally with a tradition of political and social theory in which hierarchy, order, and differentiation are fundamental ideas: a tradition as old as political thought itself and as recent as modern sociology. The mass, in contrast, is undifferentiated, amorphous, banal in its tastes, lacking in a defined role and conscious purpose, the unattractive deposit of an age of rapid social change, the lost social battalion without ties of communication, affection, and loyalty. "Mass connotes a 'glob of humanity,' as against the intricately related, institutionally bound groupings that form a healthy social organism." The "disease" of contemporary society is "mass behavior."[20]

The juxtaposition of "mass" and "elite" is highly informative of the present condition of theorizing, for it discloses that contemporary theory is, in a special sense, post-Marxian, and, in terms of mood, disenchanted. History has not only been unkind, it has been positively malicious. Instead of the highly self-conscious proletariat, the proud bearers of man's historical destiny, history has given us the vulgar mass; instead of Adonis, Quasimodo. Marx had depicted the working class as disciplined, purposeful, the symbolic representative of humanity's future triumph—"philosophy can only be realized by the abolition of the proletariat, and the proletariat can only be abolished by the realization of philosophy"—as well as the symbol of humanity's past. The proletariat had suffered on the cross of

[18] Selznick, *The Organizational Weapon*, p. 283.
[19] *Ibid.*, pp. 284, 291.
[20] Marx, *Sociology and Social Philosophy*, pp. 182–183.

history for all humanity; "its sufferings are universal"; its present misery was "not a *particular wrong* but *wrong in general*"; its future emancipation promised to be "a *total redemption of humanity.*"

Now if, instead of the proletariat, history has disgorged a "glob of humanity," it is not Marx who is teacher to the new age of mass society but Lenin; it is not the prophet of proletarian victory who speaks to the contemporary condition, but the strategist who perfects the instrument of action, the elite. If it is to be the elite, rather than the proletariat, who actually lead the way, the strategy is not to smash the pseudo-proletariat or masses, but to manipulate it. It is "our duty," Lenin wrote, "to go down *lower* and *deeper,* to the real masses."[21]

What makes Lenin a central figure for our study is that he glimpsed sooner than most writers the possibilities of organization as the action medium best suited to a mass age. Organization was to mass in Lenin's theory what idea had been to matter in Plato's: that which imparted form to the formless. Lenin was the first to seize the implications of transferring politics, political theory, political action—all that we have subsumed under the "political"—to the plane of organization. He taught that politics and the political had meaning only within an organizational setting. Industrialism and large-scale organization did not necessarily render political things unnecessary, nor did "administration" provide a complete substitute, as Saint-Simon and others had supposed. The trick was not to destroy the political, but to absorb it into organization, to create a new compound. The measure of Lenin's success is that his lessons have become the common property of the age; the irony is that his prescription for revolution has also been used to preserve giant capitalism.

The central point of Lenin's argument was the refutation of an assumption common to classical liberalism, early socialism, and Marx as well: the primordial importance of economic phenomena. While other writers, professing to follow Marx, had also expressed anxieties about the continued and stubborn vitality of capitalism, Lenin not only rendered this problem irrelevant by turning the focus of revolutionary theory upon precapitalist societies, but, above all, he taught that the greatest danger to the revolutionary movement lay in allowing the workers to become preoccupied with economic issues. If the proletariat went whoring after material class interests, its tough revolutionary temper would surely soften and victory

[21] Lenin, *Opportunism and Social Chauvinism*, Little Lenin Library (London: Lawrence and Wishart, 1914) Vol. XXII, p. 19. "I think that Bolsheviks remind us of Antaeus, the hero of Greek mythology. Like Antaeus, they are strong in keeping contact with their mother, the masses, who bore them, fed them and educated them. And as long as they keep contact with their mother, the people, they have every chance of remaining invincible." Joseph Stalin, *On Organization*, Little Stalin Library (London: Lawrence and Wishart, 1942) p. 21.

would be lost. Self-interest was self-interest, and it no more encouraged proletarian than capitalist heroics.[22]

Lenin proceeded to discard the eighteenth and nineteenth century notion that significant action meant economic action. Political action was rescued from limbo and restored to a new primacy, new because revolution was proclaimed the quintessential form of political action. "The fact that economic interests are a decisive factor *does not in the least imply* that the economic [i.e., trade union] struggle must be the main factor, for the essential and 'decisive' interests in classes can be satisfied *only* by the radical *political* changes in general."[23] For Lenin the "political" dealt with the comprehensive, with what transcended class horizons and interests; hence the workers had to rise above economic consciousness and acquire an "all-sided political consciousness" responsive to *"all cases* of tyranny, oppression, violence, and abuse, no matter *what class* is affected."[24] He insisted that "political activity had its logic quite apart" from either terrorism or economic struggle, and he accused his opponents of committing "the fundamental error" of believing it possible "to develop the class political consciousness of the workers *from within* the economic struggle."[25] "True" consciousness was political rather than economic, because revolutionary overthrow constituted a basically political act with a basically political objective.[26] The workers, therefore, had to be educated to a political consciousness, which meant, in a very ancient notion, gaining a synthetic view of the whole:

> The consciousness of the masses of the workers cannot be genuine class consciousness, unless the workers learn to observe from concrete, and above all from topical, political facts and events, *every* other social class and all the manifestations of the intellectual, ethical and political life of these classes; unless they learn to apply practically the materialist analysis

[22] The relationship between decadence and interest was one of the main themes of Lenin's contemporary and admirer, Georges Sorel. See *Réflexions sur la violence*, pp. 113–114, 115–122, 273, 315–317, 322–326 where Sorel discusses the loss of vitality on the part of the bourgeoisie and the need for an austere and heroic morality ("*la moralité de la violence"*) for the proletariat.
[23] Lenin, *Selected Works*, Vol. II, p. 68 (fn. I). In this and subsequent quotations from Lenin all italicized words are in the original.
[24] *Ibid.*, p. 88.
[25] *Ibid.*, pp. 78, 80, 88–89, 95, 98, 101.
[26] "The tasks of the Social-Democrats, however, are most exhausted by political agitation in the economic field; their task is to *convert* trade union politics into the Social-Democratic political struggle, to utilize the flashes of political consciousness which gleam in the minds of the workers during their economic struggles for the purpose of *raising* them to the level of Social-Democratic political consciousness . . . We must take upon ourselves the task of organizing a universal political struggle. We must train our Social-Democratic practical workers to become political leaders . . ." *Ibid.*, pp. 92 (fn.), 103.

and the materialist estimate of *all* aspects of the life and activity of *all* classes, strata, and groups of the population.[27]

Having asserted the primacy of political action, Lenin then turned to the question of how best to pursue it. His answer, as we have already stated, was organization, and it was a choice which symbolized a crucial turning point in the Western tradition. When we look back on the late nineteenth and early twentieth century from the vantage point of what we know about Lenin's thought, it is possible to see in a clearer light what the protests of writers like Nietzsche, Kierkegaard, and Sorel had meant. Kierkegaard's lonely, desperate "leap" to God, Nietzsche's solitary superman struggling against the toils of a mediocre, bourgeois world, Sorel's "myth" of the spontaneous general strike by a proletariat welded to unity only by an heroic impulse—these were all last-ditch efforts to secure some place for unorganized individual action. They were last gasps of a romanticism doomed to expire before the age of streamlined organizations and rationally efficient bureaucracies. Nor was this a protest confined to deformed theologians and syphilitic philosophers, for nowhere was the anguishing tension between the world of organization and the creative individual more clearly revealed than in the thought of Max Weber, perhaps the greatest of sociologists.

No one saw more clearly than he that bureaucracy and large-scale organization were the fundamental phenomena of modern political, social, and economic life. No one was more unstinting in admiration for the routinized rationality, the impersonal fairness, the high level of expertise exhibited by these structures.[28] Yet there was a strong note of ambiguity and soft whispers of pathos: "the fate of our times" is that man must dwell in the "disenchantment of the world." Mystery has been banished and "the bearing of man has been disenchanted and denuded of its mystical but inwardly genuine plasticity."[29] Yet in his famous essay, *Politics as a Vocation,* along with its clear-eyed recognition of the way bureaucracy has invaded all political realms—party, government, and legislature— Weber plaintively pleaded for a conception of political leadership cut to truly classical proportions. Weber's leader is a political hero, rising to heights of moral passion and grandeur, harried by a deep sense of responsibility. But, at bottom, he is a figure as futile and pathetic as his classical

---

[27] *Ibid.,* pp. 88–89.
[28] Weber's discussion of bureaucracy forms an interesting comparison with Hegel's admiration for this same "universal class." Compare *From Max Weber,* pp. 196 ff. with Hegel's, *Philosophy of Right,* pars. 288 ff. and see also the discussion by Michael Foster, *The Political Philosophies of Plato and Hegel* (Oxford: Clarendon, 1935) pp. 160 ff.
[29] *From Max Weber,* pp. 139, 148, 155.

counterpart. The fate of the classical hero was that he could never overcome contingency or *fortuna*; the special irony of the modern hero is that he struggles in a world where contingency has been routed by bureaucratized procedures and nothing remains for the hero to contend against. Weber's political leader is rendered superfluous by the very bureaucratic world that Weber discovered: even charisma has been bureaucratized. We are left with the ambiguity of the political man fired by deep passion— "to be passionate, *ira et studium*, is . . . the element of the political *leader*" —but facing the impersonal world of bureaucracy which lives by the passionless principle that Weber frequently cited, *sine ira et studio*, "without scorn or bias."[30]

For Weber there remained one sanctuary of personal action, one province where man could affirm himself in a world otherwise dominated by rationalized and highly intellectualized processes. The area of choice or fundamental values was one which, by nature, stubbornly resists scientific method and other techniques of objectivity; it was the last preserve of passion.[31] This casts a quite different light on Weber's endlessly labored and refined distinction between the scientifically knowable realm of "facts" and the subjective, nonscientific realm of "values." The wall between the two was not erected, as Weber's interpreters have sometimes implied, simply to shield the objective sphere of science from contamination by arbitrary values and personal idiosyncrasies. It was equally the result of a desperate effort on Weber's part to secure some sphere where affirmation was possible and, most important, where bureaucratic and scientific rationality were impossible. Yet the matter did not rest there, for Weber left a final irony for personal action to contemplate: each individual bore the awful responsibility for choice at this ultimate level but each was denied anything like the scientist's sense of certainty: "the ultimately possible attitudes towards life are irreconcilable, and hence their struggle can never be brought to a final conclusion."[32]

Nostalgias such as these had no place in Lenin's thought. The latter was mesmerized by the potentialities of organization. One does not have to supply a gloss to say that Lenin looked upon organization as the Archimedean lever for overthrowing a whole society. He himself used the metaphor.[33] "If we begin with the solid foundation of a strong organization of revolutionaries, we can guarantee the stability of the movement as a

---

[30] *Ibid.*, p. 95.

[31] *Ibid.*, pp. 139–140, 143, 145–147, 154; *Methodology of the Social Sciences*, pp. 15–19, 54–55, 76.

[32] *From Max Weber*, p. 152.

[33] ". . . paraphrasing a well-known epigram: give us an organization or revolutionaries, and we shall overturn the whole of Russia." Lenin, *Selected Works*, Vol. II, p. 141.

whole." Revolution, far from being the "spontaneous" uprising of an oppressed and exasperated mass, was an "art" requiring delicate timing; spontaneity rendered organization "more necessary."[34] Only through organizational intelligence could the revolutionaries assess "the general political situation," develop "the ability to select the proper moment for the uprising," and enforce discipline among the local organizations so that the latter would "respond simultaneously to the same political questions."[35] Thus organization provided preconceived direction and form to the bubbling ferment of "spontaneous" revolutionary forces; it maintained "a systematic plan of activity" over time and preserved "the energy, the stability and continuity of the political struggle." Through organization the revolutionaries could "concentrate all these drops and streamlets of popular excitement" into "a *single* gigantic flood."[36] Above all, the "all-sided and all-embracing political agitation" undertaken by organization helped to rivet the elite to the mass; organization brings the elite *"into closer proximity to, and merges* the elemental destructive force of the crowd with the conscious destructive force of the organization of revolutionaries."[37]

As Lenin spelled out the details of revolutionary organization, a different, almost aesthetic note, crept into his writing. He began to look upon the "apparatus" with the jealous pride of the artist, heaping scorn on those who would "degrade" the organization by turning it towards tawdry economic objectives and "immediate goals," bemoaning the "primitiveness" of the existing organization which had "lowered the prestige of revolutionaries in Russia." The task of the organization was to raise the workers "to the level of revolutionaries," not to degrade the organization to the level of "the average worker." Above all, when the revolutionary situation ripened, special care must be taken to avert the danger of the party organization being "overwhelmed" by the revolutionary wave. For its own protection, the organization must be powerful enough to master the "spontaneity" of the masses.[38]

Lenin's emphasis on the "small compact core" of professional revolutionaries as the vital cog of the organization led him to the question of what kind of democracy, and how much, could be permitted. His answer established a framework of argument that was to be duplicated by later writers concerned with the same broad question. It was the procedure

---

[34] *Ibid.*, pp. 125, 134, 138. And see the discussion in Alfred G. Meyer, *Leninism* (Cambridge, Mass.: Harvard University Press, 1957) pp. 32 ff. and Ch. 2.
[35] Lenin, *Selected Works*, Vol. II, p. 188.
[36] *Ibid.*, pp. 96, 116–117, 121, 134, 143–144; *Eve of October*, Little Lenin Library, Vol. XXIII, p. 5; *Left-Wing Communism, An Infantile Disorder*, Little Lenin Library, Vol. XVI, pp. 10–11, 75–76.
[37] Lenin, *Selected Works*, Vol. II, p. 184.
[38] *Ibid.*, pp. 122–123, 141, 145, 183–184.

adopted by Michels in his famous study of the oligarchical and bureaucratic tendencies in professedly democratic parties; by Chester Barnard in his analysis of the contradictions between the requirements of administrative leadership and democratic practices; by students of organization concerned at the way mass society, with its penchant for "radical leveling," "prevents the emergence of an effective social leadership."[39] What is important here is the way that the question is posed: how much democracy can organization endure?—never the reverse. Lenin's answer was a model of candor:

> Bureaucracy *versus* democracy is the same thing as centralism *versus* [local] autonomism, it is the same organizational principle of revolutionary political democracy as opposed to the organizational principle of the opportunists of Social Democracy. The latter want to proceed from the bottom upwards . . . The former proceed from the top, and advocate the extension of the rights and powers of the centre in respect of the parts . . . My idea . . . is "bureaucratic" in the sense that the Party is built from the top downwards . . .[40]

Democracy, therefore, had to be redefined in a way more consonant with the imperatives of organization and elitism. Membership had to be severely restricted so as not to compromise the highly professional quality of the leadership. At the same time, a type of bureaucratic democracy would encourage talented workers to rise to positions of leadership: as in the modern corporation, there was to be room at the top.[41] The "real" guarantee of democratic responsibility to the membership lay in the close-knit solidarity of the elite, the "complete, comradely, mutual confidence among revolutionaries."[42]

When Lenin came to consider the task of building the new order, he relied once more on the same prescription: construction, as well as destruction, required systematic organization and a compact leadership group. Like Calvin contending with the sectarians who believed that "enthusiasm" alone could sustain the church, Lenin had to dispose of the anarchist argument that, with the destruction of the old order, men could proceed directly to a condition where power was unnecessary. "The proletariat," Lenin asserted, "needs state power, the centralized organization of force, the organization of violence . . ."[43] To be sure, the old-style

[39] Barnard, *Dilemmas of Leadership in the Democratic Process*, pp. 10–15, 16.
[40] Lenin, *Selected Works*, Vol. II, pp. 447–448, 456 (fn. 1).
[41] *Ibid.*, pp. 138–139, 360–361, 373. "For revolution, it is essential, first that a majority of the workers (or at least a majority of the class-conscious thinking politically active workers) should fully understand the necessity for revolution and be ready to sacrifice their lives for it . . ." *Left-Wing Communism*, p. 65.
[42] Lenin, *Selected Works*, Vol. II, pp. 155–156.
[43] Lenin, *State and Revolution* (New York: International Publishers, 1932) p. 23; see also pp. 11, 17, 22.

politics would be abolished, for, thanks to the advances of capitalism, most governmental tasks had been so greatly simplified that they could be discharged by the simple routines followed in post offices. Gradually society would evolve towards the "non-political state," which, while not the final phase, would be a definite advance over the past.[44]

Lenin provided an illuminating glimpse into the workings of the organizational mentality when he turned to consider what was to be abolished of the political and what was to be retained. Politics, as represented by party rivalries, legislative maneuvers, the frictions generated between governmental units, and the struggle for group advantage, was to be suppressed: organization excluded politics. But those aspects of the political congenial or necessary to organization were to be retained. Thus the proletarian state was said to need "a certain amount of subordination" and "some authority or power." Above all, bureaucracy itself would be perpetuated: "to destroy officialdom immediately, everywhere, completely —this cannot be thought of." It was a mere "anarchist dream" to hold that "all administration" and "all subordination" could be disposed of.[45]

The affection which Lenin had lavished on the revolutionary organization was now transferred to the governmental machinery. He asserted that revolutionary society would not only exploit the advanced techniques of capitalist administration, but would perfect and purify them. No longer would public positions be degraded into being mere springboards for obtaining more lucrative posts in private industry; no longer would the careless, gentlemanly tradition of the civil service prevail. This was to be a pure organization, undisfigured by parasites. "Our problem here is only to *lop away* that which *capitalistically disfigures* this otherwise excellent apparatus . . ."[46]

In the light of his admiration for the beauties of organization and his faith in its creative power, there is small wonder that Lenin was eager to put it to the test. Like later theorists of organization, he was undismayed by the lack of resources available, the low level of skills and literacy, the appalling distance between reality and aspiration. To those faint-hearted followers who pleaded that the revolution should be postponed until human nature could be educated to the demands of the new age, Lenin replied with what was a classic statement of the faith of the new age of organization: "No, we want the Socialist revolution with human nature as

---

[44] *Ibid.*, pp. 42–44, 53.
[45] *Ibid.*, pp. 42, 43, 52–53; *Opportunism and Social-Chauvinism*, pp. 26, 29. Lenin even argued that the managerial technicians of the old system would have to be retained in the new society. The assumption that administrative and technical skills are universally applicable to any political or social system is a commonplace of recent literature.
[46] Lenin, *State and Revolution*, p. 65; *Opportunism and Social-Chauvinism*, p. 26.

it is now, with human nature that cannot do without subordination, control, and 'managers.' "⁴⁷

One final problem remained: how was organization to be squared with Marx's prophecy of a future society where the state would "wither away" and coercion would lose its rationale? For Lenin this was no problem. He agreed that ultimately there would be true or "primitive" democracy, but he conceived it to be democracy within the premises of organization, or, more accurately, he thought that the perfection of organization would be identical with true democracy. The progressive simplification of work would obviate the need for expert talents and place all functions within the reach "of every single individual." Since "democracy means equality," the development of organization could satisfy this criterion by breaking down complex jobs into simple operations. "The whole of society will have become one office and one factory, with equal work and equal pay."⁴⁸ In short, true organization *is* equality.

The prescience of Lenin's theories is confirmed by their reappearance in the conservatively-oriented literature of organization theory.⁴⁹ What Marx did to Hegel, writers like Selznick have done to Lenin; that is, turned him upside down. The new formula is not pure Leninism, but Leninism clothed in the language of Burke. The fondness for large-scale organization displayed by contemporary writers largely stems from anxieties provoked by the emergence of the mass. They see organizations as mediating institutions, shaping disoriented individuals to socially useful behavior and endowing them with a desperately needed sense of values. These large entities supply the stabilizing centers, which not only integrate and structure the amorphous masses, but control them as well.⁵⁰ The role which Selznick assigns the elite seems more indebted to Burke than to Lenin. The ruling group, he warns, is not in a position analogous to the sculptor, free "to mould the organization according to his heart's desire . . ." Instead, its posture is "essentially conservative."⁵¹ To preserve the life of the group was a task which could not be reduced to a question of balance sheets, any more than Burkean society could be treated as "a partnership agreement in a trade of pepper and coffee," or the Leninist revolutionary

⁴⁷ Lenin, *State and Revolution*, pp. 42–43.
⁴⁸ *Ibid.*, pp. 82–84.
⁴⁹ The conservative orientation of his theory is avowed by Selznick [*The Organizational Weapon*, p. 314 (fn. 28)] in a work which not only analyzes Communist theory of party organization, but extracts lessons from it for any theory of organization. The conservative cast to the thought of Selznick and, earlier, Mayo suggests how hopelessly anachronistic are the contemporary romantic conservative writers. Instead of appealing to Burke, writers like Kirk and Rossiter would be better advised to recognize their true allies.
⁵⁰ Selznick, *The Organizational Weapon*, pp. 286, 295, 313.
⁵¹ Selznick, *Leadership in Administration*, pp. 27, 149.

movement as a mere instrument to advance trade-union interests. The administrator is responsible for the life-processes of a "polity."[52] To accomplish his ends effectively it is necessary that he win the "consent" of the members. But "consent" in the age of organization does not connote self-government, much less the idea of participation as practiced in the ancient "polity." It means, instead, "commitment," which is something far different. "Commitment" is the special prescription for a mass age where men are isolated and their lives depersonalized and bleak. Their wants are psychic and hence to be satisfied by "integration" rather than made more anxious by the demands of participation.[53] The aim of the elite, therefore, is to convert "neutral men" into a "committed polity."

Now it is also true that Selznick sometimes uses commitment as a synonym for "loyalty" and "loyalty" is said to involve "rational, free-willed consent."[54] While this might appear to be either a bit of careless usage or a deceptive strategy to exploit some "hurrah-words," it is also squarely in the manipulative tradition. Selznick's notions of "commitment," "loyalty," and "rational, free-willed consent" have as much of choice and spontaneity about them as Lenin's theory of "democratic centralism" has of democracy:

> By long habituation, sometimes also as a result of aggressive indoctrination, the individual absorbs a way of perceiving and evaluating his experience. This reduces his anxiety by lending the world of fact a familiar cast; and it helps assure an easy conformity with established practice.[55]

As Selznick makes clear, "participation" is "prescribed . . . only when there is a problem of cohesion." Moreover, there is the cautionary reminder that the member must not be allowed to over-commit himself, for this builds up rigidities which limit "the freedom of the leadership to deploy its resources."[56]

Other "political" aspects of the organizational "polity" are similarly transformed into ready counters of manipulation by the leadership. The

[52] *Ibid.*, pp. 27–28, 37, 60, 147–148.
[53] *Ibid.*, pp. 90, 150. It is indicative of the modern notion of consent that even a professedly "democratic" writer like Kurt Lewin, who devoted his psychological researches to exploring the conditions conducive to a democratic group life, should have produced a theory of "acceptance" not significantly different from the more bureaucratic theories of Selznick. See *Resolving Social Conflicts*, pp. 116–117.
[54] The concern with "commitment" leads to a curious contrast between what Selznick labels the "Stalinist" and the "Stalinoid": the latter is alienated, lacking in commitment to ideals, and prone to accept expediency—"a fellow-traveler"—while the "Stalinist" has made "the fateful leap to a new set of values" and found a new source of spiritual support. *The Organizational Weapon*, pp. 298–307.
[55] Selznick, *Leadership in Administration*, p. 18.
[56] *Ibid.*, pp. 18, 116; *The Organizational Weapon*, p. 288.

rules or "laws" of the organization, the "pluralism" of its structure are all useful devices for facilitating the task of governing. The beliefs of the members are described as "ideologies," and they are the objects of a "technique" for manipulating "socially integrating myths."[57] Although at one point "administrative ideologies" are said to emerge "in spontaneous and unplanned ways," our previous discussion has prepared us for the legerdemain which transforms "spontaneity" into direction. "A well-formulated doctrine," quite unsurprisingly, is discovered to be "remarkably handy for boosting internal morale, communicating the bases for decisions, and rebuffing outside claims and criticisms."

> When we say that policy is built into the social structure of an organization, we mean that official aims and methods are *spontaneously protected or advanced*. The aspirations of individuals and groups are so stimulated and controlled . . . as to produce the desired balance of forces.[58]

REJOINDER TO WOLIN

Philip Selznick

In a wide-ranging and perceptive study of the evolution of modern political thought, Professor Wolin deplores the eclipse of political consciousness and the waning of distinctively political values. Obviously, he is well aware of the great transformations that have extended the reach, and heightened the dynamism, of modern government; he knows that hitherto isolated populations and segregated institutions have entered the mainstream of political life. But that evolution has brought with it a concern for *private* action and *segmental* interests. There has not been a genuine reassertion of the political community. Rather, he suggests, the special-purpose association is the preferred vehicle of social participation

A paper prepared especially for this book of readings.
[57] Selznick, *Leadership in Administration*, pp. 96–97, 151.
[58] *Ibid.*, pp. 14, 100.

and may become the main center of loyalty and adherence. As a result, political values are attenuated; citizenship is distracted and diffused.

For Wolin, the fragmentation of political man, and the moral impotence that goes with it, finds stimulus and support in contemporary social theory. The sociological perspective, he argues, is especially resolute in its rejection of political reality. When the political process is "group process," when political participation is molded by and directed toward parochial interests, then politics properly understood becomes unreal, epiphenomenal. And when the sociologist claims to analyze the political *dimension* of group life, he but salts an open wound.

Wolin's argument, and the warning it contains, merits our close attention. For he is right to insist that apparently technical and specialized theories are not so innocent after all. Even when clearly labeled as partial and selective treatments of an admittedly complex reality, their unspoken premises may enter historical consciousness and subtly influence emergent images of man and society. I agree that the social scientist should acknowledge responsibility for the larger implications of what he has to say.

More specifically, Wolin is right in sensing an antipolitical strand in sociology. Sociology is antiformalist in spirit, critical of received categories, always inclined to blur institutional boundaries. To study the social aspects of the political (or legal or religious or educational) realm is to place that realm "in society," to see it as part of a broader social process. An emphasis on the primacy of the social context risks offense to the separateness, the mystery, and the dignity of a specialized institution. Put another way, sociology has a tendency to level institutions by attending mainly to what they contribute to such general social processes as differentiation, control, or socialization. Perhaps more important, sociology is drawn to the concrete, problem-solving actor responding to his immediate circumstances. The result is, inevitably, a certain privatization. "Social" man pursues his own ends (or better, responds in his own organic, need-elaborating, need-reducing ways), influenced mostly by his close associates. His relation to larger, more distant, more impersonal settings is viewed as less compelling.

Yet I am puzzled by the main focus of Wolin's argument. Instead of addressing directly the antipolitical aspects of organization theory, which are real enough, he is content to take almost any blending of the organizational and the political, and especially any effort to affirm and analyze the political aspects of organizational experience, as *eo ipso* evidence of the "sublimation" of the political. Does it really follow that he who sees the public in the private, the political in the apparently technical, necessarily denies that there is a larger political community, to be addressed in its own terms? Is the effort to use political categories in fresh contexts to be taken as a rejection of them, or instead as a deeper affirmation?

In *Leadership in Administration* I located the apolitical bias of organizational theory in the tendency to focus on "neutral" organizational processes, to take ends as given, to slight the relation between structure and policy, to be insensitive to the evolution of institutional character. It is precisely when these matters are ignored that, as so often happens in institutional life, political problems are reduced to "administrative questions," to be solved by administrative methods. I was by no means suggesting, as Wolin mistakenly infers, that leadership is mostly concerned with social integration. My main emphasis was on the achievement of a *distinctive competence*. That achievement is a form of institutionalization, and therefore of social integration, but the outcome is not a neutral integration for its own sake; and the quest for it may well require periods of internal stress and disorganization.

There is indeed a Burkean strand in my view of institutional leadership; and of course Burke was an organicist of sorts. He spoke up for historicity, and he stressed the evolutionary foundations of community. But Burke understood that organic ties are not necessarily apolitical; they have political meaning when they have *content*. They then commit the community to something and that something has to be understood if it is to be nurtured or redirected. There is, I think, an important difference between the political organicism of Burke and theories of *Gemeinschaft* which detach social relations from determinate values and capabilities.

I would insist, however, that an appreciation of Burke, and more generally of the antirationalist motif in conservative thought, need not be the whole of one's social philosophy. John F. Kennedy admired that latter-day Burkean, Winston Churchill, but Kennedy did not shrink from a perspective of reform and renewal. Nor would Kennedy have gained from Churchill a mindless, contentless, apolitical image of community.

In arguing that "a political orientation is greatly needed if we are to reach a proper understanding of institutional leadership," I conceived the political, not as power conflict alone, or as the pursuit of parochial interests, but in classic terms as a realm where the ends of group existence are defined. In "high politics," if I may suggest an analogy to "high culture," what is at stake is the character of the group or community. This point of view is evident in my earlier study, *TVA and the Grass Roots*, which analyzed the organizational and political processes that determined whether the TVA could be a committed conservation agency.

In applying a political perspective to large-scale organizations, we should distinguish two issues: (1) the *appropriateness* of the political model for the case at hand, and (2) the effect of an *authoritarian context* on a purportedly political process. Wolin is properly troubled by both of these issues.

1. I do not believe that "all organizations are inevitably 'political' in character." Some are more so than others, and much depends on the narrowness or breadth of organizational ends. I have suggested that institutional leadership is dispensable when the organization's task is limited and closely defined, when technical criteria suffice for decision-making. The need for such leadership reflects the open-endedness of institutional life. To the extent that leadership can be dispensed with, by being reduced to routine management, the political perspective loses force and relevance.

Nevertheless, a close observer of complex organizations can hardly come away with the conclusion that clarity of vision, "purely technical" criteria, or singleness of purpose prevail. Many (and the most important) large businesses, trade unions, universities, and government agencies have multiple goals and commitments. Those who run such organizations discover that the "purpose" of the enterprise is a complex and subtle product of external demands, inner needs, and capabilities; they confront the problem of transforming abstract goals into living realities by building them into the social structure of the enterprise; they find that much attention has to be paid to the "integrity" of the institution, that is, to sustaining its distinctive values and competences against pressures and temptations that would weaken and distract; they learn that the group structure of the organization is a congeries of vested interests. The latter, it may be said, are only partly parochial and self-serving. A special commitment to assigned activities and values is one way of serving the enterprise as a whole; and energy is thereby generated for influence on the formulation of policy.

In this perspective, the "politicalness" of a corporate group does not depend on its being "a larger and powerful organization." Rather, it reflects the *openness* of the system, the leeway it allows for the play of interests, the opportunity it affords for meaningful participation by at least some significant number of members and subgroups. The internal nature of the group, not its external power, is the main criterion.

2. Wolin argues that the application of a political model to specialized groups is inevitably distorting because it must lead to an embrace of elitism and manipulation. Here the argument is rather strained. My own discussion of elites meant to call attention to a particular aspect of the division of labor—specialization in commitment to values. My emphasis was on the *plurality* of elites, not on a fixed establishment or hierarchy. The proliferation of elites is both a source of political process within organizations and a help in the fashioning of political community. For

example, a self-conscious group of student activists forms an elite, within the university setting, even if it has no official status.

In any human group, the process of winning consent carries the risk of manipulation. Organizations that have little leeway for self-definition, yet that must foster loyalty and commitment, are especially prone to offer symbolic substitutes for true autonomy. But that is a variable matter, and it should be recalled that the larger community is hardly free of political manipulation. To call any process of winning consent within specialized associations "manipulation" simply begs the question. Our problem is to distinguish the genuine from the sham. While it is proper to call attention to administrative pretense, co-optation, and the rest (that is another theme in *TVA and the Grass Roots*), it seems wrong, both scientifically and morally, to settle the issue by definition.

Wolin sees Lenin's preoccupation with organization as confirmation of the view that in the modern age politics is scheduled for abolition by groups that are ineluctably authoritarian and elitist. It is interesting, however, that Lenin understood how much sweat and discipline, how much unremitting struggle, would be needed to maintain the vanguard party as a pure organizational weapon. It was hardly something likely to emerge "naturally" from its historical setting. A more open, political institution was the more probable outcome. I fail to see the sense in which Lenin's ideas have been "confirmed by their reappearance in the conservatively-oriented literature of organization theory." The concept of mediating institutions goes back at least to Tocqueville and owes nothing to Lenin, who was ready to smash those institutions and create a centralized state. To make his rather fanciful point, Wolin virtually empties Leninism of any distinctive content. At most we see Leninism and organization theory sharing some common interests. The spirit of organization theory, at least as it is influenced by sociologists and political scientists, is, if anything, in full cry against Lenin's concepts of discipline and subordination.

Remarkably, Wolin sees no difference between the human relations approach represented by Elton Mayo and a more institutional and political perspective. It is as if all the criticisms of Mayo were in vain because, in the end, there is no alternative to authoritarianism in organizational life. Those criticisms centered largely on the apolitical spirit of Mayo's theories and therapies. The lack of a proper appreciation of power, and of appropriate responses to it, was the main burden of the indictment.

The critics of human relations, eager to expose a bias toward harmony and a denigration of conflict, urged that the clash of competing interests within the industrial organization could not and should not be avoided. Human relations seemed to offer a utopian and enfeebling ideal of worker-management collaboration, to be achieved by resolving tensions and sublimating aggressions. The alternative was to see labor-management relations as essentially and properly political.

The effort to restrain managerial authority, and to gain for members or employees the capacity for legitimate self-assertion, makes little sense on Wolin's premises. If there are no internal political processes, then only external control, in the name of the "comprehensive" political community, can stay the authoritarian hand. This is not only contrary to fact but a radical impoverishment of the political process.

If Wolin were to argue that special-purpose organizations have, with notable exceptions, grave limitations as potential unities of free men, or as full-blown political communities, I would agree. I would also agree that the preoccupation with special interests or intermediate associations risks diluting the "general order." But *Politics and Vision* adopts a more stringent position, one that ignores the differences among institutions and leaves the analyst helpless to deal with a significant aspect of social life.

I do not believe there is any serious disagreement over the nature of political reality. Wolin stresses the element of comprehensiveness, the function of transcending fragmented spheres and special interests "to integrate the discontinuities of group and organizational life into a common society." I would see in the political realm a somewhat richer texture. Even Wolin's definition, however, used as a tool of analysis rather than as an exercise in labeling, points to problems of responsibility and integration that beset subgroups in society. Such groups may be, at best, "quasi-polities." But the irony is that we ignore the political dimension of organization life only at the peril of sharing responsibility for just that reduction of politics to administration that Wolin himself regrets.

II

Organizational Goals

O rganizations are social units oriented toward the pursuit of specific goals. In this sense they can be conceived as tools which gain meaning and direction from their function. But one of the most important observations of students of organizations is that often the "tools" determine in part the goals to which they are applied. This process takes several forms: initial goals may prove to be "utopian," and organizational personnel may adjust these goals by making them more "realistic," or the organization's original goals may be neglected without being changed officially and the organization may develop alternative or competing goals which are more in line with the interests of its staff. Or the organization may see its predominant task as maintaining and expanding itself.

Simon explores the concept of organizational goals systematically and in depth. He first differentiates organizational goals from individual goals and motivation, and then shows that an organizational goal may be defined without reifying the concept. Simon's concept of goals as "value premises that can serve as inputs to decisions" differs from "a future state of affairs the actor is attempting to realize" by focusing on normative factors to the exclusion of all others, and by not including explicitly the notion of a commitment, which is indicated by the effort to realize.

Simon correctly pays attention to the fact that any one organization may pursue two or more goals simultaneously, and he ties the concept of organizational goals most closely to

155

that of decision-making. An actor's goals may not be what he states them to be on Sunday, but rather those that are revealed in his daily actions—goals which represent choices made between alternative routes he considered following.

A considerable number of studies on organizational goals have been conducted that seek to determine the conditions under which goals are served, in contrast to the conditions under which they are neglected or adapted. These studies have attempted to clarify the mechanisms through which goals are formulated and changed and to establish the effects of goal changes on the organization's structure and its relation to the social environment.

Sills reports the conclusion of his study on the changing goals of an organization and surveys the findings of several other studies conducted in this area. He studied the National Foundation for Infantile Paralysis which, when it came close to realizing its major goal, had to decide whether it ought to disband or whether it should persist and work toward a new goal. Since it became evident through Sills' research that the members' commitment to the organization itself was high and that it was not necessarily based on the goal of fighting polio, the organization was in a position to pursue a new, though similar, goal without risking the loss of its membership.

Sills reviews a number of other studies of voluntary associations in order to examine the conditions under which organizations abandon old goals and develop new ones. Whereas the successful attainment of the goal was a major factor in bringing about a change of goal in the case of the National Foundation for Infantile Paralysis, the lack of success in recruiting membership, funds, prestige, and public support in the case of the Woman's Christian Temperance Union and the Townsend Organization led to an abandonment of the goal. Other organizations, such as the Y.M.C.A., the Red Cross, and the Planned Parenthood Federation, increased or renewed their public appeal not by dismissing their old goals, but by reinterpreting them and adding new ones. This solution seems to allow for more organizational continuity than would a complete substitution of goals. Continuity seems to be valued because of its function in legitimating organizational activities; abrupt changes in goals seem to endanger such legitimation. Thus, Sills' analysis of goals comes full circle from considering goals as guides and ends for organizational activities to viewing them as means employed by organizations to improve their position in their social environment.

Thompson and McEwen examine the effect of interaction between organizations and their environment on organizational goals. The authors point out that the constantly changing environment requires organizations continuously to reappraise their goals. Reappraisal, in turn, depends upon the measurability of goals, organizational requirements and accomplishments. The more difficult the appraisal, the more likely it is that the organization will evade societal controls.

Thompson and McEwen also identify four forms of interaction within the organizational environment: competition, and three forms of cooperation—bargaining, co-optation, and coalition. The authors show how each form of interaction affect the way the environment influences the selection of organizational goals. Competition eliminates organizations which insist on catering to goals that society is not willing to accept. Bargaining means that representatives of the environment become actual partners in the decision-making process within the organization. Co-optation enables the organization to control those who are supposed to control it and therefore opens avenues for arbitrary or unilateral decisions. Coalition reduces the organization to the level of a committed partner in a larger unit and therefore curtails its freedom of decision.

Like the authors of the other studies, Thompson and McEwen emphasize the fact that organizations, in order to assure the realization of their goals, attempt to control the environmental factors which supposedly control them. Thus this study also underscores the major question in the analysis of organizational goals, that is, who will guard the organizations to keep them from becoming ends in themselves and who will guard the guards?

ON THE CONCEPT OF
ORGANIZATIONAL GOAL

Herbert A. Simon

Few discussions of organization theory manage to get along without introducing some concept of "organization goal." In the classical economic theory of the firm, where no distinction is made between an organization and a single entrepreneur, the organization's goal—the goal of the firm—is simply identical with the goal of the real or hypothetical entrepreneur. In general, it is thought not to be problematical to postulate that individuals have goals. If it is not, this solution raises no difficulties.

When we are interested in the internal structure of an organization, however, the problem cannot be avoided in this way. Either we must explain organizational behavior in terms of the goals of the individual members of the organization, or we must postulate the existence of one or more organization goals, over and above the goals of the individuals.[1]

The first alternative is an attractive one. It protects us from the danger of reifying the organization, of treating it as a superindividual

Reprinted from *Administrative Science Quarterly* (Ithaca, N.Y.: Graduate School of Business and Public Administration, Cornell University, June 1964), pp. 1–22, with minor omissions.

[1] The present discussion is generally compatible with, but not identical to, that of my colleagues, R. M. Cyert and J. G. March, who discuss organizational goals in ch. iii of *A Behavioral Theory of the Firm* (Englewood Cliffs, N.J., 1963). Their analysis is most germane to the paragraphs of this paper that treat of motivation for goals and organizational survival.

entity having an existence and behavior independent of the behavior of its members. The difficulty with this alternative is that it is hard to carry off. The usual way it is attempted is by identifying the phrase "organization goals" with "goals of the firm's owners" or, alternatively, "goals of the firm's top management," or "goals of those who hold legitimate authority to direct the organization."

But this solution raises new difficulties, for we often have occasion to observe that the goals that actually underlie the decisions made in an organization do not coincide with the goals of the owners, or of top management, but have been modified by managers and employees at all echelons. Must we conclude, then, that it is the goals of the latter—of subordinate managers and employees—that are governing organizational behavior? Presumably not, because the kinds of behavior taking place are not those we would expect if the managers and employees were consulting only their personal goals. The whole concept of an informal organization, modified by, but not identical with, the goals either of management or of individual employees, becomes hazy and ambiguous if we follow this path.

Let us see if we can find a way between this Scylla and the Charybdis of reification. The first step toward clarification is to maintain a distinction between goals, on the one hand, and motives, on the other. By *goals* we shall mean value premises that can serve as inputs to decisions. By *motives* we mean the causes, whatever they are, that lead individuals to select some goals rather than others as premises for their decisions. In the next section we shall develop the concept of goal, defined as above. In subsequent sections we shall undertake to explicate the notion of *organization goal* and to clarify the relations between organization goals and personal motives.

Before we can define "organization goals" we shall have to be clear on what we mean by "goals of an individual." We shall begin by considering the latter question.

GOALS AND DECISIONS: MULTIPLE CRITERIA

Our discussion of goals will be much simplified if we have a definite model before us of the situation we are considering. In recent years in the field of management science or operations research, we have learned to build formal models to characterize even quite elaborate and complex decision situations, and to use these models to reach "optimal" decisions. Since many of these models make use of the tool of linear programming, we will employ a linear programming framework to describe the decision situation. No mathematical knowledge will be assumed beyond the ability to read algebraic notation.[2]

The optimal diet problem is a typical simple linear programming problem. We are given a list of foods, and for each item on the list its price, its calory content, and its proportions of each of the minerals and vitamins relevant to nutrition. Then we are given a set of nutritional requirements, which may include statements about minimum daily intake of minerals, vitamins, and calories, and may also put limits on maximum intake of some or all of these components.

The diet problem is to find that sublist of foods and their quantities that will meet the nutritional requirements at least cost. The problem can be formalized as follows:

Let the various foods be numbered from 1 through N, and the various nutritional components from 1 through M. Let x_i be the quantity of the ith food in the diet, y_j be the total quantity of the jth nutritional component in the diet, and p_i the price of the ith food. Let a_{ij} be the amount of the jth nutritional component in a unit quantity of the ith food; let b_j be the minimum requirement of the jth nutritional component, and c_j the maximum allowance. (Some of the b_j's may be zero, and some of the c_j's infinite.) Then:

(1) $\sum_i a_{ij}x_i = y_j,$ for $j = 1, \ldots, M$;

i.e., the total consumption of the jth nutritional element is the sum of the quantities of that element for each of the foods consumed. The nutritional requirements can be stated:

(2) $c_j \geqq y_j \geqq b_j,$ for $j = 1, \ldots, M$;

i.e., the total quantity of the jth element must lie between b_j and c_j. The quantity of each food consumed must be non-negative, although it may be zero:

(3) $x_i \geqq 0,$ $i = 1, \ldots, N$.

Finally, the total cost of the diet is to be minimized; we are to find:

(4)   Min $\sum_i x_i p_i$.
          x

---

[2] There are now a substantial number of elementary discussions of linear programming in the management science literature. For a treatment that develops the point of view proposed here, see A. Charnes and W. W. Cooper, *Management Models and Industrial Applications of Linear Programming* (New York, 1961), ch. i. See also Charnes and Cooper, Deterministic Equivalents for Optimizing and Satisfying under Chance Constraints, *Operations Research*, 11 (1963), 18–39.

A diet (the solution is not necessarily unique) that satisfies all the relations (2), (3), (4) is called an *optimal* diet. A diet that satisfies the inequalities (2) and (3) (called *constraints*), but which is not necessarily a minimum cost diet, is called a *feasible* diet.

What is the goal of the diet decision? It would be an appropriate use of ordinary language to say that the goal is to minimize the cost of obtaining an adequate diet, for the condition (4) is the criterion we are minimizing. This criterion puts the emphasis on economy as the goal.

Alternatively, we might direct our attention primarily to the constraints, and in particular to the nutritional requirements (2). Then we might say that the goal is to find a nutritionally satisfactory diet that is economical. Although we still mention costs in this statement, we have clearly shifted the emphasis to the adequacy of the diet from a nutritional standpoint. The primary goal has now become good nutrition.

The relation between the criterion function (4) and the constraints (2) can be made even more symmetrical. Let us replace the criterion (4) with a new constraint:

(5) $$\sum_i x_i p_i \leqq k,$$

that is to say, with the requirement that the total cost of the diet not exceed some constant, k. Now the set of feasible diets has been restricted to those that satisfy (5) as well as (2) and (3). But since the minimization condition has been removed, there is apparently no basis for choosing one of these diets over another.

Under some circumstances, we can, however, restrict the set of diets that deserve consideration to a subset of the feasible set. Suppose that all the nutritional constraints (2) are minimal constraints, and that we would always prefer, *ceteris paribus,* a greater amount of any nutritional factor to a smaller amount. We will say that diet A is dominated by diet B if the cost of diet B is no greater than the cost of diet A, and if diet B contains at least as much of each nutritional factor as does diet A, and more of at least one factor. We will call the set of diets in the feasible set that is undominated by other diets in that set the Pareto optimal set.

Our preference for one or the other of the diets in the Pareto optimal set will depend on the relative importance we assign to cost in comparison with amounts of nutritional factors, and to the amounts of these factors in relation with each other. If cost is the most important factor, then we will again choose the diet that is selected by criterion (4). On the other hand, if we attach great importance to nutritional factor j, we will generally choose a quite different feasible diet—one in which the quantity of factor j is as great as possible. Within the limits set by the constraints, it would be quite reasonable to call whatever criterion led us to select a particular member of the Pareto optimal set our goal. But if the constraints are strong enough, so that the feasible set and, *a fortiori*, the Pareto optimal set is very small, then the constraints will have as much or more influence on what diet we finally select than will the goal, so defined. For example, if we set one or more of the nutritional requirements very high, so that only a narrow range of diets also satisfy the budget constraint (5), then introducing the cost minimization criterion as the final selection rule will have relatively little effect on what diet we choose.

Under such circumstances it might be well to give up the idea that the decision situation can be described in terms of a simple goal. Instead, it would be more reasonable to speak of a whole set of goals—the whole set, in fact, of nutritional and budgetary constraints—that the decision maker is trying to attain. To paraphrase a familiar epigram: "If you allow me to determine the constraints, I don't care who selects the optimization criterion."

MULTIPLE CRITERIA IN ORGANIZATIONS

To show the organizational relevance of our example it is only necessary to suppose that the decision we are discussing has arisen within a business firm that manufactures commercial stock feeds, that the nutritional requirements are requirements for hogs and the prices those of available feed ingredients, and that the finished feed prices facing the firm are fixed. Then minimizing the cost of feed meeting certain nutritional standards is identical with maximizing the profit from selling feed meeting those standards. Cost minimization represents the profit-maximizing goal of the company.

We can equally well say that the goal of the feed company is to provide its customers with the best feed possible, in terms of nutritional standards, at a given price, i.e., to produce feeds that are in the Pareto optimal set. Presumably this is what industry spokesmen mean when they say that the goal of business is not profit but efficient production of goods and services. If we had enlarged our model to give some of the prices that appear in it the status of constraints, instead of fixing them as constants, we could have introduced other goals, for example, the goal of suppliers' profits, or, if there were a labor input, the goal of high wages.[3]

We may summarize the discussion to this point as follows. In the

[3] See "A Comparison of Organization Theories," in my *Models of Man* (New York, 1957), pp. 170–182.

decision-making situations of real life, a course of action, to be acceptable, must satisfy a whole set of requirements, or constraints. Sometimes one of these requirements is singled out and referred to as the goal of the action. But the choice of one of the constraints, from many, is to a large extent arbitrary. For many purposes it is more meaningful to refer to the whole set of requirements as the (complex) goal of the action. This conclusion applies both to individual and organizational decision making.

SEARCH FOR A COURSE OF ACTION

Thus far, we have assumed that the set of possible actions is known in advance to the decision maker. In many, if not most, real-life situations, possible courses of action must be discovered, designed, or synthesized. In the process of searching for a satisfactory solution, the goals of the action—that is, the constraints that must be satisfied by the solution—may play a guiding role in two ways. First, the goals may be used directly to synthesize proposed solutions (*alternative generation*). Second, the goals may be used to test the satisfactoriness of a proposed solution (*alternative testing*).[4]

We may illustrate these possibilities by considering what goes on in the mind of a chess player when he is trying to choose a move in a game. One requirement of a good move is that it put pressure on the opponent by attacking him in some way or by preparing an attack. This requirement suggests possible moves to an experienced player (alternative generation). For example, if the opponent's king is not well protected, the player will search for moves that attack the king, but after a possible move has been generated in this way (and thus automatically satisfies the requirement that it put pressure on the opponent), it must be tested against other requirements (alternative testing). For example, it will not be satisfactory if it permits a counterattack that is more potent than the attack or that can be carried out more quickly.

The decisions of everyday organizational life are similar to these decisions in chess. A bank officer who is investing trust funds in stocks and bonds may, because of the terms of the trust document, take as his goal increasing the capital value of the fund. This will lead him to consider buying common stock in firms in growth industries (alternative generation). But he will check each possible purchase against other requirements: that the firm's financial structure be sound, its past earnings record

---

[4] For further discussion of the role of generators and tests in decision making and problem solving, see A. Newell and H. A. Simon, "The Processes of Creative Thinking," in H. E. Gruber, G. Terrell, and M. Wertheimer, eds., *Contemporary Approaches to Creative Thinking* (New York, 1962), particularly pp. 77–91.

satisfactory, and so on (alternative testing). All these considerations can be counted among his goals in constructing the portfolio, but some of the goals serve as generators of possible portfolios, others as checks.[5]

The process of designing courses of action provides us, then, with another source of asymmetry between the goals that guide the actual synthesis and the constraints that determine whether possible courses of action are in fact feasible. In general, the search will continue until one decision in the feasible set is found, or, at most, a very few alternatives. Which member of the feasible set is discovered and selected may depend considerably on the search process, that is, on which requirements serve as goals or generators, in the sense just defined, and which as constraints or tests.

In a multiperson situation, one man's goals may be another man's constraints. The feed manufacturer may seek to produce feed as cheaply as possible, searching, for example, for possible new ingredients. The feed, however, has to meet certain nutritional specifications. The hog farmer may seek the best quality of feed, searching, for example, for new manufacturers. The feed, however, cannot cost more than his funds allow; if it is too expensive, he must cut quality or quantity. A sale will be made when a lot of feed is feasible in terms of the requirements of both manufacturer and farmer. Do manufacturer and farmer have the same goals? In one sense, clearly not, for there is a definite conflict of interest between them: the farmer wishes to buy cheap, the manufacturer to sell dear. On the other hand, if a bargain can be struck that meets the requirements of both—if the feasible set that satisfies both sets of constraints is not empty—then there is another sense in which they do have a common goal. In the limiting case of perfect competition, the constraints imposed by the market and the technology actually narrow down the feasible set to a single point, determining uniquely the quantity of goods they will exchange and the price.

The neatness and definiteness of the limiting case of perfect competition should not blind us to the fact that most real-life situations do not fit this case exactly. Typically, the generation of alternatives (e.g., product invention, development, and design) is a laborious, costly process. Typically, also, there is a practically unlimited sea of potential alternatives. A river valley development plan that aims at the generation of electric power, subject to appropriate provision for irrigation, flood control, and recreation will generally look quite different from a plan that aims at flood control, subject to appropriate provision for the other goals mentioned. Even though the plans generated in both cases will be examined for their

[5] G. P. E. Clarkson, "A Model of Trust Investment Behavior," in Cyert and March, *op. cit.*

suitability along all the dimensions mentioned, it is almost certain that quite different plans will be devised and proposed for consideration in the two cases, and that the plans finally selected will represent quite distinct points in the feasible set.

In later paragraphs we shall state some reasons for supposing that the total sets of constraints considered by decision makers in different parts of an organization are likely to be quite similar, but that different decision makers are likely to divide the constraints between generators and tests in quite different ways. Under these circumstances, if we use the phrase organization goals broadly to denote the constraint sets, we will conclude that organizations do, indeed, have goals (widely shared constraint sets). If we use the phrase organization goals narrowly to denote the generators, we will conclude that there is little communality of goals among the several parts of large organizations and that subgoal formation and goal conflict are prominent and significant features of organizational life. The distinction we have made between generators and tests helps resolve this ambiguity, but also underlines the importance of always making explicit which sense of goal is intended.

MOTIVATION FOR GOALS

If by motivation we mean whatever it is that causes someone to follow a particular course of action, then every action is motivated—by definition. But in most human behavior the relation between motives and action is not simple; it is mediated by a whole chain of events and surrounding conditions.

We observe a man scratching his arm. His motive (or goal)? To relieve an itch.

We observe a man reaching into a medicine cabinet. His motive (or goal)? To get a bottle of lotion that, his wife has assured him, is very effective in relieving the itch of mosquito bites. Or have we misstated his motive? Is it to apply the lotion to his arm? Or, as before, to relieve the itch? But the connection between action and goal is much more complex in this case than in the previous one. There intervenes between them a means-end chain (get bottle, apply lotion, relieve itch), an expectation (that the lotion will relieve the itch), and a social belief supporting the expectation (that the wife's assurance is a reliable predictor of the lotion's efficacy). The relation between the action and the ultimate goal has become highly indirect and contingent, even in this simple case. Notice that these new complications of indirectness are superimposed on the complications we have discussed earlier—that the goal is pursued only within limits imposed by numerous side constraints (don't knock over the other bottles in the medicine cabinet, don't brush against the fresh paint, and so on).

Our point is identical with the point of the venerable story of the three bricklayers who were asked what they were doing. "Laying bricks," "Building a wall," "Helping to erect a great cathedral," were their respective answers. The investment trust officer whose behavior we considered earlier could answer in any of these modes, or others. "I am trying to select a stock for this investment portfolio." "I am assembling a portfolio that will provide retirement income for my client." "I am employed as an investment trust officer." Now it is the step of indirectness between the second and third answers that has principal interest for organization theory. The investment trust officer presumably has no "personal" interest in the retirement income of his client, only a "professional" interest in his role as trust officer and bank employee. He does have, on the other hand, a personal interest in maintaining that role and that employment status.

ROLE BEHAVIOR

Of course, in real life the line of demarcation between personal and professional interests is not a sharp one, for personal satisfactions may arise from the competent performance of a professional role, and both personal satisfactions and dissatisfactions may result from innumerable conditions that surround the employment. Nevertheless, it is exceedingly important, as a first approximation, to distinguish between the answers to two questions of motive: "Why do you keep (or take) this job?" and "Why do you make this particular investment decision?" The first question is properly answered in terms of the personal motives or goals of the occupant of the role, the second question in terms of goals that define behavior appropriate to the role itself.

Corresponding to this subdivision of goals into personal and role-defined goals, organization theory is sometimes divided into two subparts: (1) a theory of motivation explaining the decisions of people to participate in and remain in organizations; and (2) a theory of decision making within organizations comprised of such people.[6]

In the motivational theory formulated by Barnard and me, it is postulated that the motives of each group of participants can be divided into *inducements* (aspects of participation that are desired by the participants) and *contributions* (aspects of participation that are inputs to the organization's production function but that generally have negative utility to participants). Each participant is motivated to maximize, or at

[6] For further discussion and references, see J. G. March and H. A. Simon, *Organizations* (New York, 1958), ch. iv.

least increase, his inducements while decreasing his contributions, and this motivation is a crucial consideration in explaining the decision to join (or remain). But "joining" means accepting an organizational role, and hence we do not need any additional motivational assumptions beyond those of inducements-contributions theory to explain the ensuing role-enacting behavior.

I hasten to repeat the caveat, introduced a few paragraphs above, that in thus separating our consideration of organizational role-enacting behavior from our consideration of personal motivation—allowing the decision to join as the only bridge between them—we are proposing an abstraction from the complexities of real life. A good deal of the significant research on human relations and informal organization, which has contributed heavily in the last generation to our understanding of organizational behavior, has been concerned specifically with the phenomena that this abstraction excludes. Thus, desire for power and concern for personal advancement represent an intrusion of personal goals upon organizational role, as do the social and craft satisfactions and dissatisfactions associated with work.

To say that the abstraction is sometimes untenable is not to deny that there may be many situations in which it is highly useful. There are, first of all, many organizational decisions that simply do not affect personal motives at all—where organizational goals and personal goals are orthogonal, so to speak. As a trivial example, the secretary's inducement-contribution balance is generally in no whit affected by the choice between typing a letter to A or a letter to B or by the content of the letter. Second, personal motives may enter the decision process as fixed constraints (only courses of action that satisfy the constraints are considered, but the constraints have no influence on the choice of action within the set). Thus, the terms of the employment contract may limit work to a forty-hour week but may have little to say about what goes on during the forty hours.[7]

The abstraction of organizational role from personal goals turns out to be particularly useful in studying the cognitive aspects of organizational decision making, for the abstraction is consonant with some known facts about human cognitive processes. Of all the knowledge, attitudes, and values stored in a human memory, only a very small fraction are evoked in a given concrete situation. Thus, an individual can assume a wide variety of roles when these are evoked by appropriate circumstances, each of which may interact only weakly with the others. At one time he may be a father, at another a machinist, at another a chess player. Cur-

---

[7] See "A Formal Theory of Employment Relation," in *Models of Man, op. cit.*

rent information processing theories of human cognition postulate that there is only modest overlap of the subsets of memory contents—information and programs—that are evoked by these several roles. Thus, we might postulate that the day-to-day organizational environment evokes quite different associations out of the memory of the participant from those evoked when he is considering a change of jobs. To the extent this is so, it provides a further explanation of why his "personal" system of inducements and contributions, i.e., the utilities that enter into the latter decisions, will have no effect on his "organizational" decisions, i.e., those that are made while the first set is evoked.

The ability of a single individual to shift from one role to another as a function of the environment in which he finds himself thus helps explain the extent to which organizational goals become internalized, that is, are automatically evoked and applied during performance of the role. By whatever means the individual was originally motivated to adopt the role in the first place, the goals and constraints appropriate to the role become a part of the decision-making program, stored in his memory, that defines his role behavior. . . .

THE ORGANIZATIONAL
DECISION-MAKING SYSTEM

Let us limit ourselves for the present to situations where occupational roles are almost completely divorced from personal goals and pursue the implications of this factoring of the behavior of organizational participants into its personal and organizational components. If we now consider the organizational decision-making programs of all the participants, together with the connecting flow of communication, we can assemble them into a composite description of the organizational decision-making system—a system that has been largely abstracted from the individual motives that determine participation.

In the simplest case, of a small, relatively unspecialized organization, we are back to a decision-making situation not unlike that of the optimal diet problem. The language of "goals," "requirements," "constraints," that we applied there is equally applicable to similarly uncomplicated organizational situations.

In more complicated cases, abstracting out the organizational decision-making system from personal motives does not remove all aspects of interpersonal (more accurately, interrole) difference from the decision-making process. For when many persons in specialized roles participate in making an organization's decisions, the total system is not likely to be monolithic in structure. Individual roles will differ with respect to the number and kinds of communications they receive and the parts of the environment from which they receive them. They will differ with respect to the evaluative communcations they receive from other roles. They will differ in their search programs. Hence, even within our abstraction, which neglects personal motives, we can accommodate the phenomena of differential perception and subgoal formation.

To make our discussion more specific, let us again consider a specific example of an organizational decision-making system—in this case a system for controlling inventory and production. We suppose a factory in which decisions have to be made about (1) the aggregate rate of production, that is, the work force that will be employed and the hours employees will work each week, (2) the allocation of aggregate production facilities among the several products the factory makes, and (3) the scheduling of the sequence in which the individual products will be handled on the production facilities. Let us call these the aggregate production decision, item allocation decision, and scheduling decision, respectively. The three sets of decisions may be made by different roles in the organization; in general, we would expect the aggregate decision to be handled at more central levels than the others. The real world situation will always include complications beyond those we have described, for it will involve decisions with respect to shipments to warehouses, decisions as to which products to hold in warehouse inventories, and many others.

Now we could conceive of an omniscient Planner (the entrepreneur of classical economic theory) who, by solving a set of simultaneous equations, would make each and all of these interrelated decisions. Decision problems of this kind have been widely studied during the past decade by management scientists, with the result that we now know a great deal about the mathematical structures of the problems and the magnitude of the computations that would be required to solve them. We know, in particular, that discovery of the optimal solution of a complete problem of this kind is well beyond the powers of existing or prospective computational equipment.

In actual organizational practice, no one attempts to find an optimal solution for the whole problem. Instead, various particular decisions, or groups of decisions, within the whole complex are made by specialized members or units of the organization. In making these particular decisions, the specialized units do not solve the whole problem, but find a "satisfactory" solution for one or more subproblems, where some of the effects of the solution on other parts of the system are incorporated in the definition of "satisfactory."

For example, standard costs may be set as constraints for a manufacturing executive. If he finds that his operations are not meeting those constraints, he will search for ways of lowering his costs. Longer production runs may occur to him as a means for accomplishing this end. He can achieve longer production runs if the number of style variations in product is reduced, so he proposes product standardization as a solution to his cost problem. Presumably he will not implement the solution until he has tested it against constraints introduced by the sales department— objections that refusal to meet special requirements of customers will lose sales.

Anyone familiar with organizational life can multiply examples of this sort, where different problems will come to attention in different parts of the organization, or where different solutions will be generated for a problem, depending on where it arises in the organization. The important point to be noted here is that we do not have to postulate conflict in personal goals or motivations in order to explain such conflicts or discrepancies. They could, and would, equally well arise if each of the organizational decision-making roles were being enacted by digital computers, where the usual sorts of personal limits on the acceptance of organizational roles would be entirely absent. The discrepancies arise out of the cognitive inability of the decision makers to deal with the entire problem as a set of simultaneous relations, each to be treated symmetrically with the others.[8]

An aspect of the division of decision-making labor that is common to virtually all organizations is the distinction between the kinds of general, aggregative decisions that are made at high levels of the organization, and the kinds of specific, item-by-item decisions that are made at low levels. We have already alluded to this distinction in the preceding example of a system for controlling inventory and production. When executives at high levels in such a system make decisions about "aggregate inventory," this mode of factoring the decision-making problem already involves radical simplification and approximation. For example, there is no single, well-defined total cost associated with a given total value of aggregate inventories. There will generally be different costs associated with each of the different kinds of items that make up the inventory (for example, different items may have different spoilage rates or obsolescence rates), and different probabilities and costs associated with stock-outs of each kind of item. Thus, a given aggregate inventory will have different costs depending on its composition in terms of individual items.

To design a system for making decisions about the aggregate work force, production rate, and inventories requires an assumption that the

[8] For some empirical evidence, see D. C. Dearborn and H. A. Simon, "Selective Perception: A Note on the Departmental Identification of Executives," *Sociometry*, 21 (1958), 140–144.

aggregate inventory will never depart very far from a typical composition in terms of individual item types. The assumption is likely to be tolerable because subsidiary decisions are continually being made at other points in the organization about the inventories of individual items. These subsidiary decisions prevent the aggregate inventory from becoming severely unbalanced, hence make averages meaningful for the aggregate.

The assumption required for aggregation is not unlike that made by an engineer when he controls the temperature of a tank of water, with a single thermometer as indicator, knowing that sufficient mixing of the liquid in the tank is going on to maintain a stable pattern of temperature relations among its parts. Without such a stable pattern it would be infeasible to control the process by means of a measurement of the average temperature.

If one set of decisions is made, on this approximate basis, about aggregate work force, production rate, and inventories, then these decisions can be used as constraints in making detailed decisions at subsidiary levels about the inventory or production of particular items. If the aggregate decision has been reached to make one million gallons of paint next month, then other decisions can be reached as to how much paint of each kind to make, subject to the constraint that the production quotas for the individual items should, when added together, total one million gallons.[9]

This simple example serves to elucidate how the whole mass of decisions that are continually being made in a complex organization can be viewed as an organized system. They constitute a system in which (1) particular decision-making processes are aimed at finding courses of action that are feasible or satisfactory in the light of multiple goals and constraints, and (2) decisions reached in any one part of the organization enter as goals or constraints into the decisions being made in other parts of the organization.

There is no guarantee that the decisions reached will be optimal with respect to any over-all organizational goal. The system is a loosely coupled one. Nevertheless, the results of the over-all system can be measured against one or more organizational goals, and changes can be made in the decision-making structure when these results are adjudged unsatisfactory.

Further, if we look at the decision-making structure in an actual organization, we see that it is usually put together in such a way as to insure that the decisions made by specialized units will be made in cognizance of the more general goals. Individual units are linked to the

[9] A system of this kind is developed in detail in "Determining Production Quantities under Aggregate Constraints," in C. Holt, F. Modigliani, J. Muth, and H. A. Simon, *Planning Production, Inventories, and Work Force* (Englewood Cliffs, N.J., 1960).

total system by production schedules, systems of rewards and penalties based on cost and profit goals, inventory limits, and so on. The loose coupling among the parts has the positive consequence of permitting specific constraints in great variety to be imposed on subsystems without rendering their decision-making mechanisms inoperative.

THE DECISION-MAKING SYSTEM
AND ORGANIZATIONAL BEHAVIOR

In the previous sections great pains were taken to distinguish the goals and constraints (inducements and contributions) that motivate people to accept organizational roles from the goals and constraints that enter into their decision making when they are enacting those organizational roles. On the one hand, the system of personal inducements and contributions imposes constraints that the organization must satisfy if it is to survive. On the other hand, the constraints incorporated in the organizational roles, hence in what I have called here the organizational decision-making system, are the constraints that a course of action must satisfy in order for the organization to adopt it.

There is no necessary *logical* connection between these two sets of constraints. After all, organizations sometimes fail to survive, and their demise can often be attributed to failure to incorporate all the important motivational concerns of participants among the constraints in the organizational decision-making system. For example, a major cause of small business failure is working capital shortage, a result of failure to constrain actions to those that are consistent with creditors' demands for prompt payment. Similarly, new products often fail because incorrect assumptions about the inducements important to consumers are reflected in the constraints that guide product design. (It is widely believed that the troubles of the Chrysler Corporation stemmed from the design premise that car purchasers were primarily interested in buying a good piece of machinery.)

In general, however, there is a strong empirical connection between the two sets of constraints, for the organizations we will usually observe in the real world—those that have succeeded in surviving for some time—will be precisely those which have developed organizational decision-making systems whose constraints guarantee that their actions maintain a favorable balance of inducements to contributions for their participants. The argument, an evolutionary one, is the same one we can apply to biological organisms. There is no logical requirement that the temperatures, oxygen concentrations, and so on, maintained in the tissues of a bird by its physiological processes should lie within the ranges required for its survival. It is simply that we will not often have opportunities for observing birds whose physiological regulators do not reflect these external constraints. Such birds are soon extinct.[10]

Thus, what the sociologists calls the functional requisites for survival can usually give us good clues for predicting organizational goals; however, if the functional requisites resemble the goals, the similarity is empirical, not definitional. What the goals are must be inferred from observation of the organization's decision-making processes, whether these processes be directed toward survival or suicide.

CONCLUSIONS

We can now summarize our answers to the question that introduced this paper: What is the meaning of the phrase "organizational goal"? First, we discovered that it is doubtful whether decisions are generally directed toward achieving *a* goal. It is easier, and clearer, to view decisions as being concerned with discovering courses of action that satisfy a whole set of constraints. It is this set, and not any one of its members, that is most accurately viewed as the goal of the action.

If we select any of the constraints for special attention, it is (a) because of its relation to the motivations of the decision maker, or (b) because of its relation to the search process that is generating or designing particular courses of action. Those constraints that motivate the decision maker and those that guide his search for actions are sometimes regarded as more "goal-like" than those that limit the actions he may consider or those that are used to test whether a potential course of action he has designed is satisfactory. Whether we treat all the constraints symmetrically or refer to some asymmetrically as goals is largely a matter of linguistic or analytic convenience.

When we come to organizational decisions, we observe that many, if not most, of the constraints that define a satisfactory course of action are associated with an organizational role and hence only indirectly with the personal motives of the individual who assumes that role. In this situation it is convenient to use the phrase organization goal to refer to constraints, or sets of constraints, imposed by the organizational role, which has only this indirect relation to the motives of the decision makers.

If we examine the constraint set of an organizational decision-making system, we will generally find that it contains constraints that reflect virtually all the inducements and contributions important to various

[10] The relation between the functional requisites for survival and the actual constraints of the operating system is a central concept in W. R. Ashby's notion of a multistable system. See his *Design for a Brain* (2d ed; New York, 1960).

classes of participants. These constraints tend to remove from consideration possible courses of action that are inimical to survival. They do not, of course, by themselves, often fully determine the course of action.

In view of the hierarchical structure that is typical of most formal organizations, it is a reasonable use of language to employ organizational goal to refer particularly to the constraint sets and criteria of search that define roles at the upper levels. Thus it is reasonable to speak of conservation of forest resources as a principal goal of the U. S. Forest Service, or reducing fire losses as a principal goal of a city fire department. For high-level executives in these organizations will seek out and support actions that advance these goals, and subordinate employees will do the same or will at least tailor their choices to constraints established by the higher echelons with this end in view.

Finally, since there are large elements of decentralization in the decision making in any large organization, different constraints may define the decision problems of different positions or specialized units. For example, "profit" may not enter directly into the decision making of most members of a business organization. Again, this does not mean that it is improper or meaningless to regard profit as a principal goal of the business. It simply means that the decision-making mechanism is a loosely coupled system in which the profit constraint is only one among a number of constraints and enters into most subsystems only in indirect ways. It would be both legitimate and realistic to describe most business firms as directed toward profit making—subject to a number of side constraints —operating through a network of decision-making processes that introduces many gross approximations into the search for profitable courses of action. Further, the goal ascription does not imply that any employee is motivated by the firm's profit goal, although some may be.

This view of the nature of organization goals leaves us with a picture of organizational decision making that is not simple. But it provides us with an entirely operational way of showing, by describing the structure of the organizational decision-making mechanism, how and to what extent over-all goals, like "profit" or "conserving forest resources" help to determine the actual courses of action that are chosen.

THE SUCCESSION OF GOALS

David L. Sills

Any analysis of a goal-directed organization cannot be confined to things as they are, since the future state of affairs toward which the organization's activities are oriented is very much a component of the contemporary organization. It must, in the very nature of the case, inquire into the relationship of present activities to future developments.

The relevance of this statement to the present analysis is rooted in the fact that the Foundation's* major goal is by definition a finite one. A fundamental assumption underlying the original establishment of the Foundation was that infantile paralysis was a disease which medical science would eventually be able to bring under control, and a major reason for the capacity of the Foundation to maintain through the years its high ratio of goal-related activities has been the very real possibility that the organization's goal would be realized—perhaps within the lifetime of the participants. The recent development of the Salk vaccine, and its use on a nationwide scale, serve as dramatic evidence that the full achievement of the Foundation's major goal will be realized in the not too distant future. In fact, Dr. Jonas E. Salk, who developed the vaccine, and Dr. Leonard E. Scheele, former Surgeon General of the United States Public Health Service, recently reported to the American Medical Association that by the middle of 1959 paralytic polio should be completely eliminated as a threat to both children and adults.[1]

The imminence of this full achievement of its major goal naturally raises the question of what will happen to the Foundation at that time. Will it simply go out of existence, will it continue on a more limited scale, providing assistance to persons already afflicted by polio, or will

Reprinted with permission of The Macmillian Company from *The Volunteers* by David L. Sills, pp. 253–268, 270. © by The Free Press, a Corporation 1958.
* The National Foundation for Infantile Paralysis [Ed.].
[1] *New York Times*, June 12, 1956, p. 37.

it—taking advantage of experience gained in conquering polio—turn its attention to another health or welfare problem? The seriousness of these questions, as they apply to organizations generally, has been noted by a number of students of voluntary associations and social movements. Wendell King, for example, states that "an apparently unanticipated and rarely desired outcome of achieving goals can be the abrupt demolition of the whole organization. Unless additional objectives are devised, the movement lies robbed of its reason for existence."[2]

In order to achieve a perspective through which to approach the topic of the future of the Foundation it is helpful to recall the major conclusions reached by Philip Selznick in his analysis of the relationship between doctrine and action in the Tennessee Valley Authority. Organizations, Selznick notes, develop obligations over a period of time to act in a certain way, obligations which Selznick terms "commitments." He summarizes the importance of these commitments as follows:

> The systematized commitments of an organization define its character. Day-to-day decision, relevant to the actual problems met in the translation of policy into action, create precedents, alliances, effective symbols, and personal loyalties which transform the organization from a profane, manipulable instrument into something having a sacred status and thus resistant to treatment simply as a means to some external goal. That is why organizations are often cast aside when new goals are sought. . . .

> So long as goals are given, and the impulse to act persists, there will be a series of enforced lines of action demanded by the nature of the tools at hand. These commitments may lead to unanticipated consequences resulting in a deflection of original goals.[3]

Although Selznick's research was restricted to one organization, he clearly intended his conclusions to apply to other organizations as well. For this reason, it is appropriate to examine the extent to which this formulation of the consequences of organizational commitments may be said to characterize the situation which may soon confront the Foundation.

The passage cited is composed of two parts. First, it states that "day-to-day decisions" (i.e., those made in order to solve immediate and pressing problems) lead to "commitments," which in turn define the "character" of an organization. Second, it states that this process may have two consequences: an organization may be "deflected from its original goals" and it may be "cast aside when new goals are sought."

---

[2] C. Wendell King, *Social Movements in the United States* (New York: Random House, 1956), p. 114.
[3] Philip Selznick, *TVA and the Grass Roots* (Berkeley and Los Angeles: University of California Press, 1949), pp. 258–259.

Although the major focus of this study has been the current membership and activities of the Foundation, rather than the details of its history, sufficient attention has been given to the circumstances surrounding the original emergence of various features of the organization to document the first of these two statements—that decisions made for the purpose of solving immediate problems often determine the ultimate character of an organization. It has been noted, for example, that the Foundation's almost total dependence upon a fund-raising strategy based upon obtaining small gifts from large numbers of people emerged from two decisions made in the Depression year 1933: to solicit gifts from the people of Georgia in order to finance the construction of a new building at Georgia Warm Springs, and to raise funds nationally by sponsoring President's Birthday Balls; that the characteristically middle-class composition of the Foundation's Volunteer membership may be traced in large part to the decision to ask postmasters, Democrats, and persons of civic prominence generally to organize these Birthday Balls; and that the patient care program is a direct outgrowth of the decision to permit local Committees for the Celebration of the President's Birthday to retain for use in their own communities a portion of the funds raised in 1935. This brief listing of examples suggests the general applicability to the Foundation of this aspect of Selznick's thesis: the Foundation's "character" today is clearly in many respects the result of decisions made with other ends in view.

The second part of Selznick's statement concerns the consequences which may result from the emergence of organizational commitments— goal displacement and the destruction of the organization itself. Sufficient evidence from other studies has been cited throughout this volume to suggest the near-universality of the phenomenon of goal displacement within organizations, and a number of reasons underlying the Foundation's capacity to maintain itself as a goal-oriented organization have been cited. But what of the Foundation's capacity to maintain itself as an organization after its initial goals have been realized, and "new goals are sought"? Will its organizational structure be "cast aside"? It is to a consideration of these questions that the discussion now turns.

EVIDENCE FROM OTHER ORGANIZATIONS

Two important voluntary associations in our early history, the Sons of Liberty and the Committees of Correspondence, were dissolved when the anti-British purposes for which they were established culminated in the American Revolution and the establishment of the Continental Congress. Sometimes organizations decline long before their goals are achieved, as, for example, the American Anti-Slavery Society, which split through internal dissension and controversy over policy matters some twenty years before the Emancipation Proclamation. And sometimes they are dissolved when their functions are taken over by governmental bodies, as happened to the Public School Society of New York City when the public school system was established.

THE SUCCESSION OF GOALS. Dissolution, however, is not the only course of action open to an organization when its purposes are either achieved or become irrelevant because of changes in the social environment; in fact, it is equally easy to find examples of organizations which have remained intact for the purpose of working toward new or sharply modified objectives. Peter Blau has called this process the "succession of goals."[4]

The American Legion, to cite one example, was originally established in order to preserve the spirit which characterized the American Expeditionary Force in World War I, but it very soon included in its objectives the protection of the rights of veterans and, particularly among local Posts, the instigation of community service projects. Dartmouth College, to cite another example, was originally founded primarily in order to educate and Christianize the Indians of New England, but it experienced no great difficulty in transforming itself into a general liberal arts college.

Voluntary health and welfare agencies exhibit similar tendencies. The Birth Control Federation, for example, in 1942 adopted the more comprehensive name of the Planned Parenthood Federation of America, and has since that time expanded its objectives to include treatment for infertility, education for marriage, and marriage counseling.[5] The American Social Hygiene Association, which has traditionally concerned itself with combating both prostitution and venereal diseases, has in recent years adjusted to the decline in organized prostitution and the drastic lowering of the incidence of venereal diseases, and has established such new objectives as supporting family life education and preparing high school boys for the social and psychological strains which they will undergo during military service.[6] In fact, thousands of organizations of all kinds have adapted in one way or another to external conditions affecting the relevance of their objectives, but there have been very few systematic analyses of such organizations from this point of view. It is therefore

---

[4] Peter M. Blau, *The Dynamics of Bureaucracy* (Chicago: University of Chicago Press, 1955), p. 195. See also Peter M. Blau, *Bureaucracy in Modern Society* (New York: Random House, 1956), pp. 95–96.
[5] Planned Parenthood Federation of America, *Birth Control U.S.A.: Highlights of the Program*, p. 8; *The Most Important Thing*, p. 3.
[6] American Social Hygiene Association, *Social Hygiene News*, April, 1955.

instructive to examine briefly the process of organizational adaptation as it has taken place in organizations for which relatively complete information is available. Two of these organizations, the Woman's Christian Temperance Union and the Townsend Organization, have failed to adjust themselves to a changed environment, and exist today as fossil remains of their previous life. The other two, the Young Men's Christian Association and the American National Red Cross, have made highly successful adaptations.

THE YOUNG MEN'S CHRISTIAN ASSOCIATION. Although there have been a number of organizational histories of the Y.M.C.A., Owen Pence's volume, *The Y.M.C.A. and Social Need,* is most useful for an examination of the Y.M.C.A. as an illustration of the process of organizational adaptation.[7] The book is sub-titled "A Study of Institutional Adaptation"; more specifically, it is an examination of how the goals of the Y.M.C.A. have changed in response to various changes in the social environment, particularly the secularization of American society which has taken place in the past century.

Today the Y.M.C.A. places a great deal of emphasis upon the opportunities for recreation and physical exercise which it offers, but the first Association in London stated that its objective was "to improve the spiritual condition of young men engaged in the drapery and other trades"; the first Association in America, in Boston, expanded its objective to include "the improvement of the spiritual and mental condition of young men"; and the first New York Association included in its objectives the following:

> The object of this Association shall be the improvement of the spiritual, mental, and social conditions of young men . . . to bring them under moral and religious influences, by aiding them in the selection of suitable boarding places and employment. . . .[8]

With the passing years, as Pence shows, the Y.M.C.A. has devoted increasing attention to its physical and social goals, and less attention to its original religious and spiritual aims. This transition is summarized in these terms:

> In contrast with the conception of earlier years, when the principal concern of the Association was with the securing of individual commitments to the Christain life, the realization has steadily grown in recent

[7] Owen E. Pence, *The Y.M.C.A. and Social Need* (New York: Association Press, 1939).
[8] *Ibid.,* p. 12.

years that religious living and interest are so gravely conditioned by the total social experience that the two cannot be dealt with separately.[9]

And again, in more direct language:

> In time, the Associations began to take their objectives for granted. In their place activity (that is, whatever met and satisfied expressed interests of members) became the real objective.[10]

The Y.M.C.A., therefore, is an example of an organization whose goals have changed, not because they were achieved, but rather because of fundamental changes in the social environment in which its activities were carried out. . . .

THE WOMAN'S CHRISTIAN TEMPERANCE UNION. The central problem which led Joseph Gusfield to study the W.C.T.U. is the fact that changes in American drinking habits and the increased acceptance of drinking as a part of general social life "have presented the W.C.T.U. with an environment more hostile to the doctrine of total abstinence than was true in the years of the organization's formation and development."[11] In the face of this situation, Gusfield sought both to determine "whether the change in environment has led to changes in the goals and doctrine of the movement" and to explain "changes, or lack of change, in the organization."[12]

In many respects, the Y.M.C.A. and the W.C.T.U. have had similar histories. Both organizations were established at a time when a powerful middle class believed that its mission was to improve the social conditions under which the lower class lived. The Y.M.C.A. sought to improve these conditions by Christianizing and educating young men; the W.C.T.U. believed that working class people could enjoy the benefits of middle-class life if they stopped drinking—"drink is the curse of the working classes" was a popular slogan of the 19th Century temperance movement.[13] And both organizations have survived in spite of a sharp decline in the popularity of these theories of humanitarian reform. But they differ greatly in the manner in which they have survived.

As previously indicated, the Y.M.C.A.'s history has been characterized by successive adjustments to its social environment. The W.C.T.U., on the other hand, has not adjusted:

---

[9] *Ibid.*, p. 315.
[10] *Ibid.*, p. 236.
[11] Joseph R. Gusfield, "Social Structure and Moral Reform: A Study of the Woman's Christian Temperance Union," *American Journal of Sociology*, 61 (1955), pp. 221–232. The discussion in the text is based entirely upon this study.
[12] *Ibid.*, p. 222.
[13] *Ibid.*, p. 225.

Today the W.C.T.U. is an organization in retreat. Contrary to the expectations of theories of institutionalization, the movement has not acted to preserve organizational values at the expense of past doctrine.[14]

How has this been possible? As Gusfield shows, the W.C.T.U. has not abandoned its goal of establishing temperance norms, but has instead shifted its attention to a new audience. Originally the organization was composed largely of middle- and upper middle-class women who sought both to dissuade working-class people from drinking and to improve their general welfare in other ways; today it is less upper middle-class and more lower middle- and working-class in composition, and its chief target is the drinking habits of middle-class groups. In short, the W.C.T.U. has elected *not* to change its goals to meet changed conditions. Instead, the organization has changed the composition of its membership, limited its goals to the discouragement of middle-class drinking, and shifted its strategy from active campaigning against intemperance to indulging in what Gusfield terms "moral indignation."[15]

THE TOWNSEND ORGANIZATION. The Y.M.C.A. is an example of an organization which has succeeded through successive adaptations to its social environment; the W.C.T.U. is an organization which is in a state of decline because of its failure to adjust to changes in its environment; and the Townsend Organization, as Sheldon Messinger has demonstrated, is one which has nearly vanished because its major goal, alleviating or preventing economic dislocation, has at least temporarily been achieved— not, however, through the efforts of the organization.[16]

Dr. Francis E. Townsend first proposed his plan to end the Depression by retiring all United States citizens at the age of sixty on a monthly pension of $200 in September, 1933; by 1936 the Townsend Organization had 2,250,000 members. In 1935, however, the Social Security Act was passed, and by 1951 the organization had only 56,656 members, a loss of more than 97 per cent.[17] In the intervening years, the expansion of social security legislation, of pension plans by private employers, and of the national economy itself largely eliminated public interest in a program designed to end the Depression of the 1930's. In the face of these changes in

---

[14] *Ibid.*, p. 232.
[15] *Ibid.*
[16] Sheldon L. Messinger, "Organizational Transformation: A Case Study of a Declining Social Movement," *American Sociological Review*, 20 (1955), pp. 3–10. The discussion which follows is based largely upon this study. See Arnold W. Green, *Sociology* (New York: McGraw-Hill, 1956), pp. 547–555, for further details of the Townsend Movement.
[17] Messinger, *op. cit.*, p. 4.

the relevance of its original goals, how has the Townsend Organization survived at all?

Messinger outlines three organizational transformations which have taken place. First, there has been a tendency to support other measures affecting the aged, a tendency which the leaders themselves have checked since they realized it could lead only to a break-up of the organization. Second, there has been a tendency to obtain financial support by selling consumer goods of one kind or another, e.g., vitamin pills. Finally, there has been a tendency to convert membership meetings into social gatherings, and to hold other social events as well. On the basis of these tendencies, as well as of other aspects of the transformation of the Townsend Organization, Messinger draws this conclusion:

> The organized aims of declining social movements will tend to adapt to these changed conditions in characteristic ways. We can broadly describe this adaptation by asserting that the dominating orientation of leaders and members shifts *from the implementation of the values the organization is taken to represent* (by leaders, members, and public alike), *to maintaining the organizational structure as such,* even at the loss of the organization's central mission.[18]

The Townsend Organization, in short, has adjusted to changes in its environment in ways quite different from those followed by the W.C.T.U. Instead of modifying its membership and its goals, it has virtually abandoned its original goals and has concentrated its attention, not very successfully, upon maintaining its organizational structure.

THE AMERICAN NATIONAL RED CROSS.[19] Like the Y.M.C.A., the Red Cross is a highly successful organization, and for much the same reasons: it has made successive adjustments to changes in its social environment. Its initial objective, as set forth in its first constitution, was "to hold itself in readiness in the event of war or any calamity great enough to be considered national, to inaugurate such practical measures in mitigation of the suffering and for the protection and relief of sick and wounded as may be consistent with the objects of the Association. . . ."[20] The organization was small in its early years, and floods and other disasters, the Spanish-American War, and most importantly, World War I, provided sufficient challenges to its resources to make any expansion of its objectives unnecessary. The end of World War I, however, found a greatly expanded

[18] *Ibid.,* p. 10.
[19] The discussion of the Red Cross in the text is based entirely upon Foster R. Dulles, *The American Red Cross: A History* (New York: Harper & Row, 1950).
[20] Cited in Dulles, *op. cit.,* p. 16.

Red Cross without an objective of sufficient scope to maintain the organization. There was a decline in membership interest, and the leaders feared the organization would suffer. Foster Dulles has summarized this crisis in the Red Cross's history in these terms:

> The officers of the Red Cross, discouraged but not dismayed, were determined to find a way out in spite of chapter apathy. There was a natural desire on their part to see the American Red Cross maintain its position and still further broaden its field of usefulness, not only for the sake of whatever contributions could be made toward improving the conditions of American life, *but for the sake of the organization itself*.[21]

This crisis was surmounted by adopting a new program—"the preservation and improvement of the public health"[22]—and the Red Cross had no need to question the adequacy of its objectives until the Depression of the 1930's, when there was disagreement among the leaders concerning the role the organization should play in dispensing unemployment relief.[23] But the most severe test to date of the adequacy of the Red Cross's objectives came at the end of World War II, when again a greatly expanded organization found that its capacity to act outpaced its goals. Furthermore, there now existed a new threat to the organization— the increased intervention of the Government in welfare and relief activities as a result of the responsibilities it had assumed during the Depression and War years.

. . . it was necessary to establish new objectives and new activities. These were found in "the adoption of a national blood donor program as the core of its peacetime activities apart from disaster relief."[24] In this way the most recent crisis has been met, and the Red Cross has both maintained an active program and obtained adequate volunteer and public support in the postwar years. . . .

This brief review of the history of four organizations has of necessity mentioned only a few of the major conclusions reached by the authors cited. Nevertheless, it has called attention to the fact that organizations are by no means necessarily "cast aside when new goals are sought" and indicated some of the ways in which organizations have adjusted to changes in their environment and the relevancy of their goals. Furthermore, the histories of these four organizations suggest that the fate of an organization after its goals have been either achieved or rendered ir-

[21] *Ibid.*, p. 218. Italics supplied.
[22] *Ibid.*, p. 219.
[23] *Ibid.*, pp. 276–294.
[24] *Ibid.*

relevant cannot be determined on *a priori* grounds, but is rather a resultant of a given set of forces. "What," Blau asks, "determines whether displacement of goals or succession of goals predominates in an organization?"[25] Although he admits that this crucial question can be answered only in part, Blau does suggest two determining factors: "structural constraints in the organization" and acceptance on the part of the community. "When the community permits an organization . . . to become established and attain at least some of its first objectives in a relatively short period, it will probably find new fields to conquer in the course of its development."[26] It goes without saying that American society has permitted the Foundation to be established and to attain its first objectives; in fact, it has given it more encouragement and support than it has given any comparable organization. Accordingly, in order to pursue the inquiry implied in Blau's formulation of the problem of goal succession, it is necessary to examine what structural constraints might impede the Foundation from seeking new goals.

The Foundation's Structure and the Future

The relevance of the Foundation's corporate-type structure to its capacity to carry out its program has been stated in some detail throughout this volume, and need only be summarized here. Local Chapters, for example, being *ad hoc* instrumentalities of the Board of Trustees, are subject to all rules, regulations and policies of the National Headquarters —a situation which enables National Headquarters, if the need should ever arise, to exert considerable authority over the activities of a local Chapter. The March of Dimes is officially directed by National Headquarters, and local Campaign Directors are appointed by the State Chairman, who is in turn appointed by National Headquarters. Here again, the structural machinery exists through which National Headquarters can exercise control over the activities of local organizations. The patient care program, although financed largely by the 50 per cent of all campaign receipts which is retained in the local community, is dependent, for its effective operation, upon the redistribution of funds by National Headquarters. The research program is entirely under the direction of National Headquarters, and Chapters are specifically prohibited from making grants to support research projects. In short, if National Headquarters (i.e., the Board of Trustees) should decide to embark upon a new program, there is no organizational machinery to stand in the way. The new program would not need to be ratified by local Chapters, and there are no effective

[25] Blau, *Bureaucracy in Modern Society*, p. 95.
[26] *Ibid.*, pp. 95–96.

sub-groups within the organization which could offer effective resistance to it. The Foundation, in other words, has an organizational structure which would make "the succession of goals" quite feasible.

VOLUNTEERS AND THE FUTURE

The statement that the Foundation's structure would permit "the succession of goals," although true in a legal sense, does not of course acknowledge the fundamental fact that the Foundation is a voluntary association. Its members are free to leave at any time, and no one is obliged to join. For this reason, no program sponsored by National Headquarters could possibly be successful if it did not command the enthusiastic support of Volunteers throughout the country. Witness, for example, the ill-fated attempt of National Headquarters in the first year of the Foundation's existence to have full authority over the expenditure of all the funds raised during the March of Dimes. In order to examine the Foundation's future prospects it is therefore necessary to examine the potential support for a new program which exists among the Foundation's Volunteer membership. . . .

Objectively speaking, the Foundation has obviously served as an instigator of change. Not only has it pioneered in developing a coordinated mode of attack upon a specific disease, but it has also introduced new concepts of fund-raising, of patient care, and of community responsibility. The mass field trials of the Salk vaccine, which the Foundation sponsored, to cite another example of innovation, were a completely new development as far as the history of immunological verification is concerned—never before has the efficacy of a newly developed vaccine been tested on such a mass scale. It is of some interest, accordingly, to note that a considerable number of Volunteers are alert to the fact that the Foundation, in keeping with its character both as a social movement and a voluntary association, has served as a "pacesetter" in American society.

This broad theme has a number of variations. For some Volunteers, the most important precedent-setting aspect of the Foundation is the fact that it has mobilized laymen in a coordinated attack upon a disease. A March of Dimes Chairman in Defense Town, for example, adopted what he termed "the sociological viewpoint," saying "we can fight polio if we can organize people. If we can organize people like this, we can fight anything." This opinion was echoed by that of the Harbor City Campaign Director, who asked rhetorically, "Wouldn't it be a wonderful story to get polio licked, and then go on to something else and get that licked and then go on to something else?" Pausing a moment, he added the comment, "It would be a challenge, a career."

Other Volunteers focused their remarks more sharply upon specifically organizational accomplishments and potentialities. For example, after verbally exploring the possibilities of other diseases which might be conquered by techniques similar to those employed against polio, the Steamboat City Campaign Director concluded with this affirmation:

> I really believe in this type of organization when people get together and get things done. I would like to see other organizations set up or something done in other fields . . . like mental health. But no one has had the organization that the Foundation has had. . . . I don't think this unique organization should pass out of existence. It should be utilized.

. . . Finally, for some Volunteers the policy of the Foundation which permits funds to remain in the community for assisting polio victims is a precedent of such importance in terms of achieving public support that they believe it could and should be applied to the battle against other diseases. As a Wheat County March of Dimes Volunteer pointed out,

> They could take over heart and cancer and do the same thing. The money could stay in the community and that should be the basis of the talk that would be given on it. You can say, "it stays here for your protection."

Not all of the Volunteers interviewed, needless to say, were as articulate as these in expressing either their judgments of the Foundation's role as an innovating organization or their own hope that the organization would continue to exist after its objective of eliminating epidemic polio is achieved. Since Volunteers were not questioned concerning their views of the Foundation's future, only those who had given some thought to the matter prior to the interview took occasion to express their views. In fact, some Volunteers explicitly stated that in their opinion the Foundation should *not* undertake a new program. After polio has been conquered, according to the Chapter Vice-Chairman in Gas City, the Foundation "should get a big loving cup from the general population of the country and call it quits." Opinions of this kind were expressed only rarely, however, while thirty-five Volunteers— 15 per cent of those interviewed—spontaneously recommended that the Foundation should continue to exist even after its major objective had been achieved. In the light of this evidence it seems reasonable to conclude that a considerable portion of the Volunteer membership of the Foundation has found its organizational characteristics sufficiently appealing, and its activities sufficiently rewarding, to be willing and anxious to take part in the organization should it seek to realize new goals.

. . . In the final analysis, however, the most compelling reason for predicting that the Foundation will in the future make a successful adjustment to the achievement of its major goal is that the organization has in fact *already* been transformed, in large part by its Volunteers, into something other than a special purpose association. For those Volunteers who, in spite of the fact that they may initially have been recruited as Polio Veterans or Good Citizens or Joiners, have come to regard the organization as a "social movement" or a "pacesetter" have altered not only the character of their own participation but the character of the Foundation as well. Implicit in these perceptions is the notion that the Foundation has an institutionalized status which transcends its current goals. Since the Foundation includes among its Volunteers so many who are able to conceptualize their involvement in terms of its ultimate implications (for themselves, or for society as a whole), rather than only in terms of a limited, pragmatic goal, it has already become an organization as deeply committed to its mode of operation as to its current purposes. In a word, it is an organization which is as committed to a means as it is to an end.

ORGANIZATIONAL GOALS AND ENVIRONMENT

James D. Thompson and William J. McEwen

In the analysis of complex organizations the definition of organizational goals is commonly utilized as a standard for appraising organizational performance. In many such analyses the goals of the organization are often viewed as a constant. Thus a wide variety of data, such as official documents, work activity records, organizational output, or statements by organizational spokesmen, may provide the basis for the definition of

Reprinted in part from James D. Thompson and William J. McEwen, *American Sociological Review*, 23 (1958), 23–31, by permission of the authors and the publishers, The American Sociological Association.

goals. Once this definition has been accomplished, interest in goals as a dynamic aspect of organizational activity frequently ends.

It is possible, however, to view the setting of goals (i.e., major organizational purposes), not as a static element but as a necessary and recurring problem facing any organization, whether it is governmental, military, business, educational, medical, religious, or other type. The goal-setting problem as discussed here is essentially determining a relationship of the organization to the larger society, which in turn becomes a question of what the society (or elements within it) wants done or can be persuaded to support.

GOALS AS DYNAMIC VARIABLES

Because the setting of goals is essentially a problem of defining desired relationships between an organization and its environment, change in either requires review and perhaps alteration of goals. Even where the most abstract statement of goals remains constant, application requires redefinition or interpretation as changes occur in the organization, the environment, or both.

The corporation, for example, faces changing markets and develops staff specialists with responsibility for continuous study and projection of market changes and product appeal. The governmental agency, its legislative mandate notwithstanding, has need to reformulate or reinterpret its goals as other agencies are created and dissolved, as the population changes, or as non-governmental organizations appear to do the same job or to compete. The school and the university may have unchanging abstract goals, but the clientele, the needs of pupils or students, and the techniques of teaching change and bring with them redefinition and reinterpretation of those objectives. The hospital has been faced with problems requiring an expansion of goals to include consideration of preventive medicine, public health practices, and the degree to which the hospital should extend its activities out into the community. The mental hospital and the prison are changing their objectives from primary emphasis on custody to a stress on therapy. Even the church alters its pragmatic objectives as changes in the society call for new forms of social ethics, and as government and organized philanthropy take over some of the activities formerly left to organized religion.

Reappraisal of goals thus appears to be a recurrent problem for large organization, albeit a more constant problem in an unstable environment than in a stable one. Reappraisal of goals likewise appears to be more difficult as the "product" of the enterprise becomes less tangible and more difficult to measure objectively. The manufacturing firm has a relatively ready index of the acceptability of its product in sales figures; while poor sales may indicate inferior quality rather than public distaste for the commodity itself, sales totals frequently are supplemented by trade association statistics indicating the firm's "share of the market." Thus within a matter of weeks, a manufacturing firm may be able to reappraise its decision to enter the "widget" market and may therefore begin deciding how it can get out of that market with the least cost.

The governmental enterprise may have similar indicators of the acceptability of its goals if it is involved in producing an item such as electricity, but where its activity is oriented to a less tangible purpose such as maintaining favorable relations with foreign nations, the indices of effective operation are likely to be less precise and the vagaries more numerous. The degree to which a government satisfies its clientele may be reflected periodically in elections, but despite the claims of party officials, it seldom is clear just what the mandate of the people is with reference to any particular governmental enterprise. In addition, the public is not always steadfast in its mandate.

The university perhaps has even greater difficulties in evaluating its environmental situation through response to its output. Its range of "products" is enormous, extending from astronomers to zoologists. The test of a competent specialist is not always standardized and may be changing, and the university's success in turning out "educated" people is judged by many and often conflicting standards. The university's product is in process for four or more years and when it is placed on the "market" it can be only imperfectly judged. Vocational placement statistics may give some indication of the university's success in its objectives, but initial placement is no guarantee of performance at a later date. Furthermore, performance in an occupation is only one of several abilities that the university is supposed to produce in its students. Finally, any particular department of the university may find that its reputation lags far behind its performance. A "good" department may work for years before its reputation becomes "good" and a downhill department may coast for several years before the fact is realized by the professional world.

In sum, the goals of an organization, which determine the kinds of goods or services it produces and offers to the environment, often are subject to peculiar difficulties of reappraisal. Where the purpose calls for an easily identified, readily measured product, reappraisal and readjustment of goals may be accomplished rapidly. But as goals call for increasingly intangible, difficult-to-measure products, society finds it more difficult to determine and reflect its acceptability of that product, and the signals that indicate unacceptable goals are less effective and perhaps longer in coming.

ENVIRONMENTAL CONTROLS OVER GOALS

A continuing situation of necessary interaction between an organization and its environment introduces an element of environmental control into the organization. While the motives of personnel, including goal-setting officers, may be profits, prestige, votes, or the salvation of souls, their efforts must produce something useful or acceptable to at least a part of the organizational environment to win continued support.[1]

In the simpler society social control over productive activities may be exercised rather informally and directly through such means as gossip and ridicule. As a society becomes more complex and its productive activities more deliberately organized, social controls are increasingly exercised through such formal devices as contracts, legal codes, and governmental regulations. The stability of expectations provided by these devices is arrived at through interaction, and often through the exercise of power in interaction.

It is possible to conceive of a continuum of organizational power in environmental relations, ranging from the organization that dominates its environmental relations to one completely dominated by its environment. Few organizations approach either extreme. Certain gigantic industrial enterprises, such as the *Zaibatsu* in Japan or the old Standard Oil Trust in America, have approached the dominance-over-environment position at one time, but this position eventually brought about "countervailing powers."[2] Perhaps the nearest approximation to the completely powerless organization is the commuter transit system, which may be unable to cover its costs but nevertheless is regarded as a necessary utility and cannot get permission to quit business. Most complex organizations, falling somewhere between the extremes of the power continuum, must adopt strategies for coming to terms with their environments. This is not to imply that such strategies are necessarily chosen by rational or deliberate processes. An organization can survive so long as it adjusts to its situation; whether the process of adjustment is awkward or nimble becomes important in determining the organization's degree of prosperity.

However arrived at, strategies for dealing with the organizational environment may be broadly classified as either *competitive* or *cooperative*.

---

[1] This statement would seem to exclude anti-social organizations, such as crime syndicates. A detailed analysis of such organizations would be useful for many purposes; meanwhile it would appear necessary for them to acquire a clientele, suppliers, and others, in spite of the fact that their methods at times may be somewhat unique.

[2] For the *Zaibatsu* case see Japan Council, *The Control of Industry in Japan*, Tokyo: Institute of Political and Economic Research, 1953; and Edwin O. Reischauer, *The United States and Japan*, Cambridge: Harvard University Press, 1954, pp. 87–97.

Both appear to be important in a complex society—of the "free enterprise" type or other.[3] Both provide a measure of environmental control over organizations by providing for "outsiders" to enter into or limit organizational decision process.

The decision process may be viewed as a series of activities, conscious or not, culminating in a choice among alternatives. For purposes of this paper we view the decision-making process as consisting of the following activities:

1. Recognizing an occasion for decision, i.e., a need or an opportunity.
2. Analysis of the existing situation.
3. Identification of alternative courses of action.
4. Assessment of the probable consequences of each alternative.
5. Choice from among alternatives.[4]

The following discussion suggests that the potential power of an outsider increases the earlier he enters into the decision process,[5] and that competition and three sub-types of cooperative strategy—*bargaining, cooptation,* and *coalition*—differ in this respect. It is therefore possible to order these forms of interaction in terms of the degree to which they provide for environmental control over organizational goal-setting decisions.

Competition

The term "competition" implies an element of rivalry. For present purposes competition refers to that form of rivalry between two or more organizations which is mediated by a third party. In the case of the manufacturing firm the third party may be the customer, the supplier, the potential or present member of the labor force, or others. In the case of the governmental bureau, the third party through whom competition takes place may be the legislative committee, the budget bureau, or the

---

[3] For evidence on Russia see David Granick, *Management of the Industrial Firm in the U. S. S. R.*, New York: Columbia University Press, 1954; and Joseph S. Berliner, "Informal Organization of the Soviet Firm," *Quarterly Journal of Economics*, 66 (August, 1952), pp. 353–365.

[4] This particular breakdown is taken from Edward H. Litchfield, "Notes on a General Theory of Administration," *Administrative Science Quarterly*, 1 (June, 1956), pp. 3–29. We are also indebted to Robert Tannenbaum and Fred Massarik who, by breaking the decision-making process into three steps, show that subordinates can take part in the "manager's decision" even when the manager makes the final choice. See "Participation by Subordinates in the Managerial Decision-Making Process," *Canadian Journal of Economics and Political Science*, 16 (August, 1949), pp. 410–418.

[5] Robert K. Merton makes a similar point regarding the role of the intellectual in public bureaucracy. See his *Social Theory and Social Structure*, New York: The Free Press, 1949, Chapter VI.

chief executive, as well as potential clientele and potential members of the bureau.

The complexity of competition in a heterogeneous society is much greater than customary usage (with economic overtones) often suggests. Society judges the enterprise not only by the finished product but also in terms of the desirability of applying resources to that purpose. Even the organization that enjoys a product monopoly must compete for society's support. From the society it must obtain resources—personnel, finances, and materials—as well as customers or clientele. In the business sphere of a "free enterprise" economy this competition for resources and customers usually takes place in the market, but in times of crisis the society may exercise more direct controls, such as rationing or the establishment of priorities during a war. The monopoly competes with enterprises having different purposes or goals but using similar raw materials; it competes with many other enterprises, for human skills and loyalties, and it competes with many other activities for support in the money markets.

The university, customarily a non-profit organization, competes as eagerly as any business firm, although perhaps more subtly.[6] Virtually every university seeks, if not more students, better-qualified students. Publicly supported universities compete at annual budget sessions with other governmental enterprises for shares in tax revenues. Endowed universities must compete for gifts and bequests, not only with other universities but also with museums, charities, zoos, and similar non-profit enterprises. The American university is only one of many organizations competing for foundation support, and it competes with other universities and with other types of organizations for faculty.

The public school system, perhaps one of our most pervasive forms of near-monopoly, not only competes with other governmental units for funds and with different types of organizations for teachers, but current programs espoused by professional educators often compete in a very real way with a public conception of the nature of education, e.g., as the three R's, devoid of "frills."

The hospital may compete with the midwife, the faith-healer, the "quack" and the patent-medicine manufacturer, as well as with neighboring hospitals, despite the fact that general hospitals do not "advertise" and are not usually recognized as competitive.

Competition is thus a complicated network of relationships. It includes scrambling for resources as well as for customers or clients, and in a complex society it includes rivalry for potential members and their

[6] See Logan Wilson, The Academic Man, New York: Oxford University Press, 1942, especially Chapter IX. Also see Warren G. Bennis, "The Effect on Academic Goods of Their Market," American Journal of Sociology, 62 (July, 1956), pp. 28–33.

loyalties. In each case a third party makes a choice among alternatives, two or more organizations attempt to influence that choice through some type of "appeal" or offering, and choice by the third party is a "vote" of support for one of the competing organizations and a denial of support to the others involved.

Competition, then, is one process whereby the organization's choice of goals is partially controlled by the environment. It tends to prevent unilateral or arbitrary choice of organizational goals, or to correct such a choice if one is made. Competition for society's support is an important means of eliminating not only inefficient organizations but also those that seek to provide goods or services the environment is not willing to accept.

Bargaining

The term bargaining, as used here, refers to the negotiation of an agreement for the exchange of goods or services between two or more organizations. Even where fairly stable and dependable expectations have been built up with important elements of the organizational environment—with suppliers, distributors, legislators, workers and so on—the organization cannot assume that these relationships will continue. Periodic review of these relationships must be accomplished, and an important means for this is bargaining, whereby each organization, through negotiation, arrives at a decision about future behavior satisfactory to the others involved.

The need for periodic adjustment of relationships is demonstrated most dramatically in collective bargaining between labor and industrial management, in which the bases for continued support by organization members are reviewed. But bargaining occurs in other important, if less dramatic, areas of organizational endeavor. The business firm must bargain with its agents or distributors, and while this may appear at times to be one-sided and hence not much of a bargain, still even a long-standing agency agreement may be severed by competitive offers unless the agent's level of satisfaction is maintained through periodic review. Where suppliers are required to install new equipment to handle the peculiar demands of an organization, bargaining between the two is not unusual.

The university likewise must bargain. It may compete for free or unrestricted funds, but often it must compromise that ideal by bargaining away the name of a building or of a library collection, or by the conferring of an honorary degree. Graduate students and faculty members may be given financial or other concessions through bargaining, in order to prevent their loss to other institutions.

The governmental organization may also find bargaining expedient.

The police department, for example, may overlook certain violations of statutes in order to gain the support of minor violators who have channels of information not otherwise open to department members. Concessions to those who "turn state's evidence" are not unusual. Similarly, a department of state may forego or postpone recognition of a foreign power in order to gain support for other aspects of its policy, and a governmental agency may relinquish certain activities in order to gain budget bureau approval of more important goals.

While bargaining may focus on resources rather than explicitly on goals, the fact remains that it is improbable that a goal can be effective unless it is at least partially implemented. To the extent that bargaining sets limits on the amount of resources available or the ways they may be employed, it effectively sets limits on choice of goals. Hence bargaining, like competition, results in environmental control over organizational goals and reduces the probability of arbitrary, unilateral goal-setting.

Unlike competition, however, bargaining involves direct interaction with other organizations in the environment, rather than with a third party. Bargaining appears, therefore, to invade the actual decision process. To the extent that the second party's support is necessary he is in a position to exercise a veto over final choice of alternative goals, and hence takes part in the decision.

Co-optation

Co-optation has been defined as the process of absorbing new elements into the leadership or policy-determining structure of an organization as a means of averting threats to its stability or existence.[7] Co-optation makes still further inroads on the process of deciding goals; not only must the final choice be acceptable to the co-opted party or organization, but to the extent that co-optation is effective it places the representative of an "outsider" in a position to determine the occasion for a goal decision, to participate in analyzing the existing situation, to suggest alternatives, and to take part in the deliberation of consequences.

The term "co-optation" has only recently been given currency in this country, but the phenomenon it describes is neither new nor unimportant. The acceptance on a corporation's board of directors of representatives of banks or other financial institutions is a time-honored custom among firms that have large financial obligations or that may in the future want access to financial resources. The state university may find it expedient (if not mandatory) to place legislators on its board of trustees, and the

[7] Philip Selznick, *TVA and the Grass Roots*, Berkeley and Los Angeles: University of California Press, 1949.

endowed college may find that whereas the honorary degree brings forth a token gift, membership on the board may result in a more substantial bequest. The local medical society often plays a decisive role in hospital goal-setting, since the support of professional medical practitioners is urgently necessary for the hospital.

From the standpoint of society, however, co-optation is more than an expediency. By giving a potential supporter a position of power and often of responsibility in the organization, the organization gains his awareness and understanding of the problems it faces. A business advisory council may be an effective educational device for a government, and a White House conference on education may mobilize "grass roots" support in a thousand localities, both by focussing attention on the problem area and by giving key people a sense of participation in goal deliberation.

Moreover, by providing overlapping memberships, co-optation is an important social device for increasing the likelihood that organizations related to one another in complicated ways will in fact find compatible goals. By thus reducing the possibilities of antithetical actions by two or more organizations, co-optation aids in the integration of the heterogeneous parts of a complex society. By the same token, co-optation further limits the opportunity for one organization to choose its goals arbitrarily or unilaterally.

Coalition

As used here, the term coalition refers to a combination of two or more organizations for a common purpose. Coalition appears to be the ultimate or extreme form of environmental conditioning of organizational goals.[8] A coalition may be unstable, but to the extent that it is operative, two or more organizations act as one with respect to certain goals. Coalition is a means widely used when two or more enterprises wish to pursue a goal calling for more support, especially for more resources, than any one of them is able to marshall unaided. American business firms frequently resort to coalition for purposes of research or product promotion and for the construction of such gigantic facilities as dams or atomic reactors.

Coalition is not uncommon among educational organizations. Universities have established joint operations in such areas as nuclear re-

---

[8] Coalition may involve joint action toward only limited aspects of the goals of each member. It may involve the complete commitment of each member for a specific period of time or indefinitely. In either case the ultimate power to withdraw is retained by the members. We thus distinguish coalition from merger, in which two or more organizations are fused permanently. In merger one or all of the original parts may lose their identity. Goal-setting in such a situation, of course, is no longer subject to inter-organizational constraints among the components.

search, archaeological research, and even social science research. Many smaller colleges have banded together for fund-raising purposes. The consolidation of public school districts is another form of coalition (if not merger), and the fact that it does represent a sharing or "invasion" of goal-setting power is reflected in some of the bitter resistance to consolidation in tradition-oriented localities.

Coalition requires a commitment for joint decision of future activities and thus places limits on unilateral or arbitrary decisions. Furthermore, inability of an organization to find partners in a coalition venture automatically prevents pursuit of that objective, and is therefore also a form of social control. If the collective judgment is that a proposal is unworkable, a possible disaster may be escaped and unproductive allocation of resources avoided.

DEVELOPMENT OF ENVIRONMENTAL SUPPORT

Environmental control is not a one-way process limited to consequences for the organization of action in its environment. Those subject to control are also part of the larger society and hence are also agents of social control. The enterprise that competes is not only influenced in its goal-setting by what the competitor and the third party may do, but also exerts influence over both. Bargaining likewise is a form of mutual, two-way influence; co-optation affects the co-opted as well as the co-opting party; and coalition clearly sets limits on both parties.

Goals appear to grow out of interaction, both within the organization and between the organization and its environment. While every enterprise must find sufficient support for its goals, it may wield initiative in this. The difference between effective and ineffective organizations may well lie in the initiative exercised by those in the organization who are responsible for goal-setting. . . .

III

Organizational Structures

Of all the areas of organizational study, perhaps the most neglected is that of comparative study, in particular the study of organizations in the same culture and society. Most studies of organizations are case studies of a single organization, surveys of participants in a single organization, or abstract theories which presumably apply to all organizations. A careful examination of the usual generalizations applied to organizational structures would show that in fact they apply only to certain types of organizations—to economic and governmental bureaucracies, for instance—but that they are not applicable to many others.

As we suggested in detail elsewhere,* the compliance relationship of the lower and higher in rank within an organization provides a basis for comparative analysis. Organizations are social tools specializing in "getting things done" (as compared to "natural" social units, such as families, tribes, and friendships). The extraordinary capacity of an organization to act is based on the coordination of the efforts of a large number of participants and the relationships between the ranks within the organization. Those of lower rank cannot but be significantly affected by the various controls employed by those of higher rank and effective coordination depends on the orientation of the lower ranks to those in control, to the organization and its goals.

* *A Comparative Analysis of Complex Organizations* (New York: Free Press, 1961), pp. 23 ff.; see also pp. 59–76 above.

Three main types of compliance relations emerge from an analysis of both the means of control organizations use and the participants' orientations: (1) Organizations in which the higher in rank use coercion to control the lower in rank—basically negative orientations; (2) organizations in which the higher in rank use remunerative rewards and sanctions to control the lower in rank—orientations varying from negative to positive without being very intense; and (3) organizations in which the higher in rank use symbolic means such as appeals to values, persuasion, or prestige to achieve control. In these instances the orientation of the lower in rank tends, in varying degrees of intensity, to be positive, and may in fact be highly positive.

The following three studies illustrate the three archetypes of compliance: McCleery—that of coercive organizations; Blauner—the utilitarian (or remunerative) ones; and Wilson—normative organizations. Each study also serves to illustrate the tense relationship between model and data: while each study does support the basic model, and the correspondence between model and data is never exact, which in itself raises additional issues.

McCleery's study shows that while the prison is undoubtedly a coercive organization, it is less coercive than may be assumed at first sight, and in different ways than one may at first expect. Thus, in the prison studied inmate-elites were used to assist the prison management in maintaining control, an elite which was rewarded for its services by economic concessions and symbolic rewards (especially access to "limited" information). While these inmates used force to keep the other inmates "in place," and although they themselves were not in the prison quite voluntarily, the more common picture of a united inmate community facing hostile guards seems not to hold. Moreover, when the inmate-elite is "toppled" by a more liberal (less coercive-minded) prison administration, the need for coercion rises, at least temporarily.

Workers, as Blauner shows, vary significantly in their orientations. Actually, their working conditions and reactions are so divergent that at first it may seem that no generalizations are possible. Still, if we take the comparative approach, it seems quite evident that most workers are less alienated than most inmates, but more alienated than most members of normative organizations. Moreover, the factors that account for varying degrees of satisfaction among workers are precisely those that account for differences in the nature of the industrial control structures. Blauner's article may also be considered from two other perspectives: (a) the "embarrassment" that social science data and keen analysis brings to established intellectual and ideological preconceptions; (b) a revision of the conception of workers' alienation as a global attribute of modern Western society: obviously workers in the same society are alienated differentially according to the kind of organizational control system they are exposed to, which in turn is related to the kind of work they are carrying out.

Wilson studies a normative organization—a political party. Here members participate voluntarily; commitment is high, and rank differentiation small. The party under study (U.S. Democrats) is not one which generates commitment as high as do ideological parties and social movements. Also, as a normative organization it relies quite heavily on the milder variant of normative control—the "peer" social ties among members—rather than on "vertical" normative commitments. Still, the organization relies heavily on symbols and participation is largely voluntary.

Studies included in other sections of this reader cast additional light on the cross-organizational control-differential and related structural and motivational differences. See the selection by Goffman on coercive organizations (prisons and traditional mental hospitals) and by Dalton on utilitarian ones (factories). Actually, we maintain that every organization can be studied from the viewpoint of its place in the compliance scheme and the many factors which co-vary with compliance.

POLICY CHANGE IN PRISON MANAGEMENT

Richard H. McCleery

THE THEORETICAL CONTEXT

The power of man over man is the brute fact of political experience. Much of political theory is devoted to a search for the real or ideal foundations on which power is based. Depending in large part on the time in which a philosopher writes, the basis of political power may be found in force, ownership of the means of production, natural law, or divine right. Each of these bases of power may seem dominant in a culture at some stage of its historical development. As a theory for our time, this paper will suggest the role of communication patterns as a basis for a system of authority and power.

Direct application of coercive force may be regarded as the most primitive basis of power in interpersonal relations. When social affairs approach a state of anarchy, a Thomas Hobbes may take that principle as the heart of his argument. The measure of stability or even civilization, however, is the development of alternative foundations for the social order. In stable societies, a pattern of communication appears in close connection with the power structure; and the "authoritative allocation of values" becomes a matter of definition and assignment rather than snatch and grab. While abstract political theory may find an ultimate basis of

Excerpted from *Policy Change in Prison Management*, by permission of the author and the publisher, Governmental Research Bureau, Michigan State University, 1957.

authority in force, empirical research in politics often equates interaction with influence and processes of definition with power.[1]

The immediate focus of this study is on administration and the management of men in a situation which presents power relations with naked clarity—the prison. The bulk of administrative theory notwithstanding, the administrator is strictly limited in the sanctions which he can apply to sustain authority, and even the power of summary dismissal is a relic from a more primitive economic era. These limitations do not apply to prison management where force and fear stand ready as instruments of control. The task of analysis here is to weigh the role of force in comparison to the communication patterns as the basis of power. . . .

If we assume that communication patterns serve as one functional equivalent for force in sustaining the power structure of a stable society, these propositions would seem to follow:

1. Change in a formal power structure should be reflected in the patterns of communication and contact of the group.
2. Change in the patterns of communication, however instituted, should react on the system of formal power and authority, causing either its collapse or a resort to other means for its support.
3. A failure of the communication patterns to correspond to a given system of authority should result in anarchy and produce an increased resort to force.

THE RESEARCH CONTEXT

The prison, as a distinctive system of power, provides a setting in which to examine the above propositions. The present discussion is drawn from the context of a broader study of prison management in transition which compared the processes of inmate society under authoritarian and more liberal prison administrations. . . .

The prison presents special advantages as a setting for the study of communications and power. In familiar communities, power is a complex which includes large elements of habit, tradition, loyalty and even affection. Customary deference is supported by a differentiation in status symbols and by class functions accumulated over centuries. The exercise

[1] A review of the approach which identifies power structures in terms of patterns of contact and the communication of influence is found in Robert Agger, "Power Attributions in the Local Community: Theoretical and Research Considerations," *Social Forces*, 34 (May, 1956), pp. 322–331. For more general theoretical treatment, see Harold Lasswell and Abraham Kaplan, *Power and Society* (New Haven: Yale University Press, 1950).

of power in the prison, while not entirely independent of these elements, is clarified by its greater dependence on authority. The prison regime tends to suppress all class distinctions in dress and possessions and to reduce its subject to a uniform status of subordination. Hence in the relative absence of a symbolic basis of class distinction, the functional bases of those distinctions which do emerge and characterize inmate society to a marked degree become more evident. The commanding position of the "old con," his power to compel and coerce other inmates, may be traced to the process by which he creates the definitions accepted by his society.

Although the prison should not be taken uncritically as a society in microcosm, the comparative isolation of its social process from the impact of external variables provides a rare opportunity for systematic analysis. The vast majority of interaction patterns in inmate society begin and end within the walls and are subject to a measure of official control and manipulation. Finally, the identification of formal and informal systems of behavior is simplified by a sharp distinction between the ruling and subject class of the prison community.

The discussion to follow will consider the administrative and social characteristics of an authoritarian prison, certain liberal changes introduced and their consequences, and the basis of reconstruction in inmate and official societies.

THE AUTHORITARIAN PRISON

Organization and Communications

The formal organization and official policy of the traditional prison recognized industry as a goal and reform as a hope along with the objective of custodial control. However, one basic proposition emerging from this study is that formal organization is modified by the location and control of communication channels. Thus, while the prison had a work program, its inmates were sentenced to "hard labor," and the economic self-sufficiency of the institution was an ideal, the effective roles of industry and the industrial supervisor were institutionalized in their relations with the custodial force.

The Warden and his Deputy were the only policy-making officials of the institution. At the beginning of this study, the main divisions of the staff were the custodial force, organized in three watches under a Senior Captain, and the work line supervisors. Past attempts to vitalize a treatment program had atrophied by that time into a single position—

an ex-guard supervised recreation. There were other functions performed within the walls—a kitchen, an admissions and records office, and a hospital—but these seemed to have no independent organizational status. The entire staff accepted those implications for organizational structure which were institutionalized in the custodial force. The structure of that force was borrowed directly from military organization. The steps in its uniformed and disciplined hierarchy served as the measure by which those who performed non-custodial services determined their own status within the structure of formal organization. Hence the admissions officer insisted upon the rank of Captain which he had earned through many years of custodial service.

The nerve center for all institutional communication lay in the office of the Captain of the Yard. This location was dictated by the primary interest of custodial officials in the hour-by-hour reports on the location and movement of men. However, it was not just the report of counts and the time books of the work line supervisors but all orders, requests and reports which passed through this communications center. With the issuance of orders and the assignment of men channeled through a communication system controlled by custody, the perceived status of work line supervisors was below that of the guards from whom, in effect, they took their orders. . . .

Record items of costs, production, or the needs of the men might be ignored, but control information was never overlooked. The institutional pressures which dominated the office in which communication centered dictated its content and use. Custodial control of communications, and the interactional patterns thus established, imposed custodial attitudes, values and behaviors throughout the industrial program, negating its formal position and purpose.

Work supervisors had little contact with the Director of Industry but daily contact with the guards. Their ability to communicate their day-to-day needs depended on the influence involved in that contact. But contact normally involves effective communication only to the extent that shared attitudes and values are present.[2] As a result, supervisors came to think, act and dress like the guards. They justified labor in terms of

[2] There is no effective execution of orders in an agency except as some motive or sentiment appears in connection with and in support of the activity. In the absence of some more complex sentiment, the desire to earn wages may be enough to gain a tolerable level of activity, but the activity itself seems to produce sentiments in respect to the work among the employees. The manner in which the work is then carried on and the aspects of the work which gain emphasis in time are colored by the sentiments held about it and the manner of their communication. For a careful analysis of the relationships between activity, interaction and sentiment, note George Homans, *The Human Group* (New York: Harcourt, 1950).

disciplinary rather than productive or training results, maintained sharp class distinctions on the job, and repressed the rare examples of initiative which appeared among their inmate employees. Accepting that definition of labor and the status of the supervisor, inmates opposed the industrial program and gave the minimum tolerable effort to it. Supervisors, in turn, borrowed custodial attitudes which explained failures of production on the basis of the malice and incompetence of the inmates. The institutionally shared belief in the limited possibilities of prison industry further reduced its role.

The status of other functions performed in the prison was subverted in a similar way, and this may be illustrated most clearly in respect to professional services. Psychological diagnosis and medical treatment were carried on in the institution. Referral to and reports from these services were passed through custodial channels which emphasized security considerations above all else. Psychological services seemed to the inmates to be an adjunct of disciplinary control, and medical treatment appeared to be geared to the detection of malingering. Consequently, inmates believed, with some justification, that these services were subordinated to custody, and the prison community in general regarded the professional with a contempt inconsistent with his formal status and the real motive of his work.[3] The "bug doctor" was considered lower than a "screw." That contempt, in turn, reduced the actual function of professional services to insignificance.

Thus, its control of communication permitted custody to co-opt the efforts of other institutional units to the support of its own function and status. . . .

Delegating a monopoly over communication controls has different and more dictatorial power implications for a society than simply delegating a monopoly over the instruments of force. Censorship goes beyond action to control over how men think. It goes beyond overt resistance to sap the very will to resist. It removes from the universe of discourse the premises on which criticism might be based. Thus, it gains a blind and fatalistic conformity not only while the eye of authority is on the subject but even while it sleeps. Inmates regarded the traditional structures of authority in the old prison as mean, abusive and unjust; but, most important, they regarded it as inevitable. . . .

There is an anarchic tendency in the principle of backing up the

---

[3] The contrast between the formal and the effective status of professionals in penal work has been generally noted. Harvey Powelson and Reinhard Bendix discuss the conflict with custodial forces and the attitudes of inmates which negate the work of the professional in prisons. "Psychiatry in Prison," *Psychiatry*, 14 (February, 1951), pp. 73–86.

subordinate which would seem to maximize discretionary authority throughout an organization. The absence of two-way communications controlled that tendency in the authoritarian prison. All communication flowed upward, leaving each superior better informed than his subordinate and limiting the information on lower levels on which discretion could be based. Official definitions alone are not enough to establish the legitimacy of senior officials and enforce discipline in a strict hierarchy of rank. The patterns of communication in the authoritarian institution established the official hierarchy as a relative intellectual elite and legitimized the assumption that the superior was correct on any question. The superior was always better informed. . . .

Decisions are influenced as much by withholding information as by injecting it into communication channels. However, subordinate officers hesitated to stop reports or deny requests where there was any possibility of being reversed later. Each superior reinforced his place in the hierarchy with a wider sphere of movement and access to personal contact than those of his subordinates. While the fundamental basis of status in both inmate and official societies was power to command others, prestige was closely related to freedom of movement. The power to exert influence was directly proportioned to one's access to communication channels and information. . . .

Procedures of Governing

The character of the prison as a system of power may be further illustrated in the procedures of decision, control and ordinary operation. The Warden was free to express the principle of having a constructive industrial policy. Given custodial control over operational decision, however, the practice of using inmate labor only in menial tasks of no value to the inmate and little use to the state contradicted formal declarations of institutional policy but illustrated a principle of wide application in this social system. Decision reflects the interests which are communicated most effectively on the administrative level at which decisions are made. The institutional autocrat is not responsible to his subordinates, but he is no less responsive than any other executive to those who define the premises of his discretion.

In the authoritarian prison, the exercise of coercive power based essentially on force constituted one foundation of social control. But this power was, perhaps, least effective when it took the form of punitive sanctions imposed on individuals. A high degree of discipline was maintained with the minimum of direct sanctions. A vital basis of social control lay in procedures of regimentation—frequent counts and assemblies—which imposed a psychology of domination and placed the subject in a posture of silence, respect and awe. Recognition of distinctions in rank was imposed in all inmate-official contacts by the requirements of a salute and special forms of address.

More punitive forms of control rested on summary procedure and a few rules as broad in their import as the officer's sense of insubordination. Control, rather than "justice" in the familiar sense, was the object. Hence, there was no place for a body of principles or "constitutional" rights to restrain disciplinary procedure. Secret accusation was the rule, and the accused had no notice, hearing, counsel or appeal. The resulting atmosphere of "terror," produced as much by secrecy as by the actual use of informers, was vital to formal control and a key to values and social structures in inmate society. . . .

The distinguishing characteristic of ordinary operations in the authoritarian prison was the absence of alternatives for behavior permitted to or provided for the inmates. Rewards went only for ritual conformity, and initiative was as suspect to the static inmate community as to the officials. This accent on conformity did not prevent—in fact, seemed to require—the emergence of a complex organization in inmate society. Silence was imposed wherever inmates congregated, but the patterns of inmate organization and communication could not be suppressed by even the most rigid silent system. They could only be controlled. . . .

The Inmate Social System

Reason would seem to indicate what official policy assumed in the old prison: that men stripped of all but the necessities of life would be equal and that they would be ready to attack the system which reduced them to that condition. However, analysis must deal with two predominant facts of the situation. Inmate society was structured in terms of striking inequalities, and, under normal circumstances, it was geared to adjustment rather than rebellion. Only under exceptional conditions, to be examined later, did violent and aggressive men emerge to a position of leadership in prison life.

Inmate society demanded and the officials asserted, as a basic premise of prison life, that all inmates be treated alike. In spite of this, the basic interpersonal relationship in inmate society was that of dominance and subordination. The highest personal value in that system was placed on the exercise of coercive power.[4] This suggests that a fundamental goal of

[4] The apparent contradiction between the tight power hierarchy of inmate society and its constant demand for equality of treatment is discussed by Lloyd McCorkle and Richard Korn, "Resocialization Within Walls," *The Annals*, 293 (May, 1954), pp. 89 ff.

control over men was uncritically borrowed by the inmates from the administration.[5] While there are striking parallel values expressed in dress and habit between inmate and official society, the pursuit of power was not simply an end in itself.

A goal of the inmates was to achieve integrity and independence from official sanctions—to gain deliverance from perils. To gain this type of freedom, the society enforced conformity on its members by sanctions more severe than those employed by officials. In defiance of formal premises of equality, inmate society was structured in a power hierarchy at least as sharply defined and static as that of the officials. It was defended in its independence by a basic imperative of the code: "Never talk to a screw."

The absence of published regulations or official orientation for new men, the secrecy and arbitrariness of disciplinary action, the shocking unfamiliarity of the prison world to men just arrived, and the demands imposed by regimentation—all these combined to make the new inmate dependent on the experienced prisoner.[6] The old inmate knew the uncertain limits of official tolerance in a system which, of necessity, prohibited far more than it punished. He could share on his own conditions the knowledge which made life tolerable for the new man.

Knowledge of prison operations made for physical adjustment, but knowledge of explanations was required to make life psychologically tolerable. Inmates, no less than other men, needed rationalizations to give meaning to their daily lives. This was not provided by the authoritarian prison system. In the words of an old guard, "We don't have to make excuses to inmates." Senior officials dismissed the importance of the inmate grapevine because it was inaccurate, but its importance lay in its very inaccuracy. The myths and fantasies circulated by the grapevine

---

[5] Erich Fromm writes, in his study of authoritarian culture, "In any society the spirit of the whole culture is determined by the spirit of those groups that are most powerful in that society." *Escape from Freedom* (New York: Holt, Rinehart and Winston, Inc., 1941), pp. 112 f. Only the most cynical approach could apply that proposition directly to the prison and claim that the spirit of the inmate population is taken directly from its rulers. This is too uncharitable to the rulers. However, a reformulation of the proposition in more behavioral terms permits its application to the prison. The effective pursuit of security by the ruling class of the prison imposes patterns of contact and social process upon the subjects which, in turn, dictate the dominant goals and values which can emerge in their society.

[6] The complex processes by which the new inmate becomes oriented or "prisonized" in his unfamiliar setting are outlined by Donald Clemmer, "Observations on Imprisonment as a Source of Criminality," *The Journal of Criminal Law and Criminology*, 41 (September–October, 1950), pp. 311–319. For those interested in intensive study of the prison as a setting for the management of men, the most substantial work on prison government is Clemmer's *The Prison Community* (Boston: The Christopher Publishing House, 1940).

performed vital adjustive functions for inmate society, explaining events in satisfying ways, holding officials in contempt, and attributing a certain dignity to the inmate class. Initiation into these mysteries of the inmate tribe was as important as the process of physical adjustment, and it was sharing in these myths of solidarity, more than physical association, which gave a certain unity to the inmate group. . . .

Inmate society protected itself from the betrayal of both its power structure and its myths by ostracizing such men from communication and the benefits of membership. At the same time, it regarded isolates as fair game for abuse, exploitation and domination. Constant emphasis on the idea of the "rat" supported a maximal valuation of power in inmate society and still restricted the most obvious recourse to power—an appeal by informers to official sanctions. The demand for equality was not a demand against the administration but an assertion among inmates that power gained by contacts outside inmate society had no legitimacy there. Denial of validity to outside contacts protected the inmate culture from criticism and assured the stability of its social order. . . .

Inmate leaders were men able to explain, predict, or control to some degree a situation in which others were helpless and confused. Lesser men gained security and protection by attaching themselves to those leaders and supplying them the petty tribute which conveyed status.[7] This type of dominance depended on access to informal communication, contacts on the grapevine and, also, contacts with official sources. Because these men were expected to manipulate power and mediate between the forces of official action and their followers, they were given a license to talk with officials never permitted to men of unproven dependability. . . .

Under stable conditions, inmate culture supported custodial values. Its accent on conformity, on doing one's own time without fear or complaint, on avoiding behavior which would "bring on the heat," on never talking to a "screw," all these were ideally suited to custodial control. In a period of disorganization or challenge to inmate values, however, aggressiveness became the assertion of a moral independence and contempt for officials played a special, self-justifying role. The inmate whose rebellion was undeterred by the most violent official sanctions was elevated to

[7] The significance of the constant exchange of food and goods in inmate society has led to conflicting interpretation. Norman Hayner and Ellis Ash believe that "the organization of this community is primarily an economic arrangement devoted to obtaining goods and services denied by the administration." "The Prison Community as a Social Group," *American Sociological Review* 4 (June, 1949), p. 369. The present study suggests that conspicuous display of goods and privileges among inmates serves only to symbolize status which must be earned by other means. The symbols declare an ability to manipulate power, and inmate society supplies these symbols to men undergoing punishment or in death row when the only function performed by such men is to resist power bravely.

the role of a Promethean hero.[8] The utter disregard of consequences, expressed by attacks on officials or repeated attempts to escape, assumed the stature of moral courage enhanced by the disproportionate weight of the punishment resulting. Under certain conditions, the ability to resist power bravely became the equivalent of an ability to manipulate power. With the collapse of a system by which adjustive definitions of the situation were applied throughout the inmate community, the hero was called on to give violent assertion to the values of the group.

Traditional inmate culture accented the values of adjustment within the walls and the rejection of outside contacts. It supported a social hierarchy, reduced new arrivals to subordination, and adjusted its own social conflicts with sanctions more severe than those available to the guards. As will be indicated by later developments in the prison, control of a disorganized mass of men was beyond the ability of the guard force. Control of a rigid social system in which the vast majority of definitions and sanctions were informally imposed was a far more simple matter. Hence the custodial goals of peace, order and adjustment dictated an alliance between senior officers and inmate leaders in the interests of stability and to the end of minimizing the role of the hero.

In some respects it could be said that the inmates ran the authoritarian prison. Senior inmates, at least, had a voice in the assignment of men and the distribution of privileges. Integrating contacts between officials and high status inmates were conducted in a responsible way. Both groups shared a sincere contempt for "rats." Their exchanges were not moved by a desire to employ sanctions against individuals or to gain immediate private advantage so much as by a wish to maintain a condition of peace and order in which each senior group enjoyed the advantage of its position. Each group held power in its own sphere by means of ability to predict events and extended that power by intercommunication which violated the norms of both systems. In order to maintain these contacts with inmates which provided warning of danger, officials were willing to tolerate a considerable amount of rule evasion, pilfering, and petty exercises of power by inmate leaders. These privileges stabilized the inmate society. While the authoritarian prison is often accused of tolerating abuse, corruption, exploitation and inequality, such things were permitted in the interests of security and adjustment—the values most firmly institutionalized in the system.

[8] The elements of a hero-making situation are identified by Orrin Klapp, "The Creation of Popular Heroes," *The American Journal of Sociology*, 54 (September, 1948), pp. 135–141. In the prison setting, any collapse of the myths by which inmates justify themselves and their place in the world seems to demand some aggressive assertion of the idea that they are not defeated and helpless.

Summary

The analysis so far has identified systems of communication intimately allied with the structure of power in both inmate and official societies. The unit of the official system which administered communications as a means of control imposed its values and assumed a commanding role in the institution as a whole. At the same time, a power hierarchy emerged in the presumptively egalitarian inmate community which seemed directly related to its communication and informational environment.

THE LIBERAL REVOLUTION

Three phases can be distinguished in the prison's period of transition. The first runs from the death of the old Warden in 1946 to the end of 1950. In that period, a liberal group appeared in the administration, gained formal authority, and revolutionized the policies of the institution. In the next phase, from 1950 through 1953, the liberal group engaged in a contest with the guards for control over operating procedures and, in effect, for control over the population. The present section will trace these developments. A following section will outline that contest, in which control was nearly lost, to its result in the defeat of the "old guard." The final period from 1954 through 1955 was one of reconstruction, adjustment, and, as stated by the officials, "tightening up the organization."

The seeds of revolution were contained in the appointment of five men from 1946 through 1949 who had no previous penal experience and who would not or could not adjust to traditional processes by which custody had become fixed as the dominant institutional goal. While these appointments were policy acts, they did not, in themselves, indicate a policy change, and the consequences which were to follow from altered patterns of behavior were not anticipated. The extent to which these new men injected inconsistent patterns of behavior from the free community into the prison, as much as their democratic policy statements later, marks the change as a liberal or democratic revolution. . . . The tactics of their revolt were little more than the habits of open communication, concern for "justice" as well as control, and performance as well as conformity, the rejection of status differentials in social contact, and the determination to be informed of their own responsibilities—all of which they imported from free society. Yet these simple behaviors, inconsistent with the authoritarian tradition, had a direct impact on policy and organization throughout the institution.

Reformulation of Policy

The disciplined traditions of the custodial force and the attitudes toward authority held by its members blocked their access to the open door of the new Warden. Those who took advantage of that access were the new employees who were conscious of the traditional chain of command only as a device by which their functions were frustrated. Other non-custodial employees in the past had resigned in the face of these frustrations or had accepted the attitudes and goals of custody with their acceptance of its communication channels. This group was spared the custodial orientation (with its narrow definition of purposes, roles and possibilities within the prison) by a practice of turning to one another and the license it took in turning to the Warden for definitions. The new men were members of the official staff, but they were not members of the official community in the sense of sharing the goals and values which gave an integrity to that group. . . .

As the new men by-passed conventional channels and turned to the Warden for definitions, they found that officer sensitive to the limits on his discretion imposed by custodial control of communication. His efforts to inquire through the custodial force into rumors of corruption in the prison had been frustrated for a year, forcing him to employ an outside investigator. The dismissal of several guards as a result of that inquiry, based in part on testimony taken from inmates, had lowered custodial morale and strained relations with that group. In this situation, the new men were able to form themselves into a policy caucus around the Warden and participate in the making of the definitions they sought. In turn this gave the functions represented by the new men (industry, education, and treatment) a hearing in policy decisions which they had not previously enjoyed.

When other units gained a share in policy definitions, the techniques of controlling decision by controlling the information on which it was based reacted against custodial officials. The new group was able to inject a wider range of pertinent considerations for policy than had reached the Warden in the past. As officials charged with treatment responsibilities gained access to the decision-making forum, this constituted a virtual representation of the interests and welfare of the inmates. This representation was reflected in a number of minor policy changes.

One of the first projects of the liberal group was to establish a clear conception of its own functions in the institution. To that end it produced a formal diagram of the organization. In contradition to the actualities of custodial domination and the effective goals of the agency, the organizational chart placed the functions of treatment and industry on a level with the guard force. This, in itself, was a critical redefinition of roles if not of powers. Then, discarding its advisory capacity, the next step of the liberal group was to formalize its position as a policy agency for internal affairs. The guard force, the largest numerical group of employees, had only minority representation on the policy committee, and other officials of importance in the old power hierarchy were excluded altogether.

The next project of the liberal group was a Policy and Philosophy Manual. There was little formal statement of policy in the traditional prison between the establishing statute and the descriptive "wake 'em, work 'em, etc." of the guards. An authoritarian system is necessarily weak in operational ideology because it must resolve issues by appeal to the superior official rather than by appeal to principle. Authoritarian discipline is subverted by the publication of principles to which an appeal from persons can be made. Given a constitution or a law of the twelve tables, the weakest man in the community is armed with a weapon against the strongest. However, a Manual was published for the institution, and it asserted "rehabilitation through treatment and constructive industry" as the primary institutional purpose. It stated that "the democratic approach to management is the soundest" and contained commitments to:

> The delegation to lower management levels of all possible responsibility and authority commensurate with sound management.
> A practice of constant consultation, dissemination of information, and discussion of problems up and down the management chain.

These concepts were directly inconsistent with authoritarian hierarchy and control. Custodial officers were members of the council that produced the document, but they made no effective resistance to its publication. Unable to communicate effectively in the new policy forum, suspicious and on the defensive, the guard force withdrew from the area of general policy and fell back on its control over the actual operations, procedures and communications in the prison yard. The liberal group had no impact on that area until it could translate its formalized principles into operating procedures.

The Procedural Revolution

From a legalistic point of view, it would seem that the revolution in the prison had been accomplished by 1950. The liberal group had gained formal status, drafted a "constitution" and seized control of the policy-making centers thus created. In terms of the daily operating procedures of the institution, however, the change had scarcely begun. While work supervisors continued to report and take orders through the guards, their programs and the emphasis of their work continued along essentially traditional lines. The policy-making group had gained status without gaining influence. It wrote new regulations and the guards continued to enforce the old. At this point—one not uncommon in the administration of penal or other institutions—a reformulation of general policy had exerted little visible impact on actual procedures.

While efforts of the policy group to legislate patterns of behavior and standards of action were defeated in the execution, that group was able to adjust institutional patterns of communication to the new policy. The principle that all those affected by a decision should have an understanding of the issues and a voice in their determination dictated the holding of discussion meetings in several sections of the organization. Led by the treatment director, these discussions proved most effective in the newly established and more complex units of the industrial program. There they provided a means by which the interests of the work supervisors were advanced past the custodial hierarchy, and the supervisors responded briskly to the change. As an outcome of these meetings, prison rules were revised to abandon the time-honored salute in all contacts between inmate and supervisor and to give up other elements of regimentation on the work line which had hindered productivity in the past. The abandonment of these status distinctions at work opened the way to more active communication on the job, improved production, the development of workshop communities of interest, and habits of interaction quite inconsistent with the continuing demands of life in the cell blocks. The more open contacts between supervisors and inmates provided a basis for turning later to the supervisors rather than the guards for direct reports on the men. As might be expected, efforts to conduct similar discussion sessions with the custodial force brought little response.

At the start of 1951, an inmate council was established with a right to debate any issue and advance proposals for staff consideration. This Council, with an adviser from the treatment unit, formed working committees for such areas as food, hobby and craft work, education, recreation, and public relations. It would seem especially significant in terms of the type of analysis advanced here that the Council called itself "the voice of the inmates."

Later developments began to challenge the realities of custodial control in one area after another. In times past, punishment, inmate promotions, job assignments, good-time allowances, and every type of petty privilege had been administered by custody in terms of consideration of control. Seniority and the appearance of adjustment within the walls were used as a basis for the distribution of privilege. This reinforced the dominance of conservative and con-wise old prisoners. When the administration of privileges was, in effect, delegated to senior inmates, that served the interest of control as much by strengthening the inmate social structure as by applying sanctions to individuals. The administrative processes involved in this management of incentives were mainly informal and summary. That does not mean, however, that the operating decisions were not rational on the criterion of custodial control. A basic tactic of the liberal group was to alter the method and, hence, the dominant motive by which those operating decisions were made.

The treatment office claimed a voice in decisions on privilege and punishment on the grounds that privilege should be "meaningful" and that incentives should be concentrated behind their recently defined "goals of the institution." In defense of treatment-oriented personnel, it must be admitted that they had little conception of how all operations had been geared to the goals of security. By failing to share in institutional goals as defined by the guard force, they failed to comprehend the rationale of traditional procedures. They had little understanding of the economy of scarcity which prevailed in the yard or the extent to which a privilege or a larger sphere of movement extended to the "wrong" inmate could disturb the prison's social order. The philosophy of the treatment unit accented the importance of the individual, and this is the crucial basis on which the changes introduced may be called a "democratic" revolution. The focus of treatment men on the individual—a focus permitted by their lack of custodial responsibilities—was crucial in their conflict with the authoritarian tradition.

Participation in the expanding group of activities sponsored by treatment became the basis of a record. At the same time, the more complex processes of production required work supervisors to reward inmates on the basis of productivity as well as conduct. A report of the inmate's work record was channeled directly to the treatment office. Such records were inserted as relevant to daily operating decisions, and the decisions responded to the interests which were communicated most effectively. The traditional "time off for good behavior" became a committee decision in which six factors, only one of which was conduct, were weighted equally. The interest of teaching men a trade was taken as a ground for moving the administration of transfers to the treatment unit and away from custodial administration. By that time, the terminology and ideology of "individual development" rather than "good conduct" had been imposed on the reports of supervisors.

The treatment unit, armed with an expanding record, first asserted an informed interest and then assumed the management of functions in one area after another, extending finally to recreation and entertainment.

These changes in the location of effective discretion within the agency tended to leave the custodial force with nothing but its guns as a basis of control. Rising disorder in the inmate community indicated that such a basis is weak indeed. The present section has indicated that the range of discretion possessed by a unit of administration tends to be as wide and no wider than the store of information on which decision is based.

THE IMPACT OF ADMINISTRATIVE CHANGE

As new concepts of policy were incorporated into the procedures of daily administration, these had a direct effect on the patterns of communication and interpersonal contact within the prison. The communication patterns of both official and inmate societies were altered to the point that they no longer served to support the traditional power hierarchy or gain acceptance for its authority. This section will trace the development of a rebellion among members of the once disciplined custodial force and, with reference to the prison's disciplinary records, the rise in anarchy in the inmate population. . . .

The Revolt of the "Old Guard"

While significant changes took place elsewhere in the institution, the custodial force retained the traditional patterns of communication from an earlier day. Just as the new officials had avoided indoctrination with custodial attitudes, the bulk of the guard force remained isolated from the new concepts and principles of the policy manual. Three years after its publication, few of the guards knew of its existence. Written declaration from above proved incapable of challenging the rationalizations which emerged within the group. Men whose daily work required them to be constantly ready to shoot an inmate arrived at a conception of inmates as persons who might justifiably be shot.

The system of limited communication to subordinates, which supported an authoritarian hierarchy in both official and inmate groups, was supplemented by a grapevine which supplied each level of the heirarchy with self-justifying and conservative values. Acceptance of these values as legitimate was the price of peer group acceptance in all ranks. Thus, a limited communication pattern within the guard force protected the traditional set of custodial attitudes from challenge or criticism. At the same time, their isolation frequently left watch officers less well-informed than the inmates they guarded, reversing the conditions of the past and removing the legitimate basis of the guard's authority.

The guards tended to blame the treatment unit and its programs for the decline in their status which inevitably followed. The over-all consequences of procedural change were to flatten the status pyramid of the prison community by providing equal access to influence and information, narrowing the gaps of social distance which made up a formal hierarchy of authority.

In order to understand the resistance of the custodial force, it is necessary to see the situation as the guards viewed it. New officials violated the chain of command at every turn and dismissed the traditional prerogatives of rank. The failure of treatment officers to maintain distinctions of class threatened the psychology of domination so central to control, and led guards to see the treatment officials as on a level with the inmates themselves. Policy discussions with the Inmate Council challenged control based on secrecy and fear simply by supplying the rational basis for actions which had appeared to be arbitrary before. The inmates had more direct and effective representation in policy than the guards. Custodial accounting for the movement of men was confounded by the treatment activities. Finally, the guards felt with some reason that they knew far more about the behavior of prisoners in the authoritarian institution than did treatment officials. The guards were in the most favorable position to see inmates exploiting new activities in pursuit of the old goals of dominance and power. . . .

The old guard launched a counterattack with the only weapons remaining to it. The Inmate Council, meeting with its staff adviser in the yard, was free from harassment. However, completely literal enforcement of old regulations against movement and communication brought the follow-up activities of Council committees and treatment-sponsored clubs to a halt. Inmates who were "getting out of their place" through participation in new activities were the subject of disciplinary reports. Gaining access to the treatment office was made so complex and, for selected inmates, so humiliating that many who valued their self-respect in the yard abandoned the effort. Requests sent through the custodial channels to the treatment office were often lost. The custodial force perpetuated a distinction in the yard between "right inmates" and "politicians," who were assumed to be using contact with the treatment office for their own advantage. Guards manipulated traditional inmate values by asking men returning from the treatment office how much they had "beaten their time." In the face of those pressures, inmates employed in the Treatment Unit arranged for passes to work until lock-up and stayed out of the yard. In spite of the expanding number of privileges which could be manipulated by contacts in the treatment office, the influence of its inmate employees was neutralized.

By the beginning of 1953, the revolt of the old guard reached the height of its effectiveness. Conservative inmates had withdrawn from the Inmate Council, and the younger men who replaced them were exploiting the Council to an extent which challenged the faith of even the liberal officials. The inmate clubs and associations sponsored by the Treatment Unit had collapsed, and voluntary class attendance was in decline. Violence and escape had risen to a point at which new emphasis on custodial values of repression and control was required. The Deputy Warden, once a leader for liberal changes, sided with custody in the staff conferences and threatened a split in that group.

For all practical purposes, the guard force had regained control over the operation of the prison. However, it had lost control over formal policy statements as it lost its monopoly over communication channels. The old guard, ambitious for legitimacy as well as practical success, sought alliances outside the prison with men discharged earlier and with community groups which supported their position. Represented by a minority bloc in the legislature which was seeking an issue, the old guard took its policy contest into the field of politics.

Legislative hearings on the prison opened with a series of charges which indicated, by their nature, their source in the active custodial force. A stand was taken on those matters which seemed most like mismanagement to the old guard: promotion and discipline. However, what the guards called favoritism was proved to be a sound promotion on the basis of "merit." What the guards considered abuses of discipline in the failure to back up subordinates was defended as a policy of judicial fairness. The staff was able to meet the legislative inquiry with a convincing mass of records and documentary material while the guards, in making the charges, were limited to the information they could leak. Hence, the position of the old guard, which had a great deal of merit from the standpoint of authoritarian control or custody and a strong prospect of success in the conflict with the institution, was flatly rejected in the more democratic forum of the legislature. By pressing for a definition of policy in a forum beyond the range of their effective influence and communication, the guards gained only the endorsement of the liberal position and a final repudiation of their own.

The prison had changed in its character from a military dictatorship to an institution in which the role of armed forces was subordinated to the objective of treatment. While some guards persisted in their belief that all control over the inmates had been lost, a decline in escape, violence and disorder indicated, and the inmate community generally recognized, that the treatment unit had assumed control. . . .

Change and Social Disorganization

Discussion thus far has indicated that a shift in communication patterns and their control produced a drastic shift of power within a highly formalized organizational structure. The course of that change was delayed, modified, but seldom reversed by formal definitions of status and authority. The power of a unit to define a course of action for others was directly related to its store of information and capacity to transmit that information to the locale of decision. A change parallel to that in official society may be traced in the inmate community with even greater clarity in the absence of any official legitimacy for the power structure which existed there.

The first period of policy change was marked by little disturbance and relatively high morale in the yard. The investigation which crippled guard-inmate commerce brought no sanctions against the dominant inmate clique. While some activities by which inmate leadership supported its position were cut off, others appeared, and the inmate leaders were able to monopolize new privileges and claim credit for the sunshine. Control over the orientation of new men maintained the conservative inmate group in power as long as the guard force controlled the procedures of prison life. The early periods of low custodial morale and the revision of disciplinary procedures were followed by an outbreak of escape and some rise in disorder, but records show that these figures had returned to normal by 1949.

After that time, however, new activities and relationships in the treatment and production units began to create new communities of interest in the inmate body with a functional leadership of their own. As activities began to involve more and more cooperative supervision by officials, the "rat concept" of the old inmate culture and the sanctions against contact with officials were weakened. Old leaders often abandoned the opportunities for contact and information which appeared in connection with new work lines when accepting these opportunities involved accepting new relationships with officers and their fellows. The leaders drew into a more overt alliance with guard officials and sustained their position by traditional means in the prison yard. During the first part of the transition, the social consequences of the new work situations were isolated from the power structure and social processes of the prison yard, but the Council opened new avenues to recognition even there.

The old inmate leaders were like the custodial force in not being able to operate effectively in the context of group discussion and decision-making. In spite of a conservative majority of senior inmates on the first Council, a clique of new men seized the initiative in drafting the Council's constitution and bylaws, writing in provision for themselves. New officials thought the Council was a substantial privilege for the inmates, involving some small measures of control as well as a voice in prison affairs. To old inmate leaders it was a small boon in comparison to the position they had once enjoyed. The first months of the Council's operation provoked widespread inmate resistance and opposition, ending with the resignations of several old leaders. However, that move came too late to discredit the Council as a route to influence in the prison for a different class of men.

By the middle of 1951, the monolithic structure of inmate society had developed broad cracks. The marginally criminal first offenders, the lowest caste in the old prison, had found a focus of interest and organization in the Treatment Unit and the Council. As official frankness, publication of rules, and a formal orientation program made new men independent of the indoctrination by old cons, another group of tough, young, reform-school graduates declared their independence from old inmate leadership and embarked on a radical course of exploitation and troublemaking. In the following year, neither the traditional "code" nor old leadership commanded the respect which permitted them to define roles or adjust conflicts in the community. In the absence of controlling definitions, disputes were increasingly submitted to the arbitration of force, and the status of the physically powerful and aggressive men advanced.

Factions in the yard corresponded to those which split the administration in 1953. Conservative leaders allied with the old guard to neutralize the influence of inmates associated with the treatment program. However, the mounting disciplinary reports for that year did not reflect a direct conflict between those two elements. It was the young toughs, unwilling to accept definitions from any other group, who were out of control. In the face of these disturbances, created by an element of the inmate body that literally took orders from no one, the guard force and security measures were increased. The failure of these measures to restrain increasing disorder indicates the importance of informal social control, even in a society governed mainly by force and fear. . . .

This was the type of situation in which young men turned to follow "heroes" who dramatically asserted the ideals of toughness and resistance. Men made desperate by long sentences once had been absorbed into inmate society by the acceptance of values and definitions which made for adjustment. Now such men were encouraged by youthful followers to live up to newspaper reputations by sensational escapes and Promethean rebellion. It was the adverse publicity from such escapades which helped to establish the setting for the revolt of the old guard. At one critical point, a mass break-out was averted by posting machine guns on the roof and transferring inmate leaders of the younger group to another prison. Inmate society was close to a condition of anarchy in which the only recognized authority was that provided by physical force. This is not to say that attacks against officials were the rule. Official control over the instruments of force prevented this. What is significant to the analysis here is the complete failure of leadership and authority within the inmate community itself—the transfer of influence from the leader to the hero.

RECONSTRUCTION

A change in customary patterns of communication appeared to produce disorder and the collapse of authority in both official and inmate societies. This result occurred by way of the subversion of status attached to positions and conflict for the acceptance of inconsistent definitions. The emergence of a new order and stability in the prison seems anticlimactic by contrast. It involved little more than the development of patterns of communication by which all elements of the community gained the definitions on which stability is based.

Press reports of the legislative hearing which debated penal policy seem to have had a stabilizing influence on the inmates. Issues which had seemed, at first, to be little more than an administrative contest for power were defined for everyone on the level of principle. Inmates themselves entered into the debate on policy with an unprecedented interest. The position of the old guard was supported by testimony from one of the old leaders, but two of the major "heroes" of the inmate community submitted a letter to the legislative hearing in support of the new administrative position.

When the legislative debates were over, the Warden met with the inmates in a series of open discussions which are credited with a major role in restoring order. He took the lead in providing definitions and explanations of the situation so necessary to a sense of security but which no inmate group in the period of factionalism was able to supply. The role of the young toughs declined in the inmate community, and rates of escape and violence immediately dropped.

The central fact in the defeat of the old guard and those of their senior officers who remained was its recognition of the staff committee as an authoritative source of definitions for the prison. Prior to the legislative endorsement of a liberal position, the guards thought of themselves as custodians of the true or real institutional goals. It was this conviction which had armed them to circulate inconsistent definitions and also to remain aloof from the new policy centers. To the extent that the guards accepted the legitimacy of the new policy source, this acceptance worked to reduce tension in two ways. It reduced the circulation of contradictory definitions which had generated conflicts in the inmate body, but it also led the guards to a more active communication with and participation on policy councils. In the period of "tightening up the organization," policy has begun to incorporate more and more of the custodial point of view. Regular meetings between the Superintendent and the watches serve to bring considerations of security to bear on each decision.

With the defeat of the old guard, systematic efforts to isolate the influence of treatment-oriented inmates ceased, and a new social order began to emerge in the prison yard. Direct contacts between inmates and officials were taken as a matter of course. As a result, the idea of the "rat," with its implications for all inmate social process and structure, is almost forgotten at present. . . .

The transition involved a transfer of power from one unit of the agency to another. However, this change in the administration must be considered something more than simply a palace revolution. Inmate culture reflects certain qualitative differences in the present prison government. Wider access to officials constitutes a wider distribution of influence within the prison community which is reflected by a concern for inmate interests and welfare in policy. It protects against much of the exploitation and abuse which characterized inmate society in the past. While disciplinary rates have returned toward normal after the crisis, they will never be as low as was the case in the authoritarian prison. They reflect a greater initiative and a wider range of total activity in the inmate body. Even more significantly, they reflect a willingness of the inmates to accept official sanctions in the arbitration of inmate conflicts. The inmate community has abandoned many of the sanctions by which it imposed conformity on its own members.

Voluntary enrollment in treatment and education programs has shown a constant increase since the period of conflict. Such participation has become accepted as a means of gaining recognition in inmate society as well as official rewards. The programs sustain an atmosphere in which inmate attitudes are colored by ideas other than those generated within their own society and conditions in which a majority of the men are willing to accept officially sponsored ideas. An uncensored, inmate-edited newspaper, published in the treatment office, supplements the Warden's meetings with the men and prevents other inmate groups from gaining a monopoly on definition and interpretation.

Attempts by radical groups to capture the Inmate Council and to manipulate privileges administered through that agency have been defeated by inmates with little official intervention. The Council is not a strong and active organization, but it does insure that the inmates who speak with the most authority among their fellows are those in closest touch with the officials. The most striking distinction between the present inmate society and the past is the relative absence of powerful inmate leaders. Inmates elected to the Council by their fellows have less influence than the leadership which emerged in the authoritarian environment. Newly admitted inmates are no longer assigned to the lowest social status, social mobility is greater, and men with talent are recruited into activities in the yard by which status may be earned. A significant difference between past and present inmate society is indicated by the program of orientation carried on cooperatively by officials and the Council.

CONCLUSIONS

The three propositions advanced for analysis are supported by the evidence of this study. The unit which dominated the work of the old prison supported its position by control over the communication system. As those communication patterns were altered, a new policy emerged. Control over policy permitted the staff committee to formalize a drastic reassignment of roles and purposes in the institution, and this shift was followed by changes in the traditional patterns of contact for both official and inmate societies. The new principles and policy center did not become authoritative in practice until they gained the support of new communication patterns. During the interval in which communication patterns failed to correspond to the formal authority of the institution, anarchy and disorganization demanded an increased resort to force. On the basis of this evidence, it may be asserted that a pattern of communication serves as a functional equivalent for force in maintaining or subverting a stable system of authority. . . .

WORK SATISFACTION AND INDUSTRIAL TRENDS

Robert Blauner

In 1880 that famous pioneer of survey research, Karl Marx, drew up a questionnaire of 101 items, 25,000 copies of which were sent to various workers' societies and socialist circles. This long schedule, which exhorts workers to describe "with full knowledge the evils which they endure," is composed entirely of questions of *objective fact* relating to size of plant, working conditions, wages, hours, strikes, and trade unions. What appears strange in contrast with present-day surveys is the lack of questions concerning the *feelings* of the workers about their work, employers, and place in society.[1]

It is not that Marx believed that the subjective beliefs of workers were automatic and immediate reactions to their objective material conditions. He knew that workers might experience "false consciousness" instead of the "correct" awareness of their class position. But whereas the development of political class consciousness was problematic for Marx (in the short run, although not over the long haul), there seemed nothing problematic about the subjective reactions of the working class to the

Reprinted from Walter Galenson and Seymour Martin Lipset (eds.), *Labor and Trade Unionism: An Interdisciplinary Reader* (New York: Wiley, 1960), pp. 339–360, with omissions.

[1] One could argue that Marx was not only half a century ahead of his time in the use of the survey technique, but that he understood, even in 1880, the methodological difficulties in getting at subjective feelings. But then it might be retorted that he still had something to learn about eliminating bias in his questions: for example, item 59: "Have you noticed that the delay in paying your wages makes it necessary for you to resort frequently to the pawnbroker, paying a high rate of interest, and depriving yourself of things which you need; or to fall into debt to shopkeepers, becoming their victim because you are their debtor?" The entire questionnaire which was first published on April 20, 1880 in the *Revue Socialiste* appears in English in T. B. Bottomore and Maximilien Rubel, *Karl Marx, Selected Writings in Sociology and Social Philosophy* (London: Watts and Company, 1956), pp. 204–212. Bottomore and Rubel mention that very few workers took the trouble to return Marx' extremely long and difficult questionnaire and that no results were ever published.

wretched conditions of factory labor in the early industrial society of the nineteenth century. Marxists assumed that the *alienation* of labor (which referred to an objective relationship between the employee and the social organization of the work process) would have as its subjective consequence the *estrangement* of the laborers from the factory system. The worker's lack of control, epitomized in his social status as a "wage slave" and his psychotechnic status as an "appendage of the machine," would result in *feelings of dissatisfaction,* which, along with the development of the more problematic consciousness of shared class interests, would be powerful enough to launch revolutionary movements and sustain them to victory.

Two recent students of Marx have stated that "the Marxian theory of why men under capitalism would revolt was based on an assumption of what prompts men to be satisfied or dissatisfied with their work."[2] And since these expected revolts of industrial workers did not occur in many Western countries, even Marxist intellectuals in recent years have begun to look more closely at workers' subjective dispositions and attitudes. While socialists and general intellectuals were writing about the proletariat in an impressionistic fashion, sometimes without direct contact with the working classes, more empirical social researchers in industry and in the academic disciplines began to question workers directly. Systematic surveys of employee attitudes, begun in the early 1920's, developed so rapidly that in the bibliography of a recent review of research and opinion on job attitudes more than 1500 items are listed.[3]

The present paper surveys research on attitudes of workers toward their work, especially those investigations commonly called job satisfaction studies. To assess the absolute level of job satisfaction in the working population is not my aim, for this is an impossible task, but rather, my purposes are, (1) to locate differences in the incidence and intensity of work satisfaction among those in diverse occupations and work settings, and (2) to discern the factors that, in accounting for these differences, seem to indicate the important preconditions of satisfaction in work. Further, the paper considers the implications of these findings for theories of work and workers in modern society, in the light of industrial and social trends.

Although it is difficult, not to accept the proposition that at least the majority (and possibly a very large majority) of American workers are moderately satisfied in their work, such a finding is neither particularly

[2] Reinhard Bendix and Seymour Martin Lipset, "Karl Marx' Theory of Social Classes," in R. Bendix and S. M. Lipset, *Class, Status and Power* (New York: The Free Press, 1953), pp. 32 ff.

[3] Frederick Herzberg, Bernard Mausner, Richard O. Peterson, and Dora P. Capwell, *Job Attitudes: Review of Research and Opinion* (Psychological Service of Pittsburgh, 1957).

surprising nor sociologically interesting. Under "normal" conditions there is a natural tendency for people to identify with, or at least to be somewhat positively oriented toward, those social arrangements in which they are implicated. Attitude surveys show that the majority of employees like their company, that the majority of members are satisfied with their unions, and undoubtedly research would show a preponderance of positive over negative attitudes toward one's own marriage, family, religion, and nation-state. It is the presence of marked occupational *differences* in work attitudes to which I turn in the next section that is of more theoretical interest.

OCCUPATIONAL DIFFERENCES IN WORK SATISFACTION

Work satisfaction varies greatly by occupation. Highest percentages of satisfied workers are usually found among professionals and businessmen. In a given plant, the proportion satisfied is higher among clerical workers than among factory workers, just as in general labor force samples it is higher among middle-class than among manual working class occupations. Within the manual working class, job satisfaction is highest among skilled workers, lowest among unskilled laborers and workers on assembly lines.

When a scale of relative job satisfaction is formed, based on general occupational categories, the resulting rank order is almost identical with the most commonly used occupational status classification—the Edwards scale of the Bureau of the Census. For example, the mean indexes of satisfaction in Table 1 resulted from a survey of all New Hope, Pa., jobholders in 1935.

A similar rank order resulted in a national survey when the proportions of workers in each occupational group who would continue the same kind of work in the event they inherited enough money to live comfortably were computed[4] (Table 2).

TABLE 1

Occupational Group	Mean Index[5]	Number in Sample
Professional and managerial	560	23
Semiprofessional, business, and supervisory	548	32
Skilled manual and white collar	510	84
Semiskilled manual workers	483	74
Unskilled manual workers	401	55

[4] Nancy C. Morse and Robert S. Weiss, "The Function and Meaning of Work and the Job," *American Sociological Review*, **20** (1955), p. 197.
[5] In this index, the figure 100 would indicate extreme dissatisfaction, 400 indifference,

TABLE 2

Occupational Group	Percent Who Would Continue Same Kind of Work	Number in Sample
Professionals	68	28
Sales	59	22
Managers	55	22
Skilled manual	40	86
Service	33	18
Semiskilled operatives	32	80
Unskilled	16	27

The generally higher level of job satisfaction of white-collar over blue-collar workers is confirmed by a study of twelve different factories in 1934, in which the scores of clerical workers on job satisfaction were considerably higher than those of factory workers;[6] by the Centers national sample, which found that only 14 per cent of workers in middle-class occupations were dissatisfied with their jobs, compared to 21 per cent of those in working class occupations;[7] and by a 1947 *Fortune* poll, which revealed that the proportion of employees who said their jobs were interesting was 92 per cent among professionals and executives, 72 per cent among salaried employees and 54 per cent among factory workers.[8] However, a study of the Detroit area population found that only among such upper white-collar employees as secretaries, draftsmen, and book-keepers was the incidence of job satisfaction greater than among manual

and 700 extreme satisfaction. Hoppock, *op. cit.*, p. 255. A rather similar rank order was found by Donald Super. In his study, the percentages of satisfied workers were 85.6 for professionals, 74.2 for managerial, 41.9 for commercial (lowest white collar), 55.9 for skilled manual and 47.6 for semiskilled. However, Super's study has serious weaknesses: the sample was not chosen randomly but taken from members of hobby groups, and it overrepresented workers with high education and in high status occupations. D. Super, "Occupational Level and Job Satisfaction," *Journal of Applied Psychology*, 23 (1939), pp. 547–564.
[6] R. S. Uhrbock, "Attitudes of 4430 Employees," *Journal of Social Psychology*, 5 (1934), pp. 365–377.
[7] Centers, *op. cit.*, p. 134.
[8] Alexander R. Heron, *Why Men Work* (Stanford: Stanford University Press, 1948), pp. 71–72. A 1948 *Fortune* poll which asked the same question to *youth* between the ages of 18 to 25 found that the proportion of those who found their work interesting or enjoyable "all the time" was 85 per cent for professionals and executives, 64 per cent for white-collar workers, 59 per cent for non-factory manual labor and 41 per cent for factory labor. Cited in Lawrence G. Thomas, *The Occupational Structure and Education* (Englewood Cliffs, N. J.: Prentice-Hall, 1956), p. 201, whose summary of studies on the extent of, and occupational differences in, job satisfaction is one of the best in the literature.

workers; such lower white-collar employees as clerks, typists, and retail salespeople were somewhat less satisfied than blue-collar workers.[9]

Further evidence of the relation of job satisfaction to occupational status is provided by studies of retirement plans. Although there are a number of factors which affect the retirement decision, it is plausible to argue that the more satisfying a job is to the worker, the more likely he will choose not to retire. In a study of work and retirement in six occupations it was found that the proportion of men who wanted to continue working or had actually continued working after age sixty-five was more than 67 per cent for physicians, 65 per cent for department store salesmen, 49 per cent for skilled printers, 42 per cent for coal miners, and 32 per cent for unskilled and semiskilled steelworkers.[10]

As has been shown in the preceding section of this paper, the majority of workers in all occupations respond positively when asked whether or not they are satisfied with their jobs. But that does not mean they would not prefer other kinds of work. The average worker in a lower-status occupation says that he would choose another line of work if he had the chance to start his working life anew. This question then, is perhaps a more sensitive indicator of latent dissatisfactions and frustrations; the occupational differences it points to, though forming the same pattern as the other, are considerably greater. For example, when a survey of 13,000 Maryland youths was made during the depression it was found that 91 per cent of professional-technical workers preferred their own occupation to any other, compared to 45 per cent of managerial personnel and farm owners, 41 per cent of skilled manual workers, 37 per cent of domestic workers, 36 per cent of office and sales personnel, 14 per cent of unskilled, and 11 per cent of semiskilled manual workers.[11]

More detailed data for a number of professional and manual working class occupations strongly confirms these general findings. Note how for six different professions, the proportion of satisfied persons ranges from 82 per cent to 91 per cent, whereas for seven manual occupations it varies from 16 per cent for unskilled automobile workers to 52 per cent for skilled printers. (See Table 3).

To some extent, these findings on occupational differences in job satisfaction reflect not only differences in the objective conditions of work for people in various jobs, *but also occupational differences in the*

---

[9] Kornhauser, *Detroit* . . ., p. 55.
[10] E. A. Friedmann and R. J. Havighurst, *The Meaning of Work and Retirement* (Chicago: University of Chicago Press, 1954), p. 183.
[11] Howard M. Bell, *Youth Tell Their Story* (Washington: American Council on Education, 1938), p. 134.

norms with respect to work attitudes.[12] The professional is expected to be dedicated to his profession and have an intense intrinsic interest in his area of specialized competence; the white-collar employee is expected to be "company" oriented and like his work; but the loyalty of the manual worker is never taken for granted and, more than any other occupational type, cultural norms permit him the privilege of griping. In fact, it has been asserted that "the natural state of the industrial worker . . . is one of discontent."[13] The same point has been clearly made in an analysis of the latent function of the time clock:

> The office staff does not "clock-in"—ostensibly because they are not paid by the hour, but it seems likely that at least part of the reason for this is the supposition that, unlike labourers, they do not necessarily dislike work and can be placed on their honour to be punctual. The working classes, as we have seen, are supposed to dislike work and therefore need "discipline" to keep them in order. Since "clocking-in" has been abolished in many firms, it cannot be accepted as absolutely necessary.[14]

FACTORS THAT ACCOUNT FOR
OCCUPATIONAL DIFFERENCES IN SATISFACTION

The literature on work is filled with numerous attempts to list and often to estimate the relative importance of the various components, elements, or factors involved in job satisfaction. These lists do not correspond neatly with one another; they bear a large number of labels, but they all are likely to include, in one way or another, such variables as the income attached to a job, supervision, working conditions, social relations, and the variety and skill intrinsic in the work itself. The classification of these items is quite arbitrary and the number of factors considered relevant can be broken down almost indefinitely.[15]

Whereas most studies attempt to explain variations in job satisfaction among individual employees in the same company or occupation, the

[12] Theodore Caplow has pointed to the importance of this factor in his *The Sociology of Work* (Minneapolis: University of Minnesota Press, 1954), p. 133.
[13] F. H. Harbison, "Collective Bargaining and American Capitalism," in A. W. Kornhauser, Robert Dubin, and Arthur Ross, eds., *Industrial Conflict* (New York: McGraw-Hill, 1954), p. 278.
[14] J. C. Brown, *The Social Psychology of Industry* (Baltimore: Pelican), pp. 98–99.
[15] A summary of the findings of the hundreds of job factor studies is found in Chapter 3 of F. Herzberg, et al., *op. cit.*, pp. 37–94. A critical discussion of the methodological problems involved in the attempt to assess the relative saliency of various factors is A. W. Kornhauser, "Psychological Studies of Employee Attitudes," in S. D. Hoslett, ed., *Human Factors in Management* (Parkville, Mo.: Park College Press, 1946), pp. 305–319.

TABLE 3. *Proportion in Various Occupations Who Would Choose
Same Kind of Work if Beginning Career Again*

Professional Occupations (in percentages)		Working Class Occupations§ (in percentages)	
Mathematicians*	91	Skilled printers	52
Physicists*	89	Paper workers	52
Biologists*	89	Skilled automobile workers	41
Chemists*	86	Skilled steelworkers	41
Lawyers†	83	Textile workers	31
Journalists‡	82	Unskilled steelworkers	21
		Unskilled automobile workers	16

SOURCES:
* "The Scientists: A Group Portrait," *Fortune*, October 1948, pp. 106–112.
† "The U. S. Bar," *Fortune*, May 1939, p. 176.
‡ Leo Rosten, *The Washington Correspondents* (New York: Harcourt, 1938), p. 347.
§ These are unpublished data which have been computed from the IBM cards of a survey of 3,000 factory workers in 16 industries, conducted by Elmo Roper for *Fortune* magazine in 1947. A secondary analysis of this survey is being carried out by the Fund for the Republic's Trade Union Project. The general findings of the original study appeared in "The Fortune Survey," *Fortune*, May 1947, pp. 5–12, and June 1947, pp. 5–10.

interest of the present paper is to explain the gross differences in work attitudes that exist among those in *different* occupations and industries. Four factors that seem useful in accounting for these differences are discussed: occupational prestige, control, integrated work groups, and occupational communities.[16]

Occupational Prestige

Occupational prestige is the one best explanatory factor in the sense that if all occupations (for which sufficient data are available) were ranked in order of extent of typical job satisfaction, and these ranks were compared with the rank order in which they partake of public esteem, the rank-order correlations would be higher than those resulting from any other factor. This is because the prestige of any occupation depends on the level of skill the job entails, the degree of education or training necessary, the amount of control and responsibility involved in the performance

[16] Omission of other factors, such as skill, variety of operations, wages, and job security, does not suggest their lack of importance. But these are at once highly related to occupational prestige and control, and, at the same time, they do not seem as useful in explaining gross occupational differences.

of the work, the income which is typically received—to mention the most readily apparent factors. Since occupational prestige as a kind of composite index partly subsumes within itself a number of factors which contribute heavily to differences in satisfaction, it is not surprising that it should be itself the best individual measure of satisfaction.

In addition, jobs that have high prestige will tend to be valued for their status rewards even when "objective" aspects of the work are undesirable; similarly, low-status jobs will tend to be undervalued and disliked.

> . . . the lowliness or nastiness of a job are subjective estimates. . . . A doctor or a nurse, for example, or a sanitary inspector, have to do some things which would disgust the most unskilled casual laborer who did not see these actions in their social context. Yet the status and prestige of such people is generally high. . . . Above all, it is the prestige of his working group and his position in it which will influence the worker's attitude to such jobs.[17]

That the actual findings on differences in job satisfactions correspond quite closely to the scale of occupational prestige has been shown in the previous section. Professionals and business executives have the highest prestige in our society; they also consistently report the highest degree of work satisfaction. According to the most thorough occupational prestige study, doctors are the most esteemed major occupational group in the United States.[18] It is not surprising therefore that this public esteem is an important source of their satisfaction with their work:

> [For] physicians . . . work is a source of prestige. Some doctors stated that to be a physician meant that one belonged to an elite class. It meant that one associated with important people and was in a position of leadership in the community.[19]

Among non-professional or managerial employees, white-collar workers are generally more satisfied with their jobs than manual workers.

---

[17] Brown, *op. cit.*, pp. 149–150. One's prestige *within* an occupation or work group is paramount for job satisfaction; I ignore it in my discussion because it explains individual rather than group differences in satisfaction.

[18] When a national sample rated 90 occupations, doctors were second only to Supreme Court justices. National Opinion Research Center, "Jobs and Occupations: A Popular Evaluation," in Bendix and Lipset, eds., *Class, Status and Power* (New York: The Free Press, 1953), p. 412.

[19] Friedmann and Havighurst, *op. cit.*, p. 161. Thus "to be a doctor was to be doing the best of all possible jobs in the best of all possible professions." A consequence of the high satisfaction received from identifying oneself with a profession in such public esteem is that the doctor is reluctant to give up such identity: the authors found that, "except on rare occasions, physicians do not retire while they are in reasonably good physical condition."

Again status considerations play an important role. Even when white-collar work does not outrank manual jobs in income or skill, office workers are accorded higher social prestige than blue-collar personnel.[20]

Although this is so, manual work seems to be viewed with greater respect in America, with its democratic frontier traditions, than in many other nations.[21] The historic "social inferiority complex," the "sense of social subordination" of the European industrial worker, to use the words of Henri DeMan,[22] has never been well developed in the United States. We might expect, therefore, that the level of work satisfaction among manual workers would be higher in this country than in Europe.[23] With the rapidly increasing number of attitude surveys of European workers since the war, such a comparison would be of considerable interest.

Within the world of manual work, occupational differences in satisfaction are also related to the differences in prestige that exist among various working class jobs. The higher incidence of positive work attitudes consistently found among skilled workers is not only caused by the skill factor per se; the craftsman takes pride in the fact that he is looked on with more respect in the community than the factory operative or the unskilled laborer.[24] Moreover, those manual workers in occupations which are particularly looked down on will find difficulty in deriving overall positive satisfactions in their work. Interviewers of coal miners have remarked on the great pride with which they are shown various home improvements made possible by the higher wages of a period of prosperity, and on the sensitivity with which some miners react to the public image of the occupation, which has been, in part, created by the hostility of the mass media to the militancy of the union.

[20] See Lipset and Bendix, *Social Mobility in Industrial Society* (Berkeley: University of California Press, 1959), pp. 14–17.
[21] Now a rather stock generalization, Werner Sombart was evidently one of the first to state it.
[22] H. DeMan, *Joy in Work* (London: G. Allen, 1929), pp. 59–60, 208–209.
[23] On the other hand, when the norms of an "open society" encourage *all* to strive for upward advancement, large numbers of people who do not succeed will feel dissatisfied and frustrated, as the sociologist Robert Merton has emphasized in his "Social Structure and Anomie." See Merton, *Social Theory and Social Structure* (New York: The Free Press, 1957), pp. 131–160. In Europe, manual workers have more distinctive class cultures and reference groups than in America; therefore they are probably much less likely to subscribe to the advancement norms of the whole society. Consideration of this factor alone would suggest *less* dissatisfaction with jobs and occupational status in Europe.
[24] Friedmann and Havighurst found this to be true among the printers they studied, *op. cit.*, pp. 176–177. It has been noted that Chicago plumbers, who express a high level of work satisfaction, often stress their function of "protecting public sanitation" and compare their contribution to community health with that of doctors. Joel Seidman, et al., *The Worker Views His Union* (Chicago: University of Chicago Press, 1958), pp. 52–53.

I don't like to strike, because people all get mad at the miners then. I wish the people would realize that the miner has to live too, and not hate him when he tries to better conditions for himself. It bothers me the way people say bad things about the miners, and makes me ashamed of my job.[25]

An attempt has been made to illustrate the manner in which variations in work satisfaction among different occupations tend to follow variations in occupational prestige. Although this generalization is, to an impressive extent, supported by the evidence, it does not hold unfailingly. We can note occupations with relatively high prestige whose general level of satisfaction is lower than would be expected, whereas some low-status jobs seem to be highly satisfying. This suggests that in certain cases other factors play a role even more important than status. A good test of the approach applied here is to see whether the other factors which have been advanced as critical ones can indeed account for discrepancies in the generally marked association between occupational prestige and job satisfaction.

Control

In a perceptive passage, the Belgian socialist Henri DeMan remarks that "all work is felt to be coercive."[26] The fact that work inherently involves a surrender of control, a "subordination of the worker to remoter aims," is probably what makes the relative degree of control in work so important an aspect of job attitudes. As Max Weber, the German sociologist, suggested long ago, "no man easily yields to another full control over the effort, and especially over the amount of physical effort he must daily exert."[27]

---

[25] Quotation from an interview with a coal miner in Friedmann and Havighurst, *op. cit.*, pp. 73–76. I do not intend to give the impression that the above is a representative quotation; the typical reaction seems to be an overt rejection of the anti-union media and public image. However, it seems likely that such feelings as the above might still haunt the average worker who would never express them. The role of the coal miner's "occupational community" in insulating him from these derogatory evaluations is discussed later in this paper.

[26] DeMan, *op. cit.*, p. 67. "Even the worker who is free in the social sense, the peasant or the handicraftsman, feels this compulsion, were it only because while he is at work, his activities are dominated and determined by the aim of his work, by the idea of a willed or necessary creation. Work inevitably signifies subordination of the worker to remoter aims, felt to be necessary, and therefore involving a renunciation of the freedoms and enjoyments of the present for the sake of a future advantage."

[27] E. C. Hughes, *Men and Their Work* (New York: The Free Press, 1959), pp. 47–48. William Foote Whyte has put it in more general terms, "No normal person is happy in a situation which he cannot control to some extent." *Money and Motivation* (New York: Harper & Row, 1955), p. 94.

There seem to be significant cultural as well as individual differences in the need for control and independence in work. In America, where individual initiative has long been a cultural ideal, we would expect strong pressures in this direction. And we do find that surprising proportions of manual workers in this country have attempted to succeed in small business,[28] and that for many others the idea of running a gas station or a number of tourist cabins is a compelling dream.[29]

Lack of control over the conditions of work is most pronounced for industrial workers.

> The very evidence of his daily work life brings home to the manual worker the degree to which he is directed in his behavior with only limited free choices available. From the moment of starting work by punching a time clock, through work routines that are established at fixed times, until the day ends at the same mechanical time recorder, there is impressed upon the industrial worker his narrow niche in a complex and ordered system of interdependency . . . a system over which he, as an individual, exercises little direct control.[30]

The factory worker is at the bottom of the bureaucratic hierarchy; he is a person for whom action is constantly being originated, but who himself originates little activity for others.[31]

At the same time, diverse factory jobs and working class occupations vary greatly in the degree of control they permit over the conditions of work: it is these variations, of which workers are keenly aware, that are most interesting for the purpose of accounting for differences in satisfaction.

---

[28] Twenty-three per cent of the manual workers in a labor force sample in Oakland, California, had been in business at some time during their work history. Lipset and Bendix, *Social Mobility in Industrial Society*, p. 179. Cultural differences in aspirations for independence and control in work as well as differing economic opportunities are suggested in the contrast between British and American opinion poll data. Fifty-one per cent of the Americans questioned wanted to start their own business compared to only 33 per cent of the Britons; Americans were also considerably more likely to say they would actually do so. Hadley Cantril, *Public Opinion 1935-1946* (Princeton: Princeton University Press, 1951), p. 528.

[29] See especially Ely Chinoy, *Automobile Workers and the American Dream* (New York: Doubleday, 1955). He quotes a machine operator: "The main thing is to be independent and give your own orders and not have to take them from anybody else. That's the reason the fellows in the shop all want to start their own business. Then the profits are all for yourself. When you're in the shop there's nothing for yourself in it. So you just do what you have to in order to get along. A fellow would rather do it for himself. If you expend the energy, it's for your own benefit then," pp. xvi–xvii.

[30] Dubin, "Constructive Aspects of Industrial Conflict," in Kornhauser, Dubin, and Ross, *op. cit.*, p. 43.

[31] W. F. Whyte, *op. cit.*, p. 234.

The notion of control in work, as I am using it, is, of course, a vague, *sensitizing* concept which covers a wide range of phenomena rather than a concept which is precisely delimited and identifiable by precise indicators. Among its most important dimensions are control over the use of one's *time* and physical *movement,* which is fundamentally control over the *pace* of the work process, control over the *environment,* both technical and social, and control as the *freedom* from *hierarchal authority.* Naturally, these dimensions are highly interrelated; a business executive high on the occupational ladder will tend to be high in each, whereas an unskilled laborer will have little control from any of these viewpoints. *It is possible to generalize on the basis of the evidence that the greater the degree of control that a worker has (either in a single dimension or as a total composite) the greater his job satisfaction.*[32]

CONTROL OVER TIME, PHYSICAL MOVEMENT, AND PACE OF WORK. Assembly line work in the automobile industry is a good example of the almost complete absence of this aspect of control.

> Its coerced rhythms, the inability to pause at will for a moment's rest, and the need for undeviating attention to simple routines made it work to be avoided if possible and to escape from if necessary. So demanding is the line that one worker, echoing others, complained: "You get the feeling, everybody gets the feeling, whenever the line jerks everybody is wishing, 'break down, baby!' "[33]

The consensus of the work literature is that assembly line work, especially in the automobile industry, is more disliked than any other major occupation, and the prime factor in dissatisfaction with the assembly line is the lack of control over the pace of production.[34] Workers in assembly line plants have strong preferences for jobs off the line. A study of the job aspirations of 180 men on the line found that the "workers' motivations were not what might normally be expected. It was not promotion or transfer in order to improve one's economic status. Rather, it was

---

[32] Control, of course, is not independent of the other factors. The relationship between occupational status and control is particularly marked; in fact, the (status) "hierarchy is a direct reflection of freedom from control. . . ." Edward Gross, *Work and Society* (New York: Crowell, 1958), p. 428. The relationship of control to skill is intimate; in fact, skill may be conceived as a form of control over the technological process of work. Finally, control is related to integrated work teams. An important result of the pioneering research of Elton Mayo and his colleagues was the increased awareness that the informal work group, in setting and enforcing informal production standards, gives many industrial workers some control over their job situations.

[33] Chinoy, *op. cit.,* p. 71.

[34] C. R. Walker and Robert H. Guest, *Man on the Assembly Line* (Cambridge: Harvard University Press, 1952), p. 62.

primarily a desire 'to get away from the line.' " *Only 8 per cent* were satisfied, in the sense of not preferring to get an off-line job.[35] The difference between line and off-line jobs has been clearly stated by the sociologist Ely Chinoy who worked in an automobile plant and studied automobile workers:

> Work at a machine may be just as repetitive, require as few mo-
> tions and as little thought as line assembly, but men prefer it because it
> does not keep them tied as tightly to their tasks. "I can stop occasionally
> when I want to," said a machine-operator. "I couldn't do that when
> I was on the line." Production standards for a particular machine may
> be disliked and felt to be excessive, but the machine operator need only
> approximate his production quota each day. The line-tender must do
> all the work that the endless belt brings before him. . . .[36]

The greater dissatisfaction with mass production assembly line jobs is confirmed by the findings in an automobile plant that "men with highly repetitive jobs, conveyor paced, and so forth, were far more likely to take time off from work than those whose jobs did not contain such job characteristics," and that quit rates were almost twice as high among men on the assembly line as among men off the line.[37] In a study of Maryland youth during the depression, it was found that the occupation most disliked by female workers was that of operator on cannery conveyor belts. Every one of the fifty-three cannery operatives in the sample expressed a preference for different work![38] The control of these workers over the pace of production is at least as minimal as that of automobile workers, and in addition they lack even the protection of a strong union.

A machine operator may go all out in the morning to produce 100 pieces, take it easy in the afternoon, only putting out 50; at any rate, it is his own decision. In similar fashion a few assembly line workers may be able to build up a "bank" of automobile seats which they assemble to the oncoming bodies; a few try to get ahead and gain time for rest by working up the line, but for the great majority it is hopeless. Assembly line workers are "alienated," according to the researchers who have studied them. In their work they "can secure little significant experience of themselves as productive human beings." As one automobile worker put it a little wistfully:

> You understand, if you get a job that you're interested in, when you
> work you don't pay attention to the time, you don't wait for the whistle

[35] *Ibid.*, pp. 113, 110.
[36] Chinoy, *op. cit.*, pp. 71–72.
[37] Walker and Guest, *op. cit.*, pp. 120, 116–117.
[38] Bell, *op. cit.*, p. 135.

to blow to go home, you're all wrapped up in it and don't pay attention to other things. *I don't know one single job like that.*[39]

According to David Riesman, what these wage earners are deprived of is "any chance to extend themselves, to go all-out." A stark example is the worker on the packinghouse assembly line who goes home after his day's work in order to "try to accomplish something for that day."[40] How do these workers stand it? Here is the deadly answer of a Hormel meat worker: "The time passes."

> Most workers are so busily engaged in pushing the flow of work that they do not *consciously* suffer from the inherent monotony of their work. They are well adjusted, because they have reduced their level of aspirations to the rather low level of the job. They coast along, keeping busy, visiting, talking, making time go by, and getting the work done in order to get "out of there" in order to get home![41]

The great dissatisfaction with automobile assembly work is an example of a discrepancy between occupational status and job satisfaction. The status of the automobile worker is not lower than that of other semiskilled American factory workers; in fact, the level of wages would suggest that it is higher than manual workers in many other industrial occupations, especially those in non-durable goods manufacturing. But the control of the automobile assembly line worker over the work process is considerably less than in other major industrial occupations, and this is a big factor in accounting for the prevalence of job discontent.

It is interesting to contrast automobile manufacturing with mining, an occupation which, though considered lower in prestige,[42] seems to provide marked work satisfaction. Alvin Gouldner, in his study of a gypsum plant, found that although the miners had considerably less status in the community than surface workers, they showed much greater work motivation. He attributed this high job satisfaction to the fact that miners

> . . . were not "alienated" from their machines: that is, they had an unusually high degree of control over their machines' operation. The pace at which the machines worked, the corners into which they were poked, what happened to them when they broke down, was determined

---

[39] Chinoy, *op. cit.*, p. 70.
[40] Fred H. Blum, *Toward a Democratic Work Process* (New York: Harper & Row, 1953), p. 96.
[41] *Ibid.*, p. 85.
[42] In the North-Hatt occupational prestige study, "Machine operator in a factory" (the category closest in social meaning to an auto worker) ranked 65th in prestige among 90 occupations, considerably higher than "coal miner" which was ranked 77th. Most people ranked machine operator in a factory as "average" in general standing, and coal miners as "somewhat below average" or "poor."

mainly by the miners themselves. On the surface, though, the speed at which the machines worked and the procedures followed were prescribed by superiors.[43]

Finally, the higher job satisfaction of skilled workers (documented in the preceding sections of this paper) is related to the fact that they have a large measure of control over the pace of their work. The fact that craftsmen themselves largely determine the speed at which they work gives them a marked advantage over most factory workers.[44]

CONTROL OVER THE TECHNICAL AND SOCIAL ENVIRONMENT. In those occupations in which the physical environment or the technological work process is particularly challenging, control over it seems to be an important aspect of job satisfaction. Coal miners have "a very personal sense of being pitted against their environment" and express "feelings of accomplishment and pride at having conquered it."[45] That steel production is found fascinating is suggested by a mill worker: "It's sort of interesting. Sometimes you have a battle on your hands. You have to use your imagination and ability to figure out what move to make."[46] Similarly, it has been noted that railroad workers derive a sense of power in "the manipulation of many tons of railroad equipment." Engineers derive more pleasure in running large engines rather than small ones; switchmen and brakeman "give the signals that move fifty or so freight cars back and forth like so many toys."[47]

A further source of the dissatisfaction with automobile assembly, then, is the fact that these jobs provide so little scope for control over the technical environment; there is little that is challenging in the actual work operation. As a man on the line puts it:

> There is nothing more discouraging than having a barrel beside you with 10,000 bolts in it and using them all up. Then you get a barrel with another 10,000 bolts, and you know that every one of those 10,000 bolts has to be picked up and put in exactly the same place as the last 10,000 bolts.[48]

Paralleling the control of industrial workers over the technical environment is the satisfaction derived by professional and white-collar em-

[43] Alvin W. Gouldner, *Patterns of Industrial Bureaucracy* (New York: The Free Press, 1954), pp. 140–141.
[44] Seidman, et al., *op. cit.*, p. 55.
[45] Friedmann and Havighurst, *op. cit.*, p. 176.
[46] C. R. Walker, *Steeltown* (New York: Harper & Row, 1950), p. 61.
[47] John Spier, "Elements of Job Satisfaction in the Railroad Operating Crafts," unpublished paper, Berkeley, California, 1959.
[48] Walker and Guest, *op. cit.*, p. 54.

ployees from control over a social environment, namely, clients and customers. A study of salespeople concluded that "the completion of the sale, the conquering of the customer, represents the challenge or the 'meaningful life-experience' of selling."[49] As one salesclerk, contemplating the import of his retirement, said: "I think to be perfectly truthful about it, the thing I miss most is being able to project myself into a sphere, conquer it, and retire with a pleased feeling because I have conquered it."[50]

CONTROL AS THE FREEDOM FROM DIRECT SUPERVISION. On a slightly different level of analysis is this third dimension, which refers not to the aspects of the work process under control, but rather to the locus of control. One of the most consistent findings of work research is that industrial workers consider light, infrequent supervision, "foremen who aren't drivers," a crucial element in their high regard for particular jobs and companies.

The absence of close supervision in the mines has been considered an important determinant of the miners' high level of satisfaction.[51] And truck drivers and railroad workers, in explaining their preference for their own trades, stress the independence they experience in these jobs where the contact between employees and supervisor is so much less frequent than in factory work. As two railroad engineers put it:

> I'd work anywhere except at a shop or in the factory. Just don't like a place where someone is watching you do your work all the time. That's why I like my job on the railroad now.
> I wouldn't last three days working in a shop with a foreman breathing down my neck. Here I'm my own boss when I run the trains, nobody tells me what to do. . . .[52]

Such impressionistic evidence is confirmed by the more systematic comparisons of Hoppock, who found that the mean job satisfaction index of railroad employees ranked only below professional men and artists; it was higher than managers, clerical workers, small business proprietors, salesmen, and storeclerks! Although railroading is a high-status industrial occupation—railroaders have historically been part of the labor aristocracy —its occupational prestige is below most white-collar occupations. On the other hand, truck driving is a lower-status manual occupation (truck drivers are classified as semiskilled operatives by the census, and the popular stereotypes of this occupation are somewhat derogatory), and yet

[49] Friedmann and Havighurst, op. cit., p. 178.
[50] Ibid., p. 106.
[51] Gouldner, op. cit., pp. 55 ff. Seidman, et al., op. cit., p. 23.
[52] Reynolds and Shister, op. cit., pp. 13–14.

in the Hoppock survey the satisfaction of truck drivers outranked all industrial occupations except railroading and was approximately the same level as that of salesmen.[53]

It is plausible that the marked discrepancy between job satisfaction and occupational status in these industries can be explained by the high degree of control, especially as reflected in freedom from supervision, which the workers enjoy.

If control in the work process is a crucial determinant of a worker's subjective feelings of well-being on the job, as I am trying to demonstrate, the question whether industrial trends are increasing or decreasing these areas of control becomes quite significant. It is interesting that Faunce's recent study of an *automated* engine plant shows that various dimensions of control may not change in the same direction. Compared to work in a non-automated, non-assembly line engine plant, automation greatly decreased the worker's direct control over his machine and pace of work, and this was felt to be a source of serious dissatisfaction. On the other hand, the increased responsibility and control over a complex technical environment of automated equipment was seen as a source of greater satisfaction and heightened status. Thus, while Faunce was able to locate the elements which made for satisfaction and those which made for dissatisfaction in these jobs (his analysis seems very congruent with the present discussion), it was rather difficult to assess the overall effect of the change on work satisfaction.[54]

Integrated Work Groups

A third factor that is important in explaining occupational differences in work satisfaction is the nature of on-the-job social relations. The technological structure of certain industries such as steel production and mining requires that the work be carried out by *teams* of men working closely together, whereas in industries such as automobile assembly the formation of regular work groups is virtually prohibited by the organization of production. There is much evidence to support the proposition that the greater the extent to which workers are members of integrated work teams on the job, the higher the level of job satisfaction.

In a steel mill in which 85 per cent of sixty-two workers interviewed

[53] Hoppock, *op. cit.*, pp. 225 ff. In Bell's Maryland youth survey the majority in all occupational categories except professionals preferred a different kind of job. However, the proportion of truck drivers who were so "discontented" was less than that of clerks, salespersons, farm laborers, and operatives in clothing and textiles. Bell, *op. cit.*, p. 135.
[54] William A. Faunce, "Automation and the Automobile Worker," in Galenson and Lipset (eds.), *Labor and Trade Unionism* (New York: Wiley, 1960), pp. 370–379.

were satisfied with their jobs, Charles Walker found that "the source of satisfaction most often articulated or implied was that of being part of, or having membership in, the hot mill crew." As three steel workers express it:

> (A heater helper) We work for a while, it's like playing baseball. First one fellow is up and then you have your turn at bat. We can knock off every so often and take a smoke and talk. I like working with men I know and working like a team.
> (A piercer plugger) The crew I am in is very good. Our foreman likes to see his men on top and he does everything to help us . . . this attitude makes a lot of people put out more steel. . . . Over here it's teamwork. . . . You can have a lot of Hank Greenbergs on the team but if you don't work together, it isn't a team at all. And we like our work because we carry on a lot of conversation with signs and the men laugh and joke and the time passes very quick.
> (A piercer dragout worker) There's nothing like working here in this mill. Everybody cooperates. Every man works as a member of a team and every man tries to turn out as much steel as they possibly can. We work hard and get satisfaction out of working hard.[55]

While recognizing that close kinship ties and a small town atmosphere encouraged such cooperative spirit, Walker attributed the principal cause of the integrated work teams to the basic technological process of making steel, which requires small group operations. He compared this technology and its results with that of the automobile assembly plants in which the technological structure is such that the majority of workers perform their operations individually. There, the pattern of social interaction produced by the moving line is such that although workers will talk to the man in front of them, behind them, and across from them, no worker will interact with exactly the same group of men as any other worker will; therefore, no stable work groups are formed. Walker considered this a major element in the greater dissatisfaction he found among automobile workers compared to steel workers.

Mining is another occupation where technological conditions seem to favor the development of closely knit work groups. Since, as one miner expressed it, "the mines are kind of a family affair," where "the quality of the sentiment is of a depth and complexity produced only by long years of intimate association," it is not surprising that many miners feel that the loss of social contacts at work is a major disadvantage of retirement. The dangerous nature of the work is another factor that knits miners together:

55 Walker, *op. cit.*, pp. 66–67.

To be an old-timer in the mines means something more than merely knowing the technique of a particular job; it also means awareness and acceptance of the responsibility which each man has for his fellow-workers. The sense of interdependence in relation to common dangers is undoubtedly an important factor in the spirit of solidarity which has characterized miners in all countries for many generations.[56]

Within the same factory, departments and jobs vary considerably in the extent to which the work is carried out by individuals working alone or by groups; the consequences of these differences have been a major interest of the "human relations in industry" movement. A recent study of one department in a factory manufacturing rotating equipment found that the employees who were integrated members of informal work groups were, by and large, satisfied with both the intrinsic characteristics of their jobs, and such "extended characteristics" as pay, working conditions, and benefits, whereas the non-group members tended to be dissatisfied. Sixty-five per cent of "regular" group members were satisfied, compared to 43 per cent of members of groups which were deviant in accepting less fully the values of the factory community, and compared to only 28 per cent of isolated workers.[57]

The classic investigations of the functions of informal work groups in industry have been produced by the "human relations in industry" school, associated most directly with the Harvard Business School and the writings of Elton Mayo, and represented by the pioneering experiments at the Hawthorne plant of the Western Electric Company.[58] These studies have demonstrated that informal work groups establish and enforce norms which guide the productive and other behavior of workers on the job, and that such management problems as absenteeism, turnover, and morale can often be dealt with through the manipulation of work groups and supervisorial behavior. But it is striking that the human relations school has

[56] Friedmann and Havighurst, op. cit., pp. 65, 90–91.
[57] A. Zaleznik, C. R. Christensen, and F. J. Roethslisberger, The Motivation, Productivity and Satisfaction of Workers: A Prediction Study (Cambridge: Harvard University, 1958), pp. 258–277. In this factory the most important thing in accounting for group membership was ethnicity: the Irish workers tended to be the integrated members of "regular groups," while the non-Irish employees were by and large isolates or in deviant groups.
[58] The most complete account of this study appears in F. J. Roethslisberger and W. J. Dickson, Management and the Worker (Cambridge: Harvard University Press, 1939). Other accounts of the research of the Mayo school may be found in Elton Mayo and George F. Lombard, Teamwork and Labor Turnover in the Aircraft Industry of Southern California (Cambridge: Harvard University Graduate School of Business Administration, 1944); Elton Mayo, The Human Problems of an Industrial Civilization (New York: Macmillan, 1933); and The Social Problems of an Industrial Civilization (Cambridge: Harvard University Graduate School of Business Administration, 1946).

concerned itself so little with the job itself, with the relation between the worker and his work, rather than the relation between the worker and his mates.[59] A typical human relations discussion of the conditions of employee morale is likely to give all its emphasis to matters of communication, supervision, and the personality of workers and ignore almost completely intrinsic job tasks.[60] In a recent study by the Harvard Business School entitled *Worker Satisfaction and Development,* the only sources of work satisfaction discussed are those which directly concern workers' integration in work groups and cliques. Although creativity is a major concern of the author, it is the creativity of the *work group* to adapt to new circumstances, rather than the creative expression of an individual in his work, that he is interested in.[61]

In its emphasis on the importance of integrated work groups the human relations approach has made an important contribution. But "a way of seeing is a way of not seeing," and its neglect of the other factors imposes serious limitations on the usefulness of this approach, at least in providing an adequate theory of the conditions of work satisfaction.[62]

---

[59] It is difficult to determine whether this neglect stems from an implicit assumption that work tasks are sufficiently challenging for basically "non-rational" workers, or conversely, from a view that the alienation of the worker from his work is so immutable that one must concentrate instead on engineering work groups and supervision, since these are amenable to change. From a history of ideas point of view the most important source of this neglect is probably the intellectual heritage of Elton Mayo, who was greatly influenced by Emile Durkheim's theory of the increasing atomization of modern society and the consequent growth of *anomie.* Whereas Marx saw the solution to the modern social problem in the "restoration" to the worker of control over his conditions of work, Durkheim rather saw it in the reintegration of individuals into solidary social groups which could buttress the individual from the pressures of the mass state and, in addition, provide personal equilibrium and security. Mayo, in following Durkheim rather than Marx, ignores almost completely the relation of the worker to his work and concentrates instead on his integration into small work groups as a condition of industrial harmony and social health.

[60] For example, Robert N. McMurray, "Management Mentalities and Worker Reactions," in Hoslett, *op. cit.,* especially his discussion of the morale study of J. D. Houser.

[61] A. Zaleznik, *Worker Satisfaction and Development* (Cambridge: Harvard University Business School, 1956). A smiliar case in point is the excellent study of an Indian textile mill by A. K. Rice of the London Tavistock Institute. In his theoretical discussion, Rice gives equal weight to three dimensions of work satisfaction: psychological closure or the doing of a complete task, responsibility and control over the task, and work group integration. But in presenting his findings, Rice ignores almost completely the first two intrinsic job dimensions and concentrates on the work group factor. *Productivity and Social Organization: The Ahmedabad Experiment* (London: Tavistock Publications, 1958).

[62] For a summary of the major theoretical and ideological criticisms that have been made of the Mayo School, see Henry A. Landsberger, *Hawthorne Revisited* (Ithaca: Cornell University Press, 1958), especially Chapter III.

Occupational Communities

The nature of the association among workers *off-the-job* is also a factor in work satisfaction. The evidence of the work literature supports the notion that levels of work satisfaction are higher in those industries and in those kinds of jobs in which workers make up an "occupational community." One such industry is mining. Not only is the actual work carried out by solidary work groups, but, in addition, miners live in a community made up largely of fellow workers. This kind of "inbreeding" produces a devotion to the occupation which is not characteristic of many other working class jobs:

> Somehow when you get into mining and you like the men you work with, you just get to the place after a while that you don't want to leave. *Once that fever gets hold of a man, he'll never be good for anything else.*
>
> A fellow may quit the mines, but when they whistle, he goes back. I've had a lot better jobs, but I've always liked to work in the mines. I can't explain it, except I like being with the gang; I never could just sit around much.[63]

Such occupational communities are likely to develop in occupations that are isolated, either spatially or on the basis of peculiar hours of work. Coal mining and textile industries characteristically have grown up in *isolated small communities*; sailors, cowboys, and long-distance truck drivers are also isolated from contact with persons in other jobs. Similarly, *off-hours shifts* favor the development of occupational communities; this is the case with printers, a large proportion of whom work nights,[64] steelworkers, who often rotate between day, swing, and graveyard shifts, firemen, and, of course, railroad men.

The essential feature of an occupational community is that workers in their off-hours socialize more with persons in their own line of work than with a cross section of occupational types. Printers generally go to bars, movies, and baseball games with other printers.[65] In a small town

[63] Friedmann and Havighurst, *op. cit.*, pp. 70–71.
[64] The most thorough analysis of an occupational community is the study of the printers by S. M. Lipset, M. Trow, and J. Coleman, *Union Democracy* (New York: The Free Press, 1956). This section is considerably indebted to the insights of these authors. An important discussion of occupational communities in another context is C. Kerr and A. Siegel, "The Inter-Industry Propensity to Strike," in Kornhauser, Dubin, and Ross, *op. cit.*, pp. 189–212. They argue that the fact that workers in these occupations form an "isolated mass" and are not integrated into the society as a whole encourages militant strike activity.
[65] Lipset, Trow, and Coleman, *op. cit.*

steel mill, 87 per cent of the workers had spent "in the last week," at least some time off the job with other workers in their department; almost half said they had seen many or almost all of their fellow workers.[66] However, in a large tractor plant of 20,000 people only 41 per cent of the employees said that they got together socially outside the plant with employees from their own work groups.[67] *Occupational communities rarely exist among urban factory workers.*

A second characteristic of an occupational community is that its participants "talk shop" in their off-hours. That this is true of farmers, fishermen, miners, and railroaders has been described far more by novelists than by social scientists. The significance of talking about work off the job has been well expressed by Fred Blum, who notes that the assembly line workers in the meat packing plant he studied rarely do so:

> Whether they are with their family or their friends, rare are the occasions when workers feel like talking about their work. In response to the question: "Do you talk with your friends about the work you are doing?" only a very small number indicated that they do talk with their friends—or their wife—about their work. Quite a few said that they "only" talk with their friends "if they ask me" or that they talk "sometimes" or "seldom." Some workers are outspoken in saying that they do not like to talk about their work. "If we get out of there, we are through with that to the next day." Another worker said, "When I leave down there, I am through down there. I like to talk about something else." *He adds to this with some astonishment: "Railroadmen always want to talk about their work."*[68]

Third, occupational communities are little worlds in themselves. For its members the occupation itself is the reference group; its standards of behavior, its system of status and rank, guide conduct.[69]

Railroading is something more than an occupation. Like thieving and music, it is a world by itself, with its own literature and mythology, with an irrational system of status which is unintelligible to the outsider, and a complicated rule book for distributing responsibility and rewards.[70]

We can suggest a number of mechanisms by means of which occupa-

[66] Walker, *op. cit.*, pp. 111–112.
[67] Daniel Katz, "Satisfactions and Deprivations in Industrial Life," in Kornhauser, Dubin, and Ross, *op. cit.*, p. 102.
[68] Blum, *op. cit.*, pp. 96–97. My emphasis.
[69] The French sociologist Emile Durkheim felt that occupational communities which he termed "corporations" were the one agency which could provide stable norms for individuals living in an essentially normless society. See the preface to the second edition, *The Division of Labor in Society* (New York: The Free Press, 1949).
[70] Caplow, *op. cit.*, p. 96.

tional communities increase job satisfaction.[71] First, when workers know their co-workers off the job, they will derive deeper social satisfactions on the job. In the second place, an effect of the isolation of the occupation is that workers are able to develop and maintain a pride in and devotion to their line of work; at the same time, isolation insulates them from having to come to grips with the general public's image of their status, which is likely to be considerably lower than their own. Participation in an occupational community means not only the reinforcement of the group's sense of general prestige; in such worlds one's skill and expertise in doing the actual work becomes an important basis of individual status and prestige. Finally, unlike the "alienated" assembly line worker, who is characterized by a separation of his work sphere from his non-work sphere—a separation of work from life as Mills and Blum put it—the work and leisure interests of those in occupational communities are highly integrated. If the integration of work and non-work is an important element in general psychic adjustment, as some assert, then these workers should exhibit higher job satisfaction since satisfaction with life in general seems to be highly related to satisfaction in work.[72]

CONCLUSIONS

When we read modern accounts of what work and workers were like before the industrial revolution, we continually find that the dominant image of the worker of that period is the craftsman. Viewed as an independent producer in his home or small shop with complete control over the pace and scheduling of his work, making the whole product rather than a part of it, and taking pride in the creativity of his skilled tasks, his traits are typically contrasted with those of the alienated factory worker—the allegedly characteristic producer of modern society.[73]

It is remarkable what an enormous impact this *contrast* of the craftsman with the factory hand has had on intellectual discussions of work and workers in modern society, *notwithstanding its lack of correspondence to*

---

[71] The reverse process, high job satisfaction leading to high participation in an occupational community, has been described by Lipset and his colleagues in their study of union printers. Lipset, et al., *op. cit.*, pp. 124–126.

[72] Evidence on this point is reviewed in Herzberg, et al., *op. cit.*, pp. 17–20.

[73] Marx' classic characterization is the best known: "Owing to the extensive use of machinery and to the division of labor, the work of the proletarians has lost all individual character, and consequently, all charm for the workman. He becomes an appendage of the machine, and it is only the most simple, most monotonous, and most easily acquired knack, that is required of him." But almost identical accounts abound in the writings of non-Marxist intellectuals. Compare Adriano Tilgher, *Work: What It Has Meant to Men Through the Ages* (New York: Harcourt, 1930), p. 151, and Henry Durant, *The Problem of Leisure* (London: Routledge, 1938), pp. 6 ff.

present and historical realities. For, indeed, craftsmen, far from being typical workers of the past era, accounted for less than 10 per cent of the medieval labor force, and the peasant, who was actually the representative laborer, was, in the words of the Belgian socialist Henri DeMan, "practically nothing more than a working beast."[74] Furthermore, the real character of the craftsman's work has been romanticized by the prevalent tendency to idealize the past, whereas much evidence suggests that modern work does not fit the black portrait of meaningless alienation. In fact, it has been asserted "that in modern society there is far greater scope for skill and craftsmanship than in any previous society, and that far more people are in a position to use such skills.[75]

For intellectuals, it seems to be particularly difficult to grasp both the subjective and relative character of monotony and the capacity of workers to inject meaning into "objectively meaningless" work. Their strong tendency to view workers as dissatisfied suggests the idea that the alienation thesis, though a direct descendant of Marxist theory and related to a particular political posture, also reflects an intellectual perspective (in the sociology of knowledge sense) on manual work.

Surprisingly enough, business executives also tend to view manual workers as alienated. Perhaps this attitude reflects, in part, the growing influence of intellectual ideas, including neo-Marxist ones, on the more progressive business circles; perhaps, more importantly, this stems again, as in the case of the intellectual, from the middle-class businessman's separation and distance from the workaday world of his industrial employees. At any rate, such industrial spokesmen as Peter Drucker and Alexander Heron are likely to generalize much as does James Worthy of Sears Roebuck, who, in discussing "overfunctionalization," has written:

> The worker cannot see that total process, he sees only the small and uninteresting part to which he and his fellows are assigned. In a real sense, the job loses its meaning for the worker—the meaning, that is, in all terms except the pay envelope.

[74] DeMan, *op. cit.,* p. 146. The 10 per cent estimate is from Brown, *op. cit.,* p. 24.
[75] Brown, *op. cit.,* p. 207. A leading advocate of the alienation thesis, the French industrial sociologist Georges Friedmann, was unable to find any decline in the proportion of skilled workers in selected German, French, and English industries during the early years of the twentieth century. *Industrial Society* (New York: The Free Press, 1955), p. 200. Statistics of the American labor force show that the proportion of skilled workers has risen considerably since 1940 and is expected to continue rising; the proportion of unskilled laborers has been declining consistently since 1920. Semiskilled operatives, the largest manual category, increased the fastest until 1940. The increase since then has been negligible and it is expected that this group will decline in the future. *The most striking change in occupational composition, reflecting a general upgrading in skill, is the increase in the proportions of clerical and professional workers.* U. S. Department of Labor, Bureau of Labor Statistics, Bulletin 1215, *Occupational Outlook Handbook, 1957,* pp. 34–35.

Thus a very large number of employees in American industry today have been deprived of the sense of performing interesting, significant work. In consequence, they have little feeling of responsibility for the tasks to which they are assigned.[76]

But, *work has significant positive meanings to persons who do not find overall satisfaction in their immediate job.* A still viable consequence of the Protestant ethic in our society is that its work ethic (the notion of work as a calling, an obligation to one's family, society, and self-respect, if no longer to God), retains a powerful hold. This is most dramatically seen in the reactions of the retired and unemployed. The idea is quite common to American workers at all occupational levels that soon after a worker retires, he is likely to either "drop dead" or "go crazy" from sheer inactivity.[77] An English industrial psychiatrist states that this is actually a common calamity in British industry.[78] Similarly, the studies made in the 1930's of unemployed people show that the disruption of the work relationship often leads to the disruption of normal family relations, to political apathy, and to a lack of interest in social organizations and leisure-time activities.[79]

The studies of job satisfaction reviewed in this paper further question the prevailing thesis that most workers in modern society are alienated and estranged. There is a remarkable consistency in the findings that the vast majority of workers, in virtually all occupations and industries, are moderately or highly satisfied, rather than dissatisfied, with their jobs.

---

[76] James C. Worthy, "Organizational Structure and Employee Morale," *American Sociological Review*, 15 (1950), p. 175. Cf. Peter Drucker, *Concept of the Corporation* (John Day, 1946), p. 179, and Heron, *op. cit.*

[77] Morse and Weiss, *op. cit.*, p. 192; Friedmann and Havighurst, *op. cit.*, pp. 89, 162, 36 ff. Eric Hoffer notes that death rates increased among older longshoremen when a retirement plan was put into effect. A convention of general practitioners recently advised against compulsory retirement on this basis. See *SF Chronicle*, October 7, 1958. That this may be more of a stereotyped notion than a fact is suggested by the directors of the Cornell Study of Occupational Retirement who found in a panel of more than 1,000 males of the same age that those who retired were more likely to *improve* in health, while those who remained working were more likely to decline in health. Wayne E. Thompson and Gordon F. Streib, "Situational Determinants: Health and Economic Deprivation in Retirement," *Journal of Social Issues*, XIV (1958), pp. 18–34.

[78] Brown, *op. cit.*, p. 190.

[79] See E. W. Blake, *Citizens Without Work* (New Haven: Yale University Press, 1940), and *The Unemployed Man* (New York: Dutton, 1934); M. Jahoda-Lazarsfeld and H. Zeisel, *Die Arbeitslosen von Marienthal* (Leipzig: Psychologische Monographien: 1933); Mirra Komarovsky, *The Unemployed Man and His Family* (New York: Dryden Press, 1940). Daniel Bell in considering the possibilities of automation has raised the question: "Work, said Freud, was the chief means of binding an individual to reality. What will happen, then, when not only the worker but work itself is displaced by the machine?" *Work and Its Discontents* (Boston: Beacon, 1956), p. 56.

However, the marked occupational differences in work attitudes and the great significance which workers impute to being, at least to some extent, masters of their destiny in the work process, along with the fact that surrender of such control seems to be the most important condition of strong dissatisfaction are findings at least as important as the overall one of general satisfaction. Perhaps the need for autonomy and independence may be a more deep-seated human motive than is recognized by those who characterize our society in terms of crowdlike conformity and the decline of individualism.

These findings also have clear implications for industrial engineering. If industry and society have an interest in workers' experiencing satisfaction and pride in their work, a major effort must be made to increase the areas of control which employees have over the work process, especially in those industries and occupations where control is at a minimum. Charles Walker, who has written perceptively of the automobile worker's lack of control, has advocated two major solutions for humanizing repetitive assembly line work: job rotation and job enlargement. Where job rotation was introduced in one section of the automobile plant he studied, job satisfaction increased without loss of efficiency or production. The idea of recombining a number of jobs into one enlarged job seems especially to appeal to the line workers: as one man said, "I'd like to do a whole fender myself from the raw material to the finished product."[80] But such radical job enlargement would be a negation of the assembly line method of production. Therefore, we must anticipate the day when the utopian solution of eliminating assembly line production entirely will be the practical alternative for a society which is affluent and concerned at the same time that its members work with pride and human dignity.

Finally, the findings of this paper indicate a need for considerable further research on industrial statistics and industrial trends. If the evidence shows that extreme dissatisfaction is concentrated among assembly line workers, it becomes terribly important, for a total assessment of the conditions of work in modern America, to know what proportion of the labor force works on assembly lines or in other job contexts involving little control over their work activities. It is startling, considering the importance of such data, that such figures do not exist. This situation helps maintain the conventional belief that the mechanized assembly line worker is today's typical industrial worker in contrast to the craftsman of the past.

An indication that the actual proportion of assembly line workers is quite small is suggested by figures of the automobile industry, the conveyor belt industry par excellence. If we consider total employment in the indus-

[80] Walker and Guest, op. cit., p. 154.

trial groupings involved in the manufacture, sales, repair, and servicing of automobiles, we find that assembly line workers make up less than 5 per cent of all workers in this complex. There are approximately 120,000 automobile workers who are line assemblers, yet the number of skilled repair mechanics in all branches of the industry, a job which in many ways resembles the craft ideal, exceeds 500,000. In addition, the 120,000 assemblers are outnumbered by 400,000 managers who own or operate gas stations, garages, new and used car lots, and wrecking yards, and by 200,000 *skilled* workers in automobile plants.[81] Recent developments, especially automation, have served further to decrease the proportion of assembly line operatives in the industry.

If the situation in the automobile industry is at all typical, research might well show that those kinds of job contexts which are associated with high work satisfaction and control over one's time and destiny, such as skilled repair work and self-employment, are more representative than is commonly believed, and are even increasing over the long run. Such a prospect should bring considerable satisfaction to all those in the diverse intellectual traditions who have been concerned with that happens to human beings in the course of their major life activity, their work. And yet, this would not necessarily mean that the problem of the lack of fulfillment in work had become less serious. For as one industrial sociologist has suggested, this problem *may become more acute,* not because work itself has become more tedious, fractionated, and meaningless, but because the ideal of pride in creative effort is shared by an increasingly large proportion of the labor force as a result of the rise of democratic education and its emphasis on individualism and occupational mobility.

[81] The source for the estimate of 120,000 assembly line workers is a statement on page 426 of the U. S. Department of Labor's *Occupational Outlook Handbook, 1957,* which says that assembly line workers "in mid-1956 represented approximately 15 per cent of all the automobile workers." In this context all automobile workers refers to the 800,000 employed in manufacturing, 15 per cent of which is 120,000. The total employment in automobile manufacturing, automobile sales, automobile garage and repair shops, and gasoline service stations, according to 1950 census figures, is almost 2.5 million. This total was used as the base to compute the estimate of 5 per cent as the proportion of assembly line workers among all employees in the complex of automobile industries. The other figures are from the 1950 Census.

TECHNOLOGY
AND ORGANIZATION

W. J. M. Mackenzie

The puzzle which triggered off the work of Joan Woodward[1] and of Burns and Stalker[2] can be expressed in two sentences from her recent book.

> The assumption first put into words by Follett (1927) that "whatever the purpose towards which human endeavour is directed, the principles of that direction are nevertheless the same" became an accepted part of management theory (p. 35).

In the first stages of Joan Woodward's research in Essex, "the lack of any interrelationship between business success and what is generally regarded as sound organizational structure was particularly disconcerting" (p. 34).

This applied both to the classical theory of unity of command and to the human relations theory of workers' morale: in a fairly large sample of industrial organizations it was impossible to find any clear correlation between business success and the rules that were then (in the 1950s) being taught to students of management. Joan Woodward was dealing with a considerable range of firms in South-East Essex, Burns with a rather smaller range of firms, mainly in central Scotland: the field-work in both cases was circumspect and open-minded: and it led at first to the *impasse*—either go back to Square One ("good managers are born that way") or produce a new formulation.

Their formulations are similar in spirit, but differ substantially in detail, perhaps simply because of a difference of initial focus. They agree that there is no "one best way" in management; in different situations, use different tools. They differ in their analysis of the criteria for choice of tactics.

Reprinted from *Politics and Social Science* (London: Penguin Books Ltd., 1967), pp. 262–267. By permission of the publisher.

[1] *Management and Technology*, and *Industrial Organization, Theory and Practice*.
[2] *The Management of Innovation*, Tavistock Publications Ltd., 1961.

As the title of their book suggests, Burns and Stalker were primarily concerned with management facing change; the study grew out of an original concern with a state-sponsored attempt to encourage modern technologies (particularly in electronics) in an area where industrial decline was largely a reflection of early growth and obsolescent industries. He found in central Scotland and elsewhere a great variety of forms of management which were at least viable: and he arranged them on a scale between poles labelled "mechanistic" and "organismic." These terms may be misleading to the political scientist who has learnt their use from Weldon and others, because the distinction is not the same. Burns's "mechanism" and "organism" may both be artefacts, thought up by a clever boss, or they may both grow bit by bit out of a situation, because they are learnt organizationally through continuous trial and error and by piecemeal adjustments. Burns is coping not with the contrast between Bentham and Rousseau, but with the contrast between formal and informal organization; and this is one of several attempts to get round that unlucky distinction, which seemed so useful when it was new.

His theory is, in effect, that if a firm is operating a technology which is in the main known and static, it can have a proper organization chart which follows the text-book rules, and it can actually operate more or less like that, with reasonable efficiency and reasonable human comfort. But if that same firm is involved in technological change, then there will be a strain between the relations set out in the formal chart and those arising in the factory situation. Attempts to enforce the chart will make things worse; yet the chart cannot be amended fast enough to keep pace with the intake of new experience. Hence (in Burns's view) the firms which absorb innovation best have practically scrapped the rules about organization charts. They do see to it that their people know one another, in a personal sense; but they are not put out if several people seem to be doing the same job, if no one is quite sure who his boss is, if policy is changed unpredictably and no one is officially told about it. It should be added that in general (though this was not true of Burns's first group of Scottish firms) one would expect the firm plunging into innovation to be staffed by rather younger people, and by people accustomed to the shifting patterns of current technology. Furthermore, there will be a continuing process of selection: some will be sacked, some will resign, some will break under the strain, the rest will adapt themselves to the firm's adaptation.

The general point is obvious enough. The information channels of a hierarchic system have not sufficient capacity to carry the load in a period of rapid change; whereas a polycentric system has a much greater information capacity (Ashby's "Requisite Variety"), and if its members have skill and motivation (but not without these) then the system as a whole is highly adaptive. It flows through, over and around obstacles which would halt a tidier kind of organization. It also uses its men better; those who don't like it, leave, those who stay are thrown into situations of responsibility (there is no longer a visible boss), they strive to cope, and the strain of coping is mitigated by familiarity with a number of other people striving independently in the same predicament. This innovative creature is not particularly like an "organism" in the sense of "animal." Indeed, it is the formal organization chart which tries to create an artificial man or Leviathan; the innovative organization is emphatically a society, not an animal.

These correlations are not necessarily incompatible with those obtained by Joan Woodward. Much depends on the questions first asked by the investigator: and, as she insists,[3] the sociologist is never outside his or her own experiment. Questions may shape answers; a sociologist's analysis of people's own answers may persuade them that the sociologist has discovered "the truth" (which they now know that they knew all along), and so in a second stage of enquiry they may unconsciously reinforce the findings of the first stage. Given rather different questions, and rather different industries, her correlations (as distinct from those of Burns) emphasize technology more than they do innovation. Her one commandment is: Build an organization to fit your technology.

Like Burns, she ends with a simple scheme which is dramatic and teachable, and which also raises a host of new questions for investigation. She arranged her Essex firms in three technological groups, and then began to get clear correlations. There are two clear extremes, a large and difficult centre. At one extreme lies "old-fashioned" production, the organization of a group of people, each a specialist in his own line, to produce a series of objects to order, each object being unique. The making of advanced scientific instruments would be a clear case; or perhaps a medieval cathedral? At the other extreme is the sort of process typical of the large-scale chemical industry; an oil refinery, for instance, in which the "factory" is a single gigantic machine representing a very large capital investment. Production flows when one turns a switch: the job of the staff is not directly to produce, but to tend the monster and see that the flow is never interrupted by avoidable breakdowns.

Between these extremes lies the factory production of large batches of identical items by human hands using individual tools, usually machine tools. The range here is very great. Textile industries were not among these studied by Joan Woodward, but she had a range of examples extending from the machining of identical components by individual operators to the large-scale assembly line required to produce cars. Lisl Klein's book, *Multi-*

---

[3] *Industrial Organization*, p. 205.

products Ltd., gives a good picture of the former; the latter has come to stand as the paradigm case of mass production. The lines between this central area and the extremes are not sharp; and there are complex cases in which single firms combine two modes of production on the same site. But the distinctions are clear enough to ground some propositions.

First, prestige and status vary according to the character of the production. In each technology the highest status goes to the most vital man (even though this is not always explicitly recognized by salary differentials and other status badges.) In the firm producing "one off" devices by contract with individual customers, prestige goes to the development engineer; in process manufacture, prestige goes to the man who keeps the flow going, essentially the plant manager and his section heads, whether trained as chemists or as engineers (though there is—or at least there was—a certain rivalry and friction between these two professions). It is true that within a process organization as a whole, the marketing people have specially high status because the flow depends in the last resort on customers. But this is rather remote from the society grouped round the productive installations.

In batch production, the highest status is clearly that of the organizers of cheap and efficient production. But their situation itself has conflict built into it, because the flow of production is continually upset by changing demands.

Secondly, the communications systems differ in the three types, and with them the span of control. At the two extremes one has a small span of control: that is to say, a relatively high ratio of bosses to subordinates at each level. Associated with this (both cause and effect, probably) is an easy and informal system of communication, so that most people know what is going on, without having to be specially told in a formal way.

Thirdly, the two extremes, though quite different in their social composition, have this in common socially, that "what is best for production seems also to be best for people" (p. 135). At these extremes, there is a correlation between business success and social ease (it is best now to avoid words like "morale," "happiness," and "job satisfaction," which have acquired extra shades of meaning in the course of earlier studies). At one extreme, people are united by the thing they are building; at the other, by the thing they are tending. But it is not possible to say this of firms in the middle range, which constitute rather a large sector of industry at present. The mechanism (in very general terms) is that the firms have to live through a series of changing orders for production; and each change causes conflict. This may arise technologically, because there is a conflict between specialist branches of the firm about methods and priorities, and none of them has sole authority to decide. It may also arise over the distribution of pay-offs; Joan Woodward notes that the Essex workers boast of their readiness to assimilate change, yet in this type of industry each particular change breeds a row, because there is on the shop floor a tough and independent attitude—"What's in it for me if I go along?" Furthermore, these built-in conflicts are not damped down quickly by personal relationships, because (as one can envisage on an assembly line) the proportion of supervisors to operatives is relatively low, and the status of the first-line supervisor is in any case not very high, because he is bothered by continuous changes outside his control, and by "experts" of various kinds whose authority is never quite clear (and this is a built-in difficulty, not one created by a muddled organization chart).

This slender sketch may be enough to indicate what sort of theory this is. One can mutter "technological determinism," and perhaps Marx might have been interested if he were alive. The theory is "Marxist" also in that it stresses that conflict is in certain situations inevitable and even beneficial. But it is totally un-Marxist in its willingness to shut off (at least for the purpose of enquiry) social relationships outside the factory gates; and in its lack of concern with problems of power which are not simply problems of production. In a sense both of these two books are about power in action in various settings: but Joan Woodward in particular is casual in analysing "factory politics" and the "policy-making process," though she does mention them repeatedly.

THE REWARDS
OF THE AMATEUR

James Q. Wilson

. . . Most people "belong" because of the goals they feel the clubs serve rather than from any hope of material gain or because they enjoy the sociability the clubs provide. This does not mean that the goals need be specific—indeed, in many cases they are scarcely given more than the

Reprinted from James Q. Wilson, *The Amateur Democrat* (Chicago: The University of Chicago Press, 1962), pp. 164–174, with minor omissions.

most general statement. Nor does it imply that the members never derive fun, companionship, prestige, power, or even material gain from politics. What it does mean is that the amateur, unlike the professional, must feel that any rewards other than the satisfaction of serving a good cause and idealized principles are and must be secondary or derivative; mainly, one participates in politics because one ought to.

Although many clubs in various cities offer their members reduced air fares to Europe on charter flights, a full schedule of social events, forums featuring prestigious speakers, and the opportunity to play the political game, and although some members join simply to find a mate quickly or get to Paris inexpensively, if the clubs should cease to define themselves as organizations devoted to liberalism or reformism or similar worthy causes, they could not for long sustain the interest of any but the handful who simply enjoy the company of others or like being district leader.

Many members joined initially in response to the lure of a powerful national personality, such as Adlai E. Stevenson or John F. Kennedy, others in reaction against the unspecified evils of bossism and machine rule. Questionnaires returned by club members in New York and Los Angeles indicate the range of these initial motives. In New York, the most frequent answer to the question, "why did you join your club?" was a statement which related to the creed of reform. Such statements as "better politics," "good government," "increased democracy," "reform," "clean and honest government," "anti-Tammany," "rid New York of bosses," and "get rid of Tammany domination" occurred repeatedly. Far fewer mentioned any substantive goal, such as cheaper housing, improved race relations, better schools, or urban renewal. In Los Angeles, there were, in contrast, practically no references to reform in the questionnaires, but many references to the duty to participate in politics, the need for better candidates, the desire to make the party "stand for something," and the hope of forwarding the liberal cause.

The number of personal motives of the amateurs is, of course, infinite. Many volunteers are rootless, transient newcomers searching the city for a means of associating with like-minded people. Others are individuals with a deep sense of moral indignation at the corrupt and self-serving basis of city politics. They are liberals who would like to see the local Democratic party converted into their image of the national party, thereby ending the painful contrast between the national Democrats (whom they see as liberal, upright, community-regarding statesmen) and the local Democrats (whom they consider materialistic, devious, self-regarding hacks). In between can be found every variety of personal motive.[1] But the clubs are more than a

---

[1] Many politicians, both amateur and professional, delight in speculating on the motives of the amateur. Many explanations, some ingenious, are propounded, all

mixture of overeducated neurotics and party reformers, for all these personal motives are refracted through the lens of political involvement. It is with this political involvement that this study is concerned; the ultimate, deeply rooted personal motives will be left to those with a taste for mass psychiatry.

While it is true that several clubs devote a great deal of effort to holding social functions, attracting important speakers, and organizing group excursions to places of scenic or political interest, such clubs are in a minority in all three cities. In any case, only the larger clubs, like the Lexington in New York and the Beverly Hills in Los Angeles, have the resources for such programs. But no club fails to devote much of its time to the discussion of candidates and issues, passing resolutions on substantive matters as well as procedural reforms, and debates over policy. Equally important, no club fails to attempt, often to an astonishing extent, to involve the mass of the members in the work of the club; broad participation is always the desideratum and usually the reality of amateur club politics.[2]

Even for those who seem to derive satisfaction only from the social aspects of club life, it is important to remember that they choose to obtain such satisfactions from a *political* organization rather than from a Masonic order, a wine-tasting society, a country club, a Parent-Teachers' Association, or a bowling league. Some of these organizations are, of course, rejected because of class differences between Ivy League lawyers and the typical members of bowling clubs or Masonic orders, but even this choice has political implications. In effect, the person who joins an amateur political club in order to make friends and have fun is giving expression to that part of the Anglo-Saxon-Jewish ethic which says that organizations ought to have serious purposes; one ought to have fun on behalf of a worthwhile cause. A person wants friends who resemble what he would like to be: interesting and amusing, to be sure, but also idealistic and right-thinking.

Those who do join such clubs as the Beverely Hills or the Lexington for social reasons rarely become active members or do much club work. Rather, they are exploited by the active members in order to obtain resources for the club's political activities. The Beverly Hills club holds a

lacking in evidence. One Tammany supporter with an unusually abstract turn of mind suggested to me that the New York reform clubs are composed of frustrated, aggressive women who act out their hostility to males by attacking Carmine De Sapio, whom they unconsciously see as a handsome, sinister symbol of masculine virility. I shall try to avoid such unsupportable generalizations, tantalizing as they may be.
[2] "Broad" participation is a relative term, of course. Most clubs are fortunate if they can involve on a continuing basis even 15 per cent of their members. But at club elections, the turnout is much higher.

regular Sunday afternoon cocktail dance every month at a lavish nightclub on the Sunset Strip, an inaugural ball and a pre-election extravaganza at luxurious hotels, and lawn parties for candidates. Twice a year trips to Palm Springs are organized, and additional trips have been provided to Catalina Island, Las Vegas, and Mexico City. There are frequent theater parties. Large sums of money are raised by these events,[3] but relatively few politically active members or club officers attend. The affairs are designed for the socially-minded inactive members who in this way, and no other, can be induced to provide the sizable budget for the club's political work.

The politically active members heatedly deny and deeply resent the accusation that the primary reward of club politics is social.[4] "The club movement is not basically a social movement, except perhaps in Beverly Hills," said a CDC[5] officer. "My social friends are not in the clubs. I don't go to the homes of the people I know in the clubs and they don't come to mine." Leaders of such large and affluent clubs as the Beverly Hills (which has over 720 members) concede that social opportunities and parties are the primary inducement for a great many, perhaps most, members. But club leaders can be quite deliberate about this. An officer of the Schiller Banks club in Chicago, located on the Gold Coast, observed: "Knowing the snobbery of the building . . . we tried to have meetings in penthouses. We got the kind of speakers with prestige. . . . [But] it is very difficult to get people to do precinct work. We had two hundred people to [a penthouse] party. We couldn't get ten to work."

The Beverly Hills club is not typical of all or even many clubs, and even here the activists are a separate group within the club which remains apart from the fun-minded rank and file and which derives its satisfaction from aspects of club life that are unrelated to pure sociability. An officer of the Beverly Hills club described his club as "basically a social vehicle" for the average member, who is young, female, and single. But almost all the officers and activists were married. "Frankly, I prefer married people," he said. "Married people are more interested in politics and less interested in social things."

Indeed, anyone attending the meeting of a typical club would find very little of a social character that seemed attractive. Meetings are long

---

[3] These affairs are almost always a financial success. Package tours are arranged out of which the club takes a fixed percentage rebate from the commercial entrepreneur, usually amounting to $7.50 to $10.00 per person. The hotel parties can produce as much as $1,300 to $1,800, a good trip to Mexico City $1,000, and a Las Vegas excursion $700.

[4] The leading example of this interpretation is Seyom Brown, "Fun Can Be Politics," *Reporter*, November 12, 1959, pp. 27–28. It was challenged in letters to the editor written by Los Angeles club leaders.

[5] California Democratic Club.

and often dull in the extreme, with a seemingly endless agenda and inter-
minable speakers. There is much discussion from the floor, business is
transacted in minute detail, and the routine of parliamentary procedure is
constantly rehearsed. Although a handful of clubs can afford prestigious
speakers and elaborate social affairs, most simply lack the resources for
this sort of thing. It is hard to believe that many people find an average
club meeting "fun."

In understanding the rewards of politics for amateurs, the role of the
club itself is crucial. If the lure of Stevenson's personality or the force of
powerful ideals were alone sufficient to motivate political effort, then the
club would not be essential. Individuals, attracted by a candidate or cause
in which they believed, could serve as precinct workers directly under the
county central committee or under district or block captains appointed by
that body. Indeed, such tactics have been tried from time to time by the
Los Angeles County Committee, but all have met with failure. . . .

The club is the vital intervening link between the formal party and the
volunteer workers. Without it, precinct work is ineffective and whatever organization is created does not endure. With it, enthusiasm can be aroused
and effort sustained. The same county committee official observed that

> the basic organization of the County Committee depends on the club
> movement. . . . We have to have group support or consensus [for the
> members]. . . . .You've got to realize, it's not just ideals that gets people
> into politics. If it were only ideals, then the precinct system would work.
> If it were ideals simply, then you could persuade people to work
> alone in their precinct . . . in order to realize their ideals. But you
> can't persuade them to do this. You can only persuade them to work
> through a club. The club atmosphere, the "groupness," is vitally im-
> portant.

So convinced was he of this that he had become fascinated by the
theory of group dynamics in an effort better to understand the clubs' role.
The reason for the importance of the club is probably related to the character of the incentives it can distribute to members. If the County Committee had a large stock of patronage jobs, the clubs would be unnecessary
except for the convenience of decentralizing precinct operations and giving
district or ward leaders a means of exercising control over their subordinates. Workers would perform their tasks for tangible incentives, such
as jobs, because such rewards would be received regardless of the outcome
of the election so long as the worker himself performed creditably—e.g.,
by turning out a given number of Democratic voters. But if the rewards are
intangible (the lure of personality or ideals), they are not substantially
lessened if all workers do not perform ably (i.e., if the election is lost and

the candidate defeated). And if the candidate wins, even the worker who does little derives considerable satisfaction.

In brief, the crucial distinction between tangible and intangible rewards in this connection is that the former are divisible in a way the latter are not. The distinction corresponds closely to Chester Barnard's distinction between "specific" and "general" inducements.[6] The former can be offered to one person and withheld from all others; the latter cannot. Since specific or divisible incentives can be given to or withheld from individuals, a measure of control attaches to their use, such that *individual* performance can be rewarded or punished regardless of what others may do. A general or indivisible incentive lacks this element of control—its existence may depend on the efforts of many, but not on the efforts of any single individual. Everyone gets it or no one. Therefore, no person has any compelling reason to work hard for it. If he knows his candidate may win or lose regardless of what he does, he need not work at all.

Thus, the clubs intervene between the ultimate rewards (ideals, candidate personality, the national party) and individual effort by supplying a kind of inducement which these ultimate rewards, in themselves, cannot provide. The club creates a set of proximate inducements to supplement and reinforce the ultimate ones. Both are essential; neither will suffice alone. These proximate rewards derive from the act of associating together, and include the opportunities for office, power, and prestige in the club; the sense of approval from one's fellow members; and the opportunities for sociability which are in part dependent on club work and contributions of money or effort. None of these is as divisible (and hence as subject to control) as a tangible payoff, but all are more divisible than purely ideal benefactions.

The *initial* reason for joining the club is probably replaced, in most cases, by a *secondary* or supplementary motivation that produces a sustained contribution of effort. An early club organizer noted that "after the first blush of enthusiasm for Stevenson had worn off, it became evident that these people were going to stay in politics for somewhat different reasons." A leading CDC officer echoed these feelings: "The volunteer gets into this organization because he's interested in its ideals or because he's ambitious. But once this has passed—and these things always do pass—then he tends to become involved for other reasons."

These secondary motivations seem to derive from the attractions of playing the political game and shaping the course of party affairs on behalf of a liberal cause. Liberalism or reformism is the ultimate incentive (if the game were not liberal and intellectual, it would not be fun) and the game

---

[6] Chester I. Barnard, *The Functions of the Executive* (Cambridge: Harvard University Press, 1938), pp. 142 ff.

is the proximate or operative inducement. "The volunteer type soon acquires the habits of the professional without acquiring his means of livelihood," observed a former CDC president. "He tends to become involved in the campaign for the sake of winning . . . and playing the game." Playing the game includes winning club and CDC office and acquiring the prestige of political standing as well as participating in the making of club and party decisions. The fun, of course, is proportional to the intrinsic value of the game. When John F. Kennedy became the Democratic presidential nominee in 1960 despite intense pro-Stevenson feeling on the part of most club leaders in Los Angeles and New York, enthusiasm for campaign work quickly dimmed and there were muttered threats of "sitting on our hands." By and large, this did not materialize, for Kennedy, particularly in his television debates with Richard Nixon, soon began to impress many club members and, in any case, the prospect of sitting by while Nixon won was unsupportable. But many leaders, particularly at higher party levels, were eager to participate on the "inside" of the campaign regardless of who the nominee was. For a variety of reasons, including the appeal of Kennedy, the dislike of Nixon, and the irresistible lure of the game, the predicted revolt against Kennedy by the Stevenson-oriented clubs never really developed beyond scattered instances.

The importance of the lure of political activity is underscored by the failure of the DFI in Chicago. An amateur club must have something to do; it cannot be simply a debating society. Almost without exception, ex-DFI leaders blamed the organization's failure on "too much talk, not enough action." Said one leader, "We went down there [to the DFI convention] in 1958 and spent three days passing a constitution. This was fine. The next year we spent three days debating amendments." That was not enough in the absence of electoral successes. "I have been around a lot of ADA [Americans for Democratic Action] chapters but the thing that impresses me about the IVI is that we don't sit around and talk about Indonesia but we do real precinct work." These were the remarks of leaders. How the rank and file felt cannot be accurately assessed, but there was probably a good deal more enthusiasm for "talk." At a DFI convention, the hall was packed to hear Mrs. Roosevelt and Senator Gore; when they finished, so many delegates left that there was no longer a quorum for the transaction of vital organization business concerning the budget, staff, and rules.

The distinction between leader and member, and hence between initial and secondary motives, means that a good deal of what transpires publicly at club meetings or conventions is ritual. The talk on the floor of the meeting is heavily charged with slogans, references to goals and ideals, and allusions to club heroes. In the corridors and hotel rooms, however, the private conversation is almost indistinguishable (except in syntax) from that of professional politicians. The subjects are candidates, nominations, power-plays, and party gossip. But if the floor speeches are ritual, they are not meaningless ritual. The amateur politicians require a rhetoric when they are together in large numbers in public that they do not require when they are alone or in small groups.

A leader in the Riverside Democrats in New York felt that "the principal motivation for many of these people [i.e., active members and leaders] is the sheer fascination of politics. It's certainly not civic dedication. That wears thin in short order"[7] An officer of the VID shared this view:

> I think a big attraction for most people in the club is the fun of politics. I think the people who are attracted because of their interest in some goal or purpose are in the minority. The social functions are a very big part of our club, and of course, a big source of money. Many people are attracted to the club just because they're lonely and want human contact.

This fun may be nothing more than the opportunity to let off steam. "All day long," said one member of the FDR-Woodrow Wilson Club, "I can't shout back at the boss, I can't shout back at the wife, I can't shout back at the kids. But I come here in the evenings and I shout at these people, and I go away feeling like a new man."

Almost all amateur clubs endeavor to diversify their incentives such that there will be some reward in political activity for almost anybody who chooses to join. The range of club work is staggering. The Lexington Democratic Club, for example, had in 1960 thirty standing committees with a total of sixty-one chairmen and vice-chairmen. The purposes of these committees ranged from finance and campaigning to art, charter flights abroad, community affairs, and newspaper publication. (In fact, two members admitted that they had joined the club solely in order to take advantage of the cheap air travel rates provided by the charter flights committee.) Other clubs, although not so large as the Lexington, had proportionally sizable committee structures.

In addition, the club also provides for the discussion of issues and topics in current affairs. The reform clubs vary considerably in the resources they devote to such forums, and this is an important distinction among them. The Lexington Club on the East Side, the oldest, largest, and wealthiest of the reform clubs, devotes by far the most to forums; clubs

---

[7] The fun of the game attracts people into other kinds of organizations as well. Frank H. Knight asserts that it is important in the understanding of businesses. *Ethics and Competition* (New York: Harper & Row, 1935), pp. 60–61.

on the West Side and in lower Manhattan devote significantly less energy to such matters.

When Lexington Club members were asked what club activity they liked most, more answers referred to forums and the discussion of large issues than to any other activity. The club contributes amply to such interests. Scarcely a month passes in which a prominent speaker is not heard at the club. In two years (January, 1958, through January, 1960) there were twenty-eight such events, featuring such persons as Professor Arthur M. Schlesinger, Jr., Mrs. Eleanor Roosevelt, William Zeckendorf, Jr., Senator Albert Gore, Senator Harrison Williams, Thomas K. Finletter, Dr. Edward Teller, and others. The topics were almost evenly divided between local and national or international matters, and between the concern for reformism and the concern for liberalism. . . .

IV

The Organization of Knowledge

The massive use of knowledge is a new attribute of post-World War II, modern societies. The United States, for instance, spends now about 24 billion dollars a year on research and development while such expenditure totalled less than a billion before World War II. Most of this knowledge is produced within organizations or divisions within organizations devoted mainly to the knowledge function (for example, research corporations). It hence must be "transported" to other organizations (or divisions) in which it may be applied. In addition to difficulties such transportation entails, the administration of knowledge generates specific problems, because the basis of authority involved differs from the bureaucratic one.

Administration assumes a power hierarchy. Without a clear ordering of higher and lower in rank, in which the higher in rank have more power than the lower, and hence can control and coordinate the latter's activities, the basic principle of administration is violated; the organization ceases to be a coordinated tool. However, knowledge is largely an individual property; unlike other organizational means, it cannot be transferred from one person to another by decree. Creativity is basically an individual act and the individual professional has the ultimate responsibility for his professional decision, for example, the surgeon has to decide whether or not to operate. Students of the professions have pointed out that the autonomy granted to professionals who are basically responsible to their consciences (though they may be censured by their peers and in extreme cases by the courts) is necessary for effective professional work. Only when immune from ordinary social pressures and free to innovate, experiment, and take risks, without the usual social repercussions of failure, can a professional carry out his work effectively. It is this highly individualized principle which is diametrically opposed to the very essence of the organizational principle of control and coordination by superiors, that is, the principle of administrative authority. In other words, the ultimate justification for a professional act is that it is, to the best of the professional's knowledge, the right act. He might consult his colleagues before he acts, but the decision is his. If he errs, he will still be defended by his peers. The ultimate justification of an administrative act, however, is that it is in line with the organization's rules and regulations, and that it has been approved—directly or by implication—by a superior ranking official.

The question is how to create and use knowledge on a large scale, in organizations, without undermining them. Some knowledge is formulated and applied in strictly private situations. In the traditional professions of medicine and law, much work is carried out in nonorganizational contexts—in face-to-face interaction with clients. But as the need for costly resources and auxiliary staffs has grown, even the traditional professions face mounting pressures to transfer their work to organizational structures such as the hospital and the law firm. Similarly, while most artistic work is still conducted in private contexts—often in specially segregated sectors of society in which an individual's autonomy is particularly high—much of the cognitive creativity, particularly in scientific research, has become embedded in organizational structures for reasons similar to those in the case of medicine and law.*

Dalton deals with this issue in the context of three industrial corporations where production of goods takes priority over that of knowledge; knowledge is just another means of making goods—and money. Typically, the staff (the "knowledge men") are subordinated to the line-men (production and profit). The conflict between the two is reduced by this institutionalized subordination of one to the authority of the other. But other factors accentuate it, including differences in

* We draw here upon our discussion in *Modern Organizations* (Englewood Cliffs, N.J.: Prentice-Hall, 1964), especially pp. 76–77.

the social background and educational experience of the staff and line-men.

Goss deals with an organization in which knowledge is the ground of authority, namely a medical clinic. She shows various mechanisms of adaptation employed in response to bureaucratic needs such as drawing on differences in professional authority among the knowledge-men, and the administration of nonprofessional aspects of professional work by "routine" procedures, while being much less directive with regard to the professional aspects of the same work.

CONFLICT BETWEEN STAFF AND LINE MANAGERIAL OFFICERS

Melville Dalton

Industrial staff organizations are relatively new. Their appearance is a response to many complex interrelated forces, such as economic competition, scientific advance, industrial expansion, growth of the labor movement, and so on. During the last four or five decades these rapid changes and resulting unstable conditions have caused top industrial officials more and more to call in "specialists" to aid them toward the goal of greater production and efficiency. These specialists are of many kinds, including chemists, statisticians, public and industrial relations officers, personnel officers, accountants, and a great variety of engineers, such as mechanical, draughting, electrical, chemical, fuel, lubricating, and industrial engineers. In industry these individuals are usually known as "staff people." Their functions, again, for the most part are to increase and apply their specialized knowledge in problem areas, and to advise those officers who make up the "line" organization and have authority[1] over production processes.

This theoretically satisfying industrial structure of specialized experts advising busy administrators has in a number of significant cases failed to

Reprinted in part from Melville Dalton, *American Sociological Review*, 15 (1950), 342–351, by permission of the author and the publisher, The American Sociological Association.

[1] *Inside* their particular staff organization, staff officers also may have authority over their subordinates, but not over production personnel.

function as expected. The assumptions that (a) the staff specialists would be reasonably content to function without a measure of formal authority[2] over production, and that (b) their suggestions regarding improvement of processes and techniques for control over personnel and production would be welcomed by line officers and be applied, require closer examination. In practice there is often much conflict between industrial staff and line organizations and in varying degrees the members of these organizations oppose each other.

The aim of this paper is, therefore, to present and analyze data dealing with staff-line tensions.

Data were drawn from three industrial plants[3] in which the writer had been either a participating member of one or both of the groups or was intimate with reliable informants among the officers who were. . . .

For analytical convenience, staff-line friction may be examined apart from the reciprocal effects of the general conflict system. Regarded in this way, the data indicated that three conditions were basic to staff-line struggles: (1) the conspicuous ambition and "individualistic" behavior among staff officers; (2) the complication arising from staff efforts to justify its existence and get acceptance of its contributions; and, related to point two, (3) the fact that incumbency of the higher staff offices was dependent on line approval. The significance of these conditions will be discussed in order.

MOBILE BEHAVIOR OF STAFF PERSONNEL

As a group, staff personnel in the three plants were markedly ambitious, restless, and individualistic. There was much concern to win rapid promotion, to make the "right impressions," and to receive individual recognition. Data showed that the desire among staff members for personal distinctions often over-rode their sentiments of group consciousness and caused intra-staff tensions.

The relatively high turnover of staff personnel[4] quite possibly reflected the dissatisfactions and frustrations of members over inability to achieve

[2] To the extent that staff officers influence line policy they do, of course, have a certain *informal* authority.
[3] These plants were in related industries and ranged in size from 4,500 to 20,000 employees, with the managerial groups numbering from 200 to nearly 1,000. Details concerning the plants and their location are confidential. Methodological details concerning an intensive study embracing staff-line relations and several other areas of behavior in one of the plants are given in the writer's unpublished doctoral thesis, "A Study of Informal Organization Among the Managers of an Industrial Plant" (Department of Sociology, University of Chicago, 1949).
[4] During the period between 1944 and 1950 turnover of staff personnel in these plants was between two and four times as great as that of line personnel.

the distinction and status they hoped for. Several factors appeared to be of importance in this restlessness of staff personnel. Among these were age and social differences between line and staff officers, structural differences in the hierarchy of the two groups, and the staff group's lack of authority over production.

With respect to age, the staff officers were significantly younger than line officers. This would account to some extent for their restlessness. Being presumably less well-established in life in terms of material accumulations, occupational status, and security, while having greater expectations (see below), and more energy, as well as more life ahead in which to make new starts elsewhere if necessary, the staff groups were understandably more dynamic and driving.[5]

Age-conflict[6] was also significant in staff-line antagonisms. The older line officers disliked receiving what they regarded as instruction from men so much younger than themselves, and staff personnel clearly were conscious of this attitude among line officers. In staff-line meetings staff officers frequently had their ideas slighted or even treated with amusement by line incumbents. Whether such treatment was warranted or not, the effects were disillusioning to the younger, less experienced staff officers. Often selected by the organization because of their outstanding academic records, they had entered industry with the belief that they had much to contribute, and that their efforts would win early recognition and rapid advancement. Certainly they had no thought that their contributions would be in any degree unwelcome. This naiveté was apparently due to lack of earlier first-hand experience in industry (or acquaintance with those who had such experience), and to omission of realistic instruction in the social sciences from their academic training. The unsophisticated staff officer's initial contacts with the shifting, covert, expedient arrangements between members of staff and line usually gave him a severe shock. He had entered industry prepared to engage in logical, well-formulated relations with members of the managerial hierarchy, and to carry out precise, methodical functions for which his training had equipped him. Now he learned that (1) his freedom to function was snared in a web of informal commitments; (2) his

---

[5] One might also hypothesize that the drive of staff officers was reflected in the fact that the staff heads and specialists gained their positions (those held when the data were collected) in less time than did members of the line groups. E.g., the 36 staff officers discussed above had spent a median of 10 years attaining their positions, as against a median of 11 years for the first-line foremen, 17 years for the general foremen, and 19 years for the superintendents. But one must consider that some of the staff groups were relatively new (13–15 years old) and had grown rapidly, which probably accelerated their rate of promotions as compared with that of the older line organization.

[6] E. A. Ross, in *Principles of Sociology* (New York: Appleton, 1938), pp. 238–248, has some pertinent comments on age conflict.

academic specialty (on which he leaned for support in his new position) was often not relevant[7] for carrying out his formal assignments; and that (3) the important thing to do was to learn who the informally powerful line officers were and what ideas they would welcome which at the same time would be acceptable to his superiors.

Usually the staff officer's reaction to these conditions is to look elsewhere for a job or make an accommodation in the direction of protecting himself and finding a niche where he can make his existence in the plant tolerable and safe. If he chooses the latter course, he is likely to be less concerned with creative effort for his employer than with attempts to develop reliable social relations that will aid his personal advancement. The staff officer's recourse to this behavior and his use of other status-increasing devices will be discussed below in another connection.

The formal structure, or hierarchy of statuses, of the two larger plants from which data were drawn, offered a frustration to the ambitious staff officer. That is, in these plants the strata, or levels of authority, in the staff organizations ranged from three to five as against from five to ten in the line organization. Consequently there were fewer possible positions for exercise of authority into which staff personnel could move. This condition may have been an irritant to expansion among the staff groups. Unable to move vertically to the degree possible in the line organization, the ambitious staff officer could enlarge his area of authority in a given position only by lateral expansion—by increasing his personnel. Whether or not aspiring staff incumbents revolted against the relatively low hierarchy through which they could move, the fact remains that (1) they appeared eager to increase the number of personnel under their authority, (2) the personnel of staff groups *did* increase disproportionately to those of the line, and (3) there was a trend of personnel movement from staff to line, rather than the reverse, presumably (reflecting the drive and ambition of staff members) because there were more positions of authority, as well as more authority to be exercised, more prestige, and usually more income in the line.

Behavior in the plants indicated that line and staff personnel belonged to different social status groups and that line and staff antipathies were at least in part related to these social distinctions. For example, with respect to the item of formal education, the staff group stood on a higher level than members of the line. In the plant from which the age data were taken, the

---

[7] Among the staff heads and assistants referred to earlier, only 50 per cent of those with college training (32 of the 36 officers) were occupied with duties related to their specialized training. Among the college-trained of 190 line officers in the same plant, the gap between training and function was still greater, with 61 per cent in positions not related to the specialized part of their college work.

36 staff officers had a mean of 14.6 years of schooling as compared with 13.1 years for 35 line superintendents, 11.2 years for 60 general foremen, and 10.5 years for 93 first-line foremen. The difference between the mean education of the staff group and that of the highest line group (14.6–13.1) was statistically significant at better than the one per cent level. The 270 nonsupervisory staff personnel had a mean of 13.1 years—the same as that of the line superintendents. Consciousness of this difference probably contributed to a feeling of superiority among staff members, while the sentiment of line officers toward staff personnel was reflected in name-calling.

Staff members were also much concerned about their dress, a daily shave, and a weekly hair-cut. On the other hand, line officers, especially below the level of departmental superintendent, were relatively indifferent to such matters. Usually they were in such intimate contact with production processes that dirt and grime prevented the concern with meticulous dress shown by staff members. The latter also used better English in speaking and in writing reports, and were more suave and poised in social intercourse. These factors, and the recreational preferences of staff officers for night clubs and "hot parties," assisted in raising a barrier between them and most line officers.

COMPLICATIONS OF STAFF NEED TO PROVE ITS WORTH

To the thinking of many line officers, the staff functioned as an agent on trial rather than as a managerial division that might be of equal importance with the line organization in achieving production goals. Staff members were very conscious of this sentiment toward them and of their need to prove themselves. They strained to develop new techniques and to get them accepted by the line. But in doing this they frequently became impatient, and gave already suspicious line officers the impression of reaching for authority over production.

Since the line officer regards his authority over production as something sacred, and resents the implication that after many years in the line he needs the guidance of a newcomer who lacks such experience, an obstacle to staff-line cooperation develops the moment this sore spot is touched. On the other hand, the staff officer's ideology of his function leads him to precipitate a power struggle with the line organization. By and large he considers himself as an agent of top management. He feels bound to contribute something significant in the form of research or ideas helpful to management. By virtue of his greater education and intimacy with the latest theories of production, he regards himself as a managerial consultant and an expert, and feels that he must be, or appear to be, almost infallible once he has committed himself to top management on some point. With this orientation, he is usually disposed to approach middle and lower line with an attitude of condescension that often reveals itself in the heat of discussion. Consequently, many staff officers involve themselves in trouble and report their failures as due to "ignorance" and "bull-headedness" among these line officers.

On this point, relations between staff and line in all three of the plants were further irritated by a rift inside the line organization. First-line foremen were inclined to feel that top management had brought in the production planning, industrial relations, and industrial engineering staffs as clubs with which to control the lower line. Hence they frequently regarded the projects of staff personnel as manipulative devices, and reacted by cooperating with production workers and/or general foremen (whichever course was the more expedient) in order to defeat insistent and uncompromising members of the staff. Also, on occasion (see below), the lower line could cooperate evasively with lower staff personnel who were in trouble with staff superiors.

EFFECT OF LINE AUTHORITY
OVER STAFF PROMOTION

The fact that entry to the higher staff offices in the three plants was dependent on approval of top line officers had a profound effect on the behavior of staff personnel. Every member of the staff knew that if he aspired to higher office he must make a record for himself, a good part of which would be a reputation among upper line officers of ability to "understand" their informal problems without being told. This knowledge worked in varying degrees to pervert the theory of staff-line relations. Ideally the two organizations cooperate to improve existing methods of output, to introduce new methods, to plan the work, and to solve problems of production and the scheduling of orders that might arise. But when the line offers resistance to the findings and recommendations of the staff, the latter is reduced to evasive practices of getting some degree of acceptance of its programs, and at the same time of convincing top management that "good relations" exist with officers down the line. This necessity becomes even more acute when the staff officer aspires (for some of the reasons given above) to move over to the line organization, for then he must convince powerful line officers that he is worthy.

Staff personnel, particularly in the middle and lower levels, carried on expedient relations with the line that daily evaded formal rules. Even those officers most devoted to rules found that, in order not to arouse enmity in the line on a scale sufficient to be communicated *up* the line, compromising devices were frequently helpful and sometimes almost unavoidable both for organizational and career aims. The usual practice was to tolerate minor breaking of staff rules by line personnel, or even to cooperate with the line in evading rules, and in exchange lay a claim on the line for cooperation on critical issues. In some cases line aid was enlisted to conceal lower staff blunders from the upper staff and the upper line.[8]

While the staff organizations gave much time to developing new techniques, they were simultaneously thinking about how their plans would be received by the line. They knew from experience that middle and lower line officers could always give a "black eye" to staff contributions by deliberate mal-practices. Repeatedly top management had approved, and incorporated, staff proposals that had been verbally accepted down the line. Often the latter officers had privately opposed the changes, but had feared that saying so would incur the resentment of powerful superiors who could informally hurt them. Later they would seek to discredit the change by deliberate mal-practice and hope to bring a return to the former arrangement. For this reason there was a tendency for staff members to withhold improved production schemes or other plans when they knew that an attempt to introduce them might fail or even bring personal disrepute.

Line officers fear staff innovations for a number of reasons. In view of their longer experience, presumably intimate knowledge of the work, and their greater remuneration, they fear[9] being "shown up" before their line superiors for not having thought of the processual refinements themselves. They fear that changes in methods may bring personnel changes which will threaten the break-up of cliques and existing informal arrangements and quite possibly reduce their area of authority. Finally, changes in techniques may expose forbidden practices and departmental inefficiency. In some cases these fears have stimulated line officers to compromise staff

---

[8] Failure of middle and lower staff personnel to "cooperate" with line officers might cause the latter to "stand pat" in observance of line rules at a time when the pressures of a dynamic situation would make the former eager to welcome line cooperation in rule-breaking.

[9] Though there was little evidence that top management expected line officers to refine production techniques, the fear of such an expectation existed nevertheless. As noted earlier, however, some of the top executives *were* thinking that development of a "higher type" of first-line foreman might enable most of the staff groups to be eliminated.

men to the point where the latter will agree to postpone the initiation of new practices for specific periods.

In one such case an assistant staff head agreed with a line superintendent to delay the application of a bonus plan for nearly three months so that the superintendent could live up to the expedient agreement he had made earlier with his grievance committeeman to avoid a "wildcat" strike by a group of production workmen.[10] The lower engineers who had devised the plan were suspicious of the formal reasons given to them for withholding it, so the assistant staff head prevented them (by means of "busy work") from attending staff-line meetings lest they inadvertently reveal to top management that the plan was ready.

The third area of staff-line accommodations growing out of authority relations revolved around staff use of funds granted it by top management. Middle and lower line charged that staff research and experimentation was little more than "money wasted on blunders," and that various departments of the line could have "accomplished much more with less money." According to staff officers, those of their plans that failed usually did so because line personnel "sabotaged" them and refused to "cooperate." Specific costs of "crack-pot experimentation" in certain staff groups were pointed to by line officers. Whatever the truth of the charges and countercharges, evidence indicated (confidants in both groups supported this) that pressures from the line organization (below the top level) forced some of the staff groups to "kick over" parts of the funds appropriated for staff use[11] by top management. These compromises were of course hidden from top management, but the relations described were carried on to such an extent that by means of them—and line pressures for manipulation of accounts in the presumably impersonal auditing departments—certain line officers were able to show impressively low operating costs and thus win favor[12] with top management that would relieve pressures and be useful in personal advancement. In their turn the staff officers involved would receive more "cooperation" from the line and/or recommendation for transfer to the line. The data indicated that in a few such cases men from accounting and auditing staffs were given general foremanships (without previous line experience) as a reward for their understanding behavior.

[10] This case indicates the over-lapping of conflict areas referred to earlier. A later paper will deal with the area of informal union-management relations.
[11] In two of the plants a somewhat similar relation, rising from different causes, existed *inside* the line organization with the *operating* branch of the line successfully applying pressures for a share in funds assigned to the *maintenance* division of the line.
[12] The reader must appreciate the fact that constant demands are made by top management to maintain low operating costs.

SUMMARY

Research in three industrial plants showed conflict between the managerial staff and line groups that hindered the attainment of organizational goals. Privately expressed attitudes among some of the higher line executives revealed their hope that greater control of staff groups could be achieved, or that the groups might be eliminated and their functions taken over in great part by carefully selected and highly remunerated lower-line officers. On their side, staff members wanted more recognition and a greater voice in control of the plants.

All of the various functioning groups of the plants were caught up in a general conflict system; but apart from the effects of involvement in this complex, the struggles between line and staff organizations were attributable mainly to (1) functional differences between the two groups; (2) differentials in the ages, formal education, potential occupational ceilings, and status group affiliations of members of the two groups (the staff officers being younger, having more education but lower occupational potential, and forming a prestige-oriented group with distinctive dress and recreational tastes); (3) need of the staff groups to justify their existence; (4) fear in the line that staff bodies by their expansion, and well-financed research activities, would undermine line authority; and (5) the fact that aspirants to higher staff offices could gain promotion only through approval of influential line executives.

INFLUENCE AND AUTHORITY AMONG PHYSICIANS IN AN OUTPATIENT CLINIC

Mary E. W. Goss

In bureaucracy the staff is composed of trained experts and "the organization of offices follows the principle of hierarchy; that is, each lower office is under the control and supervision of a higher one."[1] Whether the hierarchical principle formulated by Weber can be applied without modification to the formal organization of experts who are professionals has been considered problematic by many sociologists.[2] For professionals require what Logan Wilson has called "individual authority": freedom to make professional decisions according to their own trained judgment rather than according to the dictates of superiors in a bureaucratic hierarchy.[3] Taking

Reprinted from *American Sociological Review*, vol. 26 (1961), pp. 39–50. By permission of the author and publisher, the American Sociological Association.

[1] A. M. Henderson and Talcott Parsons, translators, *Max Weber: The Theory of Social and Economic Organization*, New York: Oxford, 1947, p. 331. As is well known, Weber's concept of bureaucracy also has other distinctive features; see *Ibid.*, pp. 324–423, and H. H. Gerth and C. Wright Mills, translators, *From Max Weber: Essays in Sociology*, New York: Oxford, 1946, pp. 196–264.

[2] See, for example, Talcott Parsons, "Introduction" in Henderson and Parsons, *op. cit.*, pp. 58–60; Logan Wilson, *The Academic Man*, New York: Oxford, 1942, pp. 71–93; Walter I. Wardwell, "Social Integration, Bureaucratization, and the Professions," *Social Forces*, 33 (May, 1955), pp. 356–359; David N. Solomon, "Professional Persons in Bureaucratic Organizations," in *Symposium on Preventive and Social Psychiatry*, sponsored by Walter Reed Army Institute of Research, *et al.*, Washington, D. C.: U. S. Government Printing Office, 1958, pp. 253–266; Robert K. Merton, *Social Theory and Social Structure*, rev. ed.; New York: Free Press, 1957, pp. 207–224; Mary Jean Huntington, "Sociology of Professions, 1945–1955," in Hans L. Zetterberg, editor, *Sociology in the United States of America*, Paris: UNESCO, 1956, pp. 87–93.

As these writers suggest, apparent incompatibilities between bureaucratic and professional standards abound. Thus the realm of authority, with which the present paper deals, represents only one of several areas of potential strain, conflict, or adjustment that might be investigated empirically.

[3] Wilson, *op. cit.*, p. 73. This type of authority has also been described as "expert," "professional," or "functional"; see Henry G. Metcalf and L. Urwick, editors, *Dynamic Administration: The Collected Papers of Mary Parker Follett*, New York:

this requirement into account, Parsons and others have suggested that a more functionally appropriate type of formal organization for professionals would be egalitarian instead of hierarchical, and they have pointed to the strains that presumably would attend departures from organization as a "company of equals."[4] Nevertheless, available analyses and empirical studies of supervisory relationships that involve primarily non-professional personnel suggest that not all formal hierarchies are equally bureaucratic in terms of their actual operation. Should a similar situation exist for professional personnel, it would seem that hierarchical organization may, but need not, mean curtailment of individual authority and consequent organizational or individual strain.

As Gouldner,[5] Blau,[6] and others[7] have observed in various work contexts, those who hold superordinate positions in an official hierarchy may have the formal right to impose their decisions upon subordinates (that is, to exercise authority), but in fact they do not always choose to do so. Instead, they may attempt to exert influence in the desired direction through education, persuasion, or advice. Further, selection of one or another of these potential modes of control is rarely simply a function of the personal preference of the persons in charge. It is becoming increasingly clear that if such individuals are to discharge their responsibilities effectively, they are constrained in some measure to take notice of the relevant norms and values of subordinates and to act accordingly. Through being incorporated in role expectations which specify appropriate behavior patterns for supervisory relationships under various circumstances, these norms and values may set the real limits—sometimes in contrast with "official" limits—on the kinds of supervisory control that will be feasible in particular work situations.

The supervisory relationships observed among a group of physicians

---

Harper & Row, 1940, pp. 277–281; Herbert A. Simon, *Administrative Behavior*, New York: Macmillan, 1947, pp. 142–146; Talcott Parsons, *Essays in Sociological Theory: Pure and Applied*, New York: Free Press, 1949, pp. 189–191.

These terms emphasize the *basis* for authority, while "individual authority" emphasizes the *locus* and thus allows for the possibility that experts may be qualified to make independent decisions but may nevertheless not be allowed to do so under certain circumstances.

[4] See the references cited in footnote 2 above.

[5] Alvin W. Gouldner, *Patterns of Industrial Bureaucracy*, New York: Free Press, 1954, pp. 215–228.

[6] Peter M. Blau, *The Dynamics of Bureaucracy*, Chicago: University of Chicago Press, 1955, pp. 161–179.

[7] Simon, *op. cit.*, pp. 11–16 and 123–146; Chester I. Barnard, *The Functions of the Executive*, Cambridge: Harvard University Press, 1938, pp. 161–184; Metcalf and Urwick, *op. cit.*, pp. 247–294; Merton, *op. cit.*, pp. 339–340; Reinhard Bendix, "Bureaucracy: the Problem and its Setting," *American Sociological Review*, 12 (October, 1947), 493–507.

in an outpatient clinic of a large teaching hospital offer an extreme—and therefore instructive—example of this general principle. These relationships also offer suggestive evidence concerning how hierarchical organization of professionals may exist and yet be reconciled with maintenance of individual authority for each professional. Toward these ends, this paper first describes the way in which the physicians were formally organized. Then the types of supervisory control which were institutionalized among the physicians are illustrated and analyzed. Finally, the connection between type of control and sphere of work is examined, and for each sphere both observed behavior and underlying norms and values are reported. Throughout, it should be emphasized, attention is focused solely on physicians. The relationships of this professional group to patients or to the various categories of personnel in the hospital are eminently worth sociological study, as others have shown,[8] but it is *intra*-professional organization and control within a general hospital setting that is at issue in the present context.[9]

RESEARCH SETTING AND METHODS

The research site was a program of comprehensive care and teaching sponsored by the general hospital, medical school, and nursing school that together make up a major Northeastern medical center. Located mainly in the general medical clinic and the general pediatric clinic of the hospital,

[8] A relatively large body of sociological literature concerned with these relationships has accumulated, including the following representative works: Oswald Hall, "Sociological Research in the Field of Medicine: Progress and Prospects," *American Sociological Review*, 16 (October, 1951), pp. 639–643; Harvey L. Smith, "The Sociological Study of Hospitals," unpublished Ph.D. thesis, University of Chicago, 1949; Alfred H. Stanton and Morris H. Schwartz, *The Mental Hospital*, New York: Basic Books, 1954; Albert F. Wessen, "The Social Structure of a Modern Hospital," unpublished Ph.D. thesis, Yale University, 1951; Temple Burling, Edith M. Lentz, and Robert N. Wilson, *The Give and Take in Hospitals*, New York: Putnam, 1956; Mark G. Field, *Doctor and Patient in Soviet Russia*, Cambridge: Harvard University Press, 1957; Renée C. Fox, *Experiment Perilous*, New York: Free Press, 1959; E. Gartly Jaco, editor, *Patients, Physicians and Illness*, New York: Free Press, 1958; Eliot Freidson, "Client Control in Medical Practice," *American Journal of Sociology*, 65 (January, 1960), pp. 374–382; George G. Reader and Mary E. W. Goss, "Medical Sociology with Particular Reference to the Study of Hospitals," *Transactions of the Fourth World Congress of Sociology*, London: International Sociological Association, 1959, Vol. II, pp. 139–152.
[9] Cf. Oswald Hall, "The Informal Organization of the Medical Profession," *Canadian Journal of Economics and Political Science*, 12 (February, 1946), pp. 30–44, and "Stages of a Medical Career," *American Journal of Sociology*, 53 (March, 1948), pp. 327–337; Rose Laub Coser, "Authority and Decision-Making in a Hospital," *American Sociological Review*, 23 (February, 1958), pp. 56–63; Field, *op. cit.*; and Joseph Ben-David, "The Professional Role of the Physician in Bureaucratized Medicine: A Study in Role Conflict," *Human Relations*, 11 (No. 3, 1958), pp. 255–274.

the program yearly provides medical care for about 12,000 ambulant patients and clinical instruction for all fourth-year students in the medical school. Along with a small number of nurses, social workers, and other hospital personnel, some 80 physicians participate in the program. Most of these physicians serve on a part-time unpaid basis but some are salaried full-time employees; all are specialists who hold appointments on the staffs of both the hospital and the medical school.

In 1952 the Bureau of Applied Social Research, Columbia University, began a series of interlocking studies of different aspects of the program.[10] Data for the present report were gathered as part of that series, primarily through intermittent participant observation over a period of five years (1952–1957), and secondarily through study of organizational documents and questionnaires filled out by physicians. The participant observation took place mainly in the general medical clinic, where about 50 of the physicians worked; it was conducted by the author and included a total of nearly two years of attendance at staff meetings and clinical conferences as well as informal interviews with various members of the professional staff. The questionnaire survey was carried out in 1956 by another member of the research group,[11] and included all physicians then listed as members of the clinical faculty of the medical school or as residents on the hospital staff. Exactly 507 or 84 per cent of the 604 physicians filled out and returned the mailed questionnaire, which covered various features of their attitudes, values, experience, and training. Except as otherwise indicated the observations and quotations reported here are drawn from the author's field notes.

FORMAL ORGANIZATION

The overall organization of the program for comprehensive care and teaching has been described in detail elsewhere.[12] A brief account of those aspects that pertain to physicians will suffice, therefore, to indicate the general

[10] Studies of the program were, in turn, but one aspect of a larger research project concerned with the sociology of professional education, conducted by the Bureau in three medical schools over a period of several years. Although much of the information collected is still unpublished, some preliminary findings are reported in Robert K. Merton, George G. Reader, and Patricia L. Kendall, editors, *The Student-Physician*, Cambridge: Harvard University Press, 1957; see also Robert K. Merton, Samuel Bloom, and Natalie Rogoff, "Studies in the Sociology of Medical Education," *Journal of Medical Education*, 31 (August, 1956), pp. 552–564.

[11] The present paper reports only a small portion of the survey data obtained; the majority of the data are described and analyzed by David Caplovitz, "Student-Faculty Relations in Medical School: A Study of Professional Socialization," unpublished Ph.D. dissertation, Columbia University, 1960.

[12] George G. Reader, "Comprehensive Medical Care," *Journal of Medical Education*, 28 (July, 1953), pp. 34–40; Reader, "Organization and Development of a Compre-

nature of the formal hierarchy within which this professional group appeared to work without noticeable strain.

In order to "emphasize the integration necessary to the practice of comprehensive care,"[13] the program is officially conceived as a non-departmental unit of the medical center as a whole. The program is thus the ultimate responsibility of the group who makes policy for the medical center: the joint administrative board. Direct responsibility for determining general program policy, however, is the province of a formal advisory committee, appointed by the joint administrative board and consisting of the heads of the clinical departments as well as a number of other professionals who hold positions of prominence in the center.[14]

Next in line is the director of the program, a salaried internist appointed by the advisory committee. According to an official statement, he is responsible to the advisory committee for "overall supervision and coordination of the program" and "ultimately responsible to the clinical department heads for the care the patients receive." He brings to the committee "questions of policy" and keeps them "informed of general progress."[15]

Responsible to the director are four salaried assistant directors: two internists and two pediatricians. Placed in charge of the general medical clinic, the assistant director for medicine was initially "responsible to the director for the care of all adult patients under the program and the students' activities in the medical clinic and on visits to the home."[16] Subsequently the last-named responsibility was assigned to an assistant director for home care. The assistant directors for pediatrics and for pediatric home care have responsibilities that are similar but not identical to those of their counterparts in medicine.

In turn, all of the physicians who teach students and care for patients

hensive Care Program," *American Journal of Public Health*, 44 (June, 1954), pp. 760–765; Reader, "The Cornell Comprehensive Care and Teaching Program," in Merton, Reader, and Kendall, *op. cit.*, pp. 81–101; Mary E. W. Goss, "Change in the Cornell Comprehensive Care and Teaching Program," in Merton, Reader, and Kendall, *op. cit.*, pp. 249–270; David P. Barr, "The Teaching of Preventive Medicine," *Journal of Medical Education*, 28 (March, 1953), pp. 49–56; Barr, "Extramural Facilities in Medical Education," *Journal of Medical Education*, 28 (July, 1953), pp. 9–12.

[13] Reader, "Comprehensive Medical Care," *op. cit.*, p. 35.

[14] The doctors who serve as heads of the clinical departments in the medical school also hold the position of chief of the corresponding clinical service in the hospital. For example, the head of the department of medicine in the school is physician-in-chief of the hospital; the head of the department of surgery is surgeon-in-chief, and so on.

[15] Reader, "Organization and Development of a Comprehensive Care Program," *op. cit.*, p. 763.

[16] *Ibid.*

in the two clinics or in the home care services are held formally responsible for these activities to the appropriate assistant director. This group of physicians includes a small number of salaried specialty consultants and assistant residents as well as a larger number of unsalaried attending internists and pediatricians.

While medical students are in the clinics, they are viewed as junior physicians, immediately responsible to the individual physicians who serve as their instructors and ultimately responsible to those in charge of the program.

Before considering the meaning of this formal hierarchy in terms of day-to-day actions and expectations of physicians, three further facts about it should be noted. First, departures from formal organization of physicians as a "company of equals" had ample precedent in the medical center. Physicians who receive advanced training while on the house staff of the hospital are traditionally organized in hierarchical fashion; within each clinical service, interns are responsible to assistant residents, assistant residents to head resident, and head resident to the chief of the service. Correlatively, each higher level is responsible for and supervises the work of the level below.[17] Moreover, even before the program was instituted there were official—though less elaborate—lines of responsibility in the two clinics under discussion, as well as in other patient-care and teaching units of the medical center. Second, during the five-year period of observation the program as a whole underwent many changes, but the hierarchical arrangement described remained relatively stable. No trend toward a more egalitarian pattern could be discerned. Third, both positive and negative sanctioning powers remained in the hands of the advisory committee. It retained the right to appoint, dismiss, and promote physicians in the program. In this respect it also followed precedent in the medical center, where these rights are traditional prerogatives of the chief of each clinical service, subject to the final approval of the medical board of the hospital in the case of hospital appointments, and of the executive faculty of the medical school in the case of academic appointments.

TYPES OF SUPERVISORY CONTROL

Physicians who worked in the clinics recognized and distinguished between two major types of supervisory prerogatives: the right to make decisions and the right to give advice. Examination of their opinions and behavior in two specific, supervisory situations—scheduling and chart re-

[17] *Cf.* Rose Laub Coser, *op. cit.*

view—may serve as a basis for analysis of the general nature of the prerogatives.

SCHEDULING. For each session of the medical clinic the physician-in-charge—who was also the assistant director for medicine in the program—made out and posted a master schedule in which physician-instructors were paired with students and assigned patients and examining rooms. When physicians arrived at the clinic each morning or afternoon, they customarily consulted the master schedule to find out which patients they would be seeing that day and where, and to learn which students' work they would be called upon to check. "Checking" students was the main teaching activity of physicians in the clinic, and it ordinarily took place in the following manner: after a student had finished interviewing and examining his assigned patient, he reported the findings to his assigned physician-instructor, who first discussed with the student alternative probable diagnoses, possible plans for therapy, and the nature of the particular disease that seemed to be involved; then the physician-instructor proceeded to examine the patient briefly himself. Finally he conferred again with the student concerning what should be done next for the patient, and he countersigned the notes which the student had written in the patient's chart.

Occasionally a physician expressed a preference for continuing to check a particular student. When this occurred the physician-in-charge tried to take the preference into account in making future assignments though, as was generally understood, to do so was not always possible within the framework of the sometimes disparate schedules of students and physicians. There were also times when the physician assigned to a student was unavailable when that student was ready to be checked. In such instances the physician was known or assumed to be occupied elsewhere with unexpected teaching or patient care duties, and the physician-in-charge either found a substitute or checked the student himself.

But for the most part, physicians complied as a matter of course with the directives contained in the schedule, and seemed to take for granted the right of the physician-in-charge of the clinic to make decisions about these routine aspects of their work. Specific formal penalties for non-compliance did not exist, nor did they appear necessary to physicians. "*Of course* the clinic needs a schedule," an attending physician remarked, "and *naturally* we try to follow it. Otherwise the clinic would fall apart."

In this case, physicians were not particularly apt to review critically each decision made by the physician-in-charge. There were other situations, however, when they carefully examined the content of a request before they decided to comply with it. In fact, in the case of chart review they were prepared to comply *only* if they approved.

CHART REVIEW. When the physician-in-charge reviewed charts at the beginning of each clinic session, he examined the recent notes made by students and physicians[18] in the charts of patients scheduled for revisits during the session. If he had comments on the care a patient was receiving, he wrote them out in the form of suggestions and clipped them to the chart where they could be seen by the student or physician with whom the patient had an appointment. Typical of the suggestions offered were the following: "Suggest basal metabolism and serum cholesterol on this patient."; "No complete urinalysis recorded in past six months on this diabetic. How about looking for albumin and doubly-refractile bodies?"; "Occult blood in stool suggests need for barium enema and proctoscopy."; "Elderly patient with insomnia may be depressed. Psychiatric consultation?"

The director of the program, who had instituted the procedure,[19] looked on reviewing charts in this manner as a form of supervision which in the long run would aid in maintaining high standards of patient care in the medical clinic. He explained, "Going over the charts regularly lets the doctors know we're following what they're doing, and that's what counts in keeping standards up."

Apart from what could be learned through examination of successive entries in the charts themselves, no records were kept of whether or not physicians actually carried out the suggestions that were offered. However, the physician-in-charge believed that compliance with his suggestions occurred more often than not. He recognized, nevertheless, that compliance was always problematic; in accordance with the professional norms and values described more fully in a later section of this paper, physicians reserved to themselves the right to accept or reject the suggestions about patient care which the physician-in-charge might make. "I believe a doctor should always be open to advice about his patients, since no one is ever so good he can't learn something from others occasionally," said an attending physician in the clinic. However, he continued, "But it's up to the doctor who's actually taking care of the patient to make the final decisions—he's the one who's responsible for the patient, remember."

This view was shared by physicians in the clinic generally, *including* those who held supervisory positions. The director of the program himself remarked, "If you're reviewing charts *you don't expect the doctors to*

---

[18] All students cared for patients under the supervision of qualified physicians, but some patients were cared for by physicians alone. In the latter case, the physicians themselves wrote the notes for the patients' charts; when a student was also involved in caring for a patient, the student wrote the notes and his instructor countersigned them, thus signifying approval of the notes as part of the patient's permanent record.
[19] While the specific procedure was relatively new to the clinic, the principle of review as a means of maintaining standards had many precedents in the hospital as a whole.

carry out every suggestion you make. You may have a good reason for suggesting something should be done, but they may have a better reason for not doing it, since they know the patients."

In the case of chart review, then, physicians interpreted the official right to supervise as the right to advise rather than to make decisions governing their behavior. They considered it their duty to take supervisory suggestions about patient care into account, and in this sense they accepted supervision. But they also felt obliged, as responsible physicians, to examine such suggestions critically, and to follow them only if they appeared to be in the patients' best interests according to their own professional judgment. Correlatively, they would have considered it a breach of their duty as physicians to carry out a supervisory suggestion regarding the care they gave to a patient without independently evaluating its merits.

As could hardly be otherwise under such conditions, formal sanctions for non-compliance with supervisory suggestions of this sort were not in evidence. In the very infrequent instances when a supervising physician believed the well-being of a patient was seriously threatened by what he judged to be inadequate medical care, he made a point of discussing the case personally with the responsible physician. These discussions focused not on the fact that the responsible physician had failed to follow the suggestions offered, but on the technical problems presented by the patient, viewed in the light of current medical knowledge and practice. Alternatively or concomitantly, the supervising physician might arrange to have the patient presented by a student at a teaching conference, where the patient's problems and medical care were discussed by students and faculty members, presumably for the benefit of the students present. In either case, there was a strong likelihood that the responsible physician would revise his approach to the patient's care as a result of the discussion, although sometimes it was the supervising physician himself who became convinced that his suggestions had been less wise than he had originally thought.

TYPES OF CONTROL. The type of control manifested in chart review clearly differs in certain respects from that exemplified in scheduling. In the latter case, a physician who was formally in charge made a decision which indicated that one particular course of action was to be followed by other physicians. The decision was intended to leave little margin for alternative behavior on the part of those involved; compliance was expected. Physicians understood this; with respect to scheduling they believed that in making requests the physician-in-charge was within the rights attached to the supervisory status he held, and that they had an obligation to behave in accordance with the requests. Correspondingly, they complied overtly.

Thus the process of control was direct, and its outcome—overt compliance —was relatively predictable.

In chart review, on the other hand, the rights attached to the status of physician-in-charge were more limited. Consistent with professional norms, he acted as a consultant, making decisions which he intended and physicians interpreted as leaving a wide margin for alternative behavior. Accordingly, the decisions were expressed as suggestions, and overt compliance was expected and occurred only if the suggestion met with approval after independent critical evaluation. Here the process of control was indirect, and the outcome of the process was in principle unpredictable.

Obviously, the latter "indirect" process represents an institutionalized form of exercising *influence*; advice was given which, according to the norms of physicians, might legitimately be rejected by recipients.[20] In contrast, the "direct" process which was described represents the exercise of *authority*; supervisory decisions were made which, however phrased, ordinarily could not be rejected legitimately by those whose actions they concerned.

It should be noted, nevertheless, that both types of control had at least one feature in common: there were neither specific formal penalties for non-compliance nor specific formal rewards for compliance. General formal sanctions existed, of course, in the form of possible promotion or dismissal from the staff. These sanctions, however, essentially rested with the chiefs of the services, and the relationship between their application and performance in the clinic was far from obvious either to the physicians who worked in the clinic or to the observer. More apparent was the importance of anticipated informal sanctions, such as those illustrated in the case of chart review.

ACTIVITY, NORMS, AND TYPES OF CONTROL

The two normatively different types of control—influence and authority— were not confined to the instances described. Each occurred more generally among physicians in the medical center, and as this section will indicate, which one was believed appropriate in a particular situation depended immediately upon whether physicians considered the sphere of activity in question to be "administrative" or "professional" in nature, and ultimately, upon the norms and values they held regarding each sphere.

[20] *Cf.* Simon, *op. cit.:* "The characteristic which distinguishes authority from other kinds of influence is . . . that a subordinate holds in abeyance his own critical faculties for choosing between alternatives and uses the formal criterion of the receipt of a command or signal as his basis for choice. On the other hand, a person who receives a suggestion accepts it as only one of the evidential bases for making his choice—but the choice he will make depends upon conviction" (pp. 126–127).

PATIENT CARE. As the account of chart review suggests, physicians believed patient care to be a professional activity which required independence in decision making, i.e., individual authority for each doctor. Accordingly, supervising physicians generally attempted to exert influence rather than authority when they wished to affect the behavior of other physicians in this realm of activity.

Informal questioning of physicians with supervisory responsibility for patient care in various units of the hospital indicated that, except in the rare case when they found themselves dealing with an unusually stubborn and uninformed intern, they were not prepared to give anything resembling an order to another doctor concerning the care of that doctor's patient. For example, two supervising physicians acknowledged that they had the formal right to make such requests because they were officially responsible for the professional care given to patients in their units; yet both independently went on to make almost identical comments: "You just never do it, though"; "But you don't do it, of course."

Observation of interaction among doctors in the medical clinic bore out these statements, for it revealed no instance in which a supervising physician officially requested a physician on the staff to follow a particular course of action in the care he gave his patient. (Interns did not work in the clinic, and so there was no opportunity to observe whether they were in fact ever treated differently from residents and attending physicians in this respect.) However, observation did show a great many instances—apart from chart review—in which supervising physicians made some form of suggestion to those in the clinic whose work they were supervising. Space precludes description of such instances, which on the whole were most likely to occur in clinical conferences and history meetings conducted by the director of the program.

PROFESSIONAL NORMS AND VALUES. Underlying and legitimating the exercise of influence rather than authority in the realm of patient care were, of course, certain firmly institutionalized values of the medical profession: acceptance of personal responsibility for patients, together with acknowledgement of one's own potential limitations in fulfilling that responsibility.[21]

Physicians in the clinic did not often verbalize their beliefs regarding personal responsibility for patient care. Instead, such personal responsibility appeared to be a basic premise for behavior, a value which was so taken for granted that verbalization was ordinarily superfluous. By and large, only when physicians found themselves with apparently irreconcilable

[21] For an official, general statement of these values, see *Principles of Medical Ethics*, Chicago: American Medical Association, 1957, especially sections 2, 5, 6, and 8.

differences of opinion in discussions about the diagnosis or treatment of a particular patient were they likely to express themselves on the topic.

Assumption of personal responsibility for patients would seem to account in large measure for physicians' unwillingness to take or give authoritative orders concerning patient care. For once this value was accepted —as is apparently was by physicians in both supervisory and non-supervisory positions—to give an order meant usurping another doctor's professional responsibility, as well as taking over the everpresent risk of being proved wrong by later events. And to follow an order, if given, without independently evaluating it, was equivalent to being irresponsible professionally. No doctor wanted to be open to either charge—i.e., to violate these professional norms—and thus it is not surprising that no orders were given in the first place.

Nevertheless, as has been indicated, physicians were willing to give and accept *advice* in the area of patient care. The values underlying such behavior found expression in their beliefs regarding the limitations of any single doctor's medical knowledge and skill, and in the significance which they attached to possession of these attributes.

As the survey of opinions of more than five hundred physicians in the medical center indicates, almost all of the doctors queried (97 per cent) believed extensive knowledge of medical facts to be of considerable importance in judging the competence of physicians in their specialty. Moreover, they were virtually unanimous in evaluating skill in the realm of diagnosis as of great importance; fully 94 per cent of the group did so, while five per cent judged this skill to be of moderate importance and less than one per cent thought it of minor importance. But the demonstrably high value which physicians placed upon having medical knowledge and diagnostic skill did not mean they thought they could be individually omniscient in these matters. When asked how they would feel if a physician in their specialty were to "admit his uncertainties with respect to a diagnostic problem," only four per cent expressed any degree of disapproval, as contrasted with fully 86 per cent who definitely approved of admitting uncertainty when it existed. Apparently they expected to be uncertain some proportion of the time, and in accordance with the norms of medical practice, they believed in admitting it.[22]

These evaluations seem to explain at least in part why physicians would not only tolerate but, on occasion, actually welcome supervisory advise in matters of patient care, even though they would not consider the pos-

[22] For an analysis of some types of uncertainty that are inherent in medical practice, as well as an account of how medical students may learn to come to terms with such uncertainty, see Renée C. Fox, "Training for Uncertainty," in Merton, Reader, and Kendall, *op. cit.*, pp. 207–241.

sibility of orders. That is, because they had learned as professionals to place a high value upon both admitting uncertainty and being knowledgeable, it may be presumed that they were motivated to seek and accept help when they needed it as well as continually to acquire greater knowledge and skill. Advice from others clearly offered opportunities for such learning and assistance; yet, significantly, it did not jeopardize the personal responsibility for patients which physicians felt was essential to maintain.

Physicians did not invariably define advice from other physicians as a valuable learning experience, however, nor were they equally ready to accept suggestions from any physician who might conceivably be put in charge. Even though a supervising physician offers only advice rather than orders, in the nature of the supervisory situation—and in contrast with the consultation typical of private practice, where advice is given only upon request—the supervisor's advice is sometimes unsolicited. Not unlike workers in other organizations, physicians tend to interpret unsolicited advice as an adverse reflection on their professional competence.[23] Consequently if they are to accept a formal relationship involving this sort of advice and still retain their professional self-respect, they must respect the source of the advice, the supervising physician. Study of the reactions of physicians in the clinic to two successive physicians-in-charge who had differing qualifications suggested that the extent of respect accorded a supervising physician depended to a considerable extent on assessments of his professional competence, as well as on the formal rank he held in the medical school and in the immediate work context. In evaluating these characteristics the point of reference of physicians was personal: if they believed the professional competence of a supervising physician approximately equalled or exceeded their own, they were likely to respect him; and unless a supervising physician of lower rank had remarkable professional accomplishments to his credit, physicians were likely to respect him less than one whose formal rank was the same or higher than their own.[24] Thus, although giving and taking advice was a general behavior pattern among physicians which the norms and values of the medical profession not only legitimated but under certain circumstances required, translation of the pattern into effective supervisory relationships in the realm of patient care required careful "matching" of the qualifications of both parties to the relationship.

[23] *Cf.* Melville Dalton, "Conflicts Between Staff and Line Managerial Officers," *American Sociological Review*, 15 (June, 1950), pp. 342–351; Lyman Bryson, "Notes on a Theory of Advice," in Robert K. Merton, *et al.*, editors, *Reader in Bureaucracy*, New York: Free Press, 1952, pp. 202–216.
[24] Details of the data that support these statements may be found in Goss, "Physicians in Bureaucracy . . . ," pp. 79–106.

ADMINISTRATION. In contrast with patient care, the norms and values associated with the sphere of activity which physicians called "administration" permitted supervisory control through the use of authority rather than influence alone. The case of scheduling illustrates this relationship, for physicians tended to look on this activity as, in the words of one doctor, "just administrative paperwork."

Observation of physicians in the medical clinic indicated that overt compliance with administrative decisions was, in general, relatively predictable. But as might be expected, it was never completely so; deviations were also predictable, though they appeared to constitute a rather small proportion of the total behavior observed.

Physicians in the clinic, for example, did not invariably see all of the patients scheduled for them during a clinic session, or arrive exactly on time for their appointments in accordance with the administrative request that they be prompt. The reasons they gave for not complying were sometimes personal in nature, but more often they concerned an urgent professional obligation. "I'm late this morning because a patient of mine in the hospital here just died and I had to talk with the relatives," explained a physician as he came hurriedly into the clinic. Another, half an hour before the clinic session officially ended, asked the physician in charge:

> Would you see my last revisit for me today? I just heard from one of my private patients—sounds like she's in acute pulmonary edema and I think I'd better go see her right away.

Physicians in supervisory positions expected and condoned such behavior, even though it was also a source of annoyance since it meant that work had to be reallocated. As the assistant director of medicine remarked:

> Sure it's hard on us when somebody doesn't show up. But if a doctor has to see a patient who's really sick, there's nothing we can do but accept it and divide his work somehow. . . . After all, the patient does come first.

Following administrative regulations was evidently not very important to physicians when the regulations conflicted with the professional task of taking care of patients whose need they evaluated as more pressing. Consequently they felt free to disregard administrative requests on occasions when such conflicts arose.

ADMINISTRATION VERSUS PROFESSIONAL ACTIVITIES AND NORMS. That professional obligations took precedence over adhering to administrative decisions does not negate the fact that, in areas which physicians defined as "administrative," they were generally willing to grant those in charge the right to make decisions affecting their actions, a right they did not concede in the realm of patient care. Examination of the prevailing conception of administration among physicians in the medical clinic provides some explanation of this differential willingness.

By and large, physicians defined administrative activity more by exclusion than otherwise. That is, they tended to label as "administration" virtually any work in the clinic—and the medical center—that did *not* involve caring directly for patients, teaching students, doing research, or the personal planning, studying, and writing entailed in these activities.

When pressed for a positive definition, some physicians who were informally interviewed specifically cited policy-making about organizational procedures. But they were generally inclined to view administrative activity as, in the words of one of the full-time staff members, "paperwork and other housekeeping chores."

Whether identified specifically as paperwork, housekeeping, or policy-making, however, physicians seemed to agree that administrative work was relatively non-professional in character, requiring little or no medical training for its execution and bearing only indirectly on strictly medical affairs.[25] This was implicit in the way they tended to contrast administration with taking care of patients and teaching, both of which manifestly did require medical training and were obviously medical activities. As might be expected of professionally trained persons, physicians generally preferred to be doing professional work, which they valued highly, rather than administrative work which they held in less esteem.

The prevalence of this outlook is indirectly corroborated by the answers physicians gave to a question contained in the survey, which asked them to rank certain activities "in terms of the amount of interest you have in them."[26] More than half (63 per cent) of the physicians gave first place to seeing patients, and roughly two-fifths assigned this place to teaching or research (19 per cent and 17 per cent, respectively). However, practically no one (one per cent) rated administration as of primary interest, and approximately four-fifths (79 per cent) of the physicians ranked administration last in terms of the amount of interest this activity had for them.

Thus it would seem that when physicians complied with administrative decisions, they gained freedom from a responsibility—that of making the decisions—which they considered more or less onerous. Perhaps more significantly, since administrative decisions covered only activities they

---

[25] In spite of this view, there were pressures toward assigning physicians rather than lay persons to certain administrative positions. An analysis of the paradox that seems to be involved is contained in Goss, *ibid.*, pp. 107–143.

[26] Five activities were listed: "seeing patients in private practice"; "seeing patients in clinics or wards"; "teaching"; "research"; and "administration."

viewed as non-professional or ancillary to their work, the norms of professional practice were not called into question. This meant that physicians could comply with administrative requests without losing their distinctively professional prerogatives; their individual authority in the sphere of patient care remained intact and their prestige as independent professionals was not threatened.

It should also be emphasized that in the clinic and in the medical center generally, those who made administrative decisions which directly concerned the work of physicians were physicians themselves rather than lay persons. While the data reported therefore provide strong reason to believe that a physician who holds an administrative position can effectively exercise authority in administrative matters with respect to other physicians, they provide no evidence concerning what would happen if the administrator were a non-physician.

CONCLUSION

The findings that have been presented resolve certain analytic problems even while they raise others.

First, although hierarchical organization of professionals would appear to conflict with maintenance of the individual authority which is functionally required for professional work, practice in the organization that has been described indicated that it did not do so. In large measure, the potential strain implied was apparently avoided through adherence to professional norms of behavior. These norms did not require, as is sometimes thought, that each physician be autonomous in every sphere of his activity, but only that he be free to make his own decisions in professional matters as opposed to administrative concerns. Nor, even in the professional sphere, did the norms rule out the possibility of supervision; so long as supervision came from a physician and took the form of advice, it was within normatively acceptable bounds for physicians. Thus one of the organizational mechanisms for reconciling hierarchical supervision of professional activity with maintenance of individual authority in that sphere would appear to be the conception of supervision as a *formal advisory or consultation relationship*. A related structural mechanism for avoiding strain would seem to be the practice of assigning supervisory duties only to persons whose formal rank and professional qualifications are sufficient to command the respect of the professionals under their supervision.

Second, the findings suggest that supervisory relationships among physicians constitute a limiting case of the general observation that the norms and values of subordinates will affect, in greater or less degree, the extent and kinds of control which those in superordinate positions may exert with respect to subordinates. When physicians work in a formal organization they do not come as disparate individuals with vague, diverse or radically conflicting expectations regarding the nature of supervisory control they will properly exercise or submit to. Rather, as has been shown, they come as professionals, with norms and values regarding supervisory control which are relatively well defined, shared, and specific as to circumstance. Presumably this is a consequence of the similarity and intensity of their prior professional education; during the course of their successive experiences as medical student, intern, and perhaps resident, they have both the opportunity and the obligation to observe, learn, and internalize professional standards for conduct in various sorts of relationships with medical colleagues as well as with patients and ancillary personnel.[27] At any rate, the fact that physicians tend to share these standards *before* affiliating with a formal organization as fully-qualified doctors, and *regardless* of whether they hold supervisory or non-supervisory positions, is especially significant in the present connection. For it suggests that in the case of physicians, neither the norms of "superordinates" nor those of "subordinates" as such are of greatest relevance in determining the extent and kind of supervisory control that can be exercised feasibly, but rather the norms and values of the medical profession at large. When both superviser and supervised are physicians the control-oriented behavior of each is largely predetermined by established professional norms and values which both know and accept in advance. Relatively little mutual adjustment of role expectations is therefore required on the part of either person, and it is in this sense that supervisory relationships among physicians appear to constitute a limiting case of the principle cited. . . .

[27] Theoretical analysis and empirical materials bearing on the process of professional socialization among medical students are presented in Merton, Reader, and Kendall, *op. cit.*; see also Everett C. Hughes, "The Making of a Physician," *Human Organization*, 14 (Winter, 1956), pp. 21–25, and Howard S. Becker and Blanche Geer, "The Fate of Idealism in Medical School," *American Sociological Review*, 23 (February, 1958), pp. 50–56.

V

Organization and Society

Modern society is to a large degree a bureaucratic society; that is, many of its functional requirements—such as allocation of means and social integration—are carried out and controlled by complex organizations. Not only does modern society as a whole tend to be bureaucratic, but the most powerful social units of modern society are also bureaucracies. In addition to big business and big labor, which are often cited in this context, political parties, military organizations, school systems, voluntary associations, and many others make up a good part of the societal web. Finally, some organizations develop into social monsters, embracing more and more social activities and controlling so many aspects of the lives of their members that they almost become societies in themselves.

The most important organizations, from the viewpoint of the integration of society, are probably the governmental bureaucracies. Janowitz, Wright, and Delany examine the conditions for administration by consent, that is, the conditions under which the operation of a governmental bureaucracy maintains rather than decreases social and political integration. Eisenstadt examines the conditions under which societies keep control of bureaucracies, in contrast to conditions under which bureaucracies overwhelm societies. Goffman examines organizations whose control over the lives and activities of their members is so complete, they become societies of a sort in themselves. Litwak and Hylton address themselves to the relations between or-

293

ganizations which make up an important segment of the societal fabric. Crozier studies the evolution of the central organizational mechanisms of a society which is already "bureaucratized," while Brager raises the problems involved in gaining the participation of lower status groups in the organizational web of a modern society.

Janowitz, Wright, and Delany study the ways in which the public sees the local public administration. To what degree are the conditions present which enable rule by consent? Four criteria are developed: Does the public have sufficient knowledge about the administration? Does the public feel that its self-interest is preserved? Does the public regard the bureaucracy as guided by principles? And is the prestige of the Civil Service high enough, yet not too high? Forms of imbalance are discussed which arise between the public and the administration, when one or more of these bases of consent are lacking.

Eisenstadt examines the social context in which the bureaucratic sector of society emerges, develops, and expands. The major conditions seem to be a development of *Gesellschaft* orientations (universalistic, specific, and so on) and high differentiation of social systems from one another. Once the bureaucratic sector is fairly established, three forms of relationships between it and society may develop: First, one in which the bureaucracy maintains its distinct characteristics, so that it is the reliable servant of social goals and political powers; second, one in which the bureaucracy penetrates into more and more spheres of life and becomes the omnipotent organ of society; third, one in which particularistic pressures of various social groups become so intense that the conditions for effective bureaucratic activities are undermined, and the bureaucracy's value as an instrumental unit is, to a large degree, lost. The conditions are specified under which each of the three types of relationships is likely to emerge.

Goffman presents a descriptive characterization and careful analysis of "a social hybrid which is part residential community and part formal organization." The inmates live in such social establishments; in other words, many aspects of their behavior, considered "private" on the outside, are here controlled and supervised by the staff. Inmates, as a rule, do not engage in paid work; they are "taken care of." Having a family is incompatible with the organizational structure and needs of total institutions. Entrance or exit is usually not voluntary.

The interests in total organizations are many: They have intense effects on the moral orientation of their inmates; they constitute miniature totalitarian societies and as such may enhance research into the mentality and structure of totalitarian regimes. Total organizations tend, even more than other organizations, to divert means from their goals—such as therapy, rehabilitation, education, and religious service—for the purpose of promoting the fulfillment of needs of the staff and organization. Awareness of the special problems involved in these structures may lead to a reconsideration of their use in some situations, and in others to a search for mechanisms which will reduce their negative effects. Thus, while the other writers are interested in the balance between organizations and the society in which they operate, Goffman informs us about the balance between organizations and the "societies" which develop within them—a problem which is common to all organizations but which comes into especially sharp relief in total organizations.

The conceptual contribution of Litwak and Hylton lies in its extension of the analysis of interorganizational relations. The intellectual issues that are raised concern the articulation of the many simultaneous efforts in which a complex society is engaged, the use of organizations to advance particular goals, and the coordination of those goals without central control. In many ways the relations among organizations are highly "unorganizational" but a measure of coordination is nevertheless reached. As the post-modern (post-1945) society attempts to guide more and more societal processes, and as its organizational needs multiply, the problems of articulation raised by Litwak and Hylton increase in importance.

Crozier also deals with post-modern society—in particular, with postwar France. He studies various mechanisms which permit greater flexibility within the bureaucratic organization and enhance both rationality and humanity. For many, Britain is still notable for her effective civil service, while France has yet to become a fully modernized society. Crozier and other contemporary authors point out that we must now look to France for administrative innovations—innovations which many countries, including Britain, may adopt.[1] Crozier, however, may be unduly

[1] Andrew Shoenfield, *Modern Capitalism* (New York: Oxford University Press, 1965); Everett E. Hagen and Stephanie F. T. White, *Great Britain* (Syracuse, N.Y.: Syracuse University Press, 1966), especially pp. 101–128.

modest in his interpretation of recent developments in his country.

Brager deals with a topic which deserves much more attention: the organizational activities of lower status groups. In part, it is a question of the "downward" efforts of established organizations, such as school systems, welfare agencies, and medical clinics, but it is also a matter of upward mobilization, of the participation of lower status groups in political parties, labor unions, and especially social movements, in order to change society and to assure themselves of their legitimate place in it.[2]

---

[2] For our recent work on the subject, see *The Active Society* (New York: Free Press, 1968), chap. 15 and chaps. 17–18.

PUBLIC ADMINISTRATION AND THE PUBLIC

Morris Janowitz, Deil Wright, and William Delany

Our objectives were two-fold. First, we sought to describe public contact with government agencies in the metropolis and to investigate public knowledge and evaluations of the administrative process. We tried to uncover the correlates of these basic perspectives toward administrative authority. By analyzing the public's image of the administrative process we were studying by inference administrative "public relations" in its broadest context. Second, we sought to evaluate the extent to which these public perspectives were creating a political climate appropriate for administration based on consent. To this end we developed and applied four criteria with the hope that our analysis might be made relevant to the traditional interests of political theorists.

Our attention was on those administrative agencies which penetrate the daily routines of the metropolitan community. This arbitrarily neglects some crucial and controversial aspects of governmental administration. We believe, however, that the metropolitan community is the initial locus for the analysis of public administration and the public. The willingness and

Reprinted in part from Morris Janowitz, Deil Wright, and William Delany, *Public Administration and the Public: Perspectives toward Government in a Metropolitan Community,* pp. 101–114, by permission of the authors and the publisher, The University of Michigan, Institute of Public Administration. Copyright 1958.

ability of the public to support the more remote aspects of administration depend in good measure on its more direct experiences with the organs of government.

OVERVIEW OF THE FINDINGS

It became apparent from our findings in the Detroit metropolitan community that political party affiliation was not a good index to fundamental differences in public perspectives toward the administrative process. Our assumption that these perspectives would not be sharply linked to partisan party politics was repeatedly confirmed. . . .

These empirical data provide documentation of the rather pervasive acceptance of the current scope and performance of metropolitan-based administration. This is not to overlook either the small minority who object or the fact that specific operations of government may produce intense and outspoken criticism or rejection. Nor is this acceptance incompatible with the desire or even the demand for improvement. But our study did not probe willingness to support improvement. To some degree, the essential services of government are accepted simply because there is no alternative or because the public sees no possibility of alternatives. Our findings, however, underline the extent to which the new integrative functions of government, especially those connected with "service" government, have an impact on all strata throughout the social structure. All the various strata, not just the lower social groups in the metropolitan community, have developed a stake in and a reliance on these new functions of government. As a consequence, they contribute a basis for social and political consensus. For example, it should be recalled that only seven per cent of the population thought the scope of government welfare service was too broad or extensive.

These findings do not deny widespread ambivalent feelings toward the symbols of administrative authority. Ambivalence and reservation could be quickly mobilized by probing perspectives about the worth of government services and lack of principle mindedness among public servants. The fact that such negativism was less concentrated among young people may indicate a long-term trend. Generations which are growing up under the broadened scope of government are perhaps not so likely to hold the more negative orientations toward government authority historically attributed to the American public.

Also noteworthy was the finding that persons display a generalized syndrome of a tendency to accept or a tendency to reject the performance of administrative agencies. In other words, each member of the public seemed to address himself to the diffuse functions and organizations of metropolitan-based administration with some degree of self-consistency in his evaluation of its performance. Here our findings are merely compatible with the current assumptions of political behavior research which see political perspectives as being conditioned by underlying and persistent motivations. Along with the complex of perspectives concerning political partisanship we have identified another complex—that dealing with administrative authority.

For our second objective, that of evaluating the extent to which public perspectives were appropriate for administrative behavior based on consent, four categories—knowledge, self-interest redefined, principle mindedness, and prestige—formed the core of our analysis. A meaningful application of these categories would require trend data in order to establish the direction of social change. A meaningful application would also require comparative data on other nation states, such as Great Britain, to establish how much information, self-interest, principle mindedness, and prestige are required for democratic consent. For each perspective there is some optimum level, so that these four categories could be formulated into evaluative criteria and thereby constitute a bench mark for research.

First, the public failed to display extensive information about the practices of administration. The tests of the desired level of knowledge were indeed minimal. To avoid an over-intellectualized approach, a distinction was made between generalized knowledge and instrumental knowledge. *Generalized* knowledge deals with the understanding of the overall working of an agency or a system of administration. *Instrumental* knowledge deals with the information essential to an individual about his rights and obligations concerning a specific agency. Clearly, instrumental knowledge was the crucial test, and the level of instrumental knowledge was somewhat higher than that of generalized knowledge. Contact—personal or familial—with a particular agency supplied a pragmatic means for overcoming social class and educational limitations on instrumental knowledge about that agency. But even contact did not necessarily produce a very well-informed citizenry.

The heart of the matter rests in the levels of ignorance that persist even after personal and family contact. Public administrators, public affairs leaders, and communications specialists must face the reality of a relatively uninformed citizenry. The majority of the population finds it difficult to translate its self-interest into an adequate level of understanding of key social welfare programs, such as social security. This is not a matter of lower class ignorance, for lack of knowledge penetrates deeply into the middle class. Our data revealed that widespread ignorance exists about other basic functions of government enterprise. But ignorance about key social welfare benefits is likely to have greater disruptive consequences for social stability than ignorance of other governmental activity since these programs are designed to deal directly with the sources of mass insecurity in the modern metropolitan community.

Nevertheless, lack of knowledge was not associated with a pervasive feeling that the public bureaucracy was thwarting personal self-interest. To the contrary, our second criterion—that the public bureaucracy must be seen as serving personal self-interest—was operative to a considerable degree. Self-interest must operate with built-in limitations. Therefore, as a check on the disruptive consequences of self-interested demands on the bureaucracy, the public must simultaneously acknowledge the bureaucracy's capacity to act as a neutral agent in resolving social conflicts.

In applying the criterion of self-interest, three different dimensions were investigated. One dimension assumed that for self-interest to be realized there would have to be a basic and essential acceptance, rather than rejection, of the current performance of the metropolitan-based bureaucracy. A pervasive or deep-seated antagonism against the organs of government—a crude anti-bureaucratic outlook—emerged as the orientation of only a small minority. The quantitative findings, although preliminary and perhaps arbitrary, fix the size of this group at between 10 and 15 per cent of the population.

A second dimension of self-interest assumed that agreement about the desired scope of government would be a manifestation of realized, rather than thwarted, self-interest. As pointed out above, opposition to the present scope of government, in social welfare for example, was also very limited; the transformation of government over the past two decades is now an accepted event. But this consensus should not be overinterpreted. Feelings of thwarted self-interest about the scope of government bureaucracy were lodged in varying degree among those persons who demanded an expansion of government administration at the metropolitan community level. About 40 per cent of the population has such an orientation. The demand for the expansion of governmental services was most concentrated in the lower class and less prestigeful social groups.

But it was on our third dimension of self-interest—the person's estimate of the economic worth of government—that disaffection emerged most sharply. No doubt it is a chronic and perhaps superficial popular reaction to decry high taxes and red tape in public administration. But the results of our probing of these topics are too convincing to dismiss the findings that a near majority feel hostile when these standards of administrative behavior are brought into question. These negative and hostile feelings were concentrated at the bottom of the social pyramid, where simultaneously the demands for more government administration predominate. It may well be that, in our mixed economy, the cost accounting and capital funding systems that public administration is developing as techniques of internal management control may assume new functions. These techniques may produce essential material by which public information programs can demonstrate to clients and public the economic worth of government operations.

The third criterion—that the public view the bureaucracy as being guided by principles—permits no simple evaluation since beliefs about morality in government emerged as more complex than we had anticipated. We did not uncover widespread belief in active corruption among public servants. The public, however, accepted without a sense of moral indignation the perceived importance of political pull in securing aid from administrative agencies. Political pull seemed to connote little more than those advantages of personal contact and acquaintanceships which were useful in dealing with the complexity and impersonality of large organizations. This seemed to be true of both public and private organizations. It was human, so to speak, to feel defensive in dealings with an impersonal government agency. Therefore, those persons who had intimate contacts with the public bureaucracy merely had desirable advantages. The growth and persistence of such a perspective, however, cannot be viewed as compatible with administration based on consent.

The fourth criterion, or requirement, dealt with the prestige of public employment. While we were not able to study in particular the prestige of the higher civil servants, there was a marked general improvement in public attitudes toward the civil servant since 1930. The trend emerged from a comparison of our data with those of Professor L. D. White collected over a quarter of a century ago. It seems hardly likely, however, that this enhanced prestige will rise to a level at which the prestige of the civil servant would endanger administration based on consent. Certainly, impressionistic observations about the higher civil servants' prestige seem to indicate that desired levels have not yet been reached. In the particular case of the military elite, leaving aside the role of the military hero as president, this key elite continues to have relatively limited prestige.

In summary, we believe that the categories of knowledge, self-interest, principle mindedness, and prestige describe consensus about the administrative process as it actually operates in the metropolitan community setting. Thus, to point out by means of these four public perspectives the extent to which administrative behavior rests on essential consent is not to ignore more precise specification of the vulnerabilities confronting our administrative system. With insufficient information, incomplete feelings of self-interest, and considerable indifference about principle mindedness consensus remains inadequate.

IMPLICATIONS FOR BALANCED ADMINISTRATION

. . . Foreign observers have repeatedly commented on the uneasiness with which government administrative authority is exercised in the United States. This is the result not only of the organization of public administration in the United States, but also of the ambivalent public perspectives toward administrative authority in our culture and society.

Analyzing administrative behavior from the point of view of public perspectives—from the external standpoint—is almost certain to result in policy considerations pointing to the need for public informational programs. The application of our four criteria clarify, perhaps, the goals for such efforts. It is not merely a task of disseminating more information. Present efforts to increase the level of public knowledge, to project a clear image of the worth of government, and to raise the prestige of public service seem inadequate. They seem to be without focus as well. . . .

Scarcity of administrative resources is the limiting factor. Government agencies are not permitted to develop informational staffs to fill the gaps between hierarchical levels and between agency personnel and the public. Civil service managerial personnel and facilities in the agencies studied impressed us as generally inadequate for effective "community relations" programs. Given their limited resources, we were impressed however with the ingenuity used by personnel to solve these problems. The upper levels of the agencies were aware of their enforced neutrality among the competing power groups in the metropolitan community. They knew that as community-based agencies they had to make use of the imperfect, though extensive, social consensus in the community to develop their informational activities. This meant that, in large part, the task of disseminating information about their programs was assigned to voluntary associations and economic groups—business, labor, and special interest. The administrators were fully aware of the local community press and utilized it because of its emphasis on consensus in residential and suburban communities. The solutions they had to find were obviously inadequate but, just as noteworthy here, they were realistic. The problems of governmental communications with the metropolitan community will remain unsolved until organizational resources are placed at the disposal of administrative agencies.

Only by thinking in such long-range terms can progress be hoped for in the presentation of metropolitan-based government in the mass media. Perhaps the findings of this study will supply to the policy makers of the mass media a reasoned argument that a positive rather than a negative approach to the public information requirement of metropolitan-based government is very much in order. In short, leadership from the mass media is possible since the public is already prepared for leadership. . . .

To speak of the need for positive public information programs does not mean that planning and development should exclusively be preoccupied with the mass media and with mass channels. Our findings emphasize the pervasive character of "over-the-counter" activities and of the face-to-face contacts with administrative personnel. Scarcity of resources is at work here just as in the case of the bureaucracy's utilization of mass media. In a sense, the scarcity of resources is even more disruptive since inadequate mass media programs represent administrative limitations, but poorly trained and overworked contact personnel are a positive liability. To be concerned with the improvement here is not to overlook the observation that, as of the present time, a person's contact with public agencies is less important in fashioning perspectives than is his position in the social structure. Thus, we are saying that a person's perspective toward an agency is more a function of what he judges the agency contributes to his self-interest and less a function of the way in which the agency presents itself to him.

Yet it would be most misleading and incomplete if the policy implications of this research were exclusively directed to public relations and public information. This study sought to extend beyond concerns with direct internal management of pubic administration. It was a basic assumption that administrative behavior needs to be analyzed in the context of politics and the political process. The development of the public bureaucracy is in the last resort "politic" in the common sense meaning of the word. In planning the strategy of legislative reform, in developing and recruiting a civil service and in guaranteeing its accountability political issues are at stake.

It is fashionable to decry administrative reliance on voluntary associations as private co-optation of public functions. One just cannot overlook the findings of social science research in the field of communication which highlight the advantages of voluntary associations as more efficient and effective means of communication to their members than are the generalized mass vehicles. There are undoubtedly dangers when public information programs of governmental enterprise must rest exclusively on voluntary associations. But without a multiplicity of voluntary association outlets and resources a pluralistic society is impossible. The alternative would be co-optation of information activities by the political parties; and there seems to be no reasons why such an arrangement would necessarily be advantageous.

In any case, an important share of the task of informing the public will continue to fall on the general mass media over which the processes of government have no direct control. . . .

The justification of the legitimate goals of administration is a political task. It involves the election process and the deliberation of the legislature. It is not the primary or ultimate task of the public administrator to justify his own activities; this is the task of the politician and the public affairs leader—both on the national and on the metropolitan community level.

BUREAUCRACY, BUREAUCRATIZATION, AND DEBUREAUCRATIZATION

S. N. Eisenstadt

CONDITIONS OF DEVELOPMENT OF BUREAUCRATIC ORGANIZATIONS

We shall start with an analysis of the conditions of development of bureaucratic organizations and see to what extent these conditions can explain the existence of different inherent tendencies in their development and their patterns of activities. . . .

The available material suggests that bureaucratic organizations tend to develop in societies when

1. There develops extensive differentiation between major types of roles and institutional (economic, political, religious, and so forth) spheres.

2. The most important social roles are allocated not according to criteria of membership in the basic particularistic (kinship or territorial) groups, but rather according to universalistic and achievement criteria, or criteria of membership in more flexibly constituted groups such as professional, religious, vocational, or "national" groups.

Reprinted in part from S. N. Eisenstadt, *Administrative Science Quarterly*, 4 (1959), 302–320, by permission of the author and the publisher, Cornell University.

3. There evolve many functionally specific groups (economic, cultural, religious, social-integrative) that are not embedded in basic particularistic groups, as, for example, economic and professional organizations, various types of voluntary associations, clubs, and so forth.

4. The definition of the total community is not identical with, and consequently is wider than, any such basic particularistic group, as can be seen, for instance, in the definition of the Hellenic culture in Byzantium or of the Confucian cultural order.

5. The major groups and strata in the society develop, uphold, and attempt to implement numerous discrete, political, economic, and social-service goals which cannot be implemented within the limited framework of the basic particularistic groups.

6. The growing differentiation in the social structure makes for complexity in many spheres of life, such as increasing interdependence between far-off groups and growing difficulty in the assurance of supply of resources and services.

7. These developments result to some extent in "free-floating" resources, i.e., manpower and economic resources as well as commitments for political support which are neither embedded in nor assured to any primary ascriptive-particularistic groups, as, for example, monetary resources, a relatively free labor force, and a free political vote. Consequently, the various institutional units in the society have to compete for resources, manpower, and support for the implementation of their goals and provision of services; and the major social units are faced with many regulative and administrative problems.

The available material suggests that bureaucratic organizations develop in relation to such differentiation in the social system. Bureaucratic organizations can help in coping with some of the problems arising out of such differentiation, and they perform important functions in the organization of adequate services and coordination of large-scale activities, in the implementation of different goals, in the provision of resources to different groups and in the regulation of various intergroup relations and conflicts. Such bureaucratic organizations are usually created by certain elites (rulers, economic entrepreneurs, etc.) to deal with the problems outlined and to assure for these elites both the provision of such services and strategic power positions in the society.

Thus in many historical societies bureaucratic administrations were created by kings who wanted to establish their rule over feudal-aristocratic forces and who wanted, through their administration, to control the resources created by various economic and social groups and to provide these groups with political, economic, and administrative services that would make them dependent on the rulers.

In many modern societies bureaucratic organizations are created when the holders of political or economic power are faced with problems that arise because of external (war, etc.) or internal (economic development, political demands, etc.) developments. For the solution of such problems they have to mobilize adequate resources from different groups and spheres of life.

Obviously, these conclusions have to be tested and amplified. . . .

BUREAUCRATIZATION AND DEBUREAUCRATIZATION

It is through continuous interaction with its environment that a bureaucratic organization may succeed in maintaining those characteristics that distinguish it from other social groups. The most important of these characteristics, common to most bureaucratic organizations and often stressed in the literature, are specialization of roles and tasks; the prevalence of autonomous, rational, nonpersonal rules in the organization; and the general orientation to rational, efficient implementation of specific goals.[1]

These structural characteristics do not, however, develop in a social vacuum but are closely related to the functions and activities of the bureaucratic organization in its environment. The extent to which they can develop and persist in any bureaucratic organization is dependent on the type of dynamic equilibrium that the organization develops in relation to its environment. Basically, three main outcomes of such interaction or types of such dynamic equilibrium can be distinguished, although probably each of them can be further subdivided and some overlapping occurs between them.

The first type of equilibrium is one in which any given bureaucratic organization maintains its autonomy and distinctiveness. The basic structural characteristics that differentiate it from other social groups and in which it implements its goal or goals (whether its initial goal or goals are added later) are retained and it is supervised by those who are legitimately entitled to do this (holders of political power, "owners," or boards of trustees).

The second main possibility is that of bureaucratization. This is the extension of the bureaucracy's spheres of activities and power either in its own interests or those of some of its elite. It tends toward growing regimentation of different areas of social life and some extent of displacement of its service goals in favor of various power interests and orientations. Examples are military organizations that tend to impose their rule on civilian life, or political parties that exert pressure on their potential sup-

---

[1] See, for instance, P. M. Blau, *Bureaucracy in Modern Society* (New York, 1956). Blau summarizes much of the available literature on this problem.

porters in an effort to monopolize their private and occupational life and make them entirely dependent on the political party.

The third main outcome is debureaucratization. Here there is subversion of the goals and activities of the bureaucracy in the interests of different groups with which it is in close interaction (clients, patrons, interested parties). In debureaucratization the specific characteristics of the bureaucracy in terms both of its autonomy and its specific rules and goals are minimized, even up to the point where its very functions and activities are taken over by other groups or organizations. Examples of this can be found in cases when some organization (i.e., a parents' association or a religious or political group) attempts to divert the rules and working of a bureaucratic organization (school, economic agency, and so forth) for its own use or according to its own values and goals. It makes demands on the members of bureaucratic organizations to perform tasks that are obviously outside the specific scope of these organizations. . . .

Many overlappings between these various tendencies and possibilities may, of course, develop. The tendencies toward bureaucratization and debureaucratization may, in fact, develop side by side. Thus, for instance, a growing use of the bureaucratic organization and the extension of its scope of activities for purposes of political control might be accompanied by deviation from its rules for the sake of political expediency. The possibility of these tendencies occurring in the same case may be explained by the fact that a stable service-oriented bureaucracy (the type of bureaucracy depicted in the Weberian ideal type of bureaucracy) is based on the existence of some equilibrium or *modus vivendi* between professional autonomy and societal (or political) control. Once this equilibrium is severely disrupted, the outcome with respect to the bureaucracy's organization and activity may be the simultaneous development of bureaucratization and debureaucratization in different spheres of its activities, although usually one of these tendencies is more pronounced. . . .

SOME VARIABLES IN THE STUDY
OF BUREAUCRACY

It is as yet very difficult to propose any definite and systematic hypothesis about this problem since very little research is available that is specifically related to it.[2]

[2] Thus, for instance, in existing literature there is but little distinction between conditions which make for the growth of bureaucracy and those conducive to increasing bureaucratization. Gouldner's polemics against those who foresee the inevitability of bureaucratization are to some extent due to the lack of this distinction in the available literature. See his "Metaphysical Pathos and the Theory of Bureaucracy." *American Political Science Review*, 49 (1955), 496–507.

308 ORGANIZATION AND SOCIETY

What can be done at this stage is, first, to point out some variables that, on the basis of available material and the preceding discussion, seem central to this problem, and then to propose some preliminary hypotheses, which may suggest directions in which research work on this problem may be attempted.

On the basis of those discussions we would like to propose that (a) the major goals of the bureaucratic organization, (b) the place of these goals in the social structure of the society, and (c) the type of dependence of the bureaucracy on external forces (clients, holders of political power, or other prominent groups) are of great importance in influencing both its internal structure and its relation with its environment. These different variables, while to some extent interdependent, are not identical. Each brings into relief the interdependence of the bureaucratic organization with its social setting from a different point of view.

The bureaucracy's goals, as has been lately shown in great detail by Parsons,[3] are of strategic importance, because they constitute one of the most important connecting links between the given organization and the total social structure in which it is placed. That which from the point of view of the organization is the major goal is very often from the point of view of the total society the function of the organization. Hence the various interrelations between a bureaucratic organization, other groups, and the total society are largely mediated by the nature of its goals. This applies both to the resources needed by the organization and to the products it gives to the society.[4]

But it is not merely the contents of the goals, i.e., whether they are mainly political, economic, cultural, and so forth, that influence the relation of the organization with its environment, but the place of the goals in the institutional structure of the society as well. By the relative place of the specific goals of any given bureaucratic organization within the society we mean the centrality (or marginality) of these goals with respect to the society's value and power system and the extent of legitimation it affords them. Thus there would obviously be many differences between a large corporation with critical products and a small economic organization with marginal products; between a political party close to the existing government performing the functions of a "loyal opposition" and a revolutionary group; between established churches and minority or militant sects; between fully established educational institutions and sectarian study or propaganda groups.

---

[3] See T. Parsons, Suggestions for a Sociological Approach to the Theory of Organization, I and II, *Administrative Science Quarterly*, 1 (June and Sept. 1956), 63–85, 225–239.

[4] See Trend Report. *Current Sociology*, Vol. 7 (1958), 99–163.

A third variable which seems to influence the bureaucracy's structural characteristics and activities is the extent and nature of its dependence on external resources and power. This dependence or relation may be defined in terms of

1. The chief function of the organization, i.e., whether it is a service, market, or membership recruitment agency. (This definition is closely related to, but not necessarily identical with, its goals.)
2. The extent to which its clientele is entirely dependent upon its products, or conversely, the type and extent of competition between it and parallel agencies.
3. The nature and extent of the internal (ownership) and external control.
4. The criteria used to measure the success of the organization as such and its members' performance, especially the extent of changes in the behavior and membership affiliation of its clients (as, for instance, in the case of a political party).
5. The spheres of life of its personnel that the activities of a given bureaucratic organization encompass.

It is not claimed that this list is exhaustive, but it seems to provide some preliminary clues as to the possible direction of further research on the problem.

All these variables indicate the great interdependence existing between the bureaucratic organization and its social environment. Each variable points to some ways in which a bureaucratic organization attempts to control different parts of its environment and to adapt its goals to changing environment or to different ways in which groups outside the bureaucracy control it and direct its activities. The outcome of this continuous interaction varies continuously according to the constellation of these different variables.

CONDITIONS OF BUREAUCRATIZATION AND DEBUREAUCRATIZATION

On the basis of the foregoing considerations and of current research like that of Janowitz,[5] of historical research on which we have reported already, and research in progress on the relations between bureaucratic organization

[5] See M. Janowitz, D. Wright, and W. Delany, *Public Administration and the Public— Perspectives toward Government in a Metropolitan Community* (Ann Arbor, 1958), which is one of the few available works that have a bearing on this problem. We would also like to mention the work of J. A. Slesinger, who has worked with Janowitz, and who has recently proposed several hypotheses concerning some of the factors that might influence aspects of the development of bureaucracy that are of interest to us. See Slesinger, "A Model for the Comparative Study of Public Bureaucracies," Institute of Public Administration, University of Michigan, 1957 (mimeographed).

and new immigrants in Israel,[6] we propose several general hypotheses concerning the conditions that promote autonomy or, conversely, bureaucratization or debureaucratization. . . .

The first of these hypotheses proposes that the development of any given bureaucratic organization as a relatively autonomous service agency is contingent upon the following conditions obtaining in its social setting:

1. Relative predominance of universalistic elements in the orientations and goals of the groups most closely related to the bureaucracy.
2. Relatively wide distribution of power and values in the economic, cultural, and political spheres among many groups and the maintenance of continuous struggle and competition among them or, in other words, no monopoly of the major power positions by any one group.
3. A wide range of differentiation among different types of goals.
4. The continuous specialization and competition among different bureaucratic organizations and between them and other types of groups about their relative places with regard to implementation of different goals.
5. The existence of strongly articulated political groups and the maintenance of control over the implementation of the goals by the legitimate holders of political, communal, or economic power.

Thus a service bureaucracy, one that maintains both some measure of autonomy and of service orientation, tends to develop either in a society, such as the "classical" Chinese Empire or the Byzantine Empire from the sixth to the tenth century, in which there exist strong political rulers and some politically active groups, such as the urban groups, aristocracy, and the church in the Byzantine Empire, or the literati and gentry in China, whose aspirations are considered by the rulers.[7] It also tends to develop in a democratic society in which effective political power is vested in an efficient, strong, representative executive. In both cases it is the combination of relatively strong political leadership with some political articulation and activity of different strata and groups (an articulation which necessarily tends to be entirely different in expression in historical empires from modern democracies) that facilitates the maintenance of a service bureaucracy.

In some societies a group may establish a power monopoly over parts of its environment and over the definition and establishment of the society's

---

[6] See E. Katz and S. N. Eisenstadt, Some Sociological Observations on the Response of Israeli Organizations to New Immigrants, *Administrative Science Quarterly*, Vol. 5 (1960), 113–133.
[7] For a more complete discussion of some of the problems of these societies see the references in note 4.

goals and the appropriation of its resources. This group may use the bureaucracy as an instrument of power and manipulation, distort its autonomous function and service orientation, and subvert some of its echelons through various threats or inducements for personal gratification. Historically the most extreme example of such developments can be found in those societies in which the rulers developed political goals that were strongly opposed by various active groups that they tried to suppress, such as in Prussia in the seventeenth and eighteenth centuries, in many conquest empires such as the Ottoman, or in the periods of aristocratization of the Byzantine Empire.[8] Modern examples of this tendency can be found in totalitarian societies or movements. Less extreme illustrations can also be found in other societies, and it should be a major task of comparative research to specify the different possible combinations of the conditions enumerated above and their influence on the possible development of bureaucratic organizations.

The development of a bureaucratic organization in the direction of debureaucratization seems to be connected mainly with the growth of different types of *direct* dependence of the bureaucratic organization on parts of its clientele. At this stage we may propose the following preliminary hypotheses about the influence that the type of dependency of the bureaucracy on its clients has on some of its patterns of activity. First, the greater its dependence on its clientele in terms of their being able to go to a competing agency, the more it will have to develop techniques of communication and additional services to retain its clientele and the more it will be influenced by different types of demands by the clientele for services in spheres that are not directly relevant to its main goals. Second, insofar as its dependence on its clients is due to the fact that its criteria of successful organizational performance are based on the number and behavior pattern of the organization's members or clients (as is often the case in semipolitical movements, educational organizations, and so forth), it will have to take an interest in numerous spheres of its clients' activities and either establish its control over them or be subjected to their influence and direction. Finally, the greater its *direct* dependence on different participants in the political arena, and the smaller the basic economic facilities and political assurance given by the holders of political power—as is the case in some public organizations in the United States and to some extent also in different organizations in Israel[9]—the greater will be its tendency to

---

[8] Hans Rosenberg, *Bureaucracy, Aristocracy and Autocracy: The Prussian Experience, 1660–1815* (Cambridge, Mass., 1958); A. Lybyer, *The Government of the Ottoman Empire in the Time of Suleiman the Magnificent* (Cambridge, Mass., 1913); and Eisenstadt, Internal Contradictions.

[9] See Janowitz *et al., op. cit.,* pp. 107–114, and Katz and Eisenstadt, *op. cit.*

succumb to the demands of different political and economic pressure groups and to develop its activities and distort its own rules accordingly.

As already indicated, in concrete cases some overlapping between the tendencies to bureaucratization and debureaucratization may occur. Thus, for instance, when a politically monopolistic group gains control over a bureaucratic organization, it may distort the rules of this organization in order to give special benefits to the holders of political power or to maintain its hold over different segments of the population. On the other hand, when a process of debureaucratization sets in because of the growing pressure of different groups on a bureaucracy, there may also develop within the bureaucratic organization, as a sort of defense against these pressures, a tendency toward formalization and bureaucratization. This shows that the distinctive characteristics of a specific bureaucratic organization and role have been impinged upon in different directions, and one may usually discern which of these tendencies is predominant in different spheres of activity of the bureaucracy. It is the task of further research to analyze these different constellations in greater detail.

THE CHARACTERISTICS
OF TOTAL INSTITUTIONS

Erving Goffman

Social establishments—institutions in the everyday sense of that term—are buildings or plants in which activity of a particular kind regularly goes on. . . . Each captures something of the time and interest of its members and provides something of a world for them; in brief, every institution has encompassing tendencies. When we review the different institutions in our

Reprinted in part from Erving Goffman, "The Characteristics of Total Institutions," in *Symposium on Preventive and Social Psychiatry*, 15–17, April 1957, Walter Reed Army Institute of Research, Washington, D.C., by permission of the author and publisher.

Western society we find a class of them which seems to be encompassing to a degree discontinuously greater than the ones next in line. Their encompassing or total character is symbolized by the barrier to social intercourse with the outside that is often built right into the physical plant: locked doors, high walls, barbed wire, cliffs and water, open terrain, and so forth. These I am calling total institutions, and it is their general characteristics I want to explore.[1] This exploration will be phrased as if securely based on findings but will in fact be speculative.

The total institutions of our society can be listed for convenience in five rough groupings. *First,* there are institutions established to care for persons thought to be both incapable and harmless; these are the homes for the blind, the aged, the orphaned, and the indigent. *Second,* there are places established to care for persons thought to be at once incapable of looking after themselves and a threat to the community, albeit an unintended one: TB sanitariums, mental hospitals, and leprosoriums. *Third,* another type of total institution is organized to protect the community against what are thought to be intentional dangers to it; here the welfare of the persons thus sequestered is not the immediate issue. Examples are: Jails, penitentiaries, POW camps, and concentration camps. *Fourth,* we find institutions purportedly established the better to pursue some technical task and justifying themselves only on these instrumental grounds: Army barracks, ships, boarding schools, work camps, colonial compounds, large mansions from the point of view of those who live in the servants' quarters, and so forth. *Finally,* there are those establishments designed as retreats from the world or as training stations for the religious: Abbeys, monasteries, convents, and other cloisters. This sublisting of total institutions is neither neat nor exhaustive, but the listing itself provides an empirical starting point for a purely denotative definition of the category. By anchoring the initial definition of total institutions in this way, I hope to be able to discuss the general characteristics of the type without becoming tautological.

Before attempting to extract a general profile from this list of establishments, one conceptual peculiarity must be mentioned. None of the elements I will extract seems entirely exclusive to total institutions, and none seems shared by every one of them. What is shared and unique about

[1] The category of total institutions has been pointed out from time to time in the sociological literature under a variety of names, and some of the characteristics of the class have been suggested, most notably perhaps in Howard Roland's neglected paper, "Segregated Communities and Mental Health," in *Mental Health Publication of the American Association for the Advancement of Science,* No. 9, edited by F. R. Moulton, 1939. A preliminary statement of the present paper is reported in the *Third Group Processes Proceedings,* Josiah Macy Foundation, edited by Bertram Schaffner, 1957.

total institutions is that each exhibits many items in this family of attributes to an intense degree. In speaking of "common characteristics," then, I will be using this phrase in a weakened, but I think logically defensible, way.

TOTALISTIC FEATURES

A basic social arrangement in modern society is that we tend to sleep, play and work in different places, in each case with a different set of coparticipants, under a different authority, and without an over-all rational plan. The central feature of total institutions can be described as a breakdown of the kinds of barriers ordinarily separating these three spheres of life. *First,* all aspects of life are conducted in the same place and under the same single authority. *Second,* each phase of the member's daily activity will be carried out in the immediate company of a large batch of others, all of whom are treated alike and required to do the same thing together. *Third,* all phases of the day's activities are tightly scheduled, with one activity leading at a prearranged time into the next, the whole circle of activities being imposed from above through a system of explicit formal rulings and a body of officials. *Finally,* the contents of the various enforced activities are brought together as parts of a single over-all rational plan purportedly designed to fulfill the official aims of the institution.

Individually, these totalistic features are found, of course, in places other than total institutions. Increasingly, for example, our large commercial, industrial and educational establishments provide cafeterias, minor services and off-hour recreation for their members. But while this is a tendency in the direction of total institutions, these extended facilities remain voluntary in many particulars of their use, and special care is taken to see that the ordinary line of authority does not extend to these situations. Similarly, housewives or farm families can find all their major spheres of life within the same fenced-in area, but these persons are not collectively regimented and do not march through the day's steps in the immediate company of a batch of similar others.

The handling of many human needs by the bureaucratic organization of whole blocks of people—whether or not this is a necessary or effective means of social organization in the circumstances—can be taken, then, as the key fact of total institutions. From this, certain important implications can be drawn.

Given the fact that blocks of people are caused to move in time, it becomes possible to use a relatively small number of supervisory personnel where the central relationship is not guidance or periodic checking, as in many employer-employee relations, but rather surveillance—a seeing to it that everyone does what he has been clearly told is required of him, and this under conditions where one person's infraction is likely to stand out in relief against the visible, constantly examined, compliance of the others. Which comes first, the large block of managed people or the small supervisory staff, is not here at issue; the point is that each is made for the other.

In total institutions, as we would then suspect, there is a basic split between a large class of individuals who live in and who have restricted contact with the world outside the walls, conveniently called *inmates,* and the small class that supervises them, conveniently called *staff,* who often operate on an 8-hour day and are socially integrated into the outside world.[2] Each grouping tends to conceive of members of the other in terms of narrow hostile stereotypes, staff often seeing inmates as bitter, secretive and untrustworthy, while inmates often see staff as condescending, high-handed and mean. Staff tends to feel superior and righteous; inmates tend, in some ways at least, to feel inferior, weak, blameworthy and guilty.[3] Social mobility between the two strata is grossly restricted; social distance is typically great and often formally prescribed; even talk across the boundaries may be conducted in a special tone of voice. These restrictions on contact presumably help to maintain the antagonistic stereotypes.[4] In any case, two different social and cultural worlds develop, tending to jog along beside each other, with points of official contact but little mutual penetration. It is important to add that the institutional plant and name comes to be identified by both staff and inmates as somehow belonging to staff, so that when either grouping refers to the views or interests of "the institution," by implication they are referring (as I shall also) to the views and concerns of the staff.

The staff-inmate split is one major implication of the central features of total institutions; a second one pertains to work. In the ordinary arrangements of living in our society, the authority of the workplace stops with the worker's receipt of a money payment; the spending of this in a domestic and recreational setting is at the discretion of the worker and is the mechanism through which the authority of the workplace is kept within strict bounds. However, to say that inmates in total institutions have their

---

[2] The binary character of total institutions was pointed out to me by Gregory Bateson, and proves to be noted in the literature. See, for example, Lloyd E. Ohlin, *Sociology and the Field of Corrections,* Russell Sage Foundation, New York; 1956, pp. 14, 20. In those special situations where staff too is required to live in, we may expect staff members to feel they are suffering from special hardships and to have brought home to them a status-dependency on life on the inside which they did not expect. See Jane Cassels Record, "The Marine Radioman's Struggle for Status," *American Journal of Sociology,* Vol. LXII, 1957, p. 359.

[3] For the prison version, see S. Kirson Weinberg, "Aspects of the Prison's Social Structure," *American Journal of Sociology,* Vol. 47, 1942, pp. 717–726.

[4] Suggested in Ohlin, *op. cit.,* p. 20.

full day scheduled for them is to say that some version of all basic needs will have to be planned for, too. In other words, total institutions take over "responsibility" for the inmate and must guarantee to have everything that is defined as essential "layed on." It follows, then, that whatever incentive is given for work, this will not have the structural significance it has on the outside. Different attitudes and incentives regarding this central feature of our life will have to prevail.

Here, then, is one basic adjustment required of those who work in total institutions and of those who must induce these people to work. In some cases, no work or little is required, and inmates, untrained often in leisurely ways of life, suffer extremes of boredom. In other cases, some work is required but is carried on at an extremely slow pace, being geared into a system of minor, often ceremonial payments, as in the case of weekly tobacco ration and annual Christmas presents, which cause some mental patients to stay on their job. In some total institutions, such as logging camps and merchant ships, something of the usual relation to the world that money can buy is obtained through the practice of "forced saving"; all needs are organized by the institution, and payment is given only after a work season is over and the men leave the premises. And in some total institutions, of course, more than a full day's work is required and is induced not by reward, but by threat of dire punishment. In all such cases, the work-oriented individual may tend to become somewhat demoralized by the system.

In addition to the fact that total institutions are incompatible with the basic work-payment structure of our society, it must be seen that these establishments are also incompatible with another crucial element of our society, the family. The family is sometimes contrasted to solitary living, but in fact the more pertinent contrast to family life might be with batch living. For it seems that those who eat and sleep at work, with a group of fellow workers, can hardly sustain a meaningful domestic existence. Correspondingly, the extent to which a staff retains its integration in the outside community and escapes the encompassing tendencies of total institutions is often linked up with the maintenance of a family off the grounds. . . .

Total institutions, then, are social hybrids, part residential community, part formal organization, and therein lies their special sociological interest. There are other reasons, alas, for being interested in them, too. These establishments are the forcing houses for changing persons in our society. Each is a natural experiment, typically harsh, on what can be done to the self.

Having suggested some of the key features of total institutions, we can move on now to consider them from the special perspectives of the inmate world and the staff world.

THE INMATE WORLD

Mortification Processes

It is characteristic of inmates that they come to the institution as members, already full-fledged, of a *home world,* that is, a way of life and a round of activities taken for granted up to the point of admission to the institution.[5] It is useful to look at this culture that the recruit brings with him to the institution's door—his *presenting culture,* to modify a psychiatric phrase—in terms especially designed to highlight what it is the total institution will do to him. Whatever the stability of his personal organization, we can assume it was part of a wider supporting framework lodged in his current social environment, a round of experience that somewhat confirms a conception of self that is somewhat acceptable to him and a set of defensive maneuvers exercisable at his own discretion as a means of coping with conflicts, discreditings and failures.

Now it appears that total institutions do not substitute their own unique culture for something already formed. We do not deal with acculturation or assimilation but with something more restricted than these. In a sense, total institutions do not look for cultural victory. They effectively create and sustain a particular kind of tension between the home world and the institutional world and use this persistent tension as strategic leverage in the management of men. The full meaning for the inmate of being "in" or "on the inside" does not exist apart from the special meaning to him of "getting out" or "getting on the outside."

The recruit comes into the institution with a self and with attachments to supports which had allowed this self to survive. Upon entrance, he is immediately stripped of his wonted supports, and his self is systematically, if often unintentionally, mortified. In the accurate language of some of our oldest total institutions, he is led into a series of abasements, degradations, humiliations, and profanations of self. He begins, in other words, some radical shifts in his *moral career,* a career laying out the progressive changes that occur in the beliefs that he has concerning himself and significant others.

The *stripping processes* through which *mortification of the self* occurs are fairly standard in our total institutions. Personal identity equipment is removed, as well as other possessions with which the inmate may have

---

[5] There is reason then to exclude orphanages and foundling homes from the list of total institutions, except insofar as the orphan comes to be socialized into the outside world by some process of cultural osmosis, even while this world is being systematically denied him.

identified himself, there typically being a system of nonaccessible storage from which the inmate can only reobtain his effects should he leave the institution. As a substitute for what has been taken away, institutional issue is provided, but this will be the same for large categories of inmates and will be regularly repossessed by the institution. In brief, standardized defacement will occur. In addition, ego-invested separateness from fellow inmates is significantly diminished in many areas of activity, and tasks are prescribed that are *infra dignitatem*. Family, occupational, and educational career lines are chopped off, and a stigmatized status is submitted. Sources of fantasy materials which had meant momentary releases from stress in the home world are denied. Areas of autonomous decision are eliminated through the process of collective scheduling of daily activity. Many channels of communication with the outside are restricted or closed off completely. Verbal discreditings occur in many forms as a matter of course. Expressive signs of respect for the staff are coercively and continuously demanded. And the effect of each of these conditions is multiplied by having to witness the mortification of one's fellow inmates.

We must expect to find different official reasons given for these assaults upon the self. In mental hospitals there is the matter of protecting the patient from himself and from other patients. In jails there is the issue of "security" and frank punishment. In religious institutions we may find sociologically sophisticated theories about the soul's need for purification and penance through disciplining of the flesh. What all of these rationales share is the extent to which they are merely rationalizations, for the underlying force in many cases is unwittingly generated by efforts to manage the daily activity of a large number of persons in a small space with a small expenditure of resources.

In the background of the sociological stripping process, we find a characteristic authority system with three distinctive elements, each basic to total institutions.

First, to a degree, authority is of the *echelon* kind. Any member of the staff class has certain rights to discipline any member of the inmate class. This arrangement, it may be noted, is similar to the one which gives any adult in some small American towns certain rights to correct and demand small services from any child not in the immediate presence of his parents. In our society, the adult himself, however, is typically under the authority of a *single* immediate superior in connection with his work or under authority of one spouse in connection with domestic duties. The only echelon authority he must face—the police—typically are neither constantly nor relevantly present, except perhaps in the case of traffic-law enforcement.

Second, the authority of corrective sanctions is directed to a great multitude of items of conduct of the kind that are constantly occurring and constantly coming up for judgment;[6] in brief, authority is directed to matters of dress, deportment, social intercourse, manners and the like. In prisons these regulations regarding situational proprieties may even extend to a point where silence during mealtime is enforced, while in some convents explicit demands may be made concerning the custody of the eyes during prayer.

The third feature of authority in total institutions is that misbehaviors in one sphere of life are held against one's standing in other spheres. Thus, an individual who fails to participate with proper enthusiasm in sports may be brought to the attention of the person who determines where he will sleep and what kind of work task will be accorded to him.

When we combine these three aspects of authority in total institutions, we see that the inmate cannot easily escape from the press of judgmental officials and from the enveloping tissue of constraint. The system of authority undermines the basis for control that adults in our society expect to exert over their interpersonal environment and may produce the terror of feeling that one is being radically demoted in the age-grading system. On the outside, rules are sufficiently lax and the individual sufficiently agreeable to required self-discipline to insure that others will rarely have cause for pouncing on him. He need not constantly look over his shoulder to see if criticism and other sanctions are coming. On the inside, however, rulings are abundant, novel, and closely enforced so that, quite characteristically, inmates live with chronic anxiety about breaking the rules and chronic worry about the consequences of breaking them. The desire to "stay out of trouble" in a total institution is likely to require persistent conscious effort and may lead the inmate to abjure certain levels of sociability with his fellows in order to avoid the incidents that may occur in these circumstances.[7]

It should be noted finally that the mortifications to be suffered by the inmate may be purposely brought home to him in an exaggerated way during the first few days after entrance, in a form of initiation that has

---

[6] The span of time over which an employee works at his own discretion without supervision can in fact be taken as a measure of his pay and status in an organization. See Elliot Jacques, *The Measurement of Responsibility: A Study of Work, Payment, and Individual Capacity,* Harvard University Press, Cambridge, 1956. And just as "time-span of responsibility" is an index of position, so a long span of freedom from inspection is a reward of position.

[7] Staff sometimes encourages this tendency for inmates to stand clear of one another, perhaps in order to limit the dangers of organized inmate resistance to institutional rule. Through an interesting phrase, inmates may be officially encouraged to "do their own time."

been called *the welcome*. Both staff and fellow inmates may go out of their way to give the neophyte a clear notion of where he stands.[8] As part of this *rite de passage,* he may find himself called by a term such as "fish," "swab," etc., through which older inmates tell him that he is not only merely an inmate but that even within this lowly group he has a low status.

Privilege System

While the process of mortification is in progress, the inmate begins to receive formal and informal instruction in what will here be called the *privilege system.* Insofar as the inmate's self has been unsettled a little by the stripping action of the institution, it is largely around this framework that pressures are exerted, making for a reorganization of self. Three basic elements of the system may be mentioned.

First, there are the *house rules,* a relatively explicit and formal set of prescriptions and proscriptions which lay out the main requirements of inmate conduct. These regulations spell out the austere round of life in which the inmate will operate. Thus, the admission procedures through which the recruit is initially stripped of his self-supporting context can be seen as the institution's way of getting him in the position to start living by the house rules.

Second, against the stark background, a small number of clearly defined *rewards or privileges* are held out in exchange for obedience to staff in action and spirit. It is important to see that these potential gratifications are not unique to the institution but rather are ones carved out of the flow of support that the inmate previously had quite taken for granted. On the outside, for example, the inmate was likely to be able to unthinkingly exercise autonomy by deciding how much sugar and milk he wanted in his coffee, if any, or when to light up a cigarette; on the inside, this right may become quite problematic and a matter of a great deal of conscious concern. Held up to the inmate as possibilities, these few recapturings seem to have a reintegrative effect, re-establishing relationships with the whole lost world and assuaging withdrawal symptoms from it and from one's lost self.

The inmate's run of attention, then, especially at first, comes to be fixated on these supplies and obsessed with them. In the most fanatic way, he can spend the day in devoted thoughts concerning the possibility of

---

[8] For the version of this process in concentration camps, see Elie A. Cohen, *Human Behaviour in the Concentration Camp,* Jonathan Cape, n.p., 1954, p. 120. For a fictionalized treatment of the welcome in a girls' reformatory, see Sara Norris, *The Wayward Ones,* Signet Pocket Books, New York, 1952, pp. 31–34.

acquiring these gratifications or the approach of the hour at which they are scheduled to be granted. The building of a world around these minor privileges is perhaps the most important feature of inmate culture and yet is something that cannot easily be appreciated by an outsider, even one who has lived through the experience himself. This situation sometimes leads to generous sharing and almost always to a willingness to beg for things such as cigarettes, candy and newspapers. It will be understandable, then, that a constant feature of inmate discussion is the *release binge fantasy,* namely, recitals of what one will do during leave or upon release from the institution.

House rules and privileges provide the functional requirements of the third element in the privilege system: *punishments.* These are designated as the consequence of breaking the rules. One set of these punishments consists of the temporary or permanent withdrawal of privileges or abrogation of the right to try to earn them. In general, the punishments meted out in total institutions are of an order more severe than anything encountered by the inmate in his home world. An institutional arrangement which causes a small number of easily controlled privileges to have a massive significance is the same arrangement which lends a terrible significance to their withdrawal.

There are some special features of the privilege system which should be noted.

First, punishments and privileges are themselves modes of organization peculiar to total institutions. Whatever their severity, punishments are largely known in the inmate's home world as something applied to animals and children. For adults this conditioning, behavioristic model is actually not widely applied, since failure to maintain required standards typically leads to indirect disadvantageous consequences and not to specific immediate punishment at all. And privileges, it should be emphasized, are not the same as prerequisites, indulgences or values, but merely the absence of deprivations one ordinarily expects one would not have to sustain. The very notions, then, of punishments and privileges are not ones that are cut from civilian cloth.

Second, it is important to see that the question of release from the total institution is elaborated into the privilege system. Some acts will become known as ones that mean an increase or no decrease in length of stay, while others become known as means for lessening the sentence.

Third, we should also note that punishments and privileges come to be geared into a residential work system. Places to work and places to sleep become clearly defined as places where certain kinds and levels of privilege obtain, and inmates are shifted very rapidly and visibly from one place to another as the mechanisms for giving them the punishment or privilege their cooperativeness has warranted. The inmates are moved, the system is not.

This, then, is the privilege system: a relatively few components put together with some rational intent and clearly proclaimed to the participants. The overall consequence is that cooperativeness is obtained from persons who often have cause to be uncooperative.[9]

Immediately associated with the privilege system we find some standard social processes important in the life of total institutions.

We find that an *institutional lingo* develops through which inmates express the events that are crucial in their particular world. Staff too, especially its lower levels, will know this language, using it when talking to inmates, while reverting to more standardized speech when talking to superiors and outsiders. Related to this special argot, inmates will possess knowledge of the various ranks and officials, an accumulation of lore about the establishment, and some comparative information about life in other similar total institutions.

Also found among staff and inmates will be a clear awareness of the phenomenon of *messing up*, so called in mental hospitals, prisons, and barracks. This involves a complex process of engaging in forbidden activity, getting caught doing so, and receiving something like the full punishment accorded this. An alteration in privilege status is usually implied and is categorized by a phrase such as "getting busted." Typical infractions which can eventuate in messing up are: fights, drunkenness, attempted suicide, failure at examinations, gambling, insubordination, homosexuality, improper taking of leave, and participation in collective riots. While these punished infractions are typically ascribed to the offender's cussedness, villainy, or "sickness," they do in fact constitute a vocabulary of institutionalized actions, limited in such a way that the same messing up may occur for quite different reasons. Informally, inmates and staff may understand, for example, that a given messing up is a way for inmates to show resentment against a current situation felt to be unjust in terms of the informal agreements between staff and inmates,[10] or a way of postponing release without having to admit to one's fellow inmates that one really does not want to go.[11]

---

[9] An excellent description of this model universe as found in a state mental hospital may be found in Ivan Belknap, *Human Problems of a State Mental Hospital*, McGraw-Hill, New York, 1956, p. 164.

[10] For example, see Morris G. Caldwell, "Group Dynamics in the Prison Community," *Journal of Criminal Law, Criminology and Police Science*, Vol. 46, 1956, p. 656.

[11] There are some interesting incidental social functions of messings up. First, they tend to limit rigidities which might occur were seniority the only means of mobility

In total institutions there will also be a system of what might be called *secondary adjustments,* namely, technics which do not directly challenge staff management but which allow inmates to obtain disallowed satisfactions or allowed ones by disallowed means. These practices are variously referred to as: the angles, knowing the ropes, conniving, gimmicks, deals, ins, etc. Such adaptations apparently reach their finest flower in prisons, but of course other total institutions are overrun with them too.¹² It seems apparent that an important aspect of secondary adjustments is that they provide the inmate with some evidence that he is still, as it were, his own man and still has some protective distance, under his own control, between himself and the institution. In some cases, then, a secondary adjustment becomes almost a kind of lodgment for the self, a churinga in which the soul is felt to reside.¹³

The occurrence of secondary adjustments correctly allows us to assume that the inmate group will have some kind of a *code* and some means of informal social control evolved to prevent one inmate from informing staff about the secondary adjustments of another. On the same grounds we can expect that one dimension of social typing among inmates will turn upon this question of security, leading to persons defined as "squealers," "finks," or "stoolies" on one hand, and persons defined as "right guys" on the other.¹⁴ It should be added that where new inmates can play a role in the system of secondary adjustments, as in providing new faction members or new sexual objects, then their "welcome" may indeed be a sequence of initial indulgences and enticements, instead of exaggerated deprivations.¹⁵ Because of secondary adjustments we also find *kitchen strata,* namely, a kind of rudimentary, largely informal, stratification of inmates on the basis of each one's differential access to disposable illicit commodities; so also we find social typing to designate the powerful persons in the informal market system.¹⁶

---

in the privilege system. Secondly, demotion through messing up brings old-time inmates in contact with new inmates in unprivileged positions, assuring a flow of information about the system and the people in it.

¹² See, for example, Norma S. Hayner and Ellis Ash, "The Prisoner Community as a Social Group," *American Sociological Review,* Vol. 4, 1939, pp. 364 ff. under "Conniving Processes"; also, Caldwell, *op. cit.,* pp. 650–651.

¹³ See, for example, Melville's extended description of the fight his fellow seamen put up to prevent the clipping of their beards in full accordance with Navy regulations. Melville, *White Jacket* (New York: Grove Press, n.d.), pp. 333–347.

¹⁴ See, for example, Donald Clemmer, "Leadership Phenomenon in a Prison Community," *Journal of Criminal Law, Criminology and Police Science,* Vol. 28, 1938, p. 868.

¹⁵ See, for example, Ida Ann Harper, "The Role of the 'Fringer' in a State Prison for Women," *Social Forces,* Vol. 31, 1952, pp. 53–60.

¹⁶ For concentration camps, see the discussion of "Prominents" throughout Cohen, *op. cit.;* for mental hospitals, see Belknap, *op. cit.,* p. 189. For prisons, see the discus-

While the privilege system provides the chief framework within which reassembly of the self takes place, other factors characteristically lead by different routes in the same general direction. Relief from economic and social responsibilities—much touted as part of the therapy in mental hospitals—is one, although in many cases it would seem that the disorganizing effect of this moratorium is more significant than its organizing effect. More important as a reorganizing influence is the *fraternalization process,* namely, the process through which socially distant persons find themselves developing mutual support and common *counter-mores* in opposition to a system that has forced them into intimacy and into a single, equalitarian community of fate.[17] It seems that the new recruit frequently starts out with something like the staff's popular misconceptions of the character of the inmates and then comes to find that most of his fellows have all the properties of ordinary decent human beings and that the stereotypes associated with their condition or offense are not a reasonable ground for judgment of inmates.[18]

If the inmates are persons who are accused by staff and society of having committed some kind of a crime against society, then the new inmate, even though sometimes in fact quite guiltless, may come to share the guilty feelings of his fellows and, thereafter, their well-elaborated defenses against these feelings. A sense of common injustice and a sense of bitterness against the outside world tends to develop, marking an important movement in the inmate's moral career.

Adaptation Alignments

The mortifying processes that have been discussed and the privilege system represent the conditions that the inmate must adapt to in some way, but however pressing, these conditions allow for different ways of meeting them. We find, in fact, that the same inmate will employ different lines of adaptation or tacks at different phases in his moral career and may even fluctuate between different tacks at the same time.

---

sion of "Politicos" in Donald Clemmer, *The Prison Community,* Christopher Publishing House, Boston, 1940, pp. 277–279, 298–309; also Hayner, *op. cit.,* p. 367; and Caldwell, *op. cit.,* pp. 651–653.

[17] For the version of this inmate solidarity to be found in military academies, see Sanford M. Dornbusch, "The Military Academy as an Assimilating Institution," *Social Forces,* Vol. 33, 1955, p. 318.

[18] An interesting example of this re-evaluation may be found in a conscientious objector's experience with nonpolitical prisoners, see Alfred Hassler, *Diary of a Self-Made Convict,* Regnery, Chicago, 1954, pp. 74, 117. In mental hospitals, of course, the patient's antagonism to staff obtains one of its supports from the discovery that, like himself, many other patients are more like ordinary persons than like anything else.

First, there is the process of *situational withdrawal.* The inmate withdraws apparent attention from everything except events immediately around his body and sees these in a perspective not employed by others present. This drastic curtailment of involvement in interactional events is best known, of course, in mental hospitals, under the title of "regression." Aspects of "prison psychosis" or "stir simpleness" represent the same adjustment, as do some forms of "acute depersonalization" described in concentration camps. I do not think it is known whether this line of adaptation forms a single continuum of varying degrees of withdrawal or whether there are standard discontinuous plateaus of disinvolvement. It does seem to be the case, however, that, given the pressures apparently required to dislodge an inmate from this status, as well as the currently limited facilities for doing so, we frequently find here, effectively speaking, an irreversible line of adaptation.

Second, there is the *rebellious line.* The inmate intentionally challenges the institution by flagrantly refusing to cooperate with staff in almost any way.[19] The result is a constantly communicated intransigency and sometimes high rebel-morale. Most large mental hospitals, for example, seem to have wards where this spirit strongly prevails. Interestingly enough, there are many circumstances in which sustained rejection of a total institution requires sustained orientation to its formal organization and hence, paradoxically, a deep kind of commitment to the establishment. Similarly, when total institutions take the line (as they sometimes do in the case of mental hospitals prescribing lobotomy[20] or army barracks prescribing the stockade) that the recalcitrant inmate must be broken, then, in their way, they must show as much special devotion to the rebel as he has shown to them. It should be added, finally, that while prisoners of war have been known staunchly to take a rebellious stance throughout their incarceration, this stance is typically a temporary and initial phase of reaction, emerging from this to situational withdrawal or some other line of adaptation.

Third, another standard alignment in the institutional world takes the form of a kind of *colonization.* The sampling of the outside world provided by the establishment is taken by the inmate as the whole, and a stable, relatively contented existence is built up out of the maximum satisfactions procurable within the institution.[21] Experience of the outside world is used as a point of reference to demonstrate the desirability of life on the inside; and the usual tension between the two worlds collapses, thwarting the

[19] See, for example, the discussion of "The Resisters," in Edgar H. Schein, "The Chinese Indoctrination Program for Prisoners of War," *Psychiatry,* Vol. 19 (1956), pp. 160–161.
[20] See, for example, Belknap, *op. cit.,* p. 192.
[21] In the case of mental hospitals, those who take this line are sometimes called "institutional cures" or are said to suffer from "hospitalitis."

social arrangements based upon this felt discrepancy. Characteristically, the individual who too obviously takes this line may be accused by his fellow inmates of "having found a home" or of "never having had it so good." Staff itself may become vaguely embarrassed by this use that is being made of the institution, sensing that the benign possibilities in the situation are somehow being misused. Colonizers themselves may feel obliged to deny their satisfaction with the institution, if only in the interest of sustaining the counter-mores supporting inmate solidarity. They may find it necessary to mess up just prior to their slated discharge, thereby allowing themselves to present involuntary reasons for continued incarceration. It should be incidentally noted that any humanistic effort to make life in total institutions more bearable must face the possibility that doing so may increase the attractiveness and likelihood of colonization.

Fourth, one mode of adaptation to the setting of a total institution is that of *conversion.* The inmate appears to take over completely the official or staff view of himself and tries to act out the role of the perfect inmate. While the colonized inmate builds as much of a free community as possible for himself by using the limited facilities available, the convert takes a more disciplined, moralistic, monochromatic line, presenting himself as someone whose institutional enthusiasm is always at the disposal of the staff. In Chinese POW camps, we find Americans who became "pros" and fully espoused the Communist view of the world.[22] In army barracks there are enlisted men who give the impression that they are always "sucking around" and always "bucking for promotion." In prisons there are "square johns." In German concentration camps, longtime prisoners sometimes came to adopt the vocabulary, recreation, posture, expressions of aggression, and clothing style of the Gestapo, executing their role of straw-boss with military strictness.[23] Some mental hospitals have the distinction of providing two quite different conversion possibilities—one for the new admission who can see the light after an appropriate struggle and adapt the psychiatric view of himself, and another for the chronic ward patient who adopts the manner and dress of attendants while helping them to manage the other ward patients with a stringency excelling that of the attendants themselves.

Here, it should be noted, is a significant way in which total institutions differ. Many, like progressive mental hospitals, merchant ships, TB sanitariums and brain-washing camps, offer the inmate an opportunity to live

[22] Schein, *op. cit.,* pp. 167–169.
[23] See Bruno Bettelheim, "Individual and Mass Behavior in Extreme Situations," *Journal of Abnormal and Social Psychology,* Vol. 38, 1943, pp. 447–451. It should be added that in concentration camps, colonization and conversion often seemed to go together. See Cohen, *op. cit.,* pp. 200–203, where the role of the "Kapo" is discussed.

up to a model of conduct that is at once ideal and staff-sponsored—a model felt by its advocates to be in the supreme interests of the very persons to whom it is applied. Other total institutions, like some concentration camps and some prisons, do not officially sponsor an ideal that the inmate is expected to incorporate as a means of judging himself.

While the alignments that have been mentioned represent coherent courses to pursue, few inmates, it seems, carry these pursuits very far. In most total institutions, what we seem to find is that most inmates take the tack of what they call *playing it cool*. This involves a somewhat opportunistic combination of secondary adjustments, conversion, colonization and loyalty to the inmate group, so that in the particular circumstances the inmate will have a maximum chance of eventually getting out physically and psychically undamaged.[24] Typically, the inmate will support the counter-mores when with fellow inmates and be silent to them on how tractably he acts when alone in the presence of staff.[25] Inmates taking this line tend to subordinate contacts with their fellows to the higher claim of "keeping out of trouble." They tend to volunteer for nothing, and they may even learn to cut their ties to the outside world sufficiently to give cultural reality to the world inside but not enough to lead to colonization.

I have suggested some of the lines of adaptation that inmates can take to the pressures that play in total institutions. Each represents a way of managing the tension between the home world and the institutional world. However, there are circumstances in which the home world of the inmate was such, in fact, as to *immunize* him against the bleak world on the inside, and for such persons no particular scheme of adaptation need be carried very far. Thus, some lower-class mental hospital patients who have lived all their previous life in orphanages, reformatories and jails, tend to see the hospital as just another total institution to which it is possible to apply the adaptive technics learned and perfected in other total institutions. "Playing it cool" represents for such persons, not a shift in their moral career, but an alignment that is already second nature.

[24] See the discussion in Schein, *op. cit.*, pp. 165–166 of the "Get-Alongers," and Robert J. Lifton, "Home by Ship: Reaction Patterns of American Prisoners of War Repatriated from North Korea," *American Journal of Psychiatry*, Vol. 110, 1954, p. 734.

[25] This two-facedness, of course, is very commonly found in total institutions. In the state-type mental hospital studied by the writer, even the few elite patients selected for individual psychotherapy, and hence in the best position for espousal of the psychiatric approach to self, tended to present their favorable view of psychotherapy only to the members of their intimate cliques. For a report on the way in which army prisoners concealed from fellow offenders their interest in "restoration" to the army, see the comments by Richard Cloward in Session 4 of *New Perspectives for Research on Juvenile Delinquency*, ed. by Helen L. Witmer and Ruth Kotinsky, U. S. Department of Health, Education and Welfare, Children's Bureau Bulletin, 1955, especially p. 90.

The professional criminal element in the early periods of German concentration camps displayed something of the same immunity to their surroundings or even found new satisfactions through fraternization with middle-class political prisoners.[26] Similarly, Shetland youths recruited into the British merchant marine are not apparently threatened much by the cramped arduous life on board, because island life is even more stunted; they make uncomplaining sailors because from their point of view they have nothing much to complain about. Strong religious and political convictions may also serve perhaps to immunize the true believer against the assaults of a total institution, and even a failure to speak the language of the staff may cause the staff to give up its efforts at reformation, allowing the non-speaker immunity to certain pressures. . . .[27]

Consequences

Total institutions frequently claim to be concerned with rehabilitation, that is, with resetting the inmate's self-regulatory mechanisms so that he will maintain the standards of the establishment of his own accord after he leaves the setting.[28] In fact, it seems this claim is seldom realized and even when permanent alteration occurs, these changes are often not of the kind intended by the staff. With the possible exception presented by the great resocialization efficiency of religious institutions, neither the stripping processes nor the reorganizing ones seem to have a lasting effect.[29] No doubt the availability of secondary adjustments helps to account for this, as do the presence of counter-mores and the tendency for inmates to combine all strategies and "play it cool." In any case, it seems that shortly after release, the ex-inmate will have forgotten a great deal of what life was like on the inside and will have once again begun to take for granted the privileges around which life in the institution was organized. The sense of injustice, bitterness and alienation, so typically engendered by the inmate's experience and so definitely marking a stage in his moral career, seems to weaken upon graduation, even in those cases where a permanent stigma has resulted.

[26] Bettelheim, op. cit., p. 425.
[27] Thus, Schein, op. cit., p. 165 fn., suggests that Puerto Ricans and other non-English-speaking prisoners of war in China were given up on and allowed to work out a viable routine of menial chores.
[28] Interestingly enough, staff is expected to be properly self-regulating upon first coming to the total institution, sharing with members of other kinds of establishments the ideal of needing merely to learn procedure.
[29] The strongest evidence for this, perhaps, comes from our knowledge of the readjustment of repatriated brain-washed prisoners of war. See, for example, Lawrence E. Hinkle, Jr., and Harold G. Wolff, "Communist Interrogation and Indoctrination of 'Enemies of the State,'" Archives of Neurology and Psychiatry, Vol. 76, 1956, p. 174.

But what the ex-inmate does retain of his institutional experience tells us important things about total institutions. Often entrance will mean for the recruit that he has taken on what might be called a *proactive status.* Not only is his relative social position within the walls radically different from what it was on the outside, but, as he comes to learn, if and when he gets out, his social position on the outside will never again be quite what it was prior to entrance. Where the proactive status is a relatively favorable one, as it is for those who graduate from officers' training schools, elite boarding schools, ranking monasteries, etc., then the permanent alteration will be favorable, and jubilant official reunions announcing pride in one's "school" can be expected. When, as seems usually the case, the proactive status is unfavorable, as it is for those in prisons or mental hospitals, we popularly employ the term "stigmatization" and expect that the ex-inmate may make an effort to conceal his past and try to "pass."[30]

THE STAFF WORLD

Humane Standards

Most total institutions, most of the time, seem to function merely as storage dumps for inmates, but as previously suggested, they usually present themselves to the public as rational organizations designed consciously, through and through, as effective machines for producing a few officially avowed and officially approved ends. It was also suggested that one frequent official objective is the reformation of inmates in the direction of some ideal standard. This contradiction, then, between what the institution does and what its officials must say that it does, forms the central context of the staff's daily activity.

Within this context, perhaps the first thing to say about staff is that their work, and hence their world, has uniquely to do with people. This people-work is not quite like personnel work nor the work of those involved in service relationships. Staffs, after all, have objects and products to work upon, not relationships, but these objects and products are people.

As material upon which to work, people involve some of the considerations characteristic of inanimate objects. Just as an article being

---

[30] As Cloward, *op. cit.,* pp. 80–83, implies, one important kind of leverage staff has in regard to inmates and one factor leading inmates to act convertible in presence of staff is that staff can give the kind of discharge that may appear to reduce stigmatization. Prison barracks officials can hold up the possibility of the inmate's "restoration" to active duty and, potentially, an honorable discharge; mental hospital administrators can hold up the possibility of a "clean bill of health" (discharged as cured) and personal recommendations.

processed through an industrial plant must be followed by a paper shadow showing what has been done by whom, what is to be done, and who last had responsibility for it, so human objects moving, say, through a mental hospital system must be followed by a chain of informative receipts detailing what has been done to and by the patient and who had most recent responsibility for him. In his career from admission suite to burial plot, many different kinds of staff will add their official note to his case file as he temporarily passes under their jurisdiction, and long after he has died physically his marked remains will survive as an actionable entity in the hospital's bureaucratic system. Even the presence or absence of a particular patient at a given meal or for a given night may have to be recorded so that cost-accounting can be maintained and appropriate adjustments rendered in billing.

Other similarities between people-work and object-work are obvious. Just as tin mines or paint factories or chemical plants may involve special work hazards for employees, so (staffs believe at least) there are special dangers to some kinds of people-work. In mental hospitals, staffs believe that patients may strike out "for no reason" and injure an official. In army prisons, staff "is ever haunted by the spectre of riot, revolt or mutiny. . . ."[31] In TB sanitariums and in leprosoriums, staff feel they are being specially exposed to dangerous diseases.

While these similarities between people- and object-work exist, it is, I think, the unique aspects of people as material to work upon that we must look to for the crucial determinants of the work-world of staff.

Given the physiological characteristics of the human organism, it is obvious that certain requirements must be met if any continued use is to be made of people. But this, of course, is the case with inanimate objects, too; the temperature of any storehouse must be regulated, regardless of whether people or things are stored. However, persons are almost always considered to be ends in themselves, as reflected in the broad moral principles of a total institution's environing society. Almost always, then, we find that some technically unnecessary standards of handling must be maintained with human materials. This maintenance of what we can call humane standards comes to be defined as one part of the "responsibility" of the institution and presumably is one of the things the institution guarantees the inmate in exchange for his liberty. Thus, prison officials are obliged to thwart suicidal efforts of the prisoner and to give him full medical attention even though in some cases this may require postponement of his date of execution. Something similar has been reported in German

---

[31] Cloward, *op. cit.*, p. 82.

concentration camps, where inmates were sometimes given medical attention to tidy them up into a healthier shape for the gas chamber.

A second special contingency in the work-world of staff is the fact that inmates typically have statuses and relationships in the outside world that must be taken into consideration. (This consideration, of course, is related to the previously mentioned fact that the institution must respect some of the rights of inmates qua persons.) Even in the case of the committed mental patient whose civil rights are largely taken from him, a tremendous amount of mere paper-work will be involved. Of course, the rights that are denied a mental patient are usually transferred to a relation, to a committee, or to the superintendent of the hospital itself, who then becomes the legal person whose authorization must be obtained for many matters. Many issues originating outside the institution will arise: Social Security benefits, income taxes, upkeep of properties, insurance payments, old age pension, stock dividends, dental bills, legal obligations incurred prior to commitment, permission to release psychiatric case records to insurance companies or attorneys, permission for special visits from persons other than next of kin, etc. All of these issues have to be dealt with by the institution, even if only to pass the decisions on to those legally empowered to make them.

It should be noted that staff is reminded of its obligations in these matters of standards and rights, not only by its own internal superordinates, by various watchdog agencies in the wider society, and by the material itself, but also by persons on the outside who have kin ties to inmates. The latter group present a special problem because, while inmates can be educated about the price they will pay for making demands on their own behalf, relations receive less tutoring in this regard and rush in with requests for inmates that inmates would blush to make for themselves.

The multiplicity of ways in which inmates must be considered ends in themselves and the multiplicity of inmates themselves forces upon staff some of the classic dilemmas that must be faced by those who govern men. Since a total institution functions somewhat as a State, its staff must suffer somewhat from the tribulations that beset governors.

In the case of any single inmate, the assurance that certain standards will be maintained in his own interests may require sacrifice of other standards, and implied in this is a difficult weighing of ends. For example, if a suicidal inmate is to be kept alive, staff may feel it necessary to keep him under constant deprivatizing surveillance or even tied to a chair in a small locked room. If a mental patient is to be kept from tearing at grossly irritated sores and repeating time and again a cycle of curing and disorder, staff may feel it necessary to curtail the freedom of his hands. Another patient who refuses to eat may have to be humiliated by forced feeding. If inmates of TB sanitariums are to be given an opportunity to recover, it will be necessary to curtail freedom of recreation.[32]

The standards of treatment that one inmate has a right to expect may conflict, of course, with the standards desired by another, giving rise to another set of governmental problems. Thus, in mental hospitals, if the grounds gate is to be kept open out of respect for those with town parole, then some other patients who otherwise could have been trusted on the grounds may have to be kept on locked wards. And if a canteen and mailbox are to be freely available to those on the grounds, then patients on a strict diet or those who write threatening and obscene letters will have to be denied liberty on the grounds.

The obligation of staff to maintain certain humane standards of treatment for inmates represents problems in itself, as suggested above, but a further set of characteristic problems is found in the constant conflict between humane standards on one hand and institutional efficiency on the other. I will cite only one main example. The personal possessions of an individual are an important part of the materials out of which he builds a self, but as an inmate, the ease with which he can be managed by staff is likely to increase with the degree to which he is dispossessed. Thus, the remarkable efficiency with which a mental hospital ward can adjust to a daily shift in number of resident patients is related to the fact that the comers and leavers do not come or leave with any properties but themselves and do not have any right to choose where they will be located. Further, the efficiency with which the clothes of these patients can be kept clean and fresh is related to the fact that everyone's soiled clothing can be indiscriminately placed in one bundle, and laundered clothing can be redistributed not according to ownership but according to rough size. Similarly, the quickest assurance that patients going on the grounds will be warmly dressed is to march them in file past a pile of the ward's allotment of coats, requiring them for the same purposes of health to throw off these collectivized garments on returning to the ward.

Just as personal possessions may interfere with the smooth running of an institutional operation and be removed for this reason, so parts of the body itself may conflict with efficient management and the conflict

[32] Extremely useful material on TB sanitariums as total institutions will be available in the forthcoming work by Julius A. Roth, Committee on Human Development, University of Chicago. Preliminary statements may be found in his articles "What Is an Activity?" *Etc.*, Vol. XIV, Autumn 1956, pp. 54–56, and "Ritual and Magic in the Control of Contagion," *American Sociological Review*, Vol. 22, June 1957, pp. 310–314.

resolved in favor of efficiency. If the heads of inmates are to be kept clean and the possessor easily identified, then a complete head shave is efficacious, regardless of the damage this does to appearance. On similar grounds, some mental hospitals have found it useful to extract the teeth of "biters," give hysterectomies to promiscuous female patients, and perform lobotomies on chronic fighters. Flogging on men-of-war as a form of punishment expressed the same conflict between organizational and humane interests:[33]

> One of the arguments advanced by officers of the Navy in favor of corporal punishment is this: it can be inflicted in a moment; it consumes no valuable time; and when the prisoner's shirt is put on, *that* is the last of it. Whereas, if another punishment were substituted, it would probably occasion a great waste of time and trouble, besides thereby begetting in the sailor an undue idea of his importance.

I have suggested that people-work differs from other kinds because of the tangle of statuses and relationships which each inmate brings with him to the institution and because of the humane standards that must be maintained with respect to him. Another difference occurs in cases where inmates have some rights to visit off the grounds, for then the mischief they may do in civil society becomes something for which the institution has some responsibility. Given this responsibility, it is understandable that total institutions tend not to view off-grounds leave favorably. Still another type of difference between people-work and other kinds, and perhaps the most important difference of all, is that by the exercise of threat, reward or persuasion human objects can be given instructions and relied upon to carry them out on their own. The span of time during which these objects can be trusted to carry out planned actions without supervision will vary of course a great deal, but, as the social organization of back wards in mental hospitals teaches us, even in the limiting case of catatonic schizophrenics, a considerable amount of such reliance is possible. Only the most complicated electronic equipment shares this capacity.

While human materials can never be as refractory as inanimate ones, their very capacity to perceive and to follow out the plans of staff insures that they can hinder the staff more effectively than inanimate objects can. Inanimate objects cannot purposely and intelligently thwart our plans, regardless of the fact that we may momentarily react to them as if they had this capacity. Hence, in prison and on "better" wards of mental hospitals, guards have to be ready for organized efforts at escape and must constantly deal with attempts to bait them, "frame" them, and otherwise get them into trouble. This leads to a state of anxiety in the guard that is not

[33] Melville, *op. cit.*, p. 139.

alleviated by knowledge that the inmate may be acting thusly merely as a means of gaining self-respect or relieving boredom.[34] Even an old, weak, mental patient has tremendous power in this regard; for example, by the simple expedient of locking his thumbs in his trouser pockets he can remarkably frustrate the efforts of an attendant to undress him.

A third general way in which human materials are different from other kinds and hence present unique problems is that, however distant staff manages to stay from them, they can become objects of fellow-feeling and even affection. Always there is the danger that an inmate will appear human. If what are felt to be hardships must be inflicted on the inmate, then sympathetic staff will suffer. And on the other hand, if an inmate breaks a rule, staff's conceiving of him as a human being may increase their sense that injury has been done to their moral world. Expecting a "reasonable" response from a reasonable creature, staff may feel incensed, affronted and challenged when this does not occur. Staff thus finds it must maintain face not only before those who examine the product of work but before these very products themselves.

The capacity of inmates to become objects of staff's sympathetic concern is linked to what might be called an involvement cycle sometimes recorded in total institutions. Starting at a point of social distance from inmates, a point from which massive deprivation and institutional trouble cannot easily be seen, the staff person finds he has no reason not to build up a warm involvement in some inmates. The involvement, however, brings the staff members into a position to be hurt by what inmates do and by what they suffer, and also brings him to a position from which he is likely to threaten the distant stand from inmates taken by his fellow members of the staff. In response, the sympathizing staff member may feel he has been "burnt" and retreat into paper-work, committee-work or other staff-enclosed routine. Once removed from the dangers of inmate contact, he may gradually cease to feel he has reason to remain so, and thus the cycle of contact and withdrawal may be repeated again and again.

When we combine together the fact that staff is obliged to maintain certain standards of humane treatment for inmates and may come to view inmates as reasonable, responsible creatures who are fitting objects for emotional involvement, we have the background for some of the quite special difficulties of people-work. In mental hospitals, for example, there always seem to be some patients who dramatically act against their own obvious self-interest. They drink water they have themselves first polluted; they rush against the wall with their heads; they tear out their own sutures

[34] For comments on the very difficult role of guard, see McCorkle and Korn, *op. cit.*, pp. 93–94, and Gresham M. Sykes, "The Corruption of Authority and Rehabilitation," *Social Forces*, Vol. 34, 1956, pp. 257–262.

after a minor operation; they flush false teeth down the toilet, without which they cannot eat and which take months to obtain; or smash glasses, without which they cannot see. In an effort to frustrate these visibly self-destructive acts, staff may find itself forced to manhandle these patients. Staff then is forced to create an image of itself as harsh and coercive, just at the moment that it is attempting to prevent someone from doing to himself what no human being is expected to do to anyone. At such times it is extremely difficult for staff members to keep their own emotions in control, and understandably so.

Moral Climate

The special requirements of people-work establish the day's job for staff, but this job must be carried out in a special moral climate. For the staff is charged with meeting the hostility and demands of the inmates, and what it has to meet the inmate with, in general, is the rational perspective espoused by the institution. It is the role of the staff to defend the institution in the name of its avowed rational aims—to the inmate as well as to outsiders of various kinds. Thus, when inmates are allowed to have incidental face-to-face contact with staff, the contact will often take the form of "gripes" or requests on the part of the inmate and of justification for prevailing restrictive treatment on the part of the staff. Such, for example, is the general structure of staff-patient interaction in mental hospitals. Further, the privileges and punishments meted out by staff will often be couched in a language that reflects the legitimated objectives of the institution, even though this may require that inmates or low-level members of staff translate these responses into the verbal language of the privilege system.

Given the inmates over whom it has charge and the processing that must be done to these objects, staff tends to evolve what may be thought of as a *theory of human nature*. This verbalized perspective rationalizes the scene, provides a subtle means of maintaining social distance from inmates and a stereotyped view of them, and gives sanction to the treatment accorded them.[35] Typically, the theory covers the "good" and "bad" possibilities of inmate conduct, the forms that messing up take, and the instructional value of privileges and punishments. In army barracks, officers will have a theory about the relation between discipline and obedience under fire, about the qualities proper to men, about the "breaking point"

---

[35] I derive this from Everett C. Hughes' review of Leopold von Wies's *Spätlese*, in *American Journal of Sociology*, Vol. LXI, 1955, p. 182. A similar area is covered under the current anthropological term "ethnopsychology," except that the unit to which it applies is a culture, not an institution.

of men, and about the difference between mental sickness and malingering. In prisons, we find currently an interesting conflict between the psychiatric and the moral-weakness theory of crime. In convents, we find theories about the way in which the spirit can be weak and strong, and the ways its defects can be combatted. Mental hospitals, it should be noted, are especially interesting in this connection because staff members pointedly establish themselves as specialists in the knowledge of human nature who must diagnose and prescribe on the basis of this philosophy. Hence, in the standard psychiatric textbooks there are chapters on "psychodynamics" and "psychopathology" which provide charmingly explicit formulations of the "nature" of human nature.

Given the fact that the management of inmates is typically rationalized in terms of the ideal aims or functions of the establishment and that certain humane standards will form part of this ideal, we can expect that professionals ostensibly hired to service these functions will likely become dissatisfied, feeling that they are being used as "captives" to add professional sanction to the privilege system and that they cannot here properly practice their calling. And this seems to be a classic cry. At the same time, the category of staff that must keep the institution going through continuous contact with inmates may feel that they too are being set a contradictory task, having to coerce inmates into obedience while at the same time giving the impression that humane standards are being maintained and that the rational goals of the institution are being realized. . . .

INSTITUTIONAL DIFFERENCES

One important difference among total institutions is found in the spirit in which recruits enter the establishment. At one extreme we find the quite involuntary entrance of those who are sentenced to prison, committed to a mental hospital, or impressed into the crew of a ship. It is perhaps in such cases that staff's version of the ideal inmate has least chance of taking hold among the inmates. At the other extreme, we find religious institutions which deal only with those who feel they have gotten the call and, of these volunteers, take only those who seem to be the most suitable and the most serious in their intentions. In such cases, conversion seems already to have taken place, and it only remains to show the neophyte along what lines he can best discipline himself. Midway between these two extremes we find institutions like the army barracks whose inmates are required to serve, but who are given much opportunity to feel that this service is a justifiable one required in their own ultimate interests. Obviously, significant differences in tone will appear in total institutions, depending on whether recruitment is voluntary, semivoluntary or involuntary.

Another dimension of variation among total institutions is found in what might be called their *permeability,* that is, the degree to which the social standards maintained within the institution and the social standards maintained in the environing society have influenced each other sufficiently to minimize differences.[36] This issue, incidentally, gives us an opportunity to consider some of the dynamic relations between a total institution and the wider society that supports it or tolerates it.

When we examine the admission procedures of total institutions, we tend to be struck with the impermeable aspects of the establishment, since the stripping and leveling processes which occur at this time directly cut across the various social distinctions with which the recruit entered. St. Benedict's advice[37] to the abbot tends to be followed:

> Let him make no distinction of persons in the monastery. Let not one be loved more than another, unless he be found to excel in good works or in obedience. Let not one of noble birth be raised above him who was formerly a slave, unless some other reasonable cause intervene.

Thus, the new cadet in a military school finds that discussions "of wealth and family background are taboo," and that "Although the pay of the cadet is very low, he is not permitted to receive money from home."[38]

Even the age-grading system of the wider society may be stopped at the gates, as nicely suggested in a recent memoir[39] of an ex-nun:

> Gabrielle moved to the place that would ever be hers, third in line of forty postulants. She was third oldest in the group because she had been third to register on that day less than a week ago when the Order had opened its doors to new entrants. From that moment, her chronological age had ceased and the only age she would henceforth have, her age in the religious life, had started.

It is, of course, by suppressing outside distinctions that a total institution can build up an orientation to its own system of honor. There is a sense then in which the harshest total institution is the most democratic, and in fact the inmate's assurance of being treated no worse than any other of his fellows can be a source of support as well as a deprivation.

But regardless of how radical a total institution appears to be, there will always be some limits to its reshuffling tendencies and some use made

[36] If the analogy were to be carried out strictly, we would have to say of course that every total institution had a semipermeable membrane about it, since there will always be some standard equally maintained on the inside and outside, the impermeable effects being restricted to certain specifiic values and practices.
[37] St. Benedict, *Holy Rule,* Ch. 2.
[38] Dornbusch, *op. cit.,* p. 317. The classic case of this kind of echelon leveling is found perhaps in the fagging system in British public schools.
[39] Kathryn C. Hulme, *The Nun's Story,* Little, Brown, Boston, 1956, pp. 22–23.

of social distinctions already established in the environing society, if only so it can conduct necessary affairs with this society and be tolerated by it. Thus, there does not seem to be a total institution in Western society which provides batch living completely independent of sex; and ones like convents that appear to be impervious to socioeconomic gradings, in fact tend to apportion domestic roles to converts of rural peasant background, just as the patient garbage crews in our prize integrated mental hospitals tend to be wholly Negro.[40] More important, perhaps, than the fact that total institutions differ in overall permeability to outside standards, we find that each is permeable with respect to different social standards.

One of the most interesting differences among total institutions is to be found in the social fate of their graduates. Typically, these become geographically dispersed; the difference is found in the degree to which structural ties are maintained in spite of this distance. At one end of the scale we find the year's graduates of a particular Benedictine abbey, who not only keep in touch informally but find that for the rest of their life their occupation and location have been determined by their original membership. At the same end of the scale, we find ex-convicts whose stay in prison orients them to the calling and to the nationwide underworld community that will comprise their life thereafter. At the other end of the scale, we find enlisted men from the same barracks who melt into private life immediately upon demobilization and even refrain from congregating for regimental reunions. Here, too, are ex-mental patients who studiously avoid all persons and events that might connect them with the hospital. Midway between these extremes, we find "old-boy" systems in private schools and graduate universities, which function as optional communities for the distribution of life-chances among sets of fellow graduates.

---

[40] It seems to be true that within any given establishment the topmost and bottommost roles tend to be relatively permeable to wider community standards, while the impermeable tendencies seem to be focused in the middle ranges of the institution's hierarchy.

INTERORGANIZATIONAL ANALYSIS: A HYPOTHESIS ON CO-ORDINATING AGENCIES[1]

Eugene Litwak and Lydia F. Hylton

One major lacuna in current sociological study is reseach on interorganizational relations—studies which use organizations as their unit of analysis. There are some investigations, which bear tangentially on this problem, such as studies on community disasters and community power,[2] and the study of Gross and others on the school superintendency.[3] There are some explicit formulations of general rules of interorganizational analysis among some of the sociological classics of the past, such as Durkheim's discussion of organic society and, in a tangential way, Marx's analysis of class.[4] But little has been done in current sociological work to follow up the general problems of interorganizational analysis as compared to the problems of intraorganizational analysis, that is studies in bureaucracy.[5]

Reprinted from *Administrative Science Quarterly*, vol. 6 (1962), pp. 395–415, with omission.

[1] We are indebted to Henry J. Meyer for helpful comments on this paper.

[2] William H. Form and Sigmund Nosow, *Community in Disaster* (New York, 1958), pp. 243–244; Floyd Hunter, *Community and Power Structure* (Chapel Hill, N. C., 1953).

[3] Neal Gross, W. S. Mason, and A. W. McEachern, *Exploration in Role Analysis: Studies of the School Superintendency Role* (New York, 1958).

[4] Emile Durkheim, *The Division of Labor in Society* (New York, 1947). If the concept of organization is used very broadly, it could be argued that Marx provided in his theory of class conflict a view of interorganizational analysis which, according to him, explains all social behavior.

[5] The systematic study of *intra*organizational analysis has proceeded at a rapid pace since the 1940's as indicated by the many studies in bureaucracy as well as the development of industrial sociology. For a review of some of this literature, see Peter M. Blau, *Bureaucracy in Modern Society* (New York, 1956). Interorganizational analysis has received no such systematic attention. This contrasts somewhat with related social sciences, where interorganizational analysis has been a major

DIFFERENCES BETWEEN INTERORGANIZATIONAL
AND INTRAORGANIZATIONAL ANALYSIS

One of the major sociological functions of organizational independence is to promote autonomy. This is important when there is a conflict of values and the values in conflict are both desired. For instance, a society might stress both freedom and physical safety. These two values may conflict in many areas of life; yet the society seeks to maximize each. One way of assuring that each will be retained, despite the conflict, is to put them under separate organizational structures; i.e., have the police force guard physical safety and the newspapers guard freedom of the press. If both safety and freedom were the concern of a single organization, it is likely that when conflict arose, one of the values would be suppressed, as, for example, where the police have control over the press.

This conflict between organizations is taken as a given in interorganizational analysis, which starts out with the assumption that there is a situation of partial conflict and investigates the forms of social interaction designed for interaction under such conditions. From this point of view the elimination of conflict is a deviant instance and likely to lead to the disruption of interorganizational relations (i.e., organizational mergers and the like). By contrast, intraorganizational analysis assumes that conflicting values lead to a breakdown in organizational structure. Thus Weber's model of bureaucracy assumed that the organization had a homogeneous policy.[6] Blau's modification of Weber's analysis (i.e., the individual must internalize the policies of the organization) assumes that the organization has a single consistent system.[7] Selznick has pointed out that deficiencies in the Tennessee Valley Authority centered around the problem of conflicting values.[8]

By distinguishing between interorganizational and intraorganizational analysis, the investigator is sensitized to the organizational correlates of value conflict and value consistency. Without such a distinction he might concentrate on showing that value conflicts lead to organizational break-

---

concern. For some illustrations in economics see John K. Galbraith, *American Capitalism: The Concept of Countervailing Power* (Boston, 1952), pp. 117–157; Friedrich A. Hayek, *The Road to Serfdom* (Chicago, 1944), pp. 56–127; K. William Kapp, *The Social Costs of Private Enterprise* (Cambridge, Mass., 1950); E. F. M. Durbin, *Problems of Economic Planning* (London, 1949).
[6] H. H. Gerth and C. Wright Mills, eds. and tr., *From Max Weber: Essays in Sociology* (New York, 1946), pp. 196–203.
[7] *Bureaucracy in Modern Society*, pp. 57–68.
[8] Philip Selznick, *TVA and the Grass Roots: A Study in the Sociology of Formal Organization* (Berkeley, Calif., 1949).

down without appreciating that interorganizational relations permit and encourage conflict without destruction of the over-all societal relations.

Organizational independence for autonomy is functional not only in value conflict but in most forms of social conflict. For instance, values may be theoretically consistent, but limited resources force individuals to choose between them without completely rejecting either choice. (This is one of the classic problems of economics.) Or it may be that a given task requires several specialties, i.e., a division of labor, and limited resources at times of crisis force a choice between them, although all are desirable (for example, the conflicts between the various military services). In such cases organizational independence might be given to the specialties to preserve their essential core despite competition.

A second point follows from the preceding discussion. Interorganizational analysis stresses the study of social behavior under conditions of unstructured authority. International relations between nations is the polar model for interorganizational behavior,[9] a modicum of co-ordination is necessary to preserve each nation, yet there is no formal authority which can impose co-operation. By contrast, most intraorganizational analysis is made under the assumption of a fairly well-defined authority structure. As a consequence, formal authority plays a larger role in explaining behavior within the organization than it does in interorganizational analysis with exceptions, of course, as where the society has a strong monolithic power structure and is very stable. Because of this difference, interorganizational analysis will frequently use, as explanatory variables, elements that are disregarded or minimized in intraorganizational studies.

In summary, interorganizational analyses suggest two important facets of analysis which differ somewhat from intraorganizational analysis: (1) the operation of social behavior under conditions of partial conflict and (2) the stress on factors which derive equally from all units of interaction rather than being differentially weighted by authority structure.

To point out that multiple organizations are effective in situations of partial conflict is not to suggest that they necessarily arise from such situations or that conflict is the only reason for their persistence. Multiple organizations might be the consequence of social growth. Thus in one city, there may be twenty family agencies, with no rational basis for separation

---

[9] Current relations between the United States and Russia are a case in point. These two nations do not recognize any authority superior to them. Because of the potential destructive power of atomic warfare and the interrelated character of international relations they are interdependent, i.e., each can destroy the other or each must take the other into account in order to achieve its national goals. At the same time they have conflicting ideologies, which lead them to seek to maintain regions of legitimized conflict, i.e., national sovereignty.

except that their growth was an unplanned consequence of immediate social pressure. They might, indeed, be in the process of consolidation. Yet at any given time in a changing society, the investigator must expect to find multiple organizations because the processes of centralization and decentralization are slow. Culture values also condition the development of multiple organizations. In the field of business enterprise there is a tendency to argue that a competitive situation is a good per se; even where a monopoly is more efficient, society might reject it. Within the welfare field, family agencies may be separated by religious beliefs. In short, where there is a situation of partial conflict (which all societies must have because of limited resources for maximizing all values simultaneously), where a society is constantly changing, and where cultural values dictate it, the problem of multiple organizations will be an important one. Consequently there is a need for theories dealing with interorganizational analysis—situations involving partial conflict and interactions without a structure of formal authority.

THE PROBLEM OF CO-ORDINATION

One strategic problem in interorganizational analysis concerns co-ordination, a somewhat specialized co-ordination, since there is both conflict and co-operation and formal authority structure is lacking. If the conflict were complete, the issue could be settled by complete lack of interaction or by some analogue to war. Where the conflict overlaps with areas of support, however, the question arises: What procedures ensure the individual organizations their autonomy in areas of conflict while at the same time permitting their united effort in areas of agreement?

One such mechanism is the co-ordinating agency—formal organizations whose major purpose is to order behavior between two or more other formal organizations by communicating pertinent information (social service exchange and hospital agencies), by adjudicating areas of dispute (Federal Communications Commission), by providing standards of behavior (school accrediting organizations), by promoting areas of common interest (business associations, such as the National Association of Manufacturers, restaurant associations, grocery store associations), and so forth. What characterizes all these organizations is that they co-ordinate the behavior between two or more organizations. Furthermore, the organizations being co-ordinated are independent, because they have conflicting values or because the demands of efficiency suggest organizational specialization, yet share some common goal which demands co-operation.

From this reasoning we can advance the following hypothesis: Co-ordinating agencies will develop and continue in existence if formal organizations are partly interdependent; agencies are aware of this interdependence, and it can be defined in standardized units of action. What characterizes the three variables in this hypothesis (interdependence, awareness, and standardization of the units to be co-ordinated) is the extent to which they are tied to the organizations to be co-ordinated. By contrast, if this were an intraorganizational analysis, the development of co-ordinating mechanisms might be accounted for by authority structure with little concern for the awareness of the units to be co-ordinated, without standardization, and without significant variations in interdependence. For instance, the leadership might institute co-ordinating mechanisms because they are aware of interdependence where the units to be co-ordinated are unaware of this; or they might introduce co-ordinating mechanisms not to increase efficiency of the organization but to perpetuate their own authority structure; or they might introduce co-ordinating mechanisms despite lack of standardization because they feel this might speed up the process of standardization. In other words, authority structure is important in understanding intraorganizational behavior, while the variables suggested here for understanding interorganizational analysis may be insignificant.[10]

STUDY DESIGN AND DEFINITION OF TERMS

In order to provide a limited test of this hypothesis, specific attention is directed to two types of co-ordinating agencies—community chests and social service exchanges. The following nine "traditional" problems of community chest and social service exchanges will be used to show how they can be accounted for by the general hypothesis about co-ordinating agencies:

1. The emergence and continuing growth of community chest programs.
2. The fluctuations in financial campaigns of community chest programs.
3. The resistance of national agencies such as the American Cancer Society to participating in the local community chest.
4. The ability of some agencies to exclude others from the chest—Catholic agencies exclude planned-parenthood agencies.

[10] Some of the current studies in industrial organization also suggest the need to consider localized discretion and the decentralization of authority. Seymour Melman's *Decision-Making and Productivity* (Oxford, 1958), pp. 3–23, is a case in point. It is not always easy to know when a situation fits the intraorganizational or interorganizational model. Concerns such as General Electric are nominally one organization but at times resemble a series of independent ones in coalition, while the steel industry consists of formally separated groups which for many purposes tend to act as a unit (in labor bargaining, on pricing of goods, and against political pressure groups).

5. The development of dual campaigns—Jewish agencies and the Red Cross participate in local community chests as well as run independent national campaigns.
6. The decline of the social service exchange.
7. The fact that community chest agencies have adjudication functions while social service exchanges do not.
8. Principles of growth of new co-ordinating agencies.
9. The increasing encroachment of community chest agencies on member agencies' budget decisions.

If, in fact, it can be demonstrated that these diverse problems are all variations on a common theme (specified by our hypothesis), then we shall feel that our hypothesis has had initial confirmation. If nothing more, it has met the test of Ockham's razor.

To simplify the presentation, each element of the hypothesis will be examined separately. Although normally all are simultaneously involved, there are certain forms of co-ordination which more clearly represent the influence of one of these variables rather than another. In the concluding discussion, systematic consideration will be given to the simultaneous interaction among all three variables as well as alternative mechanisms of co-ordination (aside from the formal co-ordinating agency).

First it seems appropriate to define the three terms of the hypothesis— interdependence, awareness, and standardization. By interdependence is meant that two or more organizations must take each other into account if they are to accomplish their goals.[11] The definition of this term has been formally developed by Thomas who points out that there are several kinds of interdependency. The initial discussion here will concentrate on competitive interdependence (where one agency can maximize its goals only at the expense of another), while the later discussion will introduce and relate facilitative interdependence (where two or more agencies can simultaneously maximize their goals). By awareness we mean that the agency, as a matter of public policy, recognizes that a state of interdependency exists. By standardized actions we mean behavior which is reliably ascertained and repetitive in character, e.g., requests for funds, information on whether the client is served by another agency, price of goods, cost of living index, and the like.[12]

---

[11] For a more formal definition and discussion of interdependence see Edwin J. Thomas, Effects of Facilitative Role Interdependence on Group Functioning, *Human Relations*, 19 (1957), 347–366. In the definition used here the phrase "take into account" is meant in a very immediate sense for in a broad sense all organizations must take each other into account.
[12] In contrast to these illustrations the diagnosis and treatment of mental illness is nonstandardized and not public in character.

THE EVIDENCE ON INTERDEPENDENCY

Historical Emergence and Continued
Growth of Community Chests

If the factors accounting for the origin of community chest programs[13] are examined, one explanation which appears repeatedly is the complaints of donors and fund raisers that they were being confronted with too many requests for assistance and that fund raising was both time-consuming and economically wasteful.[14] It was at the urging of these donors and fund raisers that many of the community chest programs had their beginnings.

It is argued here that these complaints of the donors and their consequent demands for centralized fund raising were manifestations of the increasing interdependence of welfare agencies in the community, for what in effect had occurred was an increase in the number of agencies drawing on a limited local community fund. This meant that any given agency which drew from this common fund was depriving some other agency of a source of money, and that the same donor received many requests for funds. How much the donors' feelings of waste were a consequence of agencies' increasing interdependence on a limited and common pool of funds can be seen if one envisions the situation of few agencies and much money. In such cases no two agencies need go to the same donor. The donor, as a consequence, would not feel plagued by many requests and thus become aware of the inefficiency of many agencies carrying on independent fund raising activities.

Community chest programs have continued to grow partly because financial dependence has grown—agencies' demands for funds have grown at the same or a faster rate than national income.[15]

Fluctuations in Financial Campaigns
of Community Chest Programs

If the development of co-ordinating agencies is a function of interdependency, then any fluctuation in interdependency should lead to a fluctuation in co-ordination. If the pool of resources in the community is suddenly

---

[13] For a detailed account of the beginnings of the federation movement see: John R. Seely et al., Community Chest (Toronto, 1957), pp. 13–29; Frank J. Bruno, Trends in Social Work: 1874–1956 (New York, 1957), pp. 199–206; and William J. Norton, The Cooperative Movement in Social Work (New York, 1927), pp. 8 ff., 112 ff.

[14] Norton, op. cit., pp. 50 ff., 68 ff., 113 ff.

[15] An indirect measure of this is that for 1940–1955, where comparable figures were available, the amount collected by united funds (including Red Cross) increased at the same or slightly higher rate than disposable personal income. See Trends in

decreased while the number of agencies remains the same or increases, then the agencies' competition for funds should increase and their interdependency increase accordingly. Such limitations of community funds occur during periods of crisis—natural catastrophes, depressions, or wars. In one major historical instance, in Cincinnati, the community chest program arose not as a result of donor pressures but was formed as a consequence of a disastrous flood.[16] The same point is made in the study of a modern catastrophe by Form and Nosow, who say, "Hence [inter]organizational integration is the most crucial dimension in disaster."[17]

Co-ordination should grow both in periods of prosperity (World War II) and depression, since greater interdependency can be expected in both these periods. Figure 1 indicates that the funds raised by community chest programs rose sharply during the early thirties (prior to governmental intervention in public relief) and again during the war years of the 1940's.[18] These are peak years as compared to the years immediately preceding and following. These data suggest that the co-ordinating agencies were strengthened during these periods and that interdependency, not the level of income, was an important factor. In summary, instead of three *ad hoc* explanations, i.e., war, depression, and catastrophe, we offer one which provides a general explanation for all three.[19]

Giving, 1955 (New York, 1956), p. 3. The rate of increase of gross national product and united community funds is roughly similar between the period 1948 to 1958. See *Trends in Giving, 1958* (New York, 1959), p. 2.

[16] Norton, *op. cit.*, pp. 96 ff., 133 ff.

[17] "While in everyday affairs organizations implicitly are dependent on one another to meet routine problems, they are rarely called out in force to function effectively *together* as one unit. Yet this is precisely what is required in a disaster—the full mobilization and cooperation of interdependent organizations, which normally operate autonomously. Hence organizational integration is the most crucial dimension in disaster" (Form and Nosow, *op. cit.*, pp. 243–244).

[18] Sources of data: J. Frederic Dewhurst *et al., America's Needs and Resources* (New York, 1955), p. 437; Russel H. Kurtz, *Social Work Yearbook, 1957* (New York, 1957), p. 175; *Trends in Giving, 1957, 1958, 1959* (New York, 1958, 1959, 1960). The amount of funds raised is affected by short-term crises and is therefore a more sensitive measure of organizational strength than number of organizations, which do not reflect short-term declines because of career and job commitments. Also, when the dollar value was stabilized by computing all figures on the basis of the 1953 dollar, no significant change in the character of the fluctuations occurred.

[19] The reader can note from Figure 1 that there is a continued increase in funds following the Korean crisis. This period is marked by aggressive solicitations by national agencies in smaller communities leading to an increase in interdependency. In addition, smaller communities became aware of united giving because of its popularity among the larger cities. An examination of the *Annual Directory of Chests, United Funds and Councils* (UCFC) (1936 and 1956) shows that approximately one-third of the 429 community chests listed in 1936 were in towns of 25,000 or less population. In 1956, towns of this size represented better than half of the 1,182 community chests listed. Also see *United Giving in the Smaller Community* (New York, 1956).

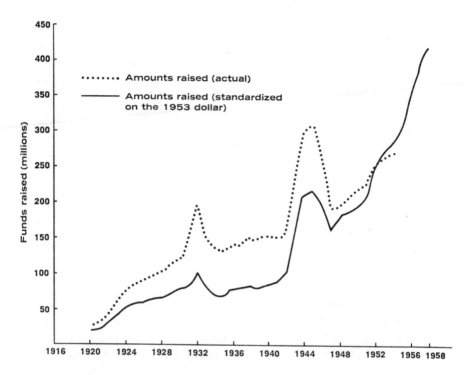

FIGURE 1.   *Federated fund raising.*

Resistance of National Agencies
to Local Community Chests—Fixed Markets

Interdependency should also be able to account for the fact that certain agencies are able to resist efforts to include them in the co-ordination process. The answer to such resistance should lie in part in the limited dependence of these agencies on other agencies in the community; i.e., they can raise money regardless of what other agencies in the community do. When examined, such agencies are seen to have "fixed markets" as far as fund raising is concerned. For instance, the American Cancer Society knows that in any open competition with other agencies, it will receive more funds than most other organizations, because of the public's tremendous concern with, and awareness of, the injurious effects of cancer.[20]

[20] For details regarding the nonparticipation of national agencies, see *Organizing a United Fund* [1953] and *United We Stand* [1958] (New York, 1954, 1959); *1958 Experience in United Funds, 1957 Experience in United Funds,* and *United Giving in the Smaller Community* (New York, 1956); and F. Emerson Andrews, *Philanthropic Giving* (New York, 1950), pp. 152 ff., 156 ff.

The Red Cross is another agency which can resist, to some extent, local community chest involvement because its historic tradition has created a following among donors which amounts to a "fixed market." Fixed markets in fund raising are also enjoyed by religious agencies in cities where their members form a large element in the local community. Such agencies can generally count on receiving priority in any competition for funds. In other words, where an agency, by virtue of cultural norms (religious), historical tradition (Red Cross), or through current interest (American Cancer Society), is able to establish a "fixed money market," it is less dependent on other agencies in the community and can resist efforts at incorporation into community chest programs.

The problem of resistance to community chest programs is a variation on the same basic theme which explains the historical emergence and the fluctuation of funds raised in community chest programs.

**Multiple Dependencies—Dual Campaigns
and Agency Exclusions**

Thus far the assumption has been that agencies are linked by one dependency relation, or if multiple dependencies exist they are consistent with each other. Where an agency has multiple relations with another and they are not consistent, i.e., some involve interdependency and some involve independence, then it will affiliate with co-ordinating agencies only on its own terms. This permits explanation of two classical problems in community chest programs—the exclusion of one agency by another and the running of dual campaigns.

For instance, Catholic agencies frequently insist that planned-parenthood agencies be excluded from community chest programs as a condition of their participation. What characterizes the Catholic agencies is mixed multiple dependencies with other agencies. Like the American Cancer Society, Catholic agencies in strong Catholic communities, have a fixed financial market. Unlike the American Cancer Society, the Catholic agencies perform services (family and recreational) that involve them in an interdependency relation with other agencies in the community. The American Cancer Society's chief service is research, which is equally valuable when done outside the confines of the community. Consequently, Catholic agencies have an incentive to join the local community chest while the Cancer Society does not. Yet, because of their financial independence, Catholic agencies can afford a policy of joining only where the situation is advantageous to them. If a Catholic agency is large, it can force the ouster of the smaller planned-parenthood organization, whose values are antithetical to theirs.

The concept of multiple and conflicting dependencies also explains why some organizations run dual campaigns. Thus Jewish agencies will frequently co-operate with the local community chest and in addition run a separate campaign. The Jewish agencies, like the Catholic agencies, may have a fixed financial market, but have local services which lead to interdependence with other agencies. In addition they have national services which are not dependent on local agencies, such as raising funds for Israel and for research on prejudice. Because of their dual service interests— local and national—their interests only partly overlap that of the local community chest. Because of their financial semi-independence they can enforce their demands for dual campaigns. Similarly, the Red Cross is also likely to run dual campaigns.

Where there are multiple dependencies, there are several possibilities which have different implications for affiliation with local co-ordination agencies. These are outlined in Table 1. Where all relations are independent of the local community, the organizations will refuse affiliation with local community chests (e.g., American Cancer Society). Where there are mixed dependencies, the organization is likely to enter the community chests only on its own terms (i.e., eliminate conflicting organizations or run dual campaigns). Where the organization has multiple dependencies and they mostly involve interdependence, there will be strong support of local co-ordinating organizations.

The Decline of Social Service Exchange

Since the 1940's there has been a steady decline in the number of social service exchanges from 320 exchanges in 1946 to 220 in 1956 to 175 in 1959.[21] If the hypothesis advanced here is correct, this decline should be a function of decreasing interdependence. To ascertain this relationship, it is necessary to know what the functions of the social service exchanges were. From the turn of the century up to the early 1930's one of the major services offered by private welfare agencies was direct material aid— money, clothing, housing, food, and the like. All agencies sought to maximize their services by providing the largest amount to the greatest number of needy. This made them interdependent, for if two agencies were both providing funds to the same individual without being aware of it, neither agency was maximizing its goals. The social service exchange served an important co-ordinating function, since any client coming to an

[21] Regarding the experiences of the exchange see *Summary Report of Research on the Social Service Exchange* (New York, 1959); *Social Work Yearbook 1957*, pp. 547 ff.; Norton, *op. cit.*, pp. 22–24.

TABLE 1. *Multiple dependencies and affiliations with community co-ordinating agencies*

Services	Financially Interdependent	Financially Independent (Fixed Markets)
Interdependent (local services)	Nondenominational family services generally have no fixed financial market and have local services which are interdependent with other agencies. They will affiliate most strongly.	Catholic family agencies in strong Catholic communities have a fixed market but are dependent for services. They will affiliate with co-ordinating agencies on their own terms, i.e., elimination of planned-parenthood groups.
Independent (national services)	National health organizations whose main activity is research but which have achieved no public acceptance of their importance will affiliate with community co-ordinating agencies.	National cancer associations have a fixed market (because of the public's fear of cancer) and have independence in services because these are mostly research. They will not affiliate with local community co-ordinating agencies.
Mixed interdependent and independent (both local and national services)	Agencies such as the Red Cross have both national and local services. They are becoming less independent because their tradition is fading. Therefore they enter into local community arrangements while insisting on maintaining their identity and the right to run national mass-media campaigns.	Jewish community councils in a strong Jewish community have a fixed market. At the same time they have both local services (family and recreation programs) and national services (i.e., research on antisemitism, aid to Israel, etc.). Hence they are likely to have dual campaigns.

agency could be checked through the exchange to see if he was receiving aid from another agency as well.

Two developments undermined the interdependence of the agencies and led to the decline of the social service exchange. First, the government in the middle 1930's took over most of the material assistance programs. Secondly, the private agencies turned their attention to other services with a strong emphasis on psychiatric casework,[22] which did not necessitate communication between agencies. First, the client was unlikely to seek duplication of service as he might seek duplication of material benefits. Secondly, it was argued that all crucial information could be secured from the client;[23] consequently it was not necessary to have any record of prior counseling by some other agency. In addition, some theorists would argue that it would be unethical to secure information from outside sources without the client's knowledge or consent.[24] In other words, old services which were co-ordinated by the social service exchange have disappeared and the new services do not result in agency interdependence,[25] and the decline of social service exchanges can therefore be explained by the decreasing interdependence of the member agencies.

Adjudicatory Functions and Types of Interdependency

Thus far the analysis has attempted to demonstrate that a series of seemingly diverse problems might all be related to the same underlying phenomenon. A simple derivative of the interdependency hypothesis might now be taken into account. If co-ordinating agencies develop when there is agency interdependency, the type of co-ordination should vary with type of dependency. Thomas points out that there is both a competitive and a noncompetitive form of interdependency.[26] In competitive interdependency an agency seeking to maximize its goal deprives another agency of doing likewise. Thus in a community chest where there is a limited amount of social welfare funds, the more one agency receives, the less another agency will receive. By contrast, the social service exchanges dealt with a noncompetitive facilitating interdependency, where maximal goal achievement by one agency was most likely when other agencies maximized their goals as well. Interdependency explains both the rise of the community chest and the decline of the social service agencies.

However, the competitive interdependency of community chests and

---

[22] See note 21 and *Budget $ in a Community Chest* (New York, 1953).
[23] See note 21.
[24] *Ibid.*
[25] More recent trends in treatment suggest that social service exchanges might be reorganized around different functions.
[26] *Op. cit.*

the facilitating interdependency of social service agencies explains one of the basic differences between these agencies—the adjudicating functions of the community chest. Where a co-ordinating agency must deal with competitive interdependence, it must have some process for adjudicating the differences which must arise. Such agencies will therefore be characterized by some judicial processes. The budget committees of community chests are frequently the core committees whose major function is to hand down judgments by approving or disapproving budget requests of competing agencies. By contrast, the social service exchanges deal with situations where member agencies have no dispute but can only increase their goal achievement by communicating through the co-ordinating agencies. This explains why social service exchanges have minor adjudicatory functions.

Growth Pattern of Co-ordinating Agencies and Some Policy Implications

Our analysis suggests that where interdependency rests on some very stable set of social relations one can anticipate the growth of the co-ordinating agencies to be constant. Since financial support is one of the most stable social conditions in a money economy such as ours, there is good reason to predict the growth and continued existence of co-ordinating agencies such as the community chest. By contrast, interdependency based on services has no such stable support, for social services frequently rest on discoveries in the social sciences. For example, psychotherapy is constantly open to the changes of scientific progress,[27] and it would be hypothesized that co-ordinating agencies dealing with such services might have a much more uncertain future. One of the policy implications which follows is that such co-ordinating agencies must be given maximum discretion to alter their functions as necessitated by new scientific developments.

SELF-AWARENESS AND CO-ORDINATING AGENCIES— THE FUTURE ROLE OF RESEARCH

Our hypothesis stated that in addition to dependency there must be self-awareness. In dealing with financial services there seems to be little problem in our moneyed economy of self-awareness. This in part explains the early emergence of the social service exchanges and the community chest. Interdependency based on services and resting on theories of social behavior might not be so easy to observe and, once observed, difficult to

---

[27] In this connection the tendency among some social workers and psychoanalysts to view principles of therapy as permanently fixed displays an attitude more akin to religious movements than to the spirit of scientific progress.

raise to agency self-awareness. To do this requires some publicly certified method such as scientific research. Thus it took a scientific survey such as Buell's[28] to raise to the agency policy level the fact that many agencies were treating different problems of the same families. By not being aware of this, the agencies frequently proposed programs of action to the client which were contradictory. As the social sciences develop, it is quite probable that agencies will increasingly turn to scientific research to see whether interdependence indeed exists.

Aside from the question of research, economic theorists suggest still another factor affecting public awareness of dependency. They point out that where there are many units in the field, e.g., farming, it is almost impossible to observe and communicate interdependency.[29] By contrast, where one has a few units, observability or interdependence is markedly increased. In the initial stages community welfare agencies were supported by a few wealthy individuals.[30] It was perhaps the small number of persons involved which contributed to their perception of the need for, and their ability to co-operate in, the development of community chest programs.[31] Whereas a large number of agencies will make observability of interdependence difficult, a small number reduces the need for formal co-ordinating agencies, since co-ordination can be handled informally.

STANDARDIZATION OF COMMUNITY CHEST AND ENCROACHMENT ON WELFARE AGENCIES

This, in turn, points out the importance of the last term of the hypothesis—standardization of social action. In order for a co-ordinating agency to operate efficiently it must develop specialists. For such specialists to develop, however, the behavior to be co-ordinated has to be standard in character—continuing and repetitive over long periods. If, for instance, social workers in family agencies needed to consult with those in childrens' agencies, and each case was unique, there would be no real way of codifying this information or developing specialists in transmitting this information, and therefore no need for formal co-ordinating agencies. The most

[28] B. Buell, *et al., Community Planning for Human Services* (New York, 1952).
[29] Galbraith, *op. cit.,* pp. 12–25, 33–53.
[30] See note 13.
[31] By contrast, current chest programs have a large mass base. However, by 1959 close to 85 per cent of the funds were collected under the aegis of business, and support for united fund drives comes from the managers of large organizations, who are relatively few in number. This estimate of 85 per cent is rough and is based on the amount given directly by corporations and the amount collected at the place of work. See *Trends in Giving, 1958,* and F. Emerson Andrews, *Corporation Giving* (New York, 1952), pp. 156–158. Like the few wealthy individuals of the past, these managers are able to see the disruptive forces in having many diverse drives.

efficient way to handle this form of interdependence might be informal mechanisms of co-ordination—telephone conversations between workers, bringing in consultants, and the like.

In short, if one is to move from mechanisms of co-ordination to formal co-ordinating agencies, it is necessary to deal with standardized units of behavior. Conversely, to increase its efficiency, a co-ordinating agency must seek to standardize the behavior which makes up interagency dependency as much as possible. In this connection the growing detailed budgetary demands made by community chests on member agencies are most instructive. From the early times, where community chests asked for a rough estimate of the agencies' current budgetary needs, to the present time, where most elaborate forms are filled out for at least one year in advance, the pressure for standardization of budgetary requests has increased. The same process can be observed in social service exchanges where the drive for standardization has led to an increasingly detailed and complex categorizing of information.

However, the relationship between standardization and co-ordinating agencies is not monotonic. Thus where extreme standardization takes place, it is frequently possible to co-ordinate activities via rules or laws rather than community organization. This is ideally what the economists mean when they speak about automatic stabilizers.[32] A good illustration of how interaction between two organizations can be co-ordinated by rules are the escalator clauses in union-management contracts. It is possible to have such rules because the computation of the living cost and wage payment is standardized—rules for computing them are readily made, publicly observable, and easily checked, and if done over and over again the same results would have a high probability of occurring.

MECHANISMS FOR PRESERVING CONFLICT

Thus far the analysis of co-ordinating mechanisms has with one exception centered on the element of co-operation or interdependence. If the interorganizational character is to be retained, there must also be some procedures for preserving autonomy and conflict. For instance, if the community chest were to concentrate just on the co-operative functions, there would be a tendency for organizational merger of member agencies or, as a minimum, the development of uniformity of services. Groups such as the community chest were originally organized around the goal of co-operation (i.e., fund raising and allocation). Group goals once set have a powerful socializing

32 E. Despres, M. Friedman, A. Hart, P. A. Samuelson, and D. H. Wallace. The Problem of Economic Instability, *American Economic Review*, 40 (1950), 505–538.

effect on members;[33] furthermore, the group tends to recruit only those who are sympathetic to its goals. Because these socialization and screening pressures for co-operation and merger have a group base, the counter-pressures for preserving organizational autonomy and conflict must have an equally pervasive influence.

One type of group mechanism designated to preserve areas of autonomy and conflict is signaled by the phrase "conflict of interest." The mechanism is a law or a professional code of ethics which says that no individual can belong to two organizations which have legitimate areas of conflict. The incipient basis for this type of mechanism can be seen in the area of welfare fund raising as well. In contrast to the community chests, community councils have in recent years more and more taken the position of defending agency autonomy (i.e., arguing that the community chest does not have the right to make the decisions about the nature and quality of services). If this incipient division of labor crystallizes, then a code of ethics might eventuate in which a person will be said to have a conflict of interest if he sits on the budget committee of the community chest and is a member of the community council committee for preserving professional control of services.

Another possible procedure for maintaining legitimate areas of conflict is to have a division of labor *within* the co-ordinating agency, with one group dealing with areas of co-operation and the other with areas of conflict and autonomy.[34] Thus the budget committee of the community chest is frequently dominated by lay people who exercise considerable control over fund raising and allocation. Problems of fund allocations frequently lead to questions about the respective merits of various services, however, and the nonprofessional members may lean heavily on their staff experts. The professional members are frequently educated to accept the legitimacy of multiple and competing forms of service and act as a barrier to demands for merger or premature resolution of conflicts.

Still another mechanism for preserving conflict is the use of the ideology of "tradition" as a decision rule. Where there has been a profusion of services in the past, such a decision rule acts to maintain existing states

[33] The socializing effects of the group on the individual has been thoroughly documented. For a recent summary see Eugene Litwak, "Some Policy Implications in Communications Theory with Emphasis on Group Factors," *Education for Social Work, Proceedings of the Seventh Annual Program Meeting* (New York, 1959), pp. 98–109.
[34] For illustrations of a division of labor as a way for maintaining legitimized conflict see Blau, *Bureaucracy in Modern Society*, pp. 64–66; James D. Thompson and Arthur Tuden, "Strategies, Structures, and Processes of Organizational Decision," in James D. Thompson et al., eds., *Comparative Studies in Administration* (Pittsburgh, 1959), pp. 200–202.

of conflict.[35] This mechanism is generally vulnerable, however, because it does not provide for innovation in a society where change is a cultural characteristic. Therefore, if this mechanism is to survive in our society, it is likely to be used as the courts use the concept of "precedent." The fiction of tradition is maintained, although, *de facto,* much innovation is permitted. There are a variety of other mechanisms of equal merit[36] which will not be explored here.

It must be pointed out that, while interorganizational co-ordination requires both co-operation and conflict, at any given time emphasis might be on one or the other. Thus, since the middle eighteen-hundreds, the major problem in welfare fund raising has been to develop co-operation between competing agencies. It is only recently, when community chests have become exceedingly strong, that attention has shifted to the problem of agency autonomy and preserving legitimate areas of conflict. By contrast, in the business world since the middle eighteen-hundreds primary attention has been paid to preserving areas of conflict between concerns (antitrust laws) and only recently has more attention been paid to the need to maintain co-operation (fair price laws, farmer subsidies, and so on). The researcher must therefore keep in mind that despite the exigencies of any particular situation, interorganizational co-ordination is characterized by the need to maintain areas both of conflict and of co-ordination. . . .

[35] The ideology of progress rather than tradition might be used to provide for legitimate areas of conflict where the past has shown a monolithic uniformity.
[36] Mechanisms might be derived by analogy from a consideration of Robert K. Merton, The Role-Set: Problems in Sociological Theory, *British Journal of Sociology,* 8 (June 1957), 106–120; and Eugene Litwak, Models of Bureaucracy Which Permit Conflict, *American Journal of Sociology,* 47 (1961), 177–184.

BUREAUCRATIC ORGANIZATIONS AND THE EVOLUTION OF INDUSTRIAL SOCIETY

Michel Crozier

Two general factors, in our opinion, influence the evolution of organizational patterns in modern society in a way Weber did not foresee. These factors, whose importance we have already stressed in our discussion of the ways in which an organization achieves conformity, are (1) the constant progress in the techniques of prediction and organization; and (2) the growing sophistication of the individual in an increasingly complex culture. Organizational progress has made it possible to be more tolerant of the personal needs and idiosyncrasies of individual members: one can obtain the wanted results from them without having to control their behavior so narrowly as before. Cultural sophistication, on the other hand, has increased the individual's capacity for accommodation and at the same time, as a consequence, his possibilities of independence. People can now measure their contribution to the organization in a more precise way; they are no longer obliged to bargain for all or nothing. Participation is much less dangerous for them, since they have learned to be more flexible and since they can participate without committing themselves quite so much. The cost of quitting and finding a substitute participation is, in any case, both psychically and materially much less heavy than before. The more tolerant modern organizations demand much less from their members, and the latters' freedom and flexibility allow them also to demand much less in return. If pressure from both sides can diminish as both parties become less demanding, rigidity will tend generally to decrease. The number and the complexity of the rules may increase tremendously—modern organizational patterns will be more flexible, much less "bureaucratic" than before.

Reprinted from Michel Crozier, *The Bureaucratic Phenomenon* (Chicago: The University of Chicago Press, 1964), pp. 296–314.

Organizations will be content with a more temporary loyalty from their members, even at the highest echelons, and individuals will not press the organization to protect them by using the rules in the most binding way. With pressures from the top and counter-pressures from below decreasing, rigidity as described in our model will tend to diminish.[1]

Many authors, we are aware, have adopted a different view of modern organizations. William H. Whyte, Jr.,[2] who has been among the more outstanding, argues, for example, that modern organization man is above all a conformist, that the new ethic which the development of large-scale organizations is creating is an ethic of conformism, in contrast to the Protestant and capitalist ethic of individual responsibility. His arguments, however, are not very convincing even if limited to the short run. It might be true that our social system still needs more individual responsibility than the present trend allows us to manifest. But this does not mean that our society is more conformist than that of even thirty years ago. The "well-rounded" personality which Whyte so attacks is the mark of a flexible individual always ready to compromise and generally more socially-minded than his more assertive counterpart of thirty years ago. Does this mean that organizational men in general are now more conformist? Certainly not; the confusion comes from Whyte's focusing on the top, successful individual. The Protestant ethic was supportive for the successful executive who could be extremely assertive in the name of individual responsibility. But this kind of independence meant more submissiveness on the part of his subordinates and the retreatism and ritualism necessary to alleviate it. The social values of today's organization man are conducive to better possibilities of adjusting in a more independent way, if not the top, but the average, member is considered.[3] Certainly, the extension of those values to other domains where individual creativity is the decisive factor can become a deterrent to progress, but in the paramount domain of social action the price which had to be paid for maintaining the authoritarian hero of former times was such that the flexible, tolerant, and well-rounded conformist manager of the organization era seems, in comparison, to be a model of efficiency.

Moreover, as Dalton has shown, the complex human relations and power relations system of a modern organization imposes on its executive

---

[1] Starting from a different point of view, the British social psychologist Tom Burns has recently presented a similar argument. For him, the growing acceleration of change in modern industrial society tends to impose a type of *organistic* management against the usual *mechanistic* type. See Tom Burns and G. M. Stalker, *The Management of Innovation* (London: Pergamon Press, 1961).

[2] William H. Whyte, Jr., *The Organization Man* (New York: Simon & Schuster, 1956).

[3] Notwithstanding the difficult situation of several layers in the hierarchical pyramid, and especially the lower supervisors and foremen.

the need to take initiative constantly and to be creative more subtly.[4] Instead of assuming the full responsibility of command in a general climate of uncertainty, they must settle conflicting claims in a maze of rules, arbitrate between opposing forms of rationality, and face the difficult moral issues of the ambiguity of means and ends. They are becoming political leaders instead of risk-taking entrepreneurs.

Considering only these general tendencies, we could conclude that bureaucratic systems founded on those vicious circles of dysfunctional elements which we have analyzed are bound to become less conspicuous. Contrary to the fear of so many humanists and revolutionary prophets of doom, we can expect more promises of liberalization than threats of standardization.

Such optimism, however, must be considerably moderated, since we must also take into account the general progress of rationalization that constantly diminishes the challenges of uncertainty, thus allowing organizations to escape reality. The existence of this long-range trend toward rationalization that so impressed Weber does not mean that organizations are becoming more "bureaucratic" in our dysfunctional sense, but that men's activities are increasingly processed through formal organizations, i.e., that bureaucratization in the Weberian sense is truly increasing, perhaps at an accelerated rate, but without entailing the dysfunctional consequences that Weber feared and all his successors prophesied. We come then to the following paradox. That greater flexibility which makes it easier for individuals to participate in the standardized and controlled activities of large-scale organizations is responsible for the development of "bureaucratization." In other words, the elimination of the "bureaucratic systems of organization" in the dysfunctional sense is the condition for the growth of "bureaucratization" in the Weberian sense.

Finally, as is most often the case, the optimist's and the pessimist's views equally should both be dismissed. Neither the logic of standardization nor the logic of liberalization is applicable alone if one tries to envisage the total picture. Both are valid at that level. Man seems to push the logic of standardization, i.e., the goals of efficiency, as much as the successes of the logic of liberalization will permit him. New equilibria are constantly formed in place of the older ones. They give man both the advantages and the burdens of greater sophistication and more complex entanglements.

Within this very general framework, it can be shown that, at the operational level, it is only when large-scale organizations become more flexible and can eliminate some of their bureaucratic vicious circles that they can overstep significant stages of growth. Recent research in the

[4] Melville Dalton, *Men Who Manage* (New York: Wiley, 1959).

field of large-scale organization history has made this point clear.[5] Decentralization now seems, to shrewd observers of the business scene, to be the necessary condition for further growth.[6]

This outcome, however, is not a simple linear process, and present systems of organization are still to a large extent "bureaucratic." Progress in the organizational field meets a strong passive resistance. Bureaucratic systems persist and always find new forms. This is the result of two opposite and yet convergent pressures. On the one side, each individual, each group and category within an organization, will always struggle to prevent the rationalization and maintain the unpredictability of their own task and function. Their power, the influence they can wield, depend, as we have demonstrated, on their amount of discretion, and, finally, on the uncertainty they have to face. One can thus understand that they will fight rationalization in their own field while trying to further it in other fields. On the other side, the constant progress of rationalization offers the possibility and the temptation, to those responsible for it, to push planning and standardization further than is rationally feasible.

Two kinds of privileges and vicious circles, therefore, tend to develop. The former correspond to the resistance of groups trying to preserve their positions of strength which can be weakened by technical progress, and the latter to the desire of other groups to impose a rationalization which is not yet warranted by this progress. Those two forces very often reinforce each other. A premature centralization can create the best protection for local privileges; conversely, a coalition of such privileges will eventually fight to impose a rationalization which will protect them and even enhance their status temporarily by eliminating other privileges.

The success of these two maneuvers depends on the organization's capacity to isolate itself from the rest of society. Since the persistence of bureaucratic vicious circles will entail, as a primary consequence, difficulty of contact with the environment, those activities in which it is easier to remain isolated from outside pressures are most likely to allow the development of bureaucratic systems of organization.

We should like thus to argue that the fears of technocracy expressed by so many authors are not founded on fact. When progress accelerates, the power of the expert is diminished and managerial power becomes more and more a political and judicial power rather than a technical one. Managers' success depends on their human qualities as leaders and not on

---

[5] See, among a number of articles published in the *Administrative Science Quarterly*, Ernest Dale, "Contribution to Administration of Alfred P. Sloan, Jr., and G. M.," I (June, 1956), 30–62.
[6] Ralph R. Cordiner, *New Frontiers for Professional Managers* (New York: McGraw-Hill, 1956).

their scientific know-how. As science invades the domain of the experts, those aspects of their roles which it affects decrease in importance.

We may emphasize, as a last paradox, that bureaucratic forms in the dysfunctional sense correspond to the impossibility of eliminating all elements of charismatic power from the functioning of large-scale organizations. Bureaucratic privileges and vicious circles follow from the necessity of resorting to charismatic-like power in an otherwise ever more rationalized world.

THE GROWING THREATS
TO THE FRENCH BUREAUCRATIC PATTERNS

Let us now analyze the place and meaning of the French model in this general context. The system as a whole seems to be functional, inasmuch as it relies on a number of cultural traits and basic patterns of behavior that have been constant throughout the modern history of French society. These traits and these behavioral patterns, however, cannot be considered as given once and for all. Whatever their stability, they have also to submit to the necessity of a minimum of equilibrium with the environment. And we now must ask ourselves whether or not, in view of the extraordinary upheaval brought about by the rise and the development of mass-consumption society, the whole complex of bureaucratic patterns, processes of change, and the basic primary traits will not finally become gravely dysfunctional and whether or not the pressure of necessity will not oblige French society to learn new patterns of behavior that will tend to influence and transform basic traits which could until now be considered immutable.

Until the present, the pressures of the outside world have led only to a reinforcement of the system. There had been constant progress in flexibility, but this was offset by a general growth of centralization and a wider diffusion of the bureaucratic patterns. French society met the challenge of the modern world by extending its own special type of organizational rationality and pushing it to the extreme. There are now signs, however, that the limit of possible developments has been reached, that the system does not have the necessary resources to solve the increasingly difficult problems which it will confront if it extends still further. We may now approach a breaking point, from which point on the basic stability of the system will be threatened.

The threat comes from two sets of convergent pressures. On the one hand, the requirements of efficiency of modern industrial society, that cannot be met as in earlier times by resorting to greater centralization, force the elimination of some of the bureaucratic rigidity. Role differentiation, the complexity of the co-operative process, and sheer organizational growth require that individuals and groups have more personal contacts, participate better in the decision-making system, and be part, finally, of more fluid equilibria of newer relationships. On the other hand, the modern mass-consumption techniques seem to present new possibilities of meeting French basic needs at lower cost and more rationally. This convergence makes it possible to meet the two basic conditions for successful change: urgent necessity and the material and moral possibility of adjusting to it.

Let us be more specific. We emphasized, in the preceding section, that the whole tendency of modern organizational development has had to be toward more flexible patterns and that decentralization at certain decisive stages has been prerequisite for further growth. This problem has been especially misunderstood in France, where modern organizational development has often been resisted under the pretext that it is bureaucratic. To be sure, many voices have denounced, time and again, the errors and failures caused by the French patterns of organization. But most of the time this has been done in a very partial and ultimately reactionary way, since the critics have refused to understand the price which would have to be paid to eliminate the dysfunctions about which they complain so bitterly. Finally, there has been a deep consensus about the relative excellence of the French system, to which most Frenchmen, revolutionaries and conservatives, radicals and moderates, alike have instinctively adhered.

They have had some justification for this opinion, since the French system has been able to claim, within the context of bourgeois and traditional Europe, all the tangible advantages that we have analyzed of stability, reliability, protection of individual independence. At the same time, it has seemed to bring, in its own way, a very sufficient measure of efficiency, while appearing, in a nation deeply influenced by the ups and downs of a turbulent history, as the best system for safeguarding the unity of purpose and the permanence of national society and insuring a quick mobilization of resources in case of war.

The consequences of the ensuing organizational lag have not been very worrying, since the lag could not be embodied in practical terms. On the contrary, most responsible Frenchmen have been very proud of the success of an organizational system that could make it possible to benefit from all the progress of modern technical civilization without having to obey the imperatives of standardization, concentration, and discipline already stifling the spirit of the other Western nations. But the lesser efficiency of French organizations can be compensated for by the gains brought by centralization, only as long as planning, prediction, and development activities remain extremely uncertain, arbitrary, and hazardous, thus making the activities of control and regulation the decisive administrative functions. Now, when a more rational view of man's influence in shaping future events can be maintained and an increasing number of organizations are becoming able to make more conscious choices, the centralized administrative state and all organizations and branches of activities influenced by bureaucratic patterns are, curiously enough, becoming more conservative than their less integrated counterparts. They may be bigger and more sophisticated, but they are paralyzed by egalitarianism, by the weight of their own impersonal rules, and, above all, they are unable to master the necessary pressure for imposing change upon resisting groups. Centralization, once a certain stage has been definitely overstepped, cannot any longer bring useful rewards. It seems even to have become self-defeating in the French cultural context, where socialist solutions are not able to escape the dilemma of stagnation or totalitarianism.[7]

At the same time, when there seems to be no escape within the system itself, pressures from without become increasingly stronger. The different para-bureaucratic systems disintegrate. The bourgeois entrepreneurial system is no longer able to compete with the more flexible modern managerial organizations. The educational system cannot any longer promote the highest learning and research achievement. The colonial system is unable to give way to another, better-adjusted type of political influence. Pressures to disrupt all these entrenched patterns are finally threatening the bureaucratic system of organization itself.

From another and perhaps more profound perspective, the possibility of the emergence of a new form of rationality not compatible with the bureaucratic tradition seems extremely difficult to discard in a country which has always prided itself in keeping in the vanguard of rational achievement.

French bureaucratic rationality has relied on individual effervescence and competition to produce new and more elaborate models of routine activities to be carried out on an egalitarian and impersonal basis after having overcome the resistance of groups. This has meant no competition and no co-operation at the group level; state and group quasi-monopolies have imposed the *one best way* through egalitarian pressures against individual resistance. This procedure makes planning extremely difficult, because planning ahead implies organizational experimentation, exchange of information, and statistical analysis—all contrary to the philosophy of the *one best way* and the negative practices of groups. It also requires a

---

[7] The model of state socialism, once rather progressive, seems now increasingly to be associated with inefficiency, corruption, and waste (the Middle East, Latin America, Spain), unless it becomes totalitarian, while the only success of socialism in modern times has been obtained in countries with strong tendencies to self-government.

co-operative attitude on the part of individuals that cannot be obtained when the dominant behavior of the central and group authorities is one of control and repression.

Now, when managerial planning for growth both in private and public organizations has definitely taken precedence over state and group attempts at controlling or regularizing the blind forces of the market, when organizations come to recognize that it is better to allow a large tolerance for calculated waste and human deviances and imperfections than to sacrifice growth to thrift and the pursuit of possible overlapping, waste, and corruption, the rationale of the traditional system of organization crumbles. The French bureaucratic system of organization, as we have described and analyzed it, cannot easily adjust to this new form of rationality. It is not fit for planning ahead, but for regularizing, after the fact, the results of group struggles over the proposals of individuals. Planned growth implies greater trust in human motivations, fostering initiative at all levels, more co-operation between individuals, and more competition between groups.

If everything is taken into account, it no longer seems possible to maintain the rate of development required by modern industrial society without resorting to this new strategy of action. And French society, as a matter of fact, has been moving steadily in this direction. The first sign of a significant change was the creation of the Planning Commission just after the Liberation, and the subsequent elaboration, in its midst, by younger higher civil servants and the most progressive business leaders, of first the practices, and then the philosophy, of *économie concertée*.[8]

Économie concertée has many weaknesses in practice and is only very partially fulfilling its ideals. It retains many of the anterior practices. The state still keeps some of its authoritarian and negative attitudes, and it is

---

[8] This is what Henry W. Ehrmann, in an otherwise extremely perceptive article on *économie concertée*, fails to understand when reviewing the theory and practice of recent French bureaucratic intervention in the economy. He is judging according to the American standards of a trust-busting and competitive philosophy. For him, therefore, *économie concertée* has much in common with the Vichy attempts at corporatism and traditional European protective tendencies. This is quite true but represents only a part of the picture. That picture may be good, but the comparisons, we believe, are not relevant. The defects of *économie concertée* to which Ehrmann is pointing concern practices that were flourishing earlier in different forms. And what is more significant for assessing the change brought by *économie concertée* is not a comparison with American but with earlier French practices which have been hampering the growth of the nation. Measured against the latter, the new attitudes toward co-operation and planning ahead, the diffusion of the new managerial rationality, are extremely important and revolutionary factors. (See Henry W. Ehrmann, "French Bureaucracy and Organized Interests," *Administrative Science Quarterly*, V, No. 4 [March, 1961], 534–553; and Club Jean Moulin, *L'Etat et le citoyen* [Paris: Le Seuil, 1961], pp. 354–370.)

only by manipulating the different pressure systems that it can succeed in obliging private groups to act. Private groups, on the other hand, maintain their infantile attitude and consent to co-operate only when they feel that the state agrees to pay a heavy price for their co-operation. Yet *économie concertée* is a significant departure, since many positive results have been achieved without the traditional controls, and both the private managerial elite and the state bureaucratic elite are gradually but definitely being won over to the new kind of rationality. These groups are thus increasingly able to bargain realistically without resorting to the traditional mixture and alternation of repressive control on the one side, and secretiveness, resistance, and apathy on the other.

While the pressures for new organizational patterns become stronger and more difficult to resist because of the lure of progress, efficiency, and a broader kind of rationality, there are also signs that the cumulative changes brought about by the emergence in France of a mass-consumption society are beginning to offer new possibilities, outside the bureaucratic system of organization, of meeting basic individual demands. In the pre-mass-consumption era, the satisfaction of the individual needs for autonomy, individual control over the environment, equality, and freedom from direct dependence relationships required the combination of a stratified society and a centralized system of decision-making. Stratification made it possible to safeguard equality, while centralization made the consequence of stratification impersonal and allowed the individual to escape the difficulties of hierarchical relationships.[9] But with mass consumption, stratification becomes less rigid. More and more people can participate in ever wider cultural influences. The greater complexity of the whole culture does not seem to entail a greater degree of hierarchy but engenders, on the contrary, greater and greater specialization and the breakdown of the old hierarchical order. Impersonality, equality, and individual autonomy, therefore, become possible outside the protection of the strata, and direct interpersonal contacts become less threatening. We do not want to imply that the pressure for avoiding face-to-face relations will cease, all at once, to be an important element of French social relations, but we do believe that the emergence of mass consumption is already lessening this pressure.

French society has resisted the diffusion of the new cultural models of mass society, which for this reason have developed less quickly in

[9] The protection brought by social stratification is still important in France. We believe one can find an indirect proof of this in the strong limitations imposed by spontaneous group references to the expectations of individuals. These limitations appear to be much greater than in America and the other Western countries closer to the model of mass society. See Stern and Keller, "Spontaneous Group References in France," *Public Opinion Quarterly*, XVII (1953), 208–217.

France than in the neighboring countries.[10] But this resistance amounts only to rearguard delaying tactics.

A national, all-encompassing market is emerging in France slowly but with increasing rapidity, in the field of culture as well as in the fields of material products and services. It may even be argued that the more rational and universalistic culture of the French has fewer possibilities of resistance than more particularistic and "deferent" cultures.[11] The open and egalitarian French culture has been able to maintain stratification only with the use of artificial distances.[12] Once such distances appear anachronistic and ludicrous, no possible basis of discrimination remains.[13]

The consequences of these new developments are already apparent. The basic rules of the game of French human relations have already changed greatly in many fields, as can readily be verified.

Changes in class relations are the most conspicuous. Social distance has diminished considerably. Class lines are increasingly blurred. Only the widest social distances are apparent. Centralization has both focused attention on them and helped to lend strategic importance to the opposition of groups at the end of the social spectrum. But the game is played, on both sides, with more sophistication and less passion than earlier. Employers and employees understand each other better and are becoming more tolerant. Parallel progress in the organizational field, finally, makes the complex game of polite avoidance and indirect bargaining seem hollow and useless.

Cultural differences, however, still remain as difficult a barrier to overcome as the traditional bureaucratic rationality; but they also are tending to crumble under the pressure of mass culture. A great loss of faith in the most discriminating aspects of bourgeois culture is already

---

[10] The temporary but important lag in the diffusion of television in France in the 1950's is a good case in point. This lag cannot be explained by economic and financial reasons, as the French standard of living in this period was high enough and still growing—it was caused by the general resistance to change generated by the French system of social relations.

[11] We use the term as suggested by S. M. Lipset in his analysis of present-day British society. See Lipset, "Democracy and the Social System," in *The First New Nation* (New York: Basic Books, 1963).

[12] Inferiors did not internalize their inferiority as in England; they were kept at a distance only by the vertical stratification of cultural patterns, the difficulty of promotion and crossing over the social barrier, and the resulting fear of face-to-face contacts and of humiliation.

[13] The disintegration of the traditional system of cultural stratification is quite apparent already when comparing the theater and movie public in Paris. The hierarchic differences in public, still very strong in the theater, have not persisted for the movies, in spite of the frantic efforts of the holders of high-brow culture to impose more sophisticated aesthetic standards. See Crozier, "Employés et petits fonctionnaires, note sur le loisir comme moyen de participation aux valeurs de la société bourgeoise," *Esprit*, June, 1959.

manifest. Even the baccalaureate, that old symbol of bourgeois status whose sacred character Goblot emphasized, is about to disappear in the relative indifference of public opinion. Correlated with this loss of faith in social discrimination, and running much deeper, is the change that is slowly gathering momentum in parent-child relationships, which will have a decisive influence upon the patterns of authority.

The impact of the mass media has already made possible the development of a youth culture outside the parental orbit, and the diminishing influence of traditional social discrimination has greatly alleviated the pressure on the younger generation. French parental authority is still far from being permissive, but the self-perpetuating conflict over authority can be expected to lose one of its indispensable sources, the family system.[14]

These new social and cultural developments may account for the emergence and the significant progress of new patterns of action opposed to the bureaucratic spirit. We shall cite only two of them. First, as we have stated, a new managerial spirit is flourishing that is breaking away from the traditional bourgeois pattern and pervades the entrepreneurial system as well as the higher strata of the Civil Service. Good observers might still find many remnants of the bourgeois patterns in this new spirit. But, here again, the important thing is the departure from entrenched patterns of action and the tendency to give more importance to the values of growth, co-operation, and service to the community than to the values of stability, individual control, and class discrimination. Another new and interesting phenomenon has been the increase in autonomous co-operative group action in a number of different domains, ranging widely in the fields of economic and political action, among students, peasants, entrepreneurs, and religious milieux. Many aspects of these new group activities, it is true, also retain some of the characteristic negative features of the French tradition.[15] Yet we believe that there has been a significant departure from the traditional group passivity of the French bureaucratic and bourgeois system. The change that is occurring in the peasantry, especially, is an extraordinary

[14] Another very important element of the French family system has changed significantly, namely, the attitude and behavior toward procreation. The change in the birth rate is not very great and may seem, at first glance, to be accounted for by too many factors to be relevant to our discussion. Yet we believe that this change is very important, because it concerns basic attitudes toward life and therefore must be associated with the general transformation of French society. The behavior of self-restraint that the French people were the first to impose on themselves in the nineteenth century was quite an unusual human achievement, and it can be considered as a milestone in human rationality typical, after all, of the bureaucratic spirit. A relaxation of this restraint is thus very significant. It corresponds in our opinion to a more trustful and future-oriented view of the human condition that is well in tune with the new forms of rationality.

[15] E.g., the activity of the students' union and of the farmers' associations in the years 1959–1961 has often been extraordinarily irresponsible.

revolution which no one would have dared to predict twenty years ago and which puts to the question many aspects of the traditional equilibrium of French bourgeois society.

All these changes and their consequences feed back vigorously on the spirit of youth and have finally brought in a new intellectual climate whose importance, although fogged by the passions and violence of the Algerian war, should not be underestimated.[16] A greater concern for empirical knowledge, a greater disregard for abstract theories, a reformist and action-oriented philosophy, have marked a student body whose enthusiasm and radiance have not been matched since the first half of the nineteenth century. The educational system has not yet changed; but the climate which is shaping the learning process of the elite of French youth[17] also calls for the acceleration of the disintegration of the traditional bourgeois and bureaucratic order.

THE MODEL'S POSSIBILITIES OF RESISTANCE: THE CASE OF FRENCH PUBLIC ADMINISTRATION

In considering the growing threat to the French bureaucratic and para-bureaucratic patterns, we have taken into account only the changes in values and modes of action effected by the accelerating development of industrial civilization. We have thus easily concluded that these patterns are likely to recede inasmuch as their latent functions lose their importance. These conclusions may be considered as probable hypotheses for the long run, but they do not seem adequately relevant to the present and the near future. For they do not give proper importance to the possibilities of resistance to change of all-encompassing and yet self-contained and tightly controlled systems of organization. It may be argued that such systems can outlive the disappearance of their traditional latent functions. Because of their possibilities of action upon their own environment, they can reshape the latter, create a new kind of equilibrium, and develop new latent functions for maintaining the basic behavioral patterns necessary to their survival.

We shall discuss these possibilities of resistance in the most central and decisive case for France, that of public administration. The bureaucratic system of organization of French public administration is certainly one of the most entrenched of such closed systems of social action that has existed in the modern world. It contributed heavily to the shaping of its own

16 The decisive breaking point seems to have been the Mendès-France experiment in 1954.
17 This climate is all the more important, since the content of the curriculum is formalistic and uninspiring.

environment in the past, and many of the patterns of action that support it at present have developed under its influence.[18] Our problem is to assess whether and to what extent it is still able to exert such influence in the mass-consumption era.

It is self-evident that most nations are now much more interdependent than they were, and that France is no longer able to pursue its own bureaucratic experiment by isolating itself from the rest of the world. Once it was possible for parallel social systems to take their own courses in a rather independent way. Today, however, there are too many organizational links and too many intellectual contacts to allow a nation to remain isolated. Only Russia and the Communist countries can preserve such isolation, but they are a world unto themselves and have to pay a heavy price for it. France, in any case, cannot conduct its bureaucratic experiment while ignoring the rest of the world. The failure of its colonial system, the end of its "civilizing mission," have taken away the last buffer against foreign contacts that it had elaborated. France has had to recognize that its organizational system is not only not universal but has proved inferior, at least in the organizational competition within the Western world.

This over-all analysis, however, is still adequate only for the long run. The relative inferiority of an organizational system does not make it impossible for this system to resist change if it is able to maintain its equilibrium or to find a new equilibrium with its environment. From this point of view, we believe that three main areas of contact are decisive for assessing the possibilities of resistance to change of the French bureaucratic system of organization: the area of policy-making (the orientation of the system); the area of personnel recruitment (the human basis of the system); and the area of the bureaucratic functions (the services given to the larger community).

The first area of contact of the bureaucracy with the outside world concerns, of course, general policy-making. We have shown how difficult this problem can be for a bureaucratic system that always tends to transfer major decisions further up. French public administration has set aside special categories of higher civil servants separately recruited and trained, relieved from the usual organizational requirements, who alone can confront these problems and thus become the system's change agents. The role of these members of the *Grands Corps* has become increasingly important as the gap between the bureaucratic system and its environment has widened,

[18] De Tocqueville has argued, for example, that the lack of independent group action and the strata isolation in French communities were due to the king's municipal and fiscal policies. See Alexis de Tocqueville, *L'ancien régime et la Révolution, passim* and especially I, 115–122.

for they have become the necessary mediators between the bureaucracy and the environment, especially at times of crisis. This is why the present change of outlook of the younger generation of higher civil servants should not be neglected. They have been deeply influenced by the new intellectual climate of the student world and by the experiments in economic action made possible by the nationalization of various enterprises and the growth of *économie concertée*.[19] As a consequence, they have lost most of their attachment to the bureaucratic system as an ideal of perfection.[20] They have become empiricists, more devoted to economic growth than to purity of style and, especially, financial purity. Their heroes are no longer the perfectionists but the doers.

This great change, however, has not as yet greatly influenced the internal functioning of the system.[21] At this level, the values and perspective of the new managerial leaders are not entirely decisive. According to the scheme we have proposed, the "directors" are all-powerful in maintaining the status quo and finding ways of readjusting the system to new conditions, but very weak in operating basic reforms or even changes affecting interrelationships between different groups. Yet it must be recognized that some margin of action is granted them, especially during crises and because of their strategic situation as mediators. In the short run, it is true, a higher civil servant who wants to initiate reform must resort to an authoritarian show of force that, in the end, defeats its own purpose and reinforces the whole system. In the long run, however, the diffusion of a reformist spirit among most of the higher civil servants must have decisive consequences. When the breaking point is reached, it will no longer be possible to maintain the bureaucratic faith in the middle ranks while the upper ranks disown it.[22] From then on, groups' resistance to reforms will be less and less easy.

The second area of contact is the domain of personnel recruitment. No organizational system can survive without achieving a proper equilibrium with the community in which it is developing and which must provide it with a reasonable flow of new members. This condition is even more restrictive for the French public service, since it relies on a tight stratifica-

---

[19] This may be only vicarious participation. The Renault experiment is considered by many younger higher civil servants as one of the outstanding successes of their new philosophy, although almost none of them has been active in it.
[20] Although, in practice, fewer of the present than of the past generations of higher civil servants leave the service.
[21] Very curious double standards seem to have emerged. The bureaucracy is progressive when dealing with the outside world and extremely conservative in regard to its own patterns of action and internal functioning.
[22] The bureaucratic faith has already much declined among young middle-rank civil servants.

tion system that functions well only if there is enough pressure for entering it at the bottom.

Yet this is now one of the weak points of the French bureaucratic system. The crisis of recruitment that began after World War II has become increasingly more acute. Contrary to a very long tradition, there seems to be a decreasing interest in state employment at the lower and middle ranks.[23] There are now fewer candidates for many competitive examinations than there are jobs offered.

This situation, which is beginning to undermine the whole system, has many causes. General factors that have devaluated the traditional advantages of the Civil Service are the universal down-grading of routine clerical occupations, the growing stability, security, and even independence guaranteed by private employment. But more specific factors may have had as much importance, especially the insistence of the French bureaucratic establishment[24] on maintaining and even extending its rigorous selective system, with its high and at times irrelevant standards, and the climate of cramped outlook and narrow bickering that has discredited petty civil servants in the community.

Here again, instead of the bureaucracy's influencing its own environment, as in earlier times, and slowly reshaping it in accord with its own wants and requirements, the community is beginning to put pressure upon the bureaucracy by refusing the bureaucratic patterns. This second area of contact is also an area where the bureaucracy is in an inferior position, more likely to be influenced than to influence.

The system has been able to maintain itself up to now by tapping new human resources. Lower civil servants, once predominantly male and recruited from all over France,[25] have become increasingly female and originate mostly from the underdeveloped Southwest. Such a new symbiosis with the community, however successful it may be in the short run, inevitably involves two risks. First, it is only temporary; the Southwest also will industrialize (it is already doing so), and there are limits to the number of women who seek employment outside the home. Second, it accentuates the inferior situation of the bureaucracy, increasingly staffed by people who are clearly ranked much lower than their counterparts in private employment.

At the same time, other pressures are exerted during the employment

---

[23] Because of their general social and intellectual prestige, the higher ranks still attract the best talent.

[24] The pressure, as we have shown, does not come from the policy-making ranks but from all the groups interested.

[25] There were, of course, already many important distortions of geographical distribution, but no such focusing on only one region as exists now.

life of civil servants. Civil servants are no longer so isolated as they once were. They are, therefore, much less committed to the Service. The rate of departure may still be low, but there is already much more alternative employment offered, and this is causing unrest. Public service will have increasingly to compete with other possible employment in order to keep its personnel. This will become extremely difficult if public service maintains the egalitarian guarantees that make it impossible to discriminate between employees.

Finally, the pressure for change we have seen developing in the higher ranks has its counterpart in the lower ranks. There, however, it is likely to be expressed through movements making rather simple claims, whose objectives are likely to be even more conservative in regard to the system. This has already been marked in the successive strikes and social movements that have plagued the Civil Service in the last fifteen years and that played their part in the troubles of the Fourth Republic.[26] But we are also close to a breaking point, inasmuch as the system is pushed into more and more contradictions and can no longer find its equilibrium.

The last and third area of contact of the bureaucracy with the outside world is the area of the bureaucratic functions. This is not so dynamic a domain as the first two, but it will also, in the long run, generate a pressure for change that will be difficult to resist. Change in this area comes from the universally increased importance of the role of the state and the growing demands of the community for public services. This trend is disturbing the traditional French equilibrium between the state and the citizen. The citizen, who once refused state intervention as much as he could, is now continually asking for more services. Thus servicing in the balance of activities of the bureaucracy is taking the precedence over controlling. Increasing numbers of new roles must therefore be created which do not fit into the old scheme. The system is tending to disintegrate because it has had to overextend. Specialization and differentiation, as we have seen, entail another logic of bureaucracy that can be reconciled with the logic of centralization only in the short run. In the long run, and we are already seeing many consequences of these new developments, the general equilibrium of the system is completely disturbed, and this engenders another kind of pressure for change.

In all three of these areas, the same scheme operates that we have so briefly reviewed. The pressure of the general community, which is much more open than the bureaucracy to the new patterns of action brought by mass production and the mass-consumption society, becomes the lead-

[26] We are still within the vicious circle. The malaise originating in the application of the system gives rise to movements that claim, and partially succeed in imposing, an extension of this system.

ing force, and the balance between the state and society is reversed. In the major areas of contact, the French Civil Service seems unable any longer to shape its own environment; it appears, on the other hand, to be fighting a rear-guard battle to escape the outside influences conveyed by this environment. The French bureaucratic system of organization is desperately trying to cope with ever expanding responsibilities, and with new functions and a new managerial spirit not easily compatible with its principles, while the community refuses to give it proper recognition and to staff it adequately.[27] In so doing, without understanding it very well, French society is paving the way for a much deeper crisis, or at least for a change of a much greater magnitude, whose repercussions will bear in their turn on the French model of change and adjustment to change and on its usual patterns of action.

THE FRENCH BUREAUCRATIC CONTRIBUTION

No such deeply stabilized system as the French bureaucratic system of organization can disappear without shaping profoundly the patterns succeeding it. The more practical question, therefore, which should be asked is not whether or not change will come, but what is likely to remain from the traditional bureaucratic system. Or, in more elaborate terms, what new equilibrium, what new system of relationships, can be evolved in, and well adjusted to, the modern world, to preserve the advantages of the original French bureaucratic contribution.[28]

We have already discussed the advantages for the individual of the French bureaucratic system, and what was at stake in the individual's attachment to it. Examining these advantages again from a general and comparative point of view, we should like to argue that the basic benefit the French bureaucratic system brought to the individual was the possibility it offered to all its members, even the most humble, of participating on a wide and egalitarian basis in a style of life that featured especially a great deal of personal independence, the possibility of detaching oneself from the pressure of circumstances, and great freedom and lucidity. These achieve-

[27] One should also take into account that the new functions and the new opportunities offered by these changes will lure away the most brilliant of the civil servants, by weakening resistance that would otherwise be very difficult to break. It can be hypothesized, finally, that resistance will come mostly from the middle and lower middle ranks that are best identified with the system and less open to exterior influences.

[28] We tend to believe that older systems influence new ones by imposing on them the requirements of securing at least equivalent benefits for most people concerned. This means that one of the decisive starting points in our prospective orientation would be to ascertain what was the basic contribution of the French bureaucratic system to the general Western culture in which it has developed.

ments should not be minimized. They may be considered as one of the best parts of the contribution of the French culture to the Western world. At different stages they have been decisive for the progress of Western civilization. They are maintained now in a very expensive and inefficient way, and the whole balance of French society is affected by the relative failure of these traditional patterns. At the same time, however, there are enough elements in modern mass production and mass-consumption society that can be utilized by French society to elaborate new patterns enabling it to maintain and to renew its traditional and necessary contribution.

Such a problem presents a very deep challenge to a society, but it is not insuperable. One should point out also that nowhere else has a satisfactory balance as yet been achieved between individual and organized activity. Modern organization man is groping for a new culture, open to all and thus a mass culture, yet lively and creative enough to encourage each individual to participate with the best of himself. It is not so surprising that France, whose bureaucratic and bourgeois system permitted the blossoming of one of the most elaborate individual cultures of the pre-industrial era, should remain attached to it somewhat longer than other nations. But we can hope that when change comes, as it now does, the challenge offered to French ingenuity may be met by a positive contribution to the new humanism that must develop in the context of the new organizational rationality.

ORGANIZING
THE UNAFFILIATED
IN A LOW-INCOME AREA

George Brager

Community organization efforts generally have one of three broad objectives. In the first instance a substantive area of community change—a needed reform—is emphasized, as, for example, attention to housing needs and inequities. Another goal is the co-ordinated and orderly development of services, as evidenced in the planning of a welfare council. The third focuses upon citizenship involvement, regardless of the issues that engage citizen attention, in order to heighten community integration. These three goals are not necessarily mutually exclusive, although it may reasonably be argued that this is more true than is generally realized. In any event, programs that do not develop objectives in some order of priority risk diffuse and ineffective performance, as well as the impossibility of focused evaluation. There is, of course, some advantage in this nondefinition. One of the three arrows may hit *some* mark, and, in any case, one need not face up to his failures if he has not specified his goals.

An encompassing delinquency prevention effort may rightly concern itself with all three objectives, although perhaps to some degree different programs need to be devised to achieve different objectives. In order to sharpen this discussion, however, focus will be placed only upon issues relating to citizenship participation.

In a study of two lower-income neighborhoods of similar socioeconomic levels it was found that in the more integrated neighborhood (in which people knew their neighbors, perceived common interests, shared common viewpoints, and felt a part of the community) delinquency rates were markedly lower.[1] Participation by adults in decision-making about

Reprinted from *Social Work*, vol. 8 (New York: Wiley, 1963), pp. 34–40, with omissions.

[1] Eleanor Maccoby *et al.*, "Community Integration and the Social Control of Delinquency," *Journal of Social Issues*, Vol. 14, No. 3 (1958), pp. 38–51.

matters that affect their interests increases their sense of identification with the community and the larger social order. People who identify with their neighborhood and share common values are more likely to try to control juvenile misbehavior. A well-integrated community can provide learning experiences for adults that enable them to serve as more adequate models and interpreters of community life for the young. In short, participation in community-oriented organizations is highly desirable in delinquency reduction efforts.

A program must, however, involve significant numbers of representative lower-class persons.[2] Such an organization ought to enable what has been called the "effective community" of working-class youth—that is, the individuals, families, and groups with whom these youth interact and identify—to exert more positive influence on them.[3] The learning that accrues from the collective process can result in better opportunities or more effective models for potential delinquents only when large numbers of working-class adults are members of community organizations.

However, such membership is not very common among the lower class. A considerable number of studies indicate that formal group membership is closely related to income, status, and education; the lower one's income status and educational level, the less likely one is to participate in formal community groups.[4]

Furthermore, in every slum neighborhood there are adults who, in attitudes, strivings, verbal skills, and possession of know-how, are oriented toward the middle class. Although their children are less likely to experience strains toward deviance, these are precisely the parents who tend to join formal community organizations and to have faith and competence in the collective solution of social problems. In most organizations, therefore, persons who are in a minority among slum dwellers (*i.e.*, the upward mobile) unfortunately represent the majority of those working-class members who participate. Because lower-class persons tend to eschew formal organizations, organizers who set out to reach the effective community of the delinquent frequently settle for those slum dwellers who are easiest to enlist.

Although reports of failure only rarely find their way into the litera-

---

[2] The word "representative" is used here in the sense of "typical of their group, *i.e.*, class" rather than in the political sense of "functioning or acting in behalf of others." Elsewhere in the literature it has been restricted to the latter use. *See* Chauncey A. Alexander and Charles McCann, "The Concept of Representativeness in Community Organization," *Social Work*, Vol. 1, No. 1 (January 1956), pp. 48–52.

[3] Derek V. Roemer, "Focus in Programming for Delinquency Reduction" (Bethesda, Md.: National Institute of Mental Health, 1961). (Mimeographed.)

[4] Morris Axelrod, "Urban Structure and Social Participation," *American Sociological Review*, Vol. 21, No. 1 (February 1956), pp. 13–18.

ture, the modesty of claims regarding the organization of the deprived population itself indicates a general lack of success. For example, in East Harlem in 1948 a five-block area was chosen for organization. Five trained social workers were assigned to organize these blocks and a program of social action was embarked upon, devoted to housing, recreational, and social needs of the neighborhood. Unfortunately, the East Harlem Neighborhood Center for Block Organization was able to attract only a limited number of participants during a three-year period. Subsequent research indicated that those who did participate were upwardly aspiring. Further, they were isolated from the rest of the community and therefore nonrepresentative.

BARRIERS TO COMMUNITY INTEGRATION

Characteristics of Community Life

Why are representative lower-income adults less likely to become closely involved in community affairs? The source of the barriers to their effective participation rests with all three elements of the interaction: the characteristics of community life, the nature of lower-income adults, and the structure of the community organization effort.

One such community characteristic is residential mobility. Local communities have been inundated by new migrants, many of them unfamiliar with the demands and opportunities of urban life. Although public housing mitigates some of the problematic aspects of slum life, the recruitment of single-family units from widely dispersed parts of the metropolitan area collects in one place thousands of deprived families, strangers to one another and to local community resources. Physical redevelopment programs and the consequent exodus of old residents have in many instances shattered existing institutions, so that they are unable to help in assimilation of the newcomers into the urban system. For example, the diminishing vitality of some local political machines, with their attentive political leaders, eliminates an important interpretive link to the new world.

Intergroup tensions are also a barrier to community integration, as are the bewildering operations of massive bureaucratic systems. The size, impersonality, concentrated power, and inflexibility of these large organizations makes them seem to local residents hardly amenable to their influence.

The community characteristic that may act as the major deterrent to involvement of lower-income people in community affairs, however, is the opposition of already entrenched organizations. New groups in a community—especially new minority groups—are often confronted with hostility from established groups whose positions of power are threatened by the possibility of forceful action by the newcomers. There is evidence, for example, that some political machines will avoid registering minority group members, even under the impetus of national campaigns. This is so even though the minority group member is assumed to support the machine's national candidates. It is recognized that the new group will inevitably challenge the dominance of incumbent leadership.

This resistance of political parties, governmental agencies, and private organizations is never directly specified. Ordinarily it takes the form of statements such as "the minority groups are not really interested," they are "not ready," "they'll take positions we don't agree with," or they will be "controlled by the left-wing agitators." Whatever its form, the opposition of established community groups is a formidable obstacle to indigenous community participation.

Lower-Income Life

The circumstances of lower-income life and the nature of lower-income persons constitute another set of obstacles. The realities of lower-class life, *i.e.*, the necessary preoccupation with the day-to-day problems of survival, hardly encourage attention to broad community matters. Furthermore, lower-class persons lack the verbal or literary requisites for organizational skills; neither do they tend to be comfortable with the formal methods of doing business in organizations. Their self-defeating attitudes also interfere with community integration. Lower-income groups tend to view life more pessimistically, with less hope of deliverance, and, as a consequence, they tend to retreat from struggle. A Gallup poll conducted in 1959 indicated that a higher percentage of respondents in the under-$3,000 income group expected World War III and a new depression than respondents in any other grouping. As one observer noted, "Seeing his chances for improvement as slim produces in the slum-dweller a psychology of listlessness, of passivity, and acceptance, which . . . reduces his chances still further."[5] Such defeatism, resulting in lack of participation, produces a loss of interest in changing their conditions.

Structure of Community Organization

The community organization itself while purportedly seeking the involvement of lower-income persons, offers certain obstacles, whether inevitable or otherwise. Most community activities, for example, are staffed by middle-class personnel. To the extent that lower-class people feel that they are

[5]Michael Harrington, "Slums, Old and New," *Commentary*, Vol. 30, No. 2 (August 1960), p. 121.

being dominated, they are likely to withdraw from collective activities. The predominance of the middle class in community organizations has a number of sources. When community problems become so severe that people are motivated to act, it is generally the middle-class element (or at least those who are oriented toward the middle class) that reacts first. Although lower-class persons may affiliate with the organization, its predominantly middle-class style soon becomes a subtle source of intimidation. Its leaders are likely to be businessmen, professionals, social welfare personnel, ministers, and other members of the middle class. The formality of the organization meetings, with predetermined agendas, concern with rules of procedure, and the like, tends to make the lower-class participant, unfamiliar with these matters, feel insecure and inferior.

Furthermore, organizers who insist on maintaining control of the activities and policies of the organization, subtly or otherwise, inevitably encourage the participation of lower-class persons whose values and skills are congenial with those of the middle-class organizer. Those whose values and skills differ, however, will gradually sense that such differences matter and that the organization exists to serve middle-class ends. They may, therefore, disassociate themselves.

It may be that, because of the disparity between lower- and middle-class "life styles," significant numbers of both groups cannot even be expected to participate together within the same organization. For example, a study conducted by the Girl Scouts, focused upon recruiting volunteers from working-class communities, was forced to conclude that the agency could offer no program suitable to both middle- and lower-class groups. As noted by the authors, lower-income adults are less interested in "the joys of fully integrated personality in a democratic society" than in the need to better their standard of living. They do not even object to their children being handled authoritatively if it serves such end.[6]

The tendency of social workers to emphasize the amelioration of conflict and the reduction of tension, while often appropriate and helpful, may, in effect, also discourage lower-income participation. With issues flattened rather than sharpened, differences minimized rather than faced, there may be little to arouse the interest of a group that already lacks the predisposition to participate. Matters sufficiently vital to engage slum residents are almost inevitably fraught with controversy or are challenging to some powerful community interest. If they are avoided by a community organization, it may be expected that the organization will be avoided in turn.

The sponsorship of the community organization effort will also affect

[6] Catherine V. Richards and Norman A. Polansky, "Reaching Working-class Youth Leaders," *Social Work*, Vol. 4, No. 4 (October 1959), p. 38.

the character of participation. The primary interests of a sponsoring group will tend to determine membership selection, organizational form, objectives, and activities. Organizational maintenance requirements of the sponsor will inevitably limit the independence of an action-oriented affiliate. Further, its responsibility to a board of directors with widely variant views and connections to numerous community interest groups will limit a sponsor's freedom to encourage a free-wheeling community action program. When the sponsoring group is an already established community organization, it is likely to contain significant representation from groups that, as noted earlier, actively oppose the effective participation of lower-income and minority group people.

The formidable array of obstacles thus cited does not permit us to be sanguine about the success potential of any program oriented toward community action by representative lower-income adults. We may conclude, as a matter of fact, that the limitations to independence inherent in sponsorship by private or public social service organizations are hardly surmountable. Or we may discover that those obstacles least accessible to the social worker's means of intervention are most centrally required for program success. However discouraging, a specification of barriers is, nevertheless, a requirement of intelligent program planning.

STIMULATING PARTICIPATION

With these points considered, a specific strategy can be developed for a specific area, such as the Organizing the Unaffiliated program of Mobilization for Youth, an experimental action-research project on Manhattan's Lower East Side in the field of juvenile delinquency prevention and control. While also offering broad-scale services in the fields of employment, education, casework, and group work, Mobilization for Youth proposes, through Organizing the Unaffiliated, to stimulate the participation of lower-income persons in attempts to resolve community problems. It is described here only because it has been designed in the context of the previous discussion, rather than because it provides ready solutions to knotty problems. As a matter of fact, plans for Organizing the Unaffiliated do not overcome a number of the obstacles cited earlier, and as such it is a ready candidate for mixed success. Whatever the risks of failure, however, attempts must be made if debilitating community conditions are to be mitigated or knowledge advanced.

Lower East Side residents who now participate in unaffiliated voluntary associations, such as storefront churches and hometown clubs, will be encouraged to plan collaborative programs of a cultural, social, and social-action nature. Although lower-class persons participate in formal group life less than do members of the middle class, urban slums do not lack indigenous social organizations. In fact, there is evidence of a proliferation of voluntary associations in depressed working-class neighborhoods. For example, in Manhattanville, a community of 100,000 within sixty city blocks, there are an estimated 400 informal groups, most of which have minimal attachments to the institutional life of the community.[7] Similarly, 300 small groups have thus far been identified in the area by Mobilization staff, each with at least a name and a designated regular meeting place.[8]

Focusing particularly upon work within the existent social structure, professionals are contacting leaders of these lower-income groups. Initial approaches have been based upon the similarities of the participants in addition to social class, *i.e.*, ethnicity, race, religion, and the like. One worker, for example, is assigned Puerto Rican hometown groups, sports, and social clubs; another has established relationships with small all-Negro social groups; a third is working with the Pentecostal churches.[9] Ways in which Organizing the Unaffiliated may relate to the group, provide specific help, and assist in the implementation of group purpose have been explored.

Issues of concern to the groups have been identified and particular interest in employment problems, housing, and youth needs has been indicated. Special efforts in these substantive areas are planned to serve the organizations in the program. In the area of employment, for example, a co-operative program with a local union, to upgrade the skills of its members, is contemplated. Programs of job-finding, English language classes, and specialized training will be developed. Finally, action will be taken to modify discriminatory employment practices or to affect legislation.

As contact is established by professionals, promising indigenous group leaders are being selected, given in-service training, and hired as part-time community organizers. Persons who represent—and can also influence— the norms of their group have been sought; the ability to handle forms and to comply with middle-class modes of behavior is considered secondary.

Because lower-income people are accustomed to performing more spontaneously, within a small, highly personal group, the organizational milieu must be informal and flexible, the structure unorthodox and unde-

---

[7] Hurley Doddy, *Informal Groups and the Community* (New York: Columbia University Press, 1952).

[8] Excluded from this definition of voluntary associations are amorphous, unattached groups, such as street-corner groups.

[9] Mobilization research indicates a low level of community integration. The small amount of interorganizational collaboration that does take place mainly involves organizations of similar type (*e.g.*, storefront church with storefront church). It would therefore probably be a mistake to attempt heterogeneous groupings in beginning the program. On the other hand, a start toward the integration of groups (and leaders) which now work separately but which have common concerns and share a desire to do something about the Lower East Side must be developed.

termined. The nature of the structure depends, of course, upon the wishes of the groups that choose to participate. Because of the wide diversity of voluntary associations and their current isolation from one another, a somewhat diffuse organizational form is anticipated. A loosely organized Council of Puerto Rican Organizations already exists. Some groups may ultimately wish to be part of a League of Storefront Churches, an Association of Tenant Councils, or an area-wide council. Those groups not prepared to join officially with others will be encouraged to maintain their ties to the programs through the community organizer and will participate on an ad hoc basis. It is also anticipated that some of the groups may ultimately wish to affiliate with a more established community organization, such as the Lower Eastside Neighborhoods Association.

Just as there is a variety of structures or groupings, so is there a wide range of readiness for programs. Some groups want to be involved only in social or cultural programs, others only in such undertakings as a large dance or a campaign against slum landlords. Still others are eager for social action on a number of issues and will concentrate on instrumental activities exclusively.

USE OF INDIGENOUS ORGANIZERS

It is hoped that the use of indigenous organizers will encourage lower-class residents to identify with the project and to perceive that the program represents their interests. In addition, it avoids the problems in communication that sometimes arise between people of different social strata. Leaders of lower-class groups will doubtless be more successful in engaging the interest and interpreting the aspirations of other residents. It is recognized, however, that the employment of these leaders may undermine their influence among group members. Since leadership adheres, in any group, to those with the power to withhold or provide items of value, the influence of indigenous organizers will be buttressed by the services provided by Organizing the Unaffiliated. To the extent possible, however, indigenous leaders will be prevented from molding themselves in the professional image.

Because of the structural and programatic diversities, these organizers have a variety of tasks. Principally, they act as a group's channel of communication with the organized community and with other small groups. If groups are informed about community developments and about the activities of others, they become a part of the community even if they remain unaffiliated. Organizers are expected to help individuals to exploit the social resources provided by other Mobilization programs, and by the settlements, churches, and other institutions.

Community organizers have often relied solely on what may be called altruism. They have offered the individual participant and the group the psychic satisfaction of contributing to communal betterment. While middle-class persons readily link social action with personal and social gain, most lower-class people have difficulty relating seemingly remote goals to their bread-and-butter problems. Organizing the Unaffiliated recognizes the immediate self-interest of the depressed population and offers members such individual benefits as free legal advice, job referrals, homemakers, and baby-sitters. Such specific aids to groups as providing meeting space and clerical assistance are also proffered. Further, organizers provide assistance in arranging social and cultural activities as well as action on social issues of meaning to the group. Although these immediate gratifications are legitimate in their own right, especially in dealing with deprived individuals, they are viewed, in addition, as an aid to organization.

Significant portions of the slum population do not, of course, belong to organizations of any kind. Another task of the organizers, then, is to encourage and assist existent social units in recruiting unaffiliated individuals. Organizers will also attempt to form new groups that can eventually be drawn into wider participation.

To be maximally effective, this requires a co-ordinated effort by a wide range of professional persons. The program of Organizing the Unaffiliated is advancing this effort in two ways. It has developed a system whereby caseworkers, group workers, and educators assess the interest in group participation of the individual with whom they have contact, for follow-up by indigenous community organizers. Further, sessions are planned to sensitize non-community organization professionals to community issues and organizational strategies, so that ultimately they may directly assist in the formation of groups around issues of community concern. This moves, of course, to the development of a generic social worker role, concerned primarily with substantive problem-solving rather than primarily with method. . . .

VI

Organizational Change

If the concept of change is loosely interpreted, most studies in this volume deal with organizational change in one way or another. Since organizations are planned social units, oriented to specific goals under relatively rational and self-conscious leadership, they are probably more given to change than any other social units. Some studies discuss changes in goals; others, changes in structure; still others discuss changes in the relationship between organizations and their social environments. But if the term "change" is conceived more strictly as change in the organization as a unit rather than as change in this or that variable; if the term "study of change" means to determine the factors which further change the conditions under which a state of equilibrium is maintained, in contrast to the conditions under which it is undermined or substituted; if it means to specify the alternative courses open to a changing structure and the conditions under which this or that path is chosen, the study of organizational change—as well as the study of change in other social units—is still a relatively undeveloped field. The following studies contribute, each in its own way, to the development of a systematic analysis of organizational change.

Bureaucracies are often regarded as conservative structures, oriented toward maintaining the external as well as the internal status quo. In an earlier section of this volume Merton examines this assumption. Blau suggests that certain external and internal factors might turn a bureaucracy into an innovating organization, interested in social change as well as in changing itself. Changes are likely to be supported by the personnel if they are aimed at satisfying organizational "needs." Such changes may in turn raise new needs calling for additional adjustments. Blau specifies some conditions under which an organization is likely to be open to internal changes. These include the actors' feelings of security, their professional orientation, and the extent of pressing organizational needs. The absence of conflict between management and personnel and cohesion among staff members are reported as factors which enhance organizational change.

Grusky studies the effects of personnel turnover on the organization. The flow of personnel, like the flow of raw material, need not affect the organization since, theoretically, a new person can be recruited for each person who leaves. Nevertheless, Grusky shows that the rate of succession and organizational effectiveness are interrelated. This, one may assume, is because rapid succession reduces effectiveness. As Grusky points out in his study of a somewhat atypical organization, the relationship may work the other way around: failures may *lead* to successions.

In their study of the control of the peasantry by the Communist Party and its response to Party control, Skinner and Winckler make the theory of compliance fully dynamic. They show how the tensions and incompatibility of each stage lead to the initiation of the next compliance pattern. In a field in which theory and data tend to follow separate routes, the authors' ability to join the two—to their mutual benefit—is rarely matched.

THE DYNAMICS
OF BUREAUCRACY

Peter M. Blau

"One cannot step twice into the same river," said Heraclitus, twenty-five centuries ago; and if one returns to the same river bed, it also has imperceptibly changed. The only permanence in bureaucratic structures is the occurrence of change in predictable patterns, and even these are not unalterably fixed.

The two government agencies studied had been established by law to achieve designated purposes. One was responsible for providing employment service, the other for enforcing legal standards of employment. The external situation in which different segments of each organization found themselves differed, and this situation continually changed. Finding jobs for accountants and finding work for day laborers called for different procedures, and practices that sufficed for enforcing the law during a war might not do so in a period of recession. In order to discharge prescribed responsibilities under varying conditions, adjustments of the bureaucratic organization were necessary.

Changes in the external situation were not the only reason for making modifications in the structure. Most procedures, even if instituted for a specific purpose, had several unintended consequences. Statistical records of performance, for example, not only furnished a means for evaluating operations but also had a variety of other effects. Some of these—latent

Reprinted in part from Peter M. Blau, *Dynamics of Bureaucracy*, pp. 201–214, 216–219, by permission of the author and publisher, The University of Chicago Press. Copyright 1955.

functions of record-keeping—furthered the achievement of organizational objectives, but others—dysfunctions—interfered with it and thus necessitated further innovations. Perfect adjustment is hardly possible, because the very practices instituted to enhance adjustment in some respects often disturb it in others. Hence the stable attainment of organizational objectives depends on perpetual change in the bureaucratic structure.

Indeed, the dynamics of bureaucratic development is not confined to the emergence of new instruments for the accomplishment of specified objectives, but in the process the objectives themselves change, too. Particularly in innovating organizations, although not only there, competent officials tend to become interested in assuming new responsibilities and in expanding the jurisdiction of the agency, since this would increase their work satisfaction and benefit their career.

EMERGENT ORGANIZATIONAL NEEDS
AND STRUCTURAL CHANGE

Weber conceived of bureaucracy as the social mechanism that maximizes efficiency in administration and also as a form of social organization with specific characteristics. Both these criteria cannot be part of the definition, since the relationship between the attributes of a social institution and its consequences is a question for empirical verification and not a matter of definition. Weber's discussion may be interpreted in one of two ways. Either he defined bureaucracy by specifying formal characteristics and hypothesized its superior operating efficiency; or he intended to define it as any administrative apparatus that maximizes efficiency and advanced hypotheses about organizational attributes that would typically have this effect.

In terms of the second alternative, bureaucracies can be looked upon as institutionalized strategies for the achievement of administrative objectives by the concerted effort of many officials. They are methods of organizing social conduct in order to transform exceptional problems into routine duties of experts and to effect the co-ordination of specialized tasks. In different cultures, different social arrangements will prove most suitable for these purposes. When an authoritarian orientation toward social relationships prevails in the family and in the society generally and when lack of education limits the qualification of subaltern officials, as in Germany at Weber's time, strict hierarchical control may be the most efficient method of bureaucratic operation. However, when equality in social relationships is highly valued and when a much higher level of popular education has been reached, as in the United States today, permitting junior officials considerable discretion in discharging their responsibilities may be a more efficient system of administration. Similarly, in a culture where people are oriented toward century-old traditions, bureaucratic efficiency probably requires less change in organization than in a young culture where progress is a central value.

Internal as well as external forces made change a recurrent phenomenon in the two organizations studied, and efficient operations depended on such readiness to reorganize. The concept of organizational need has been helpful in the analysis of these processes of bureaucratic development, since it indicates the relationship between the consequences of established practices and the emergence of new ones. Many social patterns that served important functions for operations also had some dysfunctions, that is, they produced conditions that impeded the effective attainment of organizational objectives. These emergent needs often gave rise to new practices which met them. The introduction of statistical records in the employment agency, for instance, effected needed improvements in placement operations, but it also engendered competitiveness, which interfered with service to handicapped clients and with productivity in general. In response to these two organizational needs, social innovations developed that restored operating efficiency. First, special interviewers for handicapped clients assumed duties that obligated other interviewers to help them find jobs for their clients. Second, one group of regular interviewers devised methods for discouraging competitive tendencies, and this increased productivity, as indicated by the fact that this group was more productive than the other group of regular interviewers, where competitive practices prevailed.

Contacts with clients furnish another illustration of adjustments that had dysfunctions necessitating further adjustments. Interviewers concerned with making many placements were frustrated by refusals of benefit clients to accept low-paying jobs. They often tried, therefore, to discourage such refusals by the more or less implicit threat that unemployment benefits would be discontinued. This practice, although adequate for its purpose, created conflicts with clients, which were particularly disturbing for these service-oriented interviewers. The resulting tensions constituted new obstacles to the effective performance of duties. In response to this emergent need, a custom developed that restored equanimity, namely, complaining and joking about clients in conversations with colleagues. This new pattern, in turn, had a dysfunction. It facilitated the interviewer's work, not by eliminating conflicts with clients, but by immunizing him against their disturbing effects, and consequently made inconsiderate treatment of clients more likely. Since this dysfunction, which did not directly interfere with operations, did not give rise to an organizational need, it persisted, to the detriment of clients.

Consultations in the federal agency reveal a different aspect of the same process of change in the structure. Agents, anxious to assure the accuracy of their decisions without exposing their difficulties to the supervisor, were in need of advice from another source. The practice of consulting colleagues met this need. It reduced the anxiety about making decisions which interfered with operations, and it generated social cohesion. However, it also produced needs that led to new patterns of interpersonal relationships.

To consult peers was easier than to consult the superior in the department, but if they were approached for help too often, they ceased to be peers, and this made consulting them more difficult. As the advice of some agents was in constant demand, while others recurrently requested assistance with solving their problems, status differences emerged in the group. Agents hesitated to consult expert colleagues too frequently, lest their unofficial position suffer, just as they were reluctant to ask the supervisor too many questions for fear of endangering their official position. In either case, hierarchical relations prevented free access to consultants. The resurgent need for advice from actual peers induced most agents to establish partnerships of mutual consultation and to reserve consultations with experts for their most perplexing problems.

Peer relationships rest on reciprocity in social exchange. Unilateral services engender obligations which destroy equality of status and erect barriers to the free flow of communication. This interference with egalitarian social interaction is dysfunctional for work groups. The emerging status distinctions in Department Y not only restricted the choice of consultant but even threatened the integrated position of the less competent agents. As all were attracted to popular experts, the others felt left out of group life and experienced a need for better interpersonal relationships. This need was also met by new patterns of interaction. The less competent agents tended to cultivate extensive informal relations with colleagues during the lunch period. Since this improved their popularity, it constituted an equalizing force. Although some status differences persisted, alternative mechanisms for becoming integrated in this group re-created equivalence of status in fundamental respects.

Social cohesion depends on basic equality of status. Cooperative interaction, such as the pattern of consultation, therefore affects it in two opposite ways. Cooperation is a major source of cohesion in work groups, because it unites members in the voluntary exchange of valued assistance, but it simultaneously weakens cohesion by giving rise to status distinctions which inhibit social intercourse and thus limit feelings of fellowship. As a result of these conflicting forces, cohesiveness is not a stable condition. It requires constant effort to renew the fundamental equality that makes the members of the group fully accessible to one another and permits them to become interested in one another as distinctive persons. Treatment of associates as unique individuals rather than as social types develops primarily among peers, and such an approach is a prerequisite for social interaction that is intrinsically gratifying and thereby produces strong social ties. To perpetuate group cohesion, the orientation in interpersonal relations should disallow quantitative differentiation of status but stress qualitative differentiation of persons. This orientation toward equals whose particular qualities merit consideration is also likely to enhance identification with the purposes of the group and its standards of behavior, at least in a culture where submission to authoritarian commands is negatively valued.

The significance of an egalitarian approach is not restricted to the internal structure of the work group but extends to the larger bureaucratic organization. Rational operations require the expeditious removal of obstructions to efficient performance. Effective communication in the hierarchy of authority, without which needed official innovations would not be made, is a necessary condition for this adjustment, but not a sufficient one. No system of rules and supervision can be so finely spun that it anticipates all exigencies that may arise. Moreover, some impediments to efficiency, such as the feelings of anxiety and other emotional tensions which often develop in the course of operations, cannot be eradicated by official decree. Maximum rationality in the organization, therefore, depends on the ability of operating officials to assume the initiative in establishing informal relations and instituting unofficial practices that eliminate operational difficulties as they occur. This ability, in turn, presupposes the absence of acute feelings of inequality among the members of the bureaucracy.

To be sure, the status distinctions inherent in the exercise of authority are necessary for the effective administration of a large organization, where officials in central positions must be able to direct and coordinate the work of specialized groups. However, since bureaucratic authority rests on social consensus that issuing certain directives is just as much the duty of the superior as compliance with these directives is that of subordinates, such compliance is not experienced as subjugation, while obedience to arbitrary commands of a superior would be. Hence bureaucratic authority itself does not create profound feelings of inequality, although it involves some status differences, but it often gives rise to additional hierarchical distinctions, which are not essential for systematic administration and which destroy all feelings of equality. If subaltern officials are treated as inferiors whose sole duty is to obey detailed orders of their superior, they have neither sufficient security nor incentive to cope with problems of their work on their own initiative. To supply the confidence and motivation needed for such efforts, junior officials must be considered as collaborators of administrators in the pursuit of common professional objectives. This limited type of egalitarian treatment, which is not too dissimilar from that which actually prevailed in the federal agency, is not incompatible with the exercise of bureaucratic authority. Of course, the absence of fundamental inequalities is not the only bureaucratic condition that must be met for work groups to take the initiative in making improvements when obstructions to efficient operations arise.

SOME PREREQUISITES OF ADJUSTIVE DEVELOPMENT

Spontaneous adjustments often occurred in the two agencies under consideration, that is, practices which solved incipient operational problems emerged among officials in the course of their work without being deliberately instituted by superiors. At this point, a question on the next-higher level of abstraction should be raised: What were the bureaucratic conditions that accounted for this pattern of self-adjustment, which was essential for efficiency? The exceptional cases where organizational needs persisted without evoking innovations to meet them provide some indications of these prerequisites of adjustive development in bureaucratic organizations.

Receptionists in the employment agency, quite unconsciously, treated clients of their own skin color preferentially. Since this did not disturb the work of the members of Department X, impartial treatment of applicants was not restored. However, some organizational needs that were very disturbing also persisted. When special interviewers, fearful of risking disapproval of requests to discontinue service to psychotic clients, continued to interview these clients, they found this task most irritating. In this case a conflict between this group of officials and a top administrator prevented adjustment. Still a different factor accounts for the finding that reviewers were not relieved from cross-pressures that interfered with their work, even though they allowed agents to correct most mistakes unofficially. These temporary reviewers did not constitute a distinct group, since each one remained identified with his former departmental group, and consequently were not able effectively to defend themselves against pressure from other officials. Finally, the members of Section A in the state agency, a distinct group, did not suppress competitive practices, which were disruptive and lowered productivity. Two important differences between this situation and that in Section B, where cooperative adjustment occurred, were that no common professional orientation had developed in Section A and its members had felt insecure in their job.

These cases of enduring dysfunctions suggest five prerequisites of adjustive development: first, a minimum of employment security; second, a professional orientation toward the performance of duties; third, established work groups that command the allegiance of their members; fourth, the absence of basic conflict between work group and management; fifth, organizational needs that are experienced as disturbing. Without assuming this list to be exhaustive, the following discussion will be confined to these five conditions, the absence of which was observed to obstruct the process of adjustment.

The ability to originate new patterns of adjustment and to adapt to those officially introduced presupposes relative job security. To be sure, the unemployed worker who feels he has nothing to lose may become a revolutionary, but insecurity in the bureaucratic situation, where one's job hangs in the balance, breeds ritualistic adherence to the existing order. Interviewers in Section A, while on probation for their civil service appointment, were so anxious to comply with the demands of superiors that they could not afford to discourage competitive practices. The members of Section B, who already held permanent civil service positions, felt free to cooperate in disregard of official statistical records, and they thereby improved productivity. Factory workers, who can be fired any time, resist changes in the organization, and so did officials in the federal agency whose lesser competence made them insecure in a period of reductions in staff; but the majority of agents, secure in their job, preferred frequent change to a constant routine.

Employment security engenders the psychological freedom of action that enables individuals to initiate adjustments, but it does not guarantee that these will further the objectives of the agency. Indeed, tenure may lead to private adaptations that are detrimental to the interest of the organization. To preclude this possibility, a professional orientation must prevail among officials. This involves a common identification with professional values and norms, which makes the process of attaining professional objectives a source of satisfaction.

Civil service personnel policies enhance the chances that officials will have a professional orientation toward their work. Recruitment standards assure that only applicants with the technical training required for a job are appointed. The relative security of civil service positions and the consequent long tenure of most officials encourage loyalty to the organization and its values, particularly since the specialized qualifications acquired in many years of experience in government agencies often cannot be utilized in private industry. The expert customs inspector, for instance, can hardly find a job commensurate with his skills outside the government, and even the demand for expert employment interviewers in private industry is small. Promotions in civil service, moreover, follow explicit regulations, which enable the official to predict his promotion chances with relative accuracy, in contrast to the private employee, who is promoted at the pleasure of his employer[1] and can therefore hope for a promotion at all times.[2] The system that prevents civil servants from deriving satisfaction from hopes of spectacular advancements probably also constrains them to find gratification in their work and thus invites a professional attitude toward it.

Evaluation on the basis of results achieved rather than techniques used likewise fosters a professional orientation. If interviewers in the employment agency criticized statistical records as unprofessional, it was because they felt that the indices measured only superficial accomplishments, such as the number of placements. In the federal agency, more refined statistical criteria supplemented by qualitative evaluation of results compelled agents to strive to achieve specified objectives in their work and obviated the need for many operating rules and close supervision. This external compulsion was internalized. The periodic rating by the supervisor constrained agents to adapt to their dependent position by adopting the bureaucratic system of values and norms as their own orientation toward their tasks. Moreover, the supervisor, as a means of extending his authority over subordinates, rarely enforced operating rules but relied for control on the obligations he thereby created and on his evaluation of completed cases. This put agents under further pressure to identify with professional objectives and with self-imposed standards of workmanship.

A professional orientation makes officials concerned with impediments to efficient operations and directs them to attempt adjustments, but it also engenders anxiety. The greater their interest in professional objectives and the fewer the external restraints on their method of achieving them, the more likely it is that they will experience anxiety. The bureaucratic officials observed found themselves in this predicament, although perhaps not to the same extent as independent professionals. Anxieties that persevered, whether among interviewers or department heads, agents or reviewers, led to maladaptation, rigidity, and poor performance. Adaptation to the organization in general and the ability to reorganize procedures when neces-

[1] Except in private bureaucracies that have also adopted explicit promotion procedures.

[2] None of 69 officials interviewed *aspired* to high positions in civil service within the next ten years, but 30 aspired to high positions in private industry or self-employment, although only eight *expected* to leave the government. Whether an individual directed his aspirations outside or inside civil service was not related to his work satisfaction, but simply depended on whether he expressed *any high* aspirations or not. Hopeful aspirations are not necessarily realistic, but their attainment must be conceivable, not impossible. Since officials knew that it was legally impossible for them suddenly to be promoted to, say, assistant commissioner, they either ceased to entertain hopes of this type of success or, if they wanted to indulge in wishful thinking, directed their aspirations toward careers outside the government service. One of the merits of the civil service system is that it discourages occupational aspirations which, by their very nature, must be frustrated in the majority of cases.

sary in particular depend on relatively cohesive work groups which relieve such anxiety.

Recurrent cooperative and congenial interaction with most co-workers, and not just with a few friends, gives officials a feeling of security in the work situation. This promotes assimilation in the bureaucratic structure and efficient performance of strenuous tasks, such as complex negotiations. The social support of the group also makes it easier for officials to adopt new practices, since it lessens their need to find emotional security in familiar routines. Social cohesion, therefore, paves the way for the development of new adjustments. In addition, it furnishes the group with instruments for instituting them.

To meet organizational needs requires group action. When agents found that reports of bribes by one of them endangered success in future negotiations of others, any single individual was helpless in the face of this difficulty, but the group could eliminate it by collectively discouraging every agent from making such reports. When competitive practices interfered with the work of interviewers, individual efforts to check them were ineffective, but the collective enforcement of cooperation in an entire group removed this obstacle to operations. Unofficial practices that met organizational needs were most prevalent in cohesive groups, because they alone could effectively enforce informal norms.

Most members of cohesive groups value their interpersonal relationships with one another, and this makes them subject to the control of the group. Unofficial sanctions are either indications by others that they have lost respect for a colleague and become less interested in associating with him or ostracism in miniature, signs of hostility in social situations that threaten an individual with ostracism. These sanctions, as well as the serious penalty of ostracism, are effective deterrents to deviant behavior only when an official's position in the group is important to him, and not otherwise. Social cohesion is the source of the group's power to exact obedience to its norms and thus of its ability to develop adjustive social patterns independent of official rules.

The process of enforcing norms affects the relative position of individuals within the group. Social differentiation develops, as the members of the group are especially attracted to some co-workers and seek to associate with them more than with others. Officials who received disproportionately many contacts in the course of integrative interaction occupied a superior unofficial status, which found expression in their assuming a dominant role in group situations. One major source of attraction was the possession of characteristics valued by the group, such as expert knowledge. Another basis of differential association was the degree of conformity with group norms. Deviants lost status in the group, because the others reacted, often inadvertently, to a violation of standards they valued by associating less with the offender.

Social differentiation endangered cohesiveness and optimum performance of duties, unless counterforces developed that minimized it again, as previously noted in this chapter. Continuous structural modifications, changes in relative positions as well as operating practices, occurred within the larger framework of comparatively stable hierarchical positions and specified objectives. Just as a solid body consists of moving molecules, so the bureaucratic structure is composed of constantly changing elements.

Although social cohesion cannot be officially created, conditions favorable for its development can be. Job security and the explicit promotion procedure in civil service have this function. They supply most officials with the knowledge that they will neither be promoted nor lose their job within the next few years and thus greatly lessen their need to compete with fellow-officials. Besides, the civil service system assures that most officials remain in the same group for years, usually under conditions that give rise to a common professional orientation. Daily associations between like-minded colleagues without serious conflicts for long periods of time stimulate the emergence of social cohesion.[3]

Social cohesion enables the members of a group to institute adjustments that further their interest. These adjustments will, however, not advance the objectives of the organization, if operating employees feel that their interest conflicts with that of management. This is a typical occurrence in private industry. Restriction of output among factory workers is an adjustment which is designed to protect the economic interest of workers against management and which is dysfunctional for operations. The comments and behavior of workers show that these practices are motivated by fear of losing their jobs or lowering their wages rather than by lack of professional concern with their work.[4] In contrast to those of factory

---

[3] Conditions that reduce social cohesion are, of course, dysfunctional for bureaucratic operations. This seems to be an unintended dysfunction of loyalty investigations. For example, two agents, both of whom were subsequently cleared, had been investigated. This gave rise to serious dissension in the federal agency, involving many officials aside from the two directly concerned. It stirred up political differences, which had hardly been discussed before; it produced conflict between those who testified for an innocent colleague and those who strongly disapproved of testifying for somebody under suspicion of disloyalty; it created emotional conflicts for those who were afraid to testify for a colleague whom they considered innocent, and disputes between them and those who regarded a refusal to bear witness in such a situation a betrayal; and it alienated from one another those who testified in support of and those who testified against the charges.

[4] Roy indicates that the workers he observed were professionally oriented. They derived satisfaction from working efficiently but felt they must work slowly, although they did not like to do so for fear their piece rates would be cut. See Donald Roy, "Quota Restriction and Goldbricking in a Machine Shop," *American Journal of*

workers, most unofficial practices observed in the two agencies, including some that violated official rules, contributed to operating efficiency. An important reason for this, in addition to job security, may well have been that the civil service system eliminates a basic source of conflict between operating officials and management.

Authority over personnel is split in government agencies. In private organizations, management controls employment conditions as well as operations. In government agencies, on the other hand, management controls operations, but not employment conditions. Salaries and the procedures that govern promotion and discharge are determined by the civil service commission in accordance with legal statutes. Since the rating influences advancement chances, an individual's economic interest may bring him into conflict with superiors. However, the conflict between the *collective* economic interest of operating officials and the budgetary considerations of their employer finds expression in their opposition to the civil service commission and the legislature, which set the conditions of their employment. It does not affect their relationship with the administration of the agency. On the contrary, operating officials and administrators are united by their interest in legislation that benefits civil servants.

The dominant concern of employees with their job and income may submerge a common professional interest in effective performance, but this was not characteristic of the civil servants studied. Their job was relatively secure, and they did not feel that improvements in operations would evoke managerial action detrimental to their economic welfare, as factory workers apparently do. This situation permitted officials to become and remain primarily interested in their professional responsibilities. Cohesive groups in which such a professional orientation prevailed readily initiated social practices that eliminated obstacles to efficient performance. This strain toward adjustive development in the organization greatly contributed to the achievement of its objectives.

Sociology, 57 (1952), 432. See also Mathewson, and Roethlisberger and Dickson, who observe the same phenomenon but interpret it differently; Stanley B. Mathewson, *Restriction of Output among Unorganized Workers* (New York: Viking, 1931), and F. J. Roethlisberger and W. J. Dickson, *Management and the Worker* (Cambridge: Harvard, 1939).

MANAGERIAL SUCCESSION AND ORGANIZATIONAL EFFECTIVENESS

Oscar Grusky

The major purpose of this study was to test two related hypotheses: (1) that rates of administrative succession and degree of organizational effectiveness are negatively correlated, and (2) that a change in the rate of administrative succession is negatively correlated with a change in organizational effectiveness.[1] The hypotheses are deliberately stated so as not to attribute causality solely to either succession or effectiveness. We assumed that the variables induce reciprocal effects. High rates of succession should produce declining organizational effectiveness, and low effectiveness should encourage high rates of administrative succession.

To obtain anything resembling an adequate field test of these hypotheses required a substantial number of formal organizations that, ideally, were identical in official goals, size, and authority structure. If the objectives of the organizations were not similar, then obviously it would not be feasible to compare their relative effectiveness, since this concept refers to the extent to which an organization is able to move toward the accomplishment of its official aims. We know that for business organizations and certain public agencies, and perhaps for other kinds as well, rates of succession are positively related to organizational size.[2] Therefore, we sought a sample of organizations of similar size.

Reprinted from *The American Journal of Sociology*, vol. 69 (1963), pp. 21–30, with omissions.

[1] This hypothesis was discussed in my "Administrative Succession in Formal Organizations," *Social Forces*, XXXIX (December, 1960), 105–115.

[2] See my "Corporate Size, Bureaucratization, and Managerial Succession," *American Journal of Sociology*, LXVII (November, 1961), 261–269, and L. Kriesberg, "Careers, Organization Size, and Succession," *American Journal of Sociology*, LXVIII (November, 1962), 355–359. For a comprehensive discussion of other variables related to size see T. Caplow, "Organizational Size," *Administrative Science Quarterly*, II (March, 1957), 484–505.

There is some evidence, although it is highly limited, that organizations with different types of authority structures respond in very different ways to personnel changes at top levels in the hierarchy.[3] Hence, organizations with similar types of structures of authority were desirable.

In addition, a relatively "clean" field test of the hypotheses demanded reliable and valid measures of rates of administrative succession and organizational effectiveness. Since the sixteen organizations selected for study, professional baseball teams, met all the relatively stringent requirements described, a second objective of this research was to illustrate some of the potentialities of sports organizations as objects of sociological investigation.

METHODS AND FINDINGS

All data for this study were gathered by means of secondary analysis of published documents.[4] Baseball teams and, in fact, most professional sports clubs offer the research advantages of public records of team personnel and team performance. This fact, as we shall see, also has important implications for the behavior of the organization.

Two time periods, 1921–1941 and 1951–1958, were selected for study. It was deemed wise to skip the World War II and immediate post-World War II periods.

The structure of baseball organizations is such that ultimate responsibility for the performance of the team is almost always fixed on one position, that of field manager. At the same time, official authority is generally concentrated in this position. Therefore, it was clear that personnel changes among field managers rather than club presidents, general managers, or team captains were central to the study. The number of managerial changes for each time period or the average length of managerial tenure constituted the rate of succession for each team.

The measure of organizational effectiveness was team standing, based on the number of games won and lost at the completion of the season. This might be considered analogous in some respects to productivity in

---

[3] D. L. Sills, *The Volunteers* (New York: Free Press, 1957); W. A. Lunden, "The Tenure and Turnover of State Prison Wardens," *American Journal of Corrections*, XIX (November–December, 1957), 14–15; and A. Etzioni, "Authority Structure and Organizational Effectiveness," *Administrative Science Quarterly*, IV (June, 1959), 43–67.

[4] H. Hurkin and S. C. Thompson, *The Official Encyclopedia of Baseball* (2d rev. ed.; New York: A. S. Barnes, 1959); H. Johnson, *Who's Who in Baseball* (New York: Buston Publishing Co., 1953); F. Menke, *The Encyclopedia of Sports* (2d rev. ed.; New York: A. S. Barnes, 1960); *1958 Baseball Guide and Record Book* (St. Louis, Mo.: Sporting News, 1958); T. Spink and Son, *Baseball Register*, compiled by T. Spink and P. Rickart (St. Louis, Mo.: Sporting News, 1940–1941, 1951–1958).

industrial organizations. Georgopoulos and Tannenbaum's study of thirty-two similar suborganizations or stations demonstrated significant correlations between their various measures of organizational effectiveness: expert assessment of station effectiveness, productivity, intragroup strain, and flexibility.[5] It would certainly be safe to say that, among baseball experts, team standing is the most widely accepted criterion of effectiveness. Financial profit is also an important criterion. It would appear that the profitability of a baseball club is highly related to its team standing. Consistent with this assumption, we found a strong positive correlation between team standing and yearly attendance.[6]

Table 1 presents the basic data of the study. The data for Periods I and II taken separately or together strongly supported the hypothesized negative correlation between rates of managerial succession and organizational effectiveness. The correlations were considerably greater in the second time period, 1951–1958, than in the earlier one. Rates of succession and team standing correlated —.40 in the first period and —.60 in the second. One team that contributed to the lower correlation in the earlier period was the Philadelphia Athletics. Despite the fact that the team consistently finished in the second division between 1921 and 1941, no managerial successions took place during this period. Undoubtedly, manager Connie Mack's ownership of the club assisted his long tenure. The Athletics experienced frequent managerial succession during 1951–1958 with the departure of Mack from the scene.

In contrast, the Yankees, as Table 1 suggests, contributed to the magnitude of the correlation in both time periods. Not only were they highly effective, but they also experienced few managerial changes.

The second hypothesis was tested by examining the relationship between changes from Period I to Period II in the average length of time a manager retained his position with a team and changes in the team's standing. That is, we wanted to see if teams that kept their managers for shorter periods (experienced more succession) in Period II than they had in Period I were less effective in the later period and vice versa. In fact, the average tenure for managers declined in Period II for all but two clubs.

---

[5] B. S. Georgopoulos and A. S. Tannenbaum, "A Study of Organizational Effectiveness," *American Sociological Review*, XXII (October, 1957), 534–540.

[6] Profitability, attendance, and effectiveness are related in part because prolonged increases in profits tend to yield increases in organizational control over the market for new talent and therefore tend to produce a more effective farm system. Interpretation of the correlation between team standing and attendance should be approached cautiously. Attendance may also be a function of variables such as the total population of the metropolitan area, its particular age and sex distribution, and, of course, the number of professional baseball teams in the community.

TABLE 1. *Measures of Succession and Effectiveness for Sixteen Professional Baseball Organizations over Two Time Periods**

Team	Number of Successions			Average Team Standing†		
	PERIOD I (1)	PERIOD II (2)	PERIODS I AND II (3)	PERIOD I (4)	PERIOD II (5)	PERIODS I AND II (6)
Phillies	7	3	10	7.2	4.8	6.5
Giants	1	1	2	2.7	3.4	2.9
Cardinals	10	4	14	3.0	3.8	3.2
Braves	7	3	10	6.3	6.9	5.3
Pirates	6	3	9	3.2	6.9	4.2
Cubs	8	3	11	3.5	6.2	4.4
Dodgers	4	1	5	4.9	2.2	4.2
Reds	7	3	10	4.9	4.9	4.9
Athletics	0	4	4	4.8	6.6	5.3
Nats	6	3	9	4.2	6.8	4.9
Yankees	2	0	2	1.8	1.2	1.6
White Sox	8	2	10	5.6	2.9	4.9
Red Sox	8	2	10	6.0	3.9	5.4
Indians	6	1	7	3.9	2.6	3.6
Browns (Orioles)	9	5	14	5.6	6.8	5.9
Tigers	4	4	8	3.9	5.4	4.3

* Period I, 1921–1941; Period II, 1951–1958. Rank-order correlations (Kendall's tau) and one-tail p values are: cols. (1) and (4), $-.40(p < .02)$; cols. (2) and (5), $-.60(p < .001)$; and cols. (3) and (6), $-.43(p < .001)$.

† A numerically high team standing meant low effectiveness.

As Table 2 demonstrates, our hypothesis was again strongly supported.[7] All eight teams that increased considerably their rate of managerial succession over that of the earlier period experienced a decline in average team standing. Moreover, the two clubs that decreased their rate of succession increased their effectiveness. However, it was evident that those teams

[7] We realize some of the interpretative limitations of utilizing team averages as measures of succession. A study comparing the "effectiveness" and length of tenure of the successor and his managerial predecessor is in progress. In this investigation the object of study is the manager and not the team. Some limitations in our measure of effectiveness also should be noted. Team standing may not reflect perfectly the ability of the team, just as fielding and batting averages are not ideal measures of individual performance. E.g., a team may improve over the course of a season and because of a poor start finish only second, although it is the best team by other standards. And the bias of the official scorer has a lot to do with the players' fielding and batting averages.

TABLE 2. *Relationship between Change in Average Length of Managerial Tenure and Average Team Standing from Period I to Period II for Fifteen Professional Baseball Teams**

Change in Average Managerial Tenure	Change in Average Team Standing	
	Increased Effectiveness	Decreased Effectiveness
Tenure longer	2	0
Tenure about same†	4	1
Tenure much shorter	0	8

* $P = .0014$ by Fisher's Exact Test if the categories "Tenure longer" and "Tenure about same" are combined. One team (Reds) that did not change its average team standing was excluded.

† Defined as a decrease of 0.3 year or less.

that had experienced frequent and infrequent succession in the original period needed to be analyzed separately. Therefore, we controlled for average length of managerial tenure in Period I (a control for average team standing in Period I also would have been desirable, but we did not have a sufficient number of cases). The hypothesis was supported when the relationship was examined separately for teams that were below and above the median with respect to rates of succession in the first period (Table 3). Moreover, it should be noted that the single deviant case in Table 3 (the St. Louis Cardinals) was the team with the *lowest managerial tenure of any team in Period I.* This low rate remained about the same in Period II, although team effectiveness declined somewhat. We might speculate that perhaps (1) the very slight alteration of the club's policy of frequent succession was not above the threshold necessary to raise the organization's effectiveness, and/or (2) the slight decrease in the club's effectiveness did not encourage the owners to alter their policy of frequent succession.

The findings of this study may be compared with a recent laboratory investigation by Trow.[8] Using Leavitt's Common-Symbol problem and the five-position chain organizational network, Trow found no significant linear relationship between mean rate of succession and long-run organizational performance. He did find that the mean performance of the twelve teams with the lowest replacement rates was significantly superior to the mean performance of the twelve teams with the highest rates of succession. Trow

[8] D. B. Trow, "Membership Succession and Team Performance," *Human Relations,* XIII, No. 3 (1960), 259–268.

TABLE 3. *Relationship between Change in Average Length of Managerial Tenure and Average Team Standing from Period I to Period II for Fifteen Professional Baseball Teams, Controlling for Average Length of Managerial Tenure in Period I***

	Change in Average Team Standing		
Change in Average Managerial Tenure	Increased Effectiveness	Decreased Effectiveness	One-Tail p Level†
A. Short tenure in Period I (below median):			
Tenure longer or about same‡	3	1	
			.11
Tenure much shorter	0	3	
B. Long tenure in Period I (above median):			
Tenure longer or about same	3	0	
			.018
Tenure much shorter	0	5	

* One team (Reds) that did not change its average team standing was excluded.
† By Fisher's Exact Test.
‡ "About same" was defined as a decrease of 0.3 year or less.

discovered that *variability* in the rate of succession was a more important factor in team performance, noting that "whatever the average rate of succession, an increase in the rate, i.e., a temporal clustering of succession, tends to bring about a decrease in the level of organizational performance." In addition, he found that ability of the successor was a major factor in organizational performance. Thus, despite considerable differences between the techniques of secondary analysis and contrived experimentation, the findings of the two studies appear to be consistent at least with respect to the second hypothesis.

SUCCESSION AND EFFECTIVENESS

It is apparent that theoretical explanations for the findings of this study may be pursued from two opposite directions; it may be assumed that either effectiveness or succession functions as the primary independent variable. Our data demonstrate only the existence of an association, not its cause. Logic or common knowledge will not permit us to decide the issue. However, there is no intrinsic reason why a particular variable, such as rate of succession, could not be *both* a cause and an effect of effectiveness. This may very well be so in this instance.

A common-sense explanation for our results might suggest that effectiveness alone is the cause. The manager is fired because the team performs badly. Not only is the simplicity of this explanation appealing, but the negative correlation between succession and effectiveness is fully consistent with it. However, if taken by itself, this approach possesses all the deficiencies properly attributed to orientations that rest only on common knowledge: they typically do not stimulate careful empirical test; they typically do not suggest additional propositions which might be worthy of examination; they typically do not fit in systematically to a comprehensive body of generalizations in the field of interest. Naturally, we prefer explanations that can meet these and other criteria described by Nagel somewhat more adequately.

If we assume that effectiveness and succession influence each other by contributing to managerial role strain, it is possible to formulate an alternative explanation for the major findings, one that ties in with a growing body of theory and research. It was this assumption that originally provoked this study. Succession, because it represents a universal organizational process, and effectiveness, because all formal organizations tend to strive toward the attainment of their official objectives, are strategic concepts for studying organizations within a comparative framework. Numerous studies conducted in the laboratory as well as in the field suggest that these variables produce reciprocal effects. For example, both Gouldner's and Guest's field research as well as Trow's experiment indicate that succession influences organizational effectiveness.[9] On the other hand, Hamblin's laboratory study suggests that the ineffectiveness of the group contributes to high rates of succession among the leaders. When the leader could not solve a crisis problem confronting the group, he was replaced.[10] Accordingly, the relationship between rates of succession and organizational effectiveness was analyzed within the context of a conceptual scheme that focused on their interrelationships with a number of other variables: managerial (or executive) role strain, expectation of replacement, style of

[9] A. Gouldner, *Patterns of Industrial Bureaucracy* (New York: Free Press, 1954); R. H. Guest, *Organizational Change* (Homewood, Ill.: Dorsey Press, 1962); and Trow, *op. cit.* See also W. F. Whyte, "The Social Structure of the Restaurant Industry," *American Journal of Sociology*, LIV (January, 1949), 302–310; C. R. Christiansen, *Management Succession in Small and Growing Enterprises* (Boston: Graduate School of Business Administration, Harvard University, 1953); E. Dale, "Du Pont: Pioneer in Systematic Management," *Administrative Science Quarterly*, II (June, 1957), 26–30; O. Grusky, "Role Conflict in Organization: A Study of Prison Camp Officials," *Administrative Science Quarterly*, III (March, 1959), 463–467; and R. H. McCleery, *Policy Change in Prison Management* (East Lansing: Michigan State University, 1957), pp. 10–27.
[10] R. L. Hamblin, "Leadership and Crisis," *Sociometry*, XXI (December, 1958), 322–335.

supervision, subgroup stability, morale, clientele support, degree of discrepancy between managerial authority and responsibility, and availability of objective assessment of organizational performance.

Figure 1 presents the proposed network of interrelations of the variables. The arrows indicate the direction of influence. Key propositions discussed below are followed by a numerical reference to the relevant variables. Of course, no attempt was made to exhaust the logical possibilities in the formation of propositions.

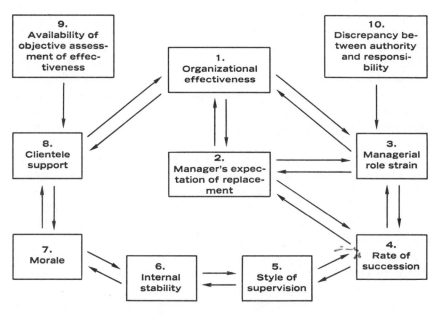

FIGURE 1.   *Organizational factors in team performance.*

The magnitude of managerial role strain is a general factor conditioning the nature of the relationship between succession and effectiveness.[11] By role strain is meant the extent to which role performance produces stress for the occupant of a position that cannot be fully relieved by institutionally

[11] Position or office refers to a category that is located in the formal social structure of an organization. In a formal organization the category is defined in terms of its relationship with other positions that in turn are organized around the official objectives of the system. By role is meant a "set of evaluative standards applied to an incumbent of a particular position" (see N. Gross, W. S. Mason, and A. W. McEachern, *Explorations in Role Analysis* [New York: Wiley, 1958], p. 60). Role strain is viewed in the present study as a more inclusive concept than role conflict. The latter is limited to situations of strain produced by incompatible expectations. W. J. Goode defines role strain as "the felt difficulty in fulfilling role obligations."

legitimated means. Hence, this concept refers to the amount of tension with which a person is confronted as a result of occupying a particular office in an organization. The sources of strain will vary, of course, with the nature of the organizational setting, rank of the position, experience of the person, and so on. In general, organizational effectiveness should be inversely related to strength of managerial role strain (*1* and *3*); high levels of effectiveness (of the manager's unit) should be associated with low managerial strain and low levels of effectiveness correlated with high managerial strain. Perhaps, however, some optimum level of managerial strain is associated with maximum organizational effectiveness. At the same time, again assuming all else equal, the magnitude of managerial role strain should be positively correlated with rates of succession (*3* and *4*). Low strain defines a position as desirable.. If the strain is too high, the manager searches for opportunities elsewhere, or redefines previous opportunities as attractive and eventually leaves the organization. Once again a simple monotonic relationship may be an oversimplification; too little strain may indicate a lack of "challenge" to the manager and thereby also stimulate turnover.

If rates of succession in a position have been high, and expectation of replacement arises, this, in turn, should contribute to managerial role strain. All else being equal, the stronger the expectation of replacement, the greater the role strain (*2* and *3*). Organizational effectiveness should be inversely related to strength of expectation of replacement; if the organization is performing well, the manager would not normally expect to be replaced (*1* and *2*). Strength of managerial role strain should also be related to style of supervision. All else being equal, the greater the role strain, the greater the likelihood that supervision will be close (*3* and *5*).[12] There are numerous studies relating closeness of supervision, morale, and organizational effectiveness (*1* and *7; 1* and *5*).[13] Judging from Guest's study, we would expect that the greater the rate of succession in an organization, the greater would be the tendency to supervise closely (*4* and *5*). There is evidence suggesting that closeness of supervision is associated with degree of internal organizational stability (*5* and *6*).[14]

Two special sources of strain seemed pertinent to the analysis of the

---

Our definition differs in that it does not require a perfect association between perceived and objective role strain ("A Theory of Role Strain," *American Sociological Review*, XXIV [August, 1960], 483–496).

[12] Guest, *op. cit.*, chap. iii.

[13] Many of these studies are discussed in P. Blau and W. R. Scott, *Formal Organizations* (San Francisco: Chandler Publishing Co., 1962), pp. 140–164.

[14] Gouldner, *op. cit.*, and R. O. Carlson, *Executive Succession and Organizational Change* (Chicago: Midwest Administrative Center, University of Chicago, 1962).

managerial role in baseball organizations: (1) the discrepancy between official responsibility and authority (we assumed that, in general, the greater this discrepancy, the greater the role strain [*3* and *10*]) and (2) the availability of objective assessment of managerial and team performance to the organization's clientele and higher levels of authority. We would expect that when objective assessment is available, the negative correlation between effectiveness and managerial role strain should be higher than when such objective assessment is not available (*8* and *9*). The first attribute concerns primarily the nature of the internal structure of baseball organizations, the second the relationship between the organization and its interested public.

Many of the role strains of the field manager emerge from the fact that he alone is acknowledged to be officially responsible for team performance. Therefore, it is defined as illegitimate for him to delegate ultimate responsibility for results either upward to the "Front Office" or downward to the coaches and individual players. At the same time, however, he depends, particularly over the long run, upon the front office for assistance by providing a strong farm system and advantageous trades, and, at all times, upon the quality of performance of the lower-level members of the hierarchy, the players. If they perform well, his position is secure; if they do not, it is in jeopardy.

However, although other managerial positions, such as those in business, often carry responsibility for results, what distinguishes the baseball manager is the fact that not only is he acknowledged to be responsible, but his superiors have objective data with which they can readily evaluate his performance. Unlike the typical business executive, for whom few clear standards of performance tend to exist, the baseball manager is exposed continually to seemingly unassailable comparative measures of effectiveness.[15] Moreover, the effects of many of the manager's daily decisions are a matter of public record. This means that every managerial decision that turns out to be an unfortunate one for the team, such as substituting in a key situation a mediocre left-hand hitting pinch batter for the team's star right-hand hitting slugger, is immediately "second-guessed" by the players, coaches, the front office, and the fans. The manager is constantly open to criticism, public and private.

The relationship between the field manager and his subordinates, upon whom he depends so heavily, is also influenced by the availability of public and objective measures of performance. Outstanding performance on the part of individual players insures their remaining with the club, and, im-

[15] See F. X. Sutton, S. E. Harris, C. Kaysen, and J. Tobin, *The American Business Creed* (New York: Schocken Books, 1962), pp. 336–338.

portantly, the evaluation of this performance rests *not* with managerial subjective judgment as it does frequently in business firms, but instead is based largely on relatively objective standards of performance. Hence, the player in many respects is independent of managerial control. Where the ballplayer tends to resemble the traditional entrepreneur, the manager resembles the bureaucrat. But the manager is a bureaucrat stripped of many vital bureaucratic controls. For example, the typical manager in a bureaucracy possesses power because he can limit the access of his subordinates to higher positions. However, the average ballplayer does not anticipate upward mobility in the ordinary sense within the structure of the professional baseball organization. In his case, upward career mobility applies primarily to the income and popularity rank systems; the players' major sources of reward are external to managerial control.

To a certain extent each manager develops his own inimitable way of handling players. After a while, the players feel comfortable with this style, and the younger ones in particular may feel that no successor can quite measure up to the standard (Willie Mays's reported fondness for Leo Durocher is a case in point). A managerial change inevitably upsets old patterns of behavior. New organizational policies, a different style of leadership, perhaps new players, and the addition of new coaches produce changes of great magnitude in the internal structure of the team. Members are forced to adapt not only to the successor's new ways of doing things but also to the new informal coalitions that inevitably develop. The recruitment of the successor from the present staff or from outside the organization may be an important factor affecting the degree of instability created by succession.[16] Moreover, a high rate of managerial succession on a team tends to generate expectations, especially during a losing streak, that the current manager's job is in danger. This may encourage dissatisfied players to challenge the manager's authority and increase even more the felt discrepancy between his responsibility and authority. The result is greater managerial role strain.

In addition to the internal sources of tension, constant pressure on both the manager and the ordinary team members emanates from the organization's clientele. Unlike many other kinds of organizations, professional baseball teams must deal with a clientele that is both highly committed and highly informed. The strong emotional identification of the fan with "his" professional baseball or football club is often a part of the resident's identification with his local community. In some locales, such as Los Angeles, comprised of a large number of suburban subcommunities, it probably represents one of the more important integrative symbols. In

---

[16] See Carlson, *op. cit.*

the Green Bay area, the Green Bay Packers football team is referred to as a "regional religion."

Not only are the clientele strongly committed but in addition, as we suggested, they can readily and continually evaluate the effectiveness of the team since performance criteria are public knowledge. In other types of organizations, the clientele cannot evaluate the effectiveness of the system with comparable precision. Consumers of an industrial corporation's products, for example, typically possess neither the propensity nor the knowledge to compare objectively the quality of the products they purchase or the "efficiency" of the corporation's employees. Accordingly, public relations and advertising men are probably able to manipulate the image of the corporation and its products much more effectively than can professional baseball teams.[17] Not even the best advertising men could have undone the damage to the Philadelphia Phillies' game attendance between 1934 and 1941 when they finished in last or next to last place every year.

Clientele support is critical because of its close relationship to morale and team effectiveness (8 and 7; 8 and 1); it is important in two ways. First, attendance is ostensibly highly related to profitability, and a drop in profitability produces strong pressures for managerial change. Second, high rates of attendance, by raising team morale, may contribute to team effectiveness as well as being affected by it. Our data revealed a strong correlation between effectiveness based on team standing and ranked yearly attendance. The zero-order correlations, by Kendall's tau, were as follows: for Period I, $T = .60$, $p < .0007$; for Period II, $T = .44$, $p < .009$; for Periods I and II combined, $T = .58$, $p < .001$. These data, of course, do not allow us to separate cause and effect. Mosteller's statistical study of the effects of playing "at home" and "away" upon winning World Series games found no significant differences in performance under the two conditions.[18] However, as he pointed out, outcomes of regular season games might still be influenced by this factor. He noted: (1) Baseball teams are often tailored to the home park because half the games are played there. Perhaps league champions are more skilful hitters and therefore less limited by the dimensions of a particular park. (2) Fatigue from excessive traveling may disadvantage the away team to a greater extent during the regular season than during the World Series. Still another possibility is that clientele support is less critical for team performance during World Series competition than during the day-in-day-out play of the regular season. The extensive publicity and assured popular interest in the World Series generates sufficient enthusiasm on the part of the player whether he is playing at home or

[17] I am indebted to Professor R. J. Murphy for this observation.
[18] F. Mosteller, "The World Series Competition," *Journal of the American Statistical Association*, XLVII (September, 1942), 355–380.

away. We suspect that the home crowd can exercise considerable influence on player performance during a regular season game. Under these conditions, enthusiastic support from the crowd may stimulate the player to "put out" more in the same way that a responsive audience can help produce scintillating dramatic performances on the stage. The ineffective team is less likely to receive this added inducement to perform well. . . .

COMPLIANCE SUCCESSION IN RURAL COMMUNIST CHINA: A CYCLICAL THEORY

G. William Skinner and Edwin A. Winckler

Analysis of the structure of compliance in Communist China reveals a regular pattern in the interaction between the Chinese Communist Party and the peasantry over the last nineteen years. Repeatedly since "liberation" the Party has shifted its primary reliance from exhortation to coercion and then to remuneration. Repeatedly the peasantry has passed from a tentative enthusiasm through disillusion to a calculative indifference. In this paper, then, we posit a compliance cycle through which the goals of the regime, its prescriptions for leadership style, the actual behavior of cadremen, and the reactions of the peasantry have run. First, we summarize the elements of compliance theory and construct a model of cycles and phases in a compliance system. Second, we trace the reordering of compliance arrangements in rural Communist China since 1949 and relate these changes to the succession of compliance cycles. Third, we summarize some of the organizational correlates of compliance cycles in the Chinese countryside.

This essay is a thorough revision of a paper entitled "Compliance and leadership in rural Communist China: a cyclical theory," presented by the first author at the 1965 annual meeting of the American Political Science Association. Copyright © 1969 by G. William Skinner and Edwin A. Winckler.

COMPLIANCE SYSTEM AND COMPLIANCE CYCLE

A compliance *relationship* is one in which "one actor behaves in accordance with a directive supported by another actor's power."[1] A compliance *system* is an assembly of such relationships seen in relation to the goals which the actors are trying to achieve. A compliance *cycle* is a recurring sequence of compliance arrangements and performance outcomes within a compliance system. This sequence may be divided into *phases* showing characteristic phenomena at the behavioral, structural, and systemic levels. In *behavioral* terms, a compliance cycle is a characteristic sequence in which goals become salient to a superordinate, types of power are applied by the superordinate, and modes of involvement are experienced by the subordinate. In *organizational* terms, a compliance cycle is the analogous sequence in the compliance structure relating an elite and lower participants, and related sequences in such organizational correlates of compliance structure as recruitment and socialization, elite structure and charisma, communication and cohesion.[2] Finally, in *systemic* terms a compliance cycle is a sequence of relationships among the external requirements and obligations of the organization, the internal arrangements through which the organization responds to these requirements, and the performance outcome, including the criteria and procedures for evaluating performance.[3] In this brief paper we limit ourselves primarily to the behavioral level of analysis, detailing the relationships among goals, power, and involvement, with only a summary statement of organizational correlates and systemic relationships.

Before presenting a detailed typology of goals, power, and involvement, it may be helpful to outline the causal relationships in the theory in general terms. The theory stipulates that certain kinds of goals are best pursued through certain types of power, because each type of power produces a given mode of involvement, and certain modes of involvement are best suited to achieving particular kinds of goals. When goals, power, and involvement are not congruent, the theory predicts that there will be a decline in performance, creating costs for the superordinates and thus a tendency for change toward congruence. There are two basic directions in which causation may flow. Moving downward, superordinates choose a set of goals, select a power mix they think will achieve those goals, and succeed in molding the involvement of the subordinates to gain compliance.

[1] Amitai Etzioni, *A Comparative Analysis of Complex Organizations* (New York: Free Press, 1961), p. 3.
[2] For an explanation of these variables, see Etzioni, Part II.
[3] For the systemic analysis on which this paper draws, see James D. Thompson, *Organizations in Action* (New York: McGraw-Hill, 1967).

Moving upward, subordinates tend uncontrollably toward a particular mode of involvement, forcing superordinates to change their power mix, and eventually also their immediate goals. Such successive changes in compliance structure are the focus of this paper.

Following the analysis of Amitai Etzioni, we distinguish among ideological goals, order goals, and economic goals. *Ideological* goals involve getting people to understand or believe the right things, or to do the right things voluntarily and for the right reasons. *Order* goals involve preventing people from doing the wrong things, more or less without regard to why they refrain from doing them, and without any expectation that they will make a positive contribution. *Economic* goals involve inducing people to produce and exchange goods and services. In similar fashion, we distinguish among normative, coercive, and remunerative power. Power is *normative* when it is based on persuasion, promises, and the manipulation of symbolic rewards. Power is *coercive* when it rests on the application or threat of physical sanctions or forceful deprivation of basic needs. Power is *remunerative* when it rests on the rationalized exchange of compliance for material rewards. To each of these kinds of power corresponds a kind of involvement. Normative power generates and is appropriate for manipulating *commitment*, or relatively intense and definitely positive involvement. Coercive power generates and is appropriate for restraining *alienation*, or relatively intense and definitely negative involvement. Remunerative power generates and is appropriate for influencing *indifference*, or involvement which is neither very positive nor very negative, and very low in intensity. Thus in this very simple typology of motivation, compliance results from either enthusiasm, fear, or acceptance of instructions within a calculatively established "zone of indifference." Each kind of goal may be pursued through the application of any kind of power, but for each kind of goal one type of power is particularly effective. Intense or prolonged application of normative power is effective in changing attitudes and is therefore fundamental to the achievement of ideological goals. Normative power will also sustain intense performance of activities for short periods of time, and is therefore useful for all kinds of goals in extraordinary compaigns or emergencies. Coercive power is relatively effective in deterring people from undesired activities, and is therefore particularly fundamental to the achievement of order goals. Coercive power will also sustain performance of activities for short periods of time, and is therefore also useful in emergencies. In the long run a steady background of coercion probably also contributes to attitude change and therefore to ideological goals. Remunerative power is particularly suited to maintaining the performance of activities over a long period of time, and is therefore particularly fundamental to the achievement of economic goals.

Quite obviously superordinates may pursue more than one kind of goal at a time, using more than one type of power, and producing mixed reactions on the part of subordinates. The possible mixed types for goals, power, and involvement may be diagrammed conveniently as shown in Figure 1. The many possible combinations among compound types of goals, power, and involvement which this typology opens up create complex problems and contradictory tendencies for managers of a compliance system. We argue that the "search" behavior of the Chinese Communist political system in

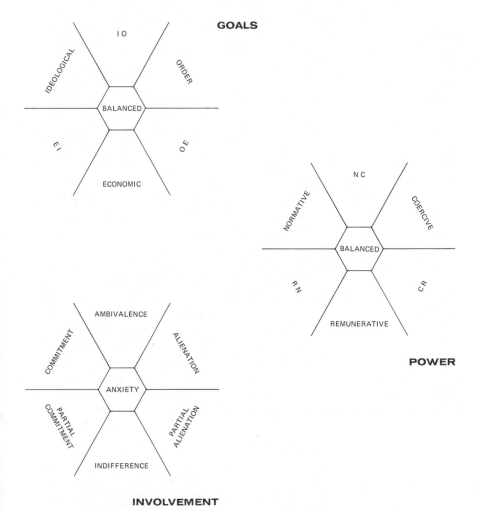

FIGURE 1.   *Typologies of goals, power, and involvement displayed on analogous fields.*

exploring after a compliance state which offers satisfactory returns on order, economic, and ideological goals is a symptom of significant contradictions among the compliance requirements of these goals, given the structure of Chinese society and the particular form of the Communist leadership's ambitions. As Cyert and March have pointed out, such contradictions are quite normal in large organizations, and are commonly handled in at least two ways: compartmentalization in space and sequential attention over time.[4] Compartmentalization in space is particularly unfeasible in a closely knit territorial system at the local level in rural Communist China, putting particular pressure on the other mechanism of adjustment, sequential attention over time. This is, in systemic terms, the basic cause of the compliance cycling we shall describe.

Having in hand definitions of the elements of a compliance system, we are now in a position to construct a formal model of compliance cycling. This may be done conveniently by constructing separate cycles for goals, power, and involvement, and then superimposing these cycles in order to study the pattern of coincidence among them. In this paper we must limit ourselves to considering the particular goal, power, and involvement cycles which we believe apply to Communist China between 1949 and 1968, and to the phases of the compliance cycle into which they concatenate.[5] These are the patterns which, in our argument, were recurrently generated by the particular distribution of power and interests which prevailed in China during this historical period.

As regards goals, the pattern of successive salience is that generated by moving clockwise around the goal field: E, EI, I, IO, O, OE. This *goal cycle* appears to be partially intentional and partially inadvertent. The exact priorities and trade-offs among these goals from the point of view of individuals or factions within the Party leadership has been both complex and inscrutable. However, the net result of the decision-making process, whatever it has been, may be described roughly as follows: While the regime (in common with all successful rulers) could not afford to ignore completely any of the three types of goals, it has, nonetheless, behaved as though when it achieved a satisfactory level of order it tried to maximize economic and ideological goals, favoring the latter whenever minimal

[4] Richard M. Cyert and James G. March, *A Behavioral Theory of the Firm* (Englewood Cliffs, N.J.: Prentice-Hall, 1963), Ch. 6.
[5] A completely general discussion would consider all the possible sequences in which goals and combinations of goals might become salient, all the possible sequences in which superordinates might shift their reliance among types and combinations of types of power, and all the possible sequences in which subordinates might move from one mode of involvement to another. Such a general discussion would also consider in detail all the possible combinations of each of these goal, power, and involvement cycles with one another.

attainment of the former permitted. Because of intervening variables in the compliance system to be described below, this tendency to sacrifice economics to ideology has led repeatedly to a crisis in the order and economic sectors. These preferences and their consequences are reflected in the formal features of the goal cycle diagrammed upper-left in Figure 2. Here rapid change in the goal mix is indicated by a thin line, slower change by a proportionately thicker line. It will be noted that the goal mix achieves relative stability during three periods of the cycle. One is seen at

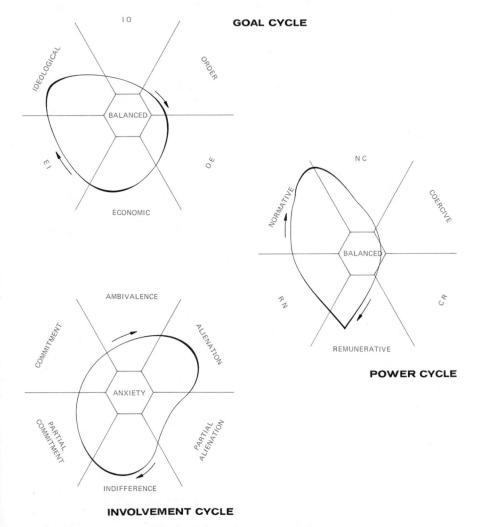

FIGURE 2.   *Models of the goal cycle, power cycle, and involvement cycle.*

the most extreme portion (i.e., that farthest from the Balanced sector) of the goal-mix trajectory, namely the tip of the "ostrich egg" in the lower portion of the I sector; it represents the goal mix which obtains during that happy portion of the upsurge when the effectiveness of the power mix and the commitment of the masses have not yet been called into question. A second temporal period during which goals change slowly comes when the trajectory is in the upper portion of the OE sector; it represents the goal mix—a relatively balanced one, it should be noted—preferred during the crisis phases. The third point of relative stability occurs during the relaxed, utilitarian phases when the goal mix settles into the left portion of the E sector.

As regards power, the pattern of successive emphasis is that generated by moving clockwise around the power field: R, RN, N, NC, C, CR. This *power cycle* appears to be generated by the alternation in power of leaders representing alternative philosophies of compliance, proponents of normative power being basically in the stronger position, but forced to accede to the proponents of remunerative power at those phases of the cycle in which economic performance and social order are dangerously impaired. Coercive power is relied upon by both sides to maintain production and order during the critical transition from the N to the R regimes. It should be stressed that the power cycle, like the goal cycle, is a matter of relative emphasis: a substantial fixed component of each kind of power is maintained throughout the cycle, with the leadership, insofar as it commands the resources, adjusting an additional variable component for particular purposes. There are two ways of looking at the power cycle, one stressing the joint effect of the three components of the power mix, the other stressing their separate movements. Stressing joint effect, the diagram at the center-right of Figure 2 shows the trajectory of the power cycle which is more or less typical for Communist China.[6] In the case of power, two periods of relative stability in the mix occur. One is seen at the most extreme (that is, the least balanced) portion of the leaf-shaped trajectory, where the tip of the leaf overlaps the N and NC sectors: this represents the power mix during the high tide of the cycle. The other period of slow change in the power mix is represented by the thickened portion of the trajectory near the stem of the leaf—the predominantly R mix, with more N than C, of the liberal phases of the cycle. Stressing movement of separate components, a generalized time-flow model of an NCR power cycle, and

---

[6] The power-mix field, it should be noted, has three coordinate axes—N, C and R— each radiating from the center of the field and bisecting its sector. The three axes, with 120 degrees between them, define a field the units of which are equilateral triangles instead of squares. The leaf-shaped curve shown in Figures 2, 4, and 5 is a plotting on this field of the values built into the time-flow diagrams in Figures 3 and 6.

the particular form approximating those which have occurred in Communist China, are both shown in Figure 3. Using the former as a foil, we may note in the latter the over-all high level of N, a relative restraint in the use of R even at its maximum, and a reluctance to employ large amounts of C (except, as we shall note below, against a small percentage of the population). Both the maximum and minimum are shown highest for N, intermediate for R, and lowest for C. The power cycle in Communist China is further defined by a "stretching out," relative to the

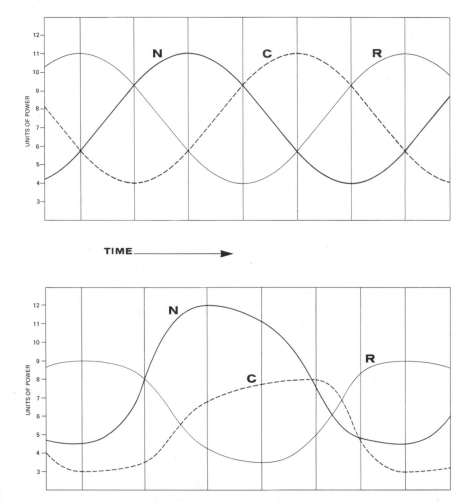

FIGURE 3.   *Top: Time-flow model of a perfectly regular power cycle. Bottom: Time-flow model of a power cycle modified to fit the Chinese case.*

generalized cycle, of the phases when N predominates in the mix, and a foreshortening of those in which the proportion of C is relatively high.

As regards involvement, the pattern of succession is that generated by moving clockwise around the involvement field: indifference, partial commitment, commitment, ambivalence, alienation, partial alienation, and back to indifference. This *involvement cycle* is, in the Chinese case, typically precipitated by an increase in normative power, applied in order to communicate and instill a new set of goals and to elicit performance in service of those goals. Most lower participants respond to this campaign with some increase in intensity and positiveness of involvement. Under successive applications of normative power, however, those who share the regime's goals are likely to move well into commitment, while those who do not will bend around into ambivalence and alienation. As the campaign comes to seem more and more shrill in its threats and promises and less and less substantial in its accomplishments, an increasing number of lower participants move over into alienation. Only when economic goals become salient again and normative power is replaced by remunerative power do these subordinates become mollified and drift back again to indifference, thereby completing the involvement cycle. A fairly typical involvement cycle is diagramed at the lower left in Figure 2.[7] Thickening in the kidney-shaped trajectory indicates the two phases of the cycle when involvement is relatively stable: during the latter stages of the crisis when alienation is great, and during the liberal phase when involvement is one of calculative indifference.

Having constructed separate cycles for goals, power, and involvement, we may now superimpose them to construct a compliance cycle. Figure 4 shows the superimposition of the power and involvement cycles. At the broadest level of analysis, this superimposition reveals three major interactions between power and involvement. During the first third of the cycle (on Figure 4, approximately from the beginning of segment 3 through segment 14) power "pulls" involvement to higher intensity, which is to say that changes in the power mix designed to induce commitment on the part of lower participants are successful. During the second third of the cycle (on Figure 4, approximately from the beginning of segment 15

---

[7] The involvement field is set apart by its formal features from the goal and power fields. It has a single vertical dimension, namely intensity of involvement, increasing from low at the bottom to high at the top. The horizontal dimension is direction of involvement, neither positive nor negative at the center of the field, increasingly positive as one moves leftward from the center, increasingly negative as one moves rightward. The typology imposed on this field, which yields 7 types of involvement, omits the two logical possibilities which are theoretically anomalous and presumably empirically rare: involvement which is at once low in intensity and extremely positive, and that which is low in intensity and extremely negative.

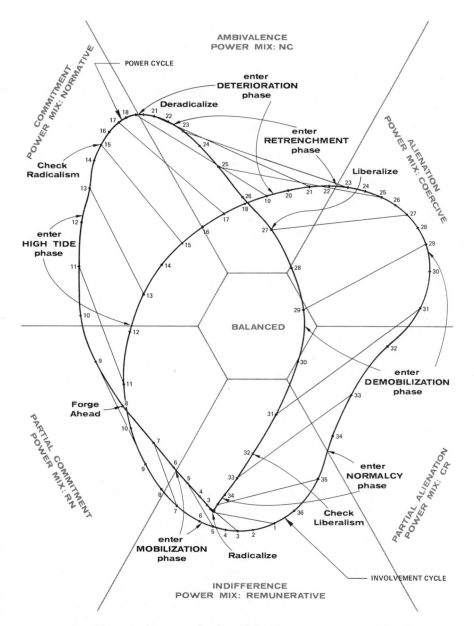

FIGURE 4. *The compliance cycle: Interaction between power and involvement and the sequence of compliance phases.*

The entire span of the power cycle has been subdivided into 36 equal time segments, defined and numbered so that Segment 1 begins when the R component of the power mix is at a minimum. The 36 segments into which the involvement and goal cycles have also been subdivided are synchronized with those of the power cycle.

420 ORGANIZATIONAL CHANGE

through segment 29), involvement begins by constraining power and eventually "pulls" it to a more balanced and more nearly congruent mix. During the last third (from the beginning of segment 29 through segment 2), power "overtakes" involvement and once again leads it, this time to lower intensity; the changes in the power mix designed to reduce alienation are successful.

While these three movements of power and involvement capture in a general way the rhythm of advance and retreat of the Chinese political system, a finer division of the cycle based on somewhat different criteria will facilitate descriptive analysis. This scheme yields six phases, of which the first, third, and fifth are inaugurated when involvement enters, respectively, the Indifference, Commitment, and Alienation sectors, while the second, fourth, and sixth begin when the power mix enters, respectively, the RN, NC, and CR sectors. The designations for these phases and for the three pairings of them which reflect the broader picture are:

P6	Demobilization	} liberal phases
P1	Normalcy	
P2	Mobilization	} radical phases
P3	High Tide	
P4	Deterioration	} crisis phases
P5	Retrenchment	
P6	Demobilization	} liberal phases
P1	Normalcy	

It may be noted that the two radical phases are that portion of the cycle when the power mix is in the RN and N sectors, the crisis phases are that portion when the power mix is in NC or C, while the liberal phases are that portion when the power mix is CR or R.

If we now superimpose the goal and power cycles, as in Figure 5, we can discern the *policy cycle* which they together define. The major point here is that for the greater part of the compliance cycle the effective power mix does not match the goals being pursued very exactly. While a moderate shift in goals during the Normalcy phase inaugurates the power cycle and goals "lead" power at an only modest distance during the first six time segments, thereafter accelerating changes in the power mix "overtake" changes in the goal mix and power remains more radical than goals until well into Demobilization. During the ascent, the power mix has a higher component of both N and C than would be appropriate for prevailing goals, while its normative component remains unsuitably high during the descent as well.

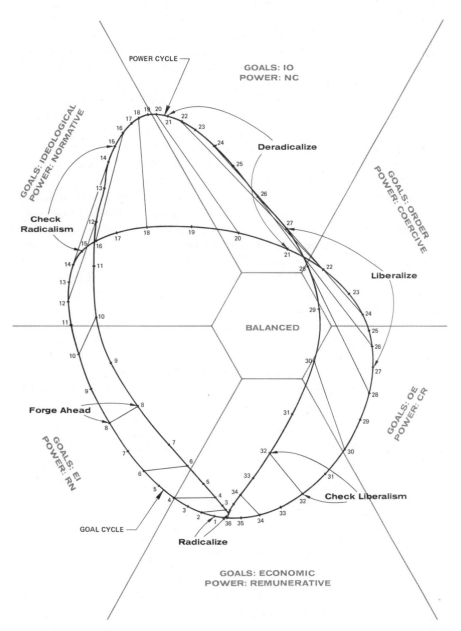

FIGURE 5. *The policy cycle: Interaction between goals and power and the sequence of policy decisions.*

These features reflect our impression of what has occurred repeatedly in Communist China. The discrepancy between power and goals which develops during the radical phases rests on an ideological tenet of the N-proponents which holds that the proper kind of normative power properly administered is more efficacious than remunerative power in achieving economic as well as ideological ends. In affirming the power of socialist thinking to achieve production victories, the regime propagates policies and encourages procedures which are unrealistically related to goals. It would appear, furthermore, that the barrage of propaganda accompanying the radical phases colors the perceptions of lower-level cadres, who begin to see miracles and report them to superiors. Others succumb to pressure for performance by consciously over-reporting, thereby further masking the discrepancy. Readjustment in the power mix during the crisis phases is slow not only because problems of face make it difficult to enunciate or implement abrupt policy changes, not only because of the lingering belief that whatever went wrong did so because of poor implementation rather than poor theory, but also because N-proponents fail to encourage feedback for fear that the full facts will discredit them. Thus, aspects of the power struggle which typically develops during the crisis phases as R-proponents challenge the incumbents further retard the reduction of power-goal discrepancy.

A formal analysis of the NCR power cycle suggests six critical turning points, each occurring when one of the components of the power mix is at its peak or its nadir in relation to the other two. It would appear that critical political decisions mark these turning points in the changing power mix, and these are incorporated into our model as the Six Decisions:

Decision to	Occurring When the Following Ratio Is at a Maximum
Radicalize	R / N+C
Forge Ahead	R+N / C
Curb Radicalism	N / C+R
Deradicalize	N+C / R
Liberalize	C / N+R
Curb Liberalism	C+R / N

We may now gather the various strands of our analysis together through a phase-by-phase tour of our generic model of the compliance cycle in Communist China. The reader may wish to refer back to the diagrammatic representations of the relationship between power and involvement in Figure 4, between goals and power in Figure 5, and to the time-flow

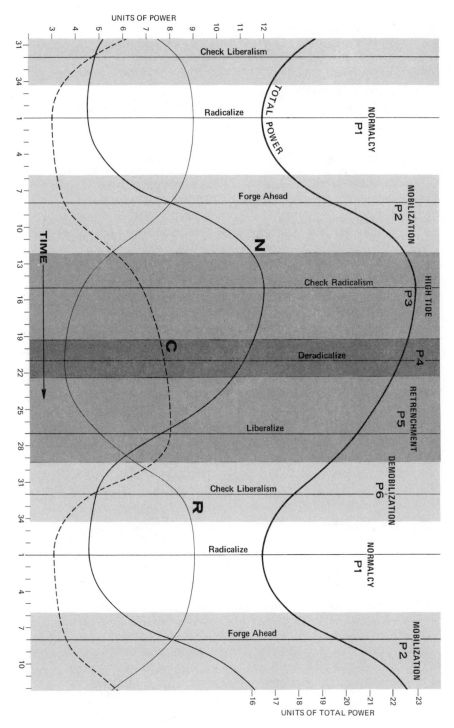

FIGURE 6. *Time-flow model of the Chinese power cycle, with policy decisions and compliance phases superimposed.*

representation in Figure 6, which displays the Six Decisions and the six compliance phases against the rising and falling curves of the N, C, and R components of the power cycle.

Phase One, Normalcy, begins when involvement, recovering from the intensity and negative feelings generated by the previous cycle, crosses again into the Indifference sector of low intensity and neutral feelings. As total power input approaches its minimum, the system settles into equilibrium. Goals, power, and involvement are roughly congruent, with none producing any significant tendencies toward change in either of the others. It is during this liberal phase that China most closely resembles a "normal" agrarian society going about its usual peasant business. With this recovery, N proponents within the elite again seize the initiative. Just as N and C reach their minimum relative to R, the atmosphere is tightened by the Decision to Radicalize, inaugurating a new cycle. Goals, in other words, move leftward toward ideology, pulling power somewhat toward the normative, which in turn has a slight positive effect on involvement.

Phase Two, Mobilization, begins as power crosses into the RN sector, R proponents having definitely lost their ability to contain the N proponents. Mobilization sees rapid changes in the power mix—changes which overshoot goals and are relatively effective in raising involvement to high positive levels. Although considerable strain between power and involvement characterizes the entire phase, the moving compliance structure approximates the congruent type whereby a predominantly RN power mix elicits partial commitment. The Decision to Forge Ahead, which determines the general goals of the big push to come and enumerates the highly normative strategies for achieving them, comes when C-power is' at a relative minimum and R-power is still being maintained at high levels. Policies which it inaugurates accelerate the ascent of C and the descent of R.

Phase Three, High Tide, begins as involvement, responding to the normative blandishments of the previous mobilization phase, moves into Commitment. Total power input reaches its maximum, C continuing to rise, R continuing to fall, and N reaching its peak. Power continues to be more radical than goals, while in the course of the phase involvement begins to constrain power. That is, the structure of compliance slips in the course of Phase Three from an effective one in which normative power and committed involvement are congruent, to a less effective one in which normative power must contend with the increasing disaffection and ambivalence of the peasantry. The Decision to Check Radicalism, which at midphase moderates the big push, leads to a downturn in the input of N power and deceleration in the rates at which R- and C-power are changing.

Phase Four, Deterioration, begins as power, responding to the growing recalcitrance of lower participants, moves over into the NC sector. Deterioration is a period of impending crisis: lower participants are becoming speedily more alienated, and in response the goal mix moves rapidly from I toward O. Change in the power mix is sluggish, however, for reasons already suggested; N power is reduced, but R remains low and steady, C high and steady. As a result, the discrepancy between power (NC) and involvement (ambivalence) widens throughout the phase. In these straits, N-proponents have no choice but to deradicalize, which decision is the R-proponents' entering wedge.

Phase Five, Retrenchment, begins as involvement, unmollified by the too little and too late curbing of radical excesses, moves squarely into alienation. During retrenchment the crisis comes to a head. Faced with serious alienation among the peasantry and shocked by production declines, the leadership forgets its scruples and effects a radical and rapid change in the power mix: N is phased out in favor of R, and with the Decision to Liberalize, C too is allowed to decline. Shortly after a period of fleeting congruence, when a maximally coercive power mix impinges on alienated peasants, power "overtakes" involvement and begins leading it to lower intensity. The crisis is then past.

Phase Six, Demobilization, begins as power, overtaking involvement and beginning to reduce alienation through a steeply rising component of remuneration, moves into the CR sector. C plummets and N eases into a less precipitous decline. The Decision to Check Liberalism slows the rate of change of all three components, setting in train the policies which cause them to level off in the subsequent phase of Normalcy.

This schematization, it should be emphasized, is specific to the temporal patterning of compliance arrangements at a particular level of periodicity and level of institutional significance in the compliance system of Communist China. Compliance cycles may occur at many levels, ranging from the diurnal, marketing-week, seasonal and annual schedules whereby work and leisure in agricultural China are arranged, through the cycles accompanying major campaigns to transform particular institutions, to the grand eras of new democratic revolution, socialist construction, and cultural revolution into which the Chinese Communists themselves periodize their own history. Such cycles may or may not be causally related to each other, they may or may not be similar in the nature and sequence of their phases, and they may or may not be related to secular change. We would argue that cycles of different lengths occur in the compliance arrangements surrounding components of the social system lying at different levels of generality. The more fundamental the component, the longer the cycle.[8]

[8] Cf. Neil J. Smelser, *Theory of Collective Behavior* (New York: Free Press, 1963), Ch. 2; and Anthony Downs, *Inside Bureaucracy* (Boston: Little, Brown, 1967), Ch. 14.

SYSTEM AND CYCLE IN CHINA

The particular level of cycling treated here is a specific consequence of the succession of campaigns through which the Chinese Communists have attempted to revolutionize Chinese society. As need hardly be said, socialism and communism are themselves prescriptive compliance theories, and these campaigns therefore have precisely to do with the alteration of compliance arrangements. As such, these campaigns and their often unanticipated compliance consequences are easy to identify, being a matter of explicit historical record. Nevertheless we feel there is something to be gained from their analysis in terms of organizational theory, in particular a more systematic analysis of the internal dynamics of each campaign, and a more complete statement of the organizational correlates of these instances of compliance cycling.

On our analysis there have been eight cycles of radicalization and deradicalization at the national level in the 19 years since the People's Republic of China was established. The dating of these cycles, which lasted two or three years each, is indicated by the following dates for the first, third, and fifth of the six decisions.

	Decision to Radicalize (Normalcy)	Decision to Check Radicalism (High Tide)	Decision to Liberalize (Retrenchment)	Decision to Radicalize (Normalcy)[9]
C1	Winter 1949–1950	Fall 1950	Spring 1951	Fall 1951
C2	Fall 1951	Summer 1952	Spring 1953	Fall 1953
C3	Fall 1953	Summer 1954	Winter 1954–1955	Spring 1955
C4	Spring 1955	Spring 1956	Fall 1956	Summer 1957
C5	Summer 1957	Winter 1958–1959	Spring 1959	Summer 1959
C6	Summer 1959	Spring 1960	Winter 1960–1961	Fall 1962
C7	Fall 1962	Winter 1963–1964	Winter 1964–1965	Fall 1965
C8	Fall 1965	Winter 1966–1967	Summer 1968	

Drastic reforms in rural society were being pushed only in cycles 1, 4, 5, and 6. Other cycles saw major developments in urban China, accompanied in the countryside by efforts to mop-up after the last major reform or prepare for the next one.

The restructuring of rural society which occurred during the first decade of Communist rule involved five stages. We shall relate these stages to cycles after briefly characterizing each stage. During the *first stage*, land reform, the entire farming population was divided into five classes: landless farmhands, "poor," "middle," and "rich" peasants, and landlords. In this

[9] The decision to radicalize is listed twice for the convenience of the reader, since it ends the previous cycle as well as inaugurating the one to come.

stage the first four categories were mobilized to struggle against the land-lords, the economic basis of whose power and prestige was destroyed through confiscation of land, livestock, and equipment. When this stage was over, some 60 million households, about half the total number of rural families, had benefited through redistribution, and the previous local elite had been eliminated as a class. The *second stage* saw the formation of mutual-aid teams, normally composed of 6–15 households. As first organized, these were usually seasonal and temporary, involving only limited reciprocity with regard to labor, draft animals and farm tools. Most teams were subsequently transformed into permanent units involving unrestricted use of these production factors. If completed everywhere, this stage would have reduced the total number of basic production units from 120 million to approximately 15 million. The *third stage* involved the formation of small agricultural producers' cooperatives, in which the peasant household invested its land, draft animals and tools, receiving dividends for their use. At the same time, the "rich-peasant economy" was brought to an end. Better-off households which prior to land reform owned more land than they tilled, the so-called "rich" peasants, were singled out as enemies of the masses and their surplus land confiscated for the new cooperative. If completed everywhere, the new cooperative production unit of 20–40 households would have numbered approximately 3.5 million. The *fourth stage* typically involved the merger of the small agricultural producers' cooperatives into larger collective farms. This stage saw massive restrictions on the family-farm economy for, in the collective, income was distributed not according to the holdings which each household had contributed but according to the labor performed by the working adults in each family. At the conclusion of this stage over 93 percent of all rural households belonged to approximately 750,000 collectives. The *fifth stage* was that of people's communes, production units so greatly enlarged that they could be merged with the basic-level units of government administration. As in the first and third stages, the topmost remaining class became the object of political and economic discrimination. At High Tide in late 1958 there were 24,000 communes.

These five stages were passed through in the course of the first five cycles. However, stage and cycle are not in perfect alignment. First, many localities and even entire regions skipped one or more stages altogether. Thus approximately two-fifths of rural households were never grouped into mutual-aid teams, while the third stage of lower-level cooperatives was skipped by a majority of both localities and households. In Szechwan and parts of other provinces, most localities went directly from cooperatives to communes, skipping the collective stage. Second, different localities passed through particular stages during different cycles. Thus, while land reform was carried out in most parts of China in C1, in many of the "old liberated areas" it had been completed in 1947–1949, while in many of the "new liberated areas" in the South and Southwest it was substantially completed only in C2. Similarly, mutual-aid teams were set up in precocious areas in C1, in most areas in C2, and in backward areas not until C3. By C5, however, most localities were on the same schedule. There remained, of course, variation in the alacrity and effectiveness with which local cadres executed directives. In general there seems to have been less variation in the timing of local policy cycles than in the extent of actual policy implementation and corresponding severity of the involvement cycle.

Let us now provide a quick review of compliance cycling in the countryside. Liberation in most parts of the country was followed by a retreat from coercion and recourse to R-power, in particular through the rent reduction program. Once the goodwill of the peasantry had been secured in this fashion (that is, as soon as their orientation to the regime had been brought around to one at least as positive as calculative involvement), mobilization for land reform (C1P2) was inaugurated. The intensity of peasant involvement was rapidly raised during P2–3, climaxing with the struggle meetings against landlords. Recourse to coercion, which began to rise with the antidespot program of P3, approached its peak when the property of landlords was confiscated in P4. Excesses in the treatment of landlords had by this time led to anxiety and revulsion on the part of many peasants (that is, their involvement had swung around to ambivalence), while fear of being stigmatized as "rich peasants" had depressed the productive zeal of many less impoverished families within the peasantry. R-power began to rise again as confiscated land was redistributed, while the concerted effort to round up "criminal and counter-revolutionary elements" was the final manifestation of C before it was allowed to plummet. With the issuance of title deeds, peasant involvement was allowed to recede to a state of low intensity, and the renewed salience of economic goals was expressed in the production drive inaugurated in P6. That the power mix had become predominantly R was apparent by July 1951, when a prominent Communist leader criticized cadres for persisting in utopianism instead of encouraging the peasants to get rich.[10]

Cycle Two, 1951–1953, was severe in the city and mild in the countryside, except of course in those areas where land reform was only then in progress. Although radicalization came in the cities in the fall of 1951, the Decision to Radicalize in rural China may be taken as the directive on formation of mutual-aid teams issued by the Central Committee of the Chinese Communist Party on 15 December 1951. A primary concern of

[10] Po I-po. Cited in Kenneth R. Walker, "Collectivization in Retrospect," *China Quarterly*, 26 (1966), p. 11.

the top leadership was the erosion of the political base built up in the villages during land reform because of the withdrawal from political involvement and preoccupation with economic gain on the part of both peasants and cadres. Mobilization was inaugurated through a transition in the emulation campaign to increase production from an emphasis on the superior moral qualities of peasant labor heroes to an emphasis on the superiority of collective organization. High Tide objectives in various areas included formation of mutual-aid teams, water conservancy projects and experiments with lower-level cooperatives. These organizational objectives were linked to such ideological campaigns as that to "aid Korea, resist America." Despite the relative modesty of these objectives and the air of caution and experiment with which they were approached, P4 saw the deterioration of cadre leadership characteristic of later, more severe cycles. Peasants were sometimes forced to join mutual-aid teams by threatening to expel them from peasant associations or by denying loans to the recalcitrant. Discrimination against individual independent farmers and violation of middle peasants' interests in teams had, as admitted by the Party in the wake of the campaign, "injured the incentive to produce." Other evidence of peasant disaffection in P5 was the "blind flow" of peasants into the cities and the rising death rate among draft animals due to overwork and neglect. P6 accordingly saw a campaign against "bureaucracy, commandism and violations of socialist laws and discipline" among cadres at the county level and above, while a milder course of education in Party principles and methods was conducted among the nascent organizations at the lowest levels. Also during C2P6, with the repudiation of coercion and renewed salience of economic goals, mutual-aid teams which had been made permanent during radicalization reverted to the seasonal type during liberalization, an early example of the two-steps-forward one-step-backward rhythm characteristic of the next three cycles as well.

The Decision to Radicalize inaugurating C3 was the introduction of state control of the purchase and sale of grain following the 1953 harvest. Mobilization began in the winter of 1953–1954, with High Tide in most areas the winter of 1954–1955. The national target for cooperatives set in the directive of December 1953 and 35,800, raised to 500,000 by September 1954, and reaching 630,000 by February 1955 when the campaign was called off. No less than a fifth of all peasant households had been organized. This effort, immense by comparison with that of C2, generated cadre "errors" and peasant disaffection on a correspondingly larger scale. As in the course of 1954 cadres felt increasingly pressed to demonstrate the superiority of cooperative organization, some forced middle peasants to join in order to appropriate their productive resources. The winter of 1954–1955 (C3P4–5) was notable for the neglect, sale, or slaughter of livestock. Other evidence of peasant alienation was reluctance during the winter slack season to improve land and maintain water-control installations, failure to collect and apply fertilizer, and a reduction in the total area sown to winter grain crops. The decision of February 1955 to liberalize was forced by a growing shortage of grain and the recognition that, in the words of the *People's Daily*, "there is nobody to take charge of spring plowing and production." Spring 1955 (C3P6) saw reintroduction of material incentives to overcome recalcitrance in spring sowing, together with a renewed emphasis on the productive significance of well-to-do peasants. Reversion to less socialist forms of organization occurred on a wide scale, Mao himself reporting that in Chekiang 15,000 out of 53,000 cooperatives had been dissolved. Normalcy extended through the autumn harvest, as provincial leaders laid plans to carry into effect Mao's dramatic Decision to Radicalize of late July.

With the lines of command to the basic levels more or less in place, in late 1955 the Party leadership was for the first time in a position to order reorganization more or less simultaneously across the entire nation. This, in the course of cycles 4 and 5, it did. Whereas only half of all peasant households had been involved in the reorganization of cycle 3, when in autumn 1955 a good harvest enabled the radicals to Forge Ahead the consequent socialist upsurge of cycle 4 carried over three-fifths of all peasant households had been involved in the reorganizations of cycle 3, tion in May 1956, less than a tenth of the peasantry remained outside either cooperatives or collectives. Given the speed, scope, and extremism of the campaign, cadres were forced to rely significantly on coercion, including arbitrary deduction of wage points, refusal to assign people jobs, increases in tax assessments, denial of access to irrigation facilities, freezing bank deposits and arbitrary increase in delivery quotas. Troops appeared to "aid agriculture," and security defense committees were established to protect from sabotage the trees, equipment, granaries, and crops now owned by the collectives. C4P4 saw indiscriminate slaughter of livestock and another mass exodus to the cities. Despite substantial evidence of peasant disaffection, the new organizational machinery was kept in place, the Decision to Check Radicalism taking the form of a stream of directives adjusting the prices for specific crops, and instructing cadres not to neglect the breeding of animals and the cultivation of crops other than grain. The fall of 1956 saw new directives "strengthening production leadership and organization construction" in the face of obvious difficulties on the part of cadres in carrying out their new managerial responsibilities, combined with some relaxation in government control of rural markets. Further concessions to liberalism followed in the spring of 1957, peaking in the rural areas in the early summer with an expansion in the size of private plots. In urban China the political pendulum had already begun to swing leftward, however, following the alarming criticism voiced during the brief liberal "100 flowers" period. A severe antirightist campaign was launched in the late spring in the urban areas, reaching rural China in the fall in the somewhat milder form of a "socialist education campaign."

Although basic decisions about the direction which Chinese agriculture should take apparently hung in the balance from the fall of 1957 until the spring of 1958, the fall and winter of 1957 was a classic mobilization phase, combining the campaign to educate the peasants in socialism with extensive mobilization of labor for work on water conservancy projects. Following hesitancy on the part of some and daring organizational innovation on the part of others, this mobilization snow-balled into the classic cycle of them all, the Great Leap Forward and communization. Between the Decision to Forge Ahead of August and the Decision to Check Radicalism of December, the enthusiasm of local cadres for their burgeoning organizational empires, and to a significant extent the enthusiasm of poor and lower-middle peasants for free supply and instant modernization, swept rural China forward to the threshold of communism. Or at least so it seemed. A bumper harvest in the fall of 1958 and a timely retrenchment in the spring of 1959 left the issue in doubt. Opponents of the strategy of mass mobilization argued at a decisive meeting in August 1959 that despite the tidying-up they had received, communes were "a mess." They lost. With preparations for the 10th anniversary of the Chinese People's Republic, with a revived stress on the significance of class struggle and the necessity for purifying the leadership cores at the basic levels, and with a renewed drive for production in both industry and agriculture, the Great Leap Forward lumbered off into a second cycle of radicalization, crisis and retreat. What exactly the involvement cycle was doing is difficult to piece together, but it is doubtful that the peasants were greatly mollified by the aborted liberalization of the spring of 1959 or greatly enthused by the exhausting reradicalization of fall 1959 to fall 1960. It is likely that some dip in their alienation did occur, however, as cadres were rectified in the winter of 1959–1960 for having pushed the peasants too hard and for having imposed collective institutions to which the peasants objected. In the fall of 1960 it became clear that, owing to bad weather, misallocation of resources and declining incentives, agricultural output was catastrophically low. In November Deradicalization was launched with a campaign to rectify the "five Communist styles" among overbearing cadres. As the countryside passed through a winter of hunger, alienation, and disorder, the 9th Plenum of January 1961 embarked on a program of full-scale liberalization.

The seventh cycle in rural Communist China began with the radicalizing communique of the 10th Plenum, held in September 1962. This cycle got off to a long slow start, reminiscent of the long transition between the land reform and collectivization cycles. An important issue was, once again, whether the basic-level cadres were sufficiently skilled to carry a mass movement to the people. Between 1952 and 1954 the Party had first rectified its special district and county organizations, educated its basic-level cadres to their tasks, and then proceeded with mass mobilization. Between 1962 and 1964 the regime, having been forced temporarily to abandon mass mobilization, tried to re-educate its basic-level cadres and, after disappointing results from both mild and severe approaches, turned again to rectify the county levels and above. The basic-level cadres, having only partially recovered from their alienation at the severe rectifications through which they were put in the course of the retreat from the Great Leap Forward, were subjected first to an educative mobilization (September 1962–September 1964), then to a sharp rectification at the hands of higher Party officials and the newly-formed Poor and Lower-Middle Peasant Associations (September 1964–January 1965), and then again to more lenient treatment. The major point for our purposes is that, for the peasantry itself, cycle 7 never really got off the ground. Except for tentative moves to restrict the free market and reduce the size of private plots, radicalization consisted only of exhortatory socialist education campaigns, and the attempt to repair the rural Party organization.

The latest cycle, and the one most obscure in its implications for the rural areas, is of course the Great Proletarian Cultural Revolution. Although the relationship among these events is unclear, it appears that Mao was disappointed in the result of various campaigns to get the country moving again, and turned to rectify the highest levels of the Party organization, while attempting to assemble the leadership for a new mass movement at the basic levels through an alliance of young radicals, disadvantaged workers, PLA personnel and the more radical "old" cadres. The countryside, largely insulated from the radical phases of the Cultural Revolution in the urban areas in 1966, became briefly involved in January 1967, and perhaps more substantially involved in the spring of 1968. Although the Cultural Revolution has clearly moved on to something of a retrenchment phase, it is too early to present a consecutive account of compliance policy in the countryside during this cycle.

THE SIX PHASES: ORGANIZATIONAL CORRELATES

Having reviewed the history of compliance cycling in Communist China, we must now turn to the organizational content and systemic context of each of the six phases of the cycle. All the elements of the generic account which follows do not necessarily occur in full or at all in all cycles, or in all phases of any cycle.

Phase One: Normalcy. During Normalcy the State and Party organizations bear their lightest loads. Projects to revolutionize rural society overnight are temporarily set aside. While economic objectives are pursued, many of the decisions and most of the tasks of agriculture are decentralized into private hands. The task environment of the organization is perceived as the routine technical inputs required for increased agricultural production. Viewing the problem under a long time horizon, policy makers apply a long-linked technology involving development of a chemical fertilizer industry, mechanization of farming, and long-term programs to raise the level of technical education of the peasants. The complex interdependencies among farming operations themselves, among the agricultural and other sectors of the economy, and among the economic and other aspects of modernization are appreciated, and coordination is attempted through standardization, planning, and mutual adjustment. The appropriate local leaders are therefore those with the relevant technical skills: the most able farmers and such government agents as agricultural extension workers. At the local level the scope (the number of activities in which lower participants jointly participate) of government-led organizations is at its most narrow, and their pervasiveness (the number of activities inside and outside the organization for which the organization tries to set norms) is at its lowest. Recruitment to positions of leadership is differentiated in both means and criteria by self-selection: the most able farmers again become the economic leaders of the natural farming community, while only the dedicated activists compete for Party membership. In regard to both instrumental and expressive activities, the role of the cadres is limited to that of officials who supervise and regulate activities which they do not organize and lead. Communication between cadres and peasants is slight and restricted to instrumental matters, a balance of upward flow of reports on tasks and output and downward flow of routine instructions and indirect incentives. Charisma in the organization is limited to the very top, to the idea of The Party and its Great Leader, Mao Tse-tung. There is little pressure for the recruitment of the population at large into collective economic organizations or into the Party and its mass organizations. Accordingly, socialization is largely informal and largely restricted to instrumental matters. The level of consensus demanded from the masses does not go actively beyond agreement on work assignments and output quotas. Cohesion in work groups of lower participants is entirely derived from extra-organization affiliations; the salience of membership in formal organizations is at a minimum in the lives of the populace. Locality-wide solidarity among peasants is defined in traditional terms, a by-product of the conflicts and alliances in the segmentary structure of a traditional Chinese community. The economic rationality of both the traditional farming methods employed and the few innovations being pushed result in an agricultural performance which is basically both efficient in its use of resources and effective in meeting the needs of the country.

  Phase Two: Mobilization. Mobilization is a period of organizational expansion. Ideological objectives are revived, and normative means are again applied to economic ends. The task environment of the organization is perceived as one of both technical and social opportunity, a promise of increased output through investment and capital formation on the one hand, and through mass mobilization on the other. To meet this medium-run opportunity a mediating technology is applied, the government acting as entrepreneur in bringing together under-utilized labor and capital. The scope of government organizations widens as they seize the initiative in capital construction projects and drives to increase production. Pervasiveness rises as socialist norms are set for these activities and for related activities outside of organization boundaries. Recruitment to leadership positions is stepped up, while both selectivity and socialization are brought to bear through a rectification of the leaders of the basic levels of the Party and mass organizations. Credentials for leadership combine the led and the expert. Cadres increase their participation in instrumental activities, mobilizing informal instrumental leaders to greater efforts. They also increase their efforts at expressive leadership, conducting campaigns among the masses to secure attitude change and increase production. With the expansion of organizational functions, the volume of communication between cadre and peasants increases through mass meetings and study sessions, becoming expressive as well as instrumental, the downward flow of ideology and instructions outweighing the upward flow of information about local conditions. Similarly, the volume of internal communication between organizational levels increases through face-to-face and telephone conferences. With the role of the Party hierarchy and Party line in directing social action again stressed, the aura of charisma surrounding the Party chain of command intensifies. As for the masses, recruitment to membership in economic and political organizations rises, becoming less selective, excluding only those with definitely bad expressive credentials. Although there is some tendency on the part of cadres to exclude from production organizations those with poor instrumental credentials (that is, the less able farmers and those without animals or equipment), the government insists on discrimination in their favor, since by and large these are the poor and lower-middle peasants who are the vanguards of socialism. The level of consensus demanded of lower participants rises to include at first the terms of participation in collective organizations, and later the new methods and goals of these organizations. With the mandatory rise in the level of collective endeavor comes an effort to define socialist norms of cohesion within work groups; with the expansion in the size of collective units comes an effort to promote solidarity within the revolutionary ranks. The government's attempt to make the performance of agriculture more effective shows real results, owing both to the rise in investment and the increase in labor input.

Phase Three: High Tide. High Tide finds the organization at its maximal expansion. Ideological goals and ideological means are both at their peak. The task environment of the organization is perceived almost entirely in terms of the manipulation of collective motivation, the seizing of the opportunity to transform both nature and society through the collective mobilization of will-power. An intensive technology is applied to these short-run problems, with little appreciation of problems of interdependence, and little effort devoted to coordination. Scope is, in principle, unlimited: as many activities as possible should be carried out through collective action. As a result, both the salience of participation in formal organization, and the tensions generated by that participation, are at their highest. However, these tensions are successfully channeled into constructive action by defining sentiments of struggle as the driving force of revolutionary accomplishment. Pervasiveness is also, in principle, unlimitedly high: there is no aspect of life which ought to be immune from the demands of socialist morality. Cadres now wholly usurp both the instrumental and expressive functions of informal leaders, the ethos of the new socialist community denying all legitimacy to the natural community and its leaders. The credentials for cadre leadership shift toward the expressive; charisma spreads across this rank of professionals in the art of sparking revolutionary transformation. Authority is decentralized so that local leaders can give full play to their charismatic powers and reap full benefit from the particular revolutionary topography of their locality. As for the masses, recruitment now aspires to the totally inclusive: even former landlords and rich peasants are now admitted. Efforts at expressive resocialization therefore continue unabated. Organizational effectiveness requires not only consensus on organizational goals, but on general values as well: in the absence of remunerative incentives, commitment to ideology is the only basis for action. Work-group cohesion is in theory absolute: there is no distinction among the role of worker, soldier, and citizen. Solidarity within the revolutionary ranks is also theoretically absolute, not only within the greatly expanded local community, but also in the nation at large. The performance outcome of these efforts is difficult to evaluate in the short run from an economic point of view, and in any case the criteria of performance applied are neither those of efficiency nor those of effectiveness, but an extrinsic standard of the socialist correctness of the productive efforts themselves. There is, indeed, progress in attitude change, in breaking through traditional habits and inhibitions, and in widening the definition of the political community.

Phase Four: Deterioration. Deterioration is a phase of incipient contraction of organizational responsibilities and energies. The task environment has become moderately unstable and moderately threatening: there are fears of both instrumental and expressive sabotage on the part of "bad elements" who have sneaked into the organization. The remedy is, however, "more of the same": purify the leadership cores by rectifying deviations, and renew the flagging campaign. Readings on most organizational variables continue to be the same as in Phase Three. However, tension, which increases under conditions of scarcity and growing problems of managing over-large collective units, begins to break out as antagonism to leaders and among subcollectivities, instead of being channeled into socialist construction. Formal leaders continue to override informal leaders in both instrumental and expressive domains, but as the upsurge of enthusiasm ebbs they become less effective in their roles. Their charisma is diminished by their association with instrumental activities, their extensive interaction with lower participants, the intimation of failure, the demands they are forced to make on lower participants, and, in some cases, their corruption and abuse of authority. Among the masses, dissensus develops as departures from traditional norms become unsettling to many, the feasibility of attaining organization goals comes to be doubted, and the unwisdom of many of the recent social and technical innovations begins to become clear. Thus dissensus focuses on organizational means, and increasingly on the terms of participation, while demands for consensus retreat to goals and increasingly to performance obligations themselves. As scarcities develop and the elan of successful reorganization dissipates, natural cohesions and local rivalries disrupt the larger solidarity of the revolutionary ranks. In communications, gaps develop both between leaders and led and between organizational levels; a rising tide of misinformation brings on an increasing distrust of upward moving reports, and an increasing irrelevance of superordinate's directives.

Phase Five: Retrenchment. With retrenchment, a sharp contraction in the ambitions and capabilities of formal organization sets in. The task environment now appears definitely threatening on both the instrumental and expressive sides. Needed on the instrumental side is the rematching of organizational units to manageable segments of the task environment, the application of technical expertise, and a major effort to re-establish coordination of a fragmented economy. Needed on the expressive side is a tightening of party discipline, a containment of alienation both among cadres and masses, and a greater severity of control until the crisis is past. The scope of activities managed by the organization and the salience of participation to lower participants both fall, reducing both the level of tension and the complexity of managerial tasks. The collaboration of informal instrumental leaders is again sought, with cadres retreating to instrumental supervision and a vain attempt to continue to provide expressive support for instrumental activities, while quietly abandoning their intervention in expressive matters. Communication between leaders and led, and between organizational levels, is at a nadir; instead of messages circulating upward to superiors, the superiors descend in waves to see what is going on and obtain reliable production information. Cadres lose an immense amount of face in the course of rectifications designed to check both over severe and over lenient leadership styles, and to transfer to the basic-level cadre the blame for failure of the mobilization strategy; it is doubtful that anyone in the organization has much charisma left, except for Mao on the wishful assumption that "he doesn't know what's really going on." As for the masses, the level of consensus demanded declines to that of performance obligations, while dissensus focuses on the demand to participate in collective organization at all. Membership becomes more selective, in fact, through the withdrawal of the most alienated members. Subcollectivities definitely split off from the socialist community, forming cohesive groups which are antagonistic to collective organization, and often to each other. It is now clear that economic performance has been poor. The State, concerned over the poor return on its investments, retrenches in its expenditures, showing an increasing concern for efficiency and a decreasing regard for effectiveness.

Phase Six: Demobilization. In the course of demobilization, government organization contracts toward its minimal role in society. The task environment is seen as less threatening, less unstable, but as more heterogeneous in both the instrumental and expressive spheres: needed are greater decentralization of tasks and minor decisions, coupled with a centralization of major decisions and supervision. With the abandonment of hopes for short-run gains in production, the time horizon expands, and serious attention is again given to developing and coordinating a long-linked agricultural technology. Although there is no formal declaration of retreat, scope and pervasiveness contract rapidly. Supervision of expressive matters is relinquished, pretensions of expressive leadership in support of production are abandoned, and cadres retreat to positional official supervisors of instrumental activities, tolerating a high degree of initiative by natural leaders. Minimal communication is restored as the pressure to achieve and report the impossible is relaxed. The charisma of even the top Party leadership passes into eclipse. More of the less committed withdraw from formal leadership positions and from membership in collective organizations. Organizational demands for consensus are limited to task performance and output quotas, while work group cohesion is again derived largely from natural affiliations. Agricultural production recovers with the restoration of incentives and the return to economically rational performance criteria.

VII

Cross-Cultural
Studies of
Organization

The comparative approach to organizational analysis helps to define the borderlines between unique items—the specific attributes of various categories—and universal ones; such an approach helps to guard against ethnocentric assumptions and enriches our sociological imagination as to the varieties possible. "Bureaucracies are modern organization"—but see the organization of the tribal society Fallers studies. "A labor union is a labor union is a labor union"—but see the significant differences in their patterns and effects despite the high similarity of culture, purpose, and environment in the two contexts studied by Richardson. "Corruption undermines effective administration"—but see the functions of corruption enumerated by Bayley.

In his study of a colonial society Fallers presents a "primitive" organization in its societal context. Both theoretical concepts and a particular "setting" are stressed. Theoretically, the study makes use of the conceptions and definitions of Max Weber—in particular his typology of authority—and illuminates a well-known source of social conflict—the attempt to institutionalize divergent sets of norms. The particular setting is British Colonial East Africa, an area in which there are few white settlers. The implications the particular setting has for the generic relations explored are the kinds of questions cross-cultural research helps to ask, and which of course a single case study can only begin to answer.

Richardson's study illustrates the value of comparing similar rather than highly divergent organizations. By studying American and British ships, which travel the same seas with the same purpose and almost identical facilities, Richardson is able to highlight the effects that differences in the cultural background of the American and British crews have on the organization of their respective ships.

Corruption, it is widely known, is the anathema of organization, above all of a rational one. The essence of organization is that participants will follow the rules of the corporate body; that the lower in rank will heed the instructions of the higher in rank; and that individual "cases" will be treated on their merit. Corruption, whatever form it takes, directly undermines these principles. Nevertheless, as Bayley shows, not all corruption is at all times "dysfunctional." For instance, a measure of corruption makes life tolerable under an overly restrictive and rigid bureaucracy. A degree of corruption serves the bureaucracy itself, not just its members' needs. Where there are no other avenues or means of adaptation, a full-scale rebellion would be likely.

Udy's selection bridges the cross-cultural and the methodological section by effectively illustrating the conceptual and methodological steps which allow the application of the tools of modern social science to the study of a large number of societies and highly divergent cultures. Udy, who studies 34 organizations in 34 societies—many of them traditional or transitional—further counters the widely held proposition that rational organization or bureaucracy is an exclusively modern feature. It remains to be seen if modern organizations can be distinguished from bureaucratic organizations of earlier periods, and what their unique attributes may be.

BUREAUCRACY IN A
PARTICULARISTIC SETTING

Lloyd A. Fallers

In modern Busoga there is, superimposed upon the traditional tension between state and lineage, a new conflict arising out of structural incompatibility between both of these institutions and the European-introduced
conception of civil service bureaucracy. The conflict springs from differing
norms concerning the exercise of authority—what Weber would have called
differing bases for the legitimation of authority. In the two traditional authority structures—lineage and state—authority relations were defined in
terms of relationships between particular persons or groups. A person was
under the authority of the members of his own lineage or the person who
was his own patron. Such criteria governing social relations I have called,
following Parsons, "particularistic."[1] In the civil service bureaucracy, on
the other hand, authority is situational. It is a property of an office, not a
person, and its validity depends upon general rules governing the office, not
upon the person who holds it. Thus, for example, whoever happens to
hold the office of Sub-County chief holds authority of a particular kind
over his area of jurisdiction. The particular person who holds the office is
irrelevant to the exercise of authority within it. This type of definition of
social relations, again following Parsons, I have called "universalistic."[2]

Reprinted from *Bantu Bureaucracy, A Century of Political Evolution Among the
Basoga of Uganda* (Chicago, Ill.: University of Chicago Press, 1965), pp. 238–247,
with minor omissions. By permission of the East African Institute of Social Research,
Uganda.

[1] Talcott Parsons, *The Social System* (New York: Free Press, 1951), pp. 61–65.
[2] *Ibid.*, pp. 61–63. These are clearly polar types rather than mutually exclusive categories. Although in traditional Busoga a man had authority relations of a special

I am arguing not merely that there is here an opposition of abstract ideal types, but rather that where such opposing authority norms are institutionalised the opposition does and must result in concrete interpersonal conflict and in instability in institutions. Thus the Soga civil-servant chief's position is defined in such a way that both sets of norms may be brought to bear upon the same situation. As regards recruitment to office, conflict may arise between the claims of kinsmen or clients and the principle of recruitment according to ability. In the daily exercise of authority, again there may be conflict between particularistic loyalties and the norm of disinterested and impartial administration. Both sets of norms cannot be satisfied, but since both are institutionalised a decision in either direction may result in interpersonal conflict and in lack of conformity with some institutionalised norms.

The tension between the introduced bureaucratic civil service pattern and the more particularistic traditional authority structures has produced different kinds of conflict at different levels within the political system. The conflict is sharpest for the civil-servant chief, for it is to him that the two sets of norms simultaneously apply with greatest immediacy. This is so because he is a specialist in the exercise of authority; authority is his profession. The traditional Soga state and the modern African Local Government organisation are specialised political rôles. Thus the norms governing the exercise of authority loom particularly large in the chief's social relations with others. Where such norms are conflicting, his rôle tends to be the focus of the conflict. Thus the chief is faced almost daily with conflicting expectations on the part of persons with whom he interacts. Furthermore, the sanctions which operate in support of the two sets of norms are such as to leave him a very small margin of error in his attempts to balance the two sets of expectations. The civil service norm is enforced by the Administration. If the chief fails to follow it closely, he may well lose his position. The particularistic demands of kinship and clientship are also, however, enforced by senior chiefs and others, who can use their influence with the Administration to punish recalcitrant juniors. The civil-servant chief must therefore steer a course which can successfully be navigated only by the most skillful.

---

kind with his lineage mates as against other persons, so that authority was from this point of view particularistic, still within the lineage his relations with all kinsmen of the same sex and generation were similar and thus, to this degree were universalistically defined. Similarly, although the African Local Government civil service to-day holds within Busoga a universalistically-defined kind of authority, still, as we have seen, the Soga are reluctant to take part in similar authority structures extending outside Busoga. To this degree, the African Local Government has particularistic elements. All concrete cases are no doubt mixed cases in terms of these categories and hence differences are differences of degree.

The conflict which centres upon the village or sub-village headman is different. He is also, though in lesser degree, a specialist in authority, but he is not a formal part of the African Local Government bureaucracy and the demands of the civil service norm consequently do not impinge upon him so directly. The difficulties of his rôle rather derive from the circumstance that, while he continues to hold his position by inheritance and to "rule" his community in large part according to traditional patterns (or, at any rate, according to what he and others believe to be traditional patterns), the upper levels of the political system have changed in such a way as to deprive him of what he sees to be the just and traditional rewards of his position. Although not directly subject to bureaucratic discipline, he has been deprived of the economic and status-enhancing rewards of personal tribute and is aware that the Administration does not approve of his rights in connection with land. Thus, though not so immediately and constantly subject to the universalistic-particularistic conflict which afflicts the civil-servant chief, he is, in a sense, punished for his refusal to adjust his position to the new civil service pattern. Thus, while continuing, as the head of his community, to participate in the wider political system as the informal local representative of the African Local Government, he does so ambivalently and may react to what he sees as his deprived position by agitating against the African Local Government and the Administration, or by withdrawing into passive inactivity.

Finally, the administrative officer is faced with still a third type of difficulty as a consequence of the structural incongruities which pervade the political system. It is his responsibility to maintain and to extend the civil service pattern of government; he is the active agent in the Westernisation of the system. At the same time, he is responsible for order—for introducing change at such a rate and in such a way that stable government is maintained. To this end he must recognise and, temporarily at any rate, accept features of the system which run counter to the civil service norms to which he is committed, since to attempt to enforce the new norms absolutely would result in disorder. To this degree he, like the Soga members of the system, must try to balance conflicting norms. He must simultaneously endeavour to further Westernisation, yield authority, and remain responsible for the exercise, according to the new norms which he is introducing, of the authority which he is yielding. He must, furthermore, carry out this complex responsibility in a situation where his knowledge of and communication with members of the system which he is endeavouring to change is severely limited, both by cultural and linguistic barriers and by the exigencies of the bureaucratic structure of which he is a part.

I suggest the hypothesis that bureaucratic structures were incompatible with the traditional Soga political structures—the corporate lineage and the patron-clientship pattern. In general, this is perhaps self-evident and hardly requires formal comparative testing. There are, however, subsidiary questions arising out of the Soga material which do seem to me worthy of comparative testing. I cannot attempt a systematic comparative analysis here, since the relevant data are widely scattered and not familiar to me. In large part they are to be found in the writings of political scientists and historians rather than in those of sociologists and social anthropologists. The reasons for this are obvious. Sociologists and social anthropologists have tended to study either modern Western societies, where bureaucratic structures are relatively well integrated with other institutions, or else non-Western societies where bureaucracy does not exist or has only recently been introduced. Data of comparative interest should soon be forthcoming as social anthropologists concern themselves more and more with contemporary political development in non-Western areas, though as yet little such data has been published.[3] Therefore, though I cannot undertake to test them systematically, I should like to note here a few points which would seem susceptible to comparative investigation.

One such concerns the apparent ease with which the traditional Soga state was transformed in a bureaucratic direction. Although there has been conflict and opposition, on the whole the process has been strikingly rapid and smooth. I have noted some of the particular historical factors which seem to have been involved here: the generally rewarding nature of the situation from the point of view of the rulers and chiefs and the early development of mission education. It is also interesting to consider, however, the degree to which the traditional state was what might be called "structurally receptive" to bureaucratisation. My earlier lumping together of the two traditional authority structures—state and lineage—as being particularistically oriented has perhaps served to obscure this point. While both structures shared this feature in opposition to bureaucratic universalism, they are in other respects not equally incompatible with bureaucratic organisation. For while the patron-client relationship was particularistic, it was also hierarchical and involved recognition of achieved status—both features which are present in bureaucratic structures. The patron-client relationship, once established, was a relationship between two persons as individuals and was often cemented by affinal ties, but in selecting clients, patrons were explicitly concerned with administrative and military ability. The relationship was also a hierarchical one, as compared with the relative egalitarianism of the lineage. One might say, therefore, that the traditional state was an "incipient bureaucracy." The general hypothesis suggests itself that societies with hierarchical, centralised political systems incorporate the Western type of civil service structure with less strain and instability than

---

[3] Again comparative data will soon be available from recent studies of other Inter-Lacustrine Bantu societies.

do societies having other types of political systems, e.g. segmentary ones. Such a hypothesis might well be tested in Uganda, where a similar African Local Government system has been introduced into both the Bantu states and the segmentary societies of the Nilotic north.

I would also suggest that the particular tension which existed in traditional Busoga between lineage and state was a contributory factor. The threat of princely revolt seems to have made Soga rulers anxious to secure more powerful allies. Both Ganda and Europeans were ready to accept such a rôle and were thus enabled to gain control over Soga states. Where the Ganda were concerned, this essentially involved merely the absorption of the Soga states into a larger unit of the same kind, but with regard to the Europeans, it meant something more; although this was undoubtedly not foreseen, it meant ultimately a commitment to a continuing process of change in kind in the political system. Rulers and chiefs, having accepted European authority in exchange for support, were committed to European policies. Generalising beyond the particular events, one might say that the conflict between lineage and state produced a kind of political opportunism in the traditional Soga authorities, and in consequence brought about a fluidity in the system, which made it vulnerable to outside penetration and to change.

I have the impression that the speed and smoothness with which Westernisation has proceeded in Busoga (and in Uganda as a whole) is rather unusual, at any rate in Africa. For example, in the Gold Coast, on the verge of self-government, Ashanti chiefs still debated whether or not to observe the traditional pagan day of rest and were in general much more traditionally-oriented than Soga chiefs, in spite of the fact that the Ashanti have had a much longer period of contact with the West than have the peoples of Uganda.[4] In Ashanti, Westernisation would appear to have proceeded to a greater extent outside of and in opposition to the traditional political hierarchy, whereas in Uganda, at any rate among the Bantu states, the traditional authorities have on the whole been its pioneers. A similar contrast would appear to hold for the Southern Bantu states referred to earlier in this chapter. The difference, perhaps, is at least partly explainable in terms of the particular tension which existed among Inter-Lacustrine Bantu between lineage and state and the consequent vulnerability of the state hierarchy to European penetration.

A second point of comparative interest arises in connection with the attempt by the Administration in Busoga to carry the bureaucratic type of authority structure down to the local community level. I have described how the village headmen resisted the attempt to transform them into salaried civil servants. I have also noted the frequent ineffectualness of the

---

[4] K. A. Busia, *The Position of the Chief in the Modern Political System of Ashanti* (London, 1951), p. 135.

Parish chief, who is a salaried and transferable civil servant but who is often overshadowed by the locally-rooted headmen. Aside from the particular circumstances of Busoga, I would suggest that there are inherent difficulties in applying the civil service conception of authority at the level of the local community. The stable local community is everywhere essentially a primary group; its members know each other as total persons as a result of long and intimate face-to-face contact. As a colleague of mine once put it: "In the village everyone is famous."[5] In the lower courts in Busoga, for example (headmen's and Parish chiefs' courts of arbitration and sometimes even Sub-County courts), procedure often assumes that the community knows, or can discover, the circumstances of the case. There is not the same obligation to tell the truth which one finds at higher levels, where anonymity is possible. Litigants and witnesses are more free to lie, since it is assumed that members of the court, knowing the persons involved, can nevertheless discover the truth. The problem is rather to find the most satisfactory means of closing a breach in the social relations of the community. The court applies substantive justice rather than a strictly-defined rule of law. The bureaucratic conception is, of course, quite different. It deals, not with relations between whole persons, but with rules governing types of situation. Acts or attributes of persons falling outside the defined situation are irrelevant. Applied to relations within the local community, however, such impersonality tends to be disruptive of the network of particularistic ties and to result in miscarriages of what the community sees as substantive justice, hence the local community's preference for a leader who knows them and is known by them.[6]

Although there would appear to be a general tendency for authority within local communities to be particularistic, the degree to which this is so is undoubtedly relative to variations in social structure. To the particularism of the primary group community, Soga society adds the particularisms of extended kinship and the patron-client relationship between the headman and his people. The resistance to bureaucracy is therefore particularly great. Comparative investigation of community authority within different types of wider social system would undoubtedly reveal other variations of this order.

In thinking comparatively about the integration of bureaucracy with other institutions, it is perhaps well to keep in mind Parsons' view that the universalistic type of orientation which bureaucracy implies is inherently unstable and difficult to institutionalise, due to the circumstance that everywhere persons tend to be socialised in particularistic situations.[7] The early

[5] Dr. Erving Goffman.
[6] A recent investigator into local government in Uganda recommended, on these grounds, that in the future Parish chiefs should be local men not subject to transfer. (See C. A. G. Wallis, *Report of an Inquiry into African Local Government in the Protectorate of Uganda*, Government Printer, Entebbe, 1953, p. 53.)
[7] T. Parsons, *op. cit.*, p. 268.

learning of social behaviour takes place in family groups and involves the building up of stable sets of mutual expectations with a relatively small group of individuals. As Freud noted, the extension of this early social learning to social relations in the larger society requires that the individual abstract general social norms from these early particularistic relationships.[8] The latter, however, tend to leave a residual tendency toward emotional attachment to individual persons which makes the learning and maintenance of universalistic orientations difficult.[9] Whatever its psychogenetic roots, such a residual tendency toward particularism has often been noted by students of modern Western societies. Such formally highly bureaucratised structures as the modern state and the business or industrial organisation are notoriously subject to nepotism and to the formation of solidary cliques.[10] The relevance of such considerations here is simply that the conflict between the civil service norm and the particularistic ties of kinship and clientship which has been observed in contemporary Soga society should perhaps not be viewed as a conflict between two equally-weighted social patterns. The special particularisms of Soga society, it would appear, have a natural ally in a universal human tendency which makes the institutionalisation of the civil service norm peculiarly difficult of achievement.

Over the long term, the bureaucratic type of authority structure will undoubtedly become more firmly institutionalised in Busoga, since both the authority of the British Administration and contemporary economic trends work in its favour, but there are various factors which, in the short term, may condition this process. One of the major obstacles to the establishment of bureaucratic structures is the kinship system involving corporate patrilineages. So long as the lineage system remains intact, it will constitute a major source of deviation from bureaucratic norms. The system of corporate lineages, however, has firm roots in the system of land holding. Though hereditary rulership has disappeared, lineage control of inheritance and succession in the local community remains undisputed and is backed by the authority of the African Local Government courts. Although lineages have broken down in some areas, there would seem to be no reason to doubt that, in the absence of further catastrophes of the order of the sleeping sickness epidemics at the turn of the century, lineage structure will remain intact throughout most parts of Busoga. A change in the direction of more individual forms of land holding would, however, undoubtedly weaken the lineage system and strengthen more universalistic orientations favourable to bureaucratic structure. A body of opinion favourable to such a change has recently appeared among persons wishing to engage in more modern forms

---

[8] Sigmund Freud, *Group Psychology and the Analysis of the Ego*, 1922.
[9] T. Parsons, *op cit.*, p. 268.
[10] See, for example, F. J. Roethlisberger, and W. J. Dickinson, *Management and the Worker*, 1939; Lincoln Steffens, *Autobiography*, 1931.

of agriculture. One might hazard the prediction that such views will gain wider support in the future with the spread, through education, of an appreciation of the economic potentialities of modern farming methods and that the result will be a situation less inimical to the development of civil service norms.

A second source of future strength for bureaucratic patterns would appear to be the growing tendency for civil-servant chiefs to form an élite sub-culture, to some degree dissociated from peasant life and institutions. I have noted the tendency for chiefs to see themselves as a solidary group and to form cliques for purposes of sociability. To the degree that this tendency is increased, it would seem to form the basis for the development of a civil service *esprit de corps,* from which the tenuously institutionalised civil service pattern might draw strength, and a defence against the particularistic demands which spring from traditional kinship and clientship institutions. This tendency is strengthened by the pattern of recruitment on the basis of ability and education. To the degree that chiefs come to feel themselves identified with the civil service as a body and to see their futures in terms of professional careers in the service, they will find it easier to commit themselves to the norms of the system.

So far I have looked at conflict within the traditional and modern Soga political systems in terms of its consequences for the particular institutions involved and for individuals playing rôles in terms of those institutions. In the case of both traditional and modern Busoga, I have centred my attention primarily upon rôle conflict—conflict of the sort which results when incompatible institutions apply to the same persons. In traditional Busoga, persons playing rôles in the state hierarchy also played rôles in the lineage organisation. In modern Busoga, members of the African Local Government hierarchy also have lineage rôles and patron-client rôles. In such situations, the conflict between institutions is, so to speak, absorbed into individual persons. Since both sets of institutional norms are accepted by the same persons, individuals are exposed to conflicting, but equally legitimate, expectations from others and have conflicting motivations within themselves. This is not to say that such conflict is never interpersonal. Interpersonal conflict often results because in a given situation one person may claim over-riding legitimacy for one of the patterns, while persons with whom he interacts may take the opposite point of view. Where conflict is of this kind, however, the positions may well be reversed in another situation. Thus the Soga chief who resists the claims of his kinsmen on one occasion may well assert the same type of claim on another occasion when it seems to him advantageous to do so. The peculiarity of this type of conflict, however, is that it does not divide persons into intransigently opposed groups. Soga society does not consist of one group wholly committed to civil service universalism and an opposed group wholly committed to kinship and clientship particularism; it consists rather of individuals attempting to follow both patterns.

This, it should be pointed out, is not the only pattern which institutional conflict may follow. Conflict between discrete groups committed to opposing norms would appear to be equally common, particularly in colonial situations. Often enough non-Western societies under Western influence become divided into such opposed groups on the basis of adherence to traditional or introduced institutions. I should not imply that inter-group conflict of this type is totally absent in Busoga. As I have noted, persons at different points in the modern political hierarchy are differently affected by institutional conflict. For the African Local Government civil-servant chief, the duality of institutional allegiance is most marked. The administrative officer, on the other hand, is more completely committed to the civil service pattern, while the village headman remains more oriented to traditional particularism. In comparative perspective, however, Busoga (and Uganda) would seem to be unusual among colonial societies in the degree to which the conflicts which inevitably arise in such societies have been confined to rôle conflict as against inter-group conflicts. . . .

ORGANIZATIONAL CONTRASTS ON BRITISH AND AMERICAN SHIPS

Stephen A. Richardson

To be effective, an organization must have a structure appropriate for the particular purpose and the resulting necessary tasks. At the same time, the form of organization and the values and needs of its members must be adapted to one another. Variations in organization, then, can be expected to follow from variations of the cultures from which members of an or-

Reprinted from Stephen A. Richardson, "Organizational Contrasts on British and American Ships," *Administrative Science Quarterly*, vol. I, 1956. (Ithaca, New York: Graduate School of Business and Public Administration, Cornell University), pp. 168–206, with minor omissions.

ganization are drawn. The effects of cultural factors can be seen in comparing organizations which function in a wide variety of countries and have identical purposes and similar environments.

The social organization on British and United States merchant ships was selected for study because cargo ships have identical purposes, closely comparable environments, and a set of conditions as near to the research ideal as is likely to be found in a natural setting without experimental manipulation. Cargo ships or freighters of approximately seven thousand tons, carrying crews of forty men, were selected for study.

We will first describe the purpose and environment which are common to foreign-going cargo ships of all nationalities. Then we will describe how British and United States seamen arrange their shipboard lives to meet these common conditions. For the purposes of this paper the description will be limited to some differences found between the two nationalities in training, social control, and stratification.

COMMON PURPOSE AND ENVIRONMENT

A merchant ship's purpose is to transport cargo and passengers. This demands three main focuses of work for the crew: (1) aiding and facilitating the loading and discharging of cargo and passengers; (2) bringing the ship and her contents safely to her appointed destination; and (3), throughout the life of the ship, maintaining and repairing her so that she will give efficient service.

A ship and her contents are a large capital investment. She is exposed frequently to such hazards as storms, collision, fire, and shipwreck. The safety of the ship depends in large measure upon the quick judgments and actions of experienced and skillful seamen. The social organization of the crew must therefore have a clearly designated hierarchy of responsibility and must make provision for rapid communication and execution of orders. Because potential hazards to the ship exist at all times, the organization must function continuously.

A ship's movements impose limitations as to when a member of the crew may form and sever connection with the ship. A seaman joins a ship when it is in his country and reasonably close to his home. With few exceptions, he must remain with the ship until it returns to his home country. This period may be from a month to two years. During the voyage, the crew therefore has a smaller turnover than any comparable organization ashore.

Members of the crew spend their working hours and leisure time at sea, isolated from other people. In foreign ports the friendships they can form ashore are limited by the brief duration of the ship's stay and by the limited channels that may be used to establish social contacts. Life at sea has in most cases been found unsuitable for families. Members of the crew must therefore be separated from their families for the duration of the voyage.

THE SOCIAL SYSTEM OF MERCHANT SHIP CREWS

To fulfill the purpose of a ship and to adapt the seaman to the environment which has been described, a clearly defined social system has been evolved through centuries of experience. This system must be sufficiently clear so that a new crew made up of men who have never before met can immediately coordinate the complex task of running a ship.

Before describing and analyzing some of the differences found in the social system on British and American merchant ships, we will outline the organization of the crews of both nationalities and the way in which the crews function. The crew is divided into four departments which work in close cooperation: deck, engineering, stewards, and radio. In this article, attention will be focused on the deck department, with other departments discussed only in relation to this department. Figure 1 shows the manning and basic working organization which with little variation is typical of British and United States cargo ships of about seven thousand tons (e.g., World War II Liberty ships).

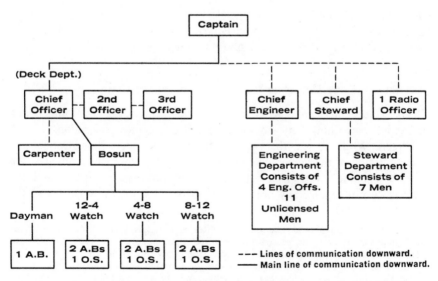

FIGURE 1.   *Typical manning and formal organization of crew of a 7,000-ton-gross United States and British merchant ship. Crew totals forty.*

There are two main categories of work for the crew while the ship is at sea. These are:

NAVIGATING AND PROPELLING THE SHIP: While at sea, a ship is continuously under way, and most members of the crew are divided into three shifts, or watches. Each watch alternates four hours on duty with eight hours off duty. A watch on deck is made up of one officer, two able-bodied seamen, and an ordinary seaman.[1] Although the deck watch-keeping officers are in full charge, the captain is at all times responsible for the safety of the ship and is on call if an unusual situation is suspected or special vigilance is required. The chief engineer is at all times responsible to the captain for the ship's machinery. Radio officers receive and transmit messages at internationally agreed-upon times. Competence of all officers is tested by a governmental examination system. The watch-keeping routine at sea is broken only in extraordinary circumstances. The entire crew is trained in the procedures to be adopted in case of emergency.

SHIP'S MAINTENANCE: During the day, the carpenter works on his own, and the bosun[2] works with any able-bodied seamen who are on day work and do not keep watch, and with the two watch members not steering the ship. Since this gives the bosun only three or four men, if any large job has to be done extra men are called out during their time off watch and paid overtime. On occasion, the bosun may be supervising ten to twelve men. Planning and supervising the deck-department work is done by the chief officer (often called the mate) during his time off watch. The captain rarely participates in this supervision but may do so if he wishes.

The Effects of the Unions on the Organization of the Crew

British and American officers and men are represented by unions, and collective bargaining between the shipping companies and unions is well accepted. While at sea, the crew must determine the administration and interpretation of the agreements without assistance from shore officials. On British ships this task is left to traditional informal practices, and the unions do not require any organized activity while the crew is aboard the

---

[1] Able-bodied seaman is a rank obtained after a man has spent three years in the deck department and has passed the required examination. The rank of ordinary seaman is given men in the deck department when they first go to sea.

[2] The position of bosun is analogous to that of foreman. It requires an able-bodied seaman's rating and sufficient sea experience and supervisory ability (as judged by competent seamen) to be responsible to the chief officer for the work of the able-bodied and ordinary seamen.

ship. On United States ships, however, unions representing the unlicensed personnel require a number of types of activity while at sea. Because of the widespread effects that union activity has had on American ships these will be described first.

At the beginning of the voyage, a meeting is called which is obligatory for all members not on duty. At the meeting, the deck, engine-room, and stewards departments each elect a delegate. The types of qualifications looked for are sea experience, education, thorough knowledge of the contract, fluency of speech, and the ability to stay sober at the pay-off at the end of the voyage. The department delegates act as official union spokesmen to the head of their department. A ship's delegate or chairman is also elected to coordinate the departments and act as delegate to the captain for all unlicensed personnel when matters arise involving more than one department. The chairman and departmental delegates constitute the ship's committee. Delegates check up on members' subscriptions, hold meetings which must be attended, educate the membership about union policies and rules, watch over members' interests, and maintain union solidarity and discipline (see Figure 2). The unions believe that any hierarchy within their ranks aboard ship might decrease their unity and strength in action; therefore union educational policies stress that all members are equals and brothers. This also tends to prevent delegates from exploiting their position for personal or political ends.

Union activity at sea is instigated mainly by the ship's committee. The union headquarters offers a wide range of suggestions and facilities, which are reflected in the agenda for union meetings of the crew. The agenda includes union business, reports from the ship's committee on the handling of complaints, education, political action, and "good and welfare." Any matter can be brought to the floor by crewmen in the form of a motion. Under the heading of "good and welfare," it is said that "everyone gets a chance to blow his top."[3] While political and educational activities take place only on some ships, the ship's committee always handles complaints, watches over living conditions, and serves a policing function in seeing that members live up to the terms of the agreement and behave in a manner which will give the shipping company no grounds for withdrawing any part of the gains won by the union. The National Maritime Union summarizes the aim of union activity aboard ship as follows: "Everyone has his special job and keeps checking with everyone else. The same policy, the same method of handling problems, the same rights apply to all. That's what makes a happy, livable, workable ship."[4]

[3] National Maritime Union, Pilot, Education and Publicity Department Publication No. 16, *Heart of the Union* (November 1947).
[4] *Ibid.*

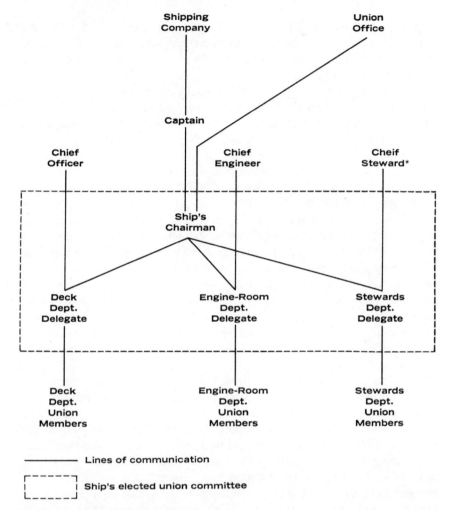

FIGURE 2. *Union organization of unlicensed personnel on United States ships.*

Union activity can have an important effect on the informal structure of the unlicensed personnel. It provides a number of positions that give prestige and leadership and an opportunity to participate in group activities. It tends to bring together the unlicensed men in the three departments, maintains union interests, gives a sense of solidarity and distinction, and provides meaningful activity in a restricted environment where men have few facilities for entertainment when not at work.

Both British and United States officers have their own unions, which have no organized activity aboard the ships while at sea.

DIFFERENCES BETWEEN THE SOCIAL SYSTEM
ON BRITISH AND UNITED STATES SHIPS

For the effective maintenance and survival of the social system on a ship there are two important requirements: (1) a continuous supply of trained men and (2) ways to control deviance from normative or ideal patterns of behavior if the degree of deviance becomes a threat to the functioning of the system. We will now focus attention on some of the national differences that appear in the way these requirements are met.

Training of Deck Department Officers

On British ships, the four-year apprenticeship for youths intending to become officers is generally spent with one company. This training begins at age sixteen or seventeen, and the company takes the responsibility of teaching the apprentice the business of a seaman and the duties of a navigating officer. The apprentice "binds and obliges himself . . . to faithfully serve [the company] and any shipmaster . . . and obey their and his lawful commands [perform various duties] . . . nor absent himself from their service without leave nor frequent taverns or alehouses, nor play at unlawful games."[5] About three-fourths of British Merchant Service officers receive their training as apprentices or cadets, and the remainder put in the required sea time as ordinary seamen and able-bodied seamen.

In the American Merchant Marine, a man is required to have three years of training before he can become an officer. Youths who train as cadets spend two of their three years at a shore-based maritime academy and two six-month periods at sea, either in maritime-academy training ships or in regular merchant ships. Training begins at eighteen or nineteen years of age.

Only about 10 per cent of the officers in the American Merchant Marine are trained as cadets. The remaining 90 per cent sail as ordinary seamen and able-bodied seamen for three years and then take the examination for their license.

Among British officers, primary loyalty is found to be to the shipping companies, and to be a "company man" is considered advantageous. Among American officers, primary loyalty is found to be to the unions. For them the expression "company man" has disparaging connotations, the most important of which is its use as an opposite to "union man."

A number of factors in the training of officers suggest an explanation for this difference in loyalty. A youth sixteen to seventeen years old is in

5 Indentures to Anchor Line Ltd., Glasgow.

the process of gaining emotional emancipation from his parents, and is doing so through increased membership in peer groups outside his family. When the British boy goes to sea as an apprentice, he is separated from his family and his friends and placed in a social structure composed almost entirely of adult men. Here the peer group is limited to one or two somewhat older apprentices, since he is not allowed to associate with able-bodied seamen or ordinary seamen. However, the captain as shipping-company representative has certain responsibilities to the youth and plays a role closely analogous to that of a father. Because the youth is in need of stability, a sense of belonging, and friendship to replace what he has lost, he is highly motivated to use the captain, who represents the company, as a substitute for his father. The company is interested in training its apprentices in its ways and follows the youth's training and development with interest because it is likely that if he shows promise he will remain with the company throughout his career. Although the apprentice is given a great deal of work that is normally done by the unlicensed personnel, he is trained to identify himself with the officers even though he does not hold officer's status.

The few American officers who are trained as cadets have little or no connection with any shipping company. Two-thirds of their training takes place ashore in schools which they enter when they are older than British apprentices, and where they associate mainly with a peer group. This type of training precludes the possibility of a relationship with a shipping company such as exists between British companies and officers. The majority of American officers spend their first three years at sea as ordinary seamen and able-bodied seamen. Although they go to sea at a somewhat older age than British seamen, they still have to make the difficult transition from shore to ship life. They have, however, a wider range of men with whom they may make friends and more chance of finding persons of their own age with whom they may associate.

The union and its elected representatives in the crew provide guidance and training for youths coming to sea as ordinary seamen. In return the youths develop a strong loyalty to the union. For American deck officers who first go to sea as ordinary seamen, the union plays a role comparable to that played by the company for British apprentices. When American able-bodied seamen become officers, it is natural for their allegiance to be transferred to the officer's union rather than to the companies, which they have been trained to consider as more unfriendly than friendly to the seaman.

Among the unlicensed personnel, the difference in loyalty may be explained in part by the greater militancy and youth of the American unions. The American union-controlled hiring halls, the union-organized activity at sea, and the union discipline, as compared to the British jointly controlled company-union hiring halls and the lack of union activity and discipline at sea result in different attitudes toward the companies and the unions.

Mechanisms of Control Used by Unlicensed Seamen

An intricate set of checks and counterchecks are continuously in play between the mate, bosun, and deck crowd.[6] The captain and officers' interest and responsibility is to initiate the work and see that it gets done. The deck crowd's interest is to control authority which is not customarily acceptable or is illegitimate. Only the differences in the kinds of controls used by the deck crowd will be examined here.

BRITISH SHIPS. When the able-bodied seamen or ordinary seamen think the mate has infringed on an official regulation (e.g., not kept an accurate check of the number of hours overtime) the offended person will generally enlist the sympathy of the deck crowd, since there is close identity of interest and a tendency to stand together for mutual protection. The first formal move generally is to take the complaint to the bosun, although this is often little more than a gesture to prevent any comeback from him that would occur if he were ignored. The deck crowd often feels that the bosun is on the chief officer's side. A direct approach to the department head would probably meet with refusal and an order to see the bosun. This was well described in two interviews:

> The bosun is rather suspect, because he works so close with the mate. The men are afraid he can be too easily called [talked around by the mate]. He is more used to acting for the mate than the men, so he may not be a good spokesman.   (British able-bodied seaman)

> Often the men try the bosun to get him to clear up the trouble and he has failed.   (British second officer)

If the complaint is not settled by the bosun himself or by his referring the matter to the mate, the second step is for the aggrieved individual, a spokesman, or a delegation to go to the mate. There is no formal way of selecting a spokesman, but one appears in almost every deck crowd. The ability to talk well and think fast seems to be the prerequisite. In interviews, an able-bodied seaman said a delegation was sent to accompany the spokesman "for moral support," and the second officer explained that the

---

[6] On U.S. ships the term "deck gang" is used. These terms, used by the men themselves, have no derogatory connotation.

delegation was sent "to give him moral courage and to see he says his piece."

If the complaint cannot be settled with the chief officer, the delegation may then go to the captain. The use of delegations for giving moral courage is evidenced by the more common usage of a delegation for the captain than for the chief officer. Omitting some of these steps may be done intentionally as a sign of hostility to or disparagement of a disliked bosun or mate.

UNITED STATES SHIPS. The unions have laid down rules for handling complaints against infringement of rules. The elected union delegate handles all grievances. This arrangement reinforces the union structure aboard the ship since it allows the ship's committee to have control and to interpret communications, and it prevents individual members from taking complaints directly to the captain and heads of departments. The discussion of any grievance centers around the interpretation of the union contract, which describes in great detail the rules and conditions of work. Having all complaints handled by the union delegate has the advantages of saving time and having an experienced man handle the disputes. It also ensures consistency in the treatment of comparable disputes. There is the disadvantage, however, that the chief officer receives complaints at second hand and has no opportunity to gauge the feelings underlying the complaint, to learn how widely those feelings are shared, and in some cases to know who instigated the complaint. The delegate system also makes it difficult for the chief officer to give a man more overtime than he has earned, a procedure sometimes used by British chief officers to reward better workers.

An American bosun has described how the procedure affects the bosun, if it is functioning well:

> The bosun likes the system of having the delegate handle all the beefs with the mate. The delegate gets the dirt and leaves the bosun clear of being involved in friction with the mate. As the bosun is clear of beefs he [is] in a more favorable position in handling the men. He keeps in touch with all beefs as these are aired at the union meetings. If the deck crowd are dissatisfied with anything the bosun does, he is talked to by the delegate and they try to straighten it out. If this is not possible the delegate takes the beef to the mate. The delegate would not go over the bosun's head.

The success of this procedure depends on its acceptance by the chief officer and on the willingness of the bosun to work in cooperation with the union. The bosun is in a difficult position, however, if the chief officer resists the union form of communication. If the chief officer is antiunion, he can weaken the union structure on board by discouraging the delegate and by encouraging communication through the bosun. In one way this strengthens the bosun's position, especially if his actions are fully backed by the chief officer, since then he is working on the side of the officers. He is, however, a union member, and by working with the officers, who tend to be identified with the company, he may antagonize the men, thus losing their support and incurring the strong controls that the union can apply to deviant members. If the bosun resists the chief officer's attempt to undermine the union communication procedure, the bosun will antagonize the chief officer. This places him in a difficult position since close cooperation between chief officer and bosun is essential in the smooth running of the crew. The difficulty of the bosun has been increased as the result of the loss of some of his traditional status symbols. Whereas he used to eat separately from the deck crowd, he now eats in the same messroom; and whereas he used to have a single cabin, he now tends to share a cabin with the deck maintenance crew. This, together with his membership in the same union as the men he supervises, has made his status less well defined and increased the difficulties of his position as "football" in the communication struggle.

It is probable that, as a result of increased experience with the union system of communication, its operation will become smoother.

The American unions have also developed a set of formal rules governing the role the deck-crowd union members should play in exercising self-regulatory controls. An able-bodied seaman outlined the delegate's job in this way:

> The delegate's job is to keep the guys in line. Charges may be brought against fellow union men for inefficiency, not cooperating, refusing work, drunkenness, being antiunion, stealing from a shipmate, pulling knives. . . . The crew tries to take care of what happens. I think the Old Man likes the men to straighten out their own troubles. All the delegates may go to the Old Man and straighten things out with him. Then the delegates will call a meeting for the membership to endorse action or decide what should be done.

Some practical difficulties which lie in the way of the delegate's carrying out his job were raised by a second officer:

> Discipline hardly lies with the union delegate. Union education is good on this matter, but one or two troublemakers are enough to wreck this. The delegate has got to live with the men, and if the trouble starts in Singapore, it is a long time for him to swim against the tide (until the end of the voyage).

The formal system of handling complaints has focused interest on the problem of formal and informal control. The subject was more often brought up by Americans than British and was spoken of at greater length. Controlling deviant behavior is a problem of great importance because it is conceived of not as a personal but as a union-owner issue. From the union's point of view, this approach has value in maintaining members' interest in the union. From the point of view of the chief officer, bosun, and deck crowd, a lack of agreement in interpreting the formal grievance rules leads to caution in adopting a flexible give-and-take system, and sometimes a struggle ensues between the chief officer and the deck crowd for the bosun's allegiance.

Informal Controls on British and United States Ships

It is possible for behavior to deviate widely from expected or ideal forms of behavior without technically infringing upon any written agreement. To counteract such deviations by officers, a number of informal controls are commonly used by crews on British and United States ships.

WORK SLOWDOWNS. Close supervision of most of the work on deck is difficult, especially if the bosun is party to the slowdowns. Slowdowns have to be very marked before the captain or chief officer can find grounds for action—great ingenuity can be exercised in doing nothing, and doing it industriously. A slowdown is most commonly used to counteract too close supervision by the mate or too rigid application of working rules without allowing for any flexibility or give-and-take. It is also used to prevent the chief officer from deviating far from the role expected of him in his relations with the men.

QUALITY OF WORK. Reduction in the quality of the work on deck serves the same purpose as work slowdowns, and these two forms of control are generally used together. Within certain limits, it is difficult for the chief officer to obtain sufficient evidence of poor workmanship, especially where the work is of such a nature or in such a position as to be difficult to check with periodic inspection.

MISUSE OF SHIP'S EQUIPMENT. This may take the form of misusing equipment or dumping overboard small articles not easily checked. The degree to which this is done will depend largely on how well equipment is watched by the chief officer. Misuse of equipment is a more destructive reaction than work slowdowns and is likely to lead to further deterioration of relations, whereas slowdowns and poor work can vary in seriousness, and any sign of improved relations instigated by the chief officer can be encouraged by increased output and quality of work.

LEAVING THE SHIP. If the work relationship has been poor between the deck officers and the men, and if the men's complaints have met with little or no satisfaction from the captain, a great deal of hostility accumulates. This is often harmlessly dissipated at the end of the voyage, but the men may all leave the ship or make a formal complaint to the union if there are grounds for action against the captain or chief officer. A complete turnover of the crew at the end of a voyage, especially if this happens on several consecutive voyages, may indicate to the shipping company's officials that the cause may be a captain or officer. The men leaving the ship spread the information of the cause for leaving, and it may in extreme cases reach the stage where the shipping company has trouble in getting a new crew so long as the officer causing the difficulty remains on the ship. A formal complaint achieves the same purpose directly.

EFFECTS OF SOCIAL STRATIFICATION ON PATTERNS OF BEHAVIOR

If the social structure of the crew is conceived as occupying a vertical scale with the captain at the top and a first-voyage ordinary seaman at the bottom, it should be possible to place all crew members on this scale and to determine the range within which groups form. This grouping may be called social stratification, and the distance along the scale may be called social distance. There are a number of indicators of social stratification and distance which are recognized implicitly or explicitly by members of British and American crews. These include wages, qualifications formally required for holding an office (such as examinations and length of sea service), number of persons supervised, food and living conditions, and such behavior as the use of titles in addressing people. Together these indicators influence the behavior of every member of the crew with respect to every other member, providing pressures toward maintaining approved patterns of behavior.

Comparison of British and American crews on indicators of social stratification and distance showed that American seamen consistently play down behavioral and physical symbols that strengthen status and social distance. Some examples of the differences will now be given.

Food and the Division of the Crew at Meals

The value of the eating arrangements aboard ship as a measure of social stratification was recognized by Herman Melville in *White Jacket* when he observed that "the dinner table is the criterion of rank in our man-of-war world."[7]

[7] *The Romances of Herman Melville* (New York, 1931), p. 1126.

The British crews have more divisions than the American. The British bosun and carpenter eat with the engine-room supervisory men; this group is often called the petty officers. The American bosun and carpenter and other petty officers eat with the able-bodied seamen and ordinary seamen, but generally at a separate table. Interviews showed a close positive relationship between status and the quality of food on British ships. The same was true of American ships in an earlier period, until unions won the right of equal food for all. This right is carefully guarded by unlicensed personnel, whose delegates compare the quality of food being served officers and men. The British able-bodied seamen and ordinary seamen collect their meals from the cook, carry food to their messroom, and after eating do their own cleaning up. American able-bodied seamen and ordinary seamen are provided with a steward, who takes orders from the men, acts as waiter, and afterward cleans up the utensils and messroom. Both British and American officers are served at meals. Whereas on British ships only officers have tablecloths at meals, on American ships tablecloths are provided for all hands.

Although union membership has had little effect on status on British ships, the American union organization among unlicensed personnel at sea has tended to decrease social distance between fellow union members of different status, because the union teachings of brotherhood and equality are in contradiction to the official social hierarchy. Social pressures are applied to the bosun, chief steward, and carpenter to make them work in close cooperation with, and give their loyalty to, the able-bodied and ordinary seamen rather than form a separate petty-officer group. Through union efforts, the pay differential and differences in living conditions have been reduced between bosun, carpenter, chief steward, and the able-bodied and ordinary seamen.

On American ships the consistent playing down of symbols that strengthen status and social distance as compared with British practice appears to be closely related to the sentiments the men have toward social distance and authority. While interviewing, I found a consistent difference between British and American seamen in the degree of awareness and acceptance of social distance between statuses. On American ships, early in the interviews, I met such expressions as:

> The bosun, he's one of the boys. He's just another fellow.
> (Able-bodied seaman)

> The mates, they just act big because they don't do no lousy jobs, and walk up and down the bridge doing nothing. I'm as good a man as any of them.
> (Able-bodied seaman)

As the interviews developed, seamen did give various reasons why there was a need for social distance, and these explanations would often be accompanied by surprise, as if these were ideas they had never before explicitly recognized.

On British ships, in contrast, social distance was accepted as a matter of course, and it was stressed among the men that one of the reasons that officers and men for the most part kept separate was that the men had no wish to mix with the officers and preferred companions from their own or a similar status.

THE EFFECTS OF CORRUPTION IN A DEVELOPING NATION

David H. Bayley

Studies of politics and administration in the developing nations, whether about Africa, Latin America, the Middle East, or South and Southeast Asia, almost invariably comment upon the prevalence of corruption on the part of both politicians and civil servants. Standards of public morality, we are told, are deplorably low. Local observers within these countries confirm this impression. Where the press is free, governmental corruption becomes a stock-in-trade of a great deal of journalistic commentary. Local authorities themselves sometimes take up the subject of venality in government in order to determine its extent and recommend measures for its eradication. Then groups within prominent political parties raise their voices in criticism, not just of politicians in other parties, but more impressively of the deteriorating standards of behavior within their own ranks. The conclusion, on the basis of all this smoke, must be that corruption certainly exists in many developing nations. It would probably not be too much to say that it forms a prominent, or at least not readily avoidable, feature of bureaucratic life in these nations.

Reprinted from *Western Political Quarterly,* vol. 19 (1966), pp. 719–732. By permission of the University of Utah, copyright owners.

Given its prevalence, whether as proven or assumed fact, it is surprising that so little attention has been given to its role and effects within the developing political situation. Western, as well as local, observers have generally been content with deploring its existence. This frequently involves taking rather perverse pleasure in dwelling upon the amount of corruption to be discovered and then asserting that elimination of corruption is a "must" for successful development. While most Western observers have manfully striven to avoid assuming a moralistic posture, they have rather uncritically assumed that the presence of corruption is an important hindrance to economic growth and progressive social change. There has been a significant absence of analysis about the effects which corruption has in fact upon economic development, nascent political institutions, and social attitudes. Unless it has been determined that a social practice, such as corruption, contributes no positive benefits, condemnation of it is really a practice at rote and is no improvement upon moralism.

The purpose of this essay is to show that corruption in developing nations is not necessarily antipathetic to the development of modern economic and social systems; that corruption serves in part at least a beneficial function in developing societies. In order to demonstrate this I shall present a list of the effects of corruption, *both* positive and negative. It will be necessary first to discuss the meaning of the word corruption, and then whether it makes sense to apply the category as defined in the West to behavior in non-Western countries. The focus of the essay will be entirely upon governmental corruption and not that within private agencies. The illustrative material will be taken overwhelmingly from Indian experience, for this is the country with which I am most familiar. I am sure, however, that the Indian situation is not atypical. Finally, it must be quite clear that in specifying the effects of corruption I am presenting hypotheses rather than proven conclusions. The arguments I make for asserting that an effect of a particular kind is present are often *a priori*. But I have carefully tried to frame my hypotheses in such a way as to highlight the empirical referents which must be studied in order to validate them.

THE DEFINITION OF CORRUPTION

Webster's Third New International Dictionary (1961) defines corruption as "inducement [as of a public official] by means of improper considerations [as bribery] to commit a violation of duty." A bribe is then defined as "a price, reward, gift or favor bestowed or promised with a view to pervert the judgment or corrupt the conduct esp. of a person in a position of trust [as a public official]." Bribery and corruption are intimately linked together, but they are not inseparable. A person bribed is a person corrupt; but a man may be corrupt who does not take bribes.[1] Corruption would surely include nepotism and misappropriation.[2] In both these cases there is "inducement by means of improper considerations." Corruption, then, while being tied particularly to the act of bribery, is a general term covering misuse of authority as a result of considerations of personal gain, which need not be monetary. This point has been well made in a recent Indian government report on corruption: "In its widest connotation, corruption includes improper and selfish exercise of power and influence attached to a public office or to the special position one occupies in public life."[3]

It is important to note that a person may be corrupt who does not in fact commit a violation of duty. Webster's definition only says that an individual must be induced to commit. The hero of the African novel, *No Longer at Ease,* which portrays the tension between the demands of traditional society and standards of a Western civil service, finally capitulates to the pressures upon him and accepts gratuities but salves his conscience with the thought that he only takes money from those whom he approves on their merits anyhow.[4] A variation of this is the civil servant who takes money from all applicants impartially but still goes ahead and decides the matter on merits. Rumor in India would have it that this is not an exceptional situation. Are such people corrupt? A strict application of Webster's definition would lead to an answer in the affirmative, and general Western usage would, I think, conform to the strict reading.

Corrupt behavior is behavior condemned and censured. "Corruption" is a pejorative term. However, applying the label to behavior on the part of public officials in many non-Western countries immediately poses a dilemma of intriguing dimensions. The man who in many non-Western countries is corrupt in Webster's sense is not condemned at all by his own society. Indeed, he may be conforming to a pattern of behavior his peers, family, and friends strongly support and applaud. For example, in both Africa and India the man who uses his official position to obtain jobs for his relatives is not considered immoral: in traditional terms, he is only doing

---

[1] In this respect there has been a change in the relation between "bribery" and "corruption" from *Webster's New International Dictionary* (2d ed., 1958). In the earlier edition the definition of corruption explicitly mentioned bribery and the definition of bribery explicitly referred to corruption.

[2] *Webster's Third New International Dictionary* defines (a) nepotism: "favoritism shown to nephews and other relatives (as by giving them positions because of their relationship rather than on their merits)"; (b) to misappropriate: "to appropriate dishonestly for one's own use: embezzle."

[3] *Report of the Committee on Prevention of Corruption* (New Delhi: Government of India, 1964), p. 5. Known as the Santhanam Committee Report, after its chairman.

[4] Chinua Achbe, *No Longer at Ease* (New York: Ivan Obolensky, 1960).

what every loyal member of an extended family is expected to do. He would be censured if he did not act in this way. The point is strongly made in the fictitious musings of a Delhi businessman in these words:

> Bribery and corruption! These were foreign words, it seemed to him, and the ideas behind them were also foreign. Here in India, he thought, one did not know such words. Giving presents and gratuities to government officers was an indispensable courtesy and a respectable, civilised way of carrying on business.[5]

It not infrequently happens, then, in developing non-Western societies that existing moral codes do not agree with Western norms as to what kinds of behavior by public servants should be condemned. The Western observer is faced with an uncomfortable choice. He can adhere to the Western definition, in which case he lays himself open to the charge of being censorious and he finds that he is condemning not aberrant behavior but normal, acceptable operating procedure. On the other hand, he may face up to the fact that corruption, if it requires moral censure, is culturally conditioned. He then argues that an act is corrupt if the surrounding society condemns it.[6] This usage, however, muddies communication, for it may be necessary then to assert in the same breath that an official accepts gratuities but is not corrupt or that an official gives preference in employment to his relatives but is not corrupt. Rather tedious explanations invariably must follow and people are left with the feeling that serious violence has been done to words.

Between these two alternatives the better choice, in my view, is to preserve the Western denotative meaning of corruption. This will be the meaning employed in this paper. If the Westerner chooses the culturally relevant definition, he will either end by abandoning the term altogether or will find it necessary to define it peculiarly, perhaps differently, for every non-Western country studied. This will present serious problems of communication with colleagues. There are other reasons as well for preserving the Western meaning. As Western observers we are interested in compara-

[5] R. Prawer Jhabvala, *The Nature of Passion* (New York: Norton, 1956), p. 56. Novels are often a forgotten key to the human problems of traditional society, and since few scholars portray social problems in intimate, biographical terms, they are indispensable sources of information to those who would seek to understand the human, motivational problems involved.
[6] This is the solution adopted by Ronald Wraith and Edgar Simpkins in *Corruption in Developing Nations* (London: G. Allen, 1963), pp. 34–35. They even go farther and say that the actor must also be afflicted with a sense of guilt. The last condition, especially, seems unduly restricting. A man may act wrongly even though he is not conscious of acting wrongly. His lack of guilt-feelings may have a bearing upon his guilt in law but surely does not affect society's definition of what constitutes improper or illicit action.

tive findings about behavior in our own and other cultures. We are familiar with the fact that even in the West there is some disagreement about standards of propriety in the dealings of public officials. This is particularly true of the activities of politicians on behalf of their constituents. It is not entirely curious then that one may speak of an act being corrupt and not find massive social censure. This being the case it is more felicitous to say that in many non-Western countries behavior X, which in the West is called corrupt, does not attract social condemnation. Other findings, predicated on the category corruption, will be that it is more or less prevalent than in the West, that it is or is not confined to different role players than in the West, that it serves the same or a different function, or that it is motivated by similar or rather different considerations.

The advantage of this solution is that we get rid of nonessentials, such as the element of social judgment, but keep the denotative core, i.e., the taking of bribes or employing of relatives. In this way, as the English would say, we do not throw out the baby with the bath water. Only minor adjustments are made, hence making possible comparative statements easily understood by colleagues.

There is another reason for keeping the Western denotative meaning. The intelligentsia, and especially top-level civil servants, in most underdeveloped nations are familiar with the Western label "corruption," and they apply it to their own countries. Since modernization around the world is most often Westernization, the standards the intelligentsia and opinion-leaders of these countries are trying to inculcate are Western ones. The premise of the Santhanam Committee was that "corruption," in the Western sense, should be eliminated. Similarly in Africa the conflict in the hearts of civil servants is precisely over which standard of morality should prevail, the Western or the traditional. Non-Westerners are acutely conscious of the Western meaning of corruption; they use it among themselves. And they are painfully aware that Western standards of governmental conduct condemn it. It is not unfair, therefore, to make comparative statements between West and non-West based upon Webster's definition. Such judgments will be readily understood by the nation-building elites in most developing nations.

An even more serious problem involves separating proper from improper behavior in the realm of politics whatever the country. It is easy to say that a civil servant should consider only the merits of a case. A politician, by the nature of his job, is a channel for the pressure of special groups within the country. It is an accepted part of his function that he garner public expenditures for his constituents or groups represented within his constituency; that he help them to gain access to government employment; that he influence administrators to locate a road through a town in his area rather than in an adjacent constituency. A politician is the instrument that makes government responsive to individuals. A civil servant who responded to his tribal or caste affiliation to secure jobs for young men would be accused of being nepotistic; a politician who secured government employ for the same group would be admired as an effective politician. Is there morally a difference between them? Clearly concepts of propriety, upon which the definition of corruption hinges, for the civil servant and politician are not coincidental; propriety is specific to roles to some extent. The latitude possessed by the politician is greater than that of the civil servant, and since the politician must respond to subnational pressure groups by the nature of his role, it follows that the boundary line between permissible and impermissible behavior on the part of politicians will be more hazy than that for civil servants. I shall not try to make this boundary more discernible, but will talk around the issue, realizing that even in the West there is apt to be substantial disagreement about where the duty of a politician lies as between his constituents and the larger interests of his country.

THE EXTENT OF CORRUPTION

Estimates of the extent of corruption practiced in underdeveloped countries are, expectedly, very imprecise. Rumor abounds, facts are scarce. Three observations may be made:

First: in many underdeveloped countries corruption is expected by the people as a part of everyday official life. Public cynicism on this score is colossal. As the *Times of India* has said, "People's acceptance of corruption as a fact of life and their general despondency need to be tackled first."[7]

Second: officials share this opinion of the people, and their opinions have at times been buttressed by government-sponsored investigations. The situation was considered sufficiently serious in India to warrant the appointment of an investigative committee by the central government. The result was the *Report of the Committee on Prevention of Corruption, 1964,* already referred to. Ronald Wraith and Edgar Simpkins in their book *Corruption in Developing Nations* cite several government studies of administrative procedures in West Africa, both under the British and after independence, which have discussed the widespread extent of corruption.

The Santhanam Committee reported that at a conservative estimate 5 per cent of the money spent during the Second Five Year Plan for construction and purchases was lost to the exchequer through corruption.[8]

[7] May 10, 1964, p. 6, editorial.
[8] P. 18.

In discussing the granting of export/import licenses the Committee said, "It is common knowledge that *each license* fetches anything between one hundred per cent to five hundred per cent of its face-value."[9] The Government of Punjab State, India, reported that in the last four years 3,000 government workers had been dismissed or punished as a result of the activities of the State Vigilance Department, which is charged with investigation of improper practices. John P. Lewis, former director of the International Development Research Center at Indiana and now A.I.D. director in India, while admitting that he cannot estimate with great accuracy the corruption at top levels in India, says that petty corruption at lower levels is immense. He also notes his impression that corruption at higher levels in India is a good deal less prevalent than in most other developing nations.[10] Read with the Santhanam Committee's assessment of the inroads corruption has made in India, this certainly does not speak well for the situation in other lands. Actually, alarming statements of the extensiveness of corrupt practices in most other developing nations could be multiplied almost indefinitely.

Wraith and Simpkins comment as follows about the African situation:

> How much is true and how much is false about corruption in high places nobody outside a small circle can ever know for certain. What *is* certain, and can be said without circumlocution, is that to wander through the corridors of power in these countries is to wander through a whispering-gallery of gossip, in which the fact of corruption at the highest levels is taken utterly for granted, and the only interest lies in capping the latest story with one that is even more startling.[11]

The same could be said of India.

Third: corruption is not confined to only a few levels of the official hierarchy, but seems to pervade the entire structure. It should also be noted that although corruption at the top attracts the most attention in public forums, and involves the largest amount of money in separate transactions, corruption at the very bottom levels is the more apparent and obvious and in total amounts of money involved may very well rival corruption at the top.

THE EFFECTS OF CORRUPTION

Corruption comes in innumerable shapes, forms, and sizes. There are as many reasons for corrupting as there are ways in which government affects individuals; there are as many avenues for corruption as there are roles

---

9 *Ibid.*, emphasis added.
10 See *Quiet Crisis in India* (New York: Doubleday, 1964), p. 145.
11 Wraith and Simpkins, *op. cit.*, pp. 15–16.

to be played in government. Corruption may be involved in the issuance of export licenses, a decision to investigate in a criminal case, obtaining of a copy of court proceedings, appointment of candidates to universities, choice of men for civil service jobs, inspection of building specifications in new housing developments, avoiding of arrest by people with defective motor vehicles, granting of contracts, and in the expediting of anything. This wealth of forms would appear to make analysis of effects formidable and perhaps impossible. The solution is to distinguish and to keep firmly in mind the essential elements of a corrupt act; that is, to establish a type-form.

Elaborating upon the definition found in Webster's, a corrupt practice will be assumed to involve the following elements: (a) a decision to depart from government-established criteria for decisions of the relevant class and (b) a monetary reward benefiting either the official directly or those related to him.

In analyzing the effects of corrupt practices two categories of generalized effects may be distinguished, apart from whether the effects are good or bad. First, there are direct, unmediated effects. These are the effects that are part of the act itself. They are the effects contained in the reasons for which the favor seeker, the corruptor, initiated the act. Second, there are indirect effects, mediated through those who perceive that an act of a certain kind—in this case a corrupt one—has taken place. There are three classes of mediating actors: the corrupted, the corruptor, and the non-participating audience.

In the discussion that follows I shall present the harmful factors first and the beneficial ones second. No attempt has been made explicitly to locate each effect within the analytic schema just presented, but it would be possible to do so. These lists are undoubtedly incomplete; the effects presented here are the more important.

Harmful Effects of Corrupt Acts

1. A corrupt act represents a failure to achieve the objectives government sought when it established criteria for decisions of various classes. To the extent that the objectives sought were worthwhile, corrupt acts exact a cost in non-achievement. For example, if the objective in hiring government employees is the obtaining of efficiency and ability in carrying out official tasks, then corruption in appointments produces inefficiency and waste. If the issuing of permits for domestic enterprises is designed to insure that scarce resources go to projects enjoying the highest priority in terms of facilitating long-run economic development, then corruption exacts a cost by inhibiting over-all economic development. Places in universities and opportunities for foreign educational experience are severely limited in

most developing nations; if corruption is present in the awards, the country fails to obtain the best result in making use of a scarce opportunity.

2. Corruption represents a rise in the price of administration. The multiple of extra cost depends on what the market will bear. The man who is both taxpayer and also forced to submit to bribing has paid several times over for the same service. Corruption is a mechanism for allocating increased amounts of resources to the performance of a single type of function, namely, government administration.

3. If corruption takes the form of a kickback, it serves to diminish the total amount expended for public purposes. It represents a diversion of resources from public purposes to private ones. For example, a civil servant may let a contract for a certain sum, but get 10 per cent back for the favor of giving the contract: 90 per cent of the allocated amount goes for the public purpose, 10 per cent goes into personal gains and acquisitions.

4. Corruption exerts a corrupting influence on other members of the administrative apparatus. This is a function of its persistence, its perceived rewards, and the impunity with which it is done. Corruption feeds upon itself and erodes the courage necessary to adhere to high standards of propriety. Morale declines, each man asking himself why he should be the sole custodian of morality.

5. Corruption in government, perceived by the people, lowers respect for constituted authority. It undercuts popular faith in government to deal even-handedly. The less a regime depends upon coercion in order to maintain itself, the more it must depend upon popular respect for it. One element in this process of legitimation is popular faith in government to deal fairly among competing claimants. Corruption weakens this element of support.

6. Politicians and civil servants constitute an elite. Their function is to give purpose to national effort. In so doing they cannot avoid setting an example others will emulate. If the elite is believed to be widely and thoroughly corrupt, the man-in-the-street will see little reason why he too should not gather what he can for himself and his loved ones. Selig Harrison has said of contemporary India:

> The old vision is gone, and there are few signs pointing to the birth of a renewed spirit of common purpose to take its place. *The mode is increasingly one of every man for himself.* This can be felt at every turn in the impatient refusal of each sector of the population to accept the disciplines of planned development. Thus a farmer who grows more food shows more determination than ever to hoard it for a time of still greater stringency or to consume it himself rather than to free it for the market in response to pleas from New Delhi. The middleman and trader reacted to the recent food price crisis by creating artificial local scarcities to push prices up, moving operations methodically from one

area to another with the police one jump behind. The low-wage consumer in the cities and towns, who has been using his increase in income in recent years to buy wheat or rice instead of coarse grains, refused to shift back during the 1964 pinch despite official exhortations. All this could also have been said of earlier food crises under Nehru, but *one detected on this occasion for the first time a note of antagonism and even of contempt toward constituted authority.*[12]

Corruption among an elite not only debases standards popularly perceived, it forces people to undertake the underhanded approach out of self-defense. They feel they must resort to corrupt practices just to get their due, not to secure inordinate returns.[13] This is a classic vicious circle.

7. An important, perhaps overwhelming, problem in those nations that have sought to develop economically within a democratic political framework has been the unwillingness of politicians to take actions which are necessary for development but unpopular with the mass of the people. Taxation is the most obvious example. A corrupt official or politician is a self-centered individual. Can such a person be expected to put country before self, to jeopardize his prospects for the sake of prosperity for the whole country in the remote future? Uncommon political courage can hardly be maintained in an atmosphere of tolerance of corruption.

8. With erosion of belief in the even-handedness of public officials comes the need to cultivate special contacts, to develop enough "pull" to offset the claims of others. In many underdeveloped countries the amount of time and human energy devoted to making these contacts is immense. The effort that might otherwise be spent in enhancing credentials, in strengthening one's case objectively, goes into the necessary task of lobbying. The loss in productive effort defies estimation.

9. Corruption, since it represents to the man-in-the-street institutionalized unfairness, inevitably leads to litigation, calumnious charges, the bitter grievances. Even the honest official may be blackmailed by the threat that unless he act unfairly he may be charged publicly with being corrupt. And there would be few to believe his disclaimer. The attention and energies of official and nonofficial alike are diverted into endless, unproductive wrangling.

10. Time is important in the making of most decisions, delays can be costly in monetary and human terms. The most ubiquitous form of corruption takes the form of what Indians call "speed money." The wheels

---

[12] "Troubled India and Her Neighbors," *Foreign Affairs*, January 1965, p. 314. Emphasis added.

[13] For an excellent description of this attitude see William and Charlotte Wiser, *Behind Mud Walls, 1930–1960* (Berkeley: University of California Press, 1963), pp. 128–129.

of the bureaucratic machine must be oiled with money, and unless this is done nothing at all will be done. Corruption causes decisions to be weighed in terms of money, not in terms of human need. The poor man with an urgent and just request gets little if any sympathy.

Beneficial Effects of Corrupt Acts

In order to sustain the points that follow, I shall present arguments sufficient to show that the effects of corruption *may* be beneficial in nature. I do not pretend that they always are, simply that it would not be unreasonable to find that they are. Nor does it follow that because the effects are good the means are either desirable or blameless.

1. There is a common assumption that corrupt acts produce effects worse than those which would have followed from an untainted decision. This assumption is only true to the extent that the government-established— or system-established—criteria for choice are better than those served by corruption. Governments have no monopoly upon correct solutions; governments are simply one among many bureaucratic institutions which may do stupid things. Both the ends and the means served by government-constricted choices may be worse than those freely chosen and finding expression through corruption. Corruption may serve as a means for impelling better choices, even in terms of government's expressed goals. Nor do I think it necessary to say that corruption only occasionally, and by chance, operates in this direction. It could systematically do so, not perhaps across the board in all decisions but certainly in all decisions of a certain kind. For example, government may desire to build a strong fertilizer industry and toward this end may have established certain requirements for the selection of firms to receive the concession. If government economists have not selected the proper indicators of efficiency, it is not far-fetched to assume that ability to offer massive bribes—bribes at least bigger than anyone else's—could be correlated with entrepreneurial efficiency. Bribes represent a peculiar element of cost, applying to all competing firms; the ability to meet it may not be unrelated to efficiency.

Corruption, then, is not an inherently defective means of arriving at decisions among competing claimants. The satisfactoriness of the inducement offered may correlate with features among claimants government would choose if it had better information or greater expertise in selecting criteria for decision-making. In order to demonstrate the effect of departing from established decision-making criteria, two general types of cases need to be analyzed, those in which the inducement is solely monetary and those in which it is something besides money such as loyalty to family, caste, tribe, and so forth. One must then ask if, for any particular group of decisions made, the absence of the extra ingredient would have made the result of the decision better? In many cases the decision probably would be unaltered; in some it might be better; but in some it could very easily have been worse. Even in the case of non-monetary inducements, it would be necessary to determine that bias across the group of decision-makers, for a particular class of choices, acted to favor persons or firms less able to carry out what government intended. It could happen that groups within a society successful in penetrating the civil service in sufficient numbers to influence decisions might for this very reason have qualities instrumental for the accomplishment of activities government wants carried out. Therefore nepotistic favoritism would lead government to rely on just those groups most capable of shouldering responsibility. In underdeveloped countries the tangle of popular pressures involving traditionally antagonistic groups frequently causes government to award contracts, scholarships, privileges, and jobs according to mechanical quota systems. Since talent and ability are very often unevenly distributed through these societies, this policy is not in the direction of optimum efficiency. Corruption of the monetary and non-monetary kind might very well offset this pervasive influence.

2. Corruption, whether in the form of kickbacks or of payments originating with the briber, may result in increased allocations of resources away from consumption and into investment. Contrary to common expectations, it may be a supplemental allocative mechanism compatible with the goals of economic development. The key elements in this determination are the marginal propensities of the corrupted and the corruptor to consume and invest. In the case of kickbacks, for example, if the kickback comes from funds designed for projects contributing little to the sum total of capital investment, then diversion of some of these to an individual who will use them for investment in productive enterprises actually results in a net accretion to the stock of capital goods. This would be the case with funds diverted from famine relief or inefficient cottage industries into the hands of civil servants backing firms manufacturing tires or machine tools. A similar instance is a bribe financed by the briber himself. His marginal propensity to consume may be greater than that of the bribed. It may even be that government servants as a whole, especially at the upper levels, representing an educated elite with unique access to information about prospects for economic development, may have a greater propensity to invest in productive enterprises of a modern kind than do a cross-section of the people who seek to bribe them. It is not indubitable, then, that corruption represents a net drain from investment into consumption or even from the modern sector of enterprise into the traditional.

3. The opportunity for corruption may actually serve to increase the

quality of public servants. If wages in government service are insufficient to meet a talented man's needs, and he has an alternate choice, he will be tempted to choose the other. On the other hand, a man anxious to serve his country through government service might opt away from non-government employment if he knew that means existed to supplement a meager salary. Even for the man with no alternative prospects for employment, security in meeting his unavoidable obligations may enhance his willingness to serve ably and loyally.

The corrupt are not always unable; nor are they always unpatriotic. These propositions seem especially true of underdeveloped countries where the rewards for government service are so piteously low. Where corruption is often necessary to provide basic necessities of life to oneself and one's family, it becomes a necessary means of ensuring a supply of able and willing public servants. Furthermore, in developing nations it is an indispensable means of reconciling insufficient wage rates with the claims of traditional society operating through extended family and clan ties. The civil servant cannot wish away these obligations. Through corruption he taxes society with preserving an important element of social continuity.

4. Nepotism in government hiring, which swells the ranks of the civil service, can be looked upon as a substitute for a public works system. It provides employment for the otherwise unemployed and by making them dependent upon government may secure a measure of support for government. Inflated civil service rolls become the price for relieving intolerable political pressure due to unemployment. To be sure, the quality of performance in government service may certainly suffer from the injection of the public works objective. The goals of each may be incompatible: relief on the one hand, efficiency in government operations on the other. But, granting the incompatibility, it is incumbent upon us to admit that to the extent that a public works program is needed corruption in hiring may serve the same end.

It is well known, for example, that in many underdeveloped countries there is a growing army of half-educated unemployed. The revolutionary potential of this mass is considerable; they gravitate to the political extremes in much greater proportions than members of other groups. In countries where the absorptive capacity of private agencies is not great enough to provide employment for the educated or half-educated, government service obtained by means of illicit considerations may provide a safety valve of considerable importance.

5. Corruption provides a means of giving those persons or groups potentially disaffected as a result of exclusion from power a stake in the system. The degree to which they can be tied to the system in this way depends upon their ability and willingness to capitalize upon the op-

portunities for corruption. A person with money who is ideologically opposed to the regime or who dislikes the personnel at the top, may nonetheless be able to make the repugnant system work for him by means of illicit influence. He is not entirely alienated.

6. In traditional societies struggling to be Western, corruption may make the new system human in traditional terms. Corruption is an understandable means of influence in most traditional societies. A transitional people may have more faith in a system they can influence in some degree through personal action than one they do not know how to manipulate by means of the institutional mechanisms provided. The human contact provided in a corrupt act may be a necessary transitional device to insure the loyalty to the new of a tradition-bound people. Perhaps it is better that people in developing nations misuse modern agencies to their own ends than they reject the new because they cannot work the handles. This argument particularly applies to countries trying to implant democratic institutions. The successor to the rejected democratic forms will not be hallowed traditional ones, whatever the people may wish, but a modern, impersonal system less subject to rejection.

7. Corruption provides a means for reducing the harshness of an elite-conceived plan for economic and social development. It supplements the political system by allowing the introduction of political considerations at the administrative level. Such access may be essential to the stability of the system. When political channels are clogged, corruption provides nonviolent entry into government affairs and administration.

8. Among politicians corruption may act as a solvent for uncompromisable issues of ideology and/or interest. Where potential schisms based upon the claims of caste, tribe, region, religion, or language are manifold, common interest in spoils may provide cement for effective political unity, especially within a single dominant party. In general, corruption should damp doctrinairism, no matter how predicated. It is the disheartened politician, cut off from power or perquisites, who is more likely to repair to the standard of factional rigidity or ideological extremism.

9. In developing nations, particularly where there is comparatively free play of political forces, there is often tension between the civil service and the politicians. The bureaucracy may develop considerable *esprit de corps* and feel impatient with the activities of politicians whose only thought seems to be to truckle to mass whims, hampering the orderly progress of the bureaucratic nation-building machine. Politicians, on the other hand, may find the civil service unresponsive, proud, and aloof, without the slightest understanding of the importance of the role politicians must play. Politicians accuse the bureaucrats of running a closed corporation; bureaucrats argue that politicians divert attention and resources from

essential tasks.[14] The practice of corruption may lessen this potentially crippling strain. It is one means of increasing the responsiveness of bureaucrats to individual and group needs. It also links the bureaucrat and the politician in an easily discerned network of self-interest. There may be a principle here: in countries where agreement upon proper relative functions has not been fixed between bureaucrats and politicians, the less amenable planning is to political pressures—due perhaps to rigid adherence to "rational" planning criteria—the greater may be the functional importance of corruption in preserving a working relationship between civil servants and popular leaders. An alternative means to the same end could be found in the imposition of sanctions by an agency capable of disciplining both sides. In this case agreement upon functions is enforced.

CONCLUSION

Because so many incommensurables are involved in the effects of corrupt practices, it is impossible to determine firmly and precisely how the positive and negative effects combine to produce an over-all thrust along either dimension. It is clear, though, that corruption is an accommodating device. Its benefits are to be seen primarily in the realm of politics. But the analysis has also shown that the net effects of corrupt practices upon economic development are not always, or necessarily, of a baneful nature. There are serious negative effects, to be sure, and these may be assessed either in terms of economic costs or of dysfunctional attitudes being formed throughout the developing society. But even if a final balance sheet cannot be constructed, it is still abundantly clear that corruption is a social practice about which there is very little accurate theoretical analysis and even less empirical research.

Research into corruption will be difficult, but ingenuity should be able to overcome many seemingly insurmountable obstacles. Analysis of indirect or mediated effects of corruption will be easier than analysis of direct effects. Mediated effects are those which depend upon someone's perceiving that an act of this particular kind has occurred. Surveys designed to touch all three acting groups—corrupted, corruptor, audience—should be able to establish, among other things, each group's opinion about improper behavior among the other groups, concept of role in society, morale, and values operating to restrain or impel behavior of various kinds. Studies of this kind yield considerable information about the mediated effects of corruption found or believed found in others. Research into the direct, unmediated effects is more difficult because it requires knowledge of how

[14] For an excellent discussion of this problem in one country, Burma, see Lucien Pye's *Politics, Personality, and Nation Building* (New Haven: Yale University Press, 1962).

many of which kinds of people are doing what in various circumstances. Precise knowledge of actors and situations is essential. By and large the researcher will have to depend upon the results of official studies; he will not have the resources, nor would it be discreet, to undertake such a survey himself—although the researcher, especially the foreign one, may find that people are distressingly willing to speak about practices engaged in by themselves which the researcher considers corrupt but the respondents do not. This is particularly true of people still substantially enmeshed in a traditional world, with little modern education, and hence unlettered in Western standards of propriety. Generally the key to unlocking tongues is to seek information about how politics works, the amount of influence various role players possess, their tactics of maneuver, and their concept of function, carefully refraining from describing behavior in pejorative terms. It must be admitted, even so, that most knowledge will be about forms of corruption and less about extent. Nonetheless, it is still possible to analyze many of the effects of corruption. Making assumptions about who corrupts and who is corrupted, describing these actors by membership in socially defined groups, one can then collect data about consumption patterns, family size, social obligations, level of remuneration, values with respect to achievement and striving, and so forth, and thereby determine either the reasons for which corruption is undertaken or the ways in which gains from it will be utilized. Moreover, it should be possible to arrive at a description of the human predicament impelling corruption. A study of this kind would underscore the root factors in corruption and thereby provide a means of gauging its function in society.

That corruption is an accommodating device has important implications. It indicates that corrupt practices are a human response to circumstances, conditioned, to be sure, by moral codes. But it also means that corruption is to some extent a creation of the very circumstances defining political and economic underdevelopment. It becomes apparent, therefore, that considerably more than exhortation may be needed in order to eliminate venality in government. It also indicates that removal of all vestiges of corruption may not be a good thing. There are three strategies that can be employed in a transitional situation to reduce corrupt practices. First, a policy may be adopted of containing the grosser forms of corruption while waiting for changing circumstance to remove the functional utility of such practices. This strategy is essentially a passive one and may be fatally flawed by the implicit assumption that corruption will not exert such harmful consequences as to jeopardize progress to a less unstable level. Second, corruption may be rooted out without hesitancy or remorse, counting upon the power of the state to contain repercussions. Coercion is used to offset the discontinuity in social accommodation which the removal of corruption may occasion. Third, the climate of opinion may be remolded so that the temptation to corruption on the part of both briber and bribed is substantially reduced. The building of a sense of national purposefulness, sacrifice, and dedication may cause the corruptor to be shunned and the potentially corrupted to be strong. This strategy relies upon psychological change and represents the substitution of one set of operational values for another. Its defect is that unless buttressed by real social change, it quickly loses force and wastes precipitously.

These three strategies are not mutually exclusive. None of them would be employed by itself. The mix of the three depends upon the character of the regime and it should also depend upon knowledge of the function corruption plays in the particular society. Corrupt practices may be more easily eradicated by exhortation and revived national morale than many suppose; corruption may also be more resistant than realized and not yield readily to such tactics. The point is that the knowledge necessary to make this judgment is now almost wholly lacking. This situation should be rapidly transformed. And this essay has sought to provide a first step, primarily by demonstrating that corruption wears two faces and not simply one. Corruption may play a useful role in transitional societies, a role which is sufficiently important that if it was not played by this device must be played by another or the consequences might severely undermine the pace, but more importantly the character, of the development effort.

ADMINISTRATIVE RATIONALITY, SOCIAL SETTING, AND ORGANIZATIONAL DEVELOPMENT

Stanley H. Udy, Jr.

Few if any concepts employed in social science are fraught with so many difficulties as is the concept "rationality." It is used in a bewildering variety of ways, each of which seems to involve its own plethora of philosophical, psychological, and sociological problems. For present purposes we shall let the chips fall where they may and consider social behavior to be *rational* insofar as it is purposefully directed toward explicit empirical objectives and planned in accordance with the best available scientific knowledge.[1] Brushing aside, for the time being, the question of uncertainty—which, though of crucial practical importance, merely complicates the problem in a formal sense—one may say that the most severe difficulties with this concept from a sociological viewpoint seem to appear in situations where it is applied simultaneously to individuals and collectivities in the same context. Historically the classic instance is perhaps the "problem of order" in utilitarian social philosophy; namely, the problem of accounting for the existence of society assuming it to be composed of discrete individuals striving rationally for the same ends in a context of scarce resources. The solution to this problem, of course, as has been widely pointed out, is that

Reprinted from Stanley H. Udy, Jr., "Administrative Rationality, Social Setting, and Organizational Development," *The American Journal of Sociology*, vol. 68, (1962) pp. 299–308, with minor omissions. By permission of the author and publisher, The University of Chicago Press.

[1] Based on Marion J. Levy, Jr., "A Note on Pareto's Logical-Nonlogical Categories," *American Sociological Review*, XIII (December, 1948), 756–757. The problem of uncertainty of information is, of course, extremely important in other contexts. See, e.g., Herbert A. Simon, *Models of Man* (New York: Wiley, 1957), pp. 241–260.

neither the individual nor society—particularly the latter—is so rational in its behavior as the utilitarians had supposed. Cultural values distribute ends among categories of persons differentiated in the social structure and, at the same time, motivate "non-rational" behavior in given circumstances. Social integration is hence possible because there is no reason to suppose that it must occur relative to explicit over-all objectives. Not all behavior need be rational; indeed, on the societal level it cannot be.[2]

In the analysis of formal organizations, however, the problem of rationality arises again in a somewhat different form. One may define a *formal organization* as any social group engaged in pursuing explicit announced empirical objectives through manifestly co-ordinated effort and, at the same time, describe an entity that appears to be culturally universal.[3] A striking feature of such organizations is that the individuals in the system qua members as well as the system as a whole are expected to behave in a rational manner. The classical "problem of order" suggests that this state of affairs is by no means easy to attain; we may reasonably expect some formal organizations to come closer to it and, in this sense, to be "more rational" than others. Such "dual rationality" can be approximated in the case of formal organization only because the members of the organization are at the same time members of a larger society where integrative values can find expression independently of administrative structure.

We may thus presume rationality to be present in a formal organization to the extent that role expectations are based on planning for organizational objectives.[4] In a more sophisticated statement, Cyert and March characterize a rational system as being oriented to produce choices through standardized search procedures in such a way as to "maximize the expected return to the system" in terms of "a well-defined preference ordering over possible future states."[5] Two major determinants of the degree of administrative rationality in an organization thus suggest themselves: The first is the extent to which the structure of the organization defines and motivates planned collective behavior; the second is the degree to which behavior in the social setting is independent of behavior in the organization, from the standpoint of the individual member. This paper will thus first attempt to isolate organizational-structural requisites of rationality and

---

[2] Talcott Parsons, *The Structure of Social Action* (New York: Free Press, 1949), pp. 87–94, 697–719.
[3] Stanley H. Udy, Jr., " 'Bureaucracy' and 'Rationality' in Weber's Organization Theory," *American Sociological Review*, XXIV (December, 1959), 792 (hereinafter cited as "*BR*").
[4] Stanley H. Udy, Jr., "Technical and Institutional Factors in Production Organization," *American Journal of Sociology*, LXVII (November, 1961), 248 (hereinafter cited as "*TI*").
[5] R. M. Cyert and J. G. March, *A Behavioral Theory of the Firm* (Englewood Cliffs, N.J.: Prentice-Hall, 1963).

to analyze their interrelations. It will be found that the requisites herein isolated form a Guttman scale in terms of which the organizations studied can be compared as to degree of rationality. Second, we shall explore relationships between the rationality scale and the institutional and social settings of the organizations studied, in an attempt to assess the independence from societal ascription of organizations lying at different points on the scale. Finally, we shall propose some hypotheses about the development of rationality in organization.[6]

DATA AND METHODS

Data are drawn from thirty-four formal organizations engaged in the production of material goods in thirty-four non-industrial societies; information is based on anthropological monographs and the Human Relations Area Files. The method of cross-cultural comparison was used in order to maximize variation in both internal structure and social setting of the organizations studied. It was also decided to limit the analysis to organizations having three or more levels of authority, inasmuch as previous work suggested that only such organizations would be of sufficient complexity to be of interest for present purposes.[7] The thirty-four organizations studied are part of a sample of 426 organizations in 150 societies assembled for an earlier, more general study of work organization in non-industrial cul-

[6] Rationality is here treated as a *function* of organizational and social structure. In two previous papers we treated rationality as a *structural* category by operationalizing it in terms of presumed structural correlates. In *BR*, Weber's conception of administrative rationality was found to involve limited objectives, a performance emphasis, and segmental participation, as those terms are defined in the present study. In *TI*, degree of rationality was operationalized in terms of the presence or absence of limited objectives and segmental participation, as those terms are herein defined. In view of present considerations these earlier characterizations seem misleading. As indicated below, orientation to limited objectives appears to be the only one of these characteristics that properly forms a part of rationality per se, functionally considered. Performance emphasis, in view of the way it is operationalized, is more properly part of the reward system, and is so considered in *TI*. Segmental participation, along with a new item herein introduced, "specificity of role assignment," may be viewed structurally as an aspect of what one might term "role differentiation and assignment."

These changes, which allow the structural requisites of rationality to cut across the scheme presented in *TI*, suggest some revisions in the model presented there. Briefly, the category "role differentiation and assignment"—with particular reference to its degree of specificity—replaces what is there termed "rationality," and is defined somewhat differently, as indicated above. Assuming more precise ways of measuring it than are presented here, "rationality" could be considered a criterion variable relative to the entire model presented in *TI*. The relationships indicated in *TI* probably remain generally the same despite the change in the one category, although the present results raise some questions about their validity under certain conditions and suggest that some of the operational items are more important than others.
[7] *TI*, pp. 247–254.

ture, and were drawn in accord with the criteria set forth by George P. Murdock for his "World Ethnographic Sample."[8] Fifty-six of the original 426 cases proved both to have three or more levels of authority and also to offer sufficient data for purposes of the present analysis. Twelve of them, however, had already been employed in an ex post facto extrapolation of a scale containing four of the seven items used in the scale developed in the present study.[9] Since one of our desires was to test the previous result, these twelve cases were dropped, leaving forty-four organizations representing thirty-four societies. Under the not entirely realistic assumption that organizations in different societies represent independent events while those in the same society do not, only one organization per society was finally used, it being drawn at random when the society offered more than one potentially usable case on the basis of a survey of pertinent ethnographic material. Of the resulting thirty-four organizations representing thirty-four societies, eleven are African, twelve North American, and the remaining eleven are distributed over the Circum-Mediterranean, Insular Pacific, East Eurasian, and South American regions.[10] The geographical distribution of the sample is therefore unfortunately somewhat unbalanced. The extent to which this imbalance reflects the actual distribution of complex production organization as opposed to complete data is not known, except that it may be noted that materials on South American societies are quite sparse.

ADMINISTRATIVE RATIONALITY
AND ITS STRUCTURAL REQUISITES

We shall assume that rationality as herein defined minimally involves orientation to *limited objectives,* defined for present purposes as objectives explicitly restricted only to the production of certain products. This simple criterion of rationality is, of course, far from ideal but represents the closest operational approach possible of our data to "explicit announced objectives" or to "a well-defined preference ordering of future states."[11] We shall thus assert that "highly rational" organizations possess limited objectives in this sense, by definition. The problem now becomes one of exploring

[8] *American Anthropologist,* LIX (August, 1957), 664–687.
[9] Stanley H. Udy, Jr., " 'Bureaucratic' Elements in Organizations," *American Sociological Review,* XXIII (August, 1958), 415–418 (hereinafter cited as "*BE*"). In this earlier study, these characteristics were termed "bureaucratic" elements. It has since seemed appropriate to refer to them as aspects of "role differentiation and assignment" associated with rationality, and to treat "bureaucracy" as another dimension of organization entirely (see *BR*).
[10] Murdock, *op. cit.*
[11] Cyert and March, *op. cit.*

the structural requisites of an organizational orientation to limited objectives. In an earlier study it had been found that all organizations with limited objectives also involved *segmental participation*—that is, explicit definition of the terms of participation by some mutual contractual agreement—but that not all organizations with segmental participation had limited objectives.[12] Since a reasonable common-sense interpretation of this relationship is at hand (unrestricted terms of participation seem likely to invite goal displacement) it was decided to hypothesize that segmental participation precedes limited objectives at the upper end of the rationality scale. Reference was then made to another previous study[13] that found (in a sample different from the present one) the following characteristics to be related to segmental participation on a scale in the following descending order: *Performance emphasis* (expected dependence of the quantity of the reward on the amount and/or quality of work done); *specialization*[14] (the concurrent performance of three or more qualitatively different operations by different members); and *compensatory rewards* (allocation of money or goods in kind by members of higher authority to members of lower authority in return for participation).[15] Reasonable theoretical interpretations seemed possible for these findings as well. Segmental participation would seem to be difficult without some explicit attention being drawn to performance. Similarly, unless roles are specialized relative to one another such that the particular content of each is stable and discretely identifiable, any emphasis on performance would seem tenuous. Specialization, in turn, is always potentially difficult to institutionalize, since it is always at least partially determined by technical considerations. Functionally, compensatory rewards constitute a mechanism whereby specialization can be "artificially" institutionalized by management through its control

---

[12] BR.

[13] BE.

[14] We have elsewhere defined "specialization" as a continuous variable (i.e., the number of different operations performed simultaneously by different members; see my *Organization of Work* [New Haven, Conn.: HRAF Press, 1959], pp. 22–23). In a social context of the type discussed here, however, it seems proper to regard specialization as discontinuous; the number "three" was chosen as the cutoff point because three is the smallest number of roles in one system wherein ego is faced with the problem of defining relationships between two alters in a way independent of ego's relationship with either of them.

[15] See Peter M. Blau and W. Richard Scott, *Formal Organizations* (San Francisco: Chandler Publishing Company, 1962), pp. 205–206, 224–225. Blau and Scott regard this characteristic as indicative of "hierarchical dependence." We find that compensatory rewards indeed do represent hierarchical dependence but only one possible form which it may take. Other possible forms would be the use or threat of force, manipulation of approval needs, etc. We would argue that if organization is to be rational it is important that hierarchical dependence be restricted to compensatory rewards.

over the reward system. Furthermore, there is some reason to believe that compensatory rewards constitute the *only* mechanism that can reliably do this. Empirically, there appear to be only two possible alternatives: manipulation of already-existing social obligations, and the use of force.[16] The first of these alternatives presupposes a fortuitous and highly improbable identity of technical activities and social roles; the second is subject to serious limitations as a continuous mode of control, particularly in organizations that are at all complex. If this line of reasoning is correct, compensatory rewards are requisite to specialization, except under extremely improbable social conditions.

A review of pertinent literature on administration revealed that the items so far mentioned are often assumed to be structural correlates of administrative rationality and suggested two further items on which data were available: *specific job assignment* (continuous assignment by management of particular people to particular roles), and *centralized management* (the existence of a single internal source of ultimate authority).[17] The former was placed on the scale between specialization and performance emphasis on the grounds that roles had to be specialized to be assigned and that particular people had to be associated with particular roles to be rewarded for performance in a consistent fashion. Centralized management was placed at the beginning of the scale on the grounds that management could not consistently allocate compensatory rewards without being centralized.

The scale suggested by the preceding arguments was tested over our sample with the results shown in Table 1: "X" denotes the presence of a characteristic, "O" its absence. In general, the results are consistent with the hypotheses proposed.

Since much of the theoretical basis of this scale is probabilistic, one would expect some exceptions. Deviant cases were thus examined in detail, and proved to be of two general types. The first involved the absence of expected specialization or performance emphasis—the apparent loci of most of the deviance. The reason why so much deviation centers on these characteristics seems to be that the presence or absence of each of them, in contrast to the other items, is in part a function of purely technical considerations. Certain kinds of tasks, as for example many involving agriculture or construction, are by nature cumulative and do not lend

[16] Udy, *Organization of Work*, chap. vii.
[17] See, e.g., Max Weber, *Theory of Social and Economic Organization* (New York: Oxford, 1947), pp. 225–226; *From Max Weber: Essays in Sociology* (New York: Oxford, 1946), pp. 196 ff.; *General Economic History* (New York: Free Press, 1950), p. 95; James G. March and Herbert A. Simon, *Organizations* (New York: Wiley, 1958), pp. 12–33; and Chris Argyris, *Understanding Organizational Behavior* (Homewood, Ill.: Dorsey Press, 1960), pp. 12–13.

TABLE 1. *Administrative Rationality in 34 Non-industrial Production Organizations**

Organization	Limited Objectives	Seg-mental Participation	Per-formance Emphasis	Specific Job Assignment	Special-ization	Compen-satory Rewards	Central Management
Iroquois	x	x	x	x	x	x	x
Navaho	x	x	x	x	x	x	x
Paiute	x	x	x	x	x	x	x
Sanpoil	x	x	x	x	x	x	x
Sinkaietk	x	x	0	x	x	x	x
Nambicuara	x	x	0	x	x	x	x
Otoro	0	x	0	x	x	x	x
Hopi	0	x	0	x	x	x	x
Tikopia	0	0	x	x	x	x	x
Kabyles	0	0	x	x	x	x	x
Jukun	0	0	x	0	x	x	x
Tallensi	0	0	x	x	0	x	x
Haida	0	0	0	x	x	x	x
Haitians	0	0	0	x	x	x	x
Dahomeans	0	0	0	x	0	x	x
Tarahumara	0	0	0	x	0	x	x
Turkana	0	0	0	x	0	x	x
Camayura	0	0	0	x	0	x	x
Betsileo	0	0	0	0	x	x	x
Trobrianders	0	0	0	0	x	x	x
Pukapukans	0	0	0	0	x	0	x
Malay	0	0	0	0	x	0	x
Bemba	0	0	0	0	0	x	x
Crow	0	0	0	0	0	x	x
Ifaluk	0	0	0	0	0	x	x
Ila	0	0	0	0	0	x	x
Kikuyu	0	0	0	0	0	x	x
Lobi	0	0	0	0	0	x	x
Papago	0	0	0	0	0	x	x
Sotho	0	0	0	0	0	x	x
Winnebago	0	0	0	0	0	x	x
Dogon	0	0	0	0	0	0	x
Tarasco	0	0	0	0	0	0	0
Tibetans	0	0	0	0	0	0	0

* Coefficient of reproducibility = .95
For references see Udy, *Organization of Work*, pp. 139–158 ff.

themselves particularly to specialization, although there is no reason why they cannot be otherwise rationally organized. The Tallensi, Tarahumara, and Camayura cases appear probably to be of this variety. They suggest that rationality involves specialization only where the latter is clearly relevant technologically. Similarly, whether or not rationality involves a performance emphasis appears to be technologically relative. Where activities are highly routinized with a minimum of uncertainty involved, performance seems less likely to be emphasized, despite the presence of other rational characteristics. The Nambicuara, Otoro, and Hopi cases may well be of this variety. In sum, it appears that specialization and a performance emphasis tend in effect not to be a part of rational administration unless their presence clearly contributes to technical efficiency in the physical sense.

The other class of exceptions may be purely a function of the research methodology and are thus possibly more apparent than real. A characteristic was coded as "absent" not only when its existence was explicitly denied but also in instances where it was simply not reported, provided the context was such that it seemed reasonable to assume that the ethnographer would have reported it had it been present. This procedure of course tended to result in "overreporting" absences. On this score the single deviant omissions for the Sinkaietk, Dahomeans, Pukapukans, and possibly the Turkana are dubious; the "absent" characteristics may actually be present. By the same token, the Betsileo case may involve specific job assignments; the description is not entirely clear on this point. General explanations for other exceptions are not apparent.

The results were adjudged to be consistent with the hypothesis, although our interpretation of some of the exceptions suggests the desirability of complicating the model with some contextual variables deriving from technology. We suggest that the scale items indicate a cumulative emphasis on specificity of organizational roles and decision rules such that (1) explicit limits for individual rationality are established and motivated, and (2) interrelated procedures relative to collective rationality are established.

THE INSTITUTIONALIZATION OF RATIONALITY

We now wish to explore and explicate the hypothesis that administrative rationality involves relative independence of the organization from its social setting. Central to this hypothesis is the idea of social involvement, developed in a previous paper. *Social involvement* is defined as the institutionalization of participation and motivation in the organization through expectations and obligations existing independently of the organization in the social setting.[18] One would expect socially involved organizations to be less rational on the grounds that they are less independent of the social setting. The presence in the organization of opportunities to express general

[18] *TI*, pp. 248–249.

social values would inhibit the development of highly specific roles and procedures. In addition, one would expect organizations that are not socially involved to be highly rational under an assumption of structural substitution: that is, if functions are not performed in the setting they would presumably have to be built into the organization.

Rationality was run against a modified version of a social involvement rank order developed in a previous study.[19] The thirty-four organizations studied were ranked in presumed order of increasing social involvement according to how participation is institutionalized as follows:

1. Participation expected on the basis of voluntary self-commitment and self-defined self-interest.
2. Participation based on voluntary self-commitment defined as a kinship or community obligation.
3. Participation required by compulsory reciprocity.
4. Participation required by compulsory kinship ascription.
5. Participation required by compulsory political ascription, usually sanctioned by bodily punishment.

Results are shown in Table 2. They are consistent with the hypothesis both as to tendency and symmetry, except that the three "compulsory" social involvement categories do not appear to differ from one another in effect.

TABLE 2.   *Rationality and Social Involvement**

| | Scale Type | | | | | | | |
Social Involvement†	0	1	2	3	4	5	6	7
Compulsory political ascription	2	0	4	3	0	0	0	0
Compulsory kinship ascription	0	1	1	0	0	0	0	0
Compulsory reciprocity	0	0	4	1	0	1	0	0
Self-commitment, kinship or community obligation	0	0	0	0	6	3	0	0
Voluntary self-commitment, self-defined self-interest	0	0	0	0	0	0	2	6

* "Compulsory" social involvement categories collapsed and scale types 0–3, 4–5, and 6–7 combined: $\chi^2 = 62.79$; $P < .001$; degrees of freedom $= 4$.
† As indicated by basis of participation.

For further exploratory purposes, the eight *most rational* organizations (those with segmental participation with or without limited objectives) were compared with all other organizations. Another measure of whether or not

[19] *Ibid.*

the organization is institutionalized as independent from its setting is the separation of ownership from management. Table 3 compares organizations having *independent proprietorship* ("ownership" separated from "management" in that control over the ultimate disposition of the means of production is not vested in management) with all other organizations with respect to rationality. All the most rational organizations in the sample have independent proprietorships; most of the other ones do not; the relationship is significant at the .05 level.

TABLE 3. *Rationality and Proprietorship**

	Most Rational Organizations	Other
Independent proprietorship	8	0
Other	7	18

$$Q = +1.00$$
$$\chi^2 = 9.93$$
$$P < .01$$

* One case was omitted owing to lack of data.

We thus conclude that the mechanisms by which rational administration is institutionalized are such as to produce an independence, or segmentation, of the organization from its social setting. As is the case with individual members relative to the organization, so is the case of the organization relative to its social setting; rational administration requires that an "area of discretion" be defined within which manipulative planning is free to occur.

**THE SOCIAL SETTING
OF RATIONAL ORGANIZATION**

The preceding discussion suggests that it is more difficult for rational administration to develop in social settings that emphasize traditional ascriptive relationships. Previous research suggests that this may be especially likely where differences of power and status are ascribed, since such differences seem particularly likely to be part of social involvement patterns.[20] Accordingly, the settings of the most rational organizations were compared with the settings of all other organizations with respect to three presumed indexes of the general presence of ascription in the society concerned: (1) the presence of a hereditary stratification system with at

[20] *Ibid.*

least three classes or castes; (2) the presence of hereditary political succession; (3) the presence of slavery in any form.[21] Combined results appear in Table 4. The hypothesis is rather weakly confirmed; none of the relationships is statistically significant at the .05 level, but all are in the expected direction, and the stratification relationship approaches significance. None of the most rational organizations in the sample existed in a setting with

TABLE 4. *Rationality and Ascriptive Elements in Social Setting**

	Complex Hereditary Stratification		Hereditary Political Succession		Slavery	
	Present	Absent	Present	Absent	Present	Absent
Most rational organizations	0	7	4	3	2	6
Other organizations	10	15	16	7	11	14
	$Q = -1.00$		$Q = -.26$		$Q = -.40$	
	$\chi^2 = 2.42$		$\chi^2 = .02$		$\chi^2 = .29$	
	$P > .10$		$P > .98$		$P > .50$	

* Cases lacking data omitted.

a complex stratification system. Furthermore, Table 5 indicates what at first glance seems to be a surprising finding—rational organization is negatively associated with the existence of a centralized government transcending the local community. The relationship, however, is not statistically significant. We report it because, in the type of society dealt with here, strong central

TABLE 5. *Rationality and General Centralized Government**

	General Centralized Government	
	Present	Absent
Most rational organizations	1	7
Other organizations	12	13
	$Q = -.73$	
	$\chi^2 = 2.33$	
	$P > .10$	

* One case omitted owing to lack of data.

[21] Data are drawn from Murdock, *op. cit.*

government indicates a hierarchical feudal order wherein political power permeates the entire social order, and is hence probably simply another index of ascription. If so, this result is consistent with our hypothesis.[22]

DEVELOPMENT OF RATIONAL ADMINISTRATION

It is very hazardous to attempt to extrapolate hypotheses concerning organizational evolution or development from cross-sectional data of the type on which this study is based. As our earlier theoretical argument indicates, a scale does suggest a structure of requisite elements. It does not, however, indicate prerequisites. One cannot conclude from our scale, for example, that centralized management must precede compensatory rewards in a temporal sequence of development. Similarly, a scale per se implies nothing about causal relationships among the items in it. It simply describes a modal static state of affairs.

One can, however, use such a scale to predict types of problems that different developmental sequences will probably entail. For example, if specialization should be the first rational characteristic to develop in an organization, the scale implies that such an organization if it is to be stable must immediately develop a centralized management and compensatory rewards. Unless it proves to be the case that rational administrative characteristics are likely to develop simultaneously—and we shall presently see that at least in many cases this is highly unlikely—one may hypothesize that a developmental sequence that follows the scale pattern will probably entail fewer problems and tensions than one which does not.[23]

It is further possible to infer certain constraints and problems that seem likely to arise at specific points in organizational development. First, the institutional system appears to be markedly discontinuous relative to administrative rationality. An increase in rationality beyond specialization evidently involves a radical change in institutional arrangements; ascriptive social involvement is abandoned in favor of self-commitment. Similarly, an increase beyond a performance emphasis involves another such change— the introduction of the norm of self-defined self-interest in commitment, as well as the separation of proprietorship from management. But between points of discontinuity, it appears possible for rationality to fluctuate independently of the institutional system, provided the requisite pattern suggested by the scale is maintained. Thus, for example, given an institutional adjustment to specific job assignments, performance can either be empha-

---

[22] It should perhaps be pointed out that political conservatives have been alleging this relationship for some time, though the applicability of the present data to such an argument is probably questionable for the reasons suggested.

[23] On the other hand it may be impossible to develop administrative rationality without generating problems and tensions.

sized or not, with no institutional implications one way or the other. By the same token an organization with no rational characteristics at all can develop a centralized management, compensatory rewards, and specialization without encountering institutional difficulties. But if either of these organizations were to proceed further in rational development, its mode of institutionalization would have to change considerably.

The fact that Table 2 is symmetrical suggests that the converse of the preceding argument may also be valid, insofar as obligation to participate is concerned. It appears that if participation is institutionalized as voluntary commitment based on self-defined self-interest, the organization must at least involve segmental participation plus, in principle, the five other characteristics lower on the scale. Also, participation based on self-commitment in a context of kinship or community obligations implies an organization at least sufficiently rational to possess specific job assignments, together with specialization, compensatory rewards, and a centralized management. On the other hand, where participation is purely ascriptive or based on compulsory reciprocity, no rational elements need necessarily be present.

One may next ask: In what kinds of societal settings is administrative rationality, together with its requisite institutional arrangements, most likely to be found? Owing to gaps in the data, our analysis at this point is necessarily quite fragmentary. In complex hereditary aristocracy, the existence of slavery, hereditary succession to political office, and complex government are viewed as rough indexes of an ascriptive emphasis in the culture concerned. Tables 4 and 5 suggest, as one might suppose, that organizations in settings where ascription is stressed are themselves likely to be highly socially involved, and hence possess non-rational administrative systems. It is particulary noteworthy that complex hereditary stratification is absent from the setting of all the most rational administrative systems. But this relationship is not symmetrical, and the situation with respect to the other social setting variables is not nearly so marked. One infers, therefore, that, to some extent at least, fairly rational organizations can be institutionalized in quite "hostile" settings. Also, it would appear that a propitious setting does not in itself guarantee rational administration. Why might this be so?

We have already seen that certain elements of rationality—notably specialization and performance emphasis—are at least partially functions of technical, as opposed to institutional, influences. If in a more general sense it is the case that administration tends to be no more rational than is technically necessary, one would indeed expect to find instances of relatively non-rational administrative systems in settings where rationality would in principle be possible, merely because in the instances concerned rationality would be technically unnecessary.

A second reason may stem from the type of ascription present in the social setting. Stinchcombe has suggested that where rationality is a general cultural value, ascription may not markedly inhibit rationality in administration, on the grounds that the major effect of ascription is to infuse the organization with general cultural values.[24] It is possible that the Iroquois case in our sample partially illustrates this type of situation. It is known that Iroquois culture placed a high valuation on efficiency and achievement, with socialization measures taken to assure the differential competence of hereditary political officials. And the Iroquois organization in our sample is highly rational, yet exists in a society with a complex government involving hereditary political officials. Complex hereditary stratification is absent, however. Furthermore, participation is based on self-defined self-interest. It may be that a general valuation of rationality simply tends to make possible non-ascriptive recruitment in otherwise ascriptive settings. Modern industrial society may largely fit in this category. For even in the presence of a high cultural valuation on efficiency and rationality, ascriptive recruitment can still be disruptive to organizational operations by introducing competing goals and loyalties, however "rationally" they are individually viewed. It would seem that there are limits to the extent to which the effects of ascription on administration can be offset by institutional arrangements. . . .

[24] Arthur L. Stinchcombe, "Comment," *American Journal of Sociology*, LXVII (November, 1961), 255–259.

VIII

Methods
for the Study
of Organization

Many areas of organizational analysis compete
for the titles of: relatively neglected, quite
neglected, and most neglected. The study of methods, on the
other hand, seems to be a field in which much work is conducted and progress constantly reported. The issues are basically
these: to learn to apply to the study of organizations methods
which have produced fruitful results in the exploration of other
fields; to adapt techniques specifically developed for the study
of other subjects as, for instance, small groups analysis; and to
establish research methods which will answer the special needs
of the field—needs generated by the "emergent properties" of
this type of social unit.

The major difficulty rests in the fact that until now the
social sciences have applied mainly qualitative research techniques, particularly the case-study method, to the study of large
social units, and quantitative techniques, such as surveys, to
the study of individuals. The problem is to bridge this gap by
applying *quantitative techniques to the study of organizations*. To
do so will require the development of methods of data collection which will make possible the gathering of quantitative materials on organizational variables, and methods of data processing
which will allow us to draw conclusions concerning the state of
organizational variables from information collected from or
about individual respondents. Until this is accomplished, quantitative studies will continue to be predominantly studies of individuals in organizations rather than studies of organizations.

Lazarsfeld and Menzel take a major step in this direction by analyzing the logical and methodological differences between the properties of individuals and those of social units. Coleman reviews applications of this kind of logic to various research and sample designs and also its applicability to the analytical methods of actual research. A major innovation is the application of the sociometric approach to the study of large social units. Barton and Anderson give two examples of another recent methodological trend in organizational analysis: the application of mathematical models to formal analysis.

Lazarsfeld and Menzel are concerned with the methodological characteristics of various statements on "collectives" and "members." These distinctions can be applied to any unit and its participants, or to any unit and its subunits. For the purpose of organizational analysis, the major interpretation would be that of seeing the organization as a "collective," and its participants or groups of participants as "members."

Analytic properties of collectives are induced from information collected from or about members themselves; "structural" properties are based on information concerning their relations and "global" properties are based on information, not on properties of members, but on collectives as such. Members' properties are "absolute" (concerning the individual alone); *relational* (his relations to others); or *comparative* (depending on the member's place in a distribution of the members); or *contextual* (following from a property of the collective). These and other conceptual distinctions differentiate and determine the nature of the various types of propositions dealt with in organizational analysis. The discussion therefore supplies a methodological paradigm for organizational analysis which may serve as a check list for the types of variables to be covered and for the classification of propositions. It gives a clear meaning to concepts, such as emergent properties, group climate, and organizational character, which are often used in a vague way. The study also discusses the kinds of measurements that may be used to determine the values of various organizational variables.

Coleman reviews the methodological innovations in statistical analysis which the study of organizations and their relationships require. New *sampling* methods have been developed which make it possible to sample individuals as parts of a context, and which take into account their relations to, and place in, the organizational structure. Coleman concludes by discussing new *analytic* methods which have been devised to establish the effect of the context, the patterns of interaction, and the heterogeneity of the unit on the single actor or for characterization of the unit as such.

Frequently, students of organizational analysis try to explain the behavior of individuals by their membership in a certain organization or organizational unit. Such an approach assumes that the member is somehow affected by the unit. The channels through which the properties of the unit affect the properties of individuals are many (although they are rarely specified). A member may *perceive* the unit realistically and thus be affected. He may be *recruited* in ways which will ensure that his properties are in line with those of the unit, or he may be *socialized* to "fit" the unit after recruitment. Often it is implicitly assumed that he is *influenced by other members* of the unit. This belief implies that the member interacts with other members and that he is emotionally attached to them and/or respects their opinions. Until recently, this was more often assumed in organizational studies than demonstrated. One of the major reasons for this tendency is that standard methods for determining patterns of interaction and inter-individual attachments were developed for the study of small groups and could not be applied to large-scale organizations. Sociograms are a typical example. However, methods have recently been developed which attempt to overcome this limitation.

Zelditch points out that the essential nature of theorizing and experimentation is to understand the relations between variables rather than to establish their distribution in the population. Once this is understood we may state that, while we do not seek to put an army (or any other large-scale organization) into a laboratory, it is possible under experimental conditions to study the relationships between organizational variables which analytically characterize an army, such as the number of ranks, formalization of integration, and so forth.

The examination of McCleery's study by Barton and Anderson is one of the relatively rare instances in the literature of social science where an empirical study is submitted to intensive methodological analysis. By showing how one would go about conducting the same study using a quantitative method, Barton and Anderson to some extent bridge the gap between qualitative and quantitative analysis. At the same time, the substantive theory developed by McCleery is given formal application through the use of a mathematical model, which makes possible a precise exposition of what is meant when one refers to the organization, or for that matter to any social unit, as a social system. Finally, an arithmetic model is presented which permits the student to study changes in organizational systems.

One of the more provocative questions implicit in the remarks by Barton and Anderson is: if extensive measurement is required in order to transform a qualitative study into a quantitative one, is not the price of this added precision too high? The authors' answer is that, even if their rigorous procedure is not adopted, qualitative analysis can be made more systematic if their model were kept in mind.

While field methods may be applied to the study of social units other than organizations, organizations are frequently studied by the use of such methods. Their application, Scott shows, gives rise to special problems, for example, the authorization to enter and explore the particular unit. While this may pose a problem in other units too, it is particularly acute in organizations which have explicit rules for conduct and authorities whom one as a rule, cannot ignore.

ON THE RELATION
BETWEEN INDIVIDUAL
AND COLLECTIVE PROPERTIES

Paul F. Lazarsfeld
and Herbert Menzel

INTRODUCTORY CONSIDERATIONS

1. Purpose

Social scientists often make use of variables to describe not only individual persons but also groups, communities, organizations, or other "collectives."[1] Thus one reads, for example, of "racially mixed census tracts," of "highly bureaucratized voluntary organizations," or of a "centrally located rooming-house district." At other times the variables, although describing individuals, are based on data about certain collectives, as in a comparison

This article is one of a series sponsored by the Documentation Project for Advanced Training in Social Research, Columbia University. It may be cited as Publication A-322 of the Bureau of Applied Social Research, Columbia University.

[1] Individuals and collectives made up of individuals do not, of course, exhaust the matters which social scientists describe. Social-science propositions may, instead, have various other units for their subjects. Not infrequently the subjects are acts, behavior patterns, customs, norms, "items of culture," and the like, as in the assertion that "items of culture that are . . . not much woven into a pattern . . . are least likely to encounter resistance to their diffusion." Ralph Linton, *The Study of Man* (New York: Appleton, 1936), 341–342. "Beliefs and practices have been sorted into four classes according to the pattern of their differential distribution among mobile and nonmobile holders of high and low positions in a stratification system."—Peter M. Blau, "Social Mobility and Interpersonal Relations," *American Sociological Review*, 21 (1956), 290–295.

of "graduates of top-ranking medical schools" with "graduates of other medical schools." This paper attempts to clarify some of the operations involved in the construction and use of such variables in empirical research, and provides a nomenclature for the different ways in which information about individuals and about collectives may be interwoven in these properties. The properties will be classified according to the measurement operations involved in their construction.

2. Some Features of Generalizing Propositions

The intended meaning of the variables often remains ambiguous if they are not examined in the context of the propositions in which they are used. It is therefore necessary at the outset to highlight certain features which are common to all generalizing propositions, whether or not they involve collectives. (As an illustration, reference is made to the proposition "Children of rich parents go to college in greater proportion than do children of poor parents.")

    a. Generalizing propositions assert something about a set of *elements* (children).

    b. For the research purposes at hand, these elements are considered *comparable*. In other words, the same set of *properties* (wealth of parents; going to college) is used to describe each element.

    c. Each element has a certain *value* on each property. The values (rich parents, poor parents; going to college, not going to college) may be quantitative or qualitative.

    d. The propositions assert interrelationships between the properties of the elements.

3. Present Concern

The propositions with which the present discussion is concerned have the additional characteristic that their elements are dealt with either as collectives or as members of collectives. An example of the first kind is "There is a negative correlation between the rate of juvenile delinquency of American cities and the proportion of their budget given over to education." An example of the second kind is "Those recognized as leaders do not deviate very far from the norms of their group."

4. Special Meaning of "Collective" and "Member"

The terms "collective" and "member" are used here in a specific sense which needs clarification. A collective may be an element of a proposition; that is, it is one of a set of units which are regarded as *comparable* in the sense specified above: the same set of properties is used to describe all the elements. These elements are *collectives* if each is considered to be composed of constituent parts, called *members,* which are regarded as comparable in their turn. "Comparable" is used in the same sense as before: all members are described by a single set of properties. (This is usually not the same set as that used to describe the collectives.)

In other instances members are the elements of the propositions. Elements will be called "members" if they are considered to be constituent parts of larger units, called "collectives," which are regarded as comparable in the same sense as before.

Thus one set of properties is always used to describe or classify all the members, and another single set of properties is used to characterize all the collectives. It is clear that under these definitions one can speak of "collectives" only when their "members" are also being referred to, and of "members" only when their "collectives" are also involved. Furthermore, there must be a multiplicity of members if the term "collective" is to be meaningful. It is perhaps less obvious but will be seen later that there must also be a multiplicity of collectives—i.e., the members of more than one collective must be referred to—if the distinctions between properties to be described below are to be relevant.

By contrast, the notion of "element" is needed to characterize any generalizing proposition whatsoever. It is applicable even in situations where the notions of "member" and "collective" are not involved at all.

5. Distinction between "Individuals" and "Members"

In the examples that come to mind most easily, the members of collectives are individual persons. Thus, for example, cities are the collectives and people are the members in the following two propositions:

(1) "The oldest settlers of cities are most likely to hold political office," or (2) "The more industry there is in a city, the higher the proportion of Democratic voters." The first proposition has members and the second has collectives as elements. In the same sense, a precinct can be treated as a collective, with the inhabitants as members. However, the members of a collective are not necessarily individual persons. A city, for example, can be described as a collective with the voting precincts as members. It follows that what appears as a collective in one context (e.g., precincts), can appear as a member in another. In any analysis of a piece of writing in which some of the elements are collectives, it is always necessary to specify clearly of what members the collectives are composed (for the purposes at hand).[2]

[2] It is, of course, also possible to make propositions about cities without reference to any members at all, just as it is possible to make propositions about individuals

The graph below will help to keep this terminology in mind. The circles symbolize the collectives, the crosses within it their members. The dots indicate that we are dealing with collectives as elements of a proposition. This is the situation with which we deal in the first part of this paper. In Sections 10 and 11 we discuss research where members are the focus of attention. They are then the elements of propositions, but their membership in one of a series of collectives is one of their characteristics.

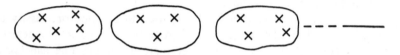

6. Possibility of "Three-Level" Propositions

In some studies, more than two levels appear: for example, inhabitants, precincts, and cities may all be elements of the same study. This whole matter could, therefore, be elaborated by pointing out the various relationships which can exist between inhabitants, precincts, and cities. The next few pages are restricted to collectives which have only one kind of member; the members in most illustrations will be individual persons, but we will also present some examples in which the members themselves are larger units. Only much later (in Section 16) will examples of "three-level" propositions be taken up, in which units, e.g., "union shops," are simultaneously considered to be both members of their locals *and* collectives of individual workers.

7. Propositions about Collectives as Substitutes and in Their Own Right

Propositions about collectives are sometimes made as substitutes for propositions about individual persons, simply because the necessary data about individual persons are not available. For example, a high Republican vote in "silk-stocking" districts is sometimes accepted to show that wealthy people are likely to vote Republican, when no records about individual votes and individual incomes are available.[3] For this reason it is often not

---

without reference to any collectives. Thus one may, e.g., correlate city size with number of churches, or location with building materials used, just as one can correlate individual income and education. In neither case are the distinctions made in the present paper relevant, because the individuals are not treated as "members" and the cities are not treated as "collectives" as here defined (i.e., as composed of "members" —constituent units described by their values on some one set of properties). It is thus clear that the typology of properties here presented is not always pertinent.

[3] This procedure can lead to very misleading statistics, as pointed out by W. S. Robinson in "Ecological Correlations and the Behavior of Individuals," *American*

realized that a large number of sociologically meaningful empirical propositions can be made of which only collectives are intended to be the elements. Thus, for example, an anthropologist may show that the political
independence of communities is correlated with their pattern of settlement.
A student of social disorganization may ask whether city zones with a high
incidence of juvenile delinquency also show a high incidence of commitments for senile dementia. A small-group experimenter may hypothesize
that "the probability of effective utilization of the insights that occur is
greater in certain communication patterns than in others."[4] Much discursive
writing also consists, in a hidden way, of such propositions.

A TYPOLOGY OF PROPERTIES DESCRIBING "COLLECTIVES" AND "MEMBERS"

8. Properties of Collectives

It is often useful to distinguish three types of properties which describe
collectives: analytical properties based on data about each member; structural properties based on data about the relations among members; and
global properties, not based on information about the properties of individual members.[5] The following examples may clarify these distinctions:

A. ANALYTICAL. These are properties of collectives which are obtained by
performing some mathematical operation upon some property of each single
member.[6]

> The average rental paid in a precinct and the proportion of its inhabitants
> who have "Old Immigrant" (English, German, Scottish, Scandinavian)
> names are analytical properties of a collective (precinct) composed of

---

Sociological Review, 15 (1950), 351–357. Sounder methods for inferring individual
correlations from ecological data are proposed by Leo A. Goodman, "Ecological
Regressions and Behavior of Individuals," *American Sociological Review,* 18 (1953),
663–664, and by Otis Dudley Duncan and Beverly Davis, "An Alternate to Ecological
Correlation," *ibid.,* pp. 665–666.

[4] For details on these and additional examples, see Paul F. Lazarsfeld and Morris
Rosenberg (eds.), *The Language of Social Research* (New York: Free Press, 1955),
pp. 302–322. Compare also Herbert Menzel, "Comment," *American Sociological
Review,* 15 (1950), 674.

[5] This classification of properties of collectives corresponds closely to the classifica-
tions presented earlier by Cattell and by Kendall and Lazarsfeld and reprinted in
Lazarsfeld and Rosenberg (eds.), *op. cit.,* pp. 291–301. Analytical properties are
Cattell's population variables and Kendall and Lazarsfeld's Types I, II, and III.
Structural properties are Cattell's structural variables and Kendall and Lazarsfeld's
Type IV. Our global properties are Cattell's syntality variables and Kendall and
Lazarsfeld's Type V. See also n. 25.

[6] It should be understood that the distinctions here proposed do not depend on who

individuals.[7] The proportion of the communities of a given state that have their own high school is an analytical property of a collective (state) the members of which are communities. The diffusion of a message in a city, defined as the per cent of the target population knowing the message, is an analytical property of the city.[8]

The standard deviation of incomes in a nation appears as an analytical property in the following example. The effect of postwar legislation in Great Britain was to make the income distribution much narrower. Economists have predicted that under these conditions people will save more, because they will spend less money on display consumption which might help them be socially acceptable in the higher strata.

Correlations are sometimes used to characterize collectives and then also constitute analytical properties. The correlation of age and prestige in a given community, for example, has been used as a measure of its norms regarding old age. Sometimes more indirect inferences are involved. MacRae shows that in urban areas voting is highly correlated with occupation, while this is not the case in rural districts. He concludes from this vote that in rural districts there is a stronger spirit of community and cohesion.[9]

B. STRUCTURAL. These are properties of collectives which are obtained by performing some operation on data about the relations of each member to some or all of the others.

Assume, for example, that a sociometrist has recorded the "best-liked classmate" of each student in a number of classes. He can then describe the classes by the degree to which all choices are concentrated upon a few "stars." Or he might, alternately, classify them according to their cliquishness, the latter being defined as the number of subgroups into which a class can be divided so that no choices cut across subgroup lines. In these examples the collective is the school class, and the members are the individual students; "concentration of choices" and "cliquishness" are structural properties of the classes.

---

performs the operations involved. For example, "average income of a city" would be classified as an analytical property regardless of whether the investigator (a) obtains individual income data from all inhabitants directly and then computes the average, (b) obtains individual income data from the files of the tax collector and then computes the average, or (c) looks up the average income in the published census reports. Compare also n. 17.

[7] Phillips Cutright and Peter H. Rossi, "Grass Roots Politicians and the Vote," *American Sociological Review*, 23 (1958), 171–179.
[8] Melvin L. DeFleur and Otto N. Larsen, *The Flow of Information* (New York: Harper & Row, 1958).
[9] Duncan MacRae, Jr., "Occupations and the Congressional Vote, 1940–1950," *American Sociological Review*, 20 (1955), 332–340. For another example, see the evidence used to demonstrate differences in the norms of two housing projects in

For an example in which the members are larger units, consider a map of the precincts of a city, which indicates the number of Negroes residing in each. Let a "Negro enclave" be defined as a precinct in which some Negroes live, but which is completely surrounded by precincts without Negroes. The proportion of the precincts of a city which are Negro enclaves would then be a structural property of the city.

C. GLOBAL. Often collectives are characterized by properties which are not based on information about the properties of individual members.

American Indian tribes have been characterized by the frequency with which themes of "achievement motive" make their appearance in their folk tales.[10] Societies have been classified as to the presence of money as a medium of exchange, of a written language, etc.[11] Nations may be characterized by the ratio of the national budget allotted to education and to armaments. Army companies may be characterized by the cleanliness of their mess equipment.

Voting precincts have been classified according to the activities and attitudes of their Republican and Democratic captains, including hours spent on party duties, number of persons known to the captain personally, and his expressed commitment to the party.[12] In experiments in message diffusion by leaflets dropped from airplanes, cities have been treated to different degrees of "stimulus intensity," defined as the per capita ratio of leaflets dropped.[13] All these are global properties.

The density of settlement is a global property of a district. Having a city manager form of government is a global property of a city. The insistence on specified initiation rites as a prerequisite to membership is a global property of a religious cult or of a college fraternity. Accessibility from the nearest big city is a global property of a village. A scale score assigned to each state according to the combination of duties assigned to the state board of education (rather than left to local authorities) is a global property of each state.[14]

Leon Festinger, Stanley Schachter, and Kurt Back, "The Operation of Group Standards," in Lazarsfeld and Rosenberg, *op. cit.*, pp. 373–377.

[10] See David C. McClelland and G. A. Friedman, "A Cross-cultural Study of the Relationship between Child Training Practices and Achievement Motivation Appearing in Folk Tales," in Guy E. Swanson, Theodore M. Newcomb, and Eugene L. Hartley (eds.), *Readings in Social Psychology* (New York: Holt, Rinehart and Winston, Inc., 1952), pp. 243–249.

[11] See, e.g., Linton C. Freeman and Robert F. Winch, "Societal Complexity: An Empirical Test of a Typology of Societies," *American Journal of Sociology*, 62 (1957), 461–466.

[12] Cutright and Rossi, *loc. cit.*

[13] DeFleur and Larsen, *op. cit.*

[14] Robert Redfield, *The Folk Culture of Yucatan* (Chicago: University of Chicago Press, 1941); and Margaret J. Hagood, and Daniel O. Price, *Statistics for Sociologists* (rev. ed.) (New York: Holt, Rinehart and Winston, Inc., 1952), pp. 144–152.

"Emergent," "integral," "syntalic" and other terms have been used in meanings very similar to that of our term "global." It is not at all certain which term is most useful.[15]

Notice that all three of the above types of properties—analytical, structural, and global—describe collectives.

9. A Subsidiary Distinction among Analytical Properties of Collectives

An interesting distinction may be made among the analytical properties. The first two examples given above were the average income of a city, and the proportion of the communities of a given state that have their own high school. These properties of collectives have what one might call a similarity of meaning to the properties of members on which they are based. The wealth of a city seems to be the same sort of thing as the wealth of an inhabitant. The endowment of a community with a high school and the rate of high-school endowed communities in a state have a parallel meaning. This is not true for the remaining examples of analytical properties given above—the standard deviation of incomes in a nation, or correlations like that between age and prestige in a given community. Correlations and standard deviations can apply only to collectives and have no parallel on the level of members. The standard deviation of incomes in a city, for example, denotes something quite different—lack of homogeneity, per- haps—from individual income, the datum from which it is computed.

Another variable of this sort is "degree of consensus." When a Demo- crat and a Republican are competing for the mayoralty, the degree of political consensus in a particular club might be measured by the extent of the club's deviation from a fifty-fifty split. In this instance the analytic property is measured by a proportion, but it is not the simple proportion of adherents of either party; clubs which are 80 per cent Democratic and those which are 20 per cent Democratic are regarded as equal in consensus.

[15] Although global properties of collectives are not based on information about members, the above examples are, of course, listed here on the assumption that assertions about the members are made somewhere in the same proposition or at least in the same body of work; otherwise the distinction between "global" and "absolute" properties would become pointless (cf. n. 2). It may also bear repeating here that any discussion of a "collective" requires clear specification of what its members are considered to be. The proportion of the buildings of a city which are devoted to cultural activities was given as an example of a "global property" of a city on the assumption that the city is treated as a collective of inhabitants; i.e., that statements involving the inhabitants are made in some connection with this measure of "cultural level." It is, of course, also possible to treat a city as a collective of buildings; then the proportion of buildings devoted to cultural activities would be- come an analytical property. Which of these two types of property it is can be judged only from the context. (See also Section 13.)

Whereas correlations, standard deviations, and similar measures always have a meaning peculiar to the group level, averages and proportions may or may not have a parallel meaning on the individual and collective levels.[16] Lack of parallel meaning is perhaps most clearly illustrated in the concept of a "hung jury," that is, a jury rendered indecisive by its inability to reach the required unanimity. Such a state of affairs is most likely when the individual jurors are most decisive and unyielding in their convictions.

10. Properties of Members

Another set of distinctions can be made between properties describing members in contexts where collectives have also been defined.

a. *Absolute* properties are characteristics of members which are obtained without making any use either of information about the characteristics of the collective, or of information about the relationships of the member being described to other members. They thus include most of the characteristics commonly used to describe individuals.

   In the proposition, "Graduates of large law schools are more likely to earn high incomes at age 40 than graduates of small law schools," income is an absolute property of the members (the individual students).

b. *Relational* properties of members are computed[17] from information about the substantive relationships between the member described and other members.

   Sociometric popularity-isolation (number of choices received) is a relational property. Many other sociometric indices fall into this category. For example, if each member of a small group has rated each other member on a 5-point scale of acceptance-rejection, each member can be characterized by the total score he received (popularity), by the total score he expressed (active sociability), by the average deviation of the scores he accorded the others (discrimina-

---

[16] Compare the notion of "counterpart" in Edgar F. Borgatta, Leonard Cottrell, Jr., and Henry J. Meyer, "On the Dimensions of Group Behavior," *Sociometry*, 19 (1956), 233.
[17] It may be worth repeating here that the distinctions proposed are independent of who performs the operations involved. Thus, e.g., "sociometric popularity" would be classified as a relational property when measured in any of the following three ways: (a) the investigator counts the number of choices accorded to a member by his colleagues in answer to a sociometric questionnaire; (b) the investigator observes the frequency of interactions between the member and his colleagues; (c) the member is asked, "How many visits did you receive from colleagues during the last week?" These distinctions are, of course, important in themselves but not relevant to the present typology (cf. n. 6).

tion in his acceptance of other members), etc.[18] In a study of the diffusion of the use of a new drug through a community of doctors, the physicians were classified according to whether or not they had a friend who had already used the new drug on a certain date.[19]

Some investigators have clarified the structure of relational properties by the use of matrices.[20] This new device can be fruitfully applied to some older papers.[21]

The distinction between relational properties of individuals and structural properties of collectives deserves emphasis. The former characterize members of collectives in their relations to one another. The latter characterize collectives and are aggregates over the relational properties of their members.

c. *Comparative* properties characterize a member by a comparison between his value on some (absolute or relational) property and the distribution of this property over the entire collective of which he is a member.

Sibling order is a comparative property of individuals in the proposition, "First-born children are more often maladjusted than intermediate and last born children." Note that each individual is characterized by comparison with the age of the other individuals in his family; in the resulting classification, many of the "last-born" will be older in years than many of the "first-born." Being a "deviate" from the majority opinion in one's housing project unit is a comparative property.[22]

Another example is contained in the following proposition: "Students who had the highest I.Q. in their respective high school classes have greater difficulty in adjusting in college than students who are not quite at the top in high school, even when their actual I.Q. score is equally high." Here the comparative property (being at the top in high school or not) is established in terms of the I.Q. distribution in each

---

[18] Some sociometric indices are listed in Hans Zeisel, *Say It with Figures* (4th ed.; New York: Harper & Row, 1957), pp. 110–114, 148–153. The list includes indices not only of relational properties but of comparative and structural properties as well.
[19] Herbert Menzel and Elihu Katz, "Social Relations and Innovation in the Medical Profession: The Epidemiology of a New Drug," *Public Opinion Quarterly*, 19 (1956), 337–352.
[20] See Zeisel, *loc. cit.*, and Leon Festinger, Stanley Schachter, and Kurt Back, "Matrix Analysis of Group Structures," in Lazarsfeld and Rosenberg, *op. cit.*, pp. 358–367. In both instances matrices are also used to develop indices for structural properties of groups.
[21] See, e.g., Robert R. Sears, "Experimental Studies of Projection," *Journal of Social Psychology*, 7 (1936), 151–163.
[22] Festinger, Schachter, and Back, *loc. cit.*, pp. 367–382.

student's respective high school; the proposition pertains to a set of college students which includes boys from several high schools (collectives).

d. *Contextual* properties describe a member by a property of his collective.

> Consider an example cited previously: "Graduates of large law schools are more likely to earn high incomes at age 40 than graduates of small law schools." In this proposition, "being a member of a large law school" is a contextual property of individuals.

> Contextual properties are also used in the following propositions: "Union members in closed shops are less militant than union members in open shops." "Residents of racially mixed districts show more racial prejudice than those of racially homogeneous districts." "The less the promotion opportunity afforded by a branch (of the army), the more favorable the opinion (of soldiers) tends to be toward promotion opportunity."[23] In these propositions, being a member of a closed shop, residing in a mixed district, or being a soldier in a branch with frequent promotions are all examples of contextual properties.

> Contextual properties are really characteristics of collectives applied to their members. Thus the classification of "collective properties" developed above could be repeated here as a subdivision of contextual "individual properties."[24] Note also that a contextual property, unlike a comparative property, has the same value for all members of a given collective.

11. Contextual and Comparative Properties Meaningful Only Where More Than One Collective Is Involved

It is not meaningful to speak of contextual or comparative properties when the elements under study are all members of the same collective—for instance, when only graduates of one law school are being studied—for the following reasons. Any *contextual* property would, in that case, have the same value for all the elements; hence nothing could be said about the interrelationship of this property and any other property. Any *comparative* property would, under these circumstances, classify the elements in exactly

[23] S. A. Stouffer, *et al., The American Soldier* (Princeton, N.J.: Princeton, 1949), I, 256.
[24] It is sometimes helpful to talk of "collective properties" instead of the cumbersome "properties of collectives"; the same holds for "individual properties." It is important, however, not to be misled by this linguistic condensation.

the same way as the absolute property from which it was derived, except that the calibration may be grosser. (If only children of one family are considered, the classification into "first-born," "intermediate," and "last-born" differs from that by age only in the grosser calibration. Similarly, if I.Q. scores of graduates of one law school are replaced by classification into lowest, second, third, and highest I.Q. quartile within their school, nothing will change except that the number of categories is reduced.)

12. Special Case Where the Typology Can Be Applied in Two Alternate Ways

A difficulty comes about when all the members of a set of collectives (or a representative sample of the members of each) constitute the elements of a proposition which includes a contextual property. Suppose, for instance, that the income ten years after graduation is recorded for all who graduate from fifty law schools in a certain year. A possible finding might be, "The income of law school graduates is correlated with the size of the school they graduated from." This is a proposition about students, relating their income (an absolute property) to the size of their law school (a contextual property). The same proposition could be interpreted also as one where the elements are the law schools; the average income of the students would then be an analytical property of each law school; its size would be a global property of these collectives.

13. The Present Classification Is Formal Rather Than Substantive

As stated at the outset, the scheme suggested above is intended for the classification of properties according to the operations involved in their measurement. Although a classification by the underlying concepts or forces that the properties may be intended to represent might have numerous parallels to the present classification, it would not be the same.[25] In

---

[25] Cattell's classification of population, structural, and syntality variables (cf. n. 5 above), which is closely paralleled in form by our analytical-structural-global distinction, seems to be based on a mixture of measurement criteria and considerations of causality. The latter gain the upper hand in the critique of Cattell's scheme by Borgatta, Cottrell, and Meyer: e.g., "Aggregate measures, to the extent that they cannot be accounted for as population variables (in direct parallel measures), may be considered syntality variables. . . . Further, changes in population variables attributable to social interaction should be regarded as syntality variables."—Borgatta, Cottrell, and Meyer, *loc. cit.*, p. 234. Peter M. Blau's "Formal Organization: Dimensions of Analysis," *American Journal of Sociology*, 63 (1957), 58–69, contains an

the present methodological context, for example, "number of libraries in a community" and "occurrence of aggressiveness themes in folk tales current in a tribe" are classified as global properties because they are not based on information about the properties of individual members. Yet it would be convincing to argue that these properties are relevant to the behavioral sciences only because properties of individuals, of the relations among individuals, or of the resulting social structures are inferred from them. Similarly, the title of office held by a person in a hierarchy would here be classified as an "absolute" property, even when the researcher is actually interested in the incumbent's power over subordinates which the title implies.

At some points arbitrary decisions have to be made. On an intuitive basis we decided to consider the number of members in a collective (e.g., population size) as a global property, although one might argue that it is analytical, obtained by counting the "existence" of each member. Even more ambiguous is the classification of rates, based on the behavior of ex-members—e.g., suicide rates. No definitive practice is proposed for such borderline cases.

COMBINATIONS OF TYPES OF PROPERTIES

The types of properties which have been defined can appear in various forms of combinations.

14. Several Types in the Same Proposition

Very commonly, as many of the above examples have shown, one proposition will make use of properties of several types. An additional illustration of this can be drawn from a study of political processes within the International Typographical Union, which has been operating under an internal two-party system for many decades. The shops of this union were classified according to their degree of "political consensus"; shops in which 67 per cent or more of the members favored the same party were regarded as

---

analysis in terms of intended underlying concepts which parallels the present discussion of measurement operations in certain respects.

In addition, the literature contains, of course, classifications of group properties which are based on quite different criteria. See, e.g., John K. Hemphill and Charles M. Westie, "The Measurement of Group Dimensions," in Lazarsfeld and Rosenberg, *op. cit.*, pp. 323–324; and Robert K. Merton, "Provisional List of Group Properties," in his *Social Theory and Social Structure* (rev. ed.; New York: Free Press, 1957), pp. 310–326. The Hemphill-Westie categories are subjected to a factor analysis and compared with certain other schemes in Borgatta, Cottrell, and Meyer, *loc. cit.*, pp. 223–240.

high in consensus, the remainder as low. Individual members were graded according to the amount of union political activity they engaged in. It was expected that men in shops where political consensus was high would be more active in politics than those in shops where consensus was low. The hypothesis, however, was borne out only in small shops (i.e., those with thirty men or less). The finding could therefore be expressed in the following proposition: "For workers in small shops, there is a correlation between consensus of the shop and degree of political activity of the men; for workers in large shops, there is no such correlation." In this proposition there appear two contextual properties (size and consensus of each man's shop) and an absolute property (political activity).[26]

The following hypothetical example again shows the use of several types of variables in one proposition—in fact, in each of several propositions. Ten preliterate tribes living in a certain country are classified according to the number of wars they have fought during the last hundred years. This characteristic, in the present terminology, is a global property of each tribe. A representative sample of one hundred men from each tribe is given a test of "aggressiveness"—an absolute property, from which a summary score for each tribe is computed, as an analytical property. At this point, the correlation between average aggressiveness and the number of wars can be computed. One may regard this computation as either a correlation between an analytical and a global property of ten collectives, or a correlation between an absolute and a contextual property of one thousand individual persons.

Now a factory is opened in the district, and some men from each of the ten tribes find employment there as laborers. Each is given the test of "aggressiveness"; each is also observed for a period of one month, and the number of fights he starts with other employees is recorded. Then the following two correlations can be computed:

    a.   The correlation between the score on the aggressiveness test and the number of fights. This is a proposition the elements of which are people and the properties of which are conventional psychological characteristics—absolute properties, in the present terminology.

    b.   The correlation between the number of fights and the number of wars reported for the tribe from which each individual came. This is again a proposition the elements of which are people. But one of the variables (number of wars) now is a contextual property.

[26] See S. M. Lipset, Martin Trow, and James Coleman, *Union Democracy: The Inside Politics of the International Typographical Union* (New York: Free Press, 1956).

The comparison between these two propositions is interesting. In proposition (a) actual fighting is related to the psychological trait of aggressiveness. In proposition (b) actual fighting is related to something that one might call the normative background of each person.

15. Properties of One Type Constructed from Properties of Another Type

The types of properties outlined can also be compounded in that a property of one type may be constructed from properties of another type. Contextual properties, for example, have been defined as properties describing a member by a property of his collective. But what property of his collective is to be used? In most of the examples given, contextual properties of members were based on global properties of their collectives, as in the phrase "men from tribes that have engaged in many wars." But contextual properties can equally well be based on any other kind of property of a collective—for example, on a structural property, as when doctors are classified according to whether or not they ever practiced in cities ridden by medical cliques. One might test whether those who formerly practiced in cliqueless cities have less tendency to form cliques in their new location.

This compounding is also illustrated by examples, cited earlier in another connection: "being a worker in a big shop" and "being a worker in a shop with high consensus." The first of these is a contextual property constructed from a global property; the second is a contextual property constructed from an analytical property.

16. Several Types from the Same Data

In some instances one body of research will construct properties of several different types from the same data, as in the following excerpts from a report on the adoption of modern farming practices by Kentucky farmers.

> 393 farm operators . . . in thirteen neighborhoods were interviewed.
> . . . Information was obtained on the extent to which each of the operators had tried and was following 21 farm practices recommended by the agricultural agencies. For each respondent, an adoption score was calculated. This score is the percentage of applicable practices which the operator had adopted. For example, if 18 of the practices applied to the farm operations being carried on and the operator had adopted 9, his score was 50. Neighborhoods varied widely in the mean adoption scores of residents, which range from a low of 25 in one neighborhood to a high of 57 in another. . . . The neighborhoods were combined . . . into three types of neighborhoods: "low adoption areas," "medium adoption areas," and "high adoption areas." . . .

The following operational hypothesis . . . is suggested: In areas of high adoption, those from whom other farmers obtain farming information have higher adoption rates than farmers in general; but, in areas of low adoption, the adoption rates of leaders are similar to adoption rates of farmers in general . . . the hypothesis is supported by data. In the "low adoption areas" the mean score of all farmers was 32 and that of the leaders 37, while in the "high adoption areas" the mean score of all farmers was 48 and that of the leaders 66.[27]

Here the farm operator's "adoption score" is used as an absolute property of information leaders and of farmers in general. It is also used as the datum from which the classification of neighborhoods into "high adoption areas" and "low adoption areas" is computed. This classification is an analytical property of the neighborhoods; when used, as in the proposition quoted, to characterize the farmers resident in the neighborhoods, it becomes a contextual property of the farmers.

17. Simultaneous Characterization of the Same Elements as Collectives and as Members

Complexity of another sort arises when one set of elements appears both as members and as collectives in the same proposition. Up to this point examples of such "three-level propositions" have deliberately been excluded. It is now appropriate to introduce such examples. Consider, for instance, the following assertion: "Women's clubs which are internally divided into cliques have less easy-going relationships with other women's clubs than have clubs which are not so divided." Here the elements (women's clubs) are first categorized according to a structural variable (internal division into cliques), and then an assertion is made about a relational property (relationship with other clubs) of the elements in each structural category.

In the study of political processes within the International Typographical Union, which was cited earlier, each printer's vote in a union election was recorded. A liberal and a conservative candidate competed for union office. Each printer's vote was compared with his own conservative-liberal predisposition, determined by an attitude scale. The individuals could thus be classified as voting according to or contrary to their own predisposition. Up to this point, no collective is involved; there is merely a combination of two absolute properties into one. This com-

---

[27] C. Paul Marsh and A. Lee Coleman, "Group Influences and Agricultural Innovations: Some Tentative Findings and Hypotheses," *American Journal of Sociology*, 61 (1956), 588–594. Other varying examples of the use of properties describing or referring to collectives will be found in Lazarsfeld and Rosenberg, *op. cit.*, pp. 287–386.

bined absolute property of each printer was then compared with two contextual properties: the majority vote in his shop, and the majority vote in the local to which his shop belonged. The question was whether the climate of opinion in a man's shop or that in his entire local is more important in affecting his decisions. The answer could be determined only by examining cases where the shop and the local were in conflict. It was found that more people voted contrary to their own predisposition when it was in conflict with the majority of their shop (but not of their local) than when it was in conflict with the majority of their local (but not of their shop). In this instance each person is first characterized as voting according to or contrary to his predisposition. This absolute variable is then correlated with two contextual variables, both describing the same members (persons), but each having reference to a different level of collectives (shops or locals).[28]

18. Outlook

The preceding analysis can be extended in many directions; three of them shall be briefly sketched. For one we can introduce status differences among the members of the collectives. Colleges have professors and administrators, factory teams have workers and foremen, platoons have soldiers and noncoms. This may call for extending the notion of structural properties if, e.g., we distinguish various types of supervision; or analytical properties may be generalized if we classify colleges according to the degree to which the administration and the faculty share the same values. Stouffer has made ingenious use of such status differences by developing what one could call partitioned analytical properties. He wanted to know whether the food provided for army units had an effect on soldiers' morale. If he had asked the soldiers to rate the food he would not have known whether their morale did not affect their rating of the food. So he asked the noncommissioned officers to judge the food and correlated their average rating with the average morale score of the soldiers; the elements of the correlation were of course the army units studied.[29]

A second line of analysis opens up if the elements of a proposition are pairs of individuals: people who are friends tend to vote the same way; egalitarian relationships are more enduring than those which are hierarchic. It would be artificial to call such notions "propositions about collectives." Obviously dyads can be characterized in an even more complex way: pairs of doctors who commonly discuss cases with each other as equals are more likely to use the same type of drug than are pairs of

[28] Adapted from Lipset, Trow, and Coleman, *op. cit.*
[29] Stouffer, *et al., op. cit.*, I, 353–358.

doctors who stand in an advisor-advisee relationship to each other.[30] A scrutiny of recent sociometric literature is likely to provide distinctions going beyond those offered in this paper.

Finally, the utility of the present approach deserves argument. Obviously no one wants to make methodological classifications for their own sake. They are, however, useful in reminding us of the variety of research operations that are possible, and in clearing up misunderstandings. It can, for example, be shown that many arguments about atomism versus "holistic" approaches in current sociological literature can be clarified by an explication of the formal types of properties which enter into speculative or empirical propositions. In another publication, the senior author has summarized passages from several recent works of social research which relate, often in quite complex ways, the characteristics and attitudes of individuals, their propensity to choose friends inside and outside of variously overlapping collectives, the composition of these collectives in terms of members' background and perceptions, and the recent occurrence of certain events in the history of the collectives. He attempted to show that such "contextual propositions" go a long way toward satisfying the frequently heard demand that social research should "consider structures" or "take the total situation into account."[31]

[30] James Coleman, Herbert Menzel, and Elihu Katz, "Social Processes in Physicians' Adoption of a New Drug," *Journal of Chronic Diseases*, 9 (1959), 18.
[31] Paul F. Lazarsfeld, "Problems in Methodology," Robert K. Merton, Leonard Broom, and Leonard S. Cottrell, Jr. (eds.), *Sociology Today* (New York: Basic Books, 1959), pp. 69–73.

RELATIONAL ANALYSIS: THE STUDY OF SOCIAL ORGANIZATIONS WITH SURVEY METHODS

James S. Coleman

Survey research methods have often led to the neglect of social structure and of the relations among individuals. On the other hand, survey methods are highly efficient in bringing in a large volume of data—amenable to statistical treatment—at a relatively low cost in time and effort. Can the student of social structure enjoy the advantages of the survey without neglecting the relationships which make up that structure? In other words, can he use a method which ordinarily treats each individual as an isolated unit in order to study social structure?

The purpose of this paper is to describe some important developments in survey research which are giving us a new way of studying social organization.

It is useful to trace briefly the history of survey research, to indicate how it has grown from "polling" to the point where it can now study problems involving complex human organization. A look at this history indicates two definite stages. The first was a polling stage which was concerned with the *distribution* of responses on any one item: What proportion favored Roosevelt in 1936? What proportion was in favor of labor unions? This type of concern continues even today among pollsters, and to the lay public it is still the function of surveys to "find out what people think" or to see just how many feel thus and so.

Among sociologists, however, this purely descriptive use of survey research was soon supplanted by an *analytical* one. First there began to be a concern with how different sub-groups in the population felt or behaved. From this, the analysts moved on to further cross-tabulations.

Reprinted from *Human Organization*, 17 (1958–1959), 28–36, by permission of the author and publisher, The Society for Applied Anthropology.

Finally, some survey analysts began, through cross-tabulations and correlations, to study complicated questions of why people behaved as they did. By relating one opinion item to another, attitude configurations and clusters of attitudes emerged; by relating background information to these attitudes, some insight was gained into the *determinants* of attitudes. It was in this analytical stage, then, beyond the simple description of a population, that survey research began to be of real use to social science.

But throughout all this one fact remained, a very disturbing one to the student of social organization. The *individual* remained the unit of analysis. No matter how complex the analysis, how numerous the correlations, the studies focused on individuals as separate and independent units. The very techniques mirrored this well: samples were random, never including (except by accident) two persons who were friends; interviews were with one individual, as an atomistic entity, and responses were coded onto separate IBM cards, one for each person. As a result, the kinds of substantive problems on which such research focused tended to be problems of "aggregate psychology," that is, *within*-individual problems, and never problems concerned with relations between people.

Now, very recently, this focus on the individual has shown signs of changing, with a shift to groups as the units of analysis, or to networks of relations among individuals. The shift is quite a difficult one to make, both conceptually and technically, and the specific methods used to date are only halting steps toward a full-fledged methodology. Nevertheless, some of these methods are outlined below, to indicate just how, taken together, they can even now provide us with an extremely fruitful research tool. This tool has sometimes been used for the study of formal organization but more often for the study of the informal organization which springs up within a formal structure. In both cases, it shows promise of opening to research, problems which have been heretofore the province of speculation.

PROBLEMS OF DESIGN AND SAMPLING

The break from the atomistic concerns of ordinary survey analysis requires taking a different perspective toward the individual interview. In usual survey research and statistical analysis, this interview is regarded as *independent* of others, as an entity in itself. All cross-tabulations and analyses relate one item in that questionnaire to another item in the same questionnaire. But, in this different approach, an individual interview is seen as a *part* of some larger structure in which the respondent finds himself: his network of friends, the shop or office where he works, the bowling team he belongs to, and so on. Thus, as a part of a larger structure, the individual is *not* treated independently. The analysis must somehow tie together and interrelate the attributes of these different parts of the structure.

So much for the basic change in perspective—away from the atomistic treatment of the individual interview, and toward the treatment of each interview as a part of some larger whole. This basic perspective has several implications for the kind of data collected and for the sample design. Perhaps the most important innovation in the kind of data collected is sociometric-type data in the interview, that is, explicit questions about the respondent's relation to other specific individuals. Each person may be asked the names of his best friends, or the names of his subordinates in the shop upon whom he depends most, or any one of a multitude of *relational* questions. For example, in a study of two housing projects by Merton, West, and Jahoda,[1] one way to map out the informal social structure in the community was to ask people who their best friends were. Having obtained such data from all the families in the project, so that each family could be located in the network of social relations in the community, it was then possible to examine the relation between this social structure, on the one hand, and various values and statuses on the other. Specifically, this information allowed these authors to show that in one housing project social ties were based very largely on similarities in background and religion; in the other, social relations were more often built around common leisure interests and participation in community organizations.

More generally, the incorporation of sociometric-type data into survey research allows the investigator to *locate* each interviewed individual within the networks of voluntary relations which surround him. In some cases, these networks of voluntary relations will be superimposed on a highly articulated formal structure. In a department of a business, for example, there are numerous hierarchical levels and there are numerous work relations which are imposed by the job itself. In such cases, sociometric-type questions can be asked relative to these formal relations, e.g.: "Which supervisor do you turn to most often?" or, "Which of the men in your own workgroup do you see most often outside of work?" or, "When you want X type of job done in a hurry to whom do you go to get it done?" or, "When you need advice on such-and-such a problem, who do you usually turn to?"

Another kind of data is that which refers to some larger social unit. For example, in some research on high schools currently being carried out at the University of Chicago, it is necessary to find the paths to prestige

[1] Robert K. Merton, Patricia S. West, and Marie Jahoda, *Patterns of Social Life: Explorations in the Sociology of Housing*, forthcoming.

within a school, so that the boys are asked: "What does it take to be important and looked up to by the other fellows here at school?" Then the responses to this question—aggregated over each school separately—can be used to characterize the *school* as well as the individual. Because of this, the question itself makes explicit reference to the school.

But apart from the kinds of data collected, there are also important *sampling* considerations. In this kind of research, it is no longer possible to pull each individual out of his social context and interview him as an independent entity. It is necessary to sample parts of that context as well or, to say it differently, to sample explicitly with reference to the social structure. There are numerous ways of doing this; only a few, which have been successfully tried, are mentioned below.

a. Snowball Sampling

One method of interviewing a man's immediate social environment is to use the sociometric questions in the interview for sampling purposes. For example, in a study of political attitudes in a New England community, Martin Trow has used this approach: first interviewing a small sample of persons, then asking these persons who their best friends are, interviewing these friends, then asking *them* their friends, interviewing these, and so on.[2] In this way, the sampling plan follows out the chains of sociometric relations in the community. In many respects, this sampling technique is like that of a good reporter who tracks down "leads" from one person to another. The difference, of course, is that snowball sampling in survey research is amenable to the same scientific sampling procedures as ordinary samples. Where the population in ordinary samples is a population of individuals, here it is two populations: one of individuals and one of *relations* among individuals.

b. Saturation Sampling

Perhaps a more obvious approach is to interview *everyone* within the relevant social structure. In a study of doctors in four communities, *all* the doctors in these communities were interviewed.[3] Sociometric-type questions were then used to lay out the professional and social relations existing among these doctors. This "saturation" method or complete census was

[2] Martin A. Trow, "Right Wing Radicalism and Political Intolerance: A Study of Support for McCarthy in a New England Town." Unpublished Ph.D. dissertation, Columbia University, 1957.
[3] J. S. Coleman, E. Katz, and H. M. Menzel, "Diffusion of an Innovation among Physicians," *Sociometry*, XX (Dec. 1957).

feasible there, because the total number of doctors in these communities was small—less than three hundred. But in the study mentioned earlier which used snowball sampling, such an approach would have been practically impossible, for the community was about 15,000 in size. Thus this "saturation sampling" is only feasible under rather special circumstances. A borderline case is the study of high schools mentioned earlier. There are 9,000 students in the ten schools being studied. Only because these students are given self-administered questionnaires, rather than interviews, is it possible to use a saturation sample, and thereby characterize the complete social structure.

c. Dense Sampling

Another approach is to sample "densely." This is a compromise between the usual thinly dispersed random sample and the saturation sample. An illustration will indicate how this may be useful. In a study of pressure upon the academic freedom of college social science teachers, carried out by Paul Lazarsfeld, at least *half* of the social science faculty in every college in the sample was interviewed.[4] Thus, by sampling densely, enough men were interviewed in each college so that the climate of the college could be characterized, as well as the attitudes of the individual respondent.

d. Multi-stage Sampling

Any of the above approaches to sampling can be combined with an element found in many sample designs: the multi-stage sample. For example, in the academic freedom study referred to above, it would have been impossible to have a dense sample of social science teachers in *all* the colleges in the United States, so a two-stage sample was used: first sampling colleges, and then teachers within colleges. In doing this, of course, the crucial question is what balance to maintain between the sampling of colleges and the sampling of teachers within colleges. Enough colleges are needed to have representativity, yet few enough so that the sampling within each one can be dense. In a study of union politics, reported in *Union Democracy*,[5] we perhaps made a wrong decision: we interviewed in 90 printing shops, spreading the interviews so thinly that only one man out of three—at most—was interviewed within the shop. This meant that we had only a very few interviews in each shop, and could not use the

---

[4] P. F. Lazarsfeld and Wagner Thielens, *The Academic Man: Social Scientists in a Time of Crisis*, The Free Press, New York, 1956.
[5] S. M. Lipset, M. A. Trow, and J. S. Coleman, *Union Democracy*, The Free Press, New York, 1956.

interview material to characterize the climate or atmosphere of the shops, except in the very largest ones.

These sampling procedures are, of course, not the only possible ones. An infinite degree of variation is possible, depending upon the problem and upon the kind of social structure involved. The most important point is that the individual interview can no longer be treated as an independent entity, but must be considered as a part of some larger whole: in the sampling, in the questions asked, and in the subsequent analysis.

ANALYTICAL METHODS

The real innovations in this new kind of research are in the techniques of analysis. I will mention several of these with which I am most familiar, to give an indication of the kinds of problems this research examines and the way it examines them.

a. Contextual Analysis

The first, and the one closest to usual survey research, might be termed contextual analysis. In essence, it consists of relating a characteristic of the respondent's social context—and the independent variable—to a characteristic of the individual himself.[6] A good example of this occurred in *The American Soldier,* where the attitudes of inexperienced men, in companies where most others were inexperienced, were compared to attitudes of similarly inexperienced men in companies where most others were veterans. It was found that inexperienced men in green companies felt very differently about themselves, and about combat, than their counterparts in veteran companies. That is, when men were characterized by both individual characteristics and by their social surroundings, the latter were found to have an important effect on their attitudes.

In the union politics study mentioned above, one of the major elements in the analysis was an examination of the effect of the shop context on the men within the shop. We had access to voting records in union political elections for these shops, and these made it possible to characterize the shop as politically radical or politically conservative and as high or low in political consensus. Then we could examine the different behavior or attitudes of men in different kinds of shops and compute a "shop effect." An example is given in Table 1. Each man is in a shop of high or low

---

[6] Peter Blau has emphasized the importance of such analysis in formal organizations for locating the "structural effects" of a situation upon the individuals in it. See his "Formal Organization: Dimensions of Analysis," *American Journal of Sociology,* LXIII (1957), 58–69.

TABLE 1

		Shops of High Political Consensus	Shops of Low Political Consensus
Percent of men active in union politics		29%	7%
	N	(125)	(28)

political consensus, depending on whether the men in the shop vote alike or are evenly split between the radical and conservative parties. And each man has a certain degree of political activity. In this table, the shop's political consensus and the man's political activity are related. The table indicates that in shops of high consensus, men are politically more active than in shops of low consensus. The inference might be that high consensus provides a kind of resonance of political beliefs which generates a greater interest in politics. In any case, the table exemplifies the use of an attribute of a *shop* related to an attribute of a *man* in the shop. This general kind of analysis, which bridges the gap between two levels of sociological units—the individual and his social context—seems to be a very basic one for this "structural" approach to survey research.

b. Boundaries of Homogeneity

A second kind of analysis attempts to answer the question: How homogeneous are various groups in some belief or attitude? In a medical school, for example, are a student's attitudes toward medicine more like those of his fraternity brothers or more like those of his laboratory partners? This question, incidentally, has been posed in a study of medical students presently being carried out at Columbia University.[7] The answer is, in the particular medical school being studied, that his attitudes are far more like those of his fraternity brothers. In other words, in this medical school, the "boundaries of homogeneity" of certain attitudes about medicine coincide very largely with fraternity boundaries.

The major problems in answering questions of group homogeneity are problems of index construction. Consider the above example: each student has twenty or thirty fraternity brothers, but only three laboratory partners in anatomy lab. How can the effects of variability between groups, due to small numbers in a group, be separated out from the actual tendency toward homogeneity of attitude? It can be done, and indices have been

[7] Some of the work in this study (though not the work mentioned here) is reported in P. F. Kendall, R. K. Merton, and G. G. Reader (eds.), *The Student Physician*, Commonwealth Fund, New York, 1957.

developed to do so. The indices, incidentally, are much like the formulas by which statisticians measure the effects of clustering in a random sample.

An example of group homogeneity may indicate more concretely how this approach can be useful in research. In the study of doctors in four communities mentioned earlier, we were interested in the social processes affecting the physicians' introduction of a new drug into their practices. Through interviewing all doctors and asking sociometric questions in the interview, we were able to delineate seven "cliques" of doctors who were sociometrically linked together. (How to reconstruct such cliques is another problem, which will be considered shortly.) The question, then, became this: At each point in time after the drug was marketed, were cliques homogeneous or not in their members' use or non-use of the drug? If they were homogeneous, then this was evidence that some kind of social influence or diffusion was going on in relation to the measured sociometric ties. If not, this indicated that the cliques delineated on the basis of questions in the interview had little relevance to drug adoption. Table 2 shows, for several time periods, just how much homogeneity there was in the cliques, beyond that which would arise by chance. An index value of 1.0 means each clique is completely homogeneous in its use or non-use of the drug. An index value of 0 means there is no more homogeneity than would arise through chance variation between groups.

TABLE 2

Months after Drug Was Marketed	Amount of Clique Homogeneity	Percent of Doctors Who Had Used the Drug
1 months	no homogeneity	14 %
3	no "	32
5	no "	49
7	.07	66
9	.12	71
11	.18	76
13	.03	83
15	no homogeneity	86

Table 2 shows that there was no homogeneity until around seven months after the drug was introduced, that is, until over 50 percent of the doctors had used the drug. The maximum homogeneity was reached at about eleven months, when three-fourths of the doctors had begun to use the drug. Then after that, the homogeneity receded to zero again.

This result helped to reinforce a conclusion derived from other findings in the study: that the social networks measured in the study were effective as paths of diffusion at certain times but not at others. However, apart from the substantive results of the study, this example indicates how such analysis of the boundaries of homogeneity may be useful for the study of the functioning of various social organizations.

c. Pair Analysis

Neither of the above kinds of analysis has required the use of sociometric-type data. An important kind of analysis which does use such direct data on relationships is the analysis of *pairs*. Here, the pair formed by A's choosing B becomes the unit of analysis. Speaking technically, "pair cards" may be constructed for each sociometric choice, and then these cards used for cross-tabulations. In other words, instead of cross-tabulating a man's attitude toward Russia with his attitude toward the United Nations, we can cross-tabulate the man's attitude toward Russia with the attitude toward Russia of the man he eats lunch with at the cafeteria.

One of the most important problems which has been studied in this way is the similarity or difference in attitudes or backgrounds between the two members of a pair. That is, do people have friendship relations with those who are like them politically, with people of the same age, with persons in the same occupation?

This kind of problem can be illustrated by Table 3, which contains hypothetical data. This table, which looks very much like an ordinary contingency table, must be treated in a slightly different fashion. It allows

TABLE 3

		Chosen		
		boy	girl	
Chooser	boy	45	15	40
	girl	20	20	60
				100

us to raise the question: do boys tend to choose boys more than would be expected by chance? and, do girls tend to choose girls more than would be expected by chance? The answer, of course, depends upon what we take as chance. However, chance models have been worked out, so that one can assign measures of the tendency to choose others of one's own kind. One of these is outlined in Appendix B. For the above example, this measure (varying between 0 and 1) says that the tendency to in-choice for boys is .38 and that for girls is .17. By comparing such indices for numerous attributes, one could get a good glimpse into the informal social organization of the group. For example, in the medical study mentioned earlier which is being carried out at Columbia University, the values of in-choice tendency for friends shown in Table 4 were found:

TABLE 4

Sub-groups	Tendencies toward In-Choice
Class in school	.92
Fraternity	.52
Sex	.33
Marital status	.20
Attitudes toward national health insurance	.37

By looking at the relative sizes of these index values, we get an idea of just how the informal social relations—that is, the friendship choices—at this medical school mesh with the formal structure, and with the distribution of attitudes.

In the study mentioned above of drug introduction by doctors, these pair relations were used as the major aspect of the analysis: by examining how close in time a doctor's first use of a new drug was to the first use of the doctor he mentioned as a friend, it was possible to infer the functioning of friendship networks in the introduction of this drug.

These examples of pair analysis give only a crude picture of the kinds of problems which can be studied in this fashion. The important matter is to break away from the analysis of *individuals* as units to the study of *pairs* of individuals. To be sure, this involves technical IBM problems and problems of index construction along with conceptual problems, but the difficulties are not great.

d. Partitioning into Cliques

Another important kind of problem is the partitioning of a larger group into cliques by use of sociometric choices. This problem is a thorny one, for it involves not only the delineation of cliques, but, even prior to this, the *definition* of what is to constitute a clique. Are cliques to be mutually exclusive in membership, or can they have overlapping memberships? Are they to consist of people who all name one another, or of people who are tied together by more tenuous connections? Such questions must be answered before the group can be partitioned into cliques.

A good review of some of the methods by which cliques and subgroups can be treated is presented in Lindzey and Borgotta.[8] The two most feasible of these are the method of matrix multiplication[9] and the method of shifting rows and columns in the sociometric choice matrix until the choices are clustered around the diagonal.[10] This last technique is by far the more feasible of the two if the groups are more than about twenty in size. When the groups are on the order of a hundred, even this method becomes clumsy. An IBM technique was successfully used in the study of doctors and the study of medical students, both mentioned above, in which the groups were 200–400 in size. At the University of Chicago, a program has been developed for Univac, using a method of shifting rows and columns in a matrix, which can handle groups up to a thousand in size.[11] The necessity for some such method becomes great when, for example, one wants to map out systematically the informal organization of a high school of a thousand students.

CONCLUSION

These four kinds of analysis, contextual analysis, boundaries of homogeneity, pair analysis, and partitioning into cliques, are only four of many possibilities. Several other approaches have been used, but these four give some idea of the way in which survey analysis can come to treat problems which involve social structure. In the long run, these modes of analysis will probably represent only the initial halting steps in the development of a kind of structural research which will represent a truly sociological methodology. In any case, these developments spell an important milestone in social research, for they help open up for systematic research those problems which have heretofore been the province of the theorist or of purely qualitative methods.

There is one new development which should be mentioned, although the frontier is just opened, and not at all explored. This development is the construction of electronic computers with immediate-access storage capacities a hundred times the size of an 80-column IBM card. Such computers make it possible, for the first time, to lay out a complex social structure for direct and systematic examination. Instead of examining the

[8] G. Lindzey (ed.), *Handbook of Social Psychology*, Addison-Wesley, Cambridge, 1956, Chap. II.
[9] See L. Festinger, "The Analysis of Sociograms Using Matrix Algebra," *Human Relations*, II, No. 2 (1949), 153–158, and R. D. Luce, "Connectivity and Generalized Cliques in Sociometric Group Structure," *Psychometrika*, XV (1950), 169–190.
[10] C. O. Beum and E. G. Brundage, "A Method for Analyzing the Sociomatrix," *Sociometry*, XIII (1950), 141–145.
[11] A description of this program, written by the author and Duncan McRae, is available upon request from the author and the program itself is available for copying, for those who have access to a Univac I or II.

similarity of attitudes between socially connected pairs, after laborious construction of "pair cards," it becomes possible to trace through a whole structural network, examining the points in the network where attitudes or actions begin to diverge. Methods for doing this have not yet been developed but, for the first time, the technical facilities exist, and it is just a matter of time until analytical methods are developed. IBM cards and counter-sorters were methodologically appropriate for the individualistic orientation which survey research has had in the past; electronic computers with large storage capacities are precisely appropriate for the statistical analysis of complex social organization.

Unfortunately, it has not been possible here to present any of the tools discussed above fully enough to show precisely how it is used. In giving a broad overview of a number of developments, my aim has been to point to an important new direction in social research, one which may aid significantly in the systematic study of social organization.

CAN YOU REALLY STUDY AN ARMY IN THE LABORATORY?

Morris Zelditch, Jr.

INTRODUCTION

No method has more influenced our conception of science than the experimental method; no method makes the contemporary sociologist more suspicious. The rapid and prolific development of the small groups field seems to argue a contrary thesis. But there is no sounder evidence of the way in which sociologists regard the experiment than the habit of calling them all "small groups" research. And because they think the laboratory group is a small group, many sociologists think that larger organizations cannot be studied in the laboratory.

If the idea is that the laboratory group resembles the smaller kinds of groups found in natural settings, then the idea is wrong. For the labora-

This article is published here for the first time.

tory group, though usually small, is no more like small groups found in natural settings than it is like a formal organization. In fact, the laboratory group is not like *any* concrete setting in society. If the laboratory group were a small group, then we would be able to equate the following group with air force flight crews:

> Two air force staff sergeants are seated on either side of an opaque partition, each under the impression that the other is an air force captain. Projected on a screen in front of them is a consecutive series of 38 large rectangles, each composed of 100 smaller black and white rectangles in varying arrangements. Every rectangle contains almost the same number of black as white rectangles, but the sergeants are to decide, for each one, whether it is more black or more white. Each sergeant makes an initial decision, exchanges opinions with the other, and makes a final decision for each repetition of the stimulus. The exchange of opinions is controlled by the experimenter: in front of each sergeant there is a console of switches and lights, which permits one sergeant to operate a switch on his own console that flashes a light on the console of the other sergeant. The circuit passes through a master control panel, permitting the experimenter to arrange any desired pattern of agreement or disagreement between the two sergeants. If the two are made to disagree, each must either *change* his initial opinion or *repeat* his initial opinion in making his final decision.
>
> In the same setting, two air force sergeants may each be made to believe that the other is an airman third class. If this condition is compared with that described above, it is found that a "captain" more readily persuades a sergeant that his initial opinion was wrong than an "airman third class."[1]

But what is studied here is no more like an air force flight crew than it is like an air force wing, or any other more complex structure. An air force flight crew has a past, a future, a system of informal social controls, and some commitment to a common goal. The two staff sergeants in the laboratory group just described are an *ad hoc* group, transitory, with no informal social system that could bring social pressures to bear on the behavior of either subject, and not much committed to the goal.

Nor is the laboratory group more like an informal peer group. Such a group is typically a primary group; the laboratory group is typically not. Both laboratory and primary groups are typically small and face-to-face, but this does not make the laboratory group a primary group. Faris made the reason perfectly clear as long ago as 1932. He insisted that size and face-to-face interaction were not the criteria that defined a primary group,

[1] J. Berger, B. P. Cohen, and M. Zelditch, *Status Conceptions in Social Interaction*, Chap. 5, forthcoming.

because a courtroom, or a housewife driving off a door-to-door salesman are both small and face-to-face, but certainly no one thinks they are primary groups. A primary group is a group having a certain system of norms,[2]— norms requiring affective, diffuse, particularistic role relations. But such norms are rarely found in laboratory groups.

The fact is that laboratory investigations are seldom efforts to study the small group *per se,* and even when they *are,* the groups studied are not often like small groups found in natural settings. But if the purpose of experiments is not to study the kinds of groups found in natural settings, just what *is* their purpose? The answer has a deceptive simplicity: *The purpose of the laboratory experiment is to create certain theoretically relevant aspects of social situations under controlled conditions.* Though the point looks simple, it has fairly profound implications for most of the issues that are most controversial about the experimental method in sociology. I will therefore first attempt to demonstrate that what I have just said is so; after which, I will point out some of its more important implications.

I will argue that the purpose of experiments is mainly to construct and test theories; that theories are necessarily abstract; and therefore experiments are also necessarily abstract. Consequently, the answer to the question which gives this paper its title is that one would not even *try* to study an army in the laboratory, if by that one means an army in the concrete sense of the term. One would try only to create those aspects of an army that were relevant to some theory. But from this it follows that, if there is any question about the possibility of studying organizations in the laboratory, the question can only be: Are there theoretically relevant aspects of organizations that cannot be created in a laboratory? To this question the answer is that nothing inherent in laboratory experiments bars us from creating many theoretically relevant aspects of organizations. But if the abstract organizations so created are not like those in natural settings, will one ever be able to generalize from the experimentally created aspect of an army to the concrete army in its natural setting? My answer is first, that the situation is no different for organizational experiments than for any other sort of analytic investigation; and second, that generalization, in the only sense meaningful in such a context, is the application of a theory supported by experiment rather than the direct extrapolation of the results of a single experiment. If the appropriate sense of "generalization" is really application of a theory in a particular setting, "application" is synonomous with the explanation or prediction of a particular event. Therefore, the widely accepted Hempel-Oppenheim para-

[2] E. Faris, "The Primary Group: Essence and Accident," *American Journal of Sociology,* 38 (1932), 41–50.

digm of explanation can be used to study what application involves.[3] From this study there are two results: On the one hand, there is no reason why experimental results *must* be directly extrapolated for them to be applied, because it is *theories* that are applied to concrete settings. On the other hand, application always involves at least some knowledge that is not guaranteed by experiment; therefore, no amount of experimental support for a theory is itself sufficient to warrant its applicability in any particular setting.

THE ABSTRACT CHARACTER
OF THEORY AND EXPERIMENT

That experiments are mainly useful in constructing and testing theory is evident from the peculiar character of some of their advantages.[4] Among the aims of an experiment are: (1) To create states of affairs difficult to discover in natural settings, for example the continual open expression of disagreement between a status inferior and his superior in an organization. (2) To produce controls and contrasts that are difficult to find *ex post facto* in natural settings, for example a high and a low status source making an identical suggestion to similar individuals. (3) To replicate events that seldom recur under the same conditions in natural settings, such as the negotiation by several foreign offices of an international disarmament treaty. (4) To isolate a process from the effects of other processes that confuse our understanding of it, such as separating the effects of power from the effects of relative competence-expectations in the study of a status superior's influence in an organization. Such concerns are mostly dictated by the desire to build and test a theory, and the special advantages of the experiment are mostly advantages from the standpoint of theorists. Experiments would make much less sense if the purpose were to describe a particular concrete situation.

That theory is necessarily abstract derives from its desire to be general. It will contain universal statements, such as, "The greater the uncertainty of an individual about his status, the greater the social distance he will maintain from status inferiors," rather than singular statements such as "John Smith is uncertain about his status." While the objective is to explain more and more, the more of one *concrete entity* a theory explains, the less it explains of any other thing, because any concrete entity is

---

[3] C. Hempel and P. Oppenheim, "Studies in the Logic of Explanation," *Philosophy of Science*, 15 (1948), 135–175.

[4] See M. Zelditch and W. Evan, "Simulated Bureaucracies: A Methodological Analysis," in H. Guetzkow, *Simulation in Social Science: Readings* (Englewood Cliffs, N.J.: Prentice-Hall, 1962), 48–60, which expands this argument.

unique.[5] If it explains everything about General Motors it will not even explain Ford Motor Company, much less an army. By a "concrete entity" I mean a particular object of the phenomenal world. To describe it, one lists its properties: Its color, mass, volume, velocity, age, gender, shape, price, status significance, purpose. . . . The list is always infinite, and the more complete it is the more it differs from any other description. By an "abstract" theory, I mean a system of properties that are thought to be related to each other dynamically. A system of abstract properties or variables will inevitably omit some of the properties of any concrete thing: it will omit precisely those properties thought to be independent of, or at least only minimally correlated with, those contained in the theoretical system. But omitting some properties, the system of abstract variables will never account for the whole of any concrete entity. It does not explain "General Motors," it explains only some property of General Motors. Economics explains General Motors' prices, sociology explains the stability of its status structure, and so on. Even the language of theory expresses this fact. Terms originally meant concretely, such as "bureaucracy," come to mean not the Pentagon or the Bureau of the Budget, but any social system that has a division of labor, a hierarchical structure, some separation from the kinship, power, and status structures of a community, and so on. Meant abstractly in this way, some things once thought to be bureaucracies come to seem less so, while others not thought of as bureaucracies at all from a phenomenal point of view come to be objects explained by the theory.[6] But often what is similar or different from the point of view of abstract theory cannot be formulated except in quite abstract terms: hence the use of expressions like "total institutions" or "utilitarian organizations" which do not even incidentally sound concrete. In no other way can the theory formulate notions that distinguish two armies, two hospitals, or two prisons from each other, while classifying *some* hospitals together with *some* armies and *some* prisons as one sort of thing.

CAN YOU REALLY STUDY AN ARMY IN THE LABORATORY?

If no theory can be concrete, and experiments are for the purpose of constructing theory, there is no basis for the common argument that an experiment ought to be as close as possible to the concrete entity it most

[5] This point, as well as the whole of the present paper, owes a great deal to the argument made in B. P. Cohen, "On the Construction of Explanations," Technical Report #19, Laboratory for Social Research, Stanford University, 1966.
[6] Cf. the argument in A. Etzioni, *A Comparative Analysis of Complex Organizations* (New York: Free Press, 1961), chap. 3.

nearly represents. An experiment aims only to reproduce that part of a concrete entity that is made relevant by some particular system of abstract variables. Therefore, we do not even *try* to study armies in the laboratory, if by that is meant an army in the concrete sense of the word. We try only to create those aspects of armies relevant to some theory.

Therefore, if it is objected that one cannot study an army in the laboratory, the objection must be that the properties of some theory relevant to the army cannot be produced under laboratory conditions. Can this objection be sustained?

Size plays an interesting and ambiguous role in such arguments. Obviously one would not bring an entire army into a laboratory, but does this mean that an army cannot be studied in the laboratory? If size is not theoretically relevant there is no reason to reproduce it in the laboratory. Therefore, the argument must be that size is, or is correlated with, a property without which a laboratory group could not simulate what is theoretically relevant about organizations. To refute such an argument, one must show that size itself is *not* relevant; that what is relevant is something else, probably complexity; and finally, that adequate degrees of complexity can be produced independently of size.[7] The rebuttal may be made a little more complicated, for propositions about organizations include some in which complexity is a variable and some in which it is not. Where complexity is not relevant, there is no need to create it even if organizations are typically complex. Where complexity *is* relevant, we face two possible situations: We may be required to produce very great degrees of complexity, say fifty different kinds of subunits and five levels of authority. In this case, it is doubtful that a laboratory group will prove adequate to the requirement. Even if one could create such an organization—and probably one could—the cost would be great, and the loss of control over the organization would ensure that the cost exceeded the return. But if something less than such great complexity will do, say three or four kinds of subunits and two or three levels of authority, then nothing precludes constructing complex laboratory organizations, and constructing fairly large numbers of them.

A process that can be studied in quite small laboratory "organizations" is the way in which stability is built into the status hierarchy of an organization. Complex organizations typically consist of at least three status classes, such as officers, noncommissioned officers, and other en-

---

[7] This part of the argument is expanded in M. Zelditch and T. K. Hopkins, "Laboratory Experiments with Organizations," in A. Etzioni (ed.), *Complex Organizations: A Sociological Reader* (First ed.), (New York: Holt, Rinehart and Winston, Inc., 1961), 465–478. There it is argued that the character of formal organizations, for example their complexity, high degree of institutionalization, and scale, do not in most circumstances preclude experimentation.

listed men in the army; or executives, supervisors, and workers in a factory. Of each status class beliefs are held about their relative abilities to perform organizational tasks. Based on these beliefs, opportunities to actually perform, evaluations of performance, and rights to influence decisions are distributed. Because it accords with the status structure, the distribution of opportunities, evaluations, and rights to exercise influence also tends to perpetuate that structure.[8] Of particular importance to the stability of the status structure is the fact that expectations embodied in status are expansive; that is, confronting a new task or activity, one not previously associated in anyone's mind with statuses in the organization, members of the organization will often behave as if superiors in the status structure were superior at the new task—providing superiority in the new activity is something the organization positively values. To understand the stability of status hierarchies, it is important to discover under what conditions status conceptions have this expansive property.

It was to study the expansive properties of status that the experiment described in the second paragraph of this paper was designed. The experiment had some additional features that it now becomes important to understand:

> The two staff sergeants were told that the task and setting of the experiment were designed to simulate a new kind of decision-making situation being studied by the air force. They were told that the decisions were difficult, but there was a correct choice in every case; that the experimenter was interested not in testing their individual abilities, but in finding out how the correct decision was made, so that it was perfectly legitimate to use advice from their co-participant; and that the co-participant, who was identified by a fictitious name, was from a different unit than the sergeant himself. Great care was taken to make sure that the task ability, called "contrast sensitivity," was not already associated with status in the air force. That is, it was not already associated with the terms "captain," "sergeant," or "airman" in the way cooking might conventionally be associated more with "female" than with "male."[9]

Thus, the sergeants were in a situation where they typically wanted to do well, but the decisions were difficult; where they had help but did not know their partner well enough to know what ability he might have; and the only cues were status cues. Under such conditions, in spite of the

---

[8] For further theoretical background, see B. Anderson, J. Berger, B. P. Cohen, and M. Zelditch, "Status Classes in Organizations," *Administrative Science Quarterly*, 11 (1966), 264–283; and J. Berger, B. P. Cohen, and M. Zelditch, "Status Characteristics and Expectation States," in J. Berger, M. Zelditch, and B. Anderson (eds.), *Sociological Theories in Progress*, vol. 1 (Boston: Houghton Mifflin, 1966), 47–73.

[9] J. Berger, B. P. Cohen, and M. Zelditch, *Status Conception in Social Interaction*, chap. 5.

irrelevance of status to the task ability, the sergeants yielded to the influence of the other participant more if he was a captain than if he was an airman.

This experiment accomplished three objectives: First, it artificially created one aspect of the organizational structure of the air force, its status structure—though only three of its status levels were used. Second, it artificially isolated one process through which status expands, separating expectations from other processes that might obscure them—such as the way in which resources, technical knowledge, or power are allocated to statuses. Third, it created those conditions, but *only* those conditions that are theoretically relevant to the way in which status-related expectations expand. It did not embody *all* the conditions that make a status structure stable, much less *all* the properties of an air force.

BRIDGING THE GAP

If armies are not really brought into the laboratory, what can be said about an army as a result of a laboratory experiment? Or, to put the question as it has been put several times in the past, how does one bridge the gap between experiment and natural setting?[10]

Usually the problem is thought to be one of *generalizing* from the experiment, and by "generalizing" people often mean equating concrete features of the experiment with concrete features of the natural setting. In this view, to generalize from the status-expansion experiment one asks if the same thing will be found true of staff sergeants outside the laboratory room. But almost certainly it will not. Equating populations in this fashion will not be sufficient to guarantee the truth of the generalization, for often the result will be false of "real live" staff sergeants. On the other hand, it is not necessary either, for often the result will be true of generals, or even college professors.

If generalization meant equating concrete features of experiment and natural setting, no bridge between the two would ever be built. But it is not concrete similarities that form the basis of generalization. One generalizes from one situation to another when both situations are described by the same abstract properties and satisfy the same conditions. For example: Instead of using staff sergeants, imagine that the status expansion experiment was run in exactly the same way with junior college students as subjects. In the same interaction conditions, given the same task, subjects

10 See B. Anderson, *The Use of Experimental Data in the Interpretation of Survey Results* (Technical Report, Bureau of Applied Social Research, Columbia University, 1961); H. Riecken, "Narrowing the Gap between Field Studies and Laboratory Experiments in Social Psychology," *Items*, 8 (1954), 37–42; and S. Verba, *Small Groups and Political Behavior* (Princeton, N.J.: Princeton University Press, 1961), 90–109.

would be told that their partner is either a high-school student or a student at a four-year college. It happens that when this is done the same result is found as in the air force experiment: subjects are much less likely to be influenced if they are told their partner has the lower state than if told that he has the higher state of a status characteristic.[11] What allows us to generalize from one experiment to the other? The task and interaction conditions are the same; and the status characteristics, though concretely very different, have the same properties from an abstract point of view. Both embody value judgments and expectations of what a person is like and how he will behave.[12] What differences there are, are not differences that are part of the system of abstract variables forming the theory of status characteristics. They are therefore differences that make no difference.

It may seem to beg the question to show that the results of one experiment generalize to the results of another *experiment,* when the issue appears to be how to generalize to a natural setting. But in fact the problem is the same: *generalization from any one situation to any other relates, not concrete settings, but abstract variables.*

But even if focus is restricted to only those abstract variables that are part of a theoretical system, the results of an experiment are not directly extrapolated, because the results of experiments are always *conditional.* One does not generalize from an experiment any claim that the *initial conditions* established by the experiment are those typically found in natural settings. That air force sergeants typically believe officers are superior to enlisted men in ability is *not* a hypothesis tested or confirmed by the status-expansion experiment. Had a sergeant not believed in the status characteristic, he would not have been a suitable subject for experiment. That the sergeants used in the experiment did believe in the characteristic proves nothing about how many sergeants in the air force believe in its status structure. What is generalized from the experiment is not the descriptive hypothesis that its initial conditions are found outside the laboratory, but the conditional law that *if* a status characteristic is present, *then* influence is distributed so as to accord with its states. It is a gross fallacy of experimental logic to generalize only the *consequent* of a conditional—the "y" in "if x, then y." For what happens then is that the result of the experiment becomes subtly transformed into a description, such as: "In an organization like the air force, one finds y." But this is not the result of the experiment. The first part of the expression is not a set of abstract conditions that form the antecedent of a conditional; instead, substituted for such conditions, one finds a concrete entity masquerading as the antecedent. The effect is

[11] J. Moore, *General Status Characteristics and Specific Performance Expectations,* unpublished Ph.D. dissertation, Stanford University, 1966.
[12] See J. Berger, *et al., op. cit.,* pp. 29–46.

to transform "y" into a descriptive claim. How often does one hear that "Asch shows most people conform," or that "Sherif shows that all groups create norms?" What one means is that *under* (*abstract*) *conditions p, q, r* . . . , people conform or make norms.

It might be supposed that one could nevertheless generalize from a single experiment to any natural setting in which the same abstract, antecedent conditions are found. But even in this sense, a single experiment is almost never meant to be directly extrapolated. Rather, one thinks of an experiment as supporting a theory. It is the *theory* that is used to make predictions about natural settings. For the fact is that almost never is a single experiment decisively informative about a theory. Therefore, any single experiment is simply one part of a larger program, each part testing a different aspect of the theory. For example, the status-expansion experiment already described is actually only one of three run at the same time in the same setting, each of which focused on a different phase of the status-expansion process. To understand what takes place in some natural setting, therefore, one must understand it in terms of the theory, not of any one experiment designed to test some aspect of the theory. It is in this sense that theory is the bridge between experiment and natural setting, and for this reason that one seldom extrapolates an experiment directly.

If generalization from an experiment comes to mean the application of a theoretical formulation supported by that experiment, and by other experiments as well, then the difficulties in generalizing from experiments are really difficulties in applying theory. There are difficulties in generalizing from experiments, but these difficulties are not peculiar to generalization from experiments. They are difficulties that attend the application of *any* theories, whether supported by experiments, or by field studies, or by surveys, or indeed by any evidence whatsoever.

"Application" here does not mean social engineering, but simply the use of an abstract theory to reason about particular settings. For example, the theory of status characteristics might be applied to questions about the status order of schools in a city school system. In this sense "application" is essentially the same as "explanation" or "prediction" of particular events in the paradigm of Hempel and Oppenheim.[13] In this paradigm, explanation or prediction is a deductive argument in which what is to be explained or predicted is shown to be a valid conclusion from two kinds of premises: (1) One or more general laws; and (2) one or more statements describing conditions in the particular setting. For example, suppose that in city school system S considerable resources are to be invested to make racially imbalanced schools equal in objective quality. The purpose is to not only

---

[13] C. Hempel and P. Oppenheim, *op. cit.*

improve their quality, but also to make "Negro" schools more attractive to teachers, parents, and students by raising their status. The theory of status characteristics implies that equalizing the objective quality of teachers, programs, and even student performance in racially imbalanced schools will not succeed in making teachers, parents, and students attribute equal quality to a "Negro" and a "white" school.[14] In fact, the status order will remain unchanged. The argument is that a status characteristic differentiates the schools; and evaluations of school quality are a function of expectations determined by status independently of their objective quality. The first statement is a statement about the particular school system S. The second is a "general law" from the theory of status characteristics.

This application assumes, first, that the ordering of schools in city school systems is a status phenomenon of the kind formulated in the theory of status characteristics; second, that particular conditions in the school system have been correctly described; and third, that important other factors, not formulated by the theory, can be safely neglected in city school systems. Each of these assumptions can be disputed. While race may satisfy the definition of a status characteristic, it is still possible that school systems fall outside the scope of the theory. This would be the case if race were an individual but not a collective property in the system.[15] In that case, schools would not be thought of as "Negro" or "white" and the theory might have nothing to say about their relative ordering. Even if race were a collective property, and the theory was applicable to schools in city school systems, the descriptive knowledge used in the application might be wrong. The schools might actually differ in objective quality, or it might be wrong to suppose that the status of schools in the system depends on the "quality" attributed by people to the schools. Even if the descriptive knowledge is accurate, the effect of interscholastic athletics has been ignored, and might be sufficiently important to change any predictions made about status ordering from a knowledge of status characteristics alone.

What is important about such disputes is that they do not simply depend on the degree to which the theory that is applied has been confirmed. They are disputes about the theory's *applicability,* not about the evidence in its favor. Some disputes about applicability can be resolved by experimental means. For example, the effect of processes that were neglected in confirming a theory but become important in some applica-

[14] B. P. Cohen, "White Expectations and Negro Aspirations: One View of *De Facto* School Segregation" (Technical Report #18, Laboratory for Social Research, Stanford University, 1965).
[15] See the paper by P. Lazarsfeld and H. Menzel, "On the Relation between Individual and Collective Properties," in this volume, pp. 499–516.

tion can sometimes be studied in the laboratory. On the other hand, some disputes about applicability cannot be resolved by such means. They depend on descriptive knowledge of the particular situation, and *no* amount of experimental investigation will provide such knowledge. *Therefore, no application can ever depend entirely on experimental investigation.*

SUMMARY

I have argued that experiments are mainly for the purpose of building and testing theories; that theories are necessarily abstract; therefore, experiments too are abstract. Neither the organizational experiment, nor any other kind of experiment, attempts to recreate a completely "real" instance of any concrete organization in the laboratory. One would not even *want* to bring an army into the laboratory, much less defend the possibility of actually doing so.

If the laboratory organization creates only the aspects of an organization relevant to some theory, then only a theory can bridge the gap between experiment and natural setting. I have rejected the view that generalization requires direct extrapolation of the results of a single experiment. In place of it I have suggested that experiments are relevant to theory, and *theory* is applied to natural settings. Two interesting consequences follow: First, if an experiment is informative for a theory, and the theory applicable in a given setting, the findings of an experiment are "generalizable" even if they bear little resemblance to the typical findings in the natural setting. For if theory is thought of as a bridge, the main requirement of the bridge is that it span both settings, not that the two settings be identical. Put a little less metaphorically, if f_1 is found in an experiment and f_2 in some natural setting, it is sufficient for some theory to imply both f_1 and f_2 for that theory to bridge the gap. It is not required that $f_1 = f_2$. But second, if the Hempel-Oppenheim paradigm is accepted as applying to an application, then application uses not only laws from some theory, but also descriptive knowledge about some domain of application. Therefore experimental support for a theory is never sufficient warrant for its applicability. But the situation is no different for theories supported by survey or other sorts of field evidence; whatever the evidence for the theory, the problem of application remains. Hence the problems of application raise no special objections to experimental studies of organizations.

CHANGE IN AN ORGANIZATIONAL SYSTEM: FORMALIZATION OF A QUALITATIVE STUDY

Allen H. Barton and Bo Anderson

Quantitative social research in the last twenty-five years has relied heavily on the sample survey. By this method very large populations can be accurately described through the study of only one or two thousand persons. The most efficient design for descriptive purposes is the random sample, with the individuals selected so as to be widely scattered among the whole population. Yet precisely this design makes it difficult to study processes which involve mutual effects among people and among groups. The atomistic survey is particularly misplaced in the study of organizations. Organizations are systems of individuals and groups which act upon one another. Changes in the behavior of one status group within an organization must affect the behavior of other groups, which in turn may have consequences feeding back to the group which changed first. The consequences of change in a system cannot be predicted by any simple two-variable notions of causation in which "A" invariably leads to "B."

The object of this paper is to see how the system aspect of organizations can be dealt with in empirical research. Progress toward methods capable of studying the operation of systems has come from several sources. One requirement is that data be gathered at several points *in time*. The technique of trend or panel studies adds this time dimension to surveys.[1]

This article is one of a series sponsored by the Documentation Project for Advanced Training in Social Research, Columbia University. It may be cited as Publication A-323 of the Bureau of Applied Social Research, Columbia University.

[1] Bernard Berelson, Paul F. Lazarsfeld, and William N. McPhee, *Voting* (Chicago: University of Chicago, 1954), is an example of the panel method applied to mass

Studies of small groups using quantified observations of behavior permit analysis of changes in different natural phases or under changing experimental conditions.[2] A few studies have traced changes in organizations over time, using such variables as could be derived from organizational records.[3]

A second requirement for system analysis is that data be obtained from the *different units* which act upon one another within the system. Some surveys have gone beyond the individual respondent by getting his description of the people with whom he interacts, for example, by asking him what the politics of his family, friends, or co-workers are.[4] Surveys have begun to use clustered samples within formal groups, such as college faculties[5] or printing shops,[6] so that the group context of individuals can be directly measured by aggregating the responses of all members. Sociometric data on contacts among group members, obtained when *all* members of a group are surveyed, provide more refined information on sets of related individuals.[7] A few studies have interviewed both sides of a role relationship, such as workers and their foreman,[8] superintendents and their school board,[9] students and faculty members.[10] These methods obtain data on related parts of a system rather than isolated individuals, although they seldom have been used to cover *all* the major parts of any system.

---

political behavior. A discussion of the method and more examples are found in Paul F. Lazarsfeld and Morris Rosenberg, *The Language of Social Research* (New York: Free Press, 1955), Section 3, "The Analysis of Change through Time."

[2] Robert F. Bales, "The Equilibrium Problem in Small Groups," in A. P. Hare, E. F. Borgatta, and R. F. Bales, *Small Groups: Studies in Social Interaction* (New York: Knopf, 1955), summarizes research along these lines done at the Harvard Laboratory of Social Relations.

Henry Lennard and Arnold Bernstein, *The Anatomy of Psychotherapy: Systems of Communication and Expectation* (New York: Columbia, 1960), studies a two-person interaction system over time in a natural situation.

[3] For example, S. M. Lipset, M. A. Trow, and J. S. Coleman, *Union Democracy* (New York: Free Press, 1956), Chaps. 3 and 17; and Julia S. Brown, "Union Size as a Function of Intra-Union Conflict," *Human Relations*, 9 (1956), 75–89.

[4] Berelson, Lazarsfeld, and McPhee (see n. 1).

[5] Paul F. Lazarsfeld and Wagner Thielens, Jr., *The Academic Mind* (New York: Free Press, 1958).

[6] Lipset, Trow, and Coleman (see n. 3).

[7] T. M. Newcomb, *Personality and Social Change* (New York: Holt, Rinehart and Winston, Inc., 1943), provides an example of this method, combined with a panel study, applied to the survey of change in attitudes of college students.

[8] Robert L. Kahn and Daniel Katz, "Leadership Practices in Relations to Productivity and Morale," in Dorwin Cartwright and Alvin Zander, *Group Dynamics: Research and Theory* (Evanston, Ill.: Row, Peterson, 1953), pp. 612–628, summarizes several such studies.

[9] Neal Gross, W. S. Mason, and A. W. McEachern, *Explorations in Role Analysis* (New York: Wiley, 1958).

[10] Newcomb (see n. 7).

What has not been done is to combine these methods in the study of an organizational system. No one has yet studied quantitatively the attitudes and behavior of different strata within an organization, at two or more time periods, with data on contacts between people and groups. We cannot therefore present a series of examples for methodological clarification. However, there are a number of *qualitative* case studies which deal with organizational processes, using largely subjective measures of the variables involved. We will examine one such study, in order to illustrate the concept of an organization as a system and to suggest how quantitative methods *might* be used to study organizations as systems. Our findings may also shed some light on the techniques of purely qualitative research.

Richard H. McCleery's *Policy Change in Prison Management*[11] is a brief report on a study of change in the social system of a prison. It describes the prison in equilibrium under an authoritarian system in which the custodial goal of strict physical orderliness was stressed above all else; the disorders and difficulties which followed a change in top personnel and policies; and the eventual restoration of equilibrium under policies which emphasized the rehabilitation function.

By observing what happened when certain features of the authoritarian regime were removed, he obtained suggestions of the functions which these features had been performing for the maintenance of order, as well as suggestions of their dysfunctions for the rehabilitation goal. Observing the growth of the new equilibrium as the "liberal" regime gradually responded to the problems of the transition period, he found evidence of the availability of alternatives to the old methods which permitted a higher achievement of the nominal goals of the prison: rehabilitation and effective custody.

THE ANATOMY OF THE SYSTEM

McCleery's first step is to describe the "anatomy" of the system, the groups or strata which formed the prison's structure. The following major status groups are distinguished: the top administration (essentially the warden, later joined by a policy committee of department heads); the custodial staff (guards and guard officers); the treatment staff (workshop supervisors, psychiatrist, and later the directors of programs of education and recreation); the inmate elite of old cons with privilege and power; and the mass of the inmates.

---

[11] Richard H. McCleery, *Policy Change in Prison Management* (East Lansing: Michigan State University, Governmental Research Bureau, 1957).

VARIABLES IN THE SYSTEM

The monograph consists of qualitative descriptions of these status groups and their relationships at various stages in the process of change. By qualitative, we mean that McCleery simply reports that a variable has a high or low value, or that it has increased or decreased.[12] The major types of variables considered are attitudes toward prison programs; the amount of communication between status groups; the degree of control over such communication held by intermediary groups; the types of sanctions employed to encourage or inhibit various behaviors; and the response of various groups to these sanctions.

TIME PERIODS

Not all variables are reported for all time periods, but generally the author uses his qualitative observations just as one would use data from a trend or panel study, or an analysis of interaction records over time. His narrative description may be summarized in a set of trend charts, with qualitative signs substituted for figures. Five main time periods seem to be distinguished: (1) the authoritarian equilibrium under the old warden, (2) the period of initiation of reforms when the new warden succeeded him, (3) a period of extension of reforms, (4) a period of sabotage by the guards and rebellion by certain groups of prisoners, and ultimately (5) a new equilibrium rather more liberal than the original one in its emphasis on fair treatment and rehabilitation.

OBSERVATIONS OF CHANGE OVER TIME

McCleery's starting point is in the communications system. The new warden's first act was to open communications channels with the treatment staff; direct communications between administration and the prisoners was expanded gradually; the preferred communications position of the custodial staff declined to a point where this group was virtually isolated, requiring a moderate rise to achieve the new equilibrium (Table 1a).

A crucial attitude area considered was the acceptance by the various groups of the goal of "treatment" or rehabilitation. The authoritarian prison gave very low priority to this goal. New personnel leading the treatment

---

[12] McCleery's monograph is based on his unpublished dissertation, *Power, Communications, and the Social Order* (Chapel Hill: University of North Carolina, 1956). Both of these reports are essentially qualitative.

TABLE 1a. *Amount of Communications between Status Groups*

	Author-itarian Equilib-rium (1)	Initia-tion of Reforms (2)	Exten-sion of Reforms (3)	Sabotage and Rebellion (4)	Liberal Equilib-rium (5)
Administration–Treatment	LOW	HIGH	HIGH	HIGH	HIGH
Administration–Custody	HIGH	MED	LOW	LOW	MED
Administration–Inmates	LOW	MED	HIGH	MED	HIGH
Custody–Treatment	HIGH	HIGH	LOW	LOW	MED
Custody–Inmate elite	HIGH	HIGH	HIGH	HIGH	*
Custody–Inmate mass	LOW	LOW	LOW	LOW	MED
Treatment–Inmates	LOW	MED	HIGH	MED	HIGH
Inmate elite–Mass	HIGH	HIGH	MED	LOW	*

* By the last period the old inmate elite had disappeared as a status group.

staff, and their new access to communications within the prison, permitted the treatment goal to be spread to the top administration, to the treatment staff, then to the mass of the prisoners and to some extent to the custodial staff (Table 1b).

TABLE 1b. *Acceptance of Treatment Goal Among Various Status Groups*

	Time Periods (1)	(2)	(3)	(4)	(5)
Administration	MED	HIGH	HIGH	LOW	HIGH
Custodial staff	LOW	LOW	LOW	LOW	MED
Treatment heads	HIGH	HIGH	HIGH	LOW	HIGH
Treatment staff	MED	HIGH	HIGH	LOW	HIGH
Inmate elite	LOW	LOW	LOW	LOW	*
Inmate mass	LOW	MED	MED	LOW	HIGH

* By the last period the old inmate elite had disappeared as a status group.

Decisive variables in achieving the prison's goals were the types of sanctions and opportunities with which the prisoners were confronted by the various staff groups. The authoritarian prison was characterized by unpredictable, arbitrary allocation of rewards and punishments; a key reform was the replacement of this arbitrariness by "due process" and full explanation. At the same time the amount of educational, recreational, and other positive activities available to the inmates was greatly increased, whereas the use of "rituals of domination" by the custodial staff was reduced. The toleration of inmate-elite privileges and positive support of their power by the custodial staff were gradually reduced to the point that the "inmate elite" in the old sense disappeared as a status group (Table 1b).

TABLE 1c. *Staff Behavior: Sanctions and Opportunities*

	Time Periods				
	(1)	(2)	(3)	(4)	(5)
Administration's arbitrariness in discipline, assignments, etc.	HIGH	MED	LOW	LOW	LOW
Rehabilitative activities offered by treatment staff	LOW	MED	HIGH	HIGH	HIGH
Custodial staff's maintenance of rituals of domination	HIGH	HIGH	MED	MED	LOW
Custodial staff's toleration of inmate-elite privileges, power, rackets, etc.	HIGH	HIGH	MED	MED	LOW

Finally we have the response of the mass of the inmates to the system—the output which the system is intended to influence. On the positive side there is the amount of inmate participation in the treatment program, which is presumably related to ultimate output of long-run change in behavior. On the negative side there is the amount of disorder within the prison—overt violence, riots, escapes, violations of rules—which threatens its custodial purpose. Both of these variables underwent wide fluctuations; the explanation of these sometimes paradoxical shifts and of the values which they achieved in the new equilibrium are the matters with which McCleery is mainly concerned (Table 1d).

TABLE 1d. *Response of Inmate Mass to Staff Behavior*

	Time Periods				
	(1)	(2)	(3)	(4)	(5)
Inmates' participation in treatment program	LOW	MED	HIGH	LOW	HIGH
Inmates' amount of disorderly behavior, violence	LOW	MED+	MED−	HIGH	MED

We will not raise here the important question of the reliability of qualitative observations—whether different observers using the same methods in the same prison would report the same things. It is important to note that all of these variables could in principle be quantitatively measured by such devices as attitude scales, sociometric questions, analysis of formal communications content, self-reports or systematic description of behavior, statistical analysis of official records, ratings by informed participants, etc. How practical such measurements would be in a prison during a crisis period is another question, but they can undoubtedly be applied to more "normal" types of organization.

SYSTEMS OF RELATIONSHIPS

On the basis of these observations of change over time, McCleery suggests a great many causal relationships which form subsystems of links and feedbacks. For example, of the authoritarian system he says,

> Custodial control of communications, and the interactional patterns thus established, imposed custodial attitudes, values and behaviors throughout the industrial program, negating its formal position and purpose (p. 11).
> Supervisors [of the work program] came to think, act and dress like the guards. They justified labor in terms of disciplinary rather than productive or training results, maintained sharp class distinction on the job, and repressed the rare examples of initiative which appeared among their inmate employees (p. 12).
> Accepting that definition of labor . . . inmates opposed the industrial program and gave the minimum tolerable effort to it. Supervisors, in turn, borrowed custodial attitudes which explained failures in production on the basis of the malice and incompetence of the inmates. The institutionally shared belief in the limited possibilities of prison industry further reduced its role (p. 12).

The operation of this set of relationships can be diagramed as in Figure 1.

This set of causal relationships might have been inferred from examining the way the authoritarian system worked; it was strongly supported by McCleery's observation of what happened when the crucial factor of control over communications was changed by the new warden, and the other factors changed thereafter.

From a number of statements in McCleery's report it is possible to reconstruct a rather intricate system of social control which served to maintain a low rate of disorderly behavior within the authoritarian prison:

> The absence of published regulations or official orientation for new men, the secrecy and arbitrariness of disciplinary action, the shocking

unfamiliarity of the prison world to men just arrived, and the demands imposed by regimentation—all these combined to make the new inmate dependent on the experienced prisoner (p. 17).

Over time, a few senior inmates proved their "rightness" to a number of primary groups. . . . Their wider range of contacts made them able to influence transfers, manipulate the system by which goods were stolen, gambled and exchanged, and give warning of official action (p. 18).

Hence the custodial goals of peace, order and adjustment dictated an alliance between senior officers and inmate leaders in the interests of stability and to the end of minimizing the role of the hero [the charismatic rebel against the prison authority]. . . . In order to maintain these contacts with inmates which provided warnings of danger, officials were willing to tolerate a considerable amount of rule evasion, pilfering, and petty exercises of power by the inmate leaders. These privileges stabilized the inmate society (pp. 19–20).

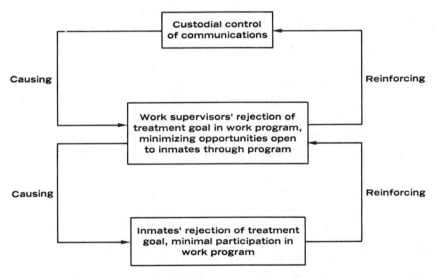

FIGURE 1. *The process of degeneration of the work program under custodial control of communications.*

Here is one of the key mechanisms by which the equilibrium of the authoritarian system was maintained—a set of relationships which permitted the maintenance of order at the expense of rendering impossible the other nominal goal of the prison, rehabilitation. This system too can be presented in the form of a flow diagram (Figure 2).

INPUTS:

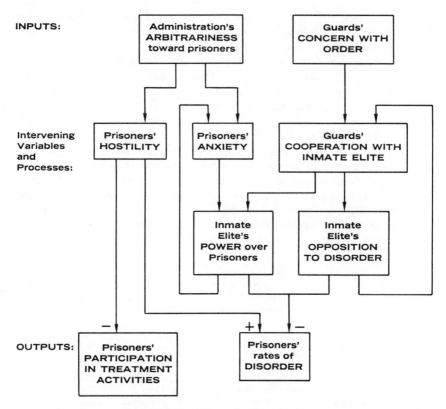

FIGURE 2.   *The system of informal control in the authoritarian state.*

In this system, the maintenance of a power elite among the prisoners is dependent on a steady input of arbitrary administrative behavior producing anxiety. The powers exercised by the inmate elite group give them something to offer the custodial staff in return for privileges, which in turn strengthen the inmate elite. The cooperation of the guards in the maintenance of their privileged position makes the inmate leadership "accommodative" rather than rebellious or reform-minded and willing to use some of their powers to hold down the rate of disorderly behavior among the prisoners. This set of conditions therefore favors a low rate of disorder. At the same time, since the arbitrariness of the administration creates a strong hostility toward the prison among the rank-and-file prisoners, their participation in treatment activities is minimized. Thus one goal of the prison is achieved, but the other is not. As long as external authorities tolerate this partial failure of output, the organization system remains balanced.

A SIMPLIFIED ARITHMETICAL MODEL
OF THE SOCIAL CONTROL SYSTEM

The ways in which the observed events are explained by the qualitative analyst may be clarified by a simplified mathematical model of the social control system of the prison. We will not consider all the many variables and stages found in the original text, and only the simplest arithmetical forms of relationships will be employed.

We will assume that the rate of prisoner Disorder (D) is increased by Hostility (H) toward the prison administration but reduced by the Power (P) exercised over the prisoners by the inmate elite.

$$(1) \qquad D = uH - vP$$

We will also assume that Hostility is created by two factors: the degree of Arbitrariness (A) of the prison authorities in administering the rules, and a constant factor, the general Frustrations (F) which are inherent in any prison, regardless of how well run.

$$(2) \qquad H = wA + F$$

We assume that the degree of Power (P) of the inmate elite to prevent Disorder is dependent on the degree of Arbitrariness (A) of the prison administration (through the mechanisms of creating anxiety and dependence on the experienced and manipulatively skilled prisoners, which will not be explicitly included here).

$$(3) \qquad P = yA$$

Finally, we will assume that the rate of prisoner participation in the rehabilitation program (R) decreases as the prisoners' Hostility (H) increases, subject to some constant factor of the attractiveness of the activities (U):

$$(4) \qquad R = U - zH$$

We have thus pulled out of the more complex model one section which illustrates the point that a given change in input can produce intervening changes which act in opposite directions on the output (Figure 3). The net result of a change in A will depend on the strength of the two opposing relationships through which it affects D.

All of these variables could be measured by various attitude scales, rating devices, behavior records, and similar measures. Let us assume for simplicity that all the relationships are linear and that our scales and measures have been so calibrated that in the equations given above all the coefficients (u, v, w, y, z) are equal to 1. The constant Frustration factor

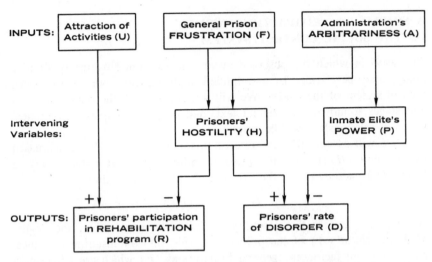

FIGURE 3. *Simplified system of informal control in the authoritarian prison.*

(F) is set equal to 20 in this example, and the constant attractiveness of the rehabilitation activities (U) equals 40. Then if we know the input values of administrative Arbitrariness, we can compute the intervening and the output variables. Table 2 shows several possible situations.

TABLE 2. *A Model of Inputs and Outputs in the Prison System*

	Inputs			Intervening Variables		Outputs	
	Adminis-tration's ARBI-TRARI-NESS (A)	Prison FRUS-TRATION Constant (F)	Activities Attrac-tion Constant (U)	Pris-oners' HOS-TILITY (H)	In-mate Elite's POWER (P)	Pris-oners' Rate of DIS-ORDER (D)	Pris-oners' REHA-BILITA-TION Activity (R)
Situation 1	20	20	40	40	20	20	0
Situation 2	10	20	40	30	10	20	10
Situation 3	0	20	40	20	0	20	20

Assumptions: $H = A + F$ $\quad P = A$ $\quad D = H - P$ $\quad R = U - H$

Given this particular system of relationships, the rate of disorder remains the same, regardless of the degree of arbitrariness of the prison administration. A reduction in arbitrariness reduces hostility and thus might be thought of as an improvement likely to reduce disorder. In fact, it also weakens the informal control mechanism just enough to allow the disorder rate to stay unchanged. If the administrator's only goal is to minimize disorder, he can choose any of the three situations. On the other hand, if he is also concerned with increasing participation in rehabilitative activities, he can do so by reducing arbitrariness without changing the rate of disorder.

As far as this model is concerned, the degree of arbitrary behavior of the administration could be increased indefinitely, thereby raising prisoner hostility higher and higher, without increasing disorder, since the increased control keeps pace. In reality such relations would hold only over a certain range, beyond which the mechanisms would break down. At some level of ruthlessness either the informal controls would fail to keep pace and a rebellion would break out or the prisoners would be so crushed that their hostility would again decline.

Suppose now that we assume a somewhat different system, in which there is a much stronger relationship between administrative arbitrariness and the inmate elite's power to control prison disorders. This can be represented by supposing that the coefficient y in the equation $P = yA$ is not 1 but 2. Then the situation will be quite different. The power of the inmate elite to hold down disorder will be much greater in Situation 1, but decreases more rapidly as administrative Arbitrariness declines (Table 3).

TABLE 3.   *A Model of the System with One Relationship Altered*

	Inputs			*Intervening Variables*		*Outputs*	
	Administration's ARBITRARINESS (A)	Prison FRUSTRATION Constant (F)	Activities Attraction Constant (U)	Prisoners' HOSTILITY (H)	Inmate Elite's POWER (P)	Prisoners' Rate of DISORDER (D)	Prisoners' REHABILITATION Activity (R)
Situation 1	20	20	40	40	40	0	0
Situation 2	10	20	40	30	20	10	10
Situation 3	0	20	40	20	0	20	20

Assumptions: $H = A + F$ $P = 2A$ $D = H - P$ $R = U - H$

Under these circumstances we obtain the apparent paradox that a greater liberalization of prison policy, reducing the prisoners' hostility, results in increased disorder. This comes about because the informal controls on the expression of hostility in the form of disorder are weakened even faster than hostility is reduced. The prison administrator who acted in

ignorance of this relationship would meet with "unanticipated consequences." If disorder is to be minimized in this system, arbitrary policies
must be maintained. On the other hand, he cannot achieve prisoner participation in rehabilitation programs without reducing administrative arbitrariness and incurring the cost of increased disorder. This dilemma will
exist unless by some *change in the structure of the system* he can create
an alternative source of control over disorder, not dependent on the inmate
elite.

THE WELFARE FUNCTION OF THE ADMINISTRATOR

If the administrator is restricted to choosing among these situations, his
choice will depend on his goals, on his weighing of different outputs. If
we assume that his only goal is to minimize disorder, he will prefer Situation 1 above. This corresponds to the actual goal of the authoritarian prison
administration, as reported by McCleery. If his only goal is participation
in rehabilitation programs, he will prefer Situation 3. If he weighs the two
goals equally, he will find all three situations equally satisfactory (or unsatisfactory).

A formal way of describing the various possible administrative preferences would be in the form of a utility function:

(5)

$$\text{Goal-attainment } (G) = pR - qD$$

With various possible functions p and q, the relative preferability of situations would be as shown in Table 4.

TABLE 4. *Alternative Measures of Goal Attainment of the Prison*

	Outputs		Various Goal-Attainment Indices			
			a. For system where P = A			
	D	R	$G_1=R$	$G_2=(-D)$	$G_3=\dfrac{R-D}{2}$	$G_4=\dfrac{R-D^2}{20}$
Situation 1	20	0	0	−20	−10	−20
Situation 2	20	10	10	−20	− 5	−10
Situation 3	20	20	20	−20	0	0
			b. For system where P = 2A			
Situation 1	0	0	0	0	0	0
Situation 2	10	10	10	−10	0	5
Situation 3	20	20	20	−20	0	0

The goal definition G_1 assumes that rehabilitation is the only goal; G_2 assumes that order is the only goal; G_3 weighs the two outputs equally. G_4 departs from the linear form; it assumes that small amounts of disorder are quite tolerable but that the undesirability of increased disorder rises very rapidly relative to the desirability of increased rehabilitation. Thus, for the system in which reduction of prisoner hostility "costs" a good deal in loss of control over prisoner behavior, this goal definition results in the best situation being a compromise.

The model so far has shown the consequences, under specified conditions, of varying administrative policies with respect to arbitrariness. If the output of the system is then related back to its input (the administration's arbitrariness), we have a closed system. By making an assumption about how the administration behaves in response to various patterns of prisoner behavior, we are able to predict which alternative situation the administration will produce. This prediction can be represented formally by saying that the administration will vary its arbitrariness to maximize its goal achievement. We assume here that the other two inputs, the general frustrations of imprisonment and the attractiveness of the rehabilitation activities, are constant; in reality, of course, they might also be variables which the administration could manipulate to achieve its goals (Figure 4).

PARTICIPANTS' PERCEPTIONS OF THE SYSTEM

There is an important assumption underlying the notion that the administrator's behavior responds in determinate ways to the output of the system. This is that he knows what the output is, and how it is related to his own acts. As was suggested above, he might be ignorant of at least some of the relationships in the system. Administrators may therefore have different policies not only because of commitment to different goals but because of different perceptions of the system. One might represent these "perceived systems" by the kind of chart used here. The processes by which perceived systems respond to reality cannot be discussed here.

This simple model has left out the behavior of the custodial staff and of the treatment staff. If such subgroups are to be covered, we should have to consider their *goal commitments,* their *perceptions* of the system, their *power* to influence different variables in the system, and the administrator's power to influence them. The behavior of the administration, the guards, and the treatment staff under the authoritarian regime is accounted for by McCleery partly in terms of their limited perception of what was possible in the prison system. Changes in their behavior were related in part to changes in perceptions and in part to the power of higher authorities.

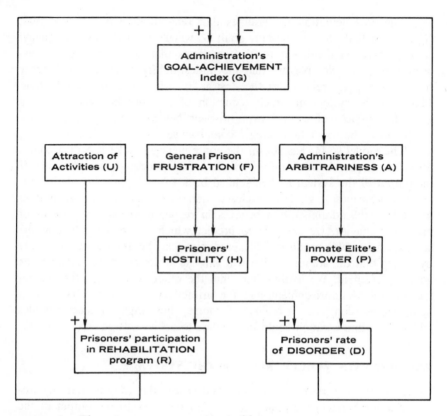

FIGURE 4.   *The prison as a system in equilibrium.*

A Dynamic Model

What actually happened in the prison was not only that a given policy change led to unanticipated results but that it led to one result in the short run and a different one in the long run. The short-run result of the liberal reforms was a great increase in disorder, but after a period of crisis the rates fell again to tolerable levels.

McCleery gives a complex explanation of this period of disorder; basically it arose because certain changes lagged behind others. The old mechanisms of informal control broke down; the new programs did not immediately create new primary group controls favorable to a more liberal prison. The result was a period during which prisoner aggressiveness broke out in a rash of disorders, against which the official controls of discipline and force were not effective. Only gradually did a new informal control through prisoner group consensus arise to hold disorder in check.

To illustrate what is involved in such a situation where lags in some variables cause short-run effects quite different from long-run effects, we will pick out certain variables involved in the process of transition and construct a simple dynamic model, using a form of period analysis. We assume, as in our static model, that disorder is increased by hostility toward the prison administration but reduced by the power exercised by the prisoner elite; that participation in rehabilitation activities is decreased by hostility; and that the degree of control of the inmate elite over disorderly behavior is dependent on the degree of arbitrariness of the prison administration in dealing with the prisoners generally.

Now, to the previous formula for hostility we add a new factor: that it is produced not only by the present state of administrative arbitrariness and the prison-frustration constant, but also by a carry-over of past hostility:

$$H_t = wA_t + F + xH_{t-1}$$

This corresponds to an assumption that it takes time for aggressiveness to be worked off even after the causes of aggressiveness are reduced.

A numerical example can be produced in which a system starts from equilibrium with a certain level of disorder, responds to the reduction of administrative arbitrariness with increased disorder, but eventually returns to the same level of disorder at which it had started—with less hostility and less power in the hands of the inmate elite. We will assume that $u = 1$, $v = 1$, $w = 1$, $z = 1$, $y = 2$, $F = 10$, $u = 40$, $x = \frac{1}{2}$.

In the example (Table 5) t_0 and t_1 are the last two periods of the authoritarian administration. The reform introduced at t_2 produces an immediate increase in the amount of disorder, which gradually falls off again to reach its former level. (We could also produce a brief lag in the increase in disorder, corresponding more closely to the actual observations in the prison, by making the power exercised by the inmate elite depend in part on past power.)

If the coefficient in the power equation were higher—for example, if $P = 3A$—the authoritarian equilibrium would involve even less disorder, reform would generate a sudden rise, and disorder would level off again somewhat higher than the original rate. If the coefficient were less than 2, the initial rate of disorder would be higher, there would be a small increase, and then it would fall to a lower level than before. In all these cases the decline in hostility follows the same curve; the difference is in how sharply the power variable drops.

If the change suggested above were reversed by a more authoritarian administration taking over, there would be a short-run fall in the rate of disorder. This "success" of old-line methods would, however, be followed by a rise to the same rate as before and accompanied by a decline in

TABLE 5.   *Short- and Long-Run Effects of Change in Administrative Arbitrariness*

	Inputs			Intervening Variables		Outputs	
	Administration ARBITRARINESS	Prison FRUSTRATION Constant (F)	Activities Attraction Constant (U)	Prisoners' HOSTILITY (H)	Inmate Elite's POWER (P)	Prisoners' Rate of DISORDER (D)	Prisoners' REHABILITATION Activity (R)
t_0: Authoritarian regime	10	10	40	40	20	20	0
t_1: Authoritarian regime	10	10	40	40	20	20	0
t_2: Reform initiated	0	10	40	30	0	30	10
t_3: Reform continued	0	10	40	25	0	25	15
t_4: Reform continued	0	10	40	22.5	0	22.5	17.5
t_5: Reform continued	0	10	40	21.25	0	21.25	18.75
t_n: New equilibrium	0	10	40	20	0	20	20

Assumptions: $H_t = A_t + F + \tfrac{1}{2}H_{t-1}$ $D_t = H_t - P_t$
$P_t = 2A_t$ $R_t = U - H_t$

participation in rehabilitation activities. If authoritarianism were continually stepped up in an effort to keep disorder below this equilibrium point, the level of hostility might get beyond the bounds within which the control mechanism can suppress its expression, and the system would break down in massive disorders.

CONCLUSION

In this paper we have attempted (a) to formalize a qualitative analysis of organizational processes, and (b) to illustrate what is meant by a *system* of relationships within an organization, in order to suggest ways in which quantitative data on organizational systems might be analyzed.

The cost of quantitatively studying a large number of "cases" is great when each case is an organization composed of many individuals and subgroups. The economy of research suggests that a few key quantitative studies should be guided and supplemented by many less expensive qualitative case analyses similar to the one discussed here. The improvement of qualitative data gathering and analysis is therefore an important methodological problem for social research. A formal analysis of what skilled practitioners actually do is one of the means by which this improvement will come about.[13] By making qualitative researchers more conscious of their operations, and more aware of the common logic which underlies both kinds of analysis, qualitative research may become more systematic and more relevant to ongoing quantitative studies. The formal devices illustrated here include the "anatomizing" of the system into subgroups characterized by a set of variables; the use of systematic tables for recording variables qualitatively observed over several time periods; the formulation of "system schemes" to portray relationships among sets of variables which are suggested by the observed changes; and the use of simple arithmetical models to explore possible consequences of change in given variables for the system.

Quantitative data on organizational systems can come from several types of studies. By *comparative studies* or *surveys of large numbers of organizational units,* in which data are gathered on all relevant status groups within the units studied rather than on just a single stratum, it should be possible to examine organizational systems in various states of equilibrium or change. By *panel or trend studies* within single organizations which obtain data from the several interacting status groups over time, the sequences of change in the system can be brought to light. Panel or trend studies conducted during periods of organizational change are especially useful for this purpose, because they permit us to observe "natural experiments." It is possible in some cases to conduct *controlled experiments* on simulated or actual organizations, which greatly facilitate the making of causal inferences.[14]

Social researchers have not generally faced the problem of analyzing quantitative data on complex systems over time. It is clear that simple methods of two-variable and three-variable analysis are not sufficient, and that some form of "models" must be used. It is not easy to say how closely such empirical data could be related to the construction of precise mathematical models.[15] The kinds of measurement used in quantitative so-

[13] Allen H. Barton and Paul F. Lazarsfeld, "Some Functions of Qualitative Analysis in Social Research," *Sociologica,* Vol. 1 of "Frankfurter Beiträge zur Soziologie" (Frankfurt: Europaeische Verlagsanstalt, 1955), 321–361. Also Howard S. Becker, "Problems of Inference and Proof in Participant Observation," *American Sociological Review,* 23 (December 1958), 652–660.

[14] Nancy Morse and E. Reimer, "The Experimental Change of a Major Organizational Variable," *Journal of Abnormal and Social Psychology,* 52 (1955), 120–129.

[15] Herbert A. Simon, *Models of Man* (New York: Wiley, 1957), Chaps. 6 and 10.

cial research are still very crude; ranking people or organizations, or locating them in a few ranked classes, is more characteristic than applying scales with equal intervals and a meaningful zero point.[16] The question of what kind of mathematics might be relevant for models of social systems and at the same time appropriate to the nature of social science measurements is a large one. The use of "simulation models" in which computers reproduce complex social processes is one promising line of development.[17]

FIELD METHODS IN THE STUDY OF ORGANIZATIONS

W. Richard Scott

Roles Permitting Sustained Participation

Although the relationship between the researcher and his subjects is a matter for concern in any situation in which social data are gathered, nowhere are the problems so acute as in the case where the two parties engage in sustained interaction over a period of time. The problem is two-sided: the presence of the observer may alter the behavior of those he studies and so bias his findings; and the observer's relationships with subjects may influence what it is he observes or the report of his observations. The particular form which the problem assumes as well as methods for dealing with it vary according to whether the researcher acknowledges his identity or conceals it from his subjects. These alternative strategies will be discussed and their strengths and weaknesses examined.

Reprinted from *Handbook of Organizations*, James G. March (ed.), Chicago, Ill.: Rand McNally & Company, pp. 272–282, with omissions.

[16] S. S. Stevens, "Mathematics Measurement, and Psychophysics," in S. S. Stevens (ed.), Handbook of Experimental Psychology (New York: Wiley, 1951). See also Bert F. Green, "Attitude Measurement," in Gardner Lindzey (ed.), *Handbook of Social Psychology* (Cambridge, Mass.: Addison-Wesley, 1954), Chap. 9.
[17] William N. McPhee, "The Uses of a Computer Model of Voting," *Public Opinion Quarterly*, 23 (Fall 1959), 440–441.

THE DISGUISED RESEARCHER. Since one-way screens cannot ordinarily be introduced into field situations, the researcher may attempt to disguise himself as a member of the subject group in order to observe their activities without raising suspicion. This approach is typically used only when the data sought are of the type which the subject group wishes to keep secret—perhaps because of their deviant nature—or when the researcher believes that his presence as a recognized observer would drastically alter the group's behavior. The study by Dalton in which he served as a staff employee in two firms in order to examine covert conflicts and coalitions among line and staff officials, exemplifies research in an organizational setting of the first type by a concealed observer.[1] And an instance of the second type is furnished by the study of interaction among patients in the ward of a mental institution in which Caudill assumed the role of a patient.[2]

An important limitation to the use of the concealed-observer role is immediately apparent: the role can only be assumed when the researcher possesses or can acquire the attributes of a subject group member. Few researchers, for example, would be qualified to assume the role of a physician in order to study instances of malpractice; likewise, it would be difficult for a white investigator to pass himself off as a Negro in order to examine minority-group reactions to discriminatory practices in industry. The lengths to which researchers will go to fit themselves for a subject role should, however, not be underestimated. An extreme instance is furnished by an investigation of the motivations and attitudes of air force personnel in a basic training program.[3] In order to prepare a twenty-six-year-old observer to play the role of recruit, the military research team felt it necessary to coach him for nine months in the ways of adolescent subculture, provide him with a fictitious biography, and even change his appearance by having him lose 35 pounds and undergo minor surgery. (The necessity for such elaborate preparations was questioned by Roth,[4] who states his belief that "the observer airman could readily have stepped into his role despite some deviations from the 'average' without any noticeable effect on his observations.")

Once the disguised researcher has gained admission to the subject group, his problems have just begun. He must not only convince his

[1] M. Dalton, *Men Who Manage* (New York: Wiley, 1959).

[2] W. Caudill, F. C. Redlich, H. R. Gilmore, and E. B Brody, "Social Structure and Interaction Processes on a Psychiatric Ward," *American Journal of Orthopsychiatry,* **22** (1952), 314–334.

[3] M. A. Sullivan, Jr., S. A. Queen, and R. C. Patrick, Jr., "Participant Observation as Employed in the Study of a Military Training Program," *American Sociological Review,* **23** (1958), 660–667.

[4] J. A. Roth, "Dangerous and Difficult Enterprise?", *American Sociological Review,* **24** (1959), 398.

subjects that he is a bona fide member of the group but must also be prepared to deal with the consequences of being accepted at face value. For obligations go with membership, and sentiments are generated in interaction. The new member is expected to carry his weight—perhaps more than his weight if there is a period of initiation and testing—and the researcher may become so self-conscious and anxious that he is unable to perform his role adequately.[5] Perhaps a more prevalent problem, however, is posed by the need for the researcher to participate without unduly influencing the activities of other participants. That this can be a difficult assignment is indicated by the experience of observers who became members of a religious sect in order to study the effect on the group of a failure to predict correctly the end of the world.[6] As the presumed day of doom approached, all members were expected to quit their jobs and participate fully in preparations. If the researchers resigned from their jobs, their action would strengthen the movement and lend confidence to other members; if they refused, their action would promote dissension and shake the conviction of the others. "In short, as members, the observers could not be neutral—any action had consequences."[7] The researchers' situation was particularly delicate here because the group was small and intense commitment was required of members, but the problem of observer influence is endemic to this method.

The observer, then, is likely to influence considerably the behavior of his subjects; but he is also likely to be influenced in turn by them. As he interacts frequently with his new associates, they will come to accept him as friend and confidant. He will find himself bound by diffuse obligations and loyalties which encroach on his original research purposes, his objectivity will be threatened, and his perceptual acuteness will be blunted as the situation becomes more familiar and as he assimilates more and more of the group's premises and values. One technique which has been recommended to deal with these difficulties is for the researcher to withdraw from the group for temporary periods so as to review his objectives—preferably with others associated in the research enterprise—and sharpen his senses. Such cooling-off periods were reported to be of great value to the observer acting as a trainee in the military camp.[8]

Other limitations of the disguised-researcher method stem from the restrictions which group membership places on the researcher's behavior. The number and kind of questions which the observer can ask of his as-

[5] R. L. Gold, "Roles in Sociological Field Observations," *Social Forces*, **36** (1958), 217–223.
[6] L. Festinger, H. W. Riecken, and S. Schachter, *When Prophecy Fails* (Minneapolis: University of Minnesota Press, 1956).
[7] *Ibid.*, p. 244.
[8] Sullivan, Queen, and Patrick, *op. cit.*

sociates without raising their suspicions as to his true identity and purposes will be limited.[9] Then, too, there are certain kinds of "naive" questions that only an outsider can ask with impunity. In addition, the researcher will probably have little opportunity to observe behavior outside the membership group or relations between this group and the larger social system.[10] Caudill, for example, reports that by assuming the role of patient he obtained a "one-sided" view of the mental hospital.[11] Finally, the researcher can expect to have great difficulty in finding opportunities to record his observations. Taking time from sleep,[12] relying on one's memory until out of the research situation,[13] and making frequent trips to the rest room for hurried note-taking,[14] are among the data-recording tactics which disguised investigators have been forced to employ.

The peculiar advantages of the disguised-researcher method are obvious and so may be discussed briefly. If the investigator is able to juggle successfully the many facets of his demanding role, he will find himself in the midst of a social group whose members are going about their business as usual, thus allowing him to observe natural situations at close range. Because he is a participant as well as an observer, and to the extent that he comes to share the perspectives of the subject group, the researcher will be able to use his own feelings and attitudes as clues in interpreting the behavior of his associates. For example, Roy,[15] who acted as a machine operator, reports that his own subjective reactions to work quotas led him to formulate the hypothesis that workers approached quotas in the spirit of a game—an exciting challenge when the odds were even, but no contest when the odds were one-sided in either direction. It would appear that the approach is particularly useful when the investigator is interested in the sentiments of his subjects, in particular, the meanings which they assign to various activities.

Apart from any discussion of the advantages or the limitations of the disguised-researcher method, some persons believe that this approach raises serious ethical problems. It is clear that the researcher is in the

[9] W. F. Whyte, "Observational Field-work Methods," in Marie Jahoda, M. Deutsch, and S. W. Cook (eds.), *Research Methods in Social Relations*, vol. II (New York: Dryden, 1951), pp. 493–513.

[10] B. H. Junker, *Field Work: An Introduction to the Social Sciences* (Chicago: University of Chicago Press, 1960).

[11] W. Caudill, *The Psychiatric Hospital as a Small Society* (Cambridge: Harvard University Press, 1958).

[12] Sullivan, Queen, and Patrick, *op. cit.*

[13] D. F. Roy, "Quota Restriction and Goldbricking in a Machine Shop," *American Journal of Sociology*, **62** (1952), 427–442.

[14] Festinger, Riecken, and Schachter, *op. cit.*

[15] D. F. Roy, "Work Satisfaction and Social Reward in Quota Achievement," *American Sociological Review*, **18** (1953), 507–514.

situation under false pretenses: he is not what he claims to be, and the reasons he gives for being there are not his real reasons. Most groups take a dim view of people who tell lies to insiders and reveal secrets to outsiders. Defenders of the method claim that although they may adopt the tactics of the spy, they do so in order to serve the objectives of science; further, identities of groups and individuals are not revealed, so that subject group members are not harmed.[16] The more serious ethical problems appear to be raised (either by the researcher himself or by others) in those cases where research in some organizational unit is undertaken either at the behest or with the knowledge of officials superior to that unit.[17] In such cases there is a greater danger that damaging information concerning subjects could fall into the hands of persons in a position to harm their interests.

THE OPEN RESEARCHER. Most field research involving sustained participation is conducted by investigators who acknowledge their identity and explain something of their purposes to the subject group. While this open approach side-steps some of the difficulties associated with maintaining a disguise, the researcher will still need "to prepare a face to meet the faces" that he meets and will, in addition, be confronted by a host of new problems.

Unlike his colleagues in disguise, who enter the research situation through the normal channels used by regular members, the open researcher must usually obtain permission from the authorities to conduct his study.[18] In the case of informal groups, the researcher will need the sponsorship of informal leaders,[19] and in the case of formal organizations, the researcher will require the approval of organizational officials. Indeed, some researchers believe that a study should not be undertaken unless key officers of the host organization are willing not simply to approve but to support enthusiastically and to participate actively in the program.[20] Even following the simple dictum that approval from organizational superiors should be obtained may raise problems for the researcher. When a complex organization, such as the military, is involved, it is often difficult to tell exactly whose permission is required, and the selection is made more difficult with

[16] Dalton, op. cit.; Sullivan, Queen, and Patrick, op. cit.

[17] Caudill, op. cit.; L. A. Coser, "A Question of Professional Ethics," American Sociological Review, 24 (1959), 397–398.

[18] B. B. Gardner and W. F. Whyte, "Methods for the Study of Human Relations in Industry," American Sociological Review, 11 (1946), 506–512.

[19] W. F. Whyte, Street Corner Society, rev. ed. (Chicago: University of Chicago Press, 1955), p. 290.

[20] F. C. Mann, "Human Relations Skills in Social Research," Human Relations, 4 (1951), 341–354; Whyte, Street Corner Society, op. cit.

the knowledge that the various "higher echelon gateways are perceived quite differently by lower echelon personnel" and hence will affect the latter's willingness to cooperate with the researcher.[21] In a loosely knit organization, such as an association where there may be conflict between national and local leaders, it may be a handicap to have the backing of top-level officers when approaching a local chapter, as Gusfield discovered in his study of the WCTU.[22] Where more than one center of authority exists, the researcher should obtain permission from each of them. Before beginning research in a housing project, for example, investigators independently obtained approval for the study from both the managers of the project and officers of the residents' association.[23]

Although gaining approval of research from top officials is usually mandatory, it creates problems for the researcher, who may become identified with management in the eyes of subordinate groups. Subordinates are also likely to feel, with some justification, that "cooperation" with the researcher is being forced upon them by higher officials, thus causing them to feel resentment and seek covert ways of scuttling the research program. One strategy, known as "contingent acceptance," has been employed by the Survey Research Center of the University of Michigan in their organizational studies to counter such identification and to facilitate acceptance by subordinates of the research.[24] The strategy calls for the investigator to solicit acceptance of the research program from the top officer and obtain his permission to approach his immediate subordinates so that their approval may be independently requested. This procedure is repeated at each level of the organization until all relevant groups have been contacted and the approval of each obtained. It is questionable, however, whether the hierarchy is so easily circumvented: only the rare subordinate will reject a research program approved by his immediate superior. Note, too, that the weight of approval accumulates as the "request" moves down the hierarchy, making it more difficult to reject at the lower than at the higher levels.

When the subject group is not merely wary of but actually hostile toward the officials of the organization—as is the case with prisoners, for example—the researcher must take great pains to disassociate himself from the hierarchy. In a study of incorrigible units in two prisons, McCleery disclaimed any official power, influence, connection, or sympathy with

[21] N. J. Demerath, "Initiating and Maintaining Research Relations in a Military Organization," *Journal of Social Issues*, **8**, No. 3 (1952), 11–23.

[22] J. R. Gusfield, "Field Work Reciprocities in Studying a Social Movement," *Human Organization*, **14**, No. 3 (1955), 29–33.

[23] R. K. Merton, "Selected Problems of Field Work in the Planned Community," *American Sociological Review*, **12** (1947), 304–312.

[24] R. L. Kahn and F. Mann, "Developing Research Relations," *Journal of Social Issues*, **8**, No. 3 (1952), 4–10.

officials and illustrated the relationship of the study to the University in every possible way. This was not a position to be asserted at the start of the sessions and ignored after that time; there was a continuing process of reinforcement throughout the study. The investigator deferred to the guard's requirements with apparent ill-will, in order to demonstrate that his power was less than that of the guard in the situation. However, he halted discussions whenever the guard came within hearing range and made obvious use of every possible technique to protect the confidence of the prisoners.[25]

Why do organizations agree to participate in research programs in which they themselves are to be the guinea pig? The reasons, of course, vary widely, from altruism and a concern with helping to advance scientific knowledge to self-interest and the hope that the investigation will uncover problems which may then be corrected. Certain specific attributes of an organization will influence the desire of its officers to cooperate in a research program. What has been called the "research maturity" of an organization— whether its members take a long-range view or are concerned largely with day-to-day problem-solving—is one such attribute; and the extent to which there are problems within the organization (if there are too few, research may seem unnecessary; if there are too many, research may appear as a luxury to be foregone) is another.[26] Organizational officials sometimes are induced to participate in the research by their belief that the researcher can perform important services for them. The services may be specific and explicitly agreed upon, such as those contributed by Mayo and Lombard[27] in examining factors affecting labor turnover in aircraft industries; or they may be diffuse and implicit. An example of the latter is furnished by Fox,[28] who ascertained that one reason for the staff's acceptance of her study of a hospital ward on which patients were being experimentally treated was that physicians perceived her research as providing "a way in which they could show—and still be thoroughly 'scientific'—how much they really cared about their patients."

In general, the researcher should realize that most organizational officials will have at best a vague notion of what social researchers do or how they do it, and many officials will be inclined to overestimate the

[25] R. H. McCleery, "Authoritarianism and the Belief System of the Incorrigible," in D. R. Cressey (ed.), *The Prison* (New York: Holt, Rinehart, and Winston, Inc., 1961), pp. 260–308, quoted from p. 273.

[26] E. Jacobson, R. Kahn, F. C. Mann, and Nancy Moore, "Research in Functioning Organization," *Journal of Social Issues*, 7, No. 3 (1951), 64–71.

[27] E. Mayo and G. F. F. Lombard, *Teamwork and Labor Turnover in the Aircraft Industry of Southern California* (Boston: Graduate School of Business Administration, Harvard University, 1944).

[28] Renee C. Fox, *Experiment Perilous* (New York: Free Press, 1959), p. 228.

practical value of the research results. Researchers must attempt to set realistic limits on these expectations. And, of course, the researcher must not make any promises on which he cannot follow through, nor should he assume specific obligations toward some members of the organizations which, if carried out, would cause him to violate his obligations to others.

One final point should be made about the types of obligations assumed by the researcher toward the host organization. Research involving sustained, open participation on the part of the investigator is more likely to be "action" research—that is, research directed in part toward solving the problems of the subject group—than is research conducted under other approaches. This association works in both directions. The sustained investigator is more likely to develop obligations to members of the subject group which he can partially repay by making available to them some of his findings. Also, his relatively closer relations with organization members will frequently result in his taking over some of their interests and concerns, so that his study becomes increasingly guided by their problems.[29] Conversely, the researcher who begins with the objective of helping the organization solve its problems will find it necessary to participate in the organization for a sustained period both in order to collect the necessary materials and to develop the kind of relationship with officials which will permit the successful communication and application of research findings.[30]

The role assumed by the sustained, open researcher is an emergent one based on his actions as well as on the actions and reactions of the subject group. Most groups will have a repertory of ready-made—and often crippling[31]—roles waiting for the stranger. In organizational settings the roles include those of management consultant (or spy), inspector, clinical psychologist, efficiency engineer, visiting expert, and student-amateur,[32] the particular assignment being a function of the researcher's actions and attributes, the research situation, and past experiences of the subject group. Unlike the disguised observer, who often must demonstrate his competence in and knowledge of the subject group's tasks in order to be accepted, the open researcher can sometimes authenticate his role by revealing ignorance

[29] J. Gullahorn and G. Strauss, "The Field Worker in Union Research," *Human Organization*, **13**, No. 3 (1954), 28–33.

[30] J. R. Gibb and R. Lippett (eds.), "Consulting with Groups and Organizations," *Journal of Social Issues*, **15**, No. 2 (1959), entire issue; Jacobson *et al.*, *op. cit.*; E. Jaques, *The Changing Culture of a Factory* (New York: Dryden, 1952); R. Lippett, Jeanne Watson, and B. Westley, *The Dynamics of Planned Change* (New York: Harcourt, 1958).

[31] Rosalie H. Wax, "Twelve Years Later: An Analysis of Field Experience," *American Journal of Sociology*, **63** (1957), 133–142.

[32] R. K. Bain, "The Researcher's Role: A Case Study," *Human Organization*, **9**, No. 1 (1950), 23–28; Demerath, *op. cit.*; W. R. Scott, "Field Work in a Formal Organization," *Human Organization*, **22**, No. 3 (1963), 162–168.

of these matters together with some knowledge of academic or scientific concerns.[33] Richardson identifies two components of role definition for the researcher: he should provide a picture of himself, of his background and interests to the subject group; and he should be able to explain his specific research purpose to them.[34] Whyte, however, reports that in his research on the informal organization of an Italian neighborhood, explanations of purpose were of little interest to his subjects (with the apparent exception of the informal leader); what mattered was their opinion of him personally.[35] J. P. Dean develops this notion into a principle: "A person becomes accepted as a participant observer more because of the kind of person he turns out to be in the eyes of the field contacts than because of what the research represents to them."[36] Whether this generalization holds in the more task-oriented formal organization is a moot question. Argyris,[37] for example, argues on the basis of his experience in studying organizations that the subjects' perception of the research itself as fulfilling some of their needs is the primary motivating factor in inducing them to participate in a study.

The researcher must seize every occasion to define and clarify his role and purposes for the subject group.[38] The officials of the host organization should not be depended on to interpret the researcher's role or purposes to subordinate members.[39] The researcher should do this himself, perhaps by describing his research interests in general meetings of all staff members affected, and by maintaining frequent informal contacts with individual staff members at all levels.[40] In a very real sense, as Wax has emphasized,[41] every researcher is a teacher, demonstrating how an investigator behaves and training members of the subject group to play the roles of respondent and informant.

Researchers may attempt to become active participants in the group

[33] P. M. Blau, *The Dynamics of Bureaucracy* (Chicago: University of Chicago Press, 1955).

[34] S. A. Richardson, "A Framework for Reporting Field Relations Experiences," *Human Organization*, 12, No. 3 (1953), 31–37.

[35] Whyte, *Street Corner Society, op. cit.*, p. 300.

[36] J. P. Dean, "Participant Observation and Interviewing," in J. T. Doby (ed.), *An Introduction to Social Research* (Harrisburg, Pa.: Stackpole, 1954), pp. 225–252, quoted from p. 233.

[37] C. Argyris, "Creating Effective Relationships in Organizations," *Human Organization*, 17, No. 1 (1958), 34–40.

[38] The general problems associated with building a consistent role and giving a convincing performance are insightfully described by Goffman (1959) and can be studied with profit by the field researcher.

[39] Bain, *op. cit.*

[40] Gardner and Whyte, *op. cit.*

[41] Wax, *op. cit.*

observed, or they may remain relatively passive.[42] The active investigator sacrifices detachment for the sake of greater control over the situation observed and greater intuitive understanding of the meaning of events to the participants; the passive researcher is better able to remain objective but as an outsider may be unaware of important events and may incur the suspicion and hostility of the subject group.

Many writers emphasize that the researcher should direct his initial energies to building relationships with subjects rather than to gathering data.[43] Often the researcher can gain acceptance more easily if he can point to some characteristic held in common with those whom he is studying. Fox, for example, reports that in her hospital study patients accepted her more readily because she had been visibly crippled by polio.[44] The characteristics involved, however, need not be so specific. Thus, having a research team composed of veterans has proved of use in gaining acceptance to both military[45] and civilian[46] organizations. Even "negative" characteristics can sometimes be turned to advantage, as when Whyte, who was known to be a college graduate, demonstrated that he did not consider this sufficient basis for looking down upon the noncollege men in the Italian slum, and so won their friendship.[47] A gambit frequently employed by the researcher to strengthen relations with subjects is to assume temporarily the humble status of student. Whether it is learning to do the work done by the respondents,[48] acquiring the language of the subject group,[49] or simply trying to discover what various persons in the group do and how they do it, this approach allows the researcher to get on more intimate terms with respondents and at the same time provides them with the ego-enhancing experience of serving as expert-teacher.

Developing working relations with subjects is beset by a basic problem: the researcher will not have equally good relations with all of his respondents. Subjects will respond to the investigator with varying degrees of interest and warmth, and the researcher, in spite of his attempts to remain impartial, will gravitate toward those individuals who make him

---

[42] M. S. Schwartz and Charlotte G. Schwartz, "Problems in Participant Observation," *American Journal of Sociology*, **60** (1955), 343–353.

[43] Dean, *op. cit.*; Gardner and Whyte, *op. cit.*; Richardson, *op. cit.*

[44] Fox, *op. cit.*, p. 214.

[45] Demerath, *op. cit.*

[46] A. W. Gouldner, *Patterns of Industrial Bureaucracy* (New York: Free Press, 1954).

[47] Whyte, "Observational Field-work. . . ," *op. cit.*

[48] Bain, *op. cit.*; F. H. Blum, "Getting Individuals to Give Information to the Outsider," *Journal of Social Issues*, **8**, No. 3 (1952), 35–42; A. B. Horsfall and C. M. Arensberg, "Teamwork and Productivity in a Shoe Factory," *Human Organization*, **8**, No. 4 (1949), 13–25.

[49] Wax, *op. cit.*; Whyte, *Street Corner Society, op. cit.*

feel welcome.[50] These processes introduce an undetermined amount of bias into the materials gathered, since the self-selected subjects may be a small or unrepresentative sample of the subject group under study. A second problem is that of overrapport between investigator and subjects. The researcher may find that his concern with protecting and developing his good relations with subjects may interfere in important ways with his collection of data. For example, a researcher who developed close ties with union leaders reported that he found himself unable to question them about their basic attitudes because, in his words, "friendship connotes an all-accepting attitude; to probe beneath the surface of long-believed values would break the friend-to-friend relationship."[51] Subject behavior may also be affected. Some respondents will distort their attitudes and actions—for example, by telling the researcher what they think he wants to hear—so as to protect or extend their relation with the researcher. A report of such distortion occurring in a community study is provided by Vidich and Bensman:

> When the Springdale community became aware that the research project was interested in "constructive" social behavior, in constructive solutions to community problems, and in organizations and organizational participation, many community members not only saw a causal relation between organizations and constructive behavior but they began to provide information on the assumption of that supposed causality.[52]

Overrapport between researcher and subjects and overinvolvement of the researcher in the situation being examined are related problems of some importance, and their nature should perhaps be somewhat amplified. The researcher enters the field situation with certain interests—he wants the answers to a set of questions that are more or less precisely formulated. To the extent that he becomes involved in or committed to the subject group or some subset of it, he assumes new interests. More generally, "the committed person has acted in such a way as to involve other interests of his, originally extraneous to the action he is engaged in, directly in that action."[53] Thus, in the example cited above, Miller discovered that his original interests in getting certain information from union leaders came into conflict with his new interest in retaining their friendship, since he did not wish to jeopardize his relation with them by asking questions which they

[50] Bain, *op. cit.*; Scott, *op. cit.*
[51] S. M. Miller, "The Participant Observer and 'Over Rapport,'" *American Sociological Review*, **17** (1952), 97–99.
[52] A. Vidich and J. Bensman, "The Validity of Field Data," *Human Organization*, **13**, No. 1 (1954), 20–27, quoted from p. 22.
[53] H. S. Becker, "Notes on the Concept of Commitment," *American Journal of Sociology*, **66** (1960), pp. 32–40, quoted from p. 35.

might find embarrassing or difficult to answer. Researchers may become committed to maintaining their relations with subjects or to the values espoused by subject group members. Gullahorn and Strauss, for example, report that during the course of their research on a union local they became active supporters of its cause.[54] Whether these new interests are ideological or interpersonal, the researcher will find them to be a handicap to his investigation to the extent that they conflict with his original objectives.

The open researcher, like his disguised colleague, is susceptible to the danger of becoming oversocialized with respect to the subject group so that he begins to see the world as his fellow participants see it.[55] That is, he finds less and less that requires explanation as he comes to share the premises and values of the group in which he is immersed. Antidotes suggested for such acculturation include reviewing early field notes, taken in a period when some of the group's ways seemed strange and inexplicable, and discussions of the research with outsiders who may be able to sensitize the researcher to blind spots in his analysis.

A particularly important problem facing the researcher engaged in sustained participation is that of maintaining a favorable balance of obligations between himself and his respondents.[56] That the researcher can offer certain incentives to the organization as a whole has already been discussed in connection with gaining access to the organization. But a distinction must be made between the rewards offered the organization or its representatives and those offered to individual respondents. The researcher asks for many things from his subjects—time, information, materials—and he must find ways of compensating them for their efforts if they are to continue to cooperate and if he is not to be burdened by unpaid social obligations. Reciprocity is called for, but with what shall the researcher reciprocate?

Only rarely does the researcher pay his subjects for their services. While field workers in underdeveloped areas sometimes rely on monetary compensation of subjects, no case was discovered of a study conducted in a modern organization in which members were paid for their participation.[57] The typical researcher, however, does have something to offer his respondents. In his scientific role, the researcher can offer them the opportunity to contribute to a scientific study, and he may hold out to them the promise that their situation will be somehow improved as a result of

[54] Gullahorn and Strauss, op. cit.

[55] Vidich and Bensman, op. cit.; Whyte, Street Corner Society, op. cit.

[56] P. M. Blau and W. R. Scott, Formal Organizations: A Comparative Approach (San Francisco: Chandler, 1962).

[57] Wax, in her studies in Japanese relocation camps, attempted to pay her respondents, but they refused her offer. Their reluctance to accept money for their participation is understandable, since in such settings, from the standpoint of subject group members, the line between "informant" and "informer" is razor thin.

his research, if this is in fact the case.[58,59] The researcher, however, seldom has the power to back up the latter offer. The major incentives stem from the researcher's nonscientific role attributes and, specifically, from his role as participant. For example, he may offer himself as an interested outsider who will listen to grievances and complaints[60] and as a person against whom aggression may be expressed without fear of reprisal.[61] And he provides an opportunity for subjects to interact with a person of considerable education and status, an experience many find gratifying.[62] As a participant, the researcher can, most simply, return the friendliness offered him. More specifically, the researcher can furnish information about himself and his background when questioned, and he can provide various kinds of favors and services to respondents. Gullahorn and Strauss, for example, performed minor clerical functions and provided transportation for union members;[63] Fox[64] and Caudill[65] helped around the hospital ward and visited with patients. The investigator can also offer his respondents a ready ear and an open mind. Wax believes that the researcher must hold out to his respondents the possibility that he will be won over by their arguments. She supports her position by analogy: "A coquette is in a much better situation to learn about men than a nun."[66] However, it would seem that the specific tactics should be determined by the over-all strategy of the study since, returning to the analogy, it could be argued that both coquettes and nuns are in a position to learn about men—although they assuredly learn very different things.

It would appear, then, that the sustained researcher has at his disposal a variety of techniques which allow him to repay his social debts and build up generalized obligations which can in turn be drawn upon as favors are asked of respondents. The researcher should understand the reasons why his subjects cooperate—as well as the reasons why they fail to do so—since these motives will influence their behavior and should be taken into account in any interpretation of it.

Finally, it must be noted that the open researcher has his share of

[58] Argyris, *op. cit.*; R. L. Kahn and C. F. Cannell, *The Dynamics of Interviewing* (New York: Wiley, 1957), pp. 45–46.

[59] Moreno, the originator of sociometric techniques, argues that his method of asking persons to name others with whom they would like to associate for specific purposes only produces valid results if the participants believe that their situation will be restructured by the investigator in the light of their choices.

[60] Rosalie H. Wax, "Reciprocity in Field Work," *Human Organization*, 11, No. 3 (1952), 34–41.

[61] Merton, *op. cit.*

[62] *Ibid.*; Scott, *op. cit.*

[63] Gullahorn and Strauss, *op. cit.*

[64] Fox, *op. cit.*

[65] Caudill, *op. cit.*

[66] Wax, "Reciprocity in Field Work," *op. cit.*, p. 37.

ethical problems. Roth correctly points out that "all research is secret in some ways and to some degree—we never tell the subjects 'everything.' "[67] Dissimulation may occur because the researcher does not wish subjects to know his true research interests for fear that this will cause them to change their behavior in the relevant areas; or because the researcher himself does not know in advance in what direction his findings will lead him; or because the subjects do not have the necessary background and knowledge to understand the full import and implications of the researcher's explanations.

Misunderstandings between the researcher and his subjects often come to the surface on the occasion when the research findings are published.[68] A widely discussed example is provided by the "Springdale Case," a community study whose publication provoked considerable hostility among the residents.[69] Members of the community studied felt that individual identities had not been properly protected and objected to the "tone" of the research report. Becker, taking a broad view of these and similar problems, has attempted to locate the primary source of trouble between field researchers and their subjects:

> Typically, the social scientist offends those he studies by describing deviations, either from some formal or informal rule, or from a strongly held ideal. The deviations reported are things which, according to the ideals of the people under study, should be punished and corrected, but about which, for various reasons that seem compelling to them, nothing can be done. In other words, the research report reveals that things are not as they ought to be and that nothing is being done about it.[70]

Much organizational research focuses on just such deviations as when, for example, the investigator concentrates attention on the operation of informal processes and structures to the neglect of the more formal and explicit ones,[71] or shows that the goals of the organization are not being realized,[72] or demonstrates that those goals strived for differ from those professed.[73] But even the researcher who does not center his analysis on deviations of

[67] J. A. Roth, "Comments on 'Secret Observation,' " *Social Problems*, **9** (1962), pp. 283–284, quoted from p. 283.

[68] W. F. Whyte, *Man and Organization* (Homewood, Ill.: Irwin, 1959), pp. 87–96.

[69] The research was reported by Vidich and Bensman (1958).

[70] H. S. Becker, "Ethical Problems in the Publication of Field Studies," in A. Vidich, J. Bensman, and M. Stein (eds.), *Reflections on Community Studies* (New York: Wiley, 1964).

[71] C. H. Page, "Bureaucracy's Other Face," *Social Forces*, **25** (1946), 88–94.

[72] P. Selznick, *TVA and the Grass Roots* (Berkeley: University of California Press, 1949).

[73] A. Etzioni, "Two Approaches to Organizational Analysis: A Critique and a Suggestion," *Administrative Science Quarterly*, **5** (1960), 257–278.

one sort or another may still offend his subjects simply by applying his particular perspective, for he attempts to take an objective and relative view of matters which from the standpoint of his subjects are value-laden and unique.[74] How much and what sorts of things to tell subjects about the research in progress and how much and what sorts of things to put into the published report—these are the kinds of ethical questions to which the open field researcher will find no easy solutions.

Some of the difficulties facing the open researcher have been described. One of the chief advantages of this approach is that it, like the role of disguised observer, permits the researcher to get a close-range view of a natural situation, although the behavior of the subject group will necessarily be somewhat affected by the presence of a recognized outsider. (The extent and nature of this influence will, of course, depend on the combined effects of factors such as those discussed above.) But the open researcher enjoys a decided advantage over his disguised counterpart in being able to collect data actively from and about the subject group. That is, his role allows him to spend relatively more time acting like a scientist and less time acting like a participant.

Roles Permitting Transitory Participation

All field study designs do not require that the researcher engage in sustained interaction with members of the subject group; many allow transitory participation on the part of the researcher. In general, these are studies in which the investigator collects data from several different organizations or from many different respondents, so that he spends relatively little time with any particular group or group member. Also, virtually all of these investigations have been conducted by open rather than disguised researchers.

One exception to the latter generalization, however, is a study on the effects of disparities in social class on the acceptance of newcomers into Alcoholics Anonymous conducted by Lofland and Lejeune.[75] In this field experiment, six graduate students each attended four open meetings of AA groups, the students posing as alcoholic newcomers. A complex research design was employed to assure that both high- and low-status newcomers (status differences effected by manipulating the type of clothing worn) were placed in groups of both high and low status (status differences determined by an observer rating scale), and to allow each student to pose, in different

[74] H. S. Becker, Blanche Geer, E. C. Hughes, and A. L. Strauss, *Boys in White* (Chicago: University of Chicago Press, 1961).
[75] J. F. Lofland and R. A. Lejeune, "Initial Interaction of Newcomers in Alcoholics Anonymous," *Social Problems*, 8 (1960), 102–111.

groups, as a person of both high and low status. This type of research role when utilized by transitory participants exhibits many of the same characteristics associated with disguised research by sustained participants. The students underwent some training designed to fit them for their role, and special data-gathering techniques had to be developed. For example, the observers secretly operated cumulative pocket stop watches to record the total time spent in interaction with members. Also, the same kinds of ethical questions concerning the use of concealed participants were raised upon the publication of the research.[76] But there are also some differences between transitory and sustained researchers using this approach. In the AA study the transient nature of the participation apparently did not allow these disguised researchers to become sufficiently involved in the subject groups to develop the sorts of loyalties and obligations which often interfere with the research orientation of the sustained participant. And the researchers, because they acted only as newcomers, were not obliged by their position in the group to initiate activity and so were less likely to influence the behavior of those they were expected to observe.

Turning to investigations undertaken by transitory researchers playing their roles openly, three examples of such studies will be briefly described. Reissman (1949) conducted interviews with 40 middle-level bureaucrats in order to investigate the nature of their role conceptions with respect to the public, their colleagues, their profession, and their employers.[77] Seashore issued questionnaires to 5,871 individuals who were members of 228 work groups in a machine company in order to examine the relation between work group cohesiveness and such variables as work-related anxiety and productivity.[78] And a questionnaire survey of 587 engineers and natural scientists employed in 19 separate work groups was conducted by Moore and Renck to determine how the job satisfaction reported by these professionals compared to that of a cross-section of American employees.[79] Obviously, in such studies as these the participant aspect of the researcher's role is minimized, while the scientific aspect of the role comes to the fore.

The open, transitory participant, however, shares many of the problems facing the open researcher engaged in sustaining interaction with his subjects. Both must gain the permission of the authorities to conduct their

[76] F. Davis, "Comment on 'Initial Interaction of Newcomers in Alcoholics Anonymous,'" *Social Problems*, **8** (1961), 364–365.
[77] L. A. Reissman, "A Study of Role Conceptions in Bureaucracy," *Social Forces*, **27** (1949), 305–310.
[78] S. E. Seashore, *Group Cohesiveness in the Industrial Work Group* (Ann Arbor: Institute for Social Research, University of Michigan, 1954).
[79] D. G. Moore and R. Renck, "The Professional Employee in Industry," *Journal of Business*, **28** (1955), 58–66.

studies and must then deal with the consequences of such sponsorship. And both must give some attention to the way in which their role and the objectives of their study are perceived by the subject group. Indeed, the problems in this area are particularly acute for the transitory participant, since he must largely rely on formal communication channels and on brief explanations of his objectives, lacking, as he does, the opportunity to clarify his role and interests in informal encounters with respondents. Sometimes, however, informal channels can be tapped. The Survey Research Center, a group which relies heavily in their organizational studies on widespread interviewing of employees, devised a technique for utilizing the informal communication networks to clarify the nature of their research objective for respondents. This procedure requires researchers to take time during the early weeks of interviewing to explain to each respondent the purpose of the research, the method of procedure, and the techniques of data analysis in the hope that these early interviewees will spread information concerning the study to others at their level.[80]

In general, relations between the transitory researcher and the members of the organization—both its officers and rank-and-file members— tend to be formalized. Agreements as to the responsibilities of each party are likely to be explicit and contractual. The investigator can usually list his needs with some precision; officials of the organization then know what is being asked of them and can propose their terms accordingly. Delany, for example, reports his experiences in gaining access to selected governmental agencies to examine the "informational perspectives" and attitudes of public officials at various organizational levels: "the research proposal must be presented to responsible officials briefly, understandably, and for the most part, accurately when requesting permission to do a study; usually the questionnaire has to be approved before a study can begin."[81] Delany also comments on the specific kinds of services he, as researcher, agreed to perform for these organizations:

> While the psychic rewards of being interviewed are usually an adequate *quid pro quo* for the cooperation of housewives and even individual public officials with social researchers, psychic rewards are not enough to win the permission of a responsible agency head to do research in his organization. In addition, the agency head must be able to see *some* definite collective gain to his organization from such cooperation, a gain that at least balances its costs and risks to the organization.

[80] Mann, *op. cit.*
[81] W. Delany, "Some Field Notes on the Problem of Access in Organizational Research," *Administrative Science Quarterly*, **5** (1960), 448–457, quoted from p. 452.

In addition to "feedback" of findings from the agency studies the author provided such a *quid pro quo* in the form of information about perspectives of agency clientele.[82]

The latter type of information was available to Delany because of a concurrent investigation of the public's understanding of and attitudes toward governmental agencies.[83] In such a bargaining situation the researcher must be certain that he does not sacrifice significant portions of his study simply in order to gain access; other organizations can be approached if necessary. And he must keep in mind his ethical responsibilities to his future respondents: he cannot promise officials information which would require him to betray the confidences of some of his subjects. Researchers, faced with the need to justify their intrusions into the affairs of others, are sometimes inclined to oversell the practical value of their research to members of the organization. This is dangerous—particularly when the expectations of many practitioners are already unrealistically high—since it can only lead to misunderstandings and disappointments.

The transitory participant is not faced with the task of attempting to cultivate strong relationships with his respondents. He asks little of them— participation in an interview or filling out a questionnaire—so he need offer them little in return. Frequently, he is allowed to question respondents on company time, making their cooperation less problematic. However, the lack of strong social ties with subjects may constitute a handicap, for the researcher has virtually no way of approaching or getting a hearing from respondents who refuse to participate out of misunderstanding or ignorance. And high-ranking officials often find themselves "too busy" to bother with an interview or questionnaire[84]—the latter is often shunted to an underling—when the request comes from a stranger.

Another kind of problem facing the transitory participant is his possible naïveté with respect to the group he confronts. He is less likely to have firsthand knowledge of the organization, and this lack renders him vulnerable to manipulation by its personnel. Dalton, for example, writes of the "frequently trivial areas to which alerted and fearful officers guided the inquiry" of naïve researchers.[85] Presumably, the investigator with more experience in the organization and stronger personal ties with respondents is less subject to such misdirection. Also, the transitory investigator who has

[82] *Ibid.*, p. 453.
[83] M. Janowitz, D. Wright, and W. Delany, *Public Administration and the Public* (Ann Arbor: Institute of Public Administration, University of Michigan, 1958).
[84] K. Eby, "Research in Labor Unions," *American Journal of Sociology*, **55** (1950), 222–228.
[85] Dalton, *op. cit.*, p. 275.

only brief contacts with members—or who communicates with them only by means of a questionnaire—is more likely to misinterpret or fail to understand their comments and responses and is more likely to himself be misunderstood by them than the researcher who has spent time "learning the language" of subject group members.[86]

While relative insulation from subjects constitutes a liability from the standpoint of effective communication with respondents, it is probably an advantage from the standpoint of allowing the researcher to maintain his detachment and objectivity and retain his original study objectives. Whether the sustained or the transitory approach results in the greater disturbance to the structure of relations among subjects or to their expressions of opinion and sentiment is impossible to determine without knowledge of the specific research situation. . . .

[86] Gold, *op. cit.*